Contents

Preface and acknowledgements   *v*

How to use this book to achieve the best results   *ix*

Learning features   *xiii*

An important note to the reader from the author   *xv*

1   Understanding the marketing process   1

2   The marketing planning process:
1 The main steps   27

3   The marketing planning process:
2 Removing the myths   77

4   Completing the marketing audit:
1 The customer and market audit   111

5   Completing the marketing audit:
2 The product audit   181

6   Setting marketing objectives and strategies   271

7   The communication plan:
1 The advertising and sales promotion plans   329

8   The communication plan:
2 The sales plan   335

9   The pricing plan   341

10   The distribution plan and customer service plan   347

11   Marketing information, forecasting and organizing
for marketing planning   353

12   Implementation issues in marketing planning   439

13   A step-by-step marketing planning system   475

Appendix A: Chapter 7   *539*

Appendix B: Chapter 8   *573*

Appendix C: Chapter 9   *603*

Appendix D: Chapter 10   *629*

Index   *667*

Preface and acknowledgements

The research on which this book is based was initiated in 1975 and has been continuously updated, not only by the author's own research but also by other scholars in universities around the world. However, rather than interrupting the flow of the text by providing individual references, readers may obtain a full bibliography of all relevant research on which this book is based from M. McDonald and B. Smith, *Strategic Marketing Planning: a domain review* (Cranfield University School of Management Research Series, 2001).

This is the Sixth Edition of a book which, since its launch in 1984, has helped and encouraged hundreds of thousands of practising managers with the difficult task of marketing planning. Many of them have been kind enough to write to me and thank me for the book's practical, no-nonsense style and approach to the subject. This has encouraged me to update the book to incorporate the findings of my latest research and experience in this difficult domain of marketing. This support also encouraged me to strengthen the book considerably by the addition of a chapter which incorporates a step-by-step, 'this is how you do it' approach to the preparation of marketing plans. The result is a book which takes the reader painstakingly through the process of marketing planning, while also providing a detailed means of implementing all the concepts and methodologies outlined. I have done this because, in working with companies ranging from world leaders in their fields to small domestic companies, there continues to be much confusion between the *process* and *methods* of marketing planning and the actual *outputs* of this process, i.e. the strategic marketing plan and the tactical marketing plan. I hope you will find this addition to the book to be of considerable value.

I have also revised the book to incorporate the latest thinking in the domain of marketing, without trying to make it a detailed, specialist book on any particular aspect of management. For example, while there are sections on customer relationship management (CRM), database marketing, integrated marketing and multi-channel integration, competitive strategies and marketing research, readers would be well advised to turn to specialist books in these subjects for detailed methodologies.

The purpose of this book is quite simply to explain and demonstrate how to prepare and use a marketing plan. It is equally relevant for consumer, service and industrial goods companies, since the process is universal, although I have now included in the CIM series specialist books on marketing planning for retailers and marketing planning for service businesses. This book, however, will serve all these different needs.

It is based on my research into the marketing planning practices of industrial, service and retail companies, which has revealed marketing planning as an area of major weakness. Almost without exception, companies that thought they were planning were in fact only forecasting and budgeting, and suffered grave operational difficulties as a result. The problem, as companies face up to the opportunities and challenges of the twenty-first century, is not that the *philosophy* of marketing is not believed; rather it is that most companies, particularly industrial goods companies and many service organizations, have difficulty in making it work.

This is largely because of ignorance about the process of planning their marketing activities, for which little help is provided in the extant body of literature. Books or articles often turn out to be about the management of the several elements of the marketing mix rather than about how the process of combining them into a coherent plan can be managed. Others treat marketing planning in such a generalized way that it is difficult to distil from them any guidance of operational significance. Finally, there are many excellent papers about individual aspects of the marketing planning process.

The truth is, of course, that the actual *process* of marketing planning is simple in outline. Any book will tell us that it consists of: a situation review; assumptions; objectives; strategies; programmes; and measurement and review. What other books *do not* tell us is that there are a number of contextual issues that have to be considered that make marketing planning one of the most baffling of all management problems.

Here are some of those issues:

- *When* should it be done, *how often*, by *whom*, and *how*?
- Is it different in a *large* and a *small* company?
- Is it different in a *diversified* and an *undiversified* company?
- Is it different in an *international* and a *domestic* company?
- What is the role of the *chief executive*?
- What is the role of the *planning department*?
- Should marketing planning be *top-down* or *bottom-up*?
- What is the relationship between *operational* (one-year) and *strategic* (longer-term) planning?

Since effective marketing planning lies at the heart of a company's revenue-earning activities, it is not surprising that there is a great demand for a guide which strips away the confusion and mystery surrounding this subject and helps firms to get to grips with it in a practical and down-to-earth manner.

This book explains what marketing is, how the marketing planning process works, how to carry out a marketing audit, how to set marketing objectives and strategies, how to schedule and cost out what has to be done to achieve the objectives, and how to design and implement a simple marketing planning system.

My approach is both logical and practical. This view has been confirmed by the hundreds of letters referred to above, and by the fact that this book is now a standard text on many marketing courses in universities, and in-company training programmes around the world.

This book includes:

● Application questions, to help you personalize the learning
● Exercises at the end of every chapter to enable practising managers to translate the theory into practice
● Mini case studies to exemplify the points being made
● A step-by-step process, with templates, for producing marketing plans.

Skill-based computer software, videos, self-assessment questionnaires and computer-based training software are also available, on request, from Butterworth-Heinemann.

Additionally, a comprehensive Tutors' Guide is available for those who wish to teach the subject to others. This Tutors' Guide contains lecture plans, PowerPoint masters, case studies, tutors' discussion points and additional assignments for use by tutors.

We have taken reasonable steps in writing this book to avoid any kind of prejudice or sexism. Where possible, for example, we have used the expression 'they' rather than 'he' or 'she'. On occasions, however, to avoid irritating the reader by unnecessary and convoluted English, we have used the word 'he'. Please be assured, however, that no deliberate offence is intended.

I should like to thank my friends and colleagues for the advice they have given me during the life of this book. To the following I am especially grateful: Professor Martin Christopher, John Leppard, Visiting Professor Simon Majaro and Professor Adrian Payne. Of all these people, I owe much to John Leppard for his creativity and innovative approach to marketing; however, I also owe a lot to the original thinking of erstwhile students of mine, Professor Hugh Wilson and Dr Brian Smith, without whom this book would not be what it is. To them I will always be grateful. Without the criticisms, suggestions and material of all of these friends and colleagues, this book would not have been the best-seller it has been since its first edition in 1984.

Finally, I should like to thank my daughter-in-law, Anne McDonald, for typing the manuscript and for her patience with me and cheerfulness throughout the whole process.

Malcolm McDonald
Cranfield University School of Management
February 2007

Note: Further details of the PhD research on which this book is based are available from m.mcdonald@cranfield.ac.uk

How to use this book to achieve the best results

Before starting this book, even if you decide to omit the Preface, *please read the section entitled 'An important note to the reader from the author' (p. xvii)* in order to get the best results from this book.

At the end of each chapter, you will find a number of application questions. More importantly, there is also a number of exercises designed to help you translate the theory into practice in the context of your own organization.

As you work through this book, you will find that some of the exercises are diagnostic and enable you to 'plot' where your company is. Some will help you to understand what might be happening to your company. Other exercises are more concerned with generating factual information about your company, its products, its markets or its planning processes. We find this combination of exercises not only provides you with insights and learning about many aspects of marketing planning, but it also helps you to assemble information which can contribute to a marketing plan for your company.

Whenever scoring and interpretation are required for an exercise, you will find the answers are provided at the end of each chapter.

This book is written to fulfil three principal needs. The first relates to the *process* of marketing planning, which, while theoretically simple, is in practice extraordinarily complex, involving, as it does, people, systems and organizational structures. One purpose, then, is to ensure that readers fully understand the process, what the pitfalls are and how to negotiate them.

The second purpose is to ensure that readers know which are the appropriate marketing diagnostic tools, structures and frameworks to use at each stage of the process.

The third and most important purpose, however, is to give both students and managers a no-nonsense, practical, step-by-step guide on how to prepare a really good, strategic marketing plan that will help their organizations to create sustainable competitive advantage for themselves and for their customers.

Marketing planning fast track

While we do not wish to discourage anyone from taking the time to understand both the process and the diagnostic tools, we can, nonetheless, suggest that readers start by quickly reading through the whole of Chapter 13, which provides a step-by-step system for producing a marketing plan.

This should ensure that everyone is fully aware of the difference between the *process* and the *output* (i.e. the strategic marketing plan), for, let no one ever forget, it is the result of the process that ultimately matters. Having this overall picture first should make Chapters 1 to 12 more meaningful and enjoyable.

Key areas for improvements in strategic marketing planning: where to look in this text for practical guidance

This help section is based on the analysis of over 700 strategic marketing plans from over fifty multinationals during a period of twenty-five years. A fee was charged for each analysis, so these comments are based on considerably more than just opinions.

Summary of the book

A strategic marketing plan should be a clear and simple summary of key market trends, key target segments, the value required by each of them, how we intend to create superior value (to competitors), with a clear prioritization of marketing objectives and strategies, together with the financial consequences.

Frequently, they are diffuse, confusing compilations of unconnected sections.

Specific problems encountered and where to look for guidance

- Market overviews contain substantially more information than is necessary, with no hint of the implications for marketing activity. See Chapters 2 and 3.
- Key segments are rarely identified. 'Segments' are often sectors or products, rather than groups of customers with similar needs. See Chapter 4.
- The competitive situation is not well analysed and plans appear to assume no activity or reaction by competitors. See Chapter 6.
- SWOT analyses rarely pin down convincingly the value that is required by segments. They are frequently too general to lead to any actionable propositions. See Chapter 5.
- Our own distinctive competences are rarely isolated and built on. See Chapters 5 and 13.
- SWOTs are rarely summarized clearly and logically in a portfolio which provides a categorization of the relative potential of each and our relative strengths in each. See Chapter 5.

- Marketing objectives are frequently confused with marketing strategies and do not follow logically from the portfolio summary. See Chapter 6.
- The resource implications of effecting the marketing plans are not always clear. See Chapter 11.

Main differences between the Sixth Edition and earlier editions

Although I am now retired from Cranfield, I am an Emeritus Professor and am still deeply involved in their research clubs that I founded when I was Chairman of the Cranfield Centre for Advanced Research in Marketing. These clubs are sponsored by some of the world's leading companies, such as IBM, GlaxoSmithKline, Cadbury Schweppes and so on, and include:

- The Strategic Marketing Planning Research Club. Its main role was to monitor successful marketing planning practices.
- The IS/Marketing Research Club. Its main role was to research best practice in improving marketing effectiveness with IT/IS.
- The Global Account Management Research Club. Its main research focus was and remains monitoring global best practice in dealing with major customers.
- The Marketing Value Added Research Club. This existed to measure quantitatively the contribution of marketing to corporate effectiveness.
- The CRM Research Forum. The objectives were to monitor best practice in conceiving, designing, implementing and measuring customer relationship management programmes.
- The New Marketing Research Club. The purpose of this club was to better understand postmodern consumer attitudes and behaviours in order to see in what ways core marketing processes need to be amended.
- The Strategic Sales Research Club. Sales management and selling are still vitally important in the twenty-first century, yet remain one of the least researched domains. This research club filled this void.
- The Multi-Channel Integration Research Club. This has been researching how new routes to market and new promotional channels can be better integrated.

Where relevant, the findings from these research clubs have been incorporated into the text. For example, there are substantial new sections on CRM, the Internet, future market mapping, integrated marketing and distribution strategies, and other technology-driven impacts in the marketing domain. Also, the dotcom revolution has come and gone, so, where appropriate, there are references to this in the new text. Readers can, then, rest assured that they are working with a thoroughly up-to-date book, which is based on deeply-researched world-class marketing.

Learning features

Marketing Plans Sixth Edition is based on the fully reworked fifth edition, with full pedagogical features as follows:

- *Summary*. Each chapter begins with bullet points which highlight the main features and learning to be covered in the chapter.
- *Key concepts*. Principal marketing ideas and themes are highlighted as snapshots throughout the text.
- *Crucial terms*. Concise definitions of important terms and vocabulary are provided in the margin to allow for a smoother, easier reading of the text.
- *Examples*. These provide additional illustrative marketing accounts to contextualize learning.
- *Marketing insights*. Real-life marketing anecdotes contextualize learning.
- *Headlines*. Highlights taken from the text as marginalized notes bring important points to the attention of the reader.
- *Case studies*. In-depth studies of marketing experiences show how the theories work in real-world companies.
- *Application questions*. These appear at the end of each chapter and relate the theory to practice by asking the reader to apply the theory to real-life situations.
- *Chapter review*. This condenses the main themes of the chapter and directs the reader to relevant exercises for each topic for them to try.
- *Exercises*. These appear at the end of each chapter and are preceded by a brief introduction which informs readers of the issues and concepts they will find within each exercise. Each exercise helps the reader to translate the theory into practice and reinforces the learning gained from each chapter. Many exercises also end with an 'interpretation' to guide readers in their workings.

An important note to the reader from the author

STOP

Producing an effective marketing plan that will give your organization competitive advantage is not easy. It takes knowledge, skills, intellect, creativity and, above all, time.

Everything you need to succeed is in this book, but you must be prepared to devote time to it. It is most definitely not a quick read!

FAST TRACK

However, for those who need a fast track to producing a marketing plan, Chapter 13 will help you. Be careful, though:

> A little learning is a dangerous thing. Drink deep, or taste not the Pierian Spring.
>
> (Alexander Pope)

INTERMEDIATE TRACK

For those interested principally in producing a strategic marketing plan, it is possible to omit Chapters 7–10, as these contain a level of detail more appropriate for the preparation of a tactical, one-year operational plan. Again, however, be careful and only omit these chapters if you feel that you already know enough about promotion, pricing, distribution and customer service to be able to outline appropriate strategies in your strategic marketing plan. Also, particularly in Chapters 8 and 10, there are some crucially important state-of-the-art developments in e-marketing described in some detail, each of which is substantially changing the face of marketing. To help readers to decide, a brief summary of Chapters 7–10 has been included and the details in each chapter have been incorporated as appendices to the main text.

An important test to help you decide which track you need

It is important that you complete the questionnaire on page *xix* before you start Chapter 1. This test was developed by the author for the President of a global IT company, who asked what he should be looking for in a world-class strategic marketing plan.

Interpretation

In our experience, it is unlikely that many readers will score above five on many of these questions. This is not the point, however. The purpose of the questionnaire is to focus your attention at the beginning of the book on what essential deliverables a marketing plan should produce. If you work carefully through this book and implement it in your organization, you will be able to give yourself high scores in all boxes. Then, you will be a truly market-driven organization!

We have just one more suggestion for readers of this book, which is that they should also complete the very last questionnaire in this book, at the end of Chapter 13. This, together with the questionnaire on page *xix*, will most certainly alert readers to the need to focus on the contents of this research-based book.

Professor Malcolm McDonald

ARE YOU GETTING THESE ESSENTIAL DELIVERABLES FROM YOUR STRATEGIC MARKETING PLAN?

Score out of 10

Market structure and segmentation

- Is there a clear and unambiguous definition of the market you are interested in serving?
- Is it clearly mapped, showing product/service flows, volumes/values in total, your shares and critical conclusions for your organization?
- Are the segments clearly described and quantified? These must be groups of customers with the same or similar needs, not sectors.
- Are the real needs of these segments properly quantified, with the relative importance of these needs clearly identified?

Differentiation

- Is there a clear and quantified analysis of how well your company satisfies these needs compared to competitors?
- Are the opportunities and threats clearly identified by segment?

Scope

- Are all the segments classified according to their relative potential for growth in profits over the next three years and according to your company's relative competitive position in each?
- Are the objectives consistent with their position in the portfolio (volume, value, market share, profit)?
- Are the strategies (including products, price, place and service) consistent with these objectives?
- Are the key issues for action for all departments clearly spelled out as key issues to be addressed?

Value capture

- Do the objectives and strategies add up to the profit goals required by your company?
- Does the budget follow on logically from all of the above, or is it merely an add on?

Total score

CHAPTER 1

Understanding the marketing process

Summary

- What marketing is
- Its role in getting the best out of an organization's asset base
- The link between the external environment, customers and their needs and the marketing mix
- Clearing up the confusion surrounding marketing's role
- Clarification of what customers look for in their suppliers
- The differences and similarities between consumer, service and industrial marketing
- Whether a marketing department is essential
- Exercises to turn the theory into actionable propositions
- Readers who are already wholly familiar with the role of marketing in organizations may wish to go straight to Chapter 2, which begins to explain the marketing planning process

■ The marketing concept[1]

In 1776, when Adam Smith said that consumption is the sole end and purpose of production, he was in fact describing what in recent years has become known as the ► **marketing concept**.

> The central idea of marketing is of a matching between a company's capabilities and the wants of customers in order to achieve the objectives of both parties.

► **DEFINITION** ◄

The marketing concept, as opposed to the marketing function, implies that all the activities of an organization are driven by a desire to satisfy customer needs

It is important at this stage to understand the difference between the marketing concept (often referred to as 'market orientation') and the marketing function, which is concerned with the management of the *marketing mix*. The management of the marketing mix involves using the various tools and techniques available to managers in order to implement the marketing concept.

For the sake of simplicity, these are often written about and referred to as the four Ps, these being Product, Price, Promotion and Place, although today many scholars include a number of additional Ps, such as People and Process.

However, before any meaningful discussion can take place about how the marketing function should be managed, it is vital to have a full understanding about the idea of marketing itself (the marketing concept), and it is this issue that we principally address in this chapter.

[1] The author would like to remind the reader that he will use the word 'product' throughout the text to avoid unnecessary references to 'services', 'not-for-profit services', 'capital goods' and 'retail'. The text is equally relevant to all of these.

■ The marketing function

There are many definitions of marketing, and much confusion about what it is. The following definition should clarify this for readers.

Marketing is a process for:

- defining markets
- quantifying the needs of the customer groups (segments) within these markets
- determining the value propositions to meet these needs
- communicating these value propositions to all those people in the organization responsible for delivering them, and getting their buy-in to their role
- playing an appropriate part in delivering these value propositions (usually only communications)
- monitoring the value actually delivered.

For this process to be effective, organizations need to be consumer–customer-driven.

This definition is represented as a 'map' in Figure 1.1.

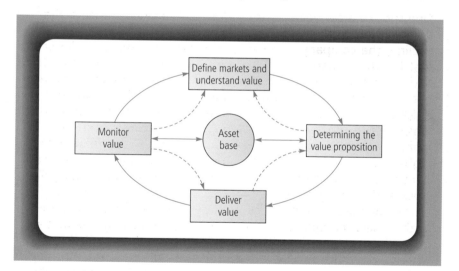

Figure 1.1

Starting at the top and moving clockwise, it should be pointed out that the first two boxes are concerned with *strategies* for markets, whereas the bottom box and the box on the left are concerned with implementing the strategies, once formulated. The fundamental difference between strategies and tactics will be expanded on in Chapter 2.

■ Company capabilities

For now, let us return to the notion of the above definition bringing about a matching between a company's capabilities and the wants of its customers. In Chapter 4 we will explain what we mean when we talk about customer wants, but for now it is important to understand what we mean when we talk about a company's capabilities. To explain this more fully, let us imagine that we have been made redundant and have decided to set ourselves up in our own business.

The first thing we would have to do is to decide what it is that we can actually *do*. In answering this question, we would quickly realize that our actual knowledge and skills restrict us very severely to certain obvious areas. For example, it would be difficult for a former sales manager to set himself up in business as an estate agent, or for an estate agent to start a marketing consultancy, unless, of course, both had the necessary skills and knowledge. A little thought will confirm that it is exactly the same for a company.

> Many commercial disasters have resulted from companies diversifying into activities for which they were basically unsuited.

One such case concerns a firm making connectors for the military and aviation markets. When these traditional markets went into decline, the company diversified into making connectors for several industrial markets such as consumer durables, automobiles and so on. Unfortunately these markets were so completely different from the ones that the company had been used to that it quickly went into a loss-making situation. Whereas the connector which the company had previously manufactured had been a highly engineered product made to the specifications of a few high-technology customers, the company now had to mass produce simple connectors for broad markets. This meant making for stock and carrying field inventory. It also meant low competitive prices. The sales force did not know how to cope with the demands of their new markets. They had been used to making one or two calls a day and to having detailed technical discussions with buyers, whereas now they were expected to make eight or nine calls a day and to sell against many competitive products. Furthermore, the company just did not have the right image to succeed in the market. The results of all this were very serious financial losses.

The lesson simply is that all firms have a unique set of capabilities in the form of resources and management skills which are not necessarily capable of taking advantage of *all* market opportunities as effectively, and hence as competitively, as other firms. To summarize, the matching process between a company's capabilities and customer wants is fundamental to commercial success. That this is so will become clearer as we get further into the task of explaining the role and the nature of marketing.

■ The role of marketing in business

What causes success in the long run, by which we mean a continuous growth in earnings per share and in the capital value of the shares, has been shown by research[2] to depend on four elements, as shown in Figure 1.2.

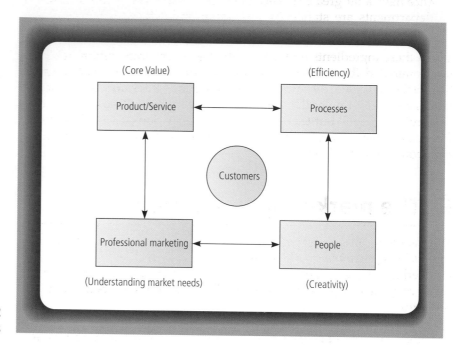

Figure 1.2
Business success

1   An excellent core product or service, and all the associated R and D, which closely matches the wants of the organization's target segments. Clearly, marketing will have a heavy input into this process. All this is showing is that companies with average products deserve average success.

2   Excellent, world-class, state-of-the-art operations. All this is saying is that inefficiency today is likely to be punished. Marketing should, of course, have an input to defining operational efficiency in customer satisfaction terms. Where it is not allowed to, because of corporate culture, quality often becomes a sterile ▶ **ISO** activity.

3   A culture that encourages and produces an infrastructure within which employees can be creative and entrepreneurial within the prescribed company procedures. Bored and boring people, for whom subservience and compliance is the norm, cause average or below-average

---

[2] V. Wong and J. Saunders (1993) 'Business orientations and corporate success', *Journal of Strategic Marketing*, 1(1); 'Marketing – The Challenge of Change. A major study into the future of marketing in British enterprises', Chartered Institute of Marketing/Cranfield University School of Management Research Report, 1994; 'The Effectiveness of Marketing Strategy Making in Medical Markets', Cranfield PhD, 2003.

performance. This is particularly important, because it is the organization's people who deliver value to customers.

4 Professional marketing departments, staffed by qualified professionals (not failures from other functions). All this means is that companies who recruit professionally qualified marketers with appropriate experience have a far greater chance of success than those whose marketing departments are staffed by just about anybody who fancies themselves as marketers.

Given these ingredients and, above all else, a corporate culture which is not dominated (because of its history) by production, or operations, or financial orientation, all the evidence shows that marketing as a function makes a contribution to the achievement of corporate objectives. Its principal role is to spell out the several value propositions demanded by different customer groups so that everyone in the organization knows what their contribution is in creating this value.

■ The marketing environment

The matching process referred to earlier takes place in what we can call the *marketing environment*, which is the milieu in which the firm is operating. Perhaps the most obvious constituent of the marketing environment is our *competitors*, for what they do vitally affects our own behaviour as a company.

The point is that, since what our competitors do so vitally affects our own decisions, it is necessary to find some way of monitoring this and other elements of the environment and of building this into our decision-making process. In Chapter 11, we show how this can be done.

The *political, fiscal, economic, social* and *legal* policies of the governments of the countries where we sell our goods also determine what we can do. For example, inflation reduces the discretionary spending power of consumers, and this can result in market decline. Legislation concerning such things as labelling, packaging, advertising, environmentalism, and so on, all affect the way we run our business, and all these things have to be taken account of when we make our plans.

Technology is constantly changing, and we can no longer assume that our current range of products will continue to be demanded by our customers. For example, the introduction of non-drip paint had a profound effect on what had traditionally been a stable market. People discovered that they could use paint without causing a mess, and eventually this product was demanded in new kinds of outlets such as supermarkets. This led to a consequent change in pricing, promotional and distribution policies. One can imagine what happened to some of those paint manufacturers who continued to make only their traditional products and to distribute them only through the more traditional outlets.

Likewise, the advent of the microprocessor revolutionized the computer industry, with a devastating effect on companies (such as IBM) who remained dependent for too long on their supremacy in mainframes. It is interesting to note that IBM is now mainly a service company, with little involvement in hardware.

Merging technologies have also revolutionized traditional industries such as telecommunications, printing, publishing, IT and many others.

The point is that the environment in which we operate is not controlled by us, and it is dynamic. Hence, it must be constantly monitored, and we must be prepared to adapt our asset base and our approach to markets. An approach for doing this is outlined in subsequent chapters.

So far, we have talked about the three constituent parts of what we have described as a matching process:

1 The capabilities of a firm
2 The wants of customers
3 The marketing environment.

Diagrammatically, this is shown in Figure 1.3.

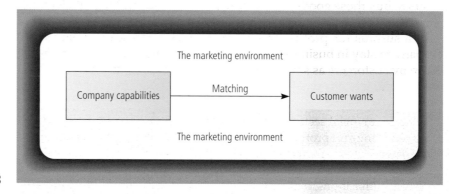

Figure 1.3

■ Customer wants

Although we shall be dealing with this subject in Chapter 4, let us briefly turn our attention to the subject of customer wants, so that we can complete our understanding of what marketing is.

Perhaps one of the greatest areas for misunderstanding in marketing concerns this question of customer wants. Companies are accused of manipulating innocent consumers by making them want things they do not really need.

If this were so, we would not have a situation in which a very high proportion of all new products launched actually fail! The fact is, people have always had needs – such as, say, for home entertainment. What changes in the course of time is the way people satisfy their needs. For example, television was only commercially viable because people needed home entertainment, and this was yet another way of fulfilling that need.

But let us not be fooled into believing that the customer, in the end, does not have the final say. All customer needs have many different ways of being satisfied, and wherever people have *choice* they will choose that product which they perceive as offering the greatest benefits to them at whatever price they are prepared to pay.

What this means, in effect, since all commercial organizations incur costs in taking goods or services to the market, is that profit, through customer satisfaction, is the only measure of efficacy or worth of what the company is doing.

> Cheapness, efficiency, quality (in the sense of international standards such as ISO) or, indeed, any other measure, are not criteria of effectiveness, since there is little point in producing anything cheaply, efficiently or perfectly if people don't actually want it and don't buy it.

Since costs are incurred in producing goods, it is necessary to find customers to buy those goods at a sufficiently high price and in sufficient volume (margin turnover) to enable the company to cover its costs and to make a surplus (or profit). This is an economic necessity to enable the company to stay in business, and means that unless what is being offered is seen by customers as satisfying their wants, they will not buy it.

> In the commercial sector, research has shown that there is a direct link between long-run profitability and the ability of a firm to understand its customers' needs and provide value for them.[3] For industries previously protected from competition, such as the airline industry and telecommunications, many now know that sustainable profitability can only come in the long run through continuous customer satisfaction.

In the not-for-profit sector, customer satisfaction is obviously a proxy for profitability. We shall say more about this important point in Chapter 4 on market segmentation.

To summarize, any organization that continues to offer something for which there is a long-term fundamental decline in demand, unless it is prepared to change so as to be more in tune with what the market wants, in the end will go out of business. Even less sensible would be for a government, or parent company, to subsidize such an operation, since we know that to go on producing what people do not want is economically inefficient, especially when people will get what they want from abroad if they cannot buy it in their home country.

---

[3] See, for example, R.D. Buzzell and B.T. Gale (1987), *The PIMS Principles Linking Strategy to Performance*, Free Press, New York.

The same line of reasoning must also apply to those who continually counsel increased productivity as the only answer to our economic problems. Unfortunately, any additional production would more than likely end up in stock unless people actually wanted what was being produced.

It would be different, of course, if there was only a temporary hiccup in demand, but unfortunately this is rarely the case, because markets are dynamic and we must learn to adapt and change as our markets mutate.

Central to this question of customer wants is an understanding that there is rarely such a thing as 'a market'. To start with, it is clear that it is customers who buy products, not markets. A market is merely an aggregation of customers sharing similar needs for which they want the products and services that best meet these needs. In reality, most markets consist of a number of sub-markets, each of which is different. For example, the airline market consists of freight and passenger transport. The passenger side can be subdivided further into VFR (visiting friends and relatives), holidays, business travel, and so on. Failure to understand the needs of these very different customer groups would result in failure to provide the desired services at an acceptable price.

Of course, it is not quite as easy as this, which is why we devote the whole of Chapter 4 to this very important aspect of what we call 'market segmentation'. But for now it is only necessary to understand that it is our ability to identify groups of customer wants which our particular company capabilities are able to satisfy profitably that is central to marketing management.

■ The marketing mix

As we have already said, managing the marketing mix involves the use of the tools and techniques of marketing. Thus, in order for the matching process to take place, we need *information*. External and internal marketing information flows (marketing research) and database management are discussed further in Chapter 11.

Having found out what customers want, we must develop products or services to satisfy those wants. This is known as 'product management', and is discussed in Chapter 5. Obviously we must charge a price for our products, and this is discussed in Chapter 9.

We must also tell our customers about our products, for we can be certain that customers will not beat a path to our door to buy whatever it is we are making. Here we must consider all forms of communication, especially advertising, personal selling and sales promotion. These are discussed in Chapters 7 and 8.

All that remains now is to get our products into our customers' hands, thus giving a time and a place utility to our product. Distribution and customer service are discussed in Chapter 10.

Finally, we must consider how to tie it all together in the form of a marketing plan. This latter point is so important that the next two chapters are devoted to a discussion of the marketing planning process.

■ Confusion about what marketing is – veneer or substance?

It is a sad reflection on the state of marketing that in spite of almost fifty years of marketing education, ignorance still abounds concerning what marketing is.

The marketing function (or department) never has been, nor ever will be, effective in an organization whose history to date is one of technical, production, operations or financial orientation. Such enterprises have long since adopted the vocabulary of marketing and applied a veneer of marketing terminology.

Thus, some of the High Street banks have spent fortunes on hiring marketing people, often from the fast-moving consumer goods sector (FMCG), producing expensive TV commercials, and creating a multiplicity of products, brochures and leaflets. Yet still most customers would have difficulty in distinguishing between the major players (so where's the competitive advantage?).

MARKETING INSIGHT

Is this marketing in the sense of understanding and meeting customers' needs better than the competition, or is it old-fashioned selling with the name changed, where we try to persuade customers to buy what we want to sell them, how, when and where we want to sell it?

> The computer industry provides perhaps even clearer examples. For years computer companies have used the word 'marketing' quite indiscriminately as they have tried to persuade customers to buy the ever more complex outpourings of their technology. At least one major hardware manufacturer used to call its Branch Sales Managers 'Marketing Managers' to create the illusion of a local process of understanding and responding to customer needs. Racked by recession, decline and huge losses, this is an industry in which most of the major players have either gone bankrupt or have changed, root and branch, their business model.

The following are the major areas of confusion regarding marketing:

1 *Confusion with sales*. One managing director aggressively announced to everyone at the beginning of a seminar in Sydney, Australia: 'There's no time for marketing in my company until sales improve!' Confusion with sales is still one of the biggest barriers to be overcome.
2 *Confusion with product management*. The belief that all a company has to do to succeed is to produce a good product also still abounds, and not Concorde, Sinclair's C5, the EMI Scanner, nor the many thousands of

brilliant products that have seen their owners or inventors go bankrupt during the past thirty years will convince such people otherwise.

3 *Confusion with advertising.* This is another popular misconception, and the annals of business are replete with examples – such as British Airways, which won awards for brilliant advertising campaigns, while failing to deliver what the advertising promised. Throwing advertising expenditure at the public is still a very popular way of tackling deep-rooted marketing problems.

4 *Confusion with customer service.* The 'Have a nice day' syndrome is still having its heyday in many countries of the world, originally popularized, of course, by Peters and Waterman in *In Search of Excellence* (Warner Books, 1982). Many organizations now know, of course, that training staff to be nice to customers does not help a lot if the basic offer is fundamentally wrong. For example, considering many railway companies around the world, while it helps to be treated nicely, it is actually much more important to get there on time! 'Stop sending me birthday cards and answer your damned phone!' is a *cri de cœur* many customers will sympathize with.

It should by now be obvious that those people who talk about 'the sharp end' – by which they usually mean personal selling – as being the only thing that matters in marketing, have probably got it wrong.

Selling is just one aspect of communication with customers, and to say that it is the only thing that matters is to ignore the importance of product management, pricing, distribution and other forms of communication in achieving profitable sales. Selling is just one part of this process, in which the transaction is actually clinched. It is the culmination of the marketing process, and success will only be possible if all the other elements of the marketing mix have been properly managed. Imagine trying to sell a horse that didn't have four legs! The more attention that is paid to finding out what customers want, to developing products to satisfy these wants, to pricing at a level consistent with the benefits offered, to gaining distribution, and to communicating effectively with our target market, the more likely we are to be able to exchange contracts through the personal selling process.

Likewise, it is naive to assume that marketing is all about advertising, since it is by now clear that advertising is only one aspect of communication. Many firms waste their advertising expenditure because they have not properly identified what their target market is.

For example, one public transport company spent half a million euros advertising how reliable their bus service was when, in reality, utilization of buses by the public was declining because they somehow felt that buses were working class! This was a classic case of believing that advertising will increase sales irrespective of what the message is. Had this company done its research, it could have decided to what extent and how advertising could be used to overcome this prejudice. As it was, the company spent a small fortune telling people something that was largely irrelevant!

In reality, many companies spend more on advertising when times are good and less on advertising when times are bad. Cutting the advertising budget is often seen as an easy way of boosting the profit and loss account when a firm is below its budgeted level of profit. This tendency is encouraged by the fact that this can be done without any apparent immediate adverse effect on sales. Unfortunately, this is just another classic piece of misunderstanding about marketing and about the role of advertising in particular. The belief here is that advertising is *caused* by sales! Also, it is naive in the extreme to assume that advertising effectiveness can be measured in terms of sales when it is only a part of the total marketing process.

■ What does the customer want?

Finally, we have to beware of what the words 'finding out what the customer wants', which appear in most definitions of marketing, really mean. The reality, of course, is that most advances in customer satisfaction are technology-driven. For example, the fabulous technological breakthroughs that occurred as a result of the Houston space programme, when the Americans put two men on the moon, have provided thousands of opportunities for commercial exploitation. The role of marketing has been to find commercial applications for the technology.

The truth, of course, is that there are two kinds of research and development:

1 Technology-driven
2 Market-driven.

From the kinds of technology-driven programmes that take place on science parks and in laboratories around the world come opportunities for commercial exploitation.

From the kinds of market-driven programmes that most companies engage in come incremental, and sometimes discontinuous, improvements to product performance. Both are legitimate activities. The former has been glamorized and popularized by companies such as 3M, which claim to encourage and institutionalize unfocused scientific research. This has led to the formation of a number of new businesses and product launches, the most famous of which is Post-It.

MARKETING INSIGHT

The main point to remember, however, is that customers do not really know what they want! All they really want are better ways of solving their problems, so one of the main tasks of marketing is to understand the customers and their problems in depth so that we can continuously work on ways of making life easier for them. Whether this happens as a result of serendipity or focused research and development is less important than the end result.

■ Are business-to-business, consumer and service marketing different?

The central ideas of marketing are universal and it makes no difference whether we are marketing furnaces, insurance policies or margarine. Yet problems sometimes arise when we try to implement marketing ideas in service companies and industrial goods companies.

A service does not lend itself to being specified in the same way as a product, as it does not have the same reproducible physical dimensions that can be measured. Thus, with the purchase of any service, there is a large element of trust on the part of the buyer, who can only be sure of the quality and performance of the service after it has been completed. Largely because of this, the salesperson actually selling the service obviously becomes part of the service, since this is one of the principal ways in which the potential efficacy of the service can be assessed. Additionally, a service product cannot be made in advance and stored for selling 'off the shelf' at some later stage. Nonetheless, apart from some differences in emphasis, the principles of marketing apply to services in exactly the same way.

Business-to-business goods are simply those goods sold to other businesses, institutional or government buyers for incorporation into their own products, to be resold, or to be used by them within their own business. Principal types of business-to-business goods are raw materials, components, capital goods, and maintenance, repair and operating goods and equipment, although even service companies sell direct to other companies rather than to consumers.

The fact that the share of world trade enjoyed by some manufacturing countries has slumped so dramatically over the past fifty years is not generally because their products were not as good as those produced by other countries, but because they failed to monitor and understand the environmental changes taking place and stuck doggedly to what had worked in the past. On the other hand, organizations that continued to thrive did do this, including, where necessary, sourcing manufacturing in countries with lower costs.

One reason for this is that many manufacturing companies naively believe that the name of the game is making well-engineered products. Making well-engineered products is all some companies are concerned about, in spite of the fact that all the evidence points to the conclusion that more often than not it is for other reasons that the final choice is actually made. Failure to understand the importance of market segmentation (to be discussed in Chapter 4), market share, service and reputation, among other things, is the principal reason why such companies fail to compete successfully in so many world markets. Making what they consider to be good products and then giving them to the sales force to get rid of is just not enough.

> Failure to understand the importance of market segmentation is the principal reason for failure to compete effectively in world markets.

But, quite apart from the fact that there appears to be a sort of status about being on the technical side of business, which sometimes acts as a barrier to the consideration of marketing issues, it is also a fact that marketing is difficult in many business-to-business markets. This makes it inevitable that managers will resort to doing things they can understand. For example, demand for all industrial products is derived from the demand for consumer products, which adds greater uncertainty to decision-making and makes forecasting extremely difficult.

It can be readily appreciated from Figure 1.4 that the further a company gets from the eventual consumer, the less control it has over demand. Take the example of brewers. They can communicate directly with their consumers, whereas the company making their plant, and, in turn, the suppliers to the plant company, are, in the final analysis, dependent on ultimate consumers and are less able to influence what they do.

Also, information about business-to-business markets is not so readily available as in consumer goods markets, which makes it more difficult to measure changes in market share. There are other difficulties, besides these, which make marketing in the business-to-business area more difficult.

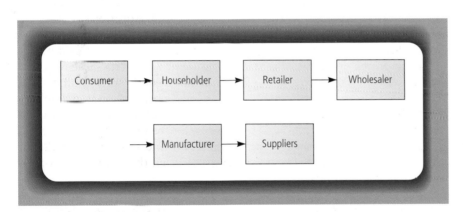

Figure 1.4

Unfortunately, the answer to this problem by many companies has been to recruit a 'marketing person' and leave that person to get on with the job of marketing. But it will now be obvious that such a solution can never work, because the marketing concept, if it is to work at all, has to be understood and practised by all executives in a firm, not just by the marketing manager. Otherwise, everyone goes on behaving just as they did before and the marketing person quickly becomes ineffective.

Again, however, the conclusion must be that, apart from differences in emphasis, the principles of marketing apply in exactly the same way.

■ Do you need a marketing department?

This brings us finally to the question of whether it is necessary for a company to have a marketing department.

It is not essential to have a formalized marketing department for the analysis, planning and control of the matching process. This is particularly so in small, undiversified companies where the chief executive has an in-depth understanding of customers' needs. Even in large companies it is not necessary to have a marketing department, because the management of products can be left to the engineers, pricing can be managed by the accountants, distribution can be managed by distribution specialists, and selling and advertising can be managed by the sales manager.

The dangers in this approach, however, are obvious. Technicians often place too much emphasis on the physical aspects of the products, accountants can be too concerned with costs rather than with market values, distribution people can often succeed in optimizing their own objectives for stock while at the same time sub-optimizing other more important aspects of the business (such as customer service), and selling and promotion can often be carried out in a way which may not be in the best interests of the firm's overall goals.

However, as a company's product range and customer types grow, and as competitive pressures and environmental turbulence increase, so it often becomes necessary to organize the management of marketing under one central control function, otherwise there is a danger of ending up with the kind of product which is brilliant technically but disastrous commercially.

In professional organizations, great care is necessary in thinking about the appropriate organizational form for marketing. For example, in a postgraduate business school the major role of the marketing department has traditionally been in the domain of promotion and information coordination. Whilst it does obviously act as a facilitator for strategy development, it is intellectually simplistic to imagine that it could be the originator of strategy. In some other service organizations the central marketing function might also provide the systems to enable others to carry out effective marketing, but in such organizations marketing departments never have actually *done* marketing, nor ever will.

The reasons are obvious. If the term 'marketing' is intended to embrace all those activities related to demand creation and satisfaction, and the associated intelligence, then it is clear that most marketing takes place during the service delivery and customer contact process, in all its forms. Marketing, then, reflects this process, and it is absurd to believe that it is the sole domain of those people in the organization who happen to belong to the marketing department.

As Alan Mitchell, a freelance journalist for *Marketing Business*, said: 'To say the Marketing Department is responsible for marketing is like saying love is the responsibility of one family member.'

It is equally absurd to suggest that the personnel department should actually emphasize personnel management, with all other managers in the organization having nothing to do with people. The same could be said for finance and information systems. Indeed, it is such myopic functional separation that got most struggling organizations into the mess they are in today.

Much more important, however, than who is responsible for marketing in an organization is the question of its marketing orientation – i.e. the

> It is absurd to believe that marketing is the sole domain of those people in the organization who happen to belong to the marketing department.

degree to which the company as a whole understands the importance of finding out what customer groups want, and of organizing all the company's resources to satisfy those wants at a profit.

Nonetheless, given the definition of marketing supplied earlier, Figure 1.1 is repeated here (as Figure 1.5) as a diagram of this definition, which we shall return to later.

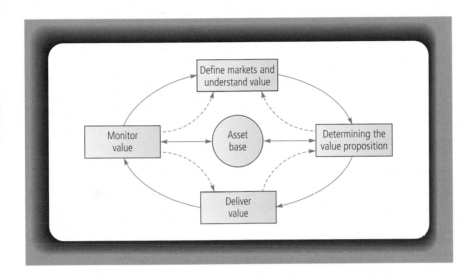

Figure 1.5

■ Application questions

1 Describe as best you can what you think marketing means in your company.
2 Describe the role of your marketing department, if you have one.
3 If you do not have a marketing department, describe how decisions are made in respect of the following:
   ● the product itself
   ● price
   ● customer service levels
   ● physical distribution
   ● advertising sales promotion
   ● the sales force
   ● information about markets.
4 How do you distinguish between marketing, promotion and selling in your organization?
5 Would you say your products are what the market wants, or what you prefer to produce?
6 Do you start your planning process with a sales forecast and then work out a budget, or do you start by setting marketing objectives which are based on a thorough review of the previous year's performance? If the former, describe why you think this is better than the latter.

Chapter 1 review

The marketing concept

Providing goods or services for which there is a known customer demand, as opposed to selling what the company likes to produce. By focusing on customers and their wants the company is better positioned to make a profit. The company is then said to be market-led, or to have a 'market orientation'.

The marketing function

There are many definitions of marketing and much confusion about what it is. The following definition should clarify this for readers:

Marketing is a process for:

- defining markets
- quantifying the needs of the customer groups (segments) within these markets
- determining the value propositions to meet these needs
- communicating these value propositions to all those people in the organization responsible for delivering them, and getting their buy-in to their role
- playing an appropriate part in delivering these value propositions (usually only communications)
- monitoring the value actually delivered.

For this process to be effective, organizations need to be consumer–customer-driven.

This definition is represented as a 'map' in Figure 1.1, repeated here as Figure 1.6.

Starting at the top and moving clockwise, it should be pointed out that the first two boxes are concerned with *strategies* for markets, whereas the bottom box and the box on the left are concerned with implementing the strategies, once formulated. The fundamental difference between strategies and tactics will be expanded on in Chapter 2.   *Try Exercise 1.1*

Figure 1.6

Company capabilities

The company will not be equally good at all things. It will have strengths and weaknesses. The astute company tries to identify customer wants that best match its own strengths, be they its product range, relations with customers, technical expertise, flexibility, or whatever. Inevitably there is an element of compromise in the matching process, but successful companies strive to build on their strengths and reduce their weaknesses.   *Try Exercise 1.2*

The marketing environment

No business operates in a vacuum; it has an environment which not only contains all its existing and potential customers and its competitors, but also many factors outside its control. Changes in the environment in terms of

- customer wants
- fashions
- technology
- environmental concerns
- legislation
- economic climate
- competition, etc.

present the company with both opportunities and threats. Keeping a finger on the pulse of the environment is essential for the successful company.   *Try Exercise 1.3*

Questions raised for the company

1 Q: Is it different marketing a product or a service?
   A: The central ideas of marketing are universal.
2 Q: What do customers want?
   A: They don't always know, but dialogue with them and intelligent research can help to answer this question.
3 Q: Do we need to bother with marketing?
   A: Some companies are very successful by chance. They happen to be in the right place at the right time. Most other companies need to plan their marketing.
                                                                              Try Exercise 1.4
4 Q: Do we need a marketing department?
   A: Not necessarily. It will depend upon the size and complexity of the company's range of products and services. The higher the complexity, the more difficult it is to coordinate activities and achieve the 'matching' of a company to its customers.

EXERCISES

Introduction to Chapter 1 exercises

The exercises are intended to give you an opportunity to explore ways of looking at marketing. Exercise 1.1 enables you to make an assessment of your own beliefs about marketing; the remaining exercises can be applied to your organization.

Exercise 1.1
Marketing orientation

Below are a number of definitions of marketing that have appeared in books and journals over the last twenty or so years. Read through them carefully and note on a piece of paper the numbers of those which most accurately reflect your own views.

   While there is no upper limit to the number of definitions you can choose, try, if you can, to limit your choice to a maximum of nine or ten definitions.

1   'The planning and execution of all aspects and activities of a product so as to exert optimum influence on the consumer, to result in maximum consumption at the optimum price and thereby producing the maximum long-term profit.'

2   'Deciding what the customer wants; arranging to make it; distributing and selling it at a profit.'

3   'Marketing perceives consumption as a democratic process in which consumers have the right to select preferred candidates. They elect them by casting their money votes to those who supply the goods or services that satisfy their needs.'

4   'The planning, executing and evaluating of the external factors related to a company's profit objectives.'

5   'Adjusting the whole activity of a business to the needs of the customer or potential customer.'

6   '. . . marketing is concerned with the idea of satisfying the needs of customers by means of the product and a whole cluster of things associated with creating, delivering and, finally, consuming it.'

7   'The total system of interacting business activities designed to plan, price, promote and distribute products and services to present and potential customers.'

8   '{Marketing is} the world of business seen from the point of view of its final result, that is from the customer's viewpoint. Concern and responsibility for marketing must therefore permeate all areas of the enterprise.'

9   'The activity that can keep in constant touch with an organization's consumers, read their needs and build a programme of communications to express the organization's purposes.'

10   'The management function which organizes and directs all those business activities involved in assessing and converting customer purchasing power into effective demand for a specific product or service and moving the product or service to the final customer or user so as to achieve the profit target or other objectives set by the company.'

11   'The marketing concept emphasizes the vital importance to effective corporate planning and control, of monitoring both the environment in which the offering is made and the needs of the customers, in order that the process may operate as effectively as is humanly possible.'

12   'The organization and performance of those business activities that facilitate the exchange of goods and services between maker and user.'

13   'The process of: (1) Identifying customer needs, (2) Conceptualizing these needs in terms of the organization's capacity to produce, (3) Communicating

that conceptualization to the appropriate locus of power in the organization, (4) Conceptualizing the consequent output in terms of the customer
needs earlier identified, (5) Communicating that conceptualization to the
customer.'

14 '{In a marketing company} all activities – from finance to production to
marketing – should be geared to profitable consumer satisfaction.'
15 'The performance of those business activities that direct the flow of goods
from producer to consumer or user.'
16 'The skill of selecting and fulfilling consumer wants so as to maximize the
profitability per unit of capital employed in the enterprise.'
17 'The economic process by means of which goods and services are
exchanged and their values determined in terms of money prices.'
18 'The performance of business activities that direct the flow of goods and
services from producer to consumer in order to accomplish the firm's
objectives.'
19 'Marketing is concerned with preventing the accumulation of non-moving
stocks.'
20 'The process of understanding markets and the present and future value
required by the different groups within these markets, of communicating
it to all customer-impacting functions within the organization and of
measuring the value actually delivered.'

Scoring for Exercise 1.1

You should have selected a number of definitions that you identify with. To
work out your score, tick the boxes in the table below which equate to your
chosen statements. Now add the number of ticks in each group and enter the
total in the boxes at the end of each row.

For example, if you selected definitions 1, 3, 5, 6, 10 and 14, then 1 and 10
would score a total of 2 in Group A, and 3, 5, 6 and 14 would score a total of
4 in Group B.

Group A	1	2	4	7	10	12	15	17	18	19	
Group B	3	5	6	8	9	11	13	14	16	20	

Interpretation of Exercise 1.1

If you study the various definitions, you will find that the essential difference
between those in Group A and those in Group B is that *Group B definitions
make an unambiguous reference about identifying and satisfying customer
needs and building systems around this principle*. This is generally accepted as
true marketing orientation, and is the stance taken throughout this book
about marketing.

Group A definitions tend to focus far less on the customer (unless it is to
decide what customers want, or to *exert influence* on the customer – i.e. to do
things to the customer) and more on the company's own systems and profit
motives. Thus Group A definitions could be described as being more traditional views about managing a business. Therefore the more Group B and the
fewer Group A answers you have, then the higher your marketing orientation
and the less at odds you should be with the ideas put forward in this book.

Please note that this is your personal orientation towards marketing, and
nothing to do with your company.

Exercise 1.2

Company capabilities and the matching process

1 Reflect on your company's recent history, say the last five years. Over that period, what would you say have been the key strengths that have carried the company to its present position?

   (a) Make a list of these below. *Note*: In a small company, among the strengths might be listed key people. Where this happens, expand on what the person actually brings to the organization, e.g. sales director – his/her contacts in the industry.

     (i) _____

     (ii) _____

     (iii) _____

   (b) What would you say are the three main weaknesses at present?

     (i) _____

     (ii) _____

     (iii) _____

2 Again, considering the last five-year period, has the company got better at matching its strengths to customers and to its business environment, or worse? Often there are both positive and negative forces at work.

   (a) Make a note of the factors which led to improvements, in the space below.

   (b) Make a note of the factors which led to a deterioration, in the space below.

At this stage you do not need to draw any specific conclusions from this exercise, although you will probably find it useful to return to this information as you progress through the book.

Exercise 1.3

The marketing environment

You will be asked to consider the marketing environment in more detail later. For now, think back over the last five years of the company's history and answer these questions:

1 Which were the three most significant *opportunities* in the environment which contributed to the company's success/present situation?

   (a) _____ ( )

   (b) _____ ( )

   (c) _____ ( )

Put a score against each factor listed, in the brackets, using a 1–10 scale (where 10 is extremely significant).

2 Which were the three most significant *threats* which operated against the company over this period and which inhibited its success?

   (a) _____ ( )

   (b) _____ ( )

   (c) _____ ( )

Again, score these threats on a 1–10 scale as above.

3 Reflect on what you have written above and consider whether or not these opportunities and threats are increasing or decreasing in significance, or if new ones are on the horizon. Make notes below, looking ahead for, say, the next three years.

Opportunities → _____

Threats   → _____

Again, at this stage, you do not need to draw any specific conclusions from this exercise, although you will probably find it useful to return to this information as you progress through the book.

Place a tick after each statement in the column which most accurately describes your company situation.

Exercise 1.4
Marketing quiz[4]

	Very true	True	Don't know	Untrue	Very untrue
1 (a) Our return on invested capital is satisfactory					
(b) There is good evidence it will stay that way for the next five years					
(c) Detailed analysis indicates that it is probably incapable of being materially improved					
2 (a) Our market share is not declining					
(b) This is a fact, based on objective evidence					
(c) There is objective evidence that it will stay that way					
3 (a) Our turnover is increasing					
(b) At a rate faster than inflation					
(c) But not at the expense of profitability					
4 I know for sure that our sales organization is only allowed to push less profitable lines at the expense of more profitable ones if there are rational reasons for doing so					
5 (a) I understand why the company has performed the way it has during the past five years					
(b) I know (apart from hoping) where it is heading during the next five years					

[4] Adapted by Professor Malcolm McDonald from a questionnaire devised by Harry Henry Associates in 1971.

	Very true	True	Don't know	Untrue	Very untrue
6 (a) I am wholly satisfied that we make what the market wants, not what we prefer to produce					
(b) Our functional strategies (such as production, finance, IT, HR, operations, R and D, etc.) are based on a clear understanding of the required customer value, rather than for self-serving functional reasons					
(c) I am satisfied that we do not use short-term tactics which are injurious to our long-term interests					
7 (a) I know that sales and profit forecasts presented by operating management are realistic					
(b) I know they are as exacting as they can reasonably be					
(c) If anyone insists that they are raised, it is because a higher level is attainable not just because a better-looking budget is required					
8 (a) The detailed data generated internally are analysed to provide timely information about what is happening in the key areas of the business					
(b) Marketing research data which operating management acquires is synthesized into plain English and is actually needed and used in the key decision-making process					
9 (a) We do not sell unprofitably to any customer					
(b) We analyse our figures to be sure of this					
(c) If we do, it is for rational reasons known to us all					
10 Our marketing policies are based on market-centred opportunities which we have fully researched, not on vague hopes of doing better					

Join up the ticks down the page and count how many are to the left of the *don't know* position, and how many are at the *Don't know* position or to the right of it.

Interpretation of Exercise 1.4
If you have 11 or more answers in the *Don't know* position or to the right of it, then the chances are that your company isn't very marketing orientated. It needs to take a closer look at itself in the ways suggested by this book.

Scores between 12 and 20 to the left of the *Don't know* position indicate an organization that appears to have reasonable control of many of the significant ingredients of commercial success. Nonetheless, there is clearly still room for improvement, and this book should be useful in bringing about such an improvement.

Scores above 20 to the left of the *Don't know* position indicate an organization completely in command of the key success variables. Are you *certain* that this is a true reflection of your organization's situation? If you are, then the chances are that its marketing skills are already highly developed. However, this book will still be useful for newcomers to the marketing function who wish to learn about the marketing process, and it will certainly help to maintain your high standards.

CHAPTER 2

The marketing planning process: 1 The main steps

Summary

- What marketing planning is
- Why it is essential
- The difference and the connection between a strategic and a tactical marketing plan
- Budgets and associated problems
- The marketing planning process
- What a marketing audit is
- Why marketing audits are essential
- Their place in organizational planning
- Who should carry out marketing audits
- What should be done with the audit results
- What the relationship is between strategic marketing planning and corporate planning
- Positioning marketing planning within marketing
- What the key components of the strategic marketing plan are
- How strategic marketing plans should be used
- What the link is to the budget
- Exercises to turn the theory into actionable propositions

■ Introduction

Although marketing planning would appear to be a simple, step-by-step process, in reality it is a multifaceted, complex, cross-functional activity that touches every aspect of organizational life. This chapter explains and explores some of these pan-company issues by focusing on the process of marketing planning. It is not an attempt to suggest that the model outlined here is the only one that can be implemented. Indeed, other models are discussed. However, the one we select to concentrate on is the one most widely used and accepted by both academics and practitioners.

■ What is marketing planning?

Any manager will readily agree that a sensible way to manage the sales and marketing function is to find a systematic way of identifying a range of options, to choose one or more of them, then to schedule and cost out what has to be done to achieve the objectives.

> This process can be defined as *marketing planning*, which is the planned application of marketing resources to achieve marketing objectives.

Marketing planning, then, is simply a logical sequence and a series of activities leading to the setting of marketing objectives and the formulation of plans for achieving them. Companies generally go through some kind of management process in developing marketing plans. In small, undiversified companies, this process is usually informal. In larger, more diversified organizations, the process is often systematized. Conceptually this process is very simple, and involves a situation review, the formulation of some basic assumptions, setting objectives for what is being sold and to whom, deciding on how the objectives are to be achieved, and scheduling and costing out the actions necessary for implementation.

> The problem is that, while as a process it is intellectually simple to understand, in practice it is the most difficult of all marketing tasks.

The reason is that it involves bringing together into one coherent plan all the elements of marketing, and in order to do this at least some degree of institutionalized procedures is necessary. It is this which seems to cause so much difficulty for companies.

Another difficulty concerns the cultural, organizational and political problems that surround the process itself. This will be dealt with in Chapter 3.

▶ **DEFINITION** ◀

Revenue is the monetary value received by a company for its goods or services. It is the net price received, i.e. the price less any discounts

▶ **DEFINITION** ◀

Profit cannot be simply defined, as different organizations define it in different ways and use different terminology. It can, for example, be trading profit, return on sales, return on investment, shareholder value added (SVA) and many other measures. In this book the term is used as a measure of shareholder satisfaction with the financial return made by a commercial organization in which they have an interest

▶ **DEFINITION** ◀

Costs are charges incurred in running an enterprise. They can take many forms including overhead, direct, indirect, attributable, avoidable and others. In this book the type of costs will be defined when the term is used

■ Why is marketing planning essential?

There can be little doubt that marketing planning is essential when we consider the increasingly hostile and complex environment in which companies operate. Hundreds of external and internal factors interact in a bafflingly complex way to affect our ability to achieve profitable sales. Also, let us consider for a moment the four typical objectives which companies set: maximizing ▶ **revenue**; maximizing ▶ **profits**; maximizing return on investment; and minimizing ▶ **costs**. Each one of these has its own special appeal to different managers within the company, depending on the nature of their particular function. In reality, the best that can ever be achieved is a kind of 'optimum compromise', because each of these objectives could be considered to be in conflict in terms of equivalences.

> Managers of a company have to have some understanding or view about how all these variables interact, and managers must try to be rational about their business decisions, no matter how important intuition, feel and experience are as contributory factors in this process of rationality.

Most managers accept that some kind of formalized procedure for marketing planning helps sharpen this rationality so as to reduce the complexity of business operations and add a dimension of realism to the company's hopes for the future. Because it is so difficult, however, most companies rely only on sales forecasting and budgeting systems. It is a well-known fact that any fool can write figures down! All too frequently, however, they bear little relationship to the real opportunities and problems facing a company. It is far more difficult to write down marketing objectives and strategies that relate to known opportunities in the market. Take the hypothetical example, shown in Figure 2.1.

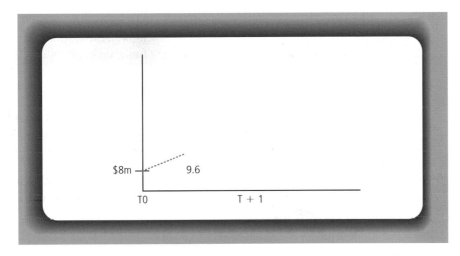

Figure 2.1

From Figure 2.1 it can be seen that in the current year this company achieved a 15 per cent increase in sales revenue over the previous year. But, being optimistic, the chief marketing officer set a so-called 'stretch' target of plus 20 per cent for next year, giving a target of 9.6 million which, if achieved, would satisfy the budget holder.

However, consider for a moment a different and more professional way of setting an objective for next year. If the market addressed were a growing market, a strategic objective might be 'to be market leader in three years' time'. In order to achieve such an objective, the chief marketing officer would need an assessment of market size in three years' time – say 100 million. Market leadership in this particular market would be, say, 25 per cent. So, representing this in Figure 2.2 and extrapolating *backwards* from this target would give a target of 15 million next year and not the backwards looking historical target of 20 per cent (9.6 million).

Were the target to be set at 15 million as opposed to 9.6 million, everything the company planned to do for the following year in order to achieve 15 million as opposed to 9.6 million would be different, including R&D, Operations, IT, HR, etc.

Also, consider for a moment the possibility that the trend in the previous year (T − 1 to T0) had occurred in a growth market, with little effort on the part of the sales force. In such circumstances, it is not uncommon to find

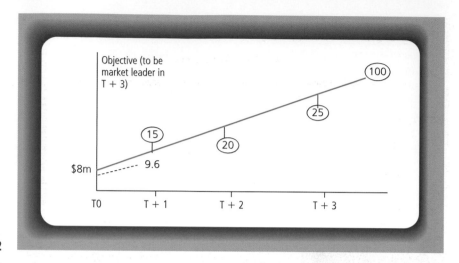

Figure 2.2

complacent sales forces selling the products that are easiest to sell to those customers who treat them most nicely, with the resultant sales going into the company's database. Also, it is not uncommon to find senior managers setting challenging targets, such as a reduction in working capital, which often find their way down to logistics managers. Such managers, in a desperate attempt to achieve their reduced inventory goal, may well find themselves having to turn away legitimate demand in order to achieve their budget target. The result is, of course, the company's *database*, and in such a system, it is clear that to use it as a basis for forecasting is tantamount to extrapolating its own inefficiencies and has little to do with market reality.

Here, it is worth pointing out why forecasts and budgets can never be a substitute for the kind of planning which is the subject of this book:

> The information appearing in the majority of boardrooms remains predominantly financial in nature. Without (additional) information on value-creating activities management are typically flying blind – when financials tell them there is a problem management have already missed the optimal point for taking appropriate corrective action.
>
> (*Transparency in Corporate Reporting*, Pricewaterhouse Coopers' Value Reporting Review 2003, p. 25)

Figure 2.3 shows that, whilst share prices rose for a number of years, underlying customer service and perceived value for money declined until eventually the shares, together with company confidence, collapsed. For a number of years, this retailer has been struggling to recover.

Table 2.1 shows a real company (whose identity has been disguised) which appears to be doing extremely well financially. Again, it is important to stress that this is the kind of financial information typically discussed at board meetings, most of which is based on forecasts and budgets.

A glance at Table 2.2, however, shows that on every market-based dimension the company is losing ground dramatically and it is likely to suffer serious consequences the moment the market stops growing.

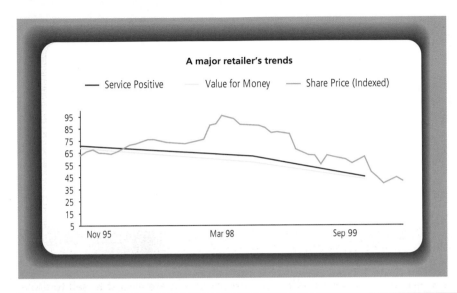

Figure 2.3
A major retailer's trends

Table 2.1 InterTech's five-year performance

Performance (£million)	Base year	1	2	3	4	5
Sales revenue	254	293	318	387	431	454
■ Cost of goods sold	135	152	167	201	224	236
Gross contribution	119	141	151	186	207	218
■ Manufacturing overhead	48	58	63	82	90	95
■ Marketing & sales	18	23	24	26	27	28
■ Research and development	22	23	23	25	24	24
Net profit	16	22	26	37	50	55
Return on sales (%)	6.3	7.5	8.2	9.6	11.6	12.1
Assets	141	162	167	194	205	206
Assets (% of sales)	56	55	53	50	48	45
Return on assets (%)	11.3	13.5	15.6	19.1	24.2	26.7

Table 2.2 InterTech's five-year market-based performance

Performance	Base year	1	2	3	4	5
Market growth (%)	18.3	23.4	17.6	34.4	24.0	17.9
InterTech sales growth (%)	12.8	17.4	11.2	27.1	16.5	10.9
Market share (%)	20.3	19.1	18.4	17.1	16.3	14.9
Customer retention (%)	88.2	87.1	85.0	82.2	80.9	80.0
New customers (%)	11.7	12.9	14.9	24.1	22.5	29.2
Dissatisfied customers (%)	13.6	14.3	16.1	17.3	18.9	19.6
Relative product quality (%)	+10	+8	+5	+3	+1	+0
Relative service quality (%)	+0	+0	−20	−3	−5	−8
Relative new product sales (%)	+8	+8	+7	+5	+1	−4

Here are some recent quotations from well-known sources:

Improvements in a short-term financial measure such as economic profit can be achieved through postponing capital investments, reducing marketing and training expenditures, or by divesting assets, each of which may have a positive effect on near-term performance but could adversely affect long-term value creation performance. Nevertheless, when incentivized with bonuses to 'manage for the measure' this is exactly what many managers will do irrespective of the consequences on shareholder value.

(Why Value Based Management Goes Wrong, Simon Court, Market Leader, 2002)

- 90% of USA and European firms think budgets are cumbersome and unreliable, providing neither predictability nor control.
- They are backward-looking and inflexible. Instead of focusing managers' time on the customers, the real source of income, they focus their attention on satisfying the boss, i.e. the budget becomes the purpose.
- Cheating is endemic in all budget regimes. The result is fear, inefficiency, suboptimization and waste.
- In companies like Enron, the pressure to make the numbers was so great that managers didn't just doctor a few numbers, they *broke the law*.
- People with targets and jobs dependent on meeting them will probably meet the targets, even if they have to destroy the enterprise to do it.

(S. Caulkin (2005) 'Escape from the budget straitjacket', *Management Today*, January, pp. 47–49)

Finally, on budgets, a major bank has been criticized for its contribution to personal debt of £1 trillion in the UK:

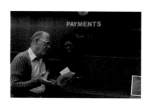

Employees are set tough targets for selling loans and double their low salaries, which encourages customer abuse and leaves many borrowers facing ruin.

    Banks are no longer there to help customers find the most suitable solution.

('We have a target-driven culture that staff must hit targets', A Major Bank, 10 May 2005)

Apart from the need to cope with increasing turbulence, environmental complexity, more intense competitive pressures, and the sheer speed of technological change, a marketing plan is useful:

- for *the marketer*
- for *superiors*
- for *non-marketing functions*
- for *subordinates*
- to help identify sources of competitive advantage
- to force an organized approach
- to develop specificity
- to ensure consistent relationships
- to inform

- to get resources
- to get support
- to gain commitment
- to set objectives and strategies.

Finally, there are some other pragmatic, profit-related reasons for needing to prepare a strategic marketing plan.

All organizations have a mix of different types of market. Figure 2.4 shows a version of Michael Porter's generic strategies matrix (M.E. Porter, *Competitive Strategy*, Free Press, New York, 1980).

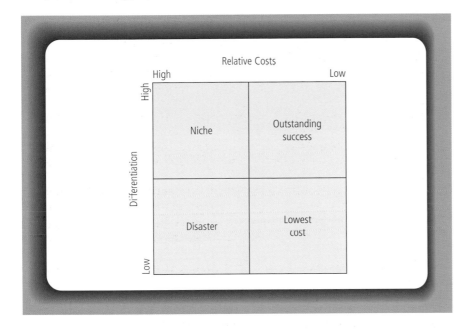

Figure 2.4

The matrix shows that some markets are inherently more prone to lack of differentiation in products and services. It is obvious that products such as flat glass, chlorine, car insurance policies and the like are harder to differentiate than, say, perfume, beer, clothes and so on. In such cases the attainment of low costs must be a corporate goal, otherwise lack of adequate margins may result. Equally, if an organization's products or services are substantially different from another's, costs are rarely the principal driving force.

In reality, in their different ways, most organizations have a mix of products or services that could be classified in all four boxes. All organizations have some 'disaster' products, some 'lowest cost' products, some 'niche' products and some 'outstanding success' products.

For example, Canada Dry used to have to sell 'pop' products, such as large bottles of lemonade, in order to have a full line of soft drinks, even though they made their profits on 'mixer' drinks such as tonic water and ginger ale. It was a requirement to have a full line in order to be a serious player in the market.

MARKETING INSIGHT

Likewise, whilst it is tempting for accountants to want to delete products like this, it is essential to understand the role they play in making profits. Consequently, it is the role of the strategic marketing plan to spell out at least three years in advance what the mix will be between products and services in each of the four boxes in Figure 2.4.

Also, all organizations have products and services that produce different levels of sales and profit margins. Figure 2.5 shows the make-up of RONA, and it is clear from this that profit occurs because of a mix of different margin products and different levels of turnover for each of these products. It is the purpose of the marketing plan to spell out at least three years in advance what the desired mix is of low margin/high turnover, high margin/high turnover products and all variations in between. It isn't enough just to do the accounts at the end of the fiscal year and hope the right net profit occurs. How the plan should do this is explained clearly in Chapter 6.

Figure 2.5

■ Are we talking about a tactical or a strategic marketing plan?

The author's own research has shown that, in peering into the murky depths of organizational behaviour in relation to marketing planning, confusion reigns supreme – and nowhere more than over the terminology of marketing.

> Few practising marketers understand the real significance of a ▶ **strategic** marketing plan as opposed to a ▶ **tactical**, or operational marketing plan.

Why should this be so? For an answer, we need to look at some of the changes that have taken place during the past three decades. For example, the simple environment of the 1970s and early 1980s, characterized by growth and the easy marketability of products and services, has now been replaced by an increasingly complex and abrasive environment, often made worse by static or declining markets. For most, the days have gone when it was only necessary to ride the tidal wave of growth. There wasn't the same need for a disciplined, systematic approach to the market. A tactical, short-term approach to marketing planning seemed to work perfectly well in such conditions. But, by failing to grasp the nettle of strategic orientation in plans that identify and develop their distinctive competence, companies became casualties in the 1990s and will increasingly become so in the first decade of the twenty-first century (evidence of this will be provided in Chapter 3).

The problem is really quite simple.

> Most managers prefer to sell the products they find easiest to sell to those customers who offer the least line of resistance. By developing short-term, tactical marketing plans first and then extrapolating them, managers merely succeed in extrapolating their own shortcomings, as was illustrated in Figures 2.1 and 2.2.

It is a bit like steering from the wake – all right in calm, clear waters, but not so sensible in busy and choppy waters! Preoccupation with preparing a detailed one-year plan first is typical of those many companies who confuse sales forecasting and budgeting with strategic marketing planning – in our experience, the most common mistake of all.

It is interesting to note that, of Tom Peters' original 43 so-called 'excellent companies in 1982', very few would be classed as excellent today, whilst many have disappeared altogether because of a fixation with excellent tactics at the expense of strategy.

Richard T. Pascale, *Managing on the Edge*, Simon and Schuster, 1990

MARKETING INSIGHT

This brings us to the starting point in marketing planning – an understanding of the difference between strategy and tactics and the association with the relevant adjectives, 'effective' and 'efficient'. This point is expanded on in Figure 2.6, which shows a matrix in which the horizontal axis represents strategy as a continuum from ineffective to effective. The vertical axis represents tactics on a continuum from inefficient to efficient. Those firms with an effective strategy (Box 1) continue to thrive. Those with an effective strategy but inefficient tactics (Box 2) have merely survived. Those firms to the left of the matrix are destined to die, as too much emphasis is placed on tactics, so avoiding the underlying strategic issues surrounding changing market needs. Any organization doing the wrong things more efficiently (Box 3) is destined to die more quickly than their less efficient counterparts. It is a bit like making a stupid manager work harder, thus doubling the chaos and probably offending twice as many customers!

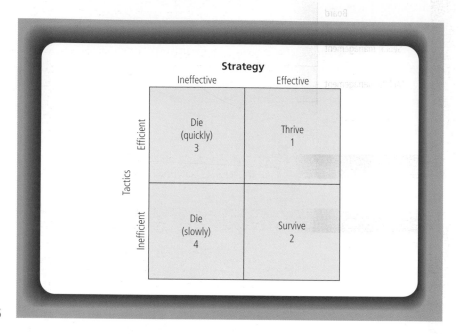

Figure 2.6

Already, companies led by chief executives with a proactive orientation that stretches beyond the end of the current fiscal year have begun to show results visibly better than the old reactive companies with only a short-term vision.

> One Scandinavian capital goods manufacturer was devoting its energies to stock control, headcount reduction, cash flow and the like. The problem, however, was one of falling demand. Had it not been pointed out to the Board that this underlying marketing issue had to be addressed, it is easy to imagine how *anorexia industrialosa* could have resulted (an excessive desire to be leaner and fitter, leading to emaciation and, eventually, death).

Figure 2.7 shows the old style of company in which very little attention is paid to strategy by any level of management. It will be seen that lower levels of management do not get involved at all, while the directors spend most of their time on operational/tactical issues.

Figure 2.8 is a representation of those companies that recognize the importance of strategy and who manage to involve all levels of management in strategy formulation.

Figure 2.7

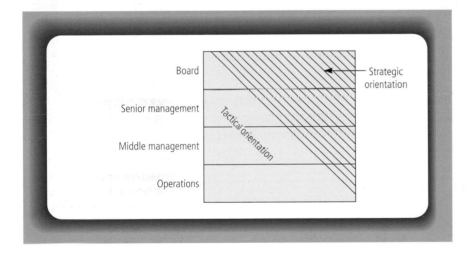

Figure 2.8

The rule, then, is simple:

- Develop the *strategic* marketing plan first. This entails greater emphasis on scanning the external environment, the early identification of forces emanating from it, and developing appropriate strategic responses, involving all levels of management in the process.
- A strategic plan should cover a period of between three and five years, and only when this has been developed and agreed should the one-year operational marketing plan be developed. Never write the one-year plan first and extrapolate it.

> The emphasis throughout this book is on the preparation of a *strategic* marketing plan. The format for an operational or tactical plan is exactly the same, except for the amount of detail. This will be dealt with in Chapter 13.

■ The effectiveness of marketing planning

Research into the efficacy of formalized marketing planning[1] has shown that marketing planning can make a significant contribution to commercial success. The main effects within organizations are:

- the systematic identification of emerging opportunities and threats
- preparedness to meet change
- the specification of sustainable competitive advantage
- improved communication among executives
- reduction of conflicts between individuals and departments
- the involvement of all levels of management in the planning process
- more appropriate allocation of scarce resources
- consistency of approach across the organization
- a more market-focused orientation across the organization.

However, although it can bring many benefits, a strategic marketing plan is mainly concerned with competitive advantage – that is to say, establishing, building, defending and maintaining it.

In order to be realistic, it must take into account the organization's existing competitive position, where it wants to be in the future, its capabilities and the competitive environment it faces. This means that the marketing planner must learn to use the various available processes and techniques which help to make sense of external trends, and to understand the organization's traditional ways of responding to these.

However, this poses the problem regarding which are the most relevant and useful tools and techniques, for each has strengths and weaknesses, and no individual concept or technique can satisfactorily describe and illuminate the whole picture. As with a jigsaw puzzle, a sense of unity only emerges as the various pieces are connected together.

The links between strategy and performance (referred to in Chapter 1) have been the subject of detailed statistical analysis by the Strategic Planning Institute. The PIMS (Profit Impact of Market Strategy) project identified, from 2600 businesses, six major links (Buzzell and Gale, 1987[2]).

---

[1] S. Thompson (1962) *How Companies Plan*, AMA Research Study No. 54, Chicago; D.S.R. Leighton (1966) *International Marketing Text and Cases*, McGraw Hill, New York; D.J. Kollatt, R.D. Blackwell and J.F. Robeson (1972) *Strategic Marketing*, Hold, Rinehart and Winston, New York; H.I. Ansoff (1977) 'The state and practice of planning systems', *Sloan Management Review*, 18(20), 1–24; G. Greenley (1984) 'An exposition into empirical research into marketing planning', *Journal of Marketing Management*, 3(1), 83–102; M. McDonald (1982) 'The Theory and Practice of Marketing Planning for Industrial Goods in Internal Markets', PhD thesis, Cranfield Institute of Technology; N.F. Piercy (2000) *Market-led Strategic Change – Transforming the Process of Going to Market*, 3rd edn, Butterworth-Heinemann, Oxford; B.D. Smith (2003) 'The Effectiveness of Marketing Strategy Making in Medical Markets', PhD thesis, Cranfield University School of Management.

[2] R.D. Buzzell and B.T. Gale (1987) *The PIMS Principles: Linking Strategy to Performance*, Free Press, New York.

From this analysis, principles have been derived for the selection of different strategies according to industry type, market conditions and the competitive position of the company.

However, not all observers are prepared to take these conclusions at face value. Like strategy consultants Lubatkin and Pitts (1985)[3], who believe that all businesses are unique, they are suspicious that something as critical as competitive advantage can be the outcome of a few specific formulae. For them, the PIMS perspective is too mechanistic and glosses over the complex managerial and organizational problems which beset most businesses.

What is agreed, however, is that strategic marketing planning presents a useful process by which an organization formulates its strategies, *providing it is adapted* to the organization and its environment.

■ How marketing planning fits in with corporate planning and other functions

First of all, it is necessary to position marketing planning firmly within the context of strategic planning generally. Strategic decisions are concerned with:

- the long-term direction of the organization, as opposed to day-to-day management issues
- defining the scope of the organization's activities in terms of what it will and will not do
- matching the activities of the organization to the environment in which it operates, so that it optimizes opportunities and minimizes threats
- matching the organization's activities to its resource capacity, be it finance, manpower, technology or skill levels.

Strategic management is characteristically dealing with an uncertain future and new initiatives. As a result of this, it is often the harbinger of change. Organizations build their business strategies in a number of different ways.

There are six accepted strategy-forming models:

1 *A Planning Model.* Strategic decisions are reached by use of a sequential, planned search for optimum solutions to defined problems. This process is highly rational and is fuelled by concrete data.

---

[3] M. Lubatkin and M. Pitts (1985) 'The PIMS and the policy perspective: a rebuttal', *Journal of Business Strategy*, Summer, 85–92.

2 *An Interpretative Model.* The organization is regarded as a collection of associations, sharing similar values, beliefs and perceptions. These 'frames of reference' enable the stakeholders to interpret the organization and the environment in which it operates, cultivating the emergence of an organizational culture particular to that company. Strategy thus becomes the product, not of defined aims and objectives, but of the prevailing values, attitudes and ideas in the organization.

3 *A Political Model.* Strategy is not chosen directly, but emerges through compromise, conflict and consensus-seeking among interested stakeholders. Since the strategy is the outcome of negotiation, bargaining and confrontation, those with the most power have the greatest influence.

4 *A Logical Incremental Model.* Strategies emerge from 'strategic sub-systems', each concerned with a different type of strategic issue. Strategic goals are based on an awareness of needs, rather than the highly structured analytical process of the planning model. Often, due to a lack of necessary information, such goals can be vague, general and non-rigid in nature until such a time when events unfold and more information becomes known.

5 *An Ecological Model.* In this perspective, the environment impinges on the organization in such a way that strategies are virtually prescribed and there is little or no free choice. In this model, the organization which adapts most successfully to its environment will survive in a way which mirrors Darwin's theory of natural selection.

6 *A Visionary Leadership Model.* Strategy emerges as the result of the leader's vision, enforced by their commitment to it, their personal credibility, and how they articulate it to others.

(Based on research by A. Bailey and J. Johnson,
Cranfield University School of Management)

It is unlikely that an organization will use a pure version of any of these models. In all probability, its strategic decision-making model will be a hybrid of some of them. However, it is possible that one or two of these will predominate and thereby give strategic decision-making a distinct 'flavour'.

Whilst academics cannot seem to agree on a single, best approach, company executives have to get on with strategy formulation as best they can, using a combination of experience, intuition and hope. One of the earliest PhDs in the domain of marketing planning (the author's) came to the conclusion that the process they go through is some sort of a logical sequence leading to the setting of objectives and the formulation of strategies and tactics for achieving them, together with the associated financial consequences. The formality of this process will be a function of the degree of product/ market complexity, organizational size and the degree of environmental turbulence. In other words, the degree of formality will be driven in part by the dominant decision-making model in the organization.

Strategic marketing planning obviously cannot be discussed in isolation from the above strategic planning models, and it is likely that the way in which an organization's marketing planning is carried out will be a microcosm of the principal mode used by a company for its corporate planning. Whilst marketing planning is based on markets, customers and products, business planning involves other corporate resources, which will have a bearing on the identified markets. Corporate planning usually involves applying business planning to several different units of the business aggregate.

> For the purpose of this book, however, the Planning Model will be used, as elements of this will underpin all marketing planning processes.

Before turning our attention to the steps in the marketing planning process, it would be useful to discuss how marketing planning relates to the corporate planning process.

There are five steps in the corporate planning process. As can be seen from Table 2.3, the starting point is usually a statement of *corporate financial objectives* for the long-range planning period of the company, which are often expressed in terms of turnover, profit before tax, and return on investment.

Table 2.3 Marketing planning and its place in the corporate cycle

Step 1 Corporate financial objectives	2 Management audit	3 Objective and strategy setting	4 Plans	5 Corporate plans
	Marketing audit: Marketing	Marketing objectives, strategies	Marketing plan	
	Distribution audit: Stocks and control; transportation; warehousing	Distribution objectives, strategies	Distribution plan	
Corporate financial objectives	*Operations audit*: Value analysis; engineering development; work study; quality control; labour; materials, plant and space utilization; production planning; factories; R&D; information technology, etc.	Operations objectives, strategies	Operations plan	Issue of corporate plan, to include corporate objectives and strategies; operations objectives and strategies, etc.; long-range profit and loss accounts; balance sheets
	Financial audit: Credit, debt, cash flow and budgetary control; resource allocation; capital expenditure; long-term finance	Financial objectives, strategies	Financial plan	
	Personnel audit: Management, technical and administrative ability, etc.	Personnel objectives, strategies	Personnel plan	

More often than not this long-range planning horizon is five years, although, more recently, three years is becoming increasingly the norm. However, the precise period should be determined by the nature of the markets in which the company operates. For example, five years would not be a long enough period for a glass manufacturer, since it takes that period of time to commission new capital plant, whereas in some fashion industries five years would be too long. A useful guideline in determining the planning horizon is that there should be a market for the company's products for long enough at least to amortize any new capital investment associated with those products.

> Nonetheless, for the purpose of putting in sufficient detail for a strategic plan to be of any practical use, it is advisable to keep the period down to three years if possible, since beyond this period detail of any kind is likely to become pointless. There can certainly be scenarios for five to ten years, but not a plan in the sense intended by this book.

The next step is the *management audit*. This is an obvious activity to follow on with, since a thorough situation review, particularly in the area of marketing, should enable the company to determine whether it will be able to meet the long-range financial targets with its current range of products in its current markets. Any projected gap can be filled by the various methods of product development or market extension.

> Undoubtedly the most important and difficult of all stages in the corporate planning process is the third step, *objective and strategy setting*, since if this is not done properly everything that follows is of little value.

Later on, we will discuss marketing objectives and strategies in more detail. For now, the important point to make is that this is the time in the planning cycle when a compromise has to be reached between what is wanted by the several functional departments and what is practicable, given all the constraints that any company has. For example, it is no good setting a marketing objective of penetrating a new market if the company does not have the production capacity to cope with the new business, and if capital is not available for whatever investment is necessary in additional capacity. At this stage, objectives and strategies will be set for three years, or for whatever the planning horizon is.

Step 4 involves producing detailed *plans* for one year, containing the responsibilities, timing and costs of carrying out the first year's objectives, and broad plans for the following years.

These plans can then be incorporated into the *corporate plan*, which will contain long-range corporate objectives, strategies, plans, profit and loss accounts, and balance sheets.

At this point it is worth noting that one of the main purposes of a corporate plan is to provide a long-term vision of what the company is or is striving to become, taking account of shareholder expectations, environmental trends, resource market trends, consumption market trends, and the distinctive competence of the company as revealed by the management audit.

What this means in practice is that the corporate plan will usually contain at least the following elements:
1　The desired level of profitability
2　Business boundaries
- what kinds of products will be sold to what kinds of markets (marketing)
- what kinds of facilities will be developed (operations, R&D, information systems, distribution, etc.)
- the size and character of the labour force (personnel)
- funding (finance)
3　Other corporate objectives, such as social responsibility, corporate image, stock market image, employer image, etc.

Such a corporate plan, containing projected profit and loss accounts and balance sheets, being the result of the process described above, is more likely to provide long-term stability for a company than plans based on a more intuitive process and containing forecasts which tend to be little more than extrapolations of previous trends. This process is further summarized in Figure 2.9.

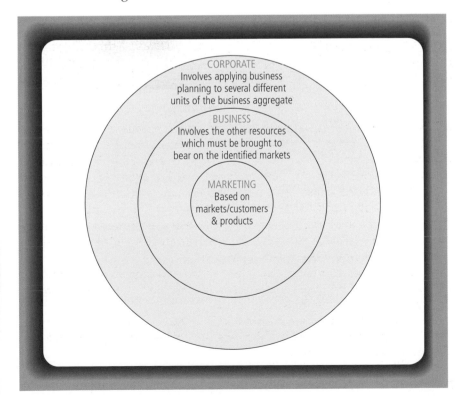

Figure 2.9

> One of the main purposes of a corporate plan is to provide a long-term vision of what the company is or is striving to become.

MARKETING INSIGHT

The headquarters of one major multinational company with a sophisticated budgeting system used to receive 'plans' from all over the world and coordinate them in quantitative and cross-functional terms such as numbers of employees, units of sales, items of plant, square feet of production area, and so on, together with the associated financial implications. The trouble was that the whole complicated edifice was built on the initial sales forecasts, which were themselves little more than a time-consuming numbers game. The really key strategic issues relating to products and markets were lost in all the financial activity, which eventually resulted in grave operational and profitability problems.

Positioning marketing planning within marketing

Smith's PhD thesis (2003) proved a direct link between organizational success and marketing strategies that conforms to what previous scholars have agreed constitutes strategy quality, which was shown to be independent of variables such as size, sector, market conditions and so on.

This thesis linked superior performance to strategies with the following qualities:

1 Homogenous market segment definition
2 Segment-specific propositions
3 Strategy uniqueness
4 Strength leverage and weakness minimization
5 Creation of internal and external synergies
6 Provision of tactical guidance
7 Alignment to objectives
8 Alignment to market trends
9 Appropriate resourcing
10 Clear basis of competition.

Let us first, however, position strategic marketing planning firmly within the context of marketing itself.

As can be deduced from Chapter 1, marketing is a process for:

● defining markets
● quantifying the needs of the customer groups (segments) within these markets
● determining the value propositions to meet these needs
● communicating these value propositions to all those people in the organization responsible for delivering them and getting their buy-in to their role

- playing an appropriate part in delivering these value propositions to the chosen market segments
- monitoring the value actually delivered.

For this process to be effective, we have also seen that organizations need to be consumer/customer-driven.

The map of this process is repeated in Figure 2.10. This process is clearly cyclical, in that monitoring the value delivered will update the organization's understanding of the value that is required by its customers. The cycle is predominantly an annual one, with a marketing plan documenting the output from the 'understand value' and 'determine value proposition' processes; however, equally, changes throughout the year may involve fast iterations around the cycle to respond to particular opportunities or problems.

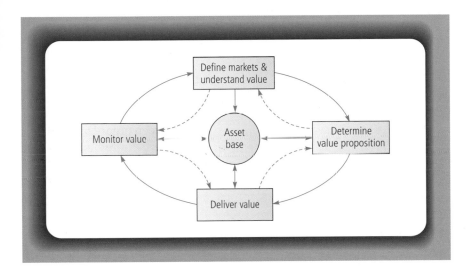

Figure 2.10
Map of the marketing process

It is well known that not all of the value proposition delivering processes will be under the control of the marketing department, whose role varies considerably between organizations.

The marketing department is likely to be responsible for the first two processes, 'Understand value' and 'Determine value proposition', although even these need to involve numerous functions, albeit coordinated by specialist marketing personnel. The 'Deliver value' process is the role of the whole company, including, for example, product development, manufacturing, purchasing, sales promotion, direct mail, distribution, sales, and customer service. The marketing department will also be responsible for monitoring the effectiveness of the value delivered.

The various choices made during this marketing process are constrained and informed not just by the outside world, but also by the organization's asset base. Whereas an efficient new factory with much spare capacity might underpin a growth strategy in a particular market, a factory running at full capacity would cause more reflection on whether price should be used to control demand, unless the potential demand warranted further capital investment. As well as physical assets, choices may be influenced by financial, human resources, brand and information technology assets, to name just a few.

Thus, it can be seen that the first two boxes are concerned with strategic marketing planning processes (in other words, developing market strategies), whilst the third and fourth boxes are concerned with the actual delivery in the market of what was planned and then measuring the effect.

Input to this process will commonly include:

- the corporate mission and objectives, which will determine which particular markets are of interest
- external data such as market research
- internal data which flow from ongoing operations.

Also, it is necessary to define the markets the organization is in, or wishes to be in, and how these divide into segments of customers with similar needs. The importance of doing this correctly was emphasized earlier in the reference to Smith's 2003 PhD. The choice of markets will be influenced by the corporate objectives as well as the asset base. Information will be collected about the markets, such as the market's size and growth, with estimates for the future.

The map is inherently cross-functional. 'Deliver value proposition', for example, involves every aspect of the organization, from new product development through inbound logistics and production to outbound logistics and customer service.

The map represents best practice, not common practice. Many aspects of the map are not explicitly addressed by well-embedded processes, even in sophisticated companies.

Also, the map is changing. One-to-one communications and principles of relationship marketing demand a radically different sales process from that traditionally practised. Hence, exploiting new media such as the Internet requires a substantial shift in thinking, not just changes to IT and hard processes. An example is illuminating. Marketing managers at one company related to us their early experience with a website which was enabling them to reach new customers considerably more cost-effectively than their traditional sales force was able to do. When the website was first launched, potential customers were finding the company on the Web, deciding the products were appropriate on the basis of the website, and sending an e-mail to ask to buy. So far, so good. But stuck in a traditional model of the sales process, the company would allocate the 'lead' to a salesperson, who would phone up and make an appointment perhaps three weeks' hence. The customer would by now probably have moved on to another online supplier who could sell the product today, but those that remained were subjected to a sales pitch which was totally unnecessary, the customer having already decided to buy. Those that were not put off would proceed to be registered as able to buy over the Web, but the company had lost the opportunity to improve its margins by using the sales force more judiciously. In time the company realized its mistake: unlike those prospects which the company identified and contacted, which might indeed need 'selling' to, many new Web customers were initiating the dialogue themselves, and simply required the company to respond effectively and rapidly. The sales force was increasingly freed up to concentrate on major clients and on relationship building.

Having put marketing planning into the context of marketing and other corporate functions, we can now turn specifically to the marketing planning process, how it should be done, and what the barriers are to doing it effectively. We are, of course, referring specifically to the second box in Figure 2.10. See Chapter 4 for more detail on market segmentation.

■ The marketing planning process

Figure 2.11 illustrates the several stages that have to be gone through in order to arrive at a marketing plan. This illustrates the difference between the *process* of marketing planning and the actual plan itself, which is the *output* of the process and is discussed later in this chapter.

Each of the process stages illustrated in Figure 2.11 will be discussed in more detail in this chapter. The dotted lines joining up stages 5–8 are

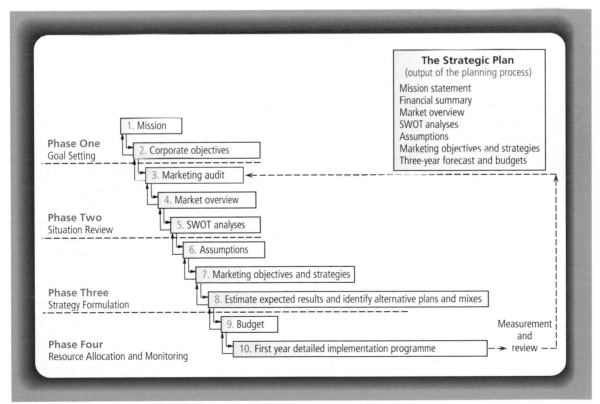

Figure 2.11
The ten steps of the strategic marketing planning process

meant to indicate the reality of the planning process, in that it is likely that each of these steps will have to be gone through more than once before final programmes can be written.

How formal should this process be?

Although research has shown these marketing planning steps to be universally applicable, the degree to which each of the separate steps in the diagram needs to be formalized depends to a large extent on the size and nature of the company. For example, an undiversified company generally uses less formalized procedures, since top management tends to have greater functional knowledge and expertise than subordinates, and because the lack of diversity of operations enables direct control to be exercised over most of the key determinants of success. Thus, situation reviews, the setting of marketing objectives, and so on, are not always made explicit in writing, although these steps have to be gone through.

In contrast, in a diversified company it is usually not possible for top management to have greater functional knowledge and expertise than subordinate management, hence planning tends to be more formalized in order to provide a consistent discipline for those who have to make the decisions throughout the organization.

Either way, there is now a substantial body of evidence to show that formalized planning procedures generally result in greater profitability and stability in the long term and also help to reduce friction and operational difficulties within organizations.

Bailey *et al.*'s (2000)[4] typology of the different styles of planning went some way to throwing light on the actual degree of formalization of marketing planning processes, although Smith's 2003 PhD thesis reduced these to three – visionary processes, rational processes and incremental processes, with most successful companies using some combination of all three.

Where marketing planning has failed, it has generally been because companies have placed too much emphasis on the procedures themselves and the resulting forecasts, rather than on generating information useful to and consumable by management – but more about reasons for failure in Chapter 3. For now, let us look at the marketing planning process in more detail, starting with the mission statement.

Step 1: Mission statement

Figure 2.11 shows that a strategic marketing plan should begin with a mission or purpose statement. This is perhaps the most difficult aspect of marketing planning for managers to master, because it is largely philosophical and qualitative in nature. Many organizations find their different departments, and sometimes even different groups in the same department,

---

[4] A. Bailey, G. Joshua and K. Daniel (2000) 'Validation of a multi-dimensional measure of strategic development process', *British Journal of Marketing*, II(22), 151–162.

pulling in different directions, often with disastrous results, simply because the organization hasn't defined the boundaries of the business and the way it wishes to do business.

Here, we can see two levels of mission. One is a *corporate* mission statement, the other is a lower level, or *purpose* statement. But there is yet another level, as shown in the following summary:

Type 1　'Motherhood' – usually found inside annual reports designed to 'stroke' shareholders; otherwise of no practical use

Type 2　The real thing – a meaningful statement, unique to the organization concerned, which 'impacts' on the behaviour of the executives at all levels

Type 3　This is a 'purpose' statement (or lower level mission statement), and is appropriate at the strategic business unit, departmental or product group level of the organization

The following is an example of a meaningless, vapid, motherhood-type mission statement, which most companies seem to have. They achieve nothing, and it is difficult to understand why these pointless statements are so popular. Employees mock them, and they rarely say anything likely to give direction to the organization. We have entitled this example 'The Generic Mission Statement' and such statements are to be avoided.

THE GENERIC MISSION STATEMENT

Our organization's primary mission is to protect and increase the value of its owners' investments while efficiently and fairly serving the needs of its customers. [. . . insert organization name . . .] seeks to accomplish this in a manner that contributes to the development and growth of its employees, and to the goals of countries and communities in which it operates.

The following should appear in a mission or purpose statement, which should normally run to no more than one page:

1　*Role or contribution*
   - profit (specify), or
   - service, or
   - opportunity seeker.
2　*Business definition* – define the business, preferably in terms of the *benefits* you provide or the *needs* you satisfy, rather than in terms of what you make.
3　*Distinctive competences* – these are the essential skills/capabilities resources that underpin whatever success has been achieved to date. Competence can consist of one particular item or the possession of a number of skills compared with competitors. If, however, you could

equally well put a competitor's name to these distinctive competences, then they are not distinctive competences.

4 *Indications for the future*
- what the firm *will* do
- what the firm *might* do
- what the firm will *never* do.

Step 2: Setting corporate objectives

What corporate objectives are, and where they fit in the total process, was discussed in the previous section.

Step 3: The marketing audit

Any plan will only be as good as the information on which it is based, and the marketing audit is the means by which information for planning is organized. There is no reason why marketing cannot be audited in the same way as accounts, in spite of its more innovative, subjective nature. A marketing audit is a systematic appraisal of all the external and internal factors that have affected a company's commercial performance over a defined period.

Given the growing turbulence of the business environment and the shorter product life-cycles that have resulted, no-one would deny the need to stop at least once a year at a particular point in the planning cycle to try to form a reasoned view of how all the many external and internal factors have influenced performance.

Sometimes, of course, a company will conduct a marketing audit because it is in financial trouble. At times like these, management often attempts to treat the wrong symptoms – most frequently by reorganizing the company. But such measures are unlikely to be effective if there are more fundamental problems which have not been identified. Of course, if the company survived for long enough, it might eventually solve its problems through a process of elimination. Essentially, though, the argument is that the problems have first to be properly defined. The audit is a means of helping to define them.

Two kinds of variable

Any company carrying out an audit will be faced with two kinds of variable. There is the kind over which the company has no direct control – for example, economic and market factors. Second, there are those over which the company has complete control, the operational variables, which are usually the firm's internal resources. This division suggests that the best way to structure an audit is in two parts, external and internal. Table 2.4 shows areas which should be investigated under both headings. Each should be examined with a view to building up an information base relevant to the company's performance.

Table 2.4 Conducting an audit	
External audit	**Internal audit**
Business and economic environment Economic, political, fiscal, legal, social, cultural Technological Intra-company	Own company Sales (total, by geographical location, by industrial type, by customer, by product) Market shares Profit margins, costs

The market
Total market, size, growth and trends (value/volume)
Market characteristics, developments and trends:
    products, prices, physical distribution, channels,
    customers, consumers, communication, industry
    practices
	Marketing information/research
	Marketing mix variables: product
	    management, price, distribution,
	    promotion, operations and resources

Competition Major competitors Size Market share/coverage Market standing and reputation Production capabilities Distribution policies Marketing methods Extent of diversification Personnel issues International links Profitability Key strengths and weaknesses	

Many people mistakenly believe that the marketing audit should be some kind of final attempt to define a company's marketing problems, or, at best, something done by an independent body from time to time to ensure that a company is on the right track. However, many highly successful companies, as well as using normal information and control procedures and marketing research throughout the year, start their planning cycle each year with a formal, audit-type process of everything that has had an important influence on marketing activities. Certainly, in many leading consumer goods companies the annual self-audit approach is a tried and tested discipline.

Objections to line managers doing their own audits usually centre on the problems of time and objectivity. In practice, a disciplined approach and thorough training will help. But the discipline must be applied from the highest to the lowest levels of management if the tunnel vision that often results from a lack of critical appraisal is to be avoided.

Where relevant, the marketing audit should contain life-cycles for major products and for market segments, for which the future shape will be predicted using the audit information. Also, major products and markets should be plotted on some kind of matrix to show their current competitive position.

The next question is: what happens to the results of the audit? Some companies consume valuable resources carrying out audits that produce very little in the way of results. The audit is simply a database, and the task remains of turning it into intelligence – that is, information essential to decision-making.

Step 4: Market overview

This step, which appears prominently in the actual strategic marketing plan, should spell out clearly:

- what the market is
- how it works
- what the key decision-making points are
- what the segments are.

Market definition is fundamental to success, and must be made in terms of need sets rather than in product/service terms. Thus, Gestetner failed by defining its markets as 'duplicators', and IBM almost failed by defining its market as 'mainframes'. Accordingly, a pension is a product, not a market, as many other products can satisfy the same or similar needs. Having done this, a 'market map' should be drawn, which plots the flow of goods or services from supplier through to user, with quantities through the chain which add up to the market size.

In the sense that if five million radiators are made or imported, then five million radiators must be distributed, five million radiators must be installed, and the decision about which radiators are to be installed must be made by someone. It is the purpose of the market map to spell all this out quantitatively.

It is at key decision points that market segmentation should take place. A segment is a group of customers or consumers that share the same (or approximately the same) needs; this is discussed in detail in Chapter 4. This step is crucial, for it is upon the key segments from the market map that SWOT analyses should be completed.

Step 5: SWOT analyses

The only remaining question is, what happens to the results of the audit? Some companies consume valuable resources carrying out audits that bring very little by way of actionable results.

Indeed, there is always the danger that, at the audit stage, insufficient attention is paid to the need to concentrate on analysis that determines which trends and developments will actually affect the company. Whilst the checklist demonstrates the completeness of logic and analysis, the people carrying out the audit should discipline themselves to omit from their audits all the information that is not central to the company's marketing problems. Thus, inclusion of research reports, or over-detailed sales performance histories by product which lead to no logical actions whatever, only serves to rob the audit of focus and reduce its relevance.

Since the objective of the audit is to indicate what a company's marketing objectives and strategies should be, it follows that it would be helpful if some format could be found for organizing the major findings.

> One useful way of doing this is in the form of a number of SWOT analyses. A SWOT is a summary of the audit under the headings, internal strengths and weaknesses as they relate to external opportunities and threats.

A SWOT should be conducted for each segment that is considered to be important in the company's future. These SWOT analyses should, if possible, contain just a few paragraphs of commentary focusing on *key* factors only. They should highlight internal *differential* strengths and weaknesses *vis-à-vis* competitors, and *key* external opportunities and threats. A summary of reasons for good or bad performance should be included. They should be interesting to read, contain concise statements, include only relevant and important data, and give greater emphasis to creative analysis.

How to conduct SWOT analyses is discussed in detail in Chapter 5.

Step 6: Assumptions

Let us now return to the preparation of the marketing plan. If we refer again to the marketing planning process, and have completed our marketing audit and SWOT analyses, assumptions now have to be written.

> There are certain key determinants of success in all companies about which assumptions have to be made before the planning process can proceed.

It is really a question of standardizing the planning environment. For example, it would be no good receiving plans from two product managers, one of whom believed the market was going to increase by 10 per cent, while the other believed the market was going to decline by 10 per cent.

Examples of assumptions might be:

'With respect to the company's industrial climate, it is assumed that:

1 Industrial overcapacity will increase from 105 per cent to 115 per cent as new industrial plants come into operation.
2 Price competition will force price levels down by 10 per cent across the board.
3 A new product in the field of *x* will be introduced by our major competitor before the end of the second quarter.'

Assumptions should be few in number, and if a plan is possible irrespective of the assumptions made, then the assumptions are unnecessary.

Step 7: Marketing objectives and strategies

The next step in marketing planning is the writing of marketing objectives and strategies – the key to the whole process.

> An *objective* is what you want to achieve. A *strategy* is how you plan to achieve your objectives.

Thus, there can be objectives and strategies at all levels in marketing. For example, there can be advertising objectives and strategies, and pricing objectives and strategies.

However, the important point to remember about marketing objectives is that they are about *products* and *markets* only. Common sense will confirm that it is only by selling something to someone that the company's financial goals can be achieved, and that advertising, pricing, service levels and so on are the means (or strategies) by which we might succeed in doing this. Thus, pricing objectives, sales promotion objectives, advertising objectives and the like should not be confused with marketing objectives.

Marketing objectives are simply about one (or more) of the following:

● Existing products for existing markets
● New products for existing markets
● Existing products for new markets
● New products for new markets.

They should be capable of measurement, otherwise they are not objectives. Directional terms such as 'maximize', minimize', penetrate', 'increase', etc. are only acceptable if quantitative measurement can be attached to them. Measurement should be in terms of some, or all, of the following: sales volume, sales value, market share, profit, percentage penetration of outlets (for example, to have 30 per cent of all retail outlets stocking our product by year 3).

> Marketing strategies are the means by which marketing objectives will be achieved, and generally are concerned with the four Ps, as follows:
>
> Product   The general policies for product deletions, modifications, additions, design, branding, positioning, packaging, etc.
>
> Price   The general pricing policies to be followed by product groups in market segments
>
> Place   The general policies for channels and customer service levels
>
> Promotion   The general policies for communicating with customers under the relevant headings, such as advertising, sales force, sales promotion, public relations, exhibitions, direct mail, etc.

Step 8: Estimate expected results and identify alternative plans and mixes

Having completed this major planning task, it is normal at this stage to employ judgement, analogous experience, field tests and so on to test out the feasibility of the objectives and strategies in terms of market share, costs, profits, etc. It is also normally at this stage that alternative plans and mixes are considered, if necessary.

Step 9: The budget

In a strategic marketing plan, these strategies would normally be costed out approximately and, if not practicable, alternative strategies would be proposed and costed out until a satisfactory solution could be reached. This would then become the budget. In most cases there would be a budget for the full three years of the strategic marketing plan, but there would also be a very detailed budget for the first year of the plan, which would be included in the one-year operational plan.

It will be obvious from all of this that not only does the setting of budgets become much easier, but the resulting budgets are more likely to be realistic and related to what the *whole* company wants to achieve, rather than just one functional department.

The problem of designing a dynamic system for budget-setting, rather than the 'tablets of stone' approach, which is more common, is a major challenge to the marketing and financial directors of all companies.

The most satisfactory approach would be for a marketing director to justify all marketing expenditure from a zero base each year against the tasks he or she wishes to accomplish. A little thought will confirm that this is exactly the approach recommended in this chapter. If these procedures are followed, a hierarchy of objectives is built up in such a way that every item of budgeted expenditure can be related directly back to the initial corporate financial objectives. For example, if sales promotion is a major means of achieving an objective in a particular market, when sales promotional items appear in the programme, each one has a specific purpose which can be related back to a major objective.

Doing it this way not only ensures that every item of expenditure is fully accounted for as part of a rational, objective and task approach, but also that when changes have to be made during the period to which the plan relates then these changes can be made in such a way that the least damage is caused to the company's long-term objectives.

> The incremental marketing expense can be considered to be all costs that are incurred after the product leaves the factory, *other than* costs involved in physical distribution, the costs of which usually represent a discrete subset.

There is, of course, no textbook answer to problems relating to questions such as whether packaging should be a marketing or a production expense, and whether some distribution costs could be considered to be marketing costs. For example, insistence on high service levels results in high inventory carrying costs. Only common sense will reveal workable solutions to issues such as these.

Under *price*, however, any form of discounting that reduces the expected gross income, such as promotional discounts, quantity discounts, royalty rebates and so on, as well as sales commission and unpaid invoices, should be given the most careful attention as incremental marketing expenses.

Most obvious incremental marketing expenses will occur, however, under the heading 'promotion', in the form of advertising, sales salaries and expenses, sales promotional expenditure, direct mail costs and so on. The important point about the measurable effects of marketing activity is that anticipated levels should be the result of the most careful analysis of what is required to take the company towards its goals, while the most careful attention should be paid to gathering all items of expenditure under appropriate headings. The healthiest way of treating these issues is a zero-based budgeting approach.

Step 10: First year detailed implementation programme

In a one-year tactical plan, the general marketing strategies would be developed into specific sub-objectives, each supported by more detailed strategy and action statements.

A company organized according to functions might have an advertising plan, a sales promotion plan, a pricing plan, and so on.

A product-based company might have a product plan, with objectives, strategies and tactics for price, place and promotion as necessary.

A market or geographically based company might have a market plan, with objectives, strategies and tactics for the four Ps as necessary.

Likewise, a company with a few major customers might have customer plans.

Any combination of the above might be suitable, depending on circumstances.

■ What should appear in a strategic marketing plan?

A written marketing plan is the backdrop against which operational decisions are taken. Consequently, too much detail should be avoided. Its major function is to determine where the company is, where it wants to go and how it can get there. It lies at the heart of a company's revenue-generating activities, such as the timing of the cash flow and the size and character of the labour force. What should actually appear in a written strategic marketing plan is shown in Table 2.5. This strategic marketing plan should be distributed only to those who need it, but it can only be an aid to effective management. It cannot be a substitute for it.

Table 2.5 What should appear in a strategic marketing plan

1 Start with a mission statement.
2 Here, include a financial summary which illustrates graphically revenue and profit for the full planning period.
3 Now do a market overview: Has the market declined or grown? How does it break down into segments? What is your share of each? Keep it simple. If you do not have the facts, make estimates. Use life-cycles, bar charts and pie charts to make it all crystal clear.
4 Now identify the key segments and do a SWOT analysis for each one: Outline the major external influences and their impact on each segment. List the key factors for success. These should be less than five. Give an assessment of the company's differential strengths and weaknesses compared with those of its competitors. Score yourself and your competitors out of 10 and then multiply each score by a weighting factor for each critical success factor (e.g. CSF 1 = 60, CSF 2 = 25, CSF 3 = 10, CSF 4 = 5).
5 Make a brief statement about the key issues that have to be addressed in the planning period.
6 Summarize the SWOTs using a portfolio matrix in order to illustrate the important relationships between your key products and markets.
7 List your assumptions.
8 Set objectives and strategies.
9 Summarize your resource requirements for the planning period in the form of a budget.

It will be obvious from Table 2.5 that not only does budget-setting become much easier and more realistic, but the resulting budgets are more likely to reflect what the whole company wants to achieve, rather than just one department.

The problem of designing a dynamic system for setting budgets is a major challenge to the marketing and financial directors of all companies. The most satisfactory approach would be for a marketing director to justify all marketing expenditure from a zero base each year against the tasks to be accomplished. If these procedures are followed, a hierarchy of objectives is built in such a way that every item of budgeted expenditure can be related directly back to the initial financial objectives.

For example, if sales promotion is a major means of achieving an objective, when a sales promotion item appears in the programme, it has a specific purpose which can be related back to a major objective. Thus every item of expenditure is fully accounted for.

> Marketing expense can be considered to be all costs that are incurred after the product leaves the 'factory', apart from those involved in physical distribution. When it comes to pricing, any form of discounting that reduces the expected gross income – such as promotional or quantity discounts, overrides, sales commission and unpaid invoices – should be given the most careful attention as marketing expenses. Most obvious marketing expenses will occur, however, under the heading of promotion, in the form of advertising, sales salaries and expenses, sales promotion and direct mail costs.

The important point about the measurable effects of marketing activity is that anticipated levels should result from careful analysis of what is required to take the company towards its goals, while the most careful attention should be paid to gathering all items of expenditure under appropriate headings. The healthiest way of treating these issues is through zero-based budgeting.

We have just described the strategic marketing plan and what it should contain. The tactical marketing plan layout and content should be similar, but the detail is much greater, as it is for one year only.

■ Marketing planning systems design and implementation

While the actual process of marketing planning is simple in outline, a number of contextual issues have to be considered that make marketing planning one of the most baffling of all management problems. The following are some of those issues:

- When should it be done, how often, by whom, and how?
- Is it different in a large and a small company? Is it different in a diversified and an undiversified company?
- What is the role of the chief executive?
- What is the role of the planning department?
- Should marketing planning be top-down or bottom-up?
- What is the relationship between operational (one-year) and strategic (longer-term) planning?

■ Requisite strategic marketing planning

Many companies with financial difficulties have recognized the need for a more structured approach to planning their marketing, and have opted for the kind of standardized, formalized procedures written about so much in textbooks. Yet these rarely bring any benefits, and often bring marketing planning itself into disrepute.

It is quite clear that any attempt at the introduction of formalized marketing planning requires a change in a company's approach to managing its business. It is also clear that unless a company recognizes these implications, and plans to seek ways of coping with them, formalized strategic planning will be ineffective.

Research (McDonald, 1982[5]) has shown that the implications are principally as follows:

1 Any closed-loop planning system (but especially one that is essentially a forecasting and budgeting system) will lead to dull and ineffective

[5] M. McDonald (1982) 'The Theory and Practice of Industrial Marketing Planning', PhD thesis, Cranfield Institute of Technology.

marketing. Therefore, there has to be some mechanism for preventing inertia from setting in through the over-bureaucratization of the system.

2 Planning undertaken at the functional level of marketing, in the absence of a means of integration with other functional areas of the business at general management level, will be largely ineffective.

3 The separation of responsibility for operational and strategic planning will lead to a divergence of the short-term thrust of a business at the operational level from the long-term objectives of the enterprise as a whole. This will encourage preoccupation with short-term results at operational level, which normally makes the firm less effective in the longer term.

4 Unless the chief executive understands and takes an active role in strategic marketing planning, it will never be an effective system.

5 A period of up to three years is necessary (especially in large firms) for the successful introduction of an effective strategic marketing planning system.

The same PhD thesis (McDonald, 1982) also found that the principal barriers to implementing marketing planning are those listed in Table 2.6.

Table 2.6 Barriers to the integration of strategic marketing planning

1 Weak support from the chief executive and top management.
2 Lack of a plan for planning.
3 Lack of line management support due to any of the following, either singly or in combination:
   ■ hostility
   ■ lack of skills
   ■ lack of information
   ■ lack of resources
   ■ inadequate organizational structure.
4 Confusion over planning terms.
5 Numbers in lieu of written objectives and strategies.
6 Too much detail, too far ahead.
7 Once-a-year ritual.
8 Separation of operational planning from strategic planning.
9 Failure to integrate marketing planning into total corporate planning system.
10 Delegation of planning to a planner.

Let us be dogmatic about requisite planning levels. First, in a large, diversified group, irrespective of such organizational issues, anything other than a systematic approach approximating to a formalized marketing planning system is unlikely to enable the necessary control to be exercised over the corporate identity. Second, unnecessary planning, or over-planning, could easily result from an inadequate or indiscriminate consideration of the real planning needs at the different levels in the hierarchical chain.

This process and its relationship to the other issues discussed in this chapter are summarized in Figure 2.12.

Figure 2.12

Figure 2.13 is another way of illustrating the total corporate strategic and marketing planning process. This time, however, a time element is

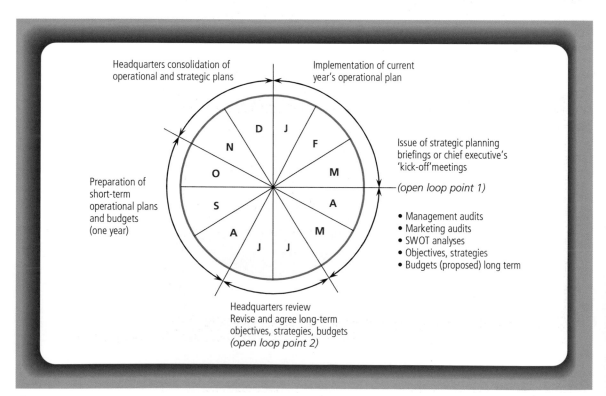

Figure 2.13
Strategic and operational planning – timing

added, and the relationship between strategic planning briefing, long-term strategic plans and short-term operational plans is clarified.

◼ The position of key account planning in the cycle

There is much debate about this, but it will be clear from looking at the planning cycle in Figure 2.13 that ▶ **key account** planning must take place at the same time as, or even before, draft plans are prepared for a strategic business unit.

If this is not clear, let us give an example of a supplies company servicing the needs of a national health service. It will be seen that there are four 'markets' within hospitals to be served. These are:

● Medical
● Administration
● Catering
● Energy.

There will be a number of key accounts, or hospital groups, referred to here as Hospital Groups A, B, C, D, etc. Each of these hospital groups may well have its own key account manager who has to plan for it. Figure 2.14 illustrates this.

▶ **DEFINITION** ◀

A key account is a major customer considered by the supplying company to be of strategic importance to the achievement of its own objectives. Hence, such a customer is singled out for special treatment

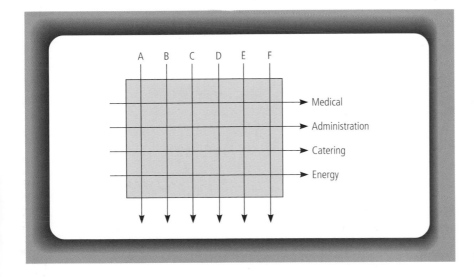

Figure 2.14

Thus, for example, the Key Account Manager for Hospital A has to prepare a draft plan across all four 'markets' and this would clearly be a key input to the planning process shown in Figure 2.13.

The position of key account planning in strategic marketing planning

As a general principle, planning should start in the market where the customers are. Indeed, in anything other than small organizations, it is clearly absurd to think that any kind of meaningful planning can take place without the committed inputs of those who operate where the customers are.

Figure 2.15 shows a hierarchy of strategic planning starting with key account planning. Every principle outlined in this chapter applies right down to the individual key account. Thus, the planning process shown in Figure 2.11 would start with key accounts. This book, however, does not deal specifically with key account planning, which is dealt with in detail in another book of the author's (*Key Account Management: the definitive guide*, Butterworth-Heinemann, Oxford, 2006).

Figure 2.15
A hierarchy of plan

■ Application questions

1 Describe your company's marketing planning system in detail.
2 List the *good* things and the *bad* things about it.
3 Say how you think it could be improved.

Chapter 2 review

What is marketing planning?

Marketing planning is a logical sequence of events leading to the setting of marketing objectives and the formulation of plans for achieving them.

The sequence is:

1 Mission statement
2 Set corporate objectives

3   Conduct marketing audit
4   Conduct market overview
5   Conduct SWOT analyses
6   Make assumptions
7   Set marketing objectives and strategies
8   Estimate expected results and identify alternative plans and mixes
9   Set the budget
10   Establish first-year implementation programmes.   *Try Exercise 2.1*

The plan itself contains:

1   Mission statement
2   Financial summary
3   Market overview
4   SWOT analyses
5   Portfolio summary
6   Assumptions
7   Marketing objectives and strategies
8   Forecasts and budgets.   *Try Exercise 2.2*

Why do it?

As business becomes increasingly complex and competition increases, a marketing plan is essential.

The benefits are as follows:

1   It allows better coordination of activities.
2   It identifies expected developments.
3   It increases organizational preparedness to change.
4   It minimizes non-rational responses to the unexpected.
5   It reduces conflicts about where the company should be going.
6   It improves communications.
7   Management is forced to think ahead systematically.
8   Available resources can be better matched to opportunities.
9   The plan provides a framework for the continuing review of operations.
10   A systematic approach to strategy formulation leads to a higher return on investment.

Try Exercise 2.3

Will it help us to survive?

All companies need to have a longer-term (strategic) marketing view as well as a short-term (tactical) marketing operation. Often the most potent short-term tactic is the use of the sales force. These can combine thus:

Market planning

	Poor	Excellent
Good	Die quickly	Thrive
Poor	Die slowly	Survive

Sales performance

From this, it can be seen that being good at implementing the wrong strategy can lead to a very quick death!

Try Exercise 2.4

Questions raised for the company

1 Q: Can we 'buy' an 'off-the-peg' planning system?
   A: Since all companies are different, the process has to be 'tailored' to fit individual requirements.
2 Q: Are we talking about tactics or strategy?
   A: A strategic marketing plan takes a long-term look (say three years) and is therefore strategic. A tactical, or operational, marketing plan is a detailed scheduling and costing out of the *first* year of the strategic marketing plan.
3 Q: How is the marketing plan used?
   A: The plan determines where the company is now, where it wants to go and how to get there. It therefore should be the backdrop against which all organizational decisions are made.
4 Q: Does the plan have to be written?
   A: The planning sequence is really a thinking process. However, key pieces of information are worth writing down because they reduce confusion and aid communication. The degree of formality depends on the size of the company and the complexity of its business.
5 Q: How detailed should it be?
   A: Enough to be useful.

EXERCISES

Introduction to Chapter 2 exercises

The first exercise enables you to make an objective analysis of your company's marketing planning process. If you choose, you can then take matters further by working out in what ways the planning process might be improved.

The second exercise helps to clarify an often misunderstood issue, that of the company's mission statement.

The third exercise explores the extent to which your company is receiving the benefits that are usually attributed to a marketing planning process.

The final exercise will enable you to plot your company's position on the 'survival matrix'. There are several benefits to be derived from knowing this:

1 It infers the relation between your company's focus on long-term versus short-term issues.
2 It can be a powerful means of communicating to your colleagues that all might not be well in the company.
3 It provides an unambiguous message about what the company needs to address for future survival.

This questionnaire enables you to make an objective assessment about the marketing planning process in your company. It is designed to enable you to take a 'helicopter view' of the way your company does its planning, and then to home in on the areas where improvements can be made. This approach will also enable you to identify information gaps that might be unknown to you at present.

Although care has been taken to use generally accepted terminology in the wording of this questionnaire, there will always be the company that uses different words. For example, when we talk about return on investment (ROI), other companies might well use other expressions or measures – such as return on capital employed, etc.

With this caveat in mind, please respond to the questionnaire by putting a tick against each question in one of the four columns provided.

Exercise 2.1
The marketing planning process questionnaire

	Yes	No	Don't know	Not applic-able
Section 1: Corporate issues				
1 Is there a corporate statement about:				
(a) The nature of the company's current business mission?				
(b) Its vision of the future?				
2 Is there a target figure for ROI?				
3 Is there a corporate plan to channel the company resources to this end?				
4 Are there defined business boundaries in terms of:				
(a) Products or services (that will be offered)?				
(b) Customers or markets (to deal with)?				
(c) Operations facilities?				
(d) Distribution facilities?				
(e) Size and character of the workforce?				
(f) Sources and levels of funding?				

	Yes	No	Don't know	Not applic-able
5 Are there objectives for promoting the corporate image with: (a) The stock market? (b) Customers? (c) The local community? (d) The employees? (e) Environmentalist/conservationist lobby? (f) Government departments? (g) Trade associations, etc.?				
Section 2: Strategic issues 1 Is there a marketing plan?				
2 Is it compatible with the corporate plan?				
3 Does it cover the same period?				
4 Is the marketing plan regularly reviewed?				
5 Is the plan based on an assessment of market potential and past performance?				
6 Will the plan close the 'gap' if carried out?				
7 Is there a marketing plan by product/ service?				
8 Do relevant managers have a copy of the marketing plan?				

9 Are the following factors monitored in a regular and conscious way, in terms of how they affect the company's business prospects?
(a) *Business environment*
  (i) Economic factors
  (ii) Political/legal factors
  (iii) Fiscal factors
  (iv) Technological developments
  (v) Social/cultural factors
  (vi) Intra-company issues
(b) *The market*
  (i) Trends in market size/growth in volume and in value				

	Yes	No	Don't know	Not applic- able
(ii) Developments/trends in product use, product demand, product presentation, accessories, substitutes				
(iii) Developments/trends in prices, terms and conditions, trade practices				
(iv) Developments/trends in physical distribution, channels of distribution, purchasing patterns, stockholding, turnover				
(v) Developments/trends in communications, use of sales force, advertising, promotions, exhibitions, the Internet				
(c) *Competition* Developments/trends of competitors, their marketing strategies, their strengths, their weaknesses, new entrants, mergers/acquisitions, their reputation				
(d) *The industry*				
(i) Activities of trade association(s)				
(ii) Inter-firm comparisons				
(iii) Industry profitability				
(iv) Investment levels of competitors				
(v) Changes in cost structure				
(vi) Investment prospects				
(vii) Technological developments				
(viii) Sources of raw materials				
(ix) Energy utilization				

Section 3: SWOT analyses

1 Is there someone (individual or group) responsible for converting the analysis of factors in Section 2 into a summary which highlights:
(a) The company's principal strengths?
(b) The company's principal weaknesses (in terms of relating to external opportunities/threats)?

2 Does this person(s) have access to the necessary information?

	Yes	No	Don't know	Not applic-able

3 Is this person(s) sufficiently senior for his or her analysis to make an impact?

4 Is the organizational climate such that a full and accurate analysis is seen as a striving for improvement rather than an attack on specific departments or vested interests?

Section 4: Assumptions
1 Is there a set of assumptions around which the marketing plan is formulated?

2 Are these assumptions made explicit to senior company personnel?

3 Do they cover:
   (a) The business environment?
   (b) The market?
   (c) The competitors?
   (d) The industry?

4 Are the assumptions valid in the light of current and predicted trading situations?

Section 5: Marketing objectives/strategies
1 Are the marketing objectives clearly stated and consistent with the corporate objectives?

2 Are there clear strategies for achieving the stated marketing objectives?

3 Are sufficient resources made available?

4 Are all responsibilities and authority clearly made known?

5 Are there agreed objectives about:
   (a) The product range?
   (b) The value of sales?
   (c) The volume of sales?
   (d) Profits?
   (e) Market share?
   (f) Market penetration?
   (g) Number of customers and retention levels?
   (h) Introducing new products/services?
   (i) Divesting of old products/services?

	Yes	No	Don't know	Not applic- able
(j) Organization changes to: (i) Develop company strengths? (ii) Reduce company weaknesses?				
Section 6: Monitoring evaluation 1 Is the planning system well conceived and effective?				
2 Do control mechanisms exist to ensure planned objectives are met?				
3 Do internal communications function effectively?				
4 Are there any problems between marketing and other corporate functions?				
5 Are people clear about their role in the planning process?				
6 Is there a procedure for dealing with non-achievement of objectives?				
7 Is there evidence that this reduces the chance of subsequent failure?				
8 Are there still unexploited opportunities?				
9 Are there still organizational weaknesses?				
10 Are the assumptions upon which the plan was based valid?				
11 Are there contingency plans in the event of objectives not being met/conditions changing?				

Scoring and interpretation for Exercise 2.1

1 Add up how many ticks were listed under 'not applicable'. It is our experience that if there are more than eight ticks, then some aspects of planning that are covered by most companies are being avoided. Reappraise those items you initially ticked as 'not applicable'. Try getting a second opinion by checking your findings with colleagues.
2 Look at those items you ticked as 'don't know'. Find out if those activities are covered in your company's planning process.
3 Having ascertained what is and what isn't done in your company, list:
   (a) the *good* things in your company's planning process
   (b) the *bad* things about it.
4 Make a note, in the space on page 72, or on a separate sheet of paper, of ways in which you think the planning process in your company could be improved.

Personal notes

Exercise 2.2
The mission statement

The following should appear in a mission statement:

1 *Role or contribution*: 'Profit' (specify), or 'Service', or 'Opportunity-seeker'.
2 *Business definition*: this should be defined in terms of the *benefits* you provide or the *needs* you satisfy, rather than in terms of what you do or what you make.
3 *Distinctive competence*: what essential skills/capabilities/resources underpin whatever success has been achieved to date? (*Note*: These factors should not apply equally to a competitor, otherwise there is no distinctive quality about them.)
4 *Indications for the future*: what the company *will* do; what the company *might* do; what the company will *never* do.

Questions
1 To what extent does your company's mission statement meet the criteria listed above?
2 If you do not have a mission statement, try writing one, following the guidelines provided here. Try it out on your colleagues and see if they agree with you or if they can find ways to improve on what you have written.

Scoring and interpretation for Exercise 2.2
Use the following to gauge whether you feel you and your colleagues have developed a mission statement that is of real value:

● What values are true priorities for the next few years?
● What would make me professionally commit my mind and heart to this vision over the next five to ten years?
● What is unique about us?
● What does the world really need that our company can and should provide?
● What do I want our company to accomplish so that I will be committed, aligned, and proud of my association with the institution?

Exercise 2.3
The benefits of marketing planning

What follows is a list of the benefits of marketing planning. With your company in mind, score each benefit by means of the scale given below.

0	1 2 3	4 5 6	7 8 9	10
Never	*Sometimes*	*Frequently*	*Most of the time*	*Always*

1 Our approach to marketing planning ensures that we get a
high level of coordination of our various marketing activities   . . . . . .

2 Our marketing planning process enables us to identify
unexpected developments in advance   . . . . . .

3 Because of the way we approach marketing planning,
there is an increased readiness for the organization to
change in response to the issues 'flagged up'   . . . . . .

4 When we are faced with the unexpected, our marketing
planning process minimizes the risk of non-rational
responses   . . . . . .

5 Having a marketing plan reduces the conflicts between
managers regarding 'where the company should
be going'   . . . . . .

6 Our marketing plan improves communications about
market-related issues   . . . . . .

7 Because of our marketing planning process, management
is forced to think ahead systematically   . . . . . .

8 Having a marketing plan enables us to match our
resources to opportunities in an effective way   . . . . . .

9 Our marketing plan provides us with a useful framework
for a continuing review of progress   . . . . . .

10 Our marketing planning has led us to develop more
profitable marketing strategies   . . . . . .

TOTAL   _____

Scoring and interpretation for Exercise 2.3
The maximum score for the exercise is 100. Check your scores below.

81–100   Marketing planning is really paying off in your company

61–80   You are not receiving the benefits you should be receiving. What's
getting in the way? (Exercise 2.1 might give some clues.)

41–60   You appear to be moving along the right lines, but there is still a
long way to go

0–40   Either your marketing planning process is inadequate, or your company is not really trying to make marketing planning work

Before you tackle this exercise, it is important to remember that profitability
and high market growth are nearly always correlated. In other words, the
higher the market growth, the higher the profitability.

This phenomenon can sometimes obscure the fact that a company that
appears to be doing well can still be losing ground in comparison with its
competitors. While apparently thriving, it is in fact dying slowly. The crunch
comes when the erstwhile buoyant market growth slows down, and the other
companies demonstrate quite clearly their superior performance.

Exercise 2.4
Survival matrix

Instructions

Before coming to the matrix, please respond to the following statements by scoring them as follows:

0	1 2 3	4 5 6	7 8 9	10
Never	*Sometimes*	*Frequently*	*Most of the time*	*Always*

1 When it comes to recruiting salespeople, we seem able to pick the best candidates in the job market   . . . . . .

2 The training we provide for salespeople is second to none   . . . . . .

3 Our salespeople consistently meet or exceed their sales targets   . . . . . .

4 Compared with our competitors, our salespeople have a better image   . . . . . .

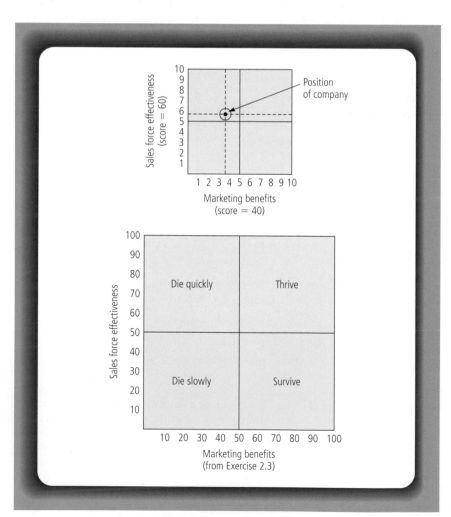

Figure 2.16
Survival matrix

5 We actually have the most appropriate number of
  salespeople employed   . . . . . .

6 Our sales staff are clear about the role they are expected
  to play   . . . . . .

7 Our sales managers are very good motivators   . . . . . .

8 Territory planning is a strong point of our sales force   . . . . . .

9 The sales force has a good conversion rate in terms of
  number of visits per order   . . . . . .

10 Our sales force is reasonably stable, i.e. there is not a
  labour turnover problem   . . . . . .

TOTAL ———

Scoring and interpretation for Exercise 2.4

Enter the sales force effectiveness score on the vertical axis on the matrix
(Figure 2.16) and then draw a horizontal dotted line across the matrix. Take
the marketing benefits score from Exercise 2.3 and enter this on the horizontal axis of the matrix. Draw a vertical dotted line up from this point. Where
the two dotted lines meet is where you position your company on the survival
matrix.

Questions

1 What are the implications for your company?
2 What actions might be required if improvements are needed?

CHAPTER 3

The marketing planning process: 2 Removing the myths

Summary

- Problems and barriers that have to be overcome to make marketing planning work
- Ignorance about the process of marketing planning and associated operational problems
- The main barriers are described and include:
  - weak support from the board of directors
  - lack of a plan for planning
  - confusion over planning terms
  - numbers in lieu of written marketing objectives and strategies
  - too much detail, too far ahead
  - once-a-year ritual
  - separation of strategic and operational planning
  - failure to integrate strategic marketing planning into corporate planning
  - delegation of planning to a planner
- These problems can be overcome by requisite systems, which are outlined
- Exercises to turn the theory into practice
- Readers who are sure these barriers do not exist in their organization may go straight to Chapter 4

Note to readers: Whilst this is an extremely important chapter, in that many excellent marketing plans fail because of the barriers and problems explained here, those readers who wish to cut to the chase, as it were, may choose to go straight to Chapter 4, although it is strongly recommended by the author that this chapter should be read before attempting to prepare a plan.

■ Introduction

In spite of the apparent simplicity and logic of the process described in the last chapter, marketing planning remains one of the most baffling subjects, for both academics and practitioners alike.

The purpose of this chapter is to remove some of the myths which surround this very complex area of marketing management and to explain why much of what passes for marketing planning is largely ineffective. These conclusions are based on a four-year study by the author into how 200 British companies carried out their marketing planning, the companies being broadly representative of the complete spectrum of type and size of business-to-business company, and 400 hundred directors were interviewed. These results have been confirmed by many other studies carried out at universities in America, Europe and Australia.

Marketing's contribution to business success in manufacturing, distribution or merchanting activities lies in its commitment to detailed analysis of future opportunities to meet customer needs and a wholly professional approach to selling to well-defined market segments those products or services that deliver the sought-after benefits. While prices and discounts are important, as are advertising and promotion, the link with operations through the product is paramount.

> Such a commitment and such activities must not be mistaken for budgets and forecasts. Those, of course, we need and have already got. Our accounting colleagues have long since seen to that.

The process of marketing planning is concerned with identifying what and to whom sales are going to be made in the longer term.

No – put quite bluntly, the process of marketing planning is concerned with identifying what and to whom sales are going to be made in the longer term to give revenue budgets and sales forecasts any chance of achievement. Furthermore, chances of achievement are a function of how good our intelligence services are, how well suited our strategies are, and how well we are led.

■ Ignorance of marketing planning and associated operational problems

> What most companies think of as planning systems are little more than ▶ **forecasting** and ▶ **budgeting** systems.

▶ **D E F I N I T I O N** ◀

A forecast in planning terms is usually associated with predicting the volume or value of sales of products and services at some future point in time

▶ **D E F I N I T I O N** ◀

A budget is the revenue and costs associated with these forecasts

These give impetus and direction to tackling the current operational problems of the business, but tend merely to project the current business unchanged into the future – something often referred to in management literature as 'tunnel vision'.

The problem with this approach is that because companies are dynamically evolving systems within a dynamically evolving business environment, some means of evaluation of the way in which the two interact has to be found in order that there should be a better matching between them. Otherwise, because of a general unpreparedness, a company will suffer increased pressures in the short term, in trying to react and to cope with environmental factors.

Many companies, having gone through various forms of rationalization or efficiency-increasing measures, become aware of the opportunities for making profit which have been lost to them because of their unpreparedness, but are confused about how to make better use of their limited resources. This problem increases in importance in relation to the size and diversity of companies.

> There is widespread awareness of lost market opportunities through unpreparedness, and real confusion over what to do about it. It is hard not to conclude, therefore, that there is a strong relationship between these two problems and the systems most widely in use at present, i.e. *sales forecasting and budgeting systems*.

Table 3.1 lists the most frequently mentioned operating problems resulting from a reliance on traditional sales forecasting and budgeting procedures in the absence of a marketing planning system.

Table 3.1 Most frequently mentioned problems

1 Lost opportunities for profit
2 Meaningless numbers in long-range plans
3 Unrealistic objectives
4 Lack of actionable market information
5 Interfunctional strife
6 Management frustration
7 Proliferation of products and markets
8 Wasted promotional expenditure
9 Pricing confusion
10 Growing vulnerability to environmental change
11 Loss of control over the business

It is not difficult to see the connection between all of these problems. However, what is perhaps not apparent from the list is that each of these operational difficulties is in fact a symptom of a much larger problem, which emanates from the way in which the objectives of a firm are set.

The meaningfulness, and hence the eventual effectiveness, of any objective is heavily dependent on the quality of the information inputs about the business environment. However, objectives also need to be realistic, and to be realistic they have to be closely related to the firm's particular capabilities in the form of its assets, competences and reputation that have evolved over a number of years.

The objective-setting process of a business, then, is central to its effectiveness.

> What the research study demonstrated conclusively is that it is inadequacies in the objective-setting process which lie at the heart of most commercial problems.

If the process by which the key function of setting objectives is performed is inadequate it follows that operational efficiency will be adversely affected.

Since companies are based on the existence of markets, and since a company's sole means of making profit is to find and maintain profitable markets, then, clearly, setting objectives in respect of these markets is a key business function. If the process by which this key function is performed is inadequate in relation to the differing organizational settings in which it takes place, it follows that operational efficiency will be adversely affected.

Some kind of appropriate system has to be used to enable meaningful and realistic marketing objectives to be set. A frequent complaint is the preoccupation with short-term thinking and an almost total lack of what has been referred to as ► **'strategic thinking'**. This was referred to briefly in Chapter 2.

► **DEFINITION** ◄

Strategic thinking is the process of considering the longer term implications of external and internal influences on the organization. It is a key part of producing a strategic marketing plan

> Another complaint is that plans consist largely of numbers, which are difficult to evaluate in any meaningful way since they do not highlight and quantify opportunities, emphasize key issues, show the company's position clearly in its markets, or delineate the means of achieving the sales forecasts.

Indeed, very often the actual numbers that are written down bear little relationship to any of these things. Sales targets for the sales force are often inflated in order to motivate them to higher achievement, while the actual budgets themselves are deflated in order to provide a safety net against shortfall. Both act as demotivators, and both lead to the frequent use of expressions such as 'ritual', 'the numbers game', 'meaningless horsetrading', and so on. It is easy to see how the problems listed in Table 3.1 begin to manifest themselves in this sort of environment. Closely allied to this is the frequent reference to profit as being the only objective necessary to successful business performance.

This theme is frequently encountered. There is in the minds of many business people the assumption that in order to be commercially successful, all that is necessary is for 'the boss' to set profit targets, to decentralize the firm into groups of similar activities, and then to make managers accountable for achieving those profits.

However, even though many companies have made the making of 'profit' almost the sole objective, many industries have gone into decline and, ironically, there has also been a decline in real profitability. As we saw earlier, most of Britain's top performing plcs in terms of return on investment during a ten-year period up to 1990 either went bankrupt or slipped into term-inal decline, according to a study by the late Professor Peter Doyle of Warwick University, and this problem got even worse in the decade up to 2000.

> There are countless examples of companies pursuing decentralized profit goals that have failed miserably.

> **Many companies appear to be bad at determining strategies for matching what the firm is good at with properly researched market-centred opportunities.**

Why should this be so? Here it is necessary to focus attention on what so many companies appear to be bad at – namely, determining strategies for matching what the firm is good at with properly researched market-centred opportunities, and then scheduling and costing out what has to be done to achieve these objectives.

> There is little evidence[1] of a deep understanding of what it is that companies can do better than their competitors, or of how their distinctive competence can be matched with the needs of certain customer groups. Instead, overall volume increases and minimum rates of return on investment are frequently applied to all products and markets, irrespective of market share, market growth rate, or the longevity of the product life-cycle.

[1] *Reminder*: For a full biography of this 'evidence', see M. McDonald and B. Smith (2002) *Strategic Marketing Planning: a domain review*, Cranfield University School of Management Research Series.

On the contrary, there is a lot of evidence to show that many companies are in trouble today precisely because their decentralized units manage their business only for the current profit and loss account, often at the expense of giving up valuable and hard-earned market share and running down the current business.

> Thus, ► **financial objectives**, while being essential measures of the desired performance of a company, are of little practical help, since they say nothing about *how* the results are to be achieved.

► **DEFINITION** ◄

Financial objectives usually use a number of measures such as return on net assets, return on sales, asset turnover, stock turnover, debtor days, liquidity, return on investment, economic value added, etc.

The same applies to sales forecasts and budgets, which are *not* marketing objectives and strategies. Understanding the real meaning and significance of marketing objectives helps managers to know what information they need to enable them to think through the implications of choosing one or more positions in the market. How to set marketing objectives and strategies is explained in detail in Chapter 6.

> Finding the right words to describe the logic of marketing objectives and strategies is infinitely more difficult than writing down numbers on a piece of paper and leaving the strategies implicit.

This lies at the heart of the problem. For, clearly, a numbers-orientated system will not encourage managers to think in a structured way about strategically relevant market segments; nor will it encourage the collection, analysis and synthesis of actionable market data. And in the absence of such activities within operating units, it is unlikely that headquarters will have much other than intuition and 'feel' to use as a basis for decisions about the management of scarce resources.

This raises the difficult question of how these very complex problems can be overcome, for this is what baffles those who have been forced by market pressures to consider different ways of coping with their environment.

The problem remains of how to get managers throughout an organization to think beyond the horizon of the current year's operations. This applies universally to all types and sizes of company. Even chief executives of small companies find difficulty in breaking out of the fetters of the current profit and loss account.

> The successes enjoyed in the past are often the result of the easy marketability of products, and during periods of high economic prosperity there was little pressure on companies to do anything other than solve operational problems as they arose.

In today's increasingly competitive markets, there is a growing realization that success in the future will only come from meticulous planning and market preparation.

The problem is that, in large companies, managers who are evaluated and rewarded on the basis of current operations find difficulty in concerning themselves about the corporate future. This is exacerbated by behavioural issues, in the sense that it is safer, and more rewarding personally, for managers to do what they know best, which in most cases is to manage their *current* range of products and customers in order to make the *current* year's budget.

MARKETING INSIGHT

Einstein wrote: 'The formulation of a problem is far more essential than its solution, which may be merely a matter of mathematical or experimental skill. To raise new questions, new possibilities, to regard old problems from a new angle, requires creative imagination.'

Unfortunately, such creativity is rare, especially when most managers are totally absorbed in managing today's business. Accordingly, they need some system which will help them to think in a structured way about problem formulation.

> It is the provision of such a rational framework to help them to make explicit their intuitive economic models of the business that is almost totally lacking from the forecasting and budgeting systems of most companies.

It is apparent that in the absence of any such synthesized and simplified views of the business, setting meaningful objectives for the future seems like an insurmountable problem, and this in turn encourages the perpetuation of systems involving merely the extrapolation of numbers.

There is also substantial evidence that those companies that provide procedures for this process, in the form of standardized methods of presentation, have gone some considerable way to overcoming this problem. Although the possible number of analyses of business situations is infinite, procedural approaches help managers throughout an organization at least to consider the essential elements of problem definition in a structured way. This applies even to difficult foreign markets, where data and information are hard to come by, and even to markets which are being managed by agents, who find that these structured approaches, properly managed, help *their* businesses as well as those of their principals.

However, there are two further major advantages enjoyed by these companies. First, the level of management frustration is lower and motivation is higher because the system provides a method of reaching agreement on such difficult matters as an assessment of the company's distinctive competence and the nature of the competitive environment. The internecine disputes and frustration which we all experience so often in our business lives is largely the result of an almost total absence of the means of discussing these issues and of reaching agreement on them. If a manager's boss does not understand what the environmental problems are, what their organizational strengths and weaknesses are, or what they are trying to achieve, and in the absence of any structured procedures and common terminology that can be used and understood by everybody, communications will be bad and the incidence of frustration will be higher.

> Secondly, some form of standardized approach which is understood by all considerably improves the ability of headquarters management not only to understand the problems of individual operating units, but also to react to them in a constructive and helpful way.

Where companies have provided a framework for problem formulation, the level of management frustration is lower and motivation is higher.

This is because they receive information in a way which enables them to form a meaningful overview of total company activities and this provides a rational basis for resource allocation.

To summarize, a structured approach to situation analysis is necessary, irrespective of the size or complexity of the organization. Such a system should:

1 Ensure that comprehensive consideration is given to the definition of opportunities and threats and strengths and weaknesses
2 Ensure that a rational process is used for the presentation of the key issues arising from this analysis.

Very few companies have planning systems which possess these characteristics. Those that do, manage to cope with their environment more effectively than those that do not. They find it easier to set meaningful marketing objectives, are more confident about the future, enjoy greater control over the business, and react less on a piecemeal basis to ongoing events. In short, they suffer fewer operational problems and are as a result more effective organizations.

■ A reminder about what marketing planning is

Let us remind ourselves of what we said in Chapter 2. Marketing planning is a logical sequence of activities leading to the setting of marketing objectives and the formulation of plans for achieving them. It is a management *process*.

Conceptually the process is very simple and, in summary, comprises the steps outlined in Chapter 2 in Figure 2.6. This process is universally agreed by the experts.

> Formalized marketing planning by means of a planning system is, *per se*, little more than a structured way of identifying a range of options for the company, of making them explicit in writing, of formulating marketing objectives which are consistent with the company's overall objectives, and of scheduling and costing out the specific activities most likely to bring about the achievement of the objectives.

It is the systematization of this process which is distinctive and was found to lie at the heart of the theory of marketing planning.

■ Naivety about marketing planning

We have just rehearsed with you the notions that any textbook would offer should you care to re-read it. We have long been bemused, however, by the fact that some meticulous marketing planning companies fare badly while the sloppy or inarticulate in marketing terms sometimes do well. Is there any real relationship between marketing planning and commercial success? And, if there is, how does that relationship work its way through?

There are, of course, many studies which identify a number of benefits to be obtained from marketing planning. However, there is little explanation for the commercial success of those companies that do *not* engage in formalized planning. Nor is there much exploration of the circumstances of those commercially unsuccessful companies that also have formalized marketing planning systems; and where the dysfunctional consequences are recognized, there is a failure to link this back to any kind of theory.

'Success' is, of course, influenced by many factors apart from just planning procedures. For example:

1 Financial performance at any one point in time is not necessarily a reflection of the adequacy or otherwise of planning procedures (*cf.* the hotel industry, location, tourism, etc.).
2 Some companies just happen to be in the right place at the right time(s).
3 Companies have many and varied objectives, such as, for example, stylistic objectives.
4 There is a proven relationship between management style and commercial success.
5 Some industries still have a quasi-monopolistic environment.
6 Some industries with few competitors happen to be in growth, and in such circumstances it is difficult not to be successful.

> Marketing planning procedures alone are not enough for success.

In other words, marketing planning procedures *alone* are not enough for success.

We have said that the process of marketing planning is conceptually very simple and universally applicable. However, it is this very simplicity and universality that make it extremely complex once a number of contextual issues are added – such as company size, degree of internationalization, management style, degree of business environmental turbulence and competitive hostility, marketing growth rate, market share, technological changes, and so on.

It is very clear that the simplistic theories do not adequately address such contextual issues in relation to marketing planning, which may well account for the fact that so few companies actually do it.

> In fact, 90 per cent of industrial goods companies in the author's study did not, by their own admission, produce anything approximating to an integrated, coordinated and internally consistent plan for their marketing activities.

This included a substantial number of companies that had highly formalized procedures for marketing planning. In six other studies in American, British and Australian universities, the highest estimate of companies getting marketing planning right was 25 per cent.

Certainly, few of these companies enjoyed the claimed benefits of formalized marketing planning, which in summary are as follows:

1 Coordination of the activities of many individuals whose actions are interrelated over time
2 Identification of expected developments
3 Preparedness to meet changes when they occur
4 Minimization of non-rational responses to the unexpected
5 Better communication among executives
6 Minimization of conflicts among individuals which would result in a subordination of the goals of the company to those of the individual.

Indeed, many companies have a lot of the trappings of sophisticated marketing planning systems but suffer as many dysfunctional consequences as those companies that have only forecasting and budgeting systems. It is clear that for any marketing planning system to be effective, certain conditions have to be satisfied, which we shall deal with in detail shortly.

It should be pointed out, however, that it is by no means essential for any company not suffering from hostile and unstable competitive and environmental conditions to have an effective marketing planning system, but there are some negative consequences.

> Without exception, all those companies in the author's study which did not have an effective marketing planning system, and which were profitable, were also operating in buoyant or high-growth markets. Such companies, though, were less successful than comparable companies with effective marketing planning systems.

Success was considered to be not only a company's financial performance over a number of years, but also the way it coped with its environment.

What this means is that, apart from profitability, a company with an effective marketing planning system is likely to have:

- widely understood objectives
- highly motivated employees
- high levels of actionable market information
- greater interfunctional coordination
- minimum waste and duplication of resources

The process of marketing planning is conceptually simple, but the contextual issues can be very complex. For this reason, 25 per cent of companies, at most, are getting marketing planning right.

- acceptance of the need for continuous change and a clear understanding of priorities
- greater control over the business and less vulnerability to the unexpected.

In the case of companies without effective marketing planning systems, while it is possible to be profitable over a number of years, especially in high-growth markets, such companies will tend to be less profitable over time and to suffer problems which are the very opposite of the benefits referred to above.

> Furthermore, companies without effective marketing planning systems tend to suffer more serious commercial organizational consequences when environmental and competitive conditions become hostile and unstable.

None of these points are new, in the sense that most of these benefits and problems are discernible to the careful observer. They are, however, actionable propositions for marketers.

■ Marketing planning systems: design and implementation problems

Many companies currently under siege have recognized the need for a more structured approach to planning their marketing and have opted for the kind of standardized, formalized procedures written about so much in textbooks. As stated above, these rarely bring the claimed benefits, and often bring marketing planning itself into disrepute.

> It is clear that any attempt at the introduction of formalized marketing planning systems has serious organizational and behavioural implications for a company, as it requires a change in its approach to managing its business.

It is also clear that unless a company recognizes these implications, and plans to seek ways of coping with them, formalized marketing planning will be ineffective.

Marketing planning is in practice a complex process, proceeding as it does from reviews to objectives, strategies, programmes, budgets and back again, until some kind of acceptable compromise is reached between what is desirable and what is practicable, given all the constraints that any company has.

It has been stated that what has been written about this topic under-estimates the operational difficulties of designing and implementing systems and procedures for marketing planning, and that the task becomes progressively more complex as the size and diversity of a company increases. Also, the literature is inadequate in the extent to which it provides practical guidance on design and implementation.

The author's research included a number of examples of companies that had been forced by market pressures to initiate procedures to help top management gain better control over the business. In all such cases, those responsible for designing the system found very little of practical help, either in the literature or in management courses. Enormous difficulties in system design and implementation were encountered in every instance.

The purpose of this section is to discuss these design and implementation problems. The most frequently encountered problems are summarized in Table 3.2.

Table 3.2 Marketing planning systems: design and implementation problems

1 Weak support from chief executive and top management
2 Lack of a plan for planning
3 Lack of line management support
- hostility
- lack of skills
- lack of information
- lack of resources
- inadequate organization structure
4 Confusion over planning terms
5 Numbers in lieu of written objectives and strategies
6 Too much detail, too far ahead
7 Once-a-year ritual
8 Separation of operational planning from strategic planning
9 Failure to integrate marketing planning into a total corporate planning system
10 Delegation of planning to a planner

Weak support from chief executive and top management

There can be no doubt that unless the chief executive sees the need for a formalized marketing planning system, understands it and shows an active interest in it, it is virtually impossible for a senior functional marketing executive to initiate procedures that will be used in a meaningful way.

This is particularly so in companies that are organized on the basis of divisional management, for which the marketing executive has no profit responsibility and in which he or she has no line management authority. In such cases, it is comparatively easy for senior operational managers to create 'political' difficulties, the most serious of which is just to ignore the new procedures entirely. Usually, however, the reasons for not participating in procedures, or for only partially following instructions, centre on the issues summarized in Table 3.2.

The vital role that the chief executive and top management *must* play in marketing planning underlines one of the key points in this section.

MARKETING INSIGHT

A multinational oil company struggled for four years to make its new marketing planning system work. It was only after the Board took an interest and the new European Chief Executive started to drive the process that any tangible results were achieved.

> This key point is that it is *people* who make systems work, and that system design and implementation have to take account of the 'personality' of both the organization and the people involved, and that these are different in all organizations.

One of the most striking features we have observed is the difference in 'personalities' between companies, and the fact that within any one company there is a marked similarity between the attitudes of executives. These attitudes vary from the impersonal, autocratic kind at one extreme to the highly personal, participative kind at the other. This is discussed further in Chapter 11.

Any system, therefore, has to be designed around the people who have to make it work, and has to take account of the prevailing traditions, attitudes, skills, resource availability and organizational constraints. Since the chief executive and top management are the key influencers of these factors, without their active support and participation any formalized marketing planning system is unlikely to work. This fact emerged very clearly from the author's research, the worst possible manifestation of which was the way in which chief executives and top managers ignored plans which emerged from the planning system and continued to make key decisions which appeared illogical to those who had participated in the production of the plans. This very quickly destroyed any credibility that the emerging plans might have had, and led to the demise of the procedures and to serious levels of frustration throughout the organization.

Indeed, there is some evidence leading to the belief that chief executives who fail first to understand the essential role of marketing in generating profitable revenue in a business, and secondly to understand how marketing can be integrated into the other functional areas of the business

> The active interest of the chief executive and top management is vital if a formalized marketing planning system is to be successful.

through marketing planning procedures, are key contributory factors in poor economic performance.

> There is a depressing preponderance of executives who live by the rule of 'the bottom line' and who apply universal financial criteria indiscriminately to all products and markets, irrespective of the long-term consequences.

There is a similar preponderance of technical managers who see marketing as an unworthy activity that is something to do with activities such as television advertising; and who think of their products only in terms of their technical features and functional characteristics, in spite of the evidence that exists that these are only a part of what a customer buys.

Not surprisingly, in companies headed by people like this marketing planning is either non-existent or, where it is tried, it fails. This is the most frequently encountered barrier to effective marketing planning.

Lack of a plan for planning

The next most common cause of the failure or partial failure of marketing planning systems is the belief that once a system is designed, it can be implemented immediately.

One company achieved virtually no improvement in the quality of the plans coming into headquarters from the operating companies over a year after the introduction of a very sophisticated system.

MARKETING INSIGHT

The evidence indicates that a period of around three years is required in a major company before a complete marketing planning system can be implemented according to its design.

Failure, or partial failure, then, is often the result of not developing a timetable for introducing a new system to take account of the following:

1 The need to communicate why a marketing planning system is necessary
2 The need to recruit top management support and participation
3 The need to test the system out on a limited basis to demonstrate its effectiveness and value
4 The need for training programmes, or workshops, to train line management in its use
5 Lack of data and information in some parts of the world
6 Shortage of resources in some parts of the world.

Above all, a resolute sense of purpose and dedication is required, tempered by patience and a willingness to appreciate the inevitable problems which will be encountered in its implementation.

This problem is closely linked with the third major reason for planning system failure, which is lack of line management support.

Lack of line management support

Hostility, lack of skills, lack of data and information, lack of resources, and an inadequate organizational structure, all add up to a failure to obtain the willing participation of operational managers.

> Hostility on the part of line managers is by far the most common reaction to the introduction of new marketing planning systems. The reasons for this are not hard to find, and are related to the system initiators' lack of a plan for planning.

New systems inevitably require considerable explanation of the procedures involved and are usually accompanied by pro formas, flow charts and the like. Often these devices are most conveniently presented in the form of a manual. When such a document arrives on the desk of busy line managers, unheralded by previous explanation or discussion, the immediate reaction often appears to be fear of their possible inability to understand it and to comply with it, followed by anger and, finally, rejection. They begin to picture headquarters as a remote 'ivory tower', totally divorced from the reality of the marketplace.

This is often exacerbated by their absorption in the current operating and reward system, which is geared to the achievement of *current* results, while the new system is geared to the future. Also, because of the trend in recent years towards the frequent movement of executives around organizations, there is less interest in planning for future business gains from which someone else is likely to benefit.

> Allied to this is the fact that many line managers are ignorant of basic marketing principles, and have never been used to breaking up their markets into strategically relevant segments, nor of collecting meaningful information about them.

This lack of skill is compounded by the fact that there are many countries in the world which cannot match the wealth of useful information and data available in the USA and Europe. This applies particularly to rapidly-growing economies, where the limited aggregate statistics are not only unreliable and incomplete, but also quickly out of date. The seriousness of this problem is highlighted by the often rigid list of corporate headquarters' informational requirements, which is based totally on the home market.

The solution to this particular problem requires a good deal of patience, common sense, ingenuity and flexibility on the part of both headquarters and operating management. This is closely connected with the need to consider resource availability and the prevailing organization structure. The problem of lack of reliable data and information can only be solved by devoting time and money to its solution, and where available resources are scarce it is unlikely that the information demands of headquarters can be met.

It is for this reason that some kind of appropriate headquarters organization has to be found for the collection and dissemination of valuable information, and that training has to be provided on ways of solving this problem.

Again, these issues are complicated by the varying degrees of size and complexity of companies. It is surprising to see the extent to which organizational structures cater inadequately for marketing as a function. In small companies there is often no-one other than the sales manager, who spends all his or her time engaged either in personal selling or in managing the sales force. Unless the chief executive is marketing-orientated, marketing planning is just not done.

In medium-sized and large companies, particularly those that are divisionalized, there is rarely any provision at board level for marketing as a discipline. Sometimes there is a commercial director, with line management responsibility for the operating divisions, but apart from sales managers at divisional level, or a marketing manager at head office level, marketing as a function is not particularly well catered for. Where there is a marketing manager, he or she tends to be somewhat isolated from the mainstream activities.

> The most successful organizations are those with a fully integrated marketing function, whether it is line management responsible for sales, or a staff function, with operating units each being a microcosm of the head office organization.

However, it is clear that without a suitable organizational structure, any attempt to implement a marketing planning system which requires the collection, analysis and synthesis of market-related information is unlikely to be successful.

> A classic example of this was a large diversified multinational, where no provision was made at headquarters for marketing, other than through the divisional directors, and where divisions also generally had no marketing function other than sales management. Their first attempt at writing a strategic plan as a result of market pressures was a complete failure.

The problem of organizing for marketing planning is discussed further in Chapter 11.

Lack of a suitable organizational structure for an integrated marketing function, compounded by lack of meaningful information about market segments, means that marketing planning is unlikely to be successful.

Confusion over planning terms

Confusion over planning terms is another reason for the failure of marketing planning systems. The initiators of these systems, often highly qualified, frequently use a form of planning terminology that is perceived by operational managers as meaningless jargon. One company even referred to the ▶ **Ansoff** Matrix, and made frequent references to other forms of matrices, missions, dimensions, quadrants, and so on.

> Those companies with successful planning systems try to use terminology which will be familiar to operational management, and, where terms such as 'objectives' and 'strategies' are used, these are clearly defined, with examples given of their practical use.

Numbers in lieu of written objectives and strategies

Most managers in operating units are accustomed to completing sales forecasts, together with the associated financial implications. They are not accustomed to considering underlying causal factors for past performance or expected results, nor of highlighting opportunities, emphasizing key issues, and so on. Their outlook is essentially parochial and short term, with a marked tendency to extrapolate numbers and to project the current business unchanged into the next fiscal year.

Thus, when a marketing planning system suddenly requires that they should make explicit their implicit economic model of the business, they cannot do it. So, instead of finding words to express the logic of their objectives and strategies, they repeat their past behaviour and fill in the data sheets provided without any narrative.

It is the provision of data sheets, and the emphasis which the system places on the physical counting of things, that encourages the questionnaire-completion mentality and hinders the development of the creative analysis so essential to effective strategic planning.

> Those companies with successful marketing planning systems ask only for essential data and place greater emphasis on narrative to explain the underlying thinking behind the objectives and strategies.

Too much detail, too far ahead

Connected with this is the problem of over-planning, usually caused by elaborate systems that demand information and data that headquarters do not need and can never use. Systems that generate vast quantities of information are generally demotivating for all concerned.

The biggest problem in this connection is undoubtedly the insistence on a detailed and thorough marketing audit. In itself this is not a bad discipline to impose on managers, but to do so without also providing some guidance on how it should be summarized to point up the key issues merely leads to the production of vast quantities of useless information. Its uselessness stems from the fact that it robs the ensuing plans of focus and confuses those who read it by the amount of detail provided.

The trouble is that few managers have the creative or analytical ability to isolate the really key issues, with the result that far more problems and opportunities are identified than the company can ever cope with. Consequently, the truly key strategic issues are buried deep in the detail and do not receive the attention they deserve until it is too late.

In an over-detailed and institutionalized planning system, the key strategic issues may be buried so deep in the detail that they get overlooked until it is too late.

> In a number of companies with highly detailed and institutionalized marketing planning systems, the resulting plans contain so much detail that it is impossible to identify what the major objectives and strategies are.

Also, the managers in these companies are rarely able to express a simplified view of the business or of the essential things that have to be done today to ensure success. Such companies are often over-extended, trying to do too many things at once. Over-diversity, and being extended in too many directions, makes control over a confusingly heterogeneous portfolio of products and markets extremely difficult.

In companies with successful planning systems, there is at all levels a widespread understanding of the key objectives that have to be achieved, and of the means of achieving them.

> In such companies, the rationale of each layer of the business is clear, and actions and decisions are disciplined by clear objectives that hang logically together as part of a rational, overall purpose.

The clarity and cohesiveness is achieved by means of a system of 'layering'. At each successive level of management throughout the organization, lower-level analyses are synthesized into a form that ensures that only the essential information needed for decision-making and control purposes reaches the next level of management. Thus, there are hierarchies of audits, SWOT analyses, assumptions, objectives, strategies and plans. This means, for example, that at conglomerate headquarters the top management have a clear understanding of the really key macro-issues of company-wide significance, while at the lower level of profit responsibility the management also have a clear understanding of the really key micro-issues of significance to the unit.

It can be concluded that a good measure of the effectiveness of a company's marketing planning system is the extent to which different managers in the organization can make a clear, lucid and logical statement about the major problems and opportunities they face, how they intend to deal with these, and how what they are doing fits in with some greater overall purpose.

Once-a-year ritual

One of the commonest weaknesses in the marketing planning systems of those companies whose planning systems fail to bring the expected benefits is the ritualistic nature of the activity. In such cases, operating managers treat the writing of the marketing plan as a thoroughly irksome and unpleasant duty.

> The pro formas are completed, not always very diligently, and the resulting plans are quickly filed away, never to be referred to again. They are seen as something which is required by headquarters rather than as an essential tool of management.

In other words, the production of the marketing plan is seen as a once-a-year ritual, a sort of game of management bluff. It is not surprising that the resulting plans are not used.

While this is obviously closely related to the explanations already given as to why some planning systems are ineffective, a common feature of companies that treat marketing planning as a once-a-year ritual is the short lead time given for the completion of the process. The problem with this approach is that, in the minds of managers, it tends to be relegated to a position of secondary importance.

In companies with effective systems, the planning cycle will start in month three or four and run through to month nine or ten, with the total twelve-month period being used to evaluate the ongoing progress of existing plans by means of the company's marketing intelligence system. Thus, by spreading the planning activity over a longer period, and by means of the active participation of all levels of management at the appropriate moment, planning becomes an accepted and integral part of management behaviour rather than an addition to it which calls for unusual behaviour. There is a much better chance that plans resulting from such a system will be formulated in the sort of form that can be converted into things that people are actually going to do.

Separation of operational planning from strategic planning

This sub-section must be seen against the background of the difficulty which the majority of companies experience in carrying out any meaningful strategic planning. In the majority of cases, the figures that appear in the long-term corporate plan are little more than statistical extrapolations that satisfy boards of directors. If they are not satisfactory the numbers are just altered, and frequently the gap between where a company gets to, compared with where it had planned to be in real terms, grows wider over time.

> Nevertheless, most companies make long-term projections. Unfortunately, in the majority of cases these are totally separate from the short-term planning activity that takes place largely in the form of forecasting and budgeting.

The view that they should be separate is supported by many of the writers in this field, who describe strategic planning as very different, and therefore divorced, from operational planning. Indeed, many stress that failure to understand the essential difference between the two leads to confusion and prevents planning from becoming an integrated part of the company's overall management system. Yet it is precisely this separation between short- and long-term plans which the author's research revealed as being the major cause of the problems experienced today by many of the respondents.

> It is the failure of long-term plans to determine the difficult choices between the emphasis to be placed on current operations and the development of new business that leads to the failure of operating management to consider any alternatives to what they are currently doing.

The almost total separation of operational or short-term planning from strategic or long-term planning is a feature of many companies whose systems are not very effective.

> The almost total separation of operational planning is a feature of many companies with ineffective systems.

More often than not, the long-term strategic plans tend to be straight-line extrapolations of past trends, and because different people are often involved (such as corporate planners) to the exclusion of some levels of operating management, the resulting plans bear virtually no relationship to the more detailed and immediate short-term plans.

This separation positively discourages operational managers from thinking strategically, with the result that detailed operational plans are completed in a vacuum. The so-called strategic plans do not provide the much-needed cohesion and logic, because they are seen as an ivory-tower exercise which contains figures in which no one really believes.

> Unless strategic plans are built up from sound strategic analysis at grass-roots level by successive layers of operational management, they have little realism as a basis for corporate decisions.

At the same time, operational plans will become increasingly parochial in their outlook and will fail to incorporate the decisions that have to be taken today to safeguard the future.

Operational planning, then, should very much be part of the strategic planning process, and *vice versa*. Indeed, wherever possible they should be completed at the same time, using the same managers and the same informational inputs.

The detailed operational plan should be the first year of the long-term plan, and operational managers should be encouraged to complete their long-term projections at the same time as their short-term projections. The advantage is that this encourages managers to think about what decisions have to be made in the current planning year, in order to achieve the long-term projections.

Failure to integrate marketing planning into a total corporate planning system

It is difficult to initiate an effective marketing planning system in the absence of a parallel corporate planning system. This is yet another facet of the separation of operational planning from strategic planning. For, unless similar processes and time-scales to those being used in the marketing planning system are also being used by other major functions such as distribution, operations, finance and personnel, the sort of trade-offs and compromises that have to be made in any company between what is wanted and what is practicable and affordable will not take place in a rational way. These trade-offs have to be made on the basis of the fullest possible understanding of the reality of the company's multifunctional strengths and weaknesses, and opportunities and threats.

One of the problems of systems in which there is either a separation of the strategic corporate planning process, or in which marketing planning is the only formalized system, is the lack of participation of key functions of the company, such as research and development (R&D), information technology (IT) or production. Where these are key determinants of success, as is frequently the case, a separate marketing planning system is virtually ineffective.

How this problem can be overcome is spelled out in Chapter 11.

However, where marketing is a major activity, as in fast-moving industrial goods companies, it is possible to initiate a separate marketing planning system. The indications are that when this happens successfully, similar systems for other functional areas of the business quickly follow suit because of the benefits which are observed by the chief executive.

Delegation of planning to a planner

The incidence of this is higher with corporate planning than with marketing planning, although where there is some kind of corporate planning function at headquarters, and no organizational function for marketing, whatever strategic marketing planning takes place is done by the corporate planners as part of a system which is divorced from the operational planning mechanism. Not surprisingly, this exacerbates the separation of operational planning from strategic planning and encourages short-term thinking in the operational units.

Very often, corporate planners are young, highly qualified people, attached to the office of the chairman or group chief executive. They appear to be widely resented and are largely ignored by the mainstream of the business. There is not much evidence that they succeed in clarifying the company's overall strategy, and there appears to be very little account taken of such strategies in the planning and thinking of operational units.

The literature sees the planner basically as a coordinator of the planning, not as an initiator of goals and strategies. It is clear that without the ability and the willingness of operational management to cooperate, a planner becomes little more than a kind of headquarters administrative assistant. In many large companies, where there is a person at headquarters with the specific title of marketing planning manager, he or she has usually been appointed as a result of the difficulty of controlling businesses that have grown rapidly in size and diversity, and which present a baffling array of new problems to deal with.

> Without the cooperation of operational management, a planner becomes little more than a headquarters administrative assistant.

The marketing planning manager's tasks are essentially those of system design and coordination of inputs, although he or she is also expected to formulate overall objectives and strategies for the board.

> In all cases, it is lack of line management skills and inadequate organizational structures that frustrates the company's marketing efforts, rather than inadequacies on the part of the planner. This puts the onus on the planner alone to do a lot of the planning, which is, not surprisingly, largely ineffective.

Two particularly interesting facts emerged from the author's research. Firstly, the marketing planning manager, as the designer and initiator of systems for marketing planning, is often in an impossibly delicate political position *vis-à-vis* both superior line managers and more junior operational managers. It is clear that not too many chief executives understand the role of planning and they have unrealistic expectations of the planner, whereas the planner cannot operate effectively without the full understanding, cooperation and participation of top management – and this rarely happens. Often, the appointment of a marketing planning manager, and sometimes of a senior marketing executive, seems to be an easier step for the chief executive and the board to take than giving serious consideration themselves to the implications of the new forces affecting the business and reformulating an overall strategy.

> The inevitable consequence of employing a marketing planning manager is the need for change in management behaviour, the implications of which may be far-reaching.

This leads on naturally to a second point. The inevitable consequence of employing a marketing planning manager is that he or she will need to initiate changes in management behaviour in order to become effective. Usually these are far-reaching in their implications, affecting training, resource allocation, and organizational structures. As the catalyst for such changes, the planner, not surprisingly, comes up against enormous political barriers, the result of which is that he or she often becomes frustrated and, eventually, ineffective. This is without doubt a major problem, particularly for big companies. The problems which are raised by a marketing planning manager occur directly as a result of the failure of top management to give thought to the formulation of overall strategies. They have not done this in the past because they have not felt the need. However, when market pressures force the emerging problems of diversity and control to the surface, without a total willingness on their part to participate in far-reaching changes, there really is not much that a planner can do.

This raises the question again of the key role of the chief executive in the whole business of marketing planning. Without his or her support and understanding of the very serious implications of initiating effective marketing planning procedures, whatever efforts are made, whether by a planner or a line manager, they will be largely ineffective.

■ Requisite marketing planning systems

The implications of all this are principally as follows:

► **DEFINITION** ◄

A closed loop system is a bureaucratic planning system that consists mainly of pro formas for completion by managers according to predetermined headings and formats. Such systems frequently degenerate into stale form-filling exercises and there is little opportunity for adding creative insights

1　Any ► **closed loop** marketing planning system (but especially one that is essentially a forecasting and budgeting system) will lead to a gradual decline of marketing and creativity. Therefore, there has to be some mechanism for preventing inertia from setting in through the over-bureaucratization of the system.

2　Marketing planning undertaken at the functional level of marketing, in the absence of a means of integration with other functional areas of the business at general management level, will be largely ineffective.

3　The separation of responsibility for operational and strategic marketing planning will lead to a divergence of the short-term thrust of a business at the operational level from the long-term objectives of the enterprise as a whole. This will encourage a preoccupation with short-term results at operational level, which normally makes the firm less effective in the long term.

4　Unless the chief executive understands and takes an active role in marketing planning, it will never be an effective system.

5　A period of up to three years is necessary (especially in large firms) for the successful introduction of an effective marketing planning system.

In Chapter 12 of this book we will explore in detail what is meant by the term 'requisite marketing planning', when we explain how to design and implement an effective marketing planning system.

For now, we believe we have given sufficient background information about the *process* of marketing planning, and why this apparently simple process requires much more perception and attention than is typically accorded it. We can now go on to explore in more detail each of the elements of this process before putting all the pieces together again in the final chapter.

■ Application question

Taking each of the issues listed in Tables 3.1 and 3.2:

1   In what ways do they apply to your company?
2   In what ways do you deal successfully with them?

Chapter 3 review

Ignorance

Most companies plan, using a combination of forecasting and budgeting systems. These tend to project current business into the future, which can work if the future is going to be the same as the present or the past. As a result of using such systems, the following problems often occur:

1   Lost opportunities for profit
2   Meaningless numbers in long-term plans
3   Unrealistic objectives
4   Lack of actionable market information
5   Interfunctional strife
6   Management frustration
7   Proliferation of products and markets
8   Wasted promotional expenditure
9   Confusion over pricing
10   Growing vulnerability to changes in the business environment
11   Loss of control over the business.

Try Exercise 3.1

Common implementation problems

1   Weak support from the chief executive and top management
2   Lack of a plan for planning

3   Lack of line management support due to:
  ■ hostility
  ■ lack of skills
  ■ lack of resources
  ■ lack of information
  ■ inadequate organization structure
4   Confusion over planning terms
5   Numbers in lieu of written objectives and strategies
6   Too much detail, too far ahead
7   Once-a-year ritual
8   Separation of operational marketing planning from strategic marketing planning
9   Failure to integrate marketing planning into the total corporate planning system
10   Delegation of planning to a planner.   *Try Exercise 3.2*

Questions raised for the company

1   Q: If we introduce marketing planning, will we automatically become more successful?
     A: No. Many other factors come into play.
2   Q: What are these factors?
     A: Here are three common factors:
       (a) Companies who by chance are in high growth markets often don't plan. They are just dragged along by the general momentum.
       (b) If the company's culture and management style are not really supportive of marketing planning (i.e. there is no real belief in it), no improvements will occur.
       (c) If the business is highly competitive, no improvement will necessarily be seen. *But* the company might fare much worse without a marketing plan.
3   Q: Is all the time and effort put into marketing planning going to be worthwhile?
     A: Only you can say. Weigh up the costs of planning against the costs of not planning.

EXERCISES

Introduction to Chapter 3 exercises

The first exercise focuses on the types of problem that your company might be experiencing because of inefficiencies in the marketing planning system. In this sense it is providing an additional diagnosis about whether or not you need to improve your system. At the same time it helps to uncover some of the areas on which any new planning process needs to make an impact.

The second exercise attempts to be quite specific in pinpointing which aspects of the company need to be addressed in order to bring about the biggest improvements in marketing planning.

Put an 'X' at the point you feel is appropriate as being descriptive of your company against each of the statements below:

Exercise 3.1
Symptoms of a lack of marketing planning

	Mainly true	Mainly untrue
1 We seem to be missing opportunities for making profit		
2 Our long-term planning seems to be nothing more than lots of meaningless numbers		
3 Looked at rationally, our marketing objectives are unreasonable		
4 We lack actionable marketing information		
5 Managers are frustrated by the inter-functional strife and rivalry which seem to exist		
6 There seems to be a steady proliferation of products and/or markets		
7 Much of our promotional expenditure is wasted		
8 There is confusion over pricing		
9 We are becoming increasingly vulnerable to changes in our business environment		
10 There is a feeling that we are not running the business, but that it and outside forces are running us		

If you find it difficult to put an 'X' against any statement, you should confer with some colleagues rather than making guesses.

Join the 'X' for statement 1 to the 'X' of statement 2 with a straight line. Then join 2 to 3, 3 to 4, etc. in a similar way down to 10.

Interpretation of Exercise 3.1

You have just drawn a 'profile' of 'marketing planning' in your company.

If your 'profile line' tends to be positioned to the right-hand side of the spectrum, then it appears that you are not experiencing many of the problems which stem from a lack of marketing planning. In other words, you appear to be doing things fairly well. If, on the other hand, your profile line tends towards the left-hand side, you are much less fortunate, and should consider reviewing your current marketing planning process, paying particular attention to the problems you wish to overcome.

Exercise 3.2

Marketing planning questionnaire – organizational issues

You are asked to answer a series of statements about your organization's approach to marketing planning. Since this quest is for useful and genuine data, please try to be as accurate and objective as you can as you complete this document.

You score the questionnaire by entering a number, 1–5, *only in the position indicated by the line next to each statement*. Choose your scores, using these criteria:

1 If you strongly disagree with statement
2 If you tend to disagree with statement
3 If you don't know whether you agree or disagree
4 If you tend to agree with statement
5 If you strongly agree with statement

	A	B	C	D	E
1 The chief executive and directors show an active interest in marketing planning					–
2 The chief executive and directors demonstrate their understanding of marketing planning	–				
3 The chief executive and directors use the marketing plan as the basis for making key marketing decisions				–	
4 The chief executive and directors allocate adequate resources to ensure the marketing plan is completed satisfactorily		–			
5 The need for a marketing plan is clearly explained to all managers	–				
6 There is adequate information/data upon which to base a marketing plan		–			
7 Our marketing plan has a good balance between short-term and long-term objectives				–	
8 People are clear about their role in the marketing planning process					–
9 Line managers are trained to understand how the marketing planning process operates	–				
10 Line operational managers believe the marketing plan is a useful document				–	
11 Enough time is allowed for the planning process		–			

	A	B	C	D	E
12 It is made easy for line managers to understand the plan	–				
13 Marketing planning is never starved for lack of resources		–			
14 It is reasonable for a company like ours to have a well-thought-out marketing plan				–	
15 Reasons for past successes or failures are analysed			–		
16 In our organization we don't leave planning just to the planners; other managers have a valuable contribution to make					–
17 Our organizational style encourages a sound marketing planning process				–	
18 There is a clear understanding of the marketing terminology we use in our organization		–			
19 Market opportunities are highlighted by the planning process			–		
20 Functional specialists contribute to the marketing planning process					–
21 We limit our activities so that we are not faced with trying to do too many things at one time		–			
22 Taking part in marketing planning in our organization holds a high prospect of being rewarded, either financially or in career terms				–	
23 Only essential data appear in our plans			–		
24 Marketing does not operate in an 'ivory tower'				–	
25 From the wealth of information available to use, we are good at picking out the key issues	–				
26 There is a balance between narrative explanation and numerical data in our plans			–		
27 Our field sales force operates in a way which is supportive to our marketing plan					–

	A	B	C	D	E
28 Our plan demonstrates a high level of awareness of the 'macro' issues facing us	–				
29 Inputs to the planning process are on the whole as accurate as we can make them		–			
30 Marketing planning is always tackled in a meaningful and serious way			–		
31 Our plan doesn't duck the major problems and opportunities faced by the organization				–	
32 There is a high awareness of 'micro' issues in our plan	–				
33 Our plans recognize that in the short term we have to match our current capabilities to the market opportunities		–			
34 Inputs to the marketing planning process are an integral part of the job of all line managers					–
35 Marketing planning is a priority issue in our organization				–	
36 Our planning inputs are not 'massaged' to satisfy senior executives		–			
37 People understand and are reasonably happy that our marketing planning process is logical and appropriate	–				
38 We use the same timescale for our marketing plans as we do for finance, distribution, production and personnel		–			
39 We view our operational plan as the first year of our long-term plan, not as a separate entity				–	
40 Senior executives do not see themselves as operating beyond the confines of the marketing plan				–	
41 The advocates of 'correct' marketing planning are senior enough in the company to make sure it happens				–	
42 People are always given clear instructions about the nature of their expected contribution to the marketing plan		–			

	A	B	C	D	E
43 We try to make data collection and retrieval as simple as possible	–				
44 Our marketing plans do not go into great detail, but usually give enough information to make any necessary point			–		
45 The role of specialists is made quite clear in our planning process					–
46 We are always prepared to learn any new techniques that will make our marketing planning process more effective	–				
47 The role of marketing planning is clearly understood in the organization					–
48 Marketing research studies (by internal staff or agencies) are often used as inputs to our marketing planning process		–			–
49 Our marketing planning is regularly evaluated in an attempt to improve the process			–		
50 The chief executive and directors receive information which enables them to assess whether or not the marketing plan is coming to fruition as expected					–
TOTAL SCORES					

Add up the total scores in each column.

The rationale behind the questionnaire

There are many ways of looking at organizations and establishing 'models' of how they operate. One very common model is the organization chart, which attempts to show how responsibility is distributed throughout the company, and to clarify the chains of command.

Other models are derived from the inputs and outputs of the company. For example, a financial model is built up by analysing all the necessary financial inputs required to conduct the business and monitoring the efficiency by which these are converted into sales revenue.

The questionnaire in Exercise 3.2 is based on a particularly useful model, one which helps us to understand the relationship between different facets of the organization. By understanding the nature of these relationships, we are better placed to introduce organizational change – in this case, an improved marketing planning system.

There are three main assumptions behind this model:

1 *That the organization today is to some extent, often very strongly, conditioned by its historical background*. For example, if historically there has never been a pressing need for a comprehensive marketing planning system because of favourable trading conditions, then this will be reflected in the current planning system and the attitudes of the company's staff.
2 *That the organization today is to some extent, sometimes strongly, conditioned and directed by its future goals*. For example, the company that senses its marketing planning processes need to improve will take steps to introduce changes. That these changes will make an impact on organizational life is self-evident. Furthermore, much of the resistance to be overcome will stem from the 'historical' forces mentioned above.
3 *What actually happens in an organization is determined by the skills, knowledge, experience and beliefs of the organization's personnel*. Thus at the heart of any organization is the collective expertise or 'knowledge' at its disposal. This will ultimately determine the success it has in any work it undertakes, whether it is making goods or providing services.

Clearly, then, the level of 'knowledge' will also be a determining factor in the quality and scope of the company's marketing planning process. These assumptions provide the 'skeleton' of our organizational model (Figure 3.1).

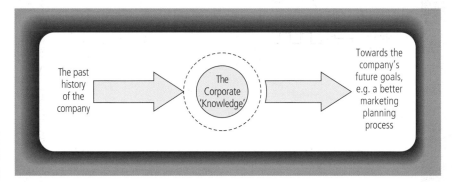

Figure 3.1
Knowledge and
marketing planning

There are still important elements missing from this model. Irrespective of the company's corporate sum of available skills and knowledge, nothing can be produced without physical *resources* being made available. The key resources required for marketing planning will be accurate data, means of storing and retrieving the data, adequate staff and time to analyse the data.

However, having the right resources isn't the whole solution; the company must also develop the best systems or *routines* to optimize the use of these resources. In marketing planning terms, concern is likely to focus on routines associated with collecting data, evaluating past performance, spotting marketing opportunities, sifting essential information from non-essential information, etc.

Routines, however, do not necessarily look after themselves. As soon as any system is set up, *roles and relationships* need to be defined. Who is going to do what to ensure that things happen?

Again, in marketing planning terms this will call into question the role of various members of staff, from the chief executive downwards. How clear are people about their role in the planning process? Should planning just be left to the planning department? What is the role of functional specialists? Who actually collects marketing data? Whom do they present it to? Many questions have to be answered if the subsequent routines are going to function smoothly.

Even this isn't the end of the story, because once roles are defined there is still the problem of setting up the right *organizational structure and climate* – one that will enable people to fulfil their roles in a productive way.

From a marketing-planning viewpoint, structure and climate issues surface in several ways – for example, the level of commitment to the planning process, the degree to which functional specialists are integrated into the planning process, the degree to which long- and short-term issues are accommodated, the extent to which the company is prepared to tackle the real and important issues it faces, the openness of communications, etc.

It is now possible to see how the completed model looks (Figure 3.2).

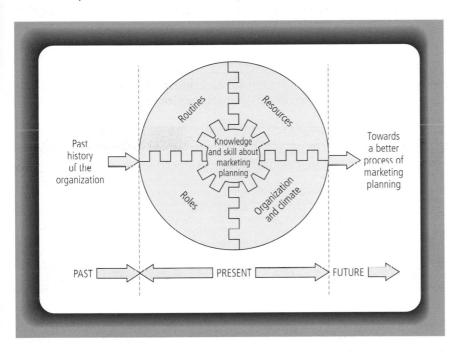

Figure 3.2
Marketing planning model

From the foregoing explanation, it is possible to see how the different facets of the organization all interrelate.

A The 'corporate knowledge', about marketing planning
B The resources allocated to planning
C The routines or systems that are used
D The roles and relationships of those engaged in marketing planning
E The organizational structure and climate, and the extent to which it supports marketing planning

Thus, to introduce an improved marketing planning system might call for changes in all these areas. Some personnel might need training, more or different resources might be required, routines or systems might need improving, roles and relationships perhaps need to be reappraised, and the structure and climate of the organization might need to be re-examined.

Conversely, only one or two of these areas might need tackling. The questionnaire is designed to provide a 'snapshot' of the company and to help you identify which areas might be the starting point for introducing improvements.

Interpretation of Exercise 3.2
Add up the scores for columns A, B, C, D and E and write them in the boxes provided. Each of the letters represents a potential barrier to marketing planning, namely:

A   Cognitive barrier, i.e. knowledge and skills
B   Resource barrier, i.e. lack of time, people, data
C   Systems/routine barrier, i.e. lack of procedures
D   Organizational climate barrier, i.e. belief and interest in marketing planning
E   Behaviour barrier, i.e. the roles people play

The maximum score for each of these areas is 50 points. The higher the score, the less that potential barrier to marketing is likely to be making an impact. In other words, the areas with low scores (below 30) will probably be the areas worth investigating initially in the search for improvement.

Personal notes
List what actions need to be taken.

CHAPTER 4

Completing the marketing audit:
1 The customer and market audit

Summary

- A discussion of whom we sell to
- The difference between consumers and customers
- Why market share is important and why the term 'market' must be carefully defined
- Pareto analysis (the 80/20 rule) and its implications
- The market segmentation process is outlined in detail. The steps are:
  - market definition
  - market mapping
  - listing who buys
  - combining into lists of who buys what
  - listing why these micro-segments buy what they buy
  - combining the micro-segments into larger segments by means of cluster analysis
- Methodologies are outlined and explained throughout
- Examples of market segmentation are provided
- Exercises to turn the theory into actionable propositions
- The next chapter focuses on what we sell to these identified markets

■ Introduction

This chapter contains some extracts from *Market Segmentation: How to do it; How to profit from it*, by Malcolm McDonald and Ian Dunbar (Butterworth-Heinemann, Oxford, 2004). These are reproduced with the permission of the authors.

Now we understand the process of marketing planning, we can begin to look in more detail at its principal components. We have, as it were, seen the picture on the front of the jigsaw puzzle; we can now examine the individual pieces with a better understanding of where they fit.

The next two chapters are designed to help us to carry out a meaningful marketing audit. We have already looked at the issues that need to be considered; what we need now are the means to help us to undertake such an analysis.

It should be stressed that, while the following two chapters deal specifically with how to carry out a customer, market, and product audit, it should not be assumed that, in carrying out a marketing audit, price, promotion, place, information and organization are unimportant. Indeed, Chapters 7–11 are devoted to these important determinants of commercial success and will provide the marketing auditor with the necessary confidence to carry out these specific parts of the audit.

> It is also important to stress that we are still dealing with steps in the marketing planning process, rather than with the all-important output of the process, the strategic marketing plan itself.

This chapter continues to explain the process of marketing planning, rather that the plan itself.

It will be recalled that the contents of the strategic marketing plan, outlined in Chapter 2, represent the summarized conclusions emanating from the marketing audit and will only be as good as the audit allows. The marketing audit itself should be a separate step in the process, and under no circumstances should voluminous data and analysis appear in the plan itself. All of this rightly belongs in the marketing audit document.

Thus, the marketing audit is a crucial stage in the marketing plan itself, the actual contents of which are set out in detail in Chapter 13.

At this point, let us revisit our earlier definition of marketing and the accompanying diagram, shown here as Figure 4.1.

The actual contents of the marketing plan itself are set out in detail in Chapter 13.

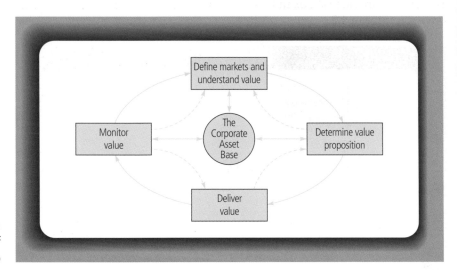

Figure 4.1
Overview of
marketing map

Marketing is a process for:

- defining markets
- quantifying the needs of the customer groups (segments) within these markets
- determining the value propositions to meet these needs
- communicating these value propositions to all those people in the organization responsible for delivering them and getting their buy-in to their role
- playing an appropriate part in delivering these value propositions (usually only communications)
- monitoring the value actually delivered.

For this process to be effective, organizations need to be consumer-/customer-driven.

This process is clearly cyclical, in that monitoring the value delivered will update the organization's understanding of the value that is required by its customers. The cycle may be predominantly an annual one, with a marketing plan documenting the output from the 'understand value' and 'create value proposition' processes, but equally changes throughout the year may involve fast iterations around the cycle to respond to particular opportunities or problems.

This chapter, and Chapter 5, describe the process involved in this first box under the headings 'The customer and market audit' and 'The product audit', both being integral to defining markets and understanding and quantifying the value required by the customer groups (segments) within these markets.

Input to this process will commonly include:

- the corporate mission and objectives, which will determine which markets are of interest
- external data such as market research
- internal data which flows from the deliver value activities.

The process in the first box in Figure 4.1 involves four major sub-processes, shown in Figure 4.2.

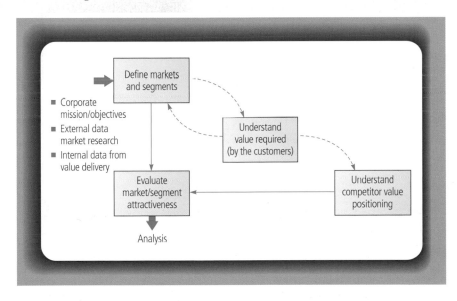

Figure 4.2
Define markets and understand value

First, it is necessary to define the markets the organization is in, or wishes to be in, and how these divide into segments of customers with similar needs. The choice of markets will be influenced by the corporate objectives as well as the asset base. Information will be collected about the markets, such as the markets' size and growth, with estimates for the future.

Once each market or segment has been defined, it is necessary to understand what value the customers within the segment want or need. This value is most simply thought of as the benefits gained from the product or service, but it can also encompass the value to the customer of surrounding services such as maintenance or information. This step also encompasses what the customer is prepared to give in exchange, in terms of price and other criteria – such as lifetime running cost or convenience of purchase. One way of expressing customer value requirements is via a critical success factor analysis which might list such criteria as product specification, quality or reliability, the quality and range of services, price and the ease of purchase, and which might also include weights to illustrate their relative importance to the customer in the buying decision.

This step of 'Understand value required' also includes predicting the value which will be required in the future.

In performing this step, it may emerge that subsets of the customers within a market have very different requirements. In this case, the market may need to be further segmented to represent these subsets. Hence there is an important feedback loop from this step to the 'Define markets' step. How markets are defined and segmented will be spelled out later in this chapter.

'Understand competitor value positioning' refers to the process of establishing how well the organization and its competitors currently deliver the value that the customers seek. To illustrate in terms of critical success factors, this process would correspond to scoring the organization and its competitors on each of the customers' success factors. Again it involves looking into the future to predict how competitors might improve – clearly a factor in planning how the organization is to respond. SWOT analysis is one tool used here, and will be explained in detail in Chapter 5.

From these three processes, the relative attractiveness of the different markets or segments can be evaluated.

The output will be some form of analysis, such as a 'marketing audit'. One way of summing up much of the key information is a portfolio matrix such as a Boston Matrix or a Directional Policy Matrix. These are explained in detail in Chapter 5.

We now turn our attention to one of the key determinants of successful marketing planning – market segmentation. This is fundamental to the matching process described in Chapter 1. But, in order to understand market segmentation, it is first necessary to appreciate the difference between ▶ **customers** and ▶ **consumers**, the meaning of market share, and the phenomenon known as the Pareto effect.

▶ **DEFINITION** ◀

The consumer is the final consumer of goods or services. Customers are people or organizations who buy directly from us

■ The difference between customers and consumers

Let us start with the difference between customers and consumers. The term 'consumer' is interpreted by most to mean the final consumer, who is not necessarily the customer. Take the example of parents who are buying breakfast cereals. The chances are that they are intermediate customers, acting as agents on behalf of the eventual consumers (their family) and, in order to market cereals effectively, it is clearly necessary to understand what the end-consumer wants, as well as what the parents want.

This is only relevant in that it is always necessary to be aware of the needs of eventual consumers down the buying chain.

Consider the case of the industrial purchasing officer buying raw materials such as wool tops for conversion into semi-finished cloths, which are then sold to other companies for incorporation into the final product – say a suit or a dress – for sale in consumer markets. Here, we can see that the requirements of those various intermediaries and the end-user are eventually translated into the specifications of the purchasing officer to the raw materials manufacturer. Consequently, the market needs that this manufacturing company is attempting to satisfy must in the last analysis be defined in terms of the requirements of the ultimate user – the consumer – even though the direct customer is quite clearly the purchasing officer.

Given that we can appreciate the distinction between customers and consumers and the need constantly to be alert to any changes in the ultimate consumption patterns of the products to which our own product contributes, the next question to be faced is: who are our customers?

Direct customers are those people or organizations who actually buy direct from us. They could, therefore, be distributors, retailers and the like. However, as intimated in the previous paragraph, there is a tendency for organizations to confine their interest, and hence their marketing, only to those who actually place orders. This can be a major mistake, as can be seen from the following case history.

A fertilizer company that had grown and prospered during the 1970s and 1980s, because of the superior nature of its products, reached its farmer consumers via merchants (wholesalers). However, as other companies copied the technology, the merchants began to stock competitive products and drove prices and margins down. Had the fertilizer company paid more attention to the needs of its different farmer groups and developed products especially for them, based on farmer segmentation, it would have continued to create demand pull through differentiation.

This company recovered its position by understanding the needs of its different farmer groups and targeting them with specific propositions, resulting in it becoming the most profitable company in its sector.

There are countless other examples of companies which, because they did not pay sufficient attention to the needs of users further down the value chain, gradually ceased to provide any real value to their direct customers and eventually went out of business.

MARKETING INSIGHT

An excellent example of good practice is Procter & Gamble in the USA supplying Wal-Mart, the giant food retailer. As can be seen from the simple diagram below, P & G creates demand pull (hence high turnover and high margins) by paying detailed attention to the needs of consumers. But it also pays detailed attention to the needs of its direct customer, Wal-Mart. Wal-Mart is able to operate on very low margins because, as the bar code goes across the till, this is when P & G invoices Walmart, produces another and activates the distribution chain, all of this being done by means of integrated IT processes. This way, it has reduced Wal-Mart's costs by hundreds of millions of dollars.

Closely related to the question of the difference between customers and consumers is the question of what our market share is.

■ Market share

Most business people already understand that there is a direct relationship between relatively high share of any market and high returns on investment, as shown in Figure 4.3.

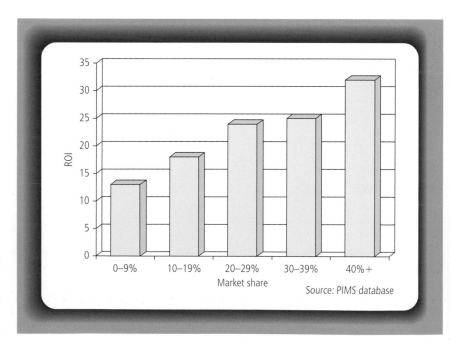

Figure 4.3
The relationship between market share and return on investment

Clearly, however, since BMW is not in the same market as Ford, for example, it is important to be most careful about how 'market' is defined. Correct market definition is crucial for: measuring market share and market growth; the specification of target customers; recognition of relevant competitors; and, most importantly of all, the formulation of marketing strategy, for it is this, above all else, that delivers differential advantage.

The general rule for ▶ **market** definition is that it should be described in terms of a customer need in a way which covers the aggregation of all the products or services which customers regard as being capable of satisfying the same need. For example, we would regard the in-company caterer as only one option when it came to satisfying lunch-time hunger. This particular need could also be satisfied at external restaurants, public houses, fast-food specialists and sandwich bars. The emphasis in the definition, therefore, is clearly on the word 'need'.

Aggregating currently available products/services is, however, simply an aid to arriving at the definition, as it is important to recognize that new products, yet to be developed, could better satisfy the users' need. For example, the button manufacturer who believed their market was the 'button market' would have been very disappointed when zips and Velcro began to satisfy the need for fastenings! A needs-based definition for this company would have enabled the management to recognize the fickleness of current products, and to accept that one of their principal tasks was to seek out better ways of satisfying their market's needs and to evolve their product offer accordingly.

The following example may help in defining the market your business is in.

▶ **DEFINITION** ◀

A market is the aggregation of all the products or services which customers regard as being capable of satisfying the same need

A company manufacturing nylon carpet for the commercial sector wanted to check that it had a realistic definition of the market it was in. The first step was to map out the total available market for all floor covering:

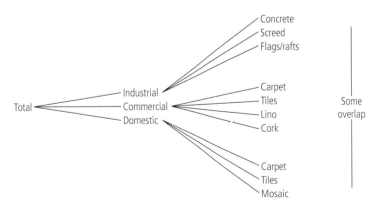

Clearly, it would be wrong to include the three types of floor covering used in the industrial sector in the company's market

definition. The qualities required from such flooring cannot hope to be matched in a carpet made from any currently known type of fibre. Similarly, in both the commercial and domestic sectors, nylon carpet is not a competitor for the luxury end of the market. This luxury part of the market buys carpet made from natural fibres, particularly wool.

This leaves the non-luxury commercial and domestic sectors which, in total, represented the company's potential available market. It was potentially available because the company could, for example, produce nylon carpet for the domestic sector and extend its market this way. Similarly, the company could move into manufacturing nylon carpet tiles and extend its operation into this product for both the domestic and commercial sectors. There was also no reason why the company should not look at replacing lino, cork or mosaic flooring with nylon carpet.

Many of the opportunities in the potentially available market, however, represent possible strategies for the future. They would be considered during the marketing planning process when the future plans for the current business activity did not achieve the required financial targets. The question now, therefore, is, what is the company's realistically available market?

To assist the company in this final stage of arriving at a market definition, the 'needs' being met by the current products, as high-lighted by the current customers, were first listed. This revealed that the company's nylon carpet was bought because:

- it fell into a particular price range
- it was quiet underfoot
- it had a life expectancy of 15 years
- it was available in pleasant colours and textures
- the market was within a 60-mile radius of the manufacturing plant.

In addition to the obvious, this list removed lino, cork and mosaic from the company's available market.

Finally, the company looked at the applicability of its current distribution and selling methods to the potentially available market, ruling out those sections of the market which required different selling *and* distribution approaches. This meant that it was unrealistic to include the domestic sector in the market definition.

Products and manufacturers which met all the criteria were then listed, along with their end users. The company had now arrived at both a market definition and a current market size, while still keeping open the option of extending it, should the need arise.

This example also illustrates the need to arrive at a meaningful balance between a broad market definition and a manageable market definition. Too narrow a definition has the pitfall of restricting the range of new opportunities that segmentation could open up for your business.

On the other hand, too broad a definition may make marketing planning meaningless. For example, the television broadcasting companies are in the 'entertainment' market, which also consists of theatres, cinemas and theme parks, to name but a few. This is a fairly broad definition. It may, therefore, be more manageable for the television broadcasters, when looking at segmenting their market, to define their market as being the 'home entertainment' market. This could then be further refined into the pre-school, child, teenager, family, or adult home entertainment market.

To help with calculating market share, the following definitions are useful:

- Product class, e.g. cigarettes, computers, fertilizers, carpets
- Product subclass, e.g. filter, personal computers, nitrogen, carpet tiles
- Product brand, e.g. Silk Cut, IBM, Intel, Heuga.

Silk Cut as a brand, for the purpose of measuring market share, is only concerned with *the aggregate of all other brands that satisfy the same group of customer wants*. Nevertheless, the manufacturer of Silk Cut also needs to be aware of the sales trends of filter cigarettes and the cigarette market in total.

One of the most frequent mistakes that is made by people who do not understand what market share really means is to assume that their company has only a small share of some market, whereas, if the company is commercially successful, it probably has a much larger share of a smaller market.

Whilst it is tempting to think that the examples given above amount to 'rigging' the definition of market and that there is the danger of fooling ourselves, we must never lose sight of the purpose of market segmentation, which is to enable us to create competitive advantage for ourselves by creating greater value for our customers.

> It is necessary to arrive at a meaningful balance between a broad market definition and a manageable market definition.

Thus, for the carpet manufacturer, or for a London orchestra that defines its market as the aggregation of all London classical orchestras rather than as all entertainment, as long as its market definition enables it to outperform its competitors and grow profitably, this is the key. Obviously, however, the definition needs to be kept under review and revised, if necessary.

MARKETING INSIGHT

To summarize, correct market definition is crucial for the purpose of:

- share measurement
- growth measurement
- the specification of target customers
- the recognition of relevant competitors
- the formulation of marketing objectives and strategies.

This brings us to another useful and fascinating observation about markets.

■ Pareto effect

It is a phenomenon commonly observed by most companies that a small
proportion of their customers accounts for a large proportion of their business. This is often referred to as the 80/20 rule, or the ► **Pareto** effect,
whereby about 20 per cent of customers account for about 80 per cent of
business.

If we graph the proportion of customers that account for a certain proportion of sales, then we might expect to find a relationship similar to that
shown in Figure 4.4. Here, customers have been categorized simply as A,
B or C according to the proportion of sales they account for. The A customers, perhaps 25 per cent of the total, account for about 70 per cent of
sales; B customers, say 55 per cent of the total, account for 20 per cent of
total sales; and C customers, 20 per cent of the total, account for the
remaining 10 per cent of sales.

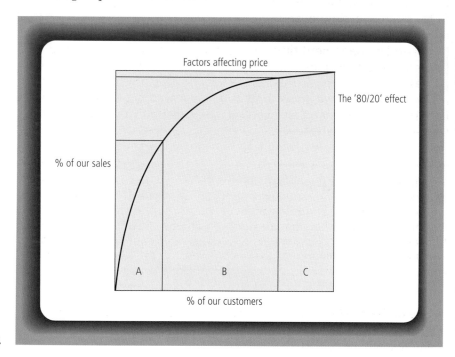

Figure 4.4

The Pareto effect is found in almost all markets, from capital industrial
goods to banking and consumer goods. What is the significance of this?
What is certain is that it does not mean that a company should drop 80 per
cent of its customers! For one thing, the sales volume bought by these customers makes a valuable contribution to overheads. For another, it is
almost certain that the 80/20 rule would still apply to the remaining 20
per cent. One could go on forever, until there was only a single customer
left! However, in carrying out this kind of analysis, it should become obvious where the company should be placing its greatest effort.

There is, however, a serious danger. This form of analysis is static. In other words, the best potential customers may well be in the 80 per cent, or even in the larger group of non-customers.

It is obvious, then, that while such analysis is vital, great care is necessary over how it is used. This is something we can now begin to discuss.

One manufacturer in the soft drinks industry did an analysis of its trade in the south-east of England and found that almost 85 per cent of its trade was coming from 20 per cent of its customers. Yet exactly the same service was being given to them all. All were receiving fortnightly calls from the sales force, all received a fortnightly delivery, and all paid the same price for the product. Not surprisingly, this led to an enormous investment in depots and vehicles, while the associated operating expenses were out of all proportion to the margins enjoyed by the company. In this case, there was a simple answer. Most of the small accounts were handed over to a grateful wholesaler, which freed valuable capital and management time to concentrate on the really important areas of the business. Meanwhile, the company's pricing policy was revised to reward those customers who bought more, and the sales force was now free to concentrate on developing its existing business and on opening new profitable outlets.

The chairman of one European airline, alas now bankrupt, told his assembled general managers that his ambition was for his airline to be the best in the world and to provide customer service to the point of obsession. The problem was that his airline didn't compete in many markets, whilst their unfocused customer obsession policy led them to give service they just couldn't afford. Heroic and unfocused statements such as this chairman's do more harm than good!

MARKETING INSIGHT

One of the most important aspects of marketing planning is being able to choose the best 20 per cent of your market to focus on. A method of doing this will be provided in Chapter 5.

■ Market segmentation

We can now begin to concentrate on a methodology for making market segmentation a reality, ▶ **market segmentation**, being the means by which any company seeks to gain a differential advantage over its competitors.

Markets usually fall into natural groups, or segments, which contain customers who exhibit a similar level of interest in the same broad requirements.

▶ **DEFINITION** ◀

A market segment consists of a group of customers within a market who share a similar level of interest in the same, or comparable, set of needs

These segments form separate markets in themselves and can often be of considerable size. Taken to its extreme, each individual consumer is a unique market segment, for all people are different in their requirements. While CRM systems (discussed in Chapter 11) have made it possible to engage in one-to-one communications, this is not viable in most organizations unless the appropriate organizational economies of scale have been obtained at a higher level of aggregation such as at segment level. Consequently, products are made to appeal to groups of customers who share approximately the same needs.

It is not surprising, then, to hear that there are certain universally accepted criteria concerning what constitutes a viable market segment:

● Segments should be of an adequate size to provide the company with the desired return for its effort.
● Members of each segment should have a high degree of similarity in their requirements, yet be distinct from the rest of the market.
● Criteria for describing segments must enable the company to communicate effectively with them.

> Unless we succeed in identifying a viable market segment for our product we will fail to achieve differential advantage and will become just another company selling 'me too' products.

While many of these criteria are obvious when we consider them, in practice market segmentation is one of the most difficult of marketing concepts to turn turn into a reality. Yet we must succeed, otherwise we become just another company selling what are called 'me too' products. In other words, what we offer the potential customer is very much the same as what any other company offers and, in such circumstances, it is likely to be the lowest priced article that is bought. This can be ruinous to our profits, unless we happen to have lower costs, hence higher margins, than our competitors. There is more about this important aspect of marketing in Chapter 5.

There are basically three stages to market segmentation, all of which have to be completed.

The first establishes the scope of the project by specifying the geographic area to be covered and defining the 'market' which is to be segmented, followed by taking a detailed look at the way this market operates and identifying where decisions are made about the competing products or services. Successful segmentation is based on a detailed understanding of decision-makers and their requirements. The second is essentially a manifestation of the way customers actually behave in the marketplace, and consists of answering the question 'Who is specifying what?'. The third stage looks at the reasons behind the behaviour of customers in the marketplace and answers the question 'Why?' and then searches for market segments based on this analysis of needs.

A detailed description of how to carry out each of these three stages, along with examples and worksheets, can be found in *Market Segmentation: How to do it; How to profit from it*, by Malcolm McDonald and Ian Dunbar (Butterworth-Heinemann, Oxford, 2004). The following sections provide an overview of the steps required to complete these three stages, and is presented in a format for conducting a segmentation project using internal resources.

■ Defining the market

The first step in market segmentation establishes the scope of the segmentation project by specifying the geographic area covered by the project and by clearly understanding from a customer's perspective the 'market' in which your products or services are competing with those of your competitors. Where necessary, the scope is modified to take into account the realistic capabilities of your organization.

A clear geographic boundary enables you to size the market, to identify the localities in which the dynamics of the market have to be understood and, once the segments have been identified, to develop the appropriate marketing objectives and strategies for those localities.

Keeping the project within the borders of a single country is a manageable starting point because the stage of market development, the available routes to market and the pattern of marketing activity will probably be the same throughout the country. Even this, however, may be too broad for some companies, simply because their geographic reach is limited by physical and/or economic considerations, or even because their appeal has a strong local sentiment attached to it.

For companies trading in numerous countries around the world, there is clearly an enormous attraction in finding a single global segmentation model that can be applied to every country. However, the experience of 'globalization' has highlighted for many of these companies that they have to 'act local' in order to succeed in their market. This doesn't mean that every country is completely unique in respect of the segments found within it. For the international company, a useful guide to predetermining which countries can be included in a single segmentation project is to ensure that in each of these countries the stage of market development, the available routes to market and the pattern of marketing activity are the same – or at least very similar.

This chapter has already addressed the issue of 'market' definition and how it should be described, the crucial point here being that it is not described in terms of what a company sells, but in terms of what customers are setting out to achieve – in other words, the 'need' they are seeking to satisfy.

An important distinction to note at this point is that, while a 'market' describes a customer need in a way which covers the aggregation of all the alternative products or services customers regard as capable of satisfying that need, 'segments' focus on specific products or services, their characteristics and properties, along with other components of the total marketing proposition, that different groups of customers are looking for in order to satisfy their particular needs within a market.

A key difference, therefore, between a 'market' and a 'segment' is that a specific marketing strategy can be defined for a segment, whereas for a market, we can only list the alternative products or services. It is simply a different level of aggregation of customer needs.

MARKETING INSIGHT

As a reminder, the general rule for 'market' definition is that it should be described in a way which covers the aggregation of all the alternative products or services which customers regard as being capable of satisfying that same need. To help, try and capture this description by completing one or the other of the following sentences with a phrase that identifies the specific purpose or intended use customers have in mind for the products or services they see as being in a competitive set, along with any relevant circumstances:

1 When choosing between these alternative products/services the need that each customer is looking to satisfy is to . . .
2 Customers acquire these products/services because they have a need to . . .

Or, more simply:

3 The customer need is to . . .

Ensure that the market definition does not refer to any particular product or service, or contains any meaningless words such as 'quality' or 'brand'. It is, however, useful to list the products or services covered by the definition.

The final consideration in defining the market is to ensure the definition is meaningful to your company. This is particularly relevant if your company is focused on a particular part of an overall market, as was the case for the manufacturer of nylon carpet presented earlier in this chapter. It may also be necessary to take into account the corporate structure of your company if the market, as defined from the customer's perspective, goes beyond the confines of a single SBU. For example, considering a market defined in terms of 'being able to secure a desired standard of living from a planned date of retirement', both pension plans and investment plans are used by customers to achieve this goal, yet these two lines are often found within two different business units.

Company structure considerations may require you initially to exclude certain product lines from your 'market'.

The preferred solution is to segment the market as defined and therefore include the competing product lines. However, it may be that in the first instance it is more pragmatic to start with your current SBU structure and segment that part of the market currently satisfied by your product line, not forgetting to monitor the trends in the use of the products or services you have excluded.

MARKETING INSIGHT

In companies consisting of a number of SBUs, it is recommended that you start segmenting markets at the lowest level of disaggregation within the organization's current structure.

Later on, it should be possible to use the same process for higher and higher levels of aggregation to check whether it may be possible to merge any of your current SBUs. Indeed, it may even be possible, eventually, to reorganize the whole company around 'new' groupings of either customers or products.

Now that the market you are segmenting has been clearly defined, a volume or value figure is required in order to size it as it is today, with estimates for the future. In most cases, the annual figure for the market would be used.

■ Market mapping

A useful way of identifying where decisions are made about competing products and services and, therefore, those who then proceed to the next stages of segmentation, is to start by drawing a 'market map'.

A ▶ **market map** defines the distribution and value-added chain between final users and suppliers of the products or services included within the scope of your segmentation project. This should take into account the various buying mechanisms found in your market, including the part played by 'influencers'.

It is useful to start your market map by plotting the various stages that occur along the distribution and value-added chain between the final users and all the suppliers of products or services competing with each other in the defined market. At the same time, indicate the particular routes to market the products are sourced through, as not all of them will necessarily involve all of these stages. An example of this starting point for market mapping is shown in Figure 4.5.

Be sure to draw a market map for the whole of the defined market rather than just the part you currently deal with. This is to ensure that you understand your market dynamics properly.

▶ **DEFINITION** ◀

A market map defines the distribution and value-added chain between final users and suppliers, which takes into account the various buying mechanisms found in a market, including the part played by influencers

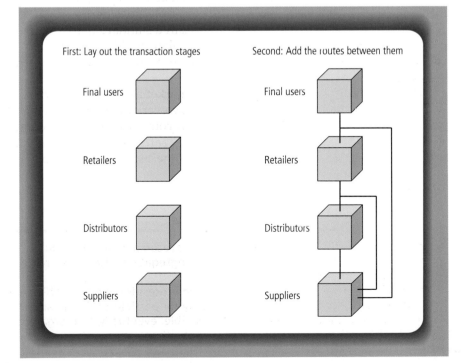

Figure 4.5
Starting a market map and adding the routes between the transaction stages

Note that this market map consists of four stages, one each for final users, retailers, distributors and suppliers. This map illustrates that products are also acquired by the final users direct from the suppliers, as well as from retailers. Some retailers also bypass distributors and acquire their stocks direct from the suppliers.

These stages (represented by the cubes in Figure 4.5) are referred to as 'junctions', with each junction on a market map positioned hierarchically, according to how close it is to the final user. The first junction along the market map would, therefore, be the final user.

It is not essential to draw the map starting from the final user; you may prefer to draw the map starting with the supplier, progressing towards the final user. Neither is it essential to draw the map down the page. You may prefer to draw the map across the page, starting with either the final user or the supplier.

> It is very important that your market map extends all the way through to the final user, even though you may not actually conduct transactions with them directly.

In some markets, the direct customer/purchaser will not always be the final user, even though that customer/purchaser may even appear to consume the product, as is illustrated in the following set of circumstances.

MARKETING INSIGHT

A company (or household) may commission a third-party contractor to carry out some redecoration, or an advertising agency to develop and conduct a promotional campaign, or a financial adviser to produce and implement a financial programme.

For all of us, the doctor we visit when seeking treatment is, in many respects, a contractor when it comes to prescribing medicine.

Although the contractor or agency is strictly the direct buyer, it is not the final user. The distinction is important because, to win the commission, the contractor would usually have needed to understand the requirements of the customer and, in carrying out the commission, would have carried out those requirements on behalf of the customer. To miss out the final user from the market map would, therefore, have ignored an array of different needs which the supplier would benefit from being aware of (and have included in its product offer) if the supplier were to ensure that its company name appeared on the contractor's 'preferred supplier list'. The inclusion of a contractor on a market map is illustrated in Figure 4.6.

Ensuring your market map continues right the way through to the final user is also appropriate in those situations where final users have their products purchased for them, for example by their parents or by their company's purchasing department. Here we would be looking to capture the decision-making and/or order-placing hierarchy that exists between

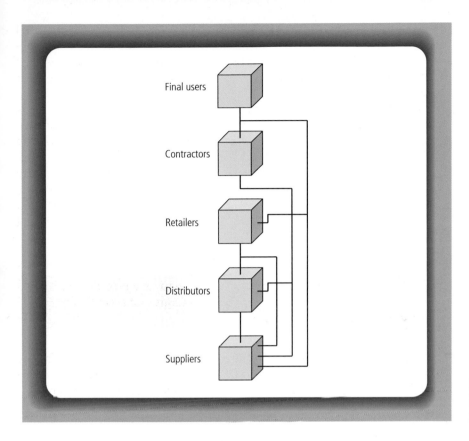

Figure 4.6
Market map with
contractor

the final user and whoever places the order. This may simply require a small change to the market map already presented in Figure 4.6, such as replacing 'Contractors' with 'Parents'. In other markets, however, especially in business-to-business markets, this will require further junctions to be added to the market map as illustrated in Figure 4.7.

A further addition to the market map in Figure 4.7, particularly in business-to-business markets, could be the inclusion of a distinct junction for the purchasing procedures that are known to take place between, say, a department's intention to buy and placing the order. In Figure 4.7 this would most likely be located between the section head and the purchasing group, the purchasing group simply carrying out instructions – though it may, of course, be involved in the purchasing procedure. Although purchasing procedures are likely to differ between companies, capture it in a single junction at this stage of constructing your market map. An opportunity to expand the detail occurs later on when we add junction types.

As the figures have illustrated, most market maps will have at least three principal junctions:

1 Final users (often referred to as 'consumers')
2 The channel (distribution channel, often referred to as 'customers')
3 Suppliers (originators of goods and services, namely the manufacturing and service industries).

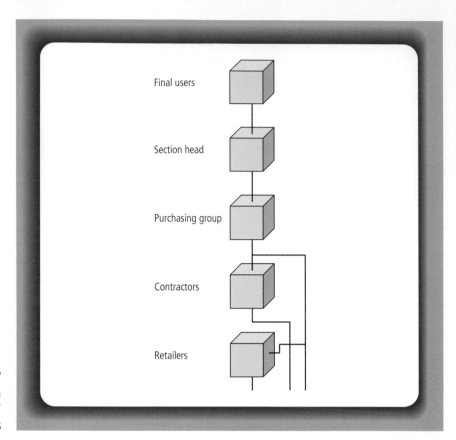

Figure 4.7
Market map with
final users 'hidden'
from the suppliers

For many markets, however, it is also essential that their maps include a fourth component, namely the stage(s) where influence and/or advice occurs (not necessarily a transaction) about which products to use:

4   Influence and advice (sources of 'information').

When referring to 'influencers', it is important to note that this does not refer to the power (or otherwise) of advertising or any other type of promotion. It is referring more to the influence of what are perceived as authoritative and independent sources of information that are deliberately sought out by some customers as part of their buying process. The important point here is that in many instances these 'influencers' are not directly featured in any transaction. These influencers should appear on the market map, as shown in Figure 4.8, just as if they were a transaction stage.

For most market maps, the decision about which junction a particular activity should be placed in will be very clear. However, there will be instances where the decision is not immediately apparent. For example, a farmer's cooperative may simply replace a retail outlet or a wholesaler, in which case it could just as easily be placed in the same junction as the retailer or wholesaler, as appropriate. Alternatively, a cooperative may source its products either from a wholesaler or direct from the manufacturer, in which

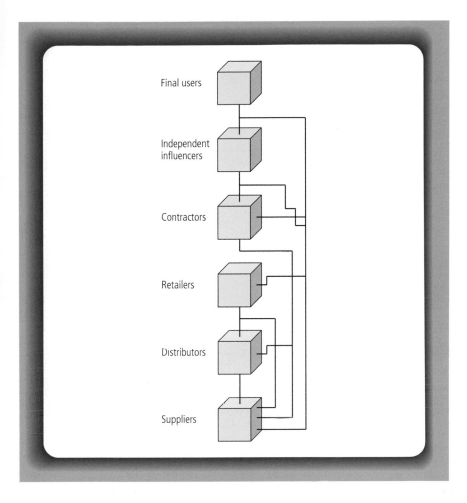

Figure 4.8
Market map with influencers

case it is clearer to position the cooperative on the market map at a stage which is nearest to the final user. Following the same guidelines, a consultant who advises the farmers on which specific product to buy would clearly be placed in a junction one stage below the farmers, and ahead of any retailers or wholesalers.

With quantification playing an important part later on in the process, mark at each junction and along each route the volumes or values dealt with by each of them. The figure used to size the market when defining the market is the base for this allocation. Where figures for this detailed breakdown of the market are not available, 'guesstimates' should be made in order to scale the role of each junction and the different routes between them. You may find it easier to start with percentages and then, when satisfied with the allocation, convert the percentages to figures. The use of figures is illustrated in Figure 4.9.

Note that the number of units 'consumed' by the final users usually equates to the number of units entering the market. Please take some time to follow the routes through the map and you will observe that, like the

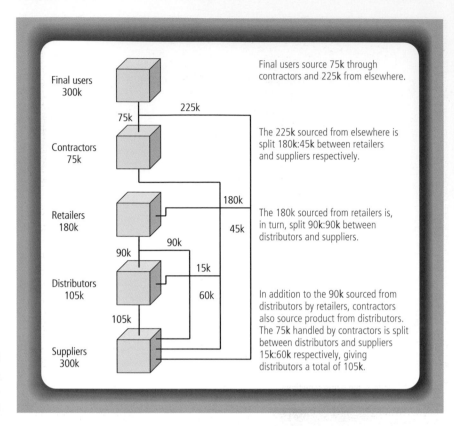

Final users source 75k through contractors and 225k from elsewhere.

The 225k sourced from elsewhere is split 180k:45k between retailers and suppliers respectively.

The 180k sourced from retailers is, in turn, split 90k:90k between distributors and suppliers.

In addition to the 90k sourced from distributors by retailers, contractors also source product from distributors. The 75k handled by contractors is split between distributors and suppliers 15k:60k respectively, giving distributors a total of 105k.

Figure 4.9
Initial quantification
of a market map –
figures

work of an accountant, it all 'balances'. The quantities are thousands (k) of units. The total number of units in this market is 300,000 (300k).

The next stage for your market map is to expand the detail it contains, as the 'top line' picture developed so far is possibly hiding some important differences between customers. These differences could provide useful information for your segmentation project.

Note at each junction on your market map, if applicable, all the different types of companies/customers that are found there, as illustrated in Figure 4.10. If you have included a junction for 'Purchase procedures', your list for this junction would consist of the different procedures that are found at this junction, such as 'Financial director and Purchasing', 'Main board and Purchasing' and so on.

Note that 'Sheds' is the name sometimes used to refer to hardware superstores.

If you already have a segmentation structure for any of these junctions and you are using this process to test its validity, you can use this structure to define the respective junction types. The market mapping routine you have followed so far could, of course, be challenging the traditional structures you have been applying to your market. In such instances, you may prefer to replace what now appears to be the out-of-date list with the new list.

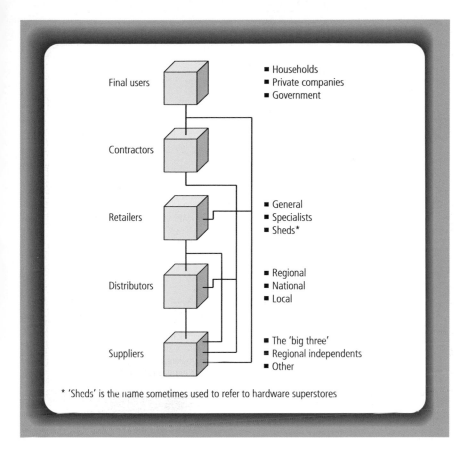

Figure 4.10
Market map listing the different junction types

A refinement which is useful at this point is to split the volume or value quantity dealt with by each junction between the junction types. Figure 4.11 illustrates how to record this for the 'Final user' types appearing in Figure 4.10. Guesstimate these figures if they are not known, and note this as a requirement for any follow-up work.

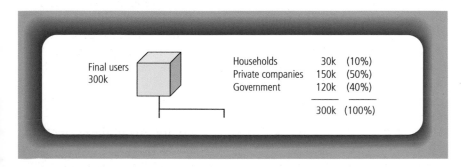

Figure 4.11
Quantities split between junction types

If easier, you can limit this level of detail to the groups you take through to the next stage of your segmentation project. This is discussed a little later in this section.

Market leverage points

Now, *highlight* those junctions where decisions are made about which of the competing products or services will be purchased. These are known as 'market leverage points'. It is not necessary for all the customers at a junction to make this decision for the junction to become a leverage point. Locating where leverage occurs in a market identifies the customer group(s) who will proceed to the next stage of the segmentation process.

The easiest junction at which to start this stage of market mapping is at the final users' junction, noting at each junction with leverage the volume/value (or percentage of the total market) that is decided there. Guesstimate these figures if they are not known, and note this as a requirement for any follow-up work generated by this first pass at segmenting your market.

The inclusion of leverage points is illustrated in Figure 4.12 (based on Figure 4.10).

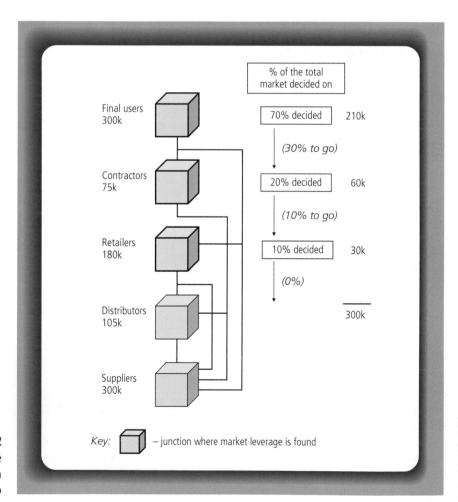

Figure 4.12
Market leverage points on a market map

In Figure 4.12, we see a market in which 30 per cent of annual sales are decided at junctions other than the final user junction.

So far, we have built a market map by tracking the distribution and value-added chain found between final users and suppliers, and shown the various routes that are taken through the map to link the two together. We then quantified the map. This was followed by expanding the detail to show the different types of companies/customers found at each junction on the map, and these were also quantified.

By then looking at where decisions are made between the products/ services of competing suppliers, we have identified a number of stages (junctions) where segmentation could occur.

For most markets it is recommended that segmentation should first take place at the final users' junction, provided it is a junction where there are decision-makers and that the quantity decided at that leverage point justifies it. Once the segmentation process has been completed for this particular junction, the process can then be repeated for each successive junction where decisions are made. It is often the case that these subsequent projects benefit from having the segmentation process completed for earlier junctions if they are sufficiently important.

Most important, however, is the fact that we now have a clearer understanding of our market and how it works.

Advanced market mapping

Before moving on to the next step of the market segmentation process it is worth noting that in addition to providing an informative picture of the distribution and value-added chain that exists between final users and suppliers, market mapping can also be used to present your own company's performance on these routes to market and to illustrate where your sales and marketing resources are allocated. In addition, after completing a segmentation project, you can then plot your segments onto the market map. How to capture these refinements on a market map can be found in *Market Segmentation: How to do it; How to profit from it*, by Malcolm McDonald and Ian Dunbar (Butterworth-Heinemann, Oxford, 2004: Chapter 11).

■ Who specifies what

In this step we are developing a representative sample of different decision-makers which identifies the characteristics and properties of a purchase on which decisions are made, along with the customer attributes that will be used to describe the decision-makers. Each constituent of this sample is called a ▶ **micro-segment**.

The uniqueness of a micro-segment is that when determining which of the alternative offers to be bought, the decision-makers it represents demonstrate a similar level of interest in a specific set of features, with the features being the characteristics and properties of 'what' is bought, 'where'

▶ **D E F I N I T I O N** ◀

A micro-segment is a group of decision-makers who share a similar level of interest in a specific set of features it is bought, 'when' it is bought and 'how' it is bought, as appropriate to the micro-segment. To this is added the descriptors which describe who the micro-segment represents, along with an estimate of the volume or value they account for in the defined market.

The principle behind this step is that by observing the purchase behaviour of decision-makers and understanding the key constituents of this behaviour, we have a platform for developing a detailed understanding of their motivations. It is, therefore, a critical link with the next step of the segmentation process, which looks at why decision-makers select the particular products and services they specify. This, in turn, becomes the basis on which the segments are formed.

What, where, when and how

The features that are of interest to a segmentation project are those which the decision-makers focus on and regard as important when they are determining which of the competing products will be bought. These features are referred to as ▶ **Key Discriminating Features** (KDFs). They are sometimes referred to as 'determiners' or 'differentiators'.

▶ **D E F I N I T I O N** ◀

Key Discriminating Features are the characteristics and properties of a purchase which customers regard as decisive when making a distinction between alternative offers

When considering 'what' is bought, we are primarily referring to the specific features of all the products and services covered by the market definition, with 'products and services', in turn, referring to the total experience of the customer when dealing with the organization. This means that both the tangible and intangible aspects have to be covered. In addition, it is important not to overlook any product or service 'add-ons' provided by any intermediaries on your market map, such as maintenance contracts, delivery services, installation and so on. These may be out of your control, but that doesn't mean they can be excluded from considering how a market splits into segments. It is also appropriate to include in 'what is bought' the role of 'influencers', as highlighted in market mapping, along with technical advisers and consultants.

Groups of features that customers could be taking into account, along with some examples of the features associated with these groups and, therefore, features that could be found in micro-segments, include:

Type of product	Cleaners, galvanizers, installed, flat-pack, ready-made, on-call engineers, resident engineers, included with a service package and so on
Specification	100% purity, 98% purity, tolerance levels, percentage failure rate and so on
Colour	Red, white, blue, pastel, garish and so on
Size of package	Single, multiple, family pack, 5-litre, 10-litre, 20-kg, bulk and so on
Area occupied by equipment (footprint)	Small, medium, large, very large, or by specific areas
Volume used	Small, medium, large, very large, or by specific quantities

Type of service	Testing service, design service, technical advice (which is sometimes, unintentionally, provided by the sales force), evaluation, evaluation analysis and so on
Brand	Innovative, youthful, sober, luxury, local, international, own-label, high-profile and so on
Country of origin	UK, German, French, European Union (EU), Scandinavian, North American, Arabian, Asian, African, Japanese and so on
Independent influencers	Advisers, consultants (complementing or competing with the technical/advisory services provided by the manufacturers/suppliers), specialist publications, consumer publications, accountants, financial advisers, financial consultants and so on
Type of delivery	Courier, first-class, within four hours, collected, automatically triggered (via links with inventory control systems) and so on
Volume of purchase	Large, medium, small, or in particular quantities
Value of purchase	High, medium, low, or in specific expenditure bands
Range bought	All, single, across the range, those at the top, middle, bottom and so on.

The resulting KDFs could be as follows:

Lawnmowers	Hover, cylinder, rotary, petrol-driven, manual, electrically-driven, 12-inch cut, 16-inch cut, engine from specialist manufacturer, extended warranty, metal structure, with after-sales service and so on
Paints	Emulsion, gloss, oil-based, water-based, non-drip, one coat, 5-litre cans, 2-litre cans, environmentally friendly, 'homely' brand, own label and so on
Petrol stations	Self-service, forecourt service, with convenience store, with 'newsagent's' products, cash-based loyalty programme, travel-based loyalty programme and so on.

In respect of where it is bought, in addition to covering all the different types of outlet from which the competing products are purchased, 'where' also includes all the different channels used to place orders, along with all the different channels used to deliver the orders. Even though outlets and channels may be run by other companies, they are an integral part of the purchase as far as the customer is concerned and could, for some of them, be differentiators.

Features that may be highlighted for where something is bought could include: direct telephone, mail order, Internet, distributor, department store, national chain, regional chain, local independent retailer, tied retailer, supermarket, wholesaler, specialist supplier, street stall, through a buying group, through a buying club, door-to-door, local/high street/out-of-town shop and so on.

Different purchase frequencies (when it is bought) may also be crucial for some decision-makers, and these could include: daily, weekly, monthly, seasonally, biannually, every two years, at 50,000 miles, occasionally, as needs, on impulse, only in emergencies, degrees of urgency, infrequently, rarely, special events, only during sales, at the bottom of the market and so on

Finally, some decision-makers may consider the availability of different methods of purchase for how they buy products or services as being very important differentiators for them. These could include: credit card, charge card, debit card, cash, direct debit, standing order, credit terms, outright purchase, lease-hire, lease-purchase, negotiated price, sealed bid and so on.

Although many of these methods of purchase will be available across the market and are therefore unlikely to act as differentiators, the ability (or otherwise) to include financing as part of the offer in some markets can still win, or lose, a sale.

Who specifies

▶ **DEFINITION** ◀

Demographics are measurable descriptions of customers

▶ **DEFINITION** ◀

Geographics are identifiable locations of customers

▶ **DEFINITION** ◀

Psychographics are a customer's inner feelings and predisposition to behave in certain ways

The profiling component of a micro-segment describes who is found within it in terms of their personal and, if appropriate, their company's characteristics. Adding details of customer attributes is important, as it seeks to find some way of describing the customers who will eventually be found in each of the concluding segments. This is essential for the successful targeting of segment-specific offers.

The standard categories of profiling information collected about customers tend to be ▶ **demographic** (sometimes referred to as 'firmographic' in business-to-business markets), ▶ **geographic**, geodemographic (which, as the name implies, is a combination of the previous two categories) and ▶ **psychographic**.

For consumer markets, demographic descriptors include: age, sex, family life-cycle, number of children, type of residence, income, occupation, qualifications, leisure interests, religion, ethnic origin and so on. Adding the applicable socio-economic groups is a popular way of classifying individuals, which, in the UK, usually sees them described as being either 'A', 'B', 'C1', 'C2', 'D' or 'E', though this was replaced in official reports in 2001 by a new eight-class occupationally-based scheme. The two schemes and their approximate alignments appear in Table 4.1. Although this example is peculiar to the UK, it will be found that there are similar groupings for many economies.

The value of such schemes, and indeed of any form of profiling, is in their practical application in isolating specific segments and in enabling you to reach them. For example, if you have a segment which consists of individuals from the professions and senior management, it is known that they tend to be light television viewers; consequently, if this is a target segment, it does not make sense to advertise your product or service heavily on television. However, they can be effectively reached by means of certain newspapers and magazines, where they comprise the principal readership.

Table 4.1 Eight-class analytic version of the 2001 socio-economic classification (UK) and its approximate relationship with the former scheme

New eight-class SEC	Former socio-economic class indicators
1 Higher managerial and professional occupations	
1.1 Large employers and higher managerial occupations	A Upper middle class
1.2 Higher professional occupations	B Middle class
2 Lower managerial and professional occupations	C1 Lower middle class
3 Intermediate occupations	
4 Small employers and own account workers	C2 Skilled working class
5 Lower supervisory and technical occupations	
6 Semi-routine occupations	D Working class
7 Routine occupations	E Subsistence level
8 Never worked and long-term unemployed	Other

Source: Based on the National Statistics website: www.statistics.gov.uk. Crown copyright material is reproduced with the permission of the Controller of HMSO and the Queen's Printer for Scotland.
Note: The alignment is only approximate due to the differences in criteria used to allocate individuals to their respective classes in the above schemes. 'Large employers' refers to individuals who employ others in enterprises employing twenty-five or more persons.

Here we are seeing a useful correlation between readership and viewing patterns and the socio-economic groups which consist of the professions and senior management, and this can be most useful in helping us to communicate cost-effectively with our target market by means of advertising.

Using consumer demographics, banks and insurance companies have realized that at different stages in the family life-cycle their customers have different needs, so this has become another most useful way of describing some of their segments. As a result, these financial institutions have been particularly adept at developing products especially for certain age categories. In this respect, because of the gradually reducing relevance of socio-economic classifications as a predictor of behaviour, there is an emerging concept of 'contexts', such as 'wellness', 'awareness', 'Euroness', 'traditionalism', 'expectism' and 'home-centredness', each one related to life stages such as 'singles', 'nesters', 'developers' and 'elders'. Thus, Laura Ashley would clearly be in the 'traditionalism' context, while Body Shop would probably be in the 'wellness' context.

For the geodemographic category, ACORN (A Classification of Residential Neighbourhoods from CACI Ltd[1]), for example, which classifies all households in Great Britain at postcode level into fifty-six different types based on key demographic variables, Census information and lifestyle data, is particularly useful for the retailing business because, when used in conjunction with market research, it can accurately predict consumption patterns in specific geographic locations.

[1] ACORN and CACI are trademarks of CACI Ltd

Psychographic profiling differences are particularly useful in the creative execution of advertising and other promotional campaigns, especially in mass markets, thereby homing the offer in on their target segment. In the market for toothpaste, for example, advertisements that play on people's concerns about the health of their teeth, especially the health of their children's teeth, have supported a number of brands targeted at the 'Worrier' segment in the second case at the end of this chapter. However, brands targeted at the 'Sociable' segment often feature young people socializing and instantly being attracted to each other simply because they use a specific toothpaste that gives them the smile that gets them noticed!

Briefly turning to business-to-business markets, ▸ **Standard Industrial Classification** (SIC) systems, number of employees, job titles, turnover and production processes have been found to be useful demographic descriptors. Stages in its business life-cycle, style of management (such as formal, authoritarian, bureaucratic, positive, cautious and so on), attitude with regard to risk, approach to technology and social policies can also be used to describe different business customers. Unfortunately, however, in business-to-business marketing the development of tools for sophisticated targeting of business customers has lagged behind the developments that have taken place in the consumer markets.

▸ **DEFINITION** ◂

Standard Industrial
Classification (SIC)
systems are lists of
business categories for
which most governments
keep production statistics

**MARKETING
INSIGHT**

On occasions, sophisticated profiling packages are seen as a method of defining segments. Segments, as has already been highlighted, are defined by their particular needs, while profiling is the means by which you identify the membership of each segment.

A selection of standard approaches to business and consumer profiling is given in the chapter review at the end of this chapter.

Developing micro-segments

When developing micro-segments it is important to bear in mind that they are based on actual decision-makers, not fictional individuals, and that they represent the defined market as a whole, not just your own customers. Each will consist of:

● a specific set of key discriminating features (KDFs) in which there is a similar level of interest shared by the decision-makers the micro-segment represents
● one or more profiling characteristics that identify who these decision-makers are
● a volume or value figure to indicate its size.

The procedure to follow when developing micro-segments can be summarized as follows:

1   Divide the market into identifiable groups of customers you can visualize and talk about, as this equips you with useful points of reference for developing micro-segments, and size each of these 'reference groups'.

2   Take one of these reference groups, familiarize yourself with the individuals it represents, and develop it into a micro-segment by carefully listing what the customers in this group regard as their KDFs, with any differences within the group captured as separate micro-segments.

3 Now attempt to indicate the relative importance of each KDF to the micro-segment(s) using a simple grading structure initially based on, for example, one to three stars.

4 Consider a cross-section of customers included in a micro-segment to confirm whether they would all generally agree with the list of KDFs and their grading, and if they wouldn't, develop additional micro-segments to cover any meaningful differences.

5 Verify each micro-segment by checking that it is based on actual decision-makers, its reality check, further verified by checking that its KDFs either represent a known transaction, or actually make sense.

6 Attach profiling characteristics to each micro-segment and use a simple grading structure to indicate what proportion of its customers each characteristic applies to with, for example, three or four tick marks identifying characteristics applicable to all of them.

7 Size each micro-segment, by referring back to the reference group it originated from and utilizing any market figures that may be available.

Steps 2–7 of this procedure are repeated for each group of customers until they have all been converted into micro-segments. On completion, review and compare the micro-segments with each other, and increase or decrease the importance of appropriate KDFs if this better reflects the differences between individual micro-segments. This may be helped by increasing the number of stars used in the grading structure, but it is best if this is limited to no more than five as this will ensure that the final picture remains visually comprehensible.

An example of how to capture the output is summarized in Table 4.2.

Table 4.2 Recording micro-segments

			Micro-segments				
			1	2	3	4	5
Feature category 'What'	**Group** Finish	**Specification** Dark hardwoods	★ ★ ★				
		Light hardwoods		★ ★			
		Pine			★ ★	★	
		To paint/stain					★ ★ ★
Profiling category Demographic	**Group** Age	**Specification** Up to 30		✓	✓	✓✓	✓✓
		31–50	✓	✓	✓✓	✓	✓
		51 and over	✓✓	✓			

Note: The most important KDFs are identified by three stars (★ ★ ★) in this table, with three tick marks (✓✓✓) used to indicate profiling characteristics applicable to all the customers represented by a micro-segment. Note the structure of features and profiling into 'Categories', then 'Groups' and finally the 'Specification'. This is a useful way of organizing the information.

This often results in around twenty or thirty micro-segments being developed. If the number becomes unmanageable, it can often be reduced by verifying that they all represent actual decision-makers in the market, that they are based on features that are true differentiators rather than basic entry requirements, and that all the features are key when they are deciding between alternative offers.

A full explanation of this procedure, along with examples and worksheets, can be found in *Market Segmentation: How to do it; How to profit from it*, by Malcolm McDonald and Ian Dunbar (Butterworth-Heinemann, Oxford, 2004: Chapter 6).

■ Why

The third stage in market segmentation begins by trying to understand why customers behave the way they do, for, surely, if we can explain the behaviour of our customers, we are in a better position to sell to them.

Basically, there are two principal theories of customer behaviour. One theory refers to the rational customer, who seeks to maximize satisfaction or utility. This customer's behaviour is determined by the utility derived from a purchase at the margin compared with the financial outlay and other opportunities foregone. While such a view of customers provides some important insights into behaviour, it must be remembered that many markets do not work this way at all, there being many examples of a growth in demand with every rise in price.

Another view of customer behaviour which helps to explain this phenomenon is that which describes the psycho-social customer, whose attitudes and behaviour are affected by family, work, prevailing cultural patterns, reference groups, perceptions, aspirations, and life style.

While such theories also provide useful insights, they rarely explain the totality of customer behaviour.

> For example, it is interesting to know that opinion leaders are often the first to adopt new ideas and new products, but unless these people can be successfully identified and communicated with, this information is of little practical use to us.

| The most useful and practical way of explaining customer behaviour has been found to be benefit segmentation.

The most useful and practical way of explaining customer behaviour has been found to be benefit segmentation, i.e. the benefits sought by customers when they buy a product. For example, some customers buy products for their functional characteristics (product), for economy (price), for convenience and availability (place), for emotional reasons (promotion), or for a combination of these reasons (a trade-off). Otherwise, how else can the success of car firms like Bentley, retailers like Harrods, and many others be explained? Understanding the benefits sought by customers helps us to organize our marketing mix in the way most likely to appeal to our target market. The importance of product benefits will become clearer in Chapter 5, in our discussion of product management.

'Customers don't buy products; they seek to acquire benefits.' This is the guiding principle of the marketing director of one of America's more innovative companies in the hair-care business. Behind that statement lies a basic principle of successful marketing.

When a customer selects a particular product or service, that customer is not motivated in the first instance by physical features, or objective attributes of the product, but by the benefit that those attributes bring with them.

To take an example from industrial marketing, a purchaser of industrial cutting oil is not buying the particular blend of chemicals sold by leading manufacturers of industrial lubricants; rather, he is buying a bundle of benefits which includes the solving of a specific lubrication problem.

MARKETING INSIGHT

The difference between benefits and products is not just a question of semantics. It is crucial to the company seeking success. Every product has its features: size, shape, performance, weight, the material from which it is made, and so on. Many companies fall into the trap of talking to customers about these features, rather than about what those features mean to the customer.

A simple formula to ensure that a benefit-orientated approach is adopted is to use the phrase 'which means that' to link a feature to the benefit it brings – for example:

- 'Maintenance time has been reduced from four to three hours, which means that most costs are reduced by . . .'
- 'The engine casing is made of aluminium, which means that six more units can be carried on a standard truck load, which means that transport costs are reduced by . . .'
- 'The size of the quench tank has been increased by 25 per cent, which means that on oil purchases alone it is possible to save . . .'
- 'The new special bearing has self-aligning symmetrical rollers, which means that the rollers find their own equilibrium, with the load always symmetrically distributed along the length of the roller, which means an extended life capacity of a year on average.'

Benefits

Benefits generally fall into one of three categories, namely 'standard' benefits, 'company' benefits and 'differential' benefits.

Standard benefits are basic benefits provided by product features but are not in any way unique to any particular manufacturer/supplier, while company benefits link customers to particular companies through their dealings with various departments or by the particular image associated with the company. However, when it comes to the detailed analysis of benefits the company must undertake, it is vital that, in doing it, the benefits that provide a competitive advantage, known as 'differential benefits', are identified – and identified not only for your own company but also for your competitors.

If a company cannot identify any differential benefits, then either what they are offering is identical to their competitors' offerings (which is unlikely), or they have not done the benefit analysis properly. It is important to make a particular note of differential benefits, for it is in these that the greatest chance of success lies. Success will only occur, however, if these differential benefits are actually wanted by the target customers.

Defining micro-segments by their needs

Here we look at your micro-segments and, by reference to the picture you have built about the individuals they represent, along with their KDFs, determine what lies behind the choices they make so that we can understand their needs-based buying requirements. The benefits that are uncovered by this analysis are referred to as ▶ **Critical Success Factors** (CSFs), a term we use to emphasize the point that it is these attributes that determine which of the alternative offers the decision-makers will choose. This is also the point at which to bring 'price' into the process, as it has an important part to play in explaining customer behaviour. 'Price' is therefore included as one of the CSFs.

▶ **DEFINITION** ◀

Critical Success Factors are the perceived or stated attributes of a purchase that customers evaluate when choosing between alternative offers

Although the principle of approaching segmentation from the customer's point of view is probably well-established by now, it is worth highlighting for this stage in the process that the benefits are for the market as a whole, not simply limited to those you deliver to your customers, and that these benefits are what the decision-makers regard as their decisive buying criteria, not what you would prefer them to see as their critical success factors.

The procedure to follow when identifying the benefits for each micro-segment can be summarized as follows:

1 Take one of your micro-segments, re-familiarize yourself with the customers it represents, and carefully list the benefits being sought from their KDFs in order to identify their decisive buying criteria or critical success factors.
2 Now attempt to indicate the importance of each CSF to this micro-segment, including the importance of price, using a simple grading structure initially based on, for example, one to three stars.
3 Consider a cross-section of customers included in the micro-segment to confirm whether they would all generally agree with the list of CSFs and their grading; if they wouldn't, develop additional micro-segments to cover any meaningful differences, redistribute the volume or value figure between them and, if required, adjust their profiling characteristics.

Repeat all three steps of this procedure for each micro-segment and, when completed, review and compare the micro-segments with each other and increase or decrease the importance of appropriate CSFs if this better reflects the differences between individual micro-segments. This may be helped by increasing the number of stars used in the grading structure, but it is best if this is limited to no more than five in order to ensure that the final picture remains visually comprehensible. Where necessary, however, use 'half' stars (⨪) if this helps better reflect the differences between micro-segments.

An example of how to capture the output is summarized in Table 4.3.

Table 4.3 Recording CSFs and indicating their relative importance to micro-segments

Features	CSFs: benefits + price	Micro-segments				
		D	E1	E2	F	G
Light-weight, mounted on wheels	Easily moved around		★ ★ ★	★ ★ ★		★
Heavy-weight	OK in production areas				★ ★ ★	
Latest technology	Innovative functionality	★ ★ ★	★			★ ★
Proven technology	Reduces training time			★ ★	★ ★ ★	
24/7 support staff	Fewer hold-ups for users	★ ★ ★			★ ★	
Staff answer calls	Faster call handling	★			★ ★	★ ★ ★
Small supplier	Personalized service			★ ★		★ ★ ★
Large supplier	Dependable back-up	★ ★	★ ★		★ ★	
	Easier approval of choice		★			
	Price	★	★	★	★ ★	★ ★

Note: While it is useful to show the link between CSFs and their KDFs, it is optional. The most important CSFs are identified by three stars (★ ★ ★) in this table. As you will see in the above, a single feature can have more than one benefit, and different features can deliver the same benefit.

It is possible, of course, to indicate the importance of CSFs numerically, and this is the approach most likely to be adopted for the quantitative stage of a segmentation research project, as it is relatively quick and easy to administer – especially if this stage is conducted over the telephone.

As before, a full explanation of this procedure, along with examples and worksheets, can be found in *Market Segmentation: How to do it; How to profit from it*.

Our segmentation is now almost complete. We have developed around twenty or around thirty micro-segments which now need to be reduced to a smaller number of ▶ **market segments** based on their CSFs.

The final step in this third stage is to look for clusters of micro-segments that share a similar level of interest in the same or comparable set of needs. This can then be used to develop the most appropriate offer for each of the segments the company chooses to target. In addition to listing the needs each cluster regards as important to the decision-makers it represents,

▶ **DEFINITION** ◀

A market segment consists of a group of customers within a market who share a similar level of interest in the same, or comparable, set of needs each cluster should also contain the profiling attributes of its decision-makers to tell us who they are, along with a volume or value figure.

With a manageable number of micro-segments, internally resourced segmentation projects can build the market segments manually. Most internally resourced projects should, therefore, be able to construct their own segments along these lines. The alternative is to build the segments with the assistance of a suitable computer-based clustering package,[2] the assistance of which will certainly be required for the quantitative stage of any follow-up market research that may be commissioned.

The general order of events in clustering can be summarized as follows:

1 Begin by looking for customers who are an exact match with each other in respect of the benefits they are looking for and the importance they give these benefits, and merge identical customers together to form some initial clusters.

2 Next, look for any customers and clusters that are a very close match with each other and merge them together to create a revised set of clusters.

3 Continue by progressively decreasing the level of similarity customers and clusters must have with each other before they can be merged together, revising the clusters until the best or desired result has been achieved, being careful to ensure that they are still sharing a similar level of interest in the same, or comparable, set of needs.

Two approaches to manual clustering are detailed in the market segmentation book referred to earlier, one which looks at visual clustering (pattern matching) along with some practical tools for doing this, the other at how this can be done mathematically.

Once the clusters have been finalized, each one needs to be sized and a profile drawn up for the decision-makers it represents by using the size and profiling information that came with each micro-segment.

This stage is completed by determining whether the clusters qualify as 'market segments' by applying the following checklist:

Volume/value	The size of each segment must be sufficient to justify the expense of developing specific offers for them and the expense of taking these offers into the market. Segments have to be measurable.
Differentiated	Is the offer required by each segment sufficiently different from that required by the other segments? This is where the marketing strategies appropriate for one segment are checked to ensure they are distinguishable from the marketing strategies developed for the other segments.
Reachable	This is where the different segments are checked to ensure that the marketing strategies appropriate for each of them can be directed towards them in some way.

[2] Details of such a package, called Market Segment Master®, can be obtained from Professor Malcolm McDonald at m.mcdonald@cranfield.ac.uk or from Ian Dunbar at ian.dunbar@market-equity.com

A fourth item to consider is:

Compatibility This is where you rigorously check your own company's ability to focus on the new segments by structuring itself around them organizationally, culturally, in its management information systems and in its decision-making processes. Such changes may not be possible immediately, therefore the organization's ability and willingness to evolve to the required structure should be tested.

Three segmentation case histories appear later in this chapter.

■ Looking to the future

One final, but crucial, step remains in this part of the marketing audit.

The essence of this stage is to revisit the market map, and consider in what ways it might be affected by e-commerce. Reconfiguring the market map involves examining the current market map, and redrawing it to take account of various anticipated effects of e-commerce.

The resulting vision of how the industry could change as a result of e-commerce presents the organization with choices as to how to position itself in the future industry structure, and how to manage the transition period. Here is a list of options based on our research of how the market map might be reconfigured.

1 *Disintermediation.* As with other IT-enabled channels, such as call centres, e-commerce can enable a link to be removed from the market map, by removing intermediaries whose primary function of information transfer can be more effectively performed using the Internet. An example is the direct sales of greetings cards to the public being trialled by a card publisher, thereby bypassing the retailer.

2 *Partial channel substitution.* This forms a halfway house towards disintermediation, in which an intermediary's role is reduced but not eliminated, through some of its value being provided remotely by the supplier to the intermediary's customer. This is the model adopted by a card manufacturer in its relationship with retailers, where its website is supplementing its agent network rather than replacing it. Similarly, a drinks manufacturer is using data gleaned from its information exchange with distributors to promote directly to retailers, providing 'pull-through' demand which the distributors perceive as of mutual benefit.

3 *Reintermediation.* In some cases, a previous intermediary is replaced by a new online intermediary, rather than bypassed, or an intermediary appears between two types of organization which previously dealt with each other directly. At the time of writing, a groceries manufacturer is having to define its strategy with respect to the various business-to-business exchanges, or e-hubs, which are appearing in its industry to link retailers to manufacturers. Similarly, the health portals such as Healtheon are forming influential intermediaries between manufacturers of drinks products with a health claim and the consumer.

Predicting what reintermediation will occur is particularly difficult, as the possibilities are numerous. Will a given relationship – say, between CTN (confectioners, tobacconists and newsagents) stores and their suppliers – be a direct one? If so, will the shops buy from a range of suppliers' websites, or will the suppliers respond to tender requests provided electronically by shops? Or will there be a new intermediary acting as a marketplace between the two? Possibilities can be placed in an approximate order, from a supplier's website (such as Japan Airlines, which puts out open invitations to tender to suppliers) at one extreme to a vendor's website (such as *Harvard Business Review*, which provides an online version at a cost) at the other. Neutral marketplaces are midway between the two. An example is an auction site, which is tied neither to the buyer nor to the seller. Somewhat closer to the vendors are intermediaries such as Auto-by-Tel, which passes on leads to a local car dealer. A more buyer-oriented intermediary is General Electric's TPN Register, a prototypical e-hub which has achieved considerable scale: set up by a consortium of buyers, it acts to ensure that they gain low prices as well as transaction-cost efficiencies through economies of scale.

Our research suggests that which of these possibilities becomes the dominant trading mechanism in a given relationship appears to depend on the number of vendors and buyers, and the relative power of suppliers and buyers. Where there are few buyers and many suppliers, or buyer power is great, the market will tend towards either individual buyer websites or buyer-oriented intermediaries such as the Covisint trading platform being set up by Ford, General Motors and Daimler Chrysler. Conversely, a small number of suppliers selling to large numbers of customers will have the power to control the market through their own websites or through supplier-oriented consortia. Large numbers of both suppliers and buyers will tend to use a neutral marketplace to reduce the search costs of both parties, though a supplier with a particularly strong brand and/or product differentiation, such as *Harvard Business Review*, may choose not to participate in such marketplaces.

To illustrate this thinking about reintermediation, consider Figure 4.13, a simplified value map from the groceries market.

The current market structure, shown in black, involves manufacturers reaching consumers via a combination of the major multiple supermarkets, independent stores and CTN stores. Our analysis suggests that because the major multiples are few in number and hold considerable buying power, their relationship with manufacturers will either continue to be a direct one, using purchasing systems dictated by the multiples, or will be mediated by a buyer-oriented intermediary, as indicated in the potential future structure shown in blue. However, the many-to-many relationship between manufacturers and independents or CTNs needs a more neutral intermediary, such as is provided currently by warehouses and wholesalers. We predict a similarly neutral online intermediary succeeding here, either through a new entrant start-up or through media addition by a wholesaler. Likewise, the relationship between manufacturers and suppliers is likely to include a neutral spot market for commodity

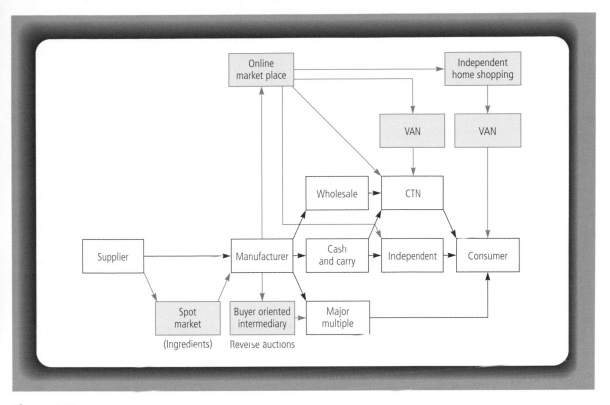

Figure 4.13
Reconfiguring the value map – groceries

ingredients. These predictions appear consistent with industry developments to date.

To reconfigure the market map, therefore, we need to consider the potential effect of each of our three broad changes in turn. In each case, we need to:

1 Sketch the effect of the possible change on the market map.
2 If the effect is positive for some segments, incorporate the transformation in a revised market map (say, for three years hence).

■ Why market segmentation is vital in marketing planning

In today's highly competitive world, few companies can afford to compete only on price, for the product has not yet been sold that someone, somewhere, cannot sell cheaper – apart from which, in many markets it is rarely the cheapest product that succeeds anyway. This is an issue we will return to in Chapter 9, dealing with the pricing plan. What this means is that we have to find some way of differentiating ourselves from the competition, and the answer lies in market segmentation.

The truth is that very few companies can afford to be 'all things to all people'. The main aim of market segmentation as part of the planning process is to enable a firm to target its effort on the most promising opportunities. But what is an opportunity for firm A is not necessarily an opportunity for firm B, depending on its strengths and weaknesses. The whole point of segmentation is that a company must either define its markets broadly enough to ensure that its costs for key activities are competitive, or define its markets in such a way that it can develop specialized skills in serving them to overcome a relative cost disadvantage.

> The typology of the customer or the segment have to be related to a firm's distinctive competence.

Both have to be related to a firm's distinctive competence and to that of its competitors.

All of this should come to the fore as a result of the marketing audit referred to previously, and should be summarized in SWOT analyses. In particular, the differential benefits of a firm's product or service should be beyond doubt to all key members of the company.

Even more important than this, however, is the issue of marketing planning and all that follows in this book. It is worth repeating why market segmentation is so important. Correct market definition is crucial for:

- share measurement
- growth measurement
- the specification of target customers
- the recognition of relevant competitors
- the formulation of marketing objectives and strategies.

To summarize, the objectives of market segmentation are:

- to help determine marketing direction through the analysis and understanding of trends and buyer behaviour
- to help determine realistic and obtainable marketing and sales objectives
- to help improve decision-making by forcing managers to consider in depth the options ahead.

■ Segmentation case histories

This chapter concludes with three case histories to illustrate how superior profitability results from successful market segmentation.

Case study

Case 1 – A national off-licence chain

In the mid-1980s, a national off-licence chain, with retail units in major shopping centres and local shopping parades, was experiencing both a decline in customer numbers and a decline in average spend. The original formula for success of design, product range and merchandising, meticulously copied in each outlet, no longer appeared to be working.

The chain had become a classic example of a business comfortably sitting in the middle ground, attempting to be all things to all people, but managing to satisfy very few of them.

Rather than sit back in the belief that the business was just passing through a difficult patch, and what worked yesterday was bound to work again, the company embarked on a project designed to understand both their actual and potential customer base.

The first stage of this study turned to one of the more sophisticated geodemographic packages in order to understand the residential profiles of each shop's catchment area. Not unexpectedly, many geodemographic differences were found, and the business quickly accepted that it was unlikely that the same retail formula would appeal to the different target markets found in them.

Rather than looking at each shop separately, the catchment area profiles for each shop were subject to a clustering routine in order to place similar catchment areas together. This resulted in twenty-one different groupings, each of which was then profiled in terms of its potential to buy different off-licence products using purchasing data from national surveys. (The company's own in-house retailing data would, of course, only reflect the purchasing pattern of their existing customers or, at worst, only a proportion of their requirements if this was limited by the company's current product range.)

However, stocking the requisite range of products in their correct geographical location would not necessarily attract their respective target markets. The chain was already associated with one type of offer which, in addition to including a particular range of drinks, also included the basic design of the shops and overall merchandising.

The project, therefore, moved into a second stage, in which the market's attitudes and motivations to drinking were explored and relative values attached to the various dimensions uncovered. This was achieved through an independently commissioned piece of market research, and resulted in the market being categorized into a number of psychographic groups. These included, amongst others, 'happy and impulsive' shoppers, 'anxious and muddled' shoppers, 'reluctant but organized' shoppers, and the 'disorganized, extravagant' shoppers.

By ensuring that this stage of the project linked the attitude and motivational findings to demographic data, the two stages could be brought together. This enabled the original twenty-one clusters to be reduced to give distinct segments, each of which required a different offer.

The company then had to decide between two alternative strategies:

1 To focus into one segment using one brand and relocate its retail outlets accordingly through a closure and opening programme; or
2 To develop a manageable portfolio of retailing brands, leave the estate relatively intact, and re-brand, re-fit and re-stock as necessary.

They decided to pursue the second strategy.

Realizing that demographic profiles in geographic areas can change over time, and that customer needs and attitudes can also evolve, the company now monitors its market quite carefully and is quite prepared to modify its brand portfolio to suit changing circumstances. In the early 1990s, however, its five retail brands of 'Bottoms Up', 'Wine Rack', 'Threshers Wine Shop', 'Drinks Store from Threshers' and 'Food and Drinks Store', sat comfortably within the five segments. They also sat comfortably together in the same shopping centre, enabling the group to meet effectively the different requirements of the segments found within that centre's catchment area.

Perhaps more importantly, this strategy sits comfortably alongside the financial targets for the business.

Source: Based on 'Market segmentation from Bottoms Up', John Thornton, Market Planning Manager, Threshers (*Research Plus*, December, 1993).

Case study

Case 2 – Sodium tri-poly phosphate!

Sodium tri-poly phosphate (STPP) was once a simple, unexciting, white chemical-cleaning agent. Today, one of its uses is as the major ingredient of a sophisticated and profitable operation, appearing under many different brand names, all competing for a share of what has become a cleverly segmented market.

Have you ever wondered how the toothpaste marketers classify you in their segmentation of the market? The following chart, adapted from R. Haley's 'Benefit segmentation: a decision-oriented research tool' (*Journal of Marketing*, Vol. 32, 1968), which presents the main segments, may assist you.

	Segment name	Worrier	Sociable	Sensory	Independent
Profile	Demographic	C1 C2 25–40 Large families	B C1 C2 Teens Young smokers	C1 C2 D Children	A B 35–40 Male
	Psychographic	conservative: hypochondriacs	high sociability: active	high self-involvement: hedonists	high autonomy: value-orientated
What is bought, where, when and how	Product examples	Signal, Mentadent P	Macleans, Ultrabrite	Colgate, Aquafresh	Own label
	Product features	large canisters	large tubes	medium tubes	small tubes
	Health properties	whitening properties	flavouring		
	Outlet	supermarket	supermarket	supermarket	independent
	Purchase frequency	weekly	monthly	monthly	quarterly
Why it is bought	Benefits sought	stop decay	attract attention	taste	functionality
	Price paid	medium	high	medium	low
	Percentage of market	50%	30%	15%	5%
Potential for growth		low	high	medium	nil

Note: 'C1', 'C2' and so on appearing in the demographic profiles of each segment represent socio-economic groups which were in use in the UK until 2001, now replaced by eight analytic classes numbered from 1 through to 8. 'Signal' and 'Mentadent P' are trademarks of Lever Fabergé; 'Macleans' and 'Aquafresh' are trademarks of GlaxoSmithKline; 'Ultrabrite' and 'Colgate' are trademarks of Colgate-Palmolive.

Case study

Case 3 – GlobalTech (service segmentation)

Summary

This case history describes the use of market segmentation to assist in the development of a service product. Customer requirements were captured via qualitative research. The segmentation was completed through the use of quantitative research. The result was a set of segments that enabled the development of a new approach to delivering service while improving customer satisfaction. GlobalTech is the fictitious name of a real company marketing high-tech and service products globally. Customers are counted in hundreds of thousands. The markets are mainly business-to-business, with a few very large customers buying thousands of items. Service is a major revenue stream measured in billions of dollars. The lessons learnt could be of interest to any organization having to care for large numbers of customers.

Background
A failed segmentation

An internal GlobalTech team tried to complete a marketing audit early in 2000. This included market definition, market segmentation and quantification. Each product division conducted their audit separately. They used mainly brainstorming techniques to define their markets and to produce the data required.

Lesson 1

Markets transcend your internally defined product divisions. Therefore it is best to understand the markets and monitor your overall performance in those markets. To reshape market information to meet the needs of internal reporting will lead to misinformation.

On completion, the results were compared across the divisions. It rapidly became apparent that each division addressed almost all the markets. However, the market definitions they produced were different, with significant bias towards just the products they offered. Similarly, the segments each division identified where in conflict with the outputs from the other divisions.

On reflection, it was agreed that the results were unreliable. They could not be used to help shape future strategies or marketing investments.

GlobalTech was now in the uncomfortable situation of being in a market information vacuum. Any confidence they had had in their understanding of the market had been destroyed. Consequently, the decision was taken that all future market analysis and understanding tasks would be supported by appropriate investments in market research.

Lesson 2

Do not rely on the internally gathered opinions of your sales and marketing staffs to define markets and identify customer requirements and attitudes. Do invest in the necessary market research to provide a reliable segmentation and support for strategy and product development.

First market segmentation

The following year the segmentation was redone, supported by extensive qualitative and quantitative market research. The objective was to understand and group into segments the product buyers in the overall market.

The qualitative study produced a very clear picture and definition of the markets addressed by GlobalTech. It also provided the customers' view of the benefits they sought from the products and the differences in their attitudes towards their suppliers. The questionnaire for the quantitative study was based on the results of the qualitative study. The result was seven clearly defined product buyer segments.

This enhanced understanding of the market assisted with hardware and software product marketing but did not address service products or customer satisfaction and loyalty issues.

The internal need

At the dawn of the twenty-first century, the market life-cycle had matured. All but the more sophisticated products were perceived as commodities. Consequentially, the opportunities for effective product differentiation had diminished. GlobalTech, in common with its competitors, was finding that customers were becoming increasingly disloyal.

For many years, product churns and upgrades from existing customers had accounted for some 70 per cent of GlobalTech's product revenues. Service and exhaust revenues[3] almost equalled total product revenues. Service was perceived to be a key influencer of loyalty, but the costs of delivering service were becoming unacceptable to customers. Concurrently, service pricing was coming under increasing competitive pressures.

The challenge was to increase loyalty while achieving a step function improvement in margins. Thus it was decided to invest in a better understanding of the service market as an enabler to delivering cost-effective differentiation and loyalty. This case history covers the project from inception to implementation.

The segmentation project
Buy-in

The GlobalTech main board director responsible for customer service sponsored the project. This was a critical prerequisite, as the outcome would have a significant impact on the organization, its processes and behaviours.

Similarly, the project team included key members of service, marketing and finance to ensure buy-in. However, at that time it was deemed inappropriate to include representatives from all but two of the countries due to travel implications, costs, and resource impacts. In retrospect, this was not a good decision.

Lesson 3

Try and anticipate the scale of organizational change that may result from a major segmentation project. Then ensure the buy-in planned from the start of the project embraces all those who will eventually have a say in the final implementation.

---

[3] Exhaust revenues are those revenues that follow on, almost automatically, from an initial product sale. These would normally include service plus training, consultancy, consumables, supplies and add-ons, etc.

Business objectives
The project team agreed the overall business objectives as:

- to develop strategies for profitable increase in market share and sustainable competitive advantage in the service markets for GlobalTech's products
- to identify opportunities for new service products and for improving customer satisfaction within the context of a robust customer needs segmentation, which can be readily applied in the marketplace
- to identify the key drivers of loyalty so that GlobalTech may take actions to increase customer loyalty significantly
- to provide the information required to help develop a new and innovative set of service products designed and tailored to meet differing customer requirements while significantly reducing internal business process costs.

Results from the qualitative study
The output from the qualitative study was a ninety-three-page report documenting the results, in line with the desired research objectives. Some of the more surprising aspects were supported by verbatims. A key output was the polarization of very different attitudes towards service requirements that some buyers had in comparison with others. For example:

- some wanted a response within a few hours, whereas many others would be equally happy with next day
- some wanted their staff thoroughly trained to take remedial actions supported by a specialist on the phone, while others did not want to know and would just wait for the service provider to fix the problem
- some wanted regular proactive communications and being kept up to date, while others wanted to be left alone
- some would willingly pay for a premium service, under a regular contract, while others would prefer to take the risk
- the attitudes of professional buyers, procuring on behalf of user departments, were consistently different from those of the user departments.

Results from the quantitative study
The output from the quantitative study was extensive. Much of the output was detailed demographic data, opportunities information and competitive positioning comparisons. However, the focus was on a fairly extensive executive summary for internal communications within GlobalTech. What follows are summarized extracts from those outputs.

The segments
Six market segments were identified as a result of iterative computer clusterings. Initially the clustering routines had identified more segments, but by careful analysis these were reduced to what was decided to be the most manageable level. Some previously very small segments were merged with very similar larger segments.

Polarizations in attitude
The computer clustering generated the segments by grouping customers with similar attitudes and requirements. This resulted in some marked differences in attitude between

segments. As illustrated below, the Koalas really did not want to know about being trained and having a go. But the Teddies, Yogis and Polars had an almost opposite attitude.

Koala Bears

Preserve their assets (however small) and use, say, an extended warranty to give them cover; won't do anything themselves, prefer to curl up and wait for someone to come and fix it.

Small offices (in small and big companies), **28% of market**

Teddy Bears

Lots of account management and love required from a single preferred supplier; will pay a premium for training and attention. If multisite, will require supplier to effectively cover these sites ('Protect me').

Larger companies, **17% of market**

Polar Bears

Like teddy bears except colder! Will shop around for cheapest service supplier, whoever that may be. Full third-party approach. 'Train me but don't expect to be paid.' Will review annually (seriously). If multisite, will require supplier to effectively cover these sites.

Larger companies, **29% of market**

Yogi Bears

'Wise' teddy or polar bears working long hours; will use trained staff to fix if possible. Needs skilled product specialist at end of phone, not a bookings clerk. Wants different service levels to match the criticality of the product to their business process.

Large and small companies, **11% of market**

Grizzly Bears

Trash them! Cheaper to replace than maintain. Besides, they're so reliable that they are probably obsolete when they bust. Expensive items will be fixed on a pay-as-when basis – if worth it. Won't pay for training.

Not small companies, **6% of market**

Andropov Big Bears

My business is totally dependent on your products. I know more about your products than you do! You will do as you are told. You will be here now! I will pay for the extra cover but you will . . . !

Not small or very large companies, **9% of market**

Satisfaction and loyalty

GlobalTech was measuring customer satisfaction for use both locally, as a business process diagnostic tool, and globally, as a management performance metric. These satisfaction metrics were averaged across all customers, both by geographic business unit and by product division to meet internal management reporting requirements.

However, the outputs from the quantitative study clearly showed that these traditionally well-accepted metrics were, in fact, almost meaningless. What delighted customers in one market segment would annoy customers in another, and *vice versa*. To make the metrics meaningful, they had to be split by key criteria and the market segments.

% very likely to repeat buy from GlobalTech

Loyalty was obviously highest where GlobalTech's 'one size fits all' service deliverable coincidently best matched a segment's requirement, as illustrated.

Correlation between loyalty and customer satisfaction

The market life-cycle for many of GlobalTech's products was moving into the commodity phase. Therefore, not surprisingly, customers were becoming less loyal.

Each percentage point increase in loyalty translated into almost the same increase in market share. Each percentage point in market share added many millions of dollars of gross revenues. The cost of reselling to a loyal customer was about one-sixth the cost of winning a new customer. Consequentially, each percentage point increase in loyalty had a significant impact on the bottom line.

Because of this, the quantitative study included correlating the key drivers of satisfaction and loyalty within each market segment. The qualitative study identified some twenty-eight key customer requirements of their service provider. The quantitative study prioritized these to provide a shorter list of seventeen common requirements. The correlation exercise reduced this to only two requirements that drew a significant correlation between satisfaction and loyalty:

1 Providing service levels that meet your needs
2 Providing consistent performance over time.

Although GlobalTech was achieving the second, it was really only delivering the first in two of the market segments.

Segment attractiveness

As an aid to deciding where best to invest, a chart of segment attractiveness was produced using attractiveness factors determined by GlobalTech. Demographic data from the quantitative study were combined with internal GlobalTech financial data.

Each factor was weighted to reflect the relative importance to GlobalTech. This highlighted quite a few issues and some opportunities. For instance, the highest margins where coming from some of the least loyal segments.

Market attractiveness factors

☐ Margin $s   ■ Market size$s   ☐ Loyalty   ■ Margin%   ☐ Market share $s
■ Market growth%   ■ No. of customers   ☐ Satisfied   ■ Very satisfied

■ The further a factor is shown to the left, the greater its importance to GlobalTech.
■ The longer the bar, the more attractive the segment is to GlobalTech.

Competitive positioning

Fortunately for GlobalTech, its competitors did not appear to have an appreciation of the market segments or the differing requirements of their customers. They were also mainly delivering a 'one size fits all' service offering. However, there were some noticeable differences in their offerings. These resulted in each major competitor being significantly stronger in just one or two market segments where their deliverable best matched the segment needs.

The quantitative study provided detailed rankings of the DBCs and CSFs for each market segment. These were to prove invaluable during the phase of designing the service products and developing the strategy to achieve competitive advantage.

> **DBCs** (decision buying criteria) are the needs (benefits) buyers are seeking to have satisfied by their choice of product or service
>
> **CSFs** (critical success factors) are the constituents of the factors required to deliver each DBC

Reachability

Key to GlobalTech successfully implementing any strategies or communications that were to be market segment-based would be being able to identify each customer by segment. As part of the quantitative study, two statistical reachability tasks were completed.

A sampling of internal GlobalTech databases showed that there was sufficient relevant data to achieve better than 70 per cent accuracy, using statistical imputation methods, to code each customer record with its market segment. This was considered to be good enough to enhance marketing communications measurably, but might not be sufficiently accurate to ensure always making the most appropriate offer. Statistical analysis identified four questions that would provide acceptable accuracy in segment identification. These questions could then be used during both inbound and outbound call centre conversations until such time as all customers had been coded.

The recommendation was to use both methods in parallel so that accuracy would improve over time. Also, the coding of larger customers should be given a priority.

> **Lesson 4**
> Understanding the different market segments helps in designing the required offers. But do not get hung-up on reachability. It is not essential to code every customer to the right segment from day one. Where you are not really sure, let them see different offers and so position themselves.
> Similarly, be willing to accept that within a large organization some buyers may fall into different market segments, though the difference will only be on one or perhaps two buying criteria rather than across all the buying criteria.

Strategy development and implementation

Market understanding and strategy development

The challenge now was for the project team to absorb and understand all the findings from the two research studies. The team then had to turn that understanding into realizable strategies. To achieve this, a workshop process covering opportunities, threats and issues (OTIs) was used.

Briefly, the process involved an extensive, but controlled, brainstorming session followed by a series of innovative strategy development workshops.

A facilitator took the team systematically through every piece of relevant information available. Using brainstorming, the team tried to identify every conceivable opportunity, threat or internal issue associated with each item of information. The information was also then tested against a predetermined list of business behaviours and processes in an endeavour to entice additional and creative ideas out of the brainstorming. Using the DBCs and CSFs from the market model, strengths and weaknesses were added, thus turning the process into a SWOT. Like ideas were merged and de-duplicated.

Each idea was given two scores in the range of 1–9. The first ranked the probable financial impact, the second ranked the probability of success. The ideas were then grouped by like activity and where they had the same or an overlapping financial impact. This ensured that double-counting was eliminated, and that opportunities and threats were offset as appropriate. Any one group of ideas would take on the highest single financial impact score and a reassessed probability of success score. If the resolution of an internal issue was a prerequisite for capturing an opportunity or overcoming a threat, then the issue plus associated costs and resources was included in the same group as the opportunity or threat. The norm was for a single issue to be attached to many groups. The groups were named and then ranked by both financial impact and probability of success. This provided a prioritized shortlist of imperatives that should deliver the maximum realizable benefits to both GlobalTech and its customers. Iterative discussions developed this into an overall strategy with a number of prioritized sub-strategies. Each sub-strategy was supported by a documented description of the opportunity. At this stage, encouragement was given to creating innovative, yet simple, implementation options that would maximize the chances of success. Each implementation option was supported by market, revenue and organizational impact data, associated issues, resources, costs, and required control metrics. Board members were involved in an option selections and investment approvals process. Finally, the implementation programmes and project plans were created.

The strategy

The overall recommendation was to create a set of service deliverables tailored to the individual needs of each segment. These would be complemented by a set of premium add-ons that could be offered to the appropriate segments. By focusing on business process simplification, during the design of the offering for each segment, redundancy was eliminated.

The objective of each offering was to increase customer satisfaction significantly, with an emphasis on those items that would most positively impact loyalty. Some offerings were quite different from others, both in terms of the deliverable and the internal processes that made it possible. This differentiation was also intended to create a measurable competitive advantage in a number of the market segments.

A key to the implementation of the project was a recommended change to the customer satisfaction metrics, so that they became an effective diagnostic tool for tuning the ongoing deliverables for each market segment.

Implementation

Throughout the project, the same core team had been intimately involved with each stage of the project. They guided the work and took on board the results. They delved deeply into the analysis and did their best to understand the markets, their customer requirements and likely competitive impacts. Finally, they worked hard at developing the proposed strategies. They thought buy-in had been achieved by being sponsored by a main board director.

The implementation roll-out across country boundaries became difficult. Each country wanted its say. Each country had different views of its customer needs and how things should be done in the country. The countries did not easily understand or even accept the findings of the research and the meaning of the outputs.

The majority of these internal barriers were eventually overcome. Inevitably, there were compromises. These led the project team into believing that not all the market segments would be fully satisfied with the new offerings in all countries.

Case history conclusion

These three case histories illustrate the importance of intelligent segmentation in guiding companies towards successful marketing strategies. However, it is easy to understand this success after the event. The problem for most of us is how to arrive at meaningful segments that will enable us to create differential advantage.

This has been the purpose of this chapter.

■ Application questions

1 Choose a major product or service. What are its features? Identify the benefits (to the customer) of each feature. Identify which of these are differential benefits.
2 If you cannot identify any differential benefits, in what ways could you develop some?
3 For those you have identified, how can they be improved on?
4 Identify your key market segments. How do you describe them?
5 If you cannot identify any distinct segments, how can you begin to identify one or more?

Chapter 4 review

Customers or consumers?

Customers are people who buy from you. Consumers are the users of your products or services – for example, a husband (customer) buys perfume for his wife (consumer). Sometimes the customer is also the consumer. Marketers need to know about the characteristics of both if they are to develop the best 'package' to meet their needs.

Market share

Market share is a key concept in marketing. It is the proportion of actual sales (either volume or value) within a defined market. How the company defines its market is extremely critical.   *Try Exercise 4.1*

Research shows that there is a direct correlation between market share and profitability.

Critical success factors

Within any given market segment there are critical success factors (CSFs) for winning the business, e.g. reliable delivery, acceptable design, low running costs, and so on. It will be essential for the company to establish what these are and how well it compares with its closest competitors, when measured against these factors.   *Try Exercise 4.2*

Market segmentation

A market segment consists of a group of customers within a market who share a similar level of interest in the same, or comparable, set of needs which can be satisfied by a distinct marketing proposition.

Each segment is sufficiently large to give the company a return for its effort. Members of each segment have a high degree of similarity. The criteria for describing segments must enable the company to communicate effectively with them.

Segmentation can be based on a combination of:

1   Analysis of customer behaviour:
- What do they buy?
  - value/volume
  - price
  - frequency
  - where they buy/outlet
  - products/services, etc.   *Try Exercise 4.3*
- Why do they buy?
  - benefits
  - lifestyle
  - fashion/novelty
  - personality types
  - peer-group pressure preferences, etc.   *Try Exercise 4.4*

2   Analysis of customer characteristics (who they are):
- customer size
- socio-economic groups
- demographic considerations
- industrial classification
- cultural/geographic factors.   *Try Exercise 4.5*

Questions raised for the company

1   Q: Why is market segmentation so important?

    A: Few companies can be 'all things to all people'. Segmentation allows the firm to target its effort on the most promising opportunities.

2   Q: How can we be expected to know our market share?

    A: The more accurately you can define your market segments, the more accurately you will find you can measure your market share. Correct market definition is also critical for:
- growth measurement
- specifying target customers
- recognizing relevant competitors
- setting marketing objectives and strategies.

3   Q: How can we keep tabs on all our competitors?

    A: You don't have to – just concentrate on your closest competitors and try to ensure that you maintain some differential advantage over them.

EXERCISES

Exercise 4.1 looks at the most crucial and complex issue in marketing, i.e. how a market is defined. Until this is clearly understood, issues such as market share, the identification of target customers and their needs, and even the recognition of competitors, will continuously cause difficulty.

Exercise 4.2 examines critical success factors. Exercise 4.3 provides a technique for auditing industrial goods and services.

Exercise 4.4 introduces another technique, benefit analysis, and this is extended and put into practice in Exercise 4.5, which provides a case study for analysis.

Often there is confusion regarding what constitutes a market. Unless such confusion is dispelled from the outset, the whole marketing edifice will be built on sand. However, as so often is the case, what on the surface appears to be a relatively simple task can prove to be extremely testing. Take the example shown in Figure 4.14, which vastly simplifies the problem.

Introduction to Chapter 4 exercises

Exercise 4.1
Market definition

Figure 4.14
Example of market definition

XYZ Ltd has five major products, A, B, C, D and E, which are sold to five different markets, as represented in Figure 4.14. Virtually all sales are achieved in the shaded areas.

Is this company's market:

(a) The shaded areas?
(b) The intersection of products A, B and C and markets 2, 3 and 4?
(c) Products A, B and C for all markets?
(d) Markets 2, 3 and 4 for all products?
(e) The entire matrix?

Scoring and Interpretation for Exercise 4.1
1 It would be possible to define our market as the shaded areas ((a) in the exercise), i.e. the product/market area currently served. The problem with this is that it might tend to close our eyes to other potential opportunities

for profitable growth and expansion, especially if there is a danger that our current markets may become mature.

2 It is also possible to define our market as the intersection of products A, B and C and markets 2, 3 and 4 ((b) in the exercise). The problem with this is that while we now have a broader vision, there may be developments in product areas D and E and markets 1 and 5 that we should be aware of.

3 To a large extent, this problem would be overcome by defining our market as products A, B and C for all markets ((c) in the exercise). The problem here is that markets 1 and 5 may not require products A, B and C, so perhaps we need to consider product development (products D and E).

4 It is certainly possible to consider our market as all products for markets 2, 3 and 4 ((d) in the exercise). The potential problem here is that we still do not have any interest in markets 1 and 3.

5 Finally, it is clearly possible to call the entire matrix our market ((e) in the exercise), with markets 1 to 5 on the vertical axis and each of products A to E on the horizontal axis. The problem with this is that we would almost certainly have too many markets, or segments, and this could lead to a costly dissipation of effort.

The answer to the conundrum therefore is that it is purely a matter of management judgement. Any combinations of (a)–(e) above could be used, as long as there is a sensible rationale to justify the choice.

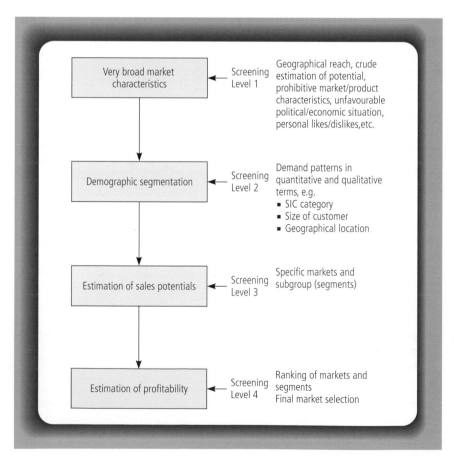

Figure 4.15
Market screening

In addition, remember the following definition of 'market':

A market is the aggregation of all the products or services which customers regard as being capable of satisfying the same need.

Remember also the following useful definition of market segmentation:

An identifiable group of customers with requirements in common that are, or may become, significant in terms of developing a separate strategy.

Often, the way a market was selected in the first instance can provide clues regarding how it can be defined. Generally, either consciously or intuitively, a screening process is used to eliminate unsuitable markets and to arrive at those with potential. This screening process often works something like that shown in Figure 4.15.

Consider one of your current markets and explain:

1 How it came to be chosen
2 How you would define it, so that it is clearly distinct from any other market.

Remember that the crude method outlined above, while working at a very general level, rarely leads to the development of differential advantage, and it is suggested that the other exercises in this chapter should be completed in order to get a better understanding of the central significance of market segmentation in marketing success.

Exercise 4.2
Critical success factors (CSFs)

Critical success factors can vary from one type of business to another, or indeed from one market segment to another. Therefore it is impossible to be prescriptive about your CSFs, and you will have to draw on the expertise you have about your business and establish which ones are correct for you.

Remember, a CSF is something which helps you to clinch the business. Thus, by definition, if it were absent, your success rate would plummet.

Normally there would only be a few CSFs – probably not more than five – although there might be many other factors which contribute to success.

Table 4.4 is an example of the way a firm of quantity surveyors analysed their business.

Table 4.4			
CSF	Weighting	Score out of 10 (10 = very high standard)	Adjusted score*
1 Reputation for on-time completion	0.5	6	30
2 Track record of quality	0.3	6	18
3 Quality of sales staff	0.2	8	16
Total	1.0		64%

*Adjusted score = score out of 10 × weighting factor.

Weighting factors are distributed to each CSF according to their relative importance. In Table 4.4, CSF1 is the most important, but the company only scores 6, just over average. In contrast, on CSF3 the company scores high, but this factor is the least critical of those listed and so the net result is diminished.

The company now repeats this process (Table 4.5), this time focusing on its nearest competitors.

Table 4.5							
CSF	Weighting	Comp. A score		Comp. B score		Comp. C score	
		Raw	Adjusted	Raw	Adjusted	Raw	Adjusted
1	0.5	9	45	5	25	7	35
2	0.3	5	15	5	15	7	21
3	0.2	6	12	5	10	5	10
Total			72%		50%		66%

On the evidence in Table 4.5, our company can see that Competitor A, even with a lower quality sales force and a slightly poorer track record, has a competitive advantage because of its ability to complete contracts on time. Similarly, Competitor C is a force to be reckoned with. In contrast, Competitor B has a lot of ground to make up in all areas.

This technique can be applied to all companies and provides three useful outcomes:

1 It forces people to think about their critical success factors.
2 It provides an overview of relative competitiveness when measured against their main competitors.
3 It highlights the areas where the most effective improvements might be made.

Now try it on your company. See Tables 4.6 and 4.7.

Table 4.6			
CSF	Weighting	Score out of 10 (10 = very high standard)	Adjusted score
CSF1			
CSF2			
CSF3			
CSF4			
CSF5			

Table 4.7

CSF	Weighting	Comp. A score		Comp. B score		Comp. C score	
		Raw	Adjusted	Raw	Adjusted	Raw	Adjusted
CSF1							
CSF2							
CSF3							
CSF4							
CSF5							

Exercise 4.3
Market audit – industrial goods and services

Using your own company as the study vehicle, complete the market audit form (Table 4.8) by following these instructions:

Step 1   In column 1, list all those industries that are consumers of your goods or services. Note that there is no need to structure this list, just write them down as they occur to you.

Step 2   In column 2, write the actual turnover figure.

Step 3   In column 3, write down the percentage value of turnover that results from each of the industries.

Step 4   In column 4, indicate whether or not this, when considered from the point of view of profitability, is high or low, by scoring 10 for high, 5 for good, and 1 for low (here, 'profitability' means whatever your company considers it to mean).

Step 5   Using column 5, consider what capacity and skills you have at your disposal to continue supplying each industry – a score of 10 would show that you have considerable capacity, with minimal interference to other products or services; 1 would indicate severe limitations.

Step 6   Using a similar scoring procedure, complete column 6. Ask yourself how confident your company is that it can supply each industry with the right quality and design of goods/services, delivered on time. Are you more confident about some than others?

Step 7   Now consider the market potential (demand) for your output in each of the listed industries. Using column 7, score 10 for high potential and 1 for low.

Step 8   Add the scores you have allocated in columns 4, 5, 6 and 7, and enter them in column 8.

Step 9   Using the information you have put together, identify your key market segments. They ought to be those industries which collected the highest aggregate scores, but for your type of business you might identify other factors that would influence your choice of market. Make a note of these in column 9. In addition, use column 9 to record any particular opportunities or threats presented in each market.

Step 10   Balancing the notes you made in column 9 against the arithmetic calculations (column 8), study the information you have assembled, and select what you regard as the best industrial market. Enter 1 against this in column 10. Continue ranking each industry, using 2 for the next best, 3 for the third, etc. until column 10 is filled.

Information from this market audit could be used at a later stage, when marketing objectives and strategies are examined (Exercises 6.6 and 6.7).

Table 4.8 Market audit industrial goods and services

1	2	3	4	5	6	7	8	9	10
Industry	Actual T/O	% T/O	Profitability, L_1 $_{10}H$	Capacity, L_1 $_{10}H$	Confidence, L_1 $_{10}H$	Potential, L_1 $_{10}H$	Total (Cols 4, 5, 6, 7)	Additional factors, opportunities/ threats	Rank

Customers buy products and services because they seek to acquire a range of benefits which go with them. In this sense, all products and services are problem-solvers. Thus, customers buy aspirin to solve the problem of headaches, they buy drills because they need holes, they buy convenience foods because they solve the problem of there not being enough hours in the day.

It is essential for providers of products or services to be aware that their output is only saleable for as long as it provides the benefits the customer requires, and for as long as it is seen by the customer to be good value when compared with other possible methods of solving their problems. Once there is a better, cheaper, quicker, tidier, more enjoyable way of putting holes in walls, the drill manufacturer will go the way of the buggy-whip maker. Therefore it is vitally important to know just as much about the benefits they supply as it is to know about the products or services themselves.

Exercise 4.4
Benefit analysis

Standard benefits

These are provided by the product but are not in any way unique – for example, 'the propellant in our aerosol does not damage the ozone layer'. Although in this respect your product might be like all others, not to make customers aware of this standard benefit could imply that you still use environmentally unfriendly materials. Clearly this would be to your disadvantage.

Company benefits

The business transaction links the customer to the company. In turn, this means that there ought to be some benefits to that customer for making that choice. Customers will prefer to deal with companies that provide better customer service, inspire confidence, have a reputation for fair trading policies, and so on. Company benefits are a means of differentiating your products or services from competing ones, if to all intents and purposes they are similar. For example, some banks are trying to establish specific identities to the benefits they supply. Hence there is 'the listening bank' and 'the bank that likes to say yes'. Perhaps eventually there will be 'the bank that is open when its customers want it to be'!

Differential benefits

These are the benefits that only your products or services provide. It is these that give the company its competitive advantage. It is these that must be identified, developed and exploited if the company is to win success. Here are some examples:

- 'We are the only company that provides a genuine 24-hour breakdown service. Therefore, any time you need us, we are there to get you moving again.'
- 'This is the only product on the market with this self-cleaning facility, so you can install it and have no maintenance worries.'

Not every benefit will have equal appeal to all customers, or groups of customers. However, by talking to them, or carrying out research, it ought to be possible to establish which are the important benefits in their eyes.

It is now possible to prepare a systematic benefit analysis along the lines shown in these examples. See Table 4.9.

Table 4.9

Customer(s) _____

Service/product _____

Customer appeal	Features	Advantages	Benefits	Proof
What issues are of particular concern to the customer, e.g. cost, reliability, safety, simplicity, etc.?	What features of the product/ service best illustrate these issues? How do they work?	What advantages do these features provide, i.e. what do they do for the customer?	How can tangible benefits be expressed to give maximum customer appeal, i.e. what does the customer get that he/she needs?	What evidence can be provided to back up the benefit and show it can be attained?
Example – saucepans				
Ease of use, ease of washing-up	Teflon-coated	This is a non-stick material	Trouble-free cooking, quicker washing-up	Results of tests
Example – office services bureau				
Accuracy and speedy turn-round of work	We use the latest equipment and very skilled staff	We are extremely versatile	Minimum of errors, cost-saving	What customers say

Note:
1 To get from a feature to an advantage, and then to a benefit, the phrase 'which means that' can be helpful – for example, 'It's coated in new formula paint (feature), which means that the colour will never fade (advantage).' If you know this is what the customer needs, then you have also arrived at a benefit.
2 To check whether you have arrived at a benefit and not just an advantage, apply the 'so what?' test. Ask this question after the benefit. If the 'so what?' prompts you to go further, the chances are you have not yet reached the real benefit – for example, 'Our products are handmade (feature), which means they are better quality than machine-made ones (benefit?)' – so what? – 'which means they last longer (the real benefit)'.

Now try producing a benefit analysis for one of your own products or services, as it impacts on a specific customer or customer group. Use Table 4.10.

Table 4.10

Customer(s) _____

Service/product _____

Customer appeal	Features	Advantages	Benefits	Proof

The customer audit applied to your own company
Working alone, and using your own company as the study vehicle:

1 Choose a major product or service, and identify:
   (a) The main customers
   (b) The features with maximum customer appeal
   (c) The benefits to the customer of each feature
   (d) Which of these benefits are differential benefits (i.e. benefits not rec-
        ognized or stressed by your major competitors).
2 If you cannot identify any differential benefits, in what ways could you
   develop them?
3 For those you have identified, how could they be improved upon?
4 Identify your key market segments. How do you describe them?
5 If you cannot readily identify any distinct segments, what would be a sensible way to segment your markets?

Personal notes

As a prerequisite to establishing marketing objectives for your company, it will
be important to analyse the customers of your products or services. For some
businesses it is adequate to focus on the needs of groups of individual customers;
for others it is more important to look at customers as being whole industries. In
this exercise, we will concentrate on the former type of customer base.

Exercise 4.5
The customer
audit – Car
Mart Ltd

The information you assemble by completing this exercise can be used at a later stage of the marketing planning process.

Types of customer audit

There are many different ways of auditing customers. Most of them work on the premise that customer needs will, to a large extent, be influenced by personal circumstances such as age, personality, occupation, lifestyle and financial situation.

The following exercise will give you an opportunity to explore the practical implications of using one such approach.

Car Mart objective

Car Mart produces a record of a series of sales transactions from which you have to identify the key market segment(s) and useful customer audit material.

Materials for Car Mart

1 *Twelve customer cards* (to be cut out from the back of the book), consisting of:
   - a lift attendant
   - a bricklayer
   - a self-employed plumber
   - a bank manager (local branch)
   - a computer programmer
   - a sales manager
   - a school teacher
   - a chairman of an industrial group
   - a senior partner in a firm of solicitors
   - a tool-maker
   - a factory machine operator
   - an elderly granny.
2 *Six product cards* – the *showroom* (to be cut out from the back of the book), consisting of:
   - economy car
   - family saloon
   - executive transport
   - estate car
   - second car
   - sports car.
3 *Car Mart sales record sheet* (see later in this exercise).
4 *Two dice.*

Assumptions

This simulation does not attempt to portray real life in accurate detail, but merely to be the vehicle for learning, and thereby provide an opportunity for experimentation. To this end, the following assumptions are made:

1 Anyone tackling this exercise will have completed Exercise 4.4 or have a clear understanding about the difference between features and benefits.
2 The 'customers' in Car Mart have the financial resources to make their purchases.

3 The 'customer needs' expressed are a genuine attempt to reflect the likely views of that particular 'customer'.
4 The car 'chosen' is in an acceptable condition for the customer, i.e. it is new if the customer wants new, or second-hand if that is what the customer is looking for.

Generating the data for Car Mart

There are two methods of developing the necessary data for this exercise.

1 *Procedure for a group of four 'players'*:
   (a) A group of four players is seated at a suitable table.
   (b) The twelve customer cards are shuffled by Player 1 and then laid face up on the table in a vertical column by one of the players. The six product cards are also placed on the table in a separate group, face upwards, to represent the Car Mart showroom.
   (c) Player 2, on the left of Player 1, shakes the two dice and uses the aggregate score to designate a customer card – for example, if the dice show 8 as a total score, Player 2 counts down the column of customer cards to the eighth card.
   (d) Player 2 then becomes this customer and improvises a realistic buying need of that person by saying, 'I'm looking for a car that (own words)' – for example, 'I'm looking for a car that will always start in the mornings'.
   (e) Player 3 responds to this by selecting one of the product cards from the table (showroom), and explains a feature of this particular car by saying 'This one has (own words)' – for example, 'This car has been on the market for many years'.
   (f) Player 4 then has to add a benefit statement to the feature raised by Player 3, by saying 'Which means that (own words)' – for example, 'Which means that it is now a very reliable vehicle'.
   (g) One of the players (probably the neatest writer) then fills in the first transaction row of the 'sales record sheet', at this stage ignoring columns 2, 4 and 9, the narrow ones.
   (h) This whole procedure is repeated, this time Player 3 shaking the dice and being the customer.
   (i) This rotation of starter continues until twenty sales transactions have been completed, i.e. the sales record sheet is filled.

2 *Procedure for individual study*:
   If it is not possible to work in a group of four as described, an individual can work through the Car Mart exercise alone. He or she will of course have to play the role of each player described above. Nevertheless, this process will produce the completed sales record sheet, which is an essential prerequisite for the rest of this exercise. If it is possible, procedure 1 is recommended, because, with other people, the exercise becomes much more creative and stimulating.
   Once the sales record sheet is completed, answer the questions in the next sections.

The customer audit (socio-economic groups and buying motives)

Imagine that the sales record sheet you have just completed was multiplied tenfold. In other words, it is a record of 200 sales transactions, which represents Car Mart's trading for the last year.

CAR MART SALES RECORD SHEET

1	2	3	4	5	6	7	8	9
Customer		Needs		Product	New or second-hand	Feature	Benefit	

Working in the same group as that which generated the data for the sales record sheet, proceed as follows:

1 Decide into which socio-economic category each customer falls. Enter your decisions in column 2 of the sales record sheet.
2 Look at customer needs (column 3) and decide which are Rational and which are more Psychological. Enter R or P in column 4.
3 Similarly, look at benefits (column 8) and enter R or P in column 9, depending on whether or not the benefit is likely to appeal to the 'rational customer' or to his/her psychological needs.
4 Tick all those benefits where the R or P in column 9 matches up with an R or P in column 4.
5 Consider the ease/difficulty of completing 1 to 4 above, and reconcile any differences that occurred between columns 4 and 9.
6 If time permits, you can discuss any interesting points which came out of the Car Mart sales record sheet.

When you have completed these tasks, proceed to the next section.

The customer audit (segmentation)

Staying in the same group as before, use the information you have collected on the completed sales record sheet and answer the following:

1 What is the key market segment(s) for Car Mart?
2 List the particular features of this or these segment(s).
3 Describe which products and benefits best meet the needs of this segment(s).
4 Suggest ways that Car Mart could exploit this information to become a more successful business.
5 Is Car Mart the best name for this company? How might it be changed to communicate more accurately its type of business or the customers it serves?
6 Consider the main learning points from Car Mart and decide how you could apply them to your own company.

You might find it useful to make notes of any interesting issues that come out of this analysis in the following space, or on a separate sheet of paper. Once you have completed those questions, proceed to the next section.

Personal notes

Interpretation of Exercise 4.5 – rationale behind Car Mart

1 The twelve customers represent two of each of the socio-economic groups:

Grade A	Chairman of industrial group
	Senior partner in firm of solicitors
Grade B	Bank manager
	Sales manager
Grade C1	Teacher
	Computer programmer
Grade C2	Tool-maker
	Plumber
Grade D	Bricklayer
	Machine operator
Grade E	Lift attendant (often a reserved occupation for the disabled)
	Elderly granny

2 The mechanism of using two dice in the way described means that, over about twenty transactions, something approaching Pareto's Law comes into play – i.e. that 20 per cent of customers account for 80 per of sales. This is because card 1 is never chosen and cards in positions 6, 7 and 8 should be prominent. But since the layout of the cards is random, there can be no pre-conceived notions about customers – it must all be interpreted from the sales analysis.

3 There are some hidden learning objectives, because, by playing the game, people become aware of, and can distinguish:
   (a) Socio-economic groupings
   (b) Differences between features and benefits
   (c) Differences between rational and psychological buying motives.

4 Car Mart provides enough data for anyone to bring to life the main points about customer analysis and segmentation.

5 Those who need to apply this learning to their own company situation will be able to proceed with more confidence.

6 Car Mart demands that there is a high level of focus on customers and ensures that there is high awareness of customer needs.

Exercise 4.6
Micro-segments

Use the form provided to work out the micro-segments found in your market. For instructions on doing this, please refer to pages 140–142.

Micro-segment	1	2	3	4	5	6	7	8	9	10
Application (if applicable)										
What is bought										
Where,										
When,										
and How										
Who										
Why (benefits sought)										

A selection of standard approaches to profiling benefits

1 *Demographic characteristics*

- Standard Industrial Classification (SIC) – the latest details are available from the appropriate statistical office. Summaries of both the UK/European and North American SIC systems appear below.

  United Kingdom and Europe

  Agriculture, Hunting and Forestry (01–02)
  Fishing (05)
  Mining and Quarrying (10–14)
  Manufacturing (15–37)
  Electricity, Gas and Water Supply (40–41)
  Construction (45)
  Wholesale and Retail Trade; Certain Repairs (50–52)
  Hotels and Restaurants (55)
  Transport, Storage and Communication (60–64)
  Financial Intermediation (65–67)
  Real Estate, Renting and Other Business Activities (70–74)
  Public Administration and Defence; Compulsory Social Security (75)
  Education (80)
  Health and Social Work (85)
  Other Community, Social and Personal Service Activities (90–93)
  Private Households with Employed Persons and Miscellaneous (95–97)
  Extra-territorial Organizations and Bodies (99)

  North America (USA, Canada and Mexico)

  Agriculture, Forestry, Fishing and Hunting (11)
  Mining (21)
  Utilities (22)
  Construction (23)
  Manufacturing (31–33)
  Wholesale Trade (42)
  Retail Trade (44–45)
  Transportation and Warehousing (48–49)
  Information (51)
  Finance and Insurance (52)
  Real Estate and Retail and Leasing (53)
  Professional, Scientific and Technical Services (54)
  Management of Companies and Enterprises (55)
  Administrative and Support and Waste Management and Remediation Services (56)
  Education Services (61)
  Health Care and Social Assistance (62)
  Arts, Entertainment and Recreation (71)
  Accommodation and Food Services (72)
  Other Services (except Public Administration) (81)
  Public Administration (92)

- Size of company – Very small, Small, Small–Medium, Medium, Medium–Large, Large, Very large, Very large+
- Department/Section – Manufacturing, Distribution, Customer Service, Sales, Marketing, Commercial, Financial, Bought Ledger, Sales Ledger, Personnel Estates, Office Services, Planning Contracts, IT
- Multidemographic – combining a selection of demographic criteria, such as size of company with job title, along with whether the company is public or private.

2 *Geographic*
- Postcode
- City, town, village, rural
- Country
- Region – frequently defined in the UK by TV region
- Country
- Economic/Political union or association (e.g. ASEAN)
- Continent.

3 *Psychographics* – buyer characteristics
- Personality – stage in its business life-cycle (start-up, growth, maturity, decline, turn-round); style/age of staff (formal, authoritarian, bureaucratic, disorganized, positive, indifferent, negative, cautious, conservative, old-fashioned, youthful)
- Attitude – risk takers or risk avoiders; innovative or cautious, and many of the adjectives used to describe different types of personality can also express a company's attitude towards your product line (as opposed to their distinctive personal character)
- Lifestyle – environmentally concerned; involved with the community; sponsor of sports/arts.

A selection of standard approaches to profiling individuals

1 *Demographic characteristics*
- Age – <3, 3–5, 6–11, 12–19, 20–34, 35–49, 50–64, 65+
- Sex – male, female
- Family life-cycle – Bachelor (young, single), split into dependants (living at home or full-time student) and those with their own household; Newly married (no children); Full nest (graded according to the number and age of children); Single parent; Empty nesters (children left home or a childless couple); Elderly single
- Family size – 1–2, 3–4, 5+
- Type of residence – Flat/house, terraced/semi-detached/detached, private/rented/council, number of rooms/bedrooms
- Income (£k) – <10, 10–15, 16–20, 21–30, 31–50, >50
- Occupation – operatives; craftsmen, foremen; managers, officials, proprietors; professional, technical; clerical, sales; farmers; retired, students; housewife; unemployed. White-collar (professional, managerial, supervisory, clerical); Blue-collar (manual)
- Education (highest level) – secondary, no qualifications; GCSE; graduate; postgraduate
- Religion – Christian, Jewish, Muslim, Buddhist, Other
- Ethnic origin – African, Asian, Caribbean, UK, Irish, Other European
- Nationality
- Socio-economic – the eight-class version of the socio-economic classification (SEC) introduced by the Office for National Statistics (UK) 2001 and the former Registrar General's 'Social Class' can be found on page 139
- Multidemographic – combining a selection of demographic criteria, such as life-cycle stages and occupation groupings, on the basis that these are indicative of different aspirations and behaviour patterns.

2 *Geographic*
- Postcode
- City, town, village, rural
- Coastal, inland
- County

- Region (frequently defined in the UK by TV areas – Anglia, Border, Carlton London, Carlton Central, Carlton West Country, Channel, Grampian, Granada, HTV, LWT, Meridian, Scottish, Tyne Tees, UTV, Yorkshire)
- Country
- Economic/Political union or association (e.g. NAFTA)
- Continent
- Population density
- Climate.

3 *Geodemographics*. A Classification of Residential Neighbourhoods (ACORN) produced by CACI Ltd[4] is one of the longer established geodemographic classifications in the UK, updated with Census information and lifestyle data. ACORN covers every street in Great Britain and classifies the whole population into fifty-six types, summarized into seventeen groups, which in turn are condensed into five broad categories. These five broad categories act as a simplified reference to the overall household classification structure and are as follows:

1 'Affluent Achievers'
2 'Urban Prosperity'
3 'Comfortably Off'
4 'Modest Means'
5 'Hard Pressed'

Geodemographic data are also combined with financial data to provide detailed information on financial product ownership. For example, Financial ACORN combines Census and financial research data into fifty-one types, twelve groups and four categories.

4 *Psychographic characteristics*
- Personality – compulsive, extrovert, gregarious, adventurous, formal, authoritarian, ambitious, enthusiastic, positive, indifferent, negative, hostile; specific ones by sex have also been developed.
- Attitude – degree of loyalty (none, total, moderate), risk takers or risk avoiders, likelihood of purchasing a new product (innovator, early adopter, early majority, late majority, laggard), and many of the adjectives used to describe different types of personality can also express an individual's attitude towards your product line (as opposed to their distinctive personal character).
- Customer status – purchase stage (aware, interested, desirous, ready for sale), user classification (non-user, lapsed user, first time, potential).
- Lifestyle – consists of three main dimensions:

  Activities Work, hobbies, social events, vacation, entertainment, club membership, community, shopping, sports

  Interests Family, home, job, community, recreation, fashion, food, media, achievements

  Opinions Selves, social issues, politics, business, economics, education, products, future, culture

  Because the data are based on individuals, variations in the attributes to be used can result in different people in the same household being selected.
- Multidimensional – combining psychographic profiles with selected demographic data and identifying geographic areas where the resulting

---

[4] 'ACORN' and 'CACI' are trademarks of CACI Ltd. Further details can be found at www.caci.co.uk

'behavioural' types are found. For example, Experían's MOSAIC[5] classifies all the households and neighbourhoods (postcodes) in Great Britain into fifty-two distinct types which describe their socio-economic and socio-cultural behaviour. These fifty-two types are aggregated into twelve broad groups:

A High Income Families	E Council Flats	I Independent Elders
B Suburban Semis	F Victorian Low Status	J Mortgaged Families
C Blue Collar Owners	G Town House and Flats	K Country Dwellers
D Low Rise Council	H Stylish Singles	L Institutional Areas

In addition to MOSAIC for Great Britain as a whole, there are separate MOSAICs for Scotland, Northern Ireland and London which identify differences only found in those areas. Experían has also extended MOSAIC to areas outside Great Britain.

---

[5] 'Experían' and 'MOSAIC' are trademarks of Experían Ltd. Further details can be found at www.micromarketing-online.com and www.experian.co.uk

CHAPTER 5

Completing the marketing audit:
2 The product audit

Summary

- What we sell to the segments identified in the last chapter
- What a 'product' is – throughout the chapter the word 'product' is used, but the guidelines provided apply equally to services
- What a brand is
- What the difference is between a successful and an unsuccessful brand
- Key diagnostic tools, specifically
  - life-cycle analysis
  - the Boston Matrix
  - the directional policy matrix
- The growing importance of category management
- Examples of all these tools in practice are provided in the form of mini case histories
- Exercises to turn the theory into actionable propositions

■ Introduction

It will be recalled that, at the beginning of the last chapter, the diagram of the marketing process – repeated here as Figure 5.1 – indicated that Chapters 4 and 5 would be concerned with Box 1, for clearly a marketing audit is concerned not just with whom we sell to but also with what we sell to them. Consequently, this chapter is concerned with this aspect of the audit.

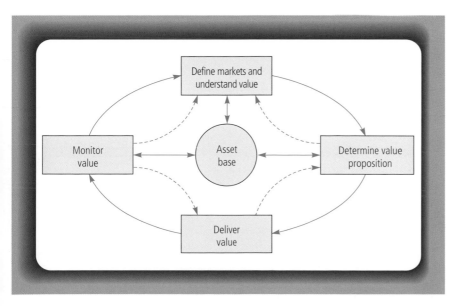

Figure 5.1
Overview of marketing map

■ What is a product?

Throughout this chapter we refer to the term 'product'. However, everything we say is equally applicable to a service.

The central role that the ► **product** plays in marketing management makes it such an important subject that mismanagement in this area is unlikely to be compensated for by good management in other areas.

The vital aspects of product management we shall discuss in this chapter are concerned with the nature of products, product life-cycles, how products make profits, the concept of the product portfolio, and new product development. The purpose of this discussion is to help us to carry out a product audit in order that we can set meaningful marketing objectives. But before we can begin a proper discussion about product management, it is necessary first to understand what a product is, since this is the root of whatever misunderstanding there is about product management.

We have already looked at customers; now we begin to look at what we sell to them (see Figure 5.2). Let us begin by explaining that a product is a problem-solver, in the sense that it solves the customers' problems, and is also the means by which the company achieves its objectives. And since it is what customers actually get for what they pay, it is clearly a subject of great importance.

The clue to what constitutes a product can be found in an examination of what it is that customers appear to buy. Customers have needs, and they buy products to satisfy them. This was made clear in the last chapter, on market segmentation. At its simplest level, someone who needs a hole may buy a drill. But if a better way of making a hole is invented – say a pocket laser – demand for drills may fall.

MARKETING INSIGHT

Some years ago, Gestetner got into serious difficulties because the company thought it was in the duplicator market, when it was clear that other solutions to the duplication problem had become available.

Figure 5.2

> The important point about this is that a company which fails to think of its business in terms of customer benefits rather than in terms of physical products or services is in danger of losing its competitive position in the market.

This is why the subject of benefit analysis was raised in Chapter 4.

But while this is important at the highest level of a company, it is also extremely relevant even at the level of the salesperson. A salesperson announcing that the quench tank on his company's furnace is three times bigger than a competitor's quench tank must not be surprised if this news is met with complete indifference, especially if this feature requires a hole to be dug in the ground three times bigger than the one the customer currently has! Much more relevant would be the fact that this larger quench tank would enable the customer to save a large amount of money each year on operating costs, which is a benefit and which is the main aspect the customer is interested in.

So far, we have not said much about service products, such as consulting, banking, insurance, and so on. The reason for this is simply that, as we said in Chapter 1, the marketing of services is not very different from the marketing of goods. The greatest difference is that a service product has benefits that cannot be stored. Thus, an airline seat, for example, if not utilized at the time of the flight, is gone forever, whereas a physical product may be stored and used at a later date.

The marketing of services is not very different from the marketing of goods.

In practice, this disadvantage makes very little difference in marketing terms. The major problem seems to lie in the difficulty many service product companies have in actually perceiving and presenting their offerings as 'products'. Consider the example of the consultant. This country is full of a constantly changing army of people who set themselves up as consultants, and it is not unusual to see people presenting themselves, for example, as marketing consultants. It would be difficult for any prospective client to glean from such a description exactly what benefits this person is offering. Yet the market for consulting is no different from any other market, and it is a simple matter to segment the market and develop 'products' which will deliver the particular package of benefits desired.

We can now begin to see that when a customer buys a product, even as an industrial buyer purchasing a piece of equipment for a company, he or she is still buying a particular bundle of benefits perceived as satisfying their own particular needs and wants.

We can now appreciate the danger of leaving product decisions entirely to technical experts. If we do, they will often assume that the only point in product management is the actual technical performance, or the functional features of the product itself.

These ideas are incorporated in Figure 5.3.

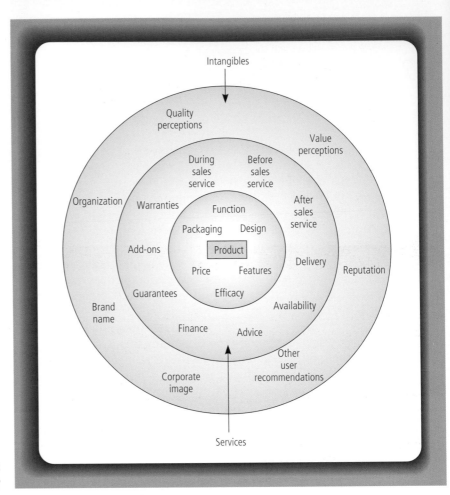

Figure 5.3
What is a product?

The two outer circles are depicted as 'product surround'. This product surround can account for as much as 80 per cent of the added values and impact of a product. Often, these only account for about 20 per cent of costs, whereas the reverse is often true of the core product. This is shown in Figure 5.4.

■ The importance of the brand

▶ **DEFINITION** ◀

A brand is a name or symbol which identifies a product. A successful brand identifies a product as having sustainable, competitive advantage

It will be clear that here we are talking about not just a physical product, but a *relationship* with the customer, a relationship that is personified either by the company's name or by the ▶ **brand name** on the product itself. IBM, BMW and Shell are excellent examples of company brand names. Persil, Coca-Cola, Fosters Lager, Dulux Paint and Castrol GTX are excellent examples of product brand names.

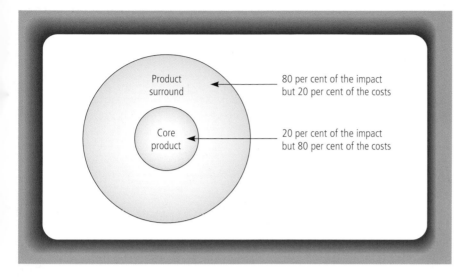

Figure 5.4

Most people are aware of the Coca-Cola/Pepsi-Cola blind-taste tests, in which little difference was perceived when the colas were drunk 'blind'. On revealing the labels, however, 65 per cent of consumers claimed to prefer Coca-Cola. This is one of the best indications of the value of what we have referred to as the 'product surround'. That it is a major determinant of commercial success there can be little doubt. When one company buys another, as in the case of Nestlé and Rowntree, it is abundantly clear that the purpose of the acquisition is not to buy the tangible assets which appear on the balance sheet, such as factories, plant, vehicles and so on, but the *brand names* owned by the company to be acquired.

> This is because it is not factories which make profits, but relationships with customers, and it is company and brand names which secure these relationships.

A recent example of this is Proctor and Gamble's purchase of Gillette for £31 billion, of which only £4 billion was for tangible assets. The bulk of the remaining £27 billion was for brand names and relationships with markets.

It is also a fact that, whenever brand names are neglected, what is known as 'the commodity slide' begins. This is because the physical characteristics of products are becoming increasingly difficult to differentiate and easy to emulate. In situations like these, purchasing decisions tend to be made on the basis of price or availability in the absence of strong brands.

Business history is replete with examples of strong brand names which have been allowed to decay through lack of attention, often because of a lack of both promotion and continuous product improvement programmes.

The fruit squash drink market is typical of this. The reverse can be seen in the case of Intel, which is a fantastic branding success story in a highly competitive global market.

Figure 5.5 depicts the process of decay from brand to commodity as the distinctive values of the brand are eroded over time, with a consequent reduction in the ability to command a premium price.

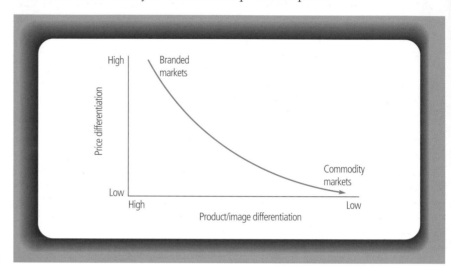

Figure 5.5

The difference between a brand and a commodity can be summed up in the term 'added values', which are the additional attributes, or intangibles, that the consumer perceives as being embodied in the product. Thus, a product with a strong brand name is more than just the sum of its component parts. The Coca-Cola example is only one of thousands of examples of the phenomenon.

In the same way, Glaxo's Zantac in the ulcer market communicates an aura of quality and reliability that enables it to protect its advantage over lesser known brands.

Research has shown that perceived product quality, as explained above, is a major determinant of profitability. This issue is further discussed in Chapter 6 under the heading 'Competitive strategies'.[1]

The difference between successful and unsuccessful brands

Successful brand building helps profitability by adding values that entice customers to buy. They also provide a firm base for expansion into product

---

[1] For further detailed discussion of branding, L. de Chernatony and M. McDonald (2003) *Creating Powerful Brands*, Butterworth-Heinemann, Oxford, 3rd edn.

improvements, variants, added services, new countries, and so on. More-over, they protect companies against the growing power of intermediaries. And last but not least, they help transform organizations from being face-less bureaucracies to ones that are attractive to work for and deal with.

We must not, however, make the mistake of confusing successful and unsuccessful 'brands'. The world is full of products and services that have brand names, but which are not successful brands. They fall down on other important criteria.

A successful brand has a name, symbol or design (or some combination) that identifies the 'product' of an organization as having a sustainable competitive advantage – for example, Coca-Cola, IBM, Tesco. A successful brand invariably results in superior profit and market performance (PIMS). Brands are only assets if they have sustainable competitive advantage. Like other assets, brands depreciate without further investment – for example, Hoover, Singer, MG, Marks & Spencer and so on.

There are many 'products' that pretend to be brands, but are not the genuine article. As the Director of Marketing at Tesco said, 'Pseudo brands are not brands. They are manufacturer's labels. They are 'me-toos' and have poor posi-tioning, poor quality and poor support. Such manufacturers no longer under-stand the consumer and see retailers solely as a channel for distribution' (reported in *Marketing Globe*, Vol. 2, No. 10, 1992).

MARKETING INSIGHT

Seen in this light, pseudo brands can never be mistaken for the real thing, because the genuine brand provides added brand values. Customers believe that the product:

- will be reliable
- is the best
- is something that will suit them better than product X
- is designed with them in mind.

These beliefs are based not only on perceptions of the brand itself relative to others, but also on customers' perceptions of the supplying company and beliefs about its reputation and integrity.

> The title 'successful brand' has to be earned. The company has to invest in everything it does so that the product meets the physical needs of customers, as well as having an image to match their emotional needs. Thus it must provide concrete and rational benefits that are sustained by a marketing mix that is compatible, believable and relevant.

By dint of considerable effort, Centrica (formerly British Gas) is close to changing from a well-known name to a successful brand. It may not quite be there yet, but it is beginning to shake off its erstwhile bureaucratic image and is getting closer to providing a consistent, high-quality service.

IBM, despite all its recent trials and tribulations, still has a substantial world market share and that three-lettered logo is still very powerful.

The components of a brand

There are three principal components: brand strategy, brand positioning, and brand personality.

The first of these, *brand strategy*, stems from the position of the brand in the portfolio of the organization that owns the brand. Later in this chapter we will see that some poor brands are competing in high-growth markets, whilst others are competing in mature or declining markets. Thus the objectives for the brand could well call for different levels and types of investment (invest or harvest), innovation (relaunch, augment, cut costs), sales and distribution patterns (extension, reduction, broad, narrow), market share, usage aims (new, existing behaviour), and so on.

> The first point to be made, then, is that an organization must be clear what the appropriate objectives are for a brand.

The second component, *brand positioning*, is concerned with what the brand actually *does* and with what it competes. In other words, brand positioning starts with the physical, or functional, aspects of the brand (the centre circle in Figure 5.3). For instance, Canada Dry is positioned in the UK as a mixer for brandies and whiskies, rather than as a soft drink competing with Coca-Cola, Pepsi-Cola and 7-Up. Tide is a tough, general-purpose detergent, rather than a powder for woollens. Tesco is a high-quality grocer rather than a low-price supermarket. SAS is positioned as the business person's airline.

There are usually several main motivators in any market, only one or two of which are of real importance. These dimensions are best seen as bipolar scales along which brands can be positioned – for example:

- expensive/inexpensive
- strong/mild
- big/small
- hot/cold
- fast/slow
- male/female.

Because they are so obvious, they are easy to research in order to establish which are those that people regard as the most fundamental basis for buying. It will be obvious that not all consumers look for the same functional performance, so market segmentation becomes important at this stage. A useful starting point in this kind of primary market interpretation is to draw a bipolar map, as shown in Figure 5.6. Figure 5.7 shows an actual bipolar map for detergents.

Clearly the physical dimensions of any market will change over time, so this kind of basic research should be conducted on a regular basis to

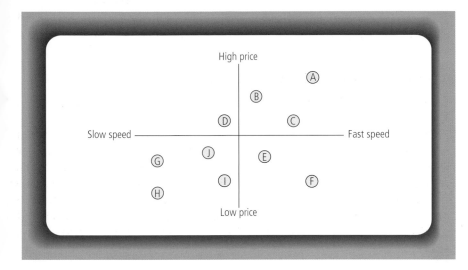

Figure 5.6
A brand position
map

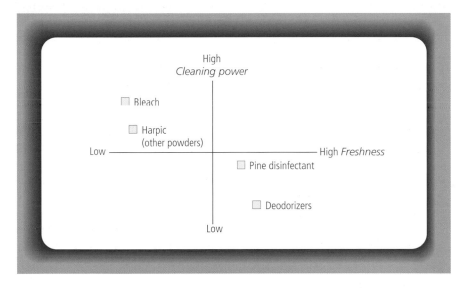

Figure 5.7
Bipolar map for
detergents

establish, firstly, what the main dimensions are and, secondly, whether the position of any competing product has changed.

In highly mature markets, brands are likely to be positioned close to one another, thus indicating that the basic functional or physical characteristics are less likely to be the sole basis on which a product or service is selected.

This brings us to the final component, *brand personality*. The late Stephen King said that a product is something that is made in a factory; a brand is something that is bought by a consumer. A product can be copied, but a successful brand is *unique* and, particularly in mature markets, is a key discriminator in the marketplace.

MARKETING INSIGHT

Brand personality is a useful descriptor for the total impression that consumers have of brands, and in many ways brands are like people, with their own physical, emotional and personality characteristics. Brands are very similar, in that they are a complex blend of physical, emotional and personality characteristics. Thus two brands can be very similar in terms of their functions, but have very different personalities.

MARKETING INSIGHT

For example, small Fords, Peugeots, VWs and Fiats all perform about the same along the functional dimensions of size, speed and price. Yet each one has a totally different personality, which is the result of a blend of three sorts of appeal: sensual, rational and emotional.

Sensual appeal, that is, how the product or service looks, feels, sounds and so on, can have an important influence on buying behaviour. It is easy to imagine how this appeal can differ in the case of, say, cigarettes, or cars.

Rational appeal, that is, how the product or service performs, what it contains and so on, can also have an important influence on buying behaviour.

Emotional appeal, however, is perhaps the most important, and has a lot to do with the psychological rewards the product or service offers, the mood it conjures up, the associations it evokes and so on. It is easy to imagine the overt appeal of certain products as being particularly masculine, or feminine, or chic, or workmanlike, or flashy.

The point is that for any brand to be successful, all these elements have to be consistent, as they will all affect the brand's personality – and it is this personality, above all else, that represents the brand's totality and makes one brand more desirable, or appealing, than another.

> Put at its simplest, it is a brand's personality that converts a commodity into something unique and enables a higher price to be charged for it.

Figure 5.8 combines brand functionality and personality in a matrix. The vertical axis refers to a brand's ability to satisfy utilitarian needs, such as quality, reliability, effectiveness and so on, where the consumer's need for such benefits is high. The horizontal axis represents the brand's ability to help consumers express something about themselves, be it, for example, their mood, their membership of a particular social group, their status and so on. Brands are chosen on this dimension because they have values that exist over and above their physical values. We call this dimension representationality. For example, products such as Yves St Laurent neckties are effective brands for expressing particular personality types and roles, with functional attributes being secondary.

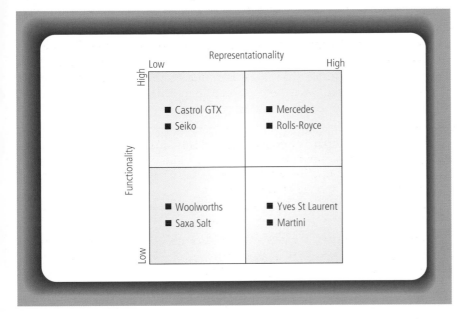

Figure 5.8
Brand functionality and personality (from *Creating Powerful Brands*, by Leslie de Chernatony and Malcolm McDonald, Butterworth-Heinemann, 3rd edn, Oxford, 2003)

It is possible, by means of ▶ **market research**, to identify the degree to which consumers perceive a brand as reflecting functionality and representationality. Having done this, it is then possible for the marketer to consider how best to use the available resources to support the brand.

For products and services in the top right-hand box (that is, ones that both provide functional excellence and are good vehicles for non-verbal communication about themselves), a creative strategy that reinforces consumers' lifestyle requirements should be adopted and communicated through appropriate media channels. Additionally, the quality of the brand needs to be maintained through high standards of quality control and continuous product development. Also, strict control over channels of distribution should be exercised.

For products and services in the top left-hand box (that is, ones bought by consumers because of a high utilitarian need rather than because of a need to say something about themselves), product superiority needs to be continuously maintained, as 'me-tooism' is a continuous threat to such brands. Also, heavy promotional support is important in communicating the functional benefits of the brand.

For products and services in the bottom right-hand box (that is, ones that are less important for their functional attributes, but which are high as symbolic devices), it is clearly important to reinforce continuously the cultural and lifestyle aspects of the brand and a heavy promotional presence is almost certainly more important than product-development issues.

For products and services in the bottom left-hand box (that is, those that are bought by consumers who are not particularly concerned about either functional differences or self-image), successful branding is more difficult, because it is likely that they must have wide distribution and be very price

▶ **DEFINITION** ◀
Market research is the collection, organization, analysis and dissemination of facts and opinions from existing or potential customers and consumers about an organization or its products

For products with high representationality, a strong creative strategy needs to be pursued. For products with high functionality, product performance strategy is very important competitive. Cost leadership, then, becomes important to the brand owner, which entails being an efficient producer. Brands in this sector are obviously vulnerable, and to succeed an attractive price proposition is usually necessary.

The company as a brand

It will, by now, be obvious that it is frequently the case that a company's name is the brand used on different products or services, as opposed to an individual brand name for each product, as in the case of, say, Persil.

> To present themselves in the most favourable way, firms develop a corporate identity programme, ensuring that all forms of external communication are coordinated and presented in the same way. Corporate identity can be a valuable asset, which, if effectively managed, can make a major contribution to brand success.

Classic examples of this include IBM, ICI, Mercedes, Sony, Yamaha, JCB, Virgin and countless others. It works well as a policy, given the prohibitive costs of building individual brands *ab inititio*, providing the product or service in question is consistent with the corporate image.

MARKETING INSIGHT

In this respect, it is easy to see why Ford has been unable to compete effectively in the high-class car market and was eventually forced to buy Jaguar in order to enter this segment. Equally, it can be seen why Mars was able to enter the ice-cream market using the Mars corporate brand name, but why it uses a totally different brand name, Pedigree, in the animal foodstuffs market.

Whilst there is a 'halo' effect of using a famous corporate name on a new product or service, there are also risks to the total portfolio should any one new product prove to be disastrous. For example, Levi Strauss was known and respected for jeans. The company's extension into Levi tailored classic suits failed because of wrong association. Adding the name 'Pierre Cardin' to bathroom tiles in Spain did little for the value of this core brand!

The late Peter Doyle developed a useful matrix for considering what an appropriate strategy might be towards corporate, as opposed to individual, product branding. This is given in Figure 5.9.

▶ DEFINITION ◀

A global brand is a product that bears the same name and logo and presents the same or similar message all over the world

Global versus local brands

So, if we can now distinguish between a brand and a pseudo brand, what is a ▶ **global brand**? Here is a definition: *a global brand is a product that bears the same name and logo and presents the same or similar message all over the world.* Usually the product is aimed at the same target market and is promoted and presented in much the same way.

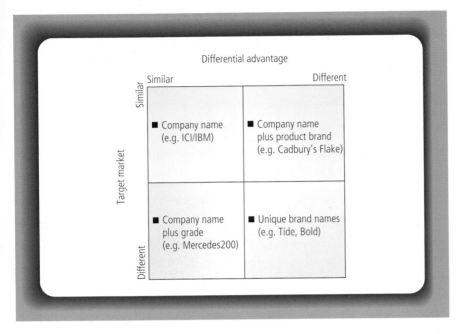

Figure 5.9
Corporate brand
positioning (Source:
Professor Peter
Doyle, reproduced
with his kind
permission)

A survey that encompassed 10,000 people in the USA, Japan and Europe discovered that the following were the ten most widely recognized brand names. Top was Coca-Cola, followed by Sony, Mercedes-Benz, Kodak, Disney, Nestlé, Toyota, McDonald's, IBM and Pepsi. Probably there are a few surprises here, but what are the alternative options to having a mass global brand?

There are only two broad options:

● develop a global brand, such as American Express, or Coca-Cola
● have a local or regional brand in each country or region of operation.

What fuels the decision-making regarding which choice? Clearly, it depends mainly upon the types of customer. However, there are some other practical considerations to take into account, such as the cost of production, the distribution costs, promotion, competitive market structure, channels, legal constraints and operational structures.

Procter & Gamble experienced major problems trying to get washing powders and liquids established under one brand name across Europe. For one thing, they had to try to accommodate different types of washing machines, different types of water, different washing habits, and different cultures. Then there was the business of getting to grips with market structures and competition, and, last but not least (because it can be the greatest barrier of all), getting its own operating structure right.

Clearly, then, the benefits to be derived from economies of scale have to be weighed very carefully against the difficulty of setting up a global brand, as the matrix in Figure 5.10 shows.

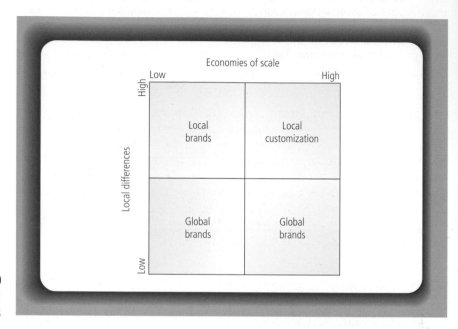

Figure 5.10
Global versus local
brands

Although three of the boxes reduce to fairly obvious choices, the top right-hand box is still something of a poser. Our own inclination is that, when faced with high difficulty but high economies of scale, we would endeavour to establish global brands.

Of course, while the matrix only represents a concept, it is possible to develop concrete data for it in much the same way as the directional policy matrix, which is described later in this chapter. For example, all the savings attributable to economies of scale could be calculated, such as manufacturing, R&D, purchasing, logistics, better management control and so on. Equally, local differences could be assessed taking into account the infrastructure of markets, demand homogeneity, culture, political/legal framework, market structure, competition and the like.

By looking at international markets in this way, the odds come out very much higher in favour of global brands as against local ones. Predictions about future trends only serve to reinforce this hypothesis. For example, in the European single market it has been predicted that:

- prices will tend to harmonize towards the lowest levels across Europe
- purchasers will tend to buy on a pan-European basis to gain maximum price advantage
- major distributors (especially importers) will operate transnationally and take advantage of remaining price differentials and low-cost suppliers.

There is much evidence to confirm that these trends are already happening.

Donald Casey of Lauder Associates asserts, 'The growth in global branding is a direct result of the explosion of media consumption amongst the young. In every country the data show that the younger consumers are significantly more aware of international brands, particularly in fields like TV, music, video and sports.' Further support is provided by Alan Woofe, who says, 'The most fundamental point of all this is that one day there will eventually be a Euro-market, and there may one day be Euro-consumers in the foreseeable future.'

MARKETING INSIGHT

The portents are clear. Already, large pan-European retailing groups are appearing, and if an organization does not have a European brand, especially if it is in fast-moving consumer goods, it does not appear to have very good prospects. It is brand names that win customers, make a profit and create customer loyalty. As stated earlier, Nestlé wanted to buy Rowntree purely for its brands, not for its factories. A good brand, at the end of the day, is the company's best marketing asset. For that reason, it is short-sighted not to invest in the brand. To allow it to slip and become a 'me-too' commodity is tantamount to commercial vandalism.

> To summarize, a successful brand is an identifiable product, service, person or place augmented in such a way that the buyer or user perceives relevant, unique added values which match their needs most closely. Its success results from being able to sustain these added values against competitors. Being able to do this on a global basis will bring great rewards, but it will not be easy.

■ Product life-cycle

Having discussed the vital factor of benefits as a part of product management, we must now ask ourselves whether one product is enough.

There are many examples of entrepreneurs who set themselves up in business to manufacture, say, toys such as 'clackers', who make their fortune and who then just as quickly lose it when this fashion-conscious market changes to its latest fad. Such examples are merely the extreme manifestation of what is known as the ▶ **product life-cycle**. This, too, is such a vital and fundamental concept that it is worth devoting some time to a discussion of the subject.

Historians of technology have observed that all technical functions grow exponentially until they come up against some natural limiting factor which causes growth to slow down and, eventually, to decline as one technology is replaced by another. There is universal agreement that the same phenomenon applies to products, so giving rise to the concept of the product life-cycle, much written about in marketing literature during the past five decades.

▶ **DEFINITION** ◀

A product life-cycle plots the volume or value of sales of a product from its launch to its decline and withdrawal

The product life-cycle postulates that if a new product is successful at the introductory stage (and many fail at this point), then gradually repeat purchase grows and spreads and the rate of sales growth increases. At this stage, competitors often enter the market and their additional promotional expenditures further expand the market. But no market is infinitely expandable, and eventually the *rate* of growth slows as the product moves into its maturity stage. Eventually, a point is reached where there are too many firms in the market, price wars break out, and some firms drop out of the market, until finally the market itself falls into decline. Figure 5.11 illustrates these apparently universal phenomena.

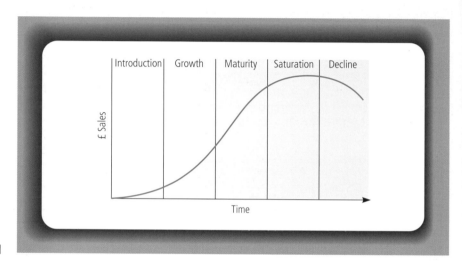

Figure 5.11

Nevertheless, while the product life-cycle may well be a useful practical generalization, it can also be argued that particular product life-cycles are determined more by the activities of the company than by any underlying 'law'.

MARKETING INSIGHT

For example, Bailey's liqueur, while exhibiting all the characteristics of the classic product life-cycle, went on to new record sales heights following the appointment of a new brand manager.

Nevertheless, while this example illustrates the dangers inherent in incorrect interpretation of life-cycle analysis, even in this case, sales will eventually mature.

From a management point of view, the product life-cycle concept is useful in that it focuses our attention on the likely future sales pattern if we take no corrective action. There are several courses of action open to us in our attempts to maintain the profitable sales of a product over its life-cycle.

Figure 5.12 illustrates the actual courses taken by an American company in the management of one of its leading industrial market products. As sales growth began to slow down, the company initiated a programme of product range extensions and market development which successfully took the brand into additional stages of growth. At the same time the company was aggressively seeking new products and even considering potential areas for diversification.

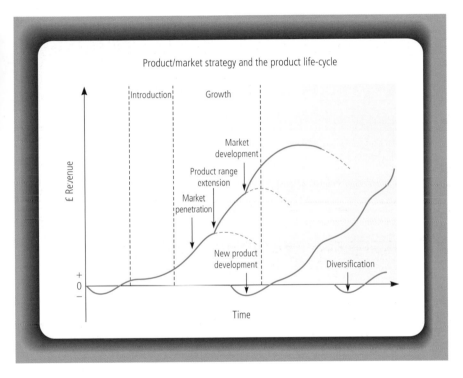

Figure 5.12

Even more important are the implications of the product life-cycle concept on every element of the marketing mix. Figure 5.13 gives some guide as to how the product has to change over its life-cycle. In addition to this, however, every other element also has to change. For example, if a company rigidly adhered to a premium pricing policy at the mature stage of the product life-cycle, when markets are often overcrowded and price wars begin, it could well lose market share. It could be regretted later on when the market has settled down, for it is often at this stage that products provide extremely profitable revenue for the company. It will become clearer later in this chapter why market share is important.

The same applies to promotion. During the early phase of product introduction, the task for advertising is often one of creating awareness, whereas during the growth phase the task may need to change to one of creating a favourable attitude towards the product. Neither should the policy towards

Key characteristics	Unique	Product differentiation	Service differentiation	'Commodity'
Marketing message	Explain	Competitive	Brand values	Corporate
Sales	Pioneering	Relative benefits Distribution support	Relationship based	Availability based
Distribution	Direct selling	Exclusive distribution	Mass distribution	80:20
Price	Very high	High	Medium	Low (consumer controlled)
Competitive intensity	None	Few	Many	Fewer, bigger, international
Costs	Very high	Medium	Medium/low	Very low
Profit	Medium/high	High	Medium/high	Medium/low
Management style	Visionary	Strategic	Operational	Cost management

The product/market life-cycle and market characteristics

Figure 5.13

channels be fixed. At first we are concerned with getting distribution for the product in the most important channels, whereas during the growth phase we have to consider ways of reaching the new channels that want our product. All of these points will become clearer in those chapters specifically concerned with the management of price, place and promotion.

MARKETING INSIGHT

The famous 3 M Post-it notes are representative of the changes which have to take place over the life of a product. At first, prices and margins were high, there were no competitors and the route to market was via direct selling. Sooner or later, new competitors entered the market. When the market reached maturity, 3 M added clearer branding to the product and the route to market changed. Today, consumers have a choice of own-label, coloured, lined, and small or large versions of the Post-it note. Faced with such a change in market circumstances, it is obvious that the key characteristics of management also had to change to ensure continued success.

MARKETING INSIGHT

Another example is Rank Xerox UK, which in 1972 had 80 per cent share of the photocopier market and a gross margin of 40 per cent. Five years later, they had 10 per cent share and a 10 per cent margin. This was because they failed to recognize that markets tend to segment as they enter the growth phase. In this case, the Japanese entered with small photocopiers.

Drawing a product life-cycle, however, can be extremely difficult, even given the availability of some form of time series analysis. This is connected with the complex question of market share measurement.

First, let us remind ourselves that a firm needs to be concerned with its share (or its proportion of volume or value) of an *actual* market, rather than with a *potential* market. The example of the carpet manufacturer given in Chapter 4 emphasized the importance of measuring the right things when determining what a company's market is.

For the purpose of helping us to draw life-cycles, it is worth repeating the definitions given in Chapter 4:

- Product class, e.g. carpets
- Product subclass, e.g. nylon rolls
- Product brand, e.g. 'X'.

> 'X' as a brand, for the purpose of measuring market share, is *concerned only with the aggregate of all other brands that satisfy the same group of customer wants.*

Nevertheless, the manufacturer of 'X' also needs to be aware of the sales trends of other kinds of carpets and floor covering in the institutional market, as well as of carpet sales overall.

One of the most frequent mistakes made by companies that do not understand what market share really means is to assume that their company has only a small share of some market, whereas if the company is commercially successful it probably has a much larger share of a smaller market segment.

The important point to remember at this stage is that the concept of the product life-cycle is not an academic figment of the imagination, but a hard reality which is ignored at great risk.

> It is interesting to see how many commercial failures can be traced back to a naive assumption on the part of managements that what was successful as a policy at one time will continue to be successful in the future.

A reference back to Figure 5.13 will immediately explain the demise of many companies, particularly in the information technology industry, who continued to pursue policies more appropriate to the second column when, in reality, the markets for some of their products had moved to the fourth column.

MARKETING INSIGHT

Table 5.1 shows a checklist used by one major company to help it determine where its markets are on the life-cycle.

Table 5.1 Guide to market maturity

Maturity stage / Factor	Embryonic	Growth	Mature	Declining
1 *Growth rate*	Normally much greater than GNP (on small base).	Sustained growth above GNP. New customers. New suppliers. Rate decelerates toward end of stage.	Approximately equals GNP.	Declining demand. Market shrinks as users' needs change.
2 *Predictability of growth potential*	Hard to define accurately. Small portion of demand being satisfied. Market forecasts differ widely.	Greater percentage of demand is met and upper limits of demand becoming clearer. Discontinuities, such as price reductions based on economies of scale, may occur.	Potential well defined. Competition specialized to satisfy needs of specific segments.	Known and limited.
3 *Product line proliferation*	Specialized lines to meet needs of early customers.	Rapid expansion.	Proliferation slows or ceases.	Lines narrow as unprofitable products dropped.
4 *Number of competitors*	Unpredictable.	Reaches maximum. New entrants attracted by growth and high margins. Some consolidation begins toward end of stage.	Entrenched positions established. Further shakeout of marginal competitors.	New entrants unlikely. Competitors continue to decline.
5 *Market share distribution*	Unstable. Shares react unpredictably to entrepreneurial insights and timing.	Increasing stability. Typically, a few competitors emerging as strong.	Stable with a few companies often controlling much of industry.	Highly concentrated or fragmented as industry segments and/or is localized.
6 *Customer stability*	Trial usage with little customer loyalty.	Some loyalty. Repeat usage with many seeking alternative suppliers.	Well-developed buying patterns with customer loyalty. Competitors understand purchase dynamics and it is difficult for a new supplier to win over accounts.	Extremely stable. Suppliers dwindle and customers less motivated to seek alternatives.
7 *Ease of entry*	Normally easy. No one dominates. Customers' expectations uncertain. If barriers exist, they are usually technology, capital or fear of the unknown.	More difficult. Market franchises and/or economies of scale may exist, yet new business is still available without directly confronting competition.	Difficult. Market leaders established. New business must be 'won' from others.	Little or no incentive to enter.
8 *Technology*	Plays an important role in matching product characteristics to market needs. Frequent product changes.	Product technology vital early, while process technology more important later in this stage.	Process and material substitution focus. Product requirements well known and relatively undemanding. May be a thrust to renew the industry via new technology.	Technological content is known, stable and accessible.

■ Diffusion of innovation

A useful explanation and extension of the product life-cycle is what is known as the 'diffusion of innovation'. This will be referred to again in Chapter 6. ▶ **Diffusion** is the adoption of new products or services over time by consumers within social systems, as encouraged by marketing. Diffusion refers to the cumulative percentage of potential adopters of a new product or service over time.

Everett Rogers examined some of the social forces that explain the product life-cycle. The body of knowledge often referred to as 'reference theory' (which incorporates work on group norms, group pressures, etc.) helps explain the snowball effect of diffusion. Rogers found that the actual rate of diffusion is a function of a product's:

- relative advantage (over existing products)
- compatibility (with lifestyles, values, etc.)
- communicability (is it easy to communicate?)
- complexity (is it complicated?)
- divisibility (can it be tried out on a small scale before commitment?).

Diffusion is also a function of the newness of the product itself, which can be classified broadly under three headings:

1 Continuous innovation (e.g. the new miracle ingredient)
2 Dynamically continuous innovation (e.g. disposable lighter)
3 Discontinuous (e.g. microwave oven).

However, Rogers found that, for all new products, not everyone adopts new products at the same time, and that a universal pattern emerges as shown in Figure 5.14.

▶ **DEFINITION** ◀
Diffusion is the adoption of new products or services over time by consumers within social systems, as encouraged by marketing. Diffusion refers to the cumulative percentage of potential adopters of a new product or service over time

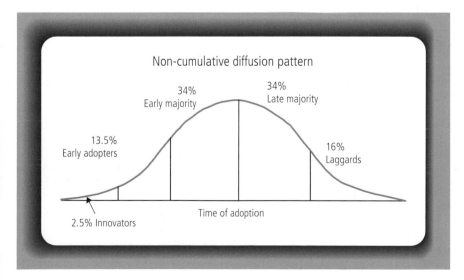

Figure 5.14
Non-cumulative diffusion pattern (Adapted from Everett Rogers, *Diffusions and Innovations*, Free Press, New York, 1976)

In general, the innovators think for themselves and try new things (where relevant); the early adopters, who have status in society, are opinion leaders and they adopt successful products, making them acceptable and respectable; the early majority, who are more conservative and who have slightly above-average status, are more deliberate and only adopt products that have social approbation; the late majority, who are below average status and sceptical, adopt products much later; the laggards, with low status, income, etc. view life 'through the rear mirror' and are the last to adopt products.

This particular piece of research can be very useful, particularly for advertising and personal selling. For example, if we can develop a typology for opinion leaders, we can target our early advertising and sales effort specifically at them. Once the first 7–8 per cent of opinion leaders have adopted our product, there is a good chance that the early majority will try it. Hence, once the 10–12 per cent point is reached the champagne can be opened, because there is a good chance that the rest will adopt our product.

We know, for example, that the general characteristics of opinion leaders are that they are venturesome, socially integrated, cosmopolitan, socially mobile, and privileged. So we need to ask ourselves what the specific characteristics of these customers are in our particular industry. We can then tailor our advertising and selling message specifically for them.

It can, however, also be both a practical diagnostic and forecasting tool. There follows a worked example of how forecasts, and eventually strategic marketing plans, were developed from the intelligent use of the diffusion of innovation curve in respect of computerized business systems for the construction industry in the UK.

1st estimate of market size		
1 Number of contracting firms (Department of Environment, Housing and Construction)	160,596	
2 Number of firms employing 4–79 direct employees	43,400	
3 Exclude painters, plasterers, etc.	6,100	
4 Conservative estimate of main target area	37,300	(1)
	or 23% of total	
2nd estimate of market size		
5 Using the Pareto (80/20 rule) likelihood that 20 per cent will be main target area, i.e. 160,596 (20%)	32,000	(2)

3rd estimate of market size

6 Total number of firms in construction
   industry (Business Statistics Office)   217,785

7 Number of firms classified by
   turnover from £100,000 to £1,000,000:
   (£K) 100–249   26,698
   (£K) 250–499   10,651
   (£K) 500–999   5,872
   (£K)   43,221   (3)

8 Company's best estimate of size of   37,300
   target market

9 Company's estimate of the number of   3,500   (9.4%)
   micro-installations in this segment

Plotting this on the diffusion of innovation curve shows:

- Penetration of innovators and early adopters has taken four
  years. Adoption rate will now accelerate. It will probably be
  complete within one year.
- *One-year* balance of early adopters = 6.6 per cent = 2,462
  firms = installed base of 5,968. Sales objective = 360 installa-
  tions plus present base of 400 = 760 – 12.7 per cent market
  share.

It will be seen from this that three independent estimates were
made of the market size in order to establish the current position on the diffusion of innovation curve.

In contrast, a Dutch computer supplier attempted to launch
hardware and software into the motor trade using an undiffer-
entiated product at a high sales price. An elementary study
would have indicated that this market is already well into the
late majority phase, when price and product features become
more important. Not surprisingly, the product launch failed.

The diffusion of innovation curve, when seen in conjunction with the
product life-cycle, helps to explain the dynamics of markets. Figure 5.15
illustrates this relationship. It shows that, when all potential users of a
product are using it, the market is a replacement market.

For example, virtually everyone in Western Europe has fridges, washing
machines, dishwashers, televisions and cars. The market is dependent on population growth or decline, so most of these are replacement markets, and most
competitors wishing to grow their sales would probably have to take it from
competitors.

**MARKETING
INSIGHT**

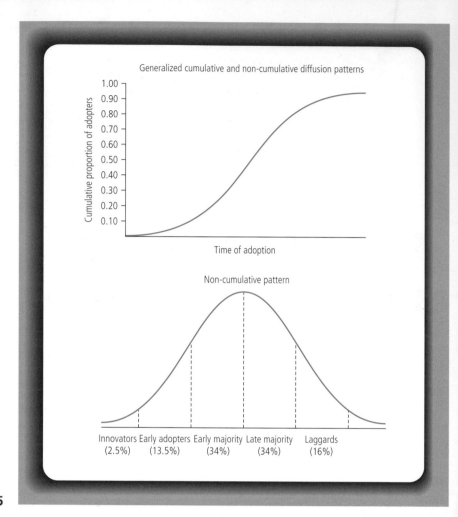

Figure 5.15

■ Product portfolio

We might well imagine that, at any point in time, a review of a company's different products would reveal different stages of growth, maturity and decline.

In Figure 5.16, the dotted line represents the time of our analysis, and this shows one product in severe decline, one product in its introductory stage, and one in the saturation stage.

If our objective is to grow in profitability over a long period of time, our analysis of our product portfolio should reveal a situation like the one in Figure 5.17, in which new product introductions are timed so as to ensure continuous sales growth.

The idea of a ▶ **portfolio** is for a company to meet its objectives by balancing sales growth, cash flow and risk. As individual products progress or decline and as markets grow or shrink, then the overall nature of the company's product portfolio will change. It is therefore essential that the

Figure 5.16

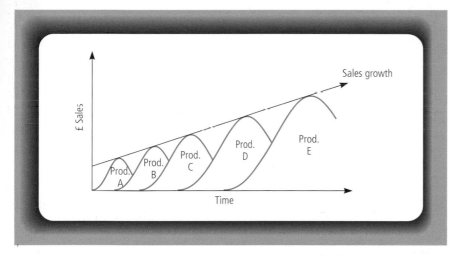

Figure 5.17

whole portfolio is reviewed regularly and that an active policy towards new product development and divestment of old products is pursued. In this respect, the work of the Boston Consulting Group, begun in the early 1960s, had a profound effect on the way managements think about this subject and about their product/market strategy.

■ Unit costs and market share

There are basically two parts to the thinking behind the work of the Boston Consulting Group (BCG). One is concerned with *market share*; the other with *market growth*.

It is a well-known fact that we become better at doing things the more we do them. This phenomenon is known as the *learning curve*. It manifests itself especially with items such as labour efficiency, work specialization and methods improvement.

► **DEFINITION** ◄

The experience effect reflects the improvements (usually resulting in lower costs) that result from economies of scale, learning and improved productivity over time

> Cost decline applies more to the value-added elements of cost than to bought-in supplies.

Such benefits are themselves a part of what we can call the ► **experience effect**, which includes such items as process innovations, better productivity from plant and equipment, product design improvements, and so on. In addition to the experience effect, and not necessarily mutually exclusive, are *economies of scale* that come with growth. For example, capital costs do not increase in direct proportion to capacity, which results in lower depreciation charges per unit of output, lower operating costs in the form of the number of operatives, lower marketing, sales, administration, and research and development costs, and lower raw materials and shipping costs. It is generally recognized, however, that cost decline applies more to the value-added elements of cost than to bought-in supplies.

In fact, the Boston Consulting Group discovered that costs decline by up to 30 per cent for every cumulative doubling of output. This phenomenon is shown in Figure 5.18. Imagine a factory producing 100 units a year for eight years. It will be seen from the following simple calculation that it becomes more difficult each year cumulatively to double output.

Year	Cumulative	Total
1	100	100
2	100	200 D
3	100	300
4	100	400 D
5	100	500
6	100	600
7	100	700
8	100	800 D

It is this phenomenon that explains the shape of the curve in Figure 5.18. The BCG used logarithmic scales on the data to enable them to make predictions about future costs at forecast output levels, a method favoured for many years by the Japanese as a way of capturing markets in America and Western Europe.

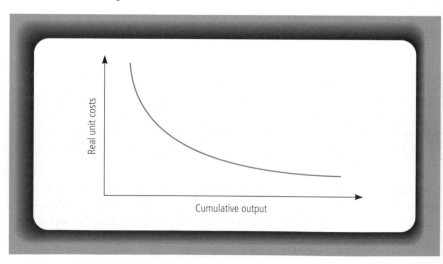

Figure 5.18

While there are many implications from this for marketing strategy, particularly in relation to pricing policy, we will confine ourselves here to a discussion of the product/market implications.

There is sufficient evidence to show that this real cost reduction actually occurs, in which case it follows that the greater your volume, the lower your unit costs should be. Thus, irrespective of what happens to the price of your product, providing you have the highest market share (hence the biggest volume), you should always be relatively more profitable than your competitors. This is illustrated in Figure 5.19.

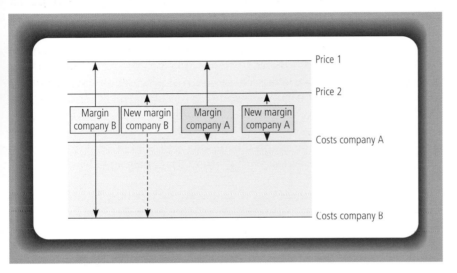

Figure 5.19

Thus, as a general rule, it can be said that market share *per se* is a desirable goal.

Indeed, the Strategic Planning Institute's Profit Impact of Market Strategies research has confirmed that market share and profitability are linearly related. However, as we made clear in Chapter 4, we have to be certain that we have carefully defined our market, or segment.

This explains why it is apparently possible for many small firms to be profitable in large markets. The reason is, of course, that, in reality, they have a large share of a smaller market segment. This is another reason why understanding market segmentation is the key to successful marketing.

It would be unusual if there were not many caveats to the above 'law', and, although what these might be are fairly obvious, nevertheless it should be noted that the evidence provided by the Boston Consulting Group shows overwhelmingly that, in general, these 'laws' apply universally, whether for consumer, industrial or service markets.

Turning now to *market growth*, we observe that, in markets which are growing at a very low rate per annum, it is extremely difficult and also very costly to increase your market share. This is usually because the market is in the steady state (possibly in the saturation phase of the product life-cycle) and is dominated by a few major firms who have probably reached a stage of equilibrium, which it is very difficult to upset.

In markets which are going through a period of high growth, it is fairly obvious that the most sensible policy would be to gain market share by taking a bigger proportion of the market growth than your competitors. However, such a policy is very costly in promotional terms. So, many companies prefer to sit tight and enjoy rates of growth lower than the market rate. The major problem with this approach is that they are, in fact, losing market share, which gives cost advantages (hence margin advantages) to competitors.

Since we know from previous experience of product life-cycles that the market growth rate will fall, when this stage is reached and the market inevitably becomes price sensitive, the product will begin to lose money and we will probably be forced out of the market. Indeed, seen in this light, it becomes easier to understand the reasons for the demise of many industries in those countries of the world where the Japanese have entered the market.

It is interesting to note, however, that even the Japanese have suffered in recent years from lower cost suppliers entering markets using lower prices than they can offer. These suppliers include the Koreans, the Chinese, and, more recently, Indians and South Americans. It is unlikely that high-cost 'Western' companies can compete on price alone in most of these markets, which is why segmentation is so important in this day and age.

MARKETING INSIGHT

Typical of this is the motorcycle industry in the UK. The output of the Japanese increased from thousands of units to millions of units during a period of market growth, while the output of the British remained steady during the same period. When the market growth rate started to decline, the inevitable happened. Even worse, it is virtually impossible to recover from such a situation, while the Japanese, with their advantageous cost position, have now dominated practically every market segment, including big bikes.

■ The Boston Matrix

The Boston Consulting Group combined these ideas in the form of a simple matrix, which has profound implications for the firm, especially in respect of *cash flow*. Profits are not always an appropriate indicator of portfolio performance, as they will often reflect changes in the liquid assets of the company, such as inventories, capital equipment, or receivables, and thus do not indicate the true scope for future development. Cash flow, on the other hand, is a key determinant of a company's ability to develop its product portfolio.

The ▶ **Boston Matrix** classifies a firm's products according to their cash usage and their cash generation along the two dimensions described above – i.e. relative market share and market growth rate. Market share is used because it is an indicator of the product's ability to generate cash; market growth is used because it is an indicator of the product's cash requirements. The measure of market share used is the product's share *relative* to the firm's largest competitor. This is important because it reflects the degree of dominance enjoyed by the product in the market. For example, if company A has 20 per cent market share and its biggest competitor also has 20 per cent market share, this position is usually less favourable than if company A had 20 per cent market share and its biggest competitor had only 10 per cent market share. The relative ratios would be 1 : 1 compared with 2 : 1. It is this ratio, or measure of market dominance, that the horizontal axis measures. This is summarized in Figure 5.20.

▶ **DEFINITION** ◀
The Boston Matrix classifies a firm's products according to their cash usage and their cash generation using market growth and relative market share to categorize them in the form of a box matrix

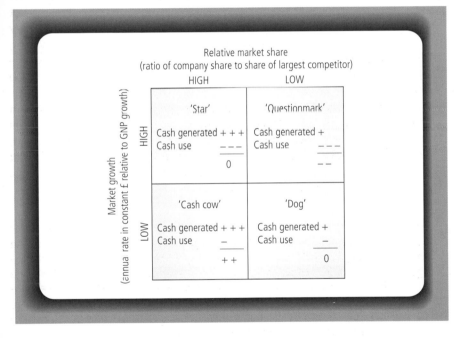

Figure 5.20

The definition of high relative market share is taken to be a ratio of one or greater than one. The cut-off point for high, as opposed to low, market growth should be defined according to the prevailing circumstances in the industry, but this is often taken as 10 per cent. There is, however, no reason why the dividing line on the vertical axis cannot be zero, or even a minus figure. It depends entirely on the industry, or segment, growth or decline. Sometimes, in very general markets, gross domestic product (GDP) can be used.

The somewhat picturesque labels attached to each of the four categories of products give some indication of the prospects for products in each quadrant. Thus, the 'question mark' is a product which has not yet achieved a dominant market position and thus a high cash flow, or perhaps it once

The picturesque labels given to the four categories in the Boston Matrix gives some indication of the prospects for products in each quadrant.

had such a position but has slipped back. It will be a high user of cash because it is in a growth market. This is also sometimes referred to as a 'wildcat'.

The 'star' is probably a newish product that has achieved a high market share and which is probably more or less self-financing in cash terms.

The 'cash cows' are leaders in markets where there is little additional growth, but a lot of stability. These are excellent generators of cash and tend to use little because of the state of the market.

'Dogs' often have little future and can be a cash drain on the company. Whilst it is possible that such products are necessary to support more successful products, they are probably candidates for divestment, although often such products fall into a category aptly described by Peter Drucker as 'investments in managerial ego'.

The art of product portfolio management now becomes a lot clearer. What we should be seeking to do is to use the surplus cash generated by the 'cash cows' to invest in our 'stars' and to invest in a selected number of 'question marks'. This is indicated in Figure 5.21.

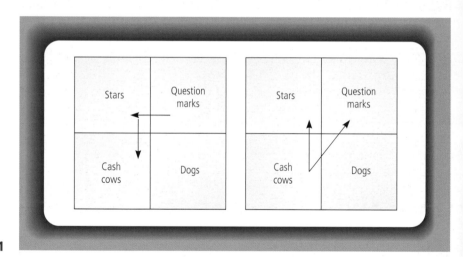

Figure 5.21

The Boston Matrix can be used to forecast the market position of our products, say, five years from now, if we continue to pursue our current policies.

Figure 5.22 illustrates this process for a manufacturer of plastic valves. The area of each circle is proportional to each product's contribution to total company sales volume. In the case of this particular company, it can be seen that they are following what could well prove to be disastrous policies in respect of their principal products. Product A, although growing, is losing market share in a high-growth market. Product D is also losing market share in a high-growth market. Products E and C are gaining market share in declining markets.

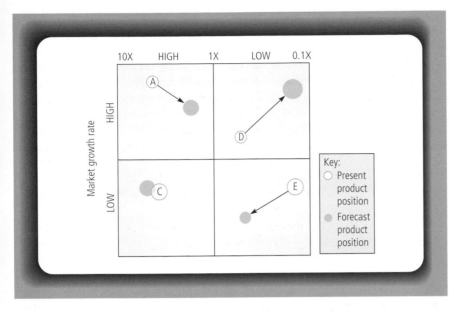

Figure 5.22

Such a framework also easily helps to explain the impracticability of marketing objectives such as 'to achieve a 10 per cent growth and a 20 per cent return on investment'. Such an objective, while fine as an *overall* policy, if applied to individual products in the portfolio, clearly becomes a nonsense and totally self-defeating. For example, to accept a 10 per cent growth rate in a market which is growing at, say, 15 per cent per annum, is likely to prove disastrous in the long run. Likewise, to go for a much higher than market growth rate in a low-growth market is certain to lead to unnecessary price wars and market disruption.

This type of framework is particularly useful to demonstrate to senior management the implications of different product/market strategies. It is also useful in formulating policies towards new product development.

Weaknesses in the Boston Matrix approach

Unfortunately, many companies started using the Boston Matrix indiscriminately during the 1970s and, as a result, it gradually lost its universal appeal. The reason, however, had more to do with lack of real understanding on the part of management than with any major defects in the methodology.[2]

[2]For readers who would like to experiment with computer software for the BCG Matrix, a computer-based training pack, by the author of this book, is available on request from Butterworth-Heinemann, Oxford.

Nonetheless, there are circumstances where great caution is required in its use. Imagine for a moment a company with 80 per cent of its products in low-growth markets, and only 20 per cent of its products market leaders. Their matrix would look as depicted in Figure 5.23. As can be seen, almost 65 per cent of the company's products are 'dogs'. To divest these may well be tantamount to throwing the baby out with the bath water!

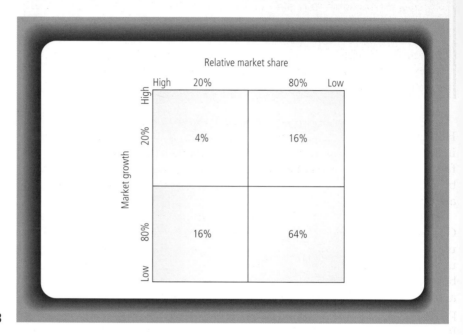

Figure 5.23

Consider, also, those industries in which market share for any single product in the range has little to do with its 'profitability'. Often a low market-share product enjoys the same production, distribution and marketing economies of scale as other products in the portfolio – as, for example, in the case of beers and chemical products.

MARKETING INSIGHT

Let us take the case of a product which is manufactured using basically the same components as other large market-share products, is manufactured in the same plant as part of a similar process, and is distributed on the same vehicles and via the same outlets. In such a case it is easy to see how this low market-share product can indeed be extremely profitable.

None of this, however, invalidates the work of the Boston Consulting Group, the principles of which can be applied to companies, divisions, subsidiaries, strategic business units, product groups, products, and so on. Providing great care is taken over the 'market share' axis, it is an extremely valuable planning tool.

Further developments of the Boston Matrix

It is complications such as those outlined above that make the Boston Matrix less relevant to certain situations. While it is impossible to give absolute rules on what these situations are, suffice it to say that great caution is necessary when dealing with such matters. In any case, two principles should always be adhered to.

> First, a business should define its markets in such a way that it can ensure that its costs for key activities will be competitive. Secondly, it should define the markets it serves in such a way that it can develop specialized skills in servicing those markets and hence overcome a relative cost disadvantage. Both, of course, have to be related to a company's *distinctive competence*.

However, the approach of the Boston Consulting Group is fairly criticized in such circumstances as those described above as relying on two single factors, i.e. relative market share and market growth. Many readers will be aware of companies with high market share in a growing market that are not profitable.

To overcome this difficulty, and to provide a more flexible approach, General Electric and McKinsey jointly developed a multifactor approach using the same fundamental ideas as the Boston Consulting Group. They used *industry attractiveness* and *business strengths* as the two main axes, and built up these dimensions from a number of variables. Using these variables, and some scheme for weighting them according to their importance, products (or businesses) are classified into one of nine cells in a 3 × 3 matrix. Thus, the same purpose is served as in the Boston Matrix (i.e. comparing investment opportunities among products or businesses), but with the difference that multiple criteria are used. These criteria vary according to circumstances, but often include those shown in Figure 5.24.

It is not necessary, however, to use a nine-box matrix, and many managers prefer to use a four-box matrix similar to the Boston box. Indeed this is the author's preferred methodology, as it seems to be more easily understood by, and useful to, practising managers.

The four-box directional policy matrix (DPM) is shown in Figure 5.25. Here, the circles represent sales into an industry, market or segment and in the same way as in the Boston Matrix, each is proportional to that segment's contribution to turnover.

The difference in this case is that, rather than using only two variables, the criteria which are used for each axis are totally relevant and specific to each company using the matrix. It shows:

- markets categorized on a scale of attractiveness to the firm
- the firm's relative strengths in each of these markets
- the relative importance of each market.

It is advisable to use no more than five or six factors for the vertical axis of the DPM, otherwise the calculations become too complex and lose focus.

Figure 5.24

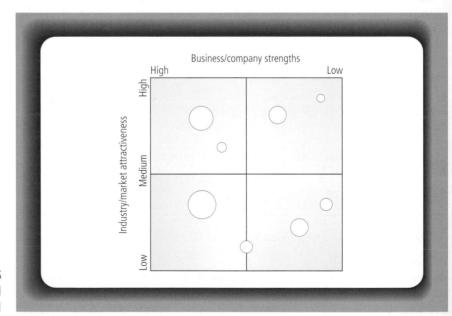

Figure 5.25
The McDonald
four-box DPM

The specific criteria to be used should be decided by key executives using the device, but a generalized list for the vertical axis is given in Table 5.2. It is advisable to use no more than five or six factors, otherwise the exercise becomes too complex and loses its focus. Read on, however, before

Table 5.2 Factors contributing to market attractiveness	
Market factors	*Financial and economic factors*
Size (money, units, or both)	Contribution margins
Size of key segments	Leveraging factors, such as economies
Growth rate per year:	of scale and experience
total	Barriers to entry or exit (both financial
segments	and non-financial)
Diversity of market	Capacity utilization
Sensitivity to price, service	
features and external factors	*Technological factors*
Cyclicality	Maturity and volatility
Seasonality	Complexity
Bargaining power of upstream	Differentiation
suppliers	Patents and copyrights
Bargaining power of	Manufacturing process technology
downstream suppliers	required
Competition	*Socio-political factors in your*
Types of competitors	*environment*
Degree of concentration	Social attitudes and trends
Changes in type and mix	Laws and government agency
Entries and exits	regulations
Changes in share	Influence with pressure groups and
Substitution by new technology	government representatives
Degrees and types of integration	Human factors, such as unionization
	and community acceptance

selecting these factors, as essential methodological instructions on the construction of a portfolio matrix follow.

■ A detailed, step-by-step approach to creating a portfolio

The strategic business unit (SBU)

Although the DPM, like other models of 'portfolio analysis', attempts to define a firm's strategic position and strategy alternatives, this objective cannot be met without considering what is meant by the term 'firm'. The accepted level at which a firm can be analysed using the DPM is that of the 'strategic business unit'.

   The most common definition of an SBU is as follows:

1 It will have common segments and competitors for most of the products.
2 It will be a competitor in an external market.

3 It is a discrete, separate and identifiable 'unit'.

4 Its manager will have control over most of the areas critical to success.

The process of defining an SBU can be applied all the way down to product or department level.

It is possible, however, to use the DPM for any unit that has in it a number of different variables that could be usefully plotted using a two-dimensional matrix.

What should be plotted on the matrix?

This is also comparatively simple to deal with, but confusion can arise because the options are rarely spelled out.

The DPM is useful where there is more than one (at least three, and a maximum of ten are suggested) 'markets' or segments between which the planner wishes to distinguish. These can be either existing or potential markets.

In order to implement the DPM, the following simple definition of 'market' and 'market segment' is offered:

> An identifiable group of customers with requirements in common that are, or may become, *significant* in determining a separate strategy.

The results from Exercise 4.1 (see previous chapter) should be plotted on the matrix.

The principal unit of analysis for the purpose of entering data will be the user's definition of 'product for market'.

Preparation

Prior to commencing analysis, the following preparation is recommended:

1 Product profiles should be available for all products/services to be scored.

2 The markets in which the products/services compete should be clearly defined.

3 Define the time period being scored – three years is recommended.

4 Define the competitors against which the products/services will be scored.

5 Ensure sufficient data are available to score the factors (where no data are available, this is no problem as long as a sensible approximation can be made for the factors).

6 Ensure up-to-date sales forecasts are available for all products/services, plus any new products/services.

Analysis team

In order to improve the quality of scoring, it is recommended that a group of people from a number of different functions takes part, as this encourages the challenging of traditional views through discussion. It is recommended that there should be no more than six people involved in the analysis.

Ten steps to producing the DPM

Step 1　Define the products/services for markets that are to be used during the analysis

Step 2　Define the criteria for market attractiveness

Step 3　Score the relevant products/services for market

Step 4　Define the organization's relative strengths for each product/service for market

Step 5　Analyse and draw conclusions from the relative position of each product/service for market

Step 6　Draw conclusions from the analysis with a view to generating objectives and strategies

Step 7　(Optional) Position the circles on the box assuming no change to current policies – that is to say, a *forecast* should be made of the future position of the circles

Step 8　Redraw the portfolio to position the circles where the organization wants them to be – that is to say, the *objectives* they wish to achieve for each product/service for market

Step 9　Detail the strategies to be implemented to achieve the objectives

Step 10　Detail the appropriate financial consequences in terms of growth rate by product/service for market and return on sales

Two key definitions

▶ **Market attractiveness** is a measure of the *potential* of the marketplace to yield growth in sales and profits. It is important to stress that this should be an objective assessment of market attractiveness using data *external* to the organization. The criteria themselves will, of course, be determined by the organization carrying out the exercise and will be relevant to the objectives the organization is trying to achieve, but it should be independent of the organization's position in its markets.

▶ **Business strengths/position** is a measure of an organization's *actual* strengths in the marketplace (i.e. the degree to which it can take advantage of a market opportunity). Thus, it is an objective assessment of an organization's ability to satisfy market needs relative to competitors.

▶ **D e f i n i t i o n** ◀
Market attractiveness is a measure of the potential of the marketplace to yield growth in sales and profits

▶ **D e f i n i t i o n** ◀
Business strengths/position is a measure of an organization's actual strengths in the marketplace (i.e. the degree to which it can take advantage of a market opportunity)

The process

Step 1　List the population of products/services for markets that you intend to include in the matrix
The list can consist of: countries, companies, subsidiaries, regions, products, markets, segments, customers, distributors, or any other unit of analysis that is important.

The DPM can be used at any level in an organization and for any kind of SBU.

Step 2   *Define market attractiveness factors*
In this step, you should list the factors you wish to consider in comparing the attractiveness of your markets.

It is also important to list the markets that you intend to apply the criteria to before deciding on the criteria themselves, since the purpose of the vertical axis is to discriminate between more and less attractive markets. The criteria themselves must be specific to the population and must not be changed for different markets in the same population.

Factors	Example weight
Growth rate	40
Accessible market size	20
Profit potential	40
Total	**100**

Note: As profit = market size × margin × growth, it would be reasonable to expect a *weighting* against each of these to be at *least* as shown, although an even higher weight on *growth* would be understandable in some circumstances (in which case, the corresponding weight for the others should be reduced).

This is a combination of a number of factors. These factors, however, can usually be summarized under three headings.

1 *Growth rate*. Average annual growth rate of revenue spent by that segment (2004 over 2003, plus % growth, 2005 over 2004, plus % growth, 2006 over 2005, plus % growth, divided by 3). If preferred, compound average growth rate could be used.
2 *Accessible market size*. An attractive market is not only large – it can also be accessed. One way of calculating this is to estimate the *total* revenue of the segment in $t + 3$, *less* revenue impossible to access, *regardless of investment made*. Alternatively, total market size can be used, which is the most frequent method, as it does not involve any managerial judgement to be made that could distort the truth. *This latter method is the preferred method.* A market size factor score is simply the score multiplied by the weight (20 as in the example above).
3 *Profit potential*. This is much more difficult to deal with, and will vary considerably, according to industry. For example,

Porter's Five Forces model could be used to estimate the profit potential of a segment, as in the following example:

Sub-factors	10 × Low 0 × High	× Weight	Weighted factor score
1 Intensity of competition	50		
2 Threat of substitute	5		
3 Threat of new entrants	5		
4 Power of suppliers	10		
5 Power of customer	30		
Profit potential factor score			

Alternatively, a combination of these and industry-specific factors could be used. In the case of the pharmaceutical industry, for example, the factors could be:

Sub-factors	High	Medium	Low × Weight	Weighted factor score
Unmet medical needs (efficacy)			30	
Unmet medical needs (safety)			25	
Unmet medical needs (convenience)			15	
Price potential			10	
Competitive intensity			10	
Cost of market entry			10	
Profit potential factor score				

These are clearly a proxy for profit potential. Each is weighted according to its importance. The weights add up to 100 in order to give a *profit potential factor score*, as in the Porter's Five Forces example above.

Note that, following this calculation, the *profit potential factor score* is simply multiplied by the weight (40 as in the example above).

Variations
Naturally, growth, size and profit will not encapsulate the requirements of all organizations. For example, in the case of an orchestra, artistic satisfaction may be an important consideration. In another case, social considerations could be important. In yet another, cyclicality may be a factor.

It is possible, then, to add another heading, such as 'Risk' or 'Other' to the three factors listed at the beginning of Step 2. In general, however, it should be possible to reduce it to just the three main ones, with sub-factors incorporated into these, as shown.

Step 3   *Score the relevant products/services for markets*
In this step you should score the products/services for markets against the criteria defined in Step 1.

Can market attractiveness factors change whilst constructing the DPM?
The answer to this is no. Once agreed, under no circumstances should market attractiveness factors be changed, otherwise the attractiveness of our markets is not being evaluated against common criteria and the matrix becomes meaningless. Scores, however, will be specific to each market.

Can the circles move vertically?
No is the obvious answer, although yes is also possible, providing the matrix shows the current level of attractiveness at the present time. This implies carrying out one set of calculations for the present time according to market attractiveness factors, in order to locate markets on the vertical axis, then carrying out another set of calculations for a future period (say, in three years' time), based on our forecasts according to the same factors. In practice, it is easier to carry out only the latter calculation, in which case the circles can only move horizontally.

Step 4   (i) *Define business strengths/position*
This is a measure of an organization's *actual* strengths in the marketplace and will differ by market/segment opportunity.

These factors will usually be a combination of an organization's relative strengths versus competitors in connection with *customer-facing* needs, i.e. those things that are required by the customer.

These can often be summarized under:

- product requirements
- price requirements
- service requirements
- promotion requirements.

The weightings given to each should be specific to each market/segment. In the same way that 'profit' on the market attractiveness axis can be broken down into sub-headings, so can each of the above be broken down further and analysed. Indeed, this is to be strongly recommended. These sub-factors should be dealt with in the same way as the sub-factors described under 'market attractiveness'.

For example, in the case of pharmaceuticals, product strengths could be represented by:

- relative product strengths
- relative product safety
- relative product convenience
- relative cost-effectiveness.

(ii) *Broadening the analysis*

It will be clear that an organization's relative strengths in meeting customer-facing needs will be a function of its *capabilities* in connection with *industry-wide success factors*. For example, if a depot is necessary in each major town/city for any organization to succeed in an industry and the organization carrying out the analysis doesn't have this, then it is likely that this will account for its poor performance under 'customer service', which is, of course, a customer requirement. Likewise, if it is necessary to have low feedstock costs for any organization to succeed in an industry and the organization carrying out the analysis doesn't have this, then it is likely that this will account for its poor performance under 'price', which is, of course, a customer requirement.

Thus, in the same way that sub-factors should be estimated in order to arrive at 'market attractiveness' factors, so an assessment of an organization's capabilities in respect of *industry-wide success factors* could be made in order to understand what needs to be done in the organization in order to satisfy customer needs better. This assessment, however, is quite separate from the quantification of the business strengths/position axis and its purpose is to translate the analysis into actionable propositions for other functions within the organization, such as purchasing, production, distribution and so on.

In the case of pharmaceuticals, for example, factors such as 'patent life' are simply an indication of an organization's capability to provide product differentiation. They are irrelevant to the doctor, but need to be taken account of by the organization carrying out the analysis.

(iii) *How to deal with business strengths/position*

The first of these concerns the quantification of business strengths within a 'market'.

Many books for the manager are not particularly useful when used to construct a marketing plan. Few of the factors they mention take account of the need for a company to make an 'offer' to a particular 'market' that has a sustainable competitive advantage over the 'offers' of relevant competitors.

The only way a company can do this is to understand the real needs and wants of the chosen customer group, find out by means of market research how well these needs are being met by the products on offer, and then seek to satisfy these needs better than their competitors.

The worked example given in the table below shows how to assess the strength of a company in a market. The following three questions are used to plot the firm's (SBU's) position on the horizontal axis (competitive position/business strengths):

1 What are the few key things that any competitor has to do right to succeed (i.e. what are the critical success factors, also known as CSFs, in this industry sector)?
2 How important is each of these critical success factors (measured comparatively using a score out of 100)?
3 How do you and each of your competitors score (out of 10) on each of the critical success factors?

These questions yield the information necessary to make an overall assessment of an SBU's competitive strengths (shown in the table below). From this it will be seen that:

● this organization is not market leader
● all competitors score more than 5.0.

Critical success factors (What are the few key things that any competition has to do right to succeed?)	Weighting (How important is each of these CSFs? Score out of 100)	Strengths/weaknesses analysis (Score yourself and each of your main competitors out of 10 on each of the CSFs, then multiply the score by the weight)			
		You	Comp. A	Comp. B	Comp. C
1 Product	20	9 = 1.8	6 = 1.2	5 = 1.0	4 = 0.8
2 Price	10	8 = 0.8	5 = 0.5	6 = 0.6	10 = 0.1
3 Service	50	5 = 2.5	9 = 4.5	7 = 3.5	6 = 3.0
4 Image	20	8 = 1.6	8 = 1.6	5 = 1.0	3 = 0.6
These should normally be viewed from the customer's point of view	Total 100 Total score × weight	6.7	7.8	6.1	5.5

The problem with this and many similar calculations is that rarely will this method discriminate sufficiently well to indicate the relative strengths of a number of products in a particular company's product/market portfolio, and many of the SBU's products would appear on the left of the matrix.

Some method is required to prevent all products appearing on the left of the matrix. This can be achieved by using a ratio, as in the Boston Matrix. This will indicate a company's position relative to the best in the market.

In the example provided, Competitor A has most strengths in the market, so our organization needs to make some improvements. To reflect this, our weighted score should be compared with that of Competitor A (the highest weighted score). Thus $6.7 : 7.8 = 0.86 : 1$.

If we were to plot this on a logarithmic scale on the horizontal axis, this would place our organization to the right of the dividing line as follows:

$$3\times \qquad\qquad 1 \qquad\qquad 0.3$$

(We should make the left hand extreme point 3 and start the scale on the right at 0.3.[3])

Step 5   *Produce the DPM*
Finally, circles should be drawn on a four-box matrix, using market size (as defined in Step 2 above) to determine the area of the circle. An organization's market share can be put in as a 'cheese' in each circle. Alternatively, an organization's own sales into each market can be used.

In practice, however, it is advisable to do both and compare them in order to see how closely actual sales match the opportunities.

Step 6   *Analysis and generation of marketing objectives and strategies*
The objective of producing the DPM is to see the portfolio of products/services for markets relative to each other in the context of the criteria used. This analysis should indicate whether the portfolio is well balanced or not and should give a clear indication of any problems.

Step 7   *(Optional) Forecasting*
The forecast position of the circles should now be made. This is simply done by re-scoring the products/services for markets in three years' time, assuming the organization doesn't change its strategies (see Step 3). This will indicate whether the position is getting worse or better.

It is not absolutely necessary to change the scores on the vertical axis (see Step 3).

---

[3] A scale of 3 to 0.3 has been chosen because such a band is likely to encapsulate most extremes of competitive advantage. If it doesn't, just change it to suit your own circumstances.

Step 8   *Setting marketing objectives*
This involves changing the volumes/values and/or market share (marketing objectives) and the scores on the horizontal axis (relative strength in market) in order to achieve the desired volumes/values. Conceptually, one is picking up the circle and moving it/revising it without specifying how this is to be achieved. Strategies are then defined, which involve words and changes to individual CSF scores (Step 9).

Step 9   *Spell out strategies*
This involves making specific statements about the marketing strategies to be employed to achieve the desired volumes/values.

Step 10   *Sales and profit forecasts*
Once this is done, organizations should be asked to do the following:

1 Plot average % growth in sales revenue by segment ($t - 3$ to $t0$); plot average % ROS by segment ($t - 3$ to $t0$).
2 Plot *forecast* average % growth in sales revenue by segment ($t0$ to $t + 3$); plot *forecast* average % ROS by segment ($t0$ to $t + 3$).

This will show clearly whether past performance and, more importantly, forecasts match the market rating exercise above. *This should preferably be done by someone else (e.g. accountants).*

One major chemical company used the directional policy matrix to select fifty distributors out of the 450 they were dealing with. They needed to do this because the market was in decline and the distributors began *buying* for customers rather than *selling* for the supplier. This led to a dramatic fall in prices. The only way the chemical company could begin to tackle the problem was by appointing a number of exclusive distributorships. The issue of which distributorships to choose was tackled using the directional policy matrix, as clearly some were more attractive than others, while the company had varying strengths in their dealings with each distributor.

Portfolio summary

The resulting portfolio summary pulls together the information from the SWOT analyses and demonstrates the overall competitive position and indicates the relative importance of each product/market segment. The four-box matrix, as in Figure 5.26, illustrates the position most effectively.

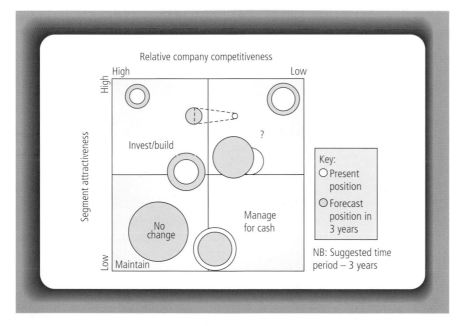

Figure 5.26
A completed DPM

Table 5.3 shows how market attractiveness was calculated for three of the segments. Table 5.4 shows how the strengths and weaknesses for one segment was calculated. These were transferred to the directional policy matrix, which shows how the circles are positioned.

Table 5.3 Establishing how attractive each segment is to your business

Attractiveness	Weight	Segment 1		Segment 2		Segment 3	
		score	total	score	total	score	total
Growth	25	6	1.5	5	1.25	10	2.5
Profitability	25	9	2.25	8	2.0	7	1.75
Size	15	6	0.9	5	0.75	8	1.2
Vulnerability	15	5	0.75	6	0.9	6	0.9
Competition	10	8	0.8	8	0.8	4	0.4
Cyclicality	10	2.5	0.25	3	0.3	2.5	0.25
Total	100		6.45		6.0		7.0

Note: This could be calculated for Year 0 and Year 3, though it is easier and quicker to carry out only the calculations for the final year.

Table 5.4 Scoring your company and your competitors

CSFs	Weight	Your company		Competitor A		Competitor B	
		score	total	score	total	score	total
1 Price	50	5	2.5	6	3.0	4	2.0
2 Product	25	6	1.5	8	2.0	10	2.5
3 Service	15	8	1.2	4	0.6	6	0.9
4 Image	10	6	0.6	5	0.5	3	0.3
Total	100		5.8		6.1		5.7

Note: Calculations are first made for Year 0 as this enables you to establish a fixed position on the portfolio matrix for your company in each segment against which the forecast outcome of alternative strategies and assumptions for the planning period can be seen when plotted onto the DPM.

The horizontal axis in Figure 5.26 reflects the scores in the strengths and weaknesses analysis, and the vertical axis quantifies the attractiveness, to the organization, of each of the important segments contained in the plan. The circle sizes are relative to the current turnover in each. The darker circles indicate forecast sales in three years' time. From this graphical representation of a portfolio of products or range of segments, a number of marketing options present themselves:

1 In the top left box, where strengths are high and markets are attractive, the probable option would be to invest heavily in these markets and increase market share.

2 In the bottom left box, where strengths are high, but markets are less attractive, a likely aim would be to maintain market share and manage for sustained earnings.

3 In the top right box, low strengths, combined with an attractive market, indicate a probable policy of selective investment, to improve competitive position.

4 Finally, in the bottom right box, low strengths allied to poor market attractiveness, point to a management for profits strategy, or even withdrawal.

This matrix gives a clear indication of the marketing objectives and strategies that should be set for each segment or product shown. This is the subject of more detailed treatment in Chapter 6.

■ Combining product life-cycles and portfolio management

Figure 5.27 illustrates the consequences of failing to appreciate the implications of both the product life-cycle concept and the dual combination of market share and market growth.

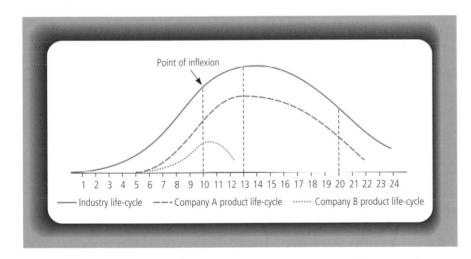

Figure 5.27
Short-term profit maximization versus market share and long-term profit maximization

Companies A and B both start out with question marks (wildcats) in years 5 and 6 in a growing market. Company A invests in building market share and quickly turns into a star. Company B, meanwhile, manages its product for profit over a four-year period so that, while still growing, it steadily loses market share (i.e. it remains a question mark or wildcat). In Year 10, when the market becomes saturated (when typically competitive pressures intensify), Company B with its low market share (hence typically higher costs and lower margins) cannot compete and quickly drops out of the market. Company A, on the other hand, aggressively defends its market share and goes on to enjoy a period of approximately ten years with a product which has become a cash cow. Thus, company B, by pursuing a policy of short-term profit maximization, lost at least ten years' profit potential.

■ Relevance of life-cycle analysis and portfolio management to the marketing audit

It will be recalled that this discussion took place against the background of the need to complete a full and detailed marketing audit prior to setting marketing objectives. Such analyses as those described in this chapter should be an integral part of the marketing audit.

The audit should contain a product life-cycle for each major product and an attempt should be made (using other audit information) to predict the future shape of the life-cycle. It should also contain a product portfolio matrix showing the present position of the products.

■ Case studies

This section concludes with some case studies showing the use and misuse of the DPM.

Case study

Case 1 – A blue-chip company

The first concerns a senior marketing manager of a blue-chip company who dismissed the DPM as irrelevant because he had only four principal products, each one of which was sold to the same customer (or market). Clearly we are talking about major capital sales in this instance.

The manager had plotted products A, B, C and D on the horizontal axis with only one 'market' on the vertical axis. The resulting matrix obviously had four circles in a straight line. Since the purpose of a matrix is to develop a relationship between two or more variables judged by the planner to be of significance in a given planning context, this matrix was clearly absurd and served no useful purpose whatever.

If this manager really wished to use the DPM, he would have to put products A, B, C and D on the vertical axis and look at their respective size and strengths on the horizontal axis. In such a case, all we have done is to change the nomenclature, making a product equivalent to a market, which is clearly acceptable. The main point is that the purpose of the DPM is to display clearly and visibly the relationship between product/market variables.

Case study

Case 2 – A Business School portfolio

This is certainly the case for a Business School portfolio. Here, the 'product' (for example, the MBA programme) equals 'market'. This is shown in Figure 5.28. (By astute management, some of these circles have since been moved to the left of the matrix, surely the purpose of using the DPM in the first place!)

Figure 5.28

Let us now look at two companies whose revenue and profits were static for two consecutive years, and both of which kept their shareholders at bay by selling off part of their assets. The boards of both companies attempted to use the DPM to help clarify the options. In both cases, the resulting matrix was not a reflection of the reality.

Case study

Case 3 – An international engineering company

Here, the Shipping, Food, Thermal and Separation Divisions were all operating in no-growth markets; only the Biotechnology Division was in a growth market. Using market growth as a factor obviously caused all divisions to appear in the bottom half of the matrix, except the Biotechnology Division. The other factor used, however, was profitability, which in the case of Shipping and Separation was high. The weighting of 60 per cent on the profit factor pulled both of these divisions into the upper part of the matrix. Strengths in each case were different, and the resulting matrix looked as shown in Figure 5.29.

However, since both the Shipping and Separation Divisions had little (if any) potential to increase their volume and profitability in mature markets, and since the Food and Biotechnology Divisions did, the circles were clearly in the wrong place. The reality facing the company was as shown in Figure 5.30.

Figure 5.29

Figure 5.30

The opportunity was clearly there for this company to invest in the Food Division, where it was comparatively weak, and also in the Thermal Division. Both of these markets provided ample opportunity for the company to improve its market share and strengths (especially if it also used productivity measures at the same time), in spite of the fact that both markets were relatively mature.

In other words, all we are really interested in is the potential for us to increase our volume and profits, and, in some instances, externally derived factors of market growth and profitability, however accurate, are not particularly useful.

Having reached the conclusion above, obviously this company then took each division in turn and completed the DPM for each of their component parts in order to decide how best to allocate resources.

Case study

Case 4 – A conglomerate with twelve separate companies

This group, although enjoying very high return on capital employed (ROCE), was also under extreme pressure from the financial institutions because its turnover and profits were static. At a directors' meeting, the DPM was used as one of the basic tools of analysis. ROCE of the companies varied between 500 per cent and 5 per cent, with seven about 50 per cent and five below 15 per cent.

Again, using market growth and industry return-on-sales (ROS) as the factors, weighted 30 and 70, not surprisingly all the high-profit companies appeared in the top left of the matrix and all the low-profit companies appeared in the bottom half of the matrix. All this did was to confirm the group's existing position, but was of little value when considering the future.

The directors were advised by the author of this book to change the factors to encapsulate *potential* for growth in volume and profits rather than the *existing* profitability of the markets themselves. The resulting DPM then showed most of the high-profit companies in the lower half of the matrix, since few of them were in growth markets and most already had high market shares.

It also demonstrated clearly another point of policy. One company enjoying a 500 per cent ROCE could grow, providing the chairperson was prepared to allow them to redefine their market more broadly and move into lower ROS segments. Such a policy move would have put this particular company back into the top part of the matrix!

But this, of course, is the whole point of using the DPM in the first place. It should raise key issues and force senior executives into thinking about the future in a structured way.

Case study

Case 5 – An Australian division of an international agrochemical company

This Australian division of an international agrochemical company was under extreme pressure to grow the revenue and profits in a declining market. At first glance, the marketing plans looked to be extremely sophisticated. The plans themselves were also well presented.

The problem was that they did not succeed in spelling out a clear strategy to achieve the corporate objectives, the individual product/market objectives appearing to be little more than 'wish lists'. On closer examination, it became clear that the underlying diagnosis was at fault.

The SWOT analysis shown in Table 5.5 is a typical example of the format used. Even a cursory glance at this shows that none of these factors are discriminators in the choice of supply. On discovering, however, that the SWOT had been done on the merchants (or channel) and that merchants were motivated mainly by price, it was easy to conclude that the three main brands were really commodities in the eyes of the merchants, albeit they were major brand names.

Table 5.5				
Critical success factors		**Success factor scores**		
	Weight	**Us**	**Comp. A**	**Comp. B**
Product efficacy	30	9	8	8
Product price	25	9	9	9
Product image	20	9	8	9
Profitability	20	8	9	6
Formulation	5	8	8	7
		8.8	**8.4**	**8.0**

The real bottom line on all of this was that the merchants were calling the shots, a situation that was bound to get worse and that would continue to drive the price down. The next obvious conclusion was that this company needed to go down the value chain to the farmer and to segment them according to need in order to enable the company to create demand pull, thus reducing the power of the channel. SWOTing at the next link in the chain quickly revealed two things:

1 There was ample opportunity for this company to create value for the farmer.
2 Not enough was known about farmers' needs to enable proper SWOTs to be done on them.

The marketing plan of this company contained what looked to be quite sophisticated DPMs. Again, however, on closer examination of the underlying data, one circle that appeared at the top of the 'market attractiveness' axis was clearly in the wrong place, as the data in Table 5.6 illustrate.

Table 5.6		
	Product 1	**Product 2**
Sales in 1996	$10 million	$5 million
Profit in 1996	$1 million	$0.5 million
Projected sales in 1999	$10 million	$7 million
Projected profit in 1999	$1 million	$0.7 million

From this, it can be seen that the product manager doing the analysis believed that Product 1 was more attractive than Product 2 because, even in 1999, the absolute dollar profits were going to be greater. Clearly, however, positioning Product 1 near the top of the vertical axis of the DPM implied an *invest* strategy, while the implied strategy for Product 2 was a *maintain* (or manage for sustained earnings) strategy. Both strategies would have been wholly inappropriate, thus reducing the value of the DPM as an analytical tool.

Even worse, since we have already seen that the CSF calculation (to derive the position on the horizontal axis of the DPM) was also wrong, the resulting DPM merely served to *confuse*, rather than to clarify and to provide valuable insights about competitive strategy.

Since then, having had the DPM properly explained to them, all of these organizations were able to develop objectives and strategies designed to grow the business and all are now thriving and prospering.

Finally, it may be useful to conclude this section with a definition of a portfolio matrix: 'The use of graphic models to develop a relationship between two or more variables judged by the planner to be of significance in the planning context.'

Whichever approach is used, it can be seen that obvious consideration should be given to marketing objectives and strategies which are appropriate to the attractiveness of a market (market growth in Boston Matrix) and the extent to which such opportunities match our capabilities (market share in Boston Matrix). What these objectives should be will be discussed in Chapter 6.

■ Category management

Finally in this chapter, a few words about category management are necessary.

Category management (CM) is a concept that has developed as a radical alternative to brand management in retail marketing since the mid-1990s. The process of CM can be summarized as:

> The strategic management of a group of products clustered around a specific customer need. This group, or category, is managed as a strategic business unit with clearly defined profitability goals.

The impact if CM is that it shifts attention from individual brands to the management of overall categories as defined by local customer needs.

CM emerged from the development of ideas within the concept of Efficient Customer Response (ECR) that was initiated industry-wide in the US from the mid-1980s onwards. The emphasis of ECR is on sales profitability rather than sales volume and spans the entire business process from the purchase of raw materials to manufacturing, distribution and sale. It is founded on the recent improvements in technology that have allowed suppliers and buyers to reduce waste and stockholding as well as reduced discounts as a means of generating sales. The focus of the concept is the business processes to be found in retail organizations.

Growth of category management

Brand management focuses on individual brands from the manufacturer's perspective, grouping all functions that affect a brand's profitability under one manager. Retailers, however, will often group brands together by product (e.g. soap powder) because that is more convenient for their customers and reflects the way in which customers shop.

The resultant categories are therefore defined by customers, but this can lead to problems of definition. For instance, when a customer wants a cleaner for the bathroom, does he or she categorize it as a bathroom product, a cleaner, or a home safety product? In addition, categories tend to vary regionally and according to customer types, rather than on a broader cross-cultural basis. In response some manufacturers have had to recast their brands for categories, but this in turn raises the question of whether some products should appear in more than one category (for instance, should herbs be categorized with fresh produce, baking goods or both?).

In the final analysis, what is important to retailers is that their shelf space sells more than it would if managed another way. Retailers' expertise lies in providing space to sell products and services to facilitate that. Sometimes, an external supplier is appointed as category manager, who is then made responsible for optimizing sales from that space. By doing so, retailers are exploiting manufacturer skills in such areas as display, sales promotion and merchandising.

The retailer will normally set minimum standards for the category, such as demanding that there must be at least one major brand name and one 'own label' product displayed. After that, the category managers make their own stocking and communications decisions on behalf of their assigned category. For example, if SmithKline Beecham were to identify opportunities for increased toothbrush sales within the oral hygiene category for which they acted as category manager, they could spend their own budget on promoting them.

CM reflects the shift of power from manufacturer to retailer.

Contrary to traditional practices, CM obliges manufacturers to consider the profitability of an entire product segment rather than that of just their own brands. The fact that retailers have forced this change is another example of the evolution of retailers from passive distributors to proactive marketers and the shift of power from manufacturer to retailer.

Where category managers are appointed internally, they usually have a similar role – i.e. the management of a partnership between a supplier or a number of suppliers with the objective of sales and profit enhancement.

The trend towards CM has also required a shift from the traditionally narrow focus of brand management. Looked at from a category perspective, it is possible to see that the consumer choice is not just about selecting from competing brands such as Coca-Cola or Pepsi, but involves an entire drinks portfolio of soft drinks, juices, beverages and alcohol. Heinz began realigning its business along category management principles in 1997, and now has eight global categories: ketchups, condiments and sauces, infant feeding, seafood (tuna), organic and nutritional food, pet food, frozen food, and convenience food (H.J. Heinz Company Corporate Profile 2000).

Rather than relying on the power of their brand names, organizations need to ensure that all of their support systems demonstrate to retailers that they are capable of managing categories to advantage. This might mean a review of all of the organization's systems for retail supply, such as the logistics of keeping the shelves fully supplied or maintaining efficient electronic data interchange systems for stocks.

Limitations of CM

Viewed purely as a strategy to reduce waste and therefore costs, CM loses its focus on the end customer as the absolute priority. Concentrating on the maximization of shelf-space profitability may not improve customer satisfaction levels and that, in the long run, may reduce profits.

One recent report concluded that the availability of a wide selection of goods is a major determinant in customers' decisions about where to shop. CM limits the product choice to those which are most profitable for the retailer, and this can have a negative impact on the customers' shopping experience. If customers feel hindered in their purchase decisions by the inability to compare prices of different brands, the CM process will ultimately rebound.

Further difficulties arise from the issue of positioning different product categories. Should paper tissues, for instance, be categorized with bathroom products, or health and beauty? And should the two categories be set next to each other or apart? In addition, different retailers and manufacturers could well work to different category definitions.

These limitations reflect the fact that much of the emphasis of CM has been on the manufacturer/retailer relationship. As far back as 1994, a *Financial Times* survey found that consumers have effectively been demoted as the focus of marketing strategy as retailers have grown in importance, with consumers attracting 30 per cent of marketing expenditure against retailers at 54 per cent.

> CM's emphasis on the manufacturer/retailer relationship can demote a customer focus.

Challenges for the future

One of the most difficult challenges facing CM is reducing the number of superfluous items on the shelves. This is in opposition to traditional brand marketing, which aims to prolong the life of the brand by extending the product range. Possible ways of evolution are demonstrated by Figure 5.31.

Mass customization has been made possible by the increased sophistication in consumer information which has allowed marketers to provide variations on the central product to suit each customer group. The growth of retailers' own-label products (e.g., Tesco's 'finest' and 'value') reflects this, but further limits the available shelf space for branded supplies.

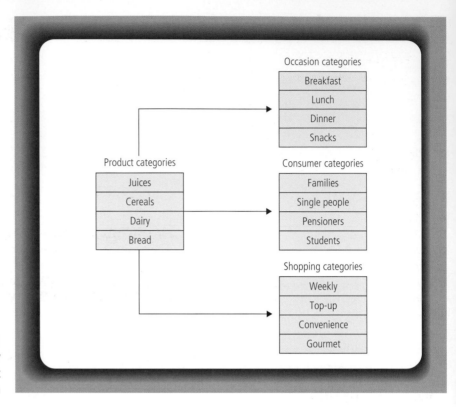

Figure 5.31
Category
management
evolution

The difficulty for retailers is ensuring that limiting consumers' brand choice is not perceived as limiting their category choice just because they cannot find their favourite products.

The future of CM must necessarily take account of the distribution systems for an increasingly 'global village' market. Many mass retailers are unable to market so many products properly, even when redefined as categories. Providing marketing expertise is therefore one way in which manufacturers can hope to retain some kind of balance in the relationship with such international retailers.

> CM can help deliver customer satisfaction by focusing retailers on customer preferences.

In order to sustain a customer focus, manufacturers need free access to customer information. This can be obtained through large panel companies such as Nielsen or Taylor Nelson Sofres (TNS), or through the development of a manufacturer's own database, such as Heinz. Manufacturers can also try to establish a reputation for themselves as leaders in ECR.

Future emphasis will probably be on targeting customer satisfaction more effectively, in order to maximize long-term profit. CM can help by focusing on the retail audience and the way in which category sales are driven. This is turn helps retailers build an effective vehicle for appealing to the variety of customers' product decisions and needs. The challenge is to make this happen on a store-by-store basis, at an affordable cost.

■ Application questions

1 Select a major product and:
- draw a life-cycle of the product itself
- draw a life-cycle of the market (segment) in which it competes
- explain why this is the shape it is
- predict the shape and length of the life-cycle in the future
- say *why* you are making these predictions.

2 Plot your products on a Boston Matrix and:
- explain their relative positions
- forecast where they will be (and why), say, five years from now.

3 List your main markets or segments.

4 List criteria for attractiveness (to you).

5 List criteria for business strengths (you *vis-à-vis* competitors).

6 Devise a scoring and weighting system for each axis.

7 Put the markets or segments through the criteria.

8 Draw circles around the coordinates. The diameter of each circle should be proportional to that segment's contribution to turnover. Is this where you want the circles to be?

Chapter 5 review

What is a product?

A product (or service) is a problem-solver, in the sense that it provides what the customer needs or wants. A product consists of:

1 A core (functional performance)
2 A surround (a bundle of features and benefits).

Usually the core product has 20 per cent of the impact, yet leads to 80 per cent of the cost. The surround is the reverse of this. *Try Exercise 5.1*

The product life-cycle

All products or services have a life-cycle which follows this pattern:

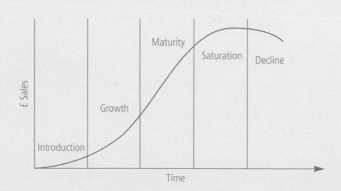

The phases of the life-cycle are:

A Introduction
B Growth
C Maturity
D Saturation
E Decline

The total life-cycle depends on the type of product or service, e.g. fashion products have short life-cycles.

There is a trend for life-cycles of most products to get shorter as changes in technology and customer expectations make greater impact. Each phase of the life-cycle calls for different management responses.

Try Exercise 5.2

Diffusion of innovation

Some people/companies are always prepared to buy new products, while others wait until things are tried and tested. All products and services have customers which fall into these categories.

A Innovators (2.5 per cent of total)
B Early adopters (13.5 per cent of total)
C Early majority (34 per cent of total).
D Late majority (34 per cent of total)
E Laggards (16 per cent of total)

Discovering a typology for innovators and early adopters can help in the promotion of new products.

Product portfolio

Ideally, a company should have a portfolio of products whose life-cycles overlap. This guarantees continuity of income and growth potential.

Time

Boston Matrix

The product portfolio can be analysed in terms of revenue-producing potential, using this technique.

Cash cows need to generate sufficient funds to sustain stars and wildcats, and make a profit.
Try Exercise 5.3

Directional policy matrix (DPM)

Not all companies possess the data required by the Boston Matrix (above). Similar results can be obtained using this technique. The axes become as shown in the figure on page 242.
Try Exercises 5.4 and 5.5

Questions raised for the company

1 Q: How useful is a brand name?
  A: Well-known brands have successfully differentiated themselves from competing products by conveying something extra. Such differentiation enables them to command a higher price than unbranded, 'commodity' products.
2 Q: How does market share relate to cash generation, as in the Boston Matrix?
  A: The higher the market share, the higher the output, and the lower the unit costs through economies of scale and the learning curve. Thus a company can command higher margins and generate more revenue.

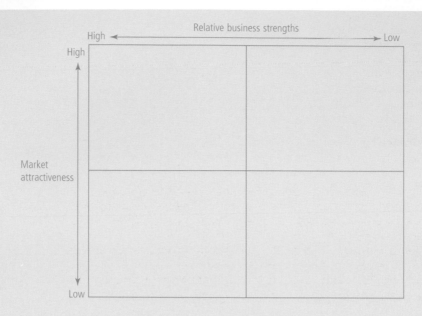

3 Q: Should 'dogs' always be killed off?
   A: It is a question of timing. It is possible sometimes to squeeze extra earnings from a 'dog'. Sometimes a 'dog' is supportive of another product. Sometimes a 'dog' product can be profitable because it shares in the economies of scale of another product in the range.

EXERCISES

Introduction to Chapter 5 exercises

The exercises are designed to help you to look at your product or service range in three different ways:

1 As a 'package' of benefits (Exercise 5.1)
2 From the point of view of their life-cycles (Exercise 5.2)
3 As a total portfolio to be developed and managed in the best possible way. There are two approaches to this idea of a portfolio:
   (a) one uses the approach developed by the Boston Consulting Group, the Boston Matrix (Exercise 5.3)
   (b) the other uses the approach developed by General Electric and McKinsey, the directional policy matrix (Exercise 5.4).

The final exercise in this section invites you to construct and interpret a directional policy matrix for your own company (Exercise 5.5).

Exercise 5.1
Benefit package analysis

It has been shown that customers buy products and services for many reasons. Different people look for different types of benefits from the product to satisfy their needs. Here are some typical sources of customer benefits:

1 Good comparative price
2 Well-known product/service

3 Good after-sales service
4 Reputable company image
5 Low after-sales costs
6 Prompt delivery
7 Efficient performance
8 Well-designed product
9 Fashionable
10 Ease of purchase
11 Good quality
12 Reliability
13 Safety factors.

Obviously, the better the products/services provide benefits to customers and match their needs, the more competitive they are going to be in the market-place. The following process is designed to help you complete a benefit analysis on your products or services.

By doing this you will discover or confirm which items of your range are the strongest on the market when compared to your competitors'. It should also provide you with insights about where attention might be paid to your products or services, either to improve existing customer benefits or to put emphasis on new ones.

Proceed as follows:

1 Study the customer benefits list above. Are these typical of the reasons why people buy your products or services? If you can think of others that are more pertinent to your particular business, write them down in the spaces provided.
2 Taking into account the market segments with which you do business, look at the customer benefits list and decide which are the three most important benefits demanded by your most important segment(s). Make a note of these.
3 Now identify the next three most important benefits demanded by these customers, and also make a note of these.
4 Finally, tick any other benefits on the list that are relevant to these customers.
5 Repeat this exercise for other important segments.
6 You are now asked to transpose this information on to Worksheet 1 (an example of a completed sheet is provided in Worksheet 2). Proceed as follows.

Step 1 In column 1 list the products or services you supply. No particular order is required.
Step 2 Take the three most important benefits that you selected above and use them as headings for columns 2, 3 and 4 on the worksheet, so that column 2 represents one benefit, column 3 another and column 4 the third.
Step 3 Fill in columns 2, 3 and 4 as follows. Starting with column 2, look at the benefit heading and work down your list of products or services scoring each one on a *1 to 10 point scale*: 1 will show that the product barely supplies this particular benefit to the customer and compares badly with competitors' performance, whereas a 10 score would

demonstrate very high meeting of customer needs, superior to that provided by competitors. For example, if the benefit heading was 'Delivery' and, working down the list of products, the first product had a good delivery record, as good as any in the trade, then it could be allocated 9 or 10 points. If the next product on the list had a very patchy record on meeting delivery, and we knew several competitors were better, then we might only allocate 4 or 5 points, and so on. Follow the same procedure for columns 3 and 4. Note that the 1–10 scoring scale is only used on columns 2, 3 and 4 because these represent the major benefits to your customers and thus need to be weighted accordingly.

Step 4   Now take the second three most important benefits and use these as headings for columns 5, 6 and 7.

Step 5   As before rate each of your products or services against each heading, in comparison with competitor performance, but this time only *use a scoring scale of 1–6*, where again 1 point represents low provision of the benefit and 6 high. The 1–6 scoring scale is in recognition of the reduced importance these benefits have for customers.

Step 6   Finally take any other benefits you ticked above and use these as headings for column 8 and onwards as far as required.

Step 7   Again work through your list of products or services comparing them against how well they meet the benefit heading of each column, but this time only *use a 1–3 points scoring scale*. The reduced scale reflects the reduced level of importance of the customer benefits in this last group.

Step 8   Aggregate the scores you have allocated to each product or service and enter the result in the Total column.

Step 9   The product or service with the highest points score is clearly that which provides most benefits to your customers and competes favourably with the competition. Therefore allocate this product with the ranking of 1 in the Ranking column. Find the next highest total score and mark that 2 and so on. You might find some total scores so close to each other that it would be helpful to rank your products or services by groups of similar scores, rather than individually, e.g. have a first 'division', second 'division', etc. of product groupings.

Step 10   On either Worksheet 1 or a separate sheet of paper, make notes about any relevant points. For example, should some scores be qualified because of recent design improvements, are some products under threat from new competition, does the ranking reflect particular strengths or weaknesses, are there any surprises?

What are the main lessons to be learned from this type of benefit analysis for your company's products/services? What steps can you recommend to improve future product development? Use the space in 'Personal notes' to record your thoughts.

Note: This analysis shows that 'containers' provide the best 'benefits package' when compared to the rest of the product range. In contrast, 'water butts' provide least benefits, falling down on price, delivery and design. This analysis enables a company to see where it needs to work at the 'product surround' to become more effective.

Worksheet 1 Benefit package analysis (Exercise 5.1)

Col. nos.1	Major benefits Low 1 – High 10			Medium benefits Low 1 – High 6			Lesser benefits Low 1 – High 3											Total	Ranking	Notes, Observations, Qualifying comments, Strengths, etc.
Customer benefits / Prods or services	2	3	4	5	6	7	8	9	10	11	12	13	14	15	16	17	18			

Worksheet 2 Benefit package analysis (Exercise 5.1)

Col. nos.1 Prods or services	Major benefits Low 1 – High 10			Medium benefits Low 1 – High 6			Lesser benefits Low 1 – High 3												Total	Ranking	Notes, Observations, Qualifying comments, Strengths, etc.
Customer benefits	Price (2)	Quality (3)	Delivery (4)	Design (5)	Safety (6)	Reliability (7)	Our image (8)	After-sales service (9)	Packaging (10)	Comprehensive range (11)	12	13	14	15	16	17	18			
Water butts	5	8	5	3	6	6	1	1	2	2								39	4	Check costing and deliveries
Containers	8	8	7	5	6	3	3	2	3	2								47	1	Again business difficult to improve except on delivery and reliability
Toy (compts)	3	8	9	5	6	5	1	1	2	2								42	2	Doesn't always mix with other work
Cones for road works, etc.	7	8	6	4	6	5	1	1	3	1								42	2	Work at price and delivery. Also need to improve designs and range

Personal notes

Exercise 5.2
Life-cycle
analysis

It is universally accepted that all products or services go through a life-cycle of five stages – introduction, growth, maturity, saturation and, ultimately, decline.

Depending upon the nature of the particular product and its market, the life-cycle can be of short or long duration. Similarly, different products will have different levels of sales. Nevertheless, allowing for these differences in 'width' and 'height', product life-cycle curves all have a remarkably similar and consistent shape. It is because of consistency of the life-cycle curve that this aspect of the product audit becomes such a powerful analytical tool.

The following exercise is designed to help you construct a life-cycle analysis for your company's products or services. By doing this it will help to focus on information that will be used in setting marketing objectives and strategies.

1 Using Worksheet 1, invent a suitable scale for the sales volume axis, i.e. one that will encompass the sales peaks you have had or are likely to experience in your business.
2 At the position marked 'Current sales', record the levels of sales volume for your products or services. You will have to select the timescale you use. If your products are short-lived, perhaps you might have to calculate sales figures in terms of days or weeks. For longer-lived products, perhaps annual sales figures will be more appropriate.
3 Taking each product in turn, plot a life-cycle curve based upon the historical data at your disposal, e.g. if in 2 above you decided that a monthly sales analysis would be necessary to capture the movement on the life-cycle curves, then check back through your sales records and plot the sales volume for each product at monthly intervals.
4 From the life-cycle curves you have drawn, extend those into the future where extrapolation looks feasible, i.e. where a distinct pattern exists. You should finish up with a worksheet looking something like Worksheet 2.
5 Make notes about your key findings from this exercise in the space below.
6 So far you have only looked at your products in isolation. Now on a separate piece of paper (or on the same worksheet if it doesn't cause too much confusion), compare each life-cycle pattern of your major products or services with the *total market* life-cycle for each one. Do your product patterns mirror the market life-cycle? Are your sales falling, while the total market sales are steady or increasing? Is the reverse happening? Many outcomes will be possible, but whatever they are, you are asked to explain them and to write in the space below what these comparisons between the total

market and your sales tell you about your product/service range and its future prospects. If you find it difficult to establish total market life-cycles then refer to the 'Guide to market maturity', later in this exercise.

7 Finally, and to demonstrate that this examination of product life-cycles is not just an intellectual exercise, prepare a short presentation for one of your senior colleagues, or, better still, your boss, following the instructions given on the 'Special project brief', at the end of this exercise.

Worksheet 1 Life-cycle analysis (Exercise 5.2)

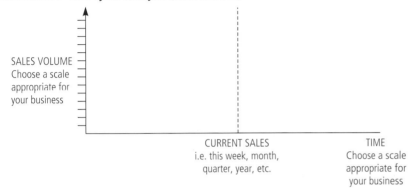

Worksheet 2 Life-cycle analysis (Exercise 5.2) a plastics processing company

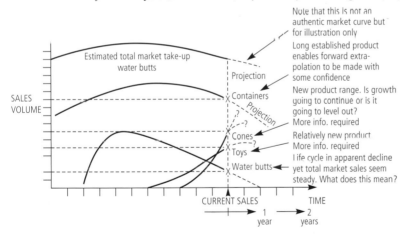

Personal notes

Guide to market maturity

The following checklist is used by one major company to help it determine where its markets are on the life-cycle (repeated from page 202).

Factor	Maturity stage			
	Embryonic	**Growth**	**Mature**	**Declining**
1 *Growth rate*	Normally much greater than GNP (on small base).	Sustained growth above GNP. New customers. New suppliers. Rate decelerates toward end of stage.	Approximately equals GNP.	Declining demand. Market shrinks as users' needs change.
2 *Predictability of growth potential*	Hard to define accurately. Small portion of demand being satisfied. Market forecasts differ widely.	Greater percentage of demand is met and upper limits of demand becoming clearer. Discontinuities, such as price reductions based on economies of scale, may occur.	Potential well defined. Competition specialized to satisfy needs of specific segments.	Known and limited.
3 *Product line proliferation*	Specialized lines to meet needs of early customers.	Rapid expansion.	Proliferation slows or ceases.	Lines narrow as unprofitable products dropped.
4 *Number of competitors*	Unpredictable.	Reaches maximum. New entrants attracted by growth and high margins. Some consolidation begins toward end of stage.	Entrenched positions established. Further shakeout of marginal competitors.	New entrants unlikely. Competitors continue to decline.
5 *Market share distribution*	Unstable. Shares react unpredictably to entrepreneurial insights and timing.	Increasing stability. Typically, a few competitors emerging as strong.	Stable with a few companies often controlling much of industry.	Highly concentrated or fragmented as industry segments and/ or is localized.
6 *Customer stability*	Trial usage with little customer loyalty.	Some loyalty. Repeat usage with many seeking alternative suppliers.	Well-developed buying patterns with customer loyalty. Competitors understand purchase dynamics and it is difficult for a new supplier to win over accounts.	Extremely stable. Suppliers dwindle and customers less motivated to seek alternatives.

(Continued)

Factor	Maturity stage			
	Embryonic	Growth	Mature	Declining
7 *Ease of entry*	Normally easy. No one dominates. Customers' expectations uncertain. If barriers exist, they are usually technology, capital or fear of the unknown.	More difficult. Market franchises and/or economies of scale may exist, yet new business is still available without directly confronting competition.	Difficult. Market leaders established. New business must be 'won' from others.	Little or no incentive to enter.
8 *Technology*	Plays an important role in matching product characteristics to market needs. Frequent product changes	Product technology vital early, while process technology more important later in this stage.	Process and material substitution focus. Product requirements well known and relatively undemanding. May be a thrust to renew the industry via new technology.	Technological content is known, stable and accessible.

Special project brief
Product life-cycles
Take any product you know well and prepare a short presentation (say 10 minutes) which covers the following areas/questions:

1 Brief product description – your definition of the market it serves
2 Your estimates of the product's current point in the life-cycle curve
3 Your reasons for believing it is at this point
4 Your estimate of the length and shape of this life-cycle
5 Your reasons for this estimate
6 Your predictions of the prospects for this product over the next three years
7 Your reasons for these predictions.

Exercise 5.3

Case study: International Bearings Ltd (IBL)

The objectives of this case study are as follows:

1 To demonstrate a useful method of reviewing, at any point in time, the commercial implications of decision-making for a company with a number of different products, in different markets, at different stages of growth, maturity or decline. This is known as a product portfolio. This method was introduced by the Boston Consulting Group and is known as the Boston Matrix.
2 To demonstrate the application of the Boston Matrix by using a case study in which an industrial company competes with a number of competitors in a number of different market segments.

3 To give the user practical experience by working through the situation analysis and decision-making process illustrated in the case study.
4 To encourage the user to apply the principles learned in the case study to his/her own commercial situation.

You are asked to write down your answers to the questions on the worksheet provided. The correct answers are given in Appendix 1 on page 257.

International Bearings Limited (IBL) sells a number of fast-moving industrial products in a market with about sixty competitors, most of whom are relatively small. Eight companies, including IBL, are significant in terms of size. IBL has seven major product groups.

The situation of IBL is shown in Table 5.7.

Table 5.7				
Product	Sales volume (units)	Relative market share	Current market growth (year 1, %)	Forecast market growth (year 3, %)
1	1,500	*	20	25
2	1,300	2 : 1	9	6
3	1,000	0.9 : 1	12	25
4	1,000	0.6 : 1	10	2
5	900	0.5 : 1	5	3
6	800	0.2 : 1	3	0
7	500	0.1 : 1	22	25
Total	7,000			

*This ratio has been omitted, as it forms part of the exercise later in this case study.

Definitions of headings in Table 5.7

Relative market share is the ratio of your market share to the share of the largest competitor in your market. Thus, if you have 10 per cent market share and your biggest competitor has 40 per cent market share, then the ratio (or relative market share) is 1 : 4. This is usually expressed as 0.25 : 1. If you have a market share of 20 per cent and your biggest competitor has a market share of 10 per cent, then the ratio would be 2 : 1.

Current market growth is the percentage growth in sales of a product in a market over the previous year's sales. Thus, if a market was 100 last year and 120 this year, then the growth would be 20 per cent.

Forecast market growth is the annual rate at which you believe the market will grow in the future. For example, you may forecast that the market will grow by 10 per cent in Year 2 and 20 per cent in Year 3. So 10 per cent forecast market growth for Year 2 is Year 1 figure of 120 × 10 per cent: answer: 132. For Year 3 it is Year 2 figure of 132 × 20: answer: 158.4.

Table 5.8 shows IBL's absolute market share, compared to that of its competitors.

Table 5.8

	Companies								
	IBL	B	C	D	E	F	G	H	Others (about 50)
Absolute market share (%)	15	10	8	8	8	7	5	5	34

IBL has 15 per cent absolute market share. Table 5.7 states that figure represents 1,500, so:

$$\frac{1500}{1} \times \frac{100}{15} \times 10,000$$

which is the current year total market size for product 1.

Definitions of headings in Table 5.8

Absolute market share is the percentage of a total market that your product enjoys. For example, total market size = 100 units per annum. Your sales are 25 per annum. Therefore you have 25 per cent absolute market share. Absolute market share is expressed as a percentage of the total market.

As defined above, relative market share is expressed as a ratio, e.g. 2 : 1. This compares your market share and degree of dominance to one other competitor.

The market forecast for IBL's product 1 is as shown in Table 5.9.

Table 5.9

	Current year (%)	Year 2 (%)	Year 3 (%)
Actual production	20		
Forecast growth		22	25

IBL's own forecast for product 1 is shown in Table 5.10.

Table 5.10

	Current year	Year 2	Year 3
Actual sales	1,500 units		
Sales forecast		1,650 units	1,815 units

Please note that the forecast market growth for product 1 in Table 5.9 is different from IBL's own forecast of product 1 in Table 5.10.

A senior executive from company B has recently joined IBL, as a result of which IBL has received some accurate market intelligence about company B's product 1, which competes with IBL's own product 1. This is shown in Table 5.11.

Table 5.11			
	Current year	**Year 2**	**Year 3**
Actual sales	1,000 units		
Sales forecast		1,500 units	1,562 units

Please answer the following questions:

Question 1
What is IBL's relative market share for product 1? Remember that relative market share is a ratio, e.g. 3.5 : 1. Write your answer to this question and all others on the answer sheet provided on page 256 (correct answers are provided on page 257).

Question 2
What will IBL's relative market share be for product 1 in Year 3? Limit your answer to two decimal places. For this question, you may need to refer to Tables 5.10 and 5.11.

Question 3
What is the annual growth of the market for product 1?

Question 4
What will be the total market volume for product 1 in year 3?

Question 5
What is the absolute market share of IBL's product 1 in year 3? Round up your answer to the nearest whole number.

Question 6
Is the market growth in the current year, high or low, relative to the industry average of 10 per cent?

Question 7
Relative market share and market growth are important factors a company should consider when appraising its product portfolio. Rather than looking at masses of figures, which are hard to interpret individually, the Boston Consulting Group (BCG), devised a matrix to show these two factors as a graphic drawing. The matrix is square and the relative market share (RMS) is placed on the horizontal axis. The imaginary lines are vertical. Market growth is measured on the vertical axis. See Figure 5.32.

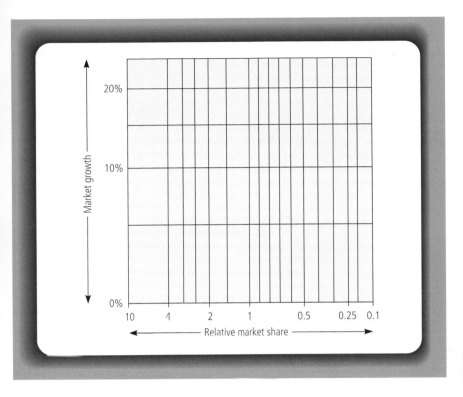

Figure 5.32
Boston Matrix

The lowest figure (usually zero) is at the bottom, and, depending on the industry, is up to 20 per cent. (This upper figure may vary – for example, an established product may be under 10 per cent or a new product may be in excess of 100 per cent.)

The decision on what constitutes 'high' or 'low' growth is thus dependent on the industry. The decision is yours. In this case we have chosen to use 10 per cent as the dividing line between high growth, i.e. greater than 10 per cent, and low growth, i.e. less than 10 per cent.

In the example, we are using a scale ending at approximately 20 per cent. The imaginary lines run horizontally across the matrix.

Take the products numbered 1 to 7 and, using Table 5.7 data, place them at the correct coordinates for relative market share and market growth. For this purpose, a matrix is provided on the answer sheet later in this exercise.

Question 8
The next stage is to make these coordinates into circles. This is necessary so that the executive completing the matrix can understand the relative importance to the company of the products which appear in the matrix. Some circles will be bigger than others, indicating a greater contribution to turnover.

It is also important because the executive can forecast the size of each circle and its likely position on the matrix in, say, three years' time. He or she could, for example, show the position and size of the circles if the company continued with its current policies, or where they will be if different policies are pursued.

In this case, the diameter of each circle represents the relative contribution of each product to the total volume of IBL. The scale adopted is your decision. It generally depends on the size of paper you are using. For example, you may choose 1 mm = 10,000 units, so a product selling 50,000 units will measure 5 mm and so on for each product. (To be technically correct, we should take the square root of each of the sales volumes to determine the proportionate area of each circle. However, for the sake of simplicity, we have used the method described above.)

On Figure 5.32, the next task is to convert the coordinates marked 1–7 into circles representing the relative contribution of each product. First, however, using a scale of 1 mm × 100 units of sales volume, calculate the correct diameter for each of the seven products and write your answers in the answer sheet provided. Next, draw circles on the matrix provided, using the answers given above for the diameters.

A short explanation of the principles behind the Boston Matrix is given in Appendix 2 (page 258). Understanding the matrix will enable you to answer the questions which follow.

Question 9
Do you think IBL currently has a well-balanced product portfolio? Give reasons for your answer.

Question 10
State the forecast position of IBL's product 1 in Year 3. Write in figures the RMS (including a decimal point and colon, e.g. 5.2 : 1). Write in figures the RMG (e.g. 50%).

Question 11
Using a scale of 1 mm = 100 units of sales volume, what will the diameter of the circle for IBL's product 1 be in Year 3? State your answer in figures to the nearest whole number.

Question 12
Are the signs ahead good, comparing the forecast position of IBL's product 1 with the current situation? Give reasons for your answer.

Question 13
What is happening to IBL's main product in the current situation? Choose from the options A–D listed below:

A   Losing market share in a declining market
B   Gaining market share in a growing market
C   Losing market share in a growing market
D   Losing profitability in a stable market

Question 14
What policy should IBL pursue for product 1? Choose from the options listed below:

A   Increase price, reduce promotion
B   Reduce price, reduce promotion

C   Hold price, reduce promotion
D   Hold price, increase promotion
E   Reduce price, increase promotion
F   Increase price, increase promotion

Question 15
In this situation it was decided to maintain product 1's market share by investing in it, to grow at the same rate of forecast market growth of 20, 22, 25 per
cent. Which other products from the list below would you invest in? Choose
from the combinations A, B, C or D:

A   Products 2 and 5
B   Products 3 and 7
C   Products 3 and 6
D   Products 4 and 7

Question 16
Select one product's position you should maintain from the options of products 2 to 7. Select product 2, 3, 4, 5, 6 or 7.

Question 17
Which combinations of products might it be appropriate to manage for cash
from the options below?

A   Products 5, 6 and 7
B   Products 3, 4 and 5
C   Products 4, 5 and 6
D   Products 4, 5 and 7

Having completed this case study, you should by now fully understand the
principles and the methodology of the Boston Matrix.

There are, of course, other approaches to portfolio management. However,
before considering these, using the methodology explained in this case study,
produce a Boston Matrix for your own company's products.

Some practical suggestions for producing your own Boston Matrix now
follow:

1 Try not to use more than ten products. If in doubt, choose the 20 per cent
  of your products that account for the majority of your turnover.
2 If this still proves to be too many, then find some way of grouping your
  products until you have a manageable number.
3 Directors and senior managers doing this additional exercise may prefer to
  use companies, divisions, countries, markets, or strategic business units
  instead of products. They all work just as well.
4 Great care is needed in defining 'market' share. Remember, a 'market' consists of all other brands that satisfy the same needs as your brand.
5 Forecast the size and position of your products in, say, three years' time.

Ask yourself:

(a) Is it a well-balanced portfolio?
(b) Are you pursuing appropriate policies for each of your products or busi-
    ness areas?

Worksheet for Answers – Case Study IBL.

Case Study (IBL)

Last name

First name

Question number	Answer
1	
2	
3	
4	Yr 1… Yr 2… Yr3…

Product	RMS	RMG
1		
2		
3		
4		
5		
6		
7		

5

6

7

1
2
3
4
5
6
7

8

9

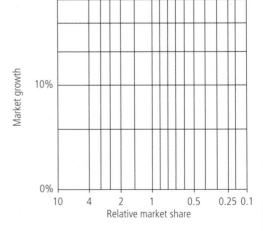

10

11

12

13

14

15

16

17

Appendix 1 Answers to the IBL Case Study

1   1.5 : 1 (1,500 ÷ 1,000)
2   1.16 : 1 (1,815 ÷ 1,562)
3   20%, 22%, 25% (from Table 5.9)
4   Table 5.7 gave product 1 sales as 1,500. Table 5.8 gave absolute market share of 15% for IBL. Market size in Year 1 is:

$$\frac{1,500}{1} \times \frac{100}{15} = 10,000$$

    Thus, market size for Year 3 is found from the % figures in Table 5.9. Thus, 10,000 × 22% × 25% = 15,250
5   12% from Table 5.9, Year 3 (1,815), divide that by the answer to question 4 (15,250) = 11.9
6   High. In each of the three years the market is forecast to grow at a higher rate than 10% (20%, 22%, 25%)
7

	RMS	RMG
1	1.5 : 1	20%
2	2 : 1	9%
3	0.9 : 1	12%
4	0.6 : 1	10%
5	0.5 : 1	5%
6	0.2 : 1	3%
7	0.1 : 1	22%

Figure 5.33 shows the coordination for the Boston Matrix.

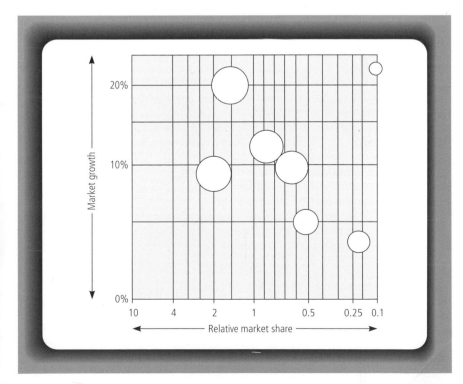

Figure 5.33
Coordinates for RMS and RMG

8 1 15 mm
   2 13 mm
   3 10 mm
   4 10 mm
   5 9 mm
   6 8 mm
   7 5 mm
9 Yes. There is one significant cash cow. 'Cash cow' product 1 is market leader in a fast-growing market (a 'star'). Product 3 is almost market leader in a fast-growing market. Product 7 is a 'question mark'. Products 4, 5 and 6 are 'dogs', but this is not a problem as long as products 2, 3 and 7 are managed appropriately.
10 1.16 : 1, 25%
11 1,815, 18
12 No. IBL's main product is losing market share in a growing market.
13 C is the best answer, but not the only one. You may wish to consider other factors, including company policy, e.g. improving the product.
14 D
15 B
16 2
17 C

Appendix 2 The principles of the Boston Matrix

The principles of the Boston Matrix can be applied to practical commercial situations for improving business planning and assisting decision-taking where a company has a number of products.

What is the Boston Matrix?

The Boston Matrix is used for what is known as product portfolio planning. It uses graphic models to develop a relationship between two or more variables known to be of significance in the corporate context.

The two main variables are relative market share and market growth. Both have been shown to be strongly related to profitability. In general, the bigger a firm's relative market share is, the lower its costs are, and the bigger its return on investment. The rate of market growth also has a significant impact on a company's performance.

The Boston Consulting Group combined these two variables in the form of a simple matrix, which has been shown to have profound implications for the firm, especially in respect of cash flow.

The Boston Matrix classifies a firm's products according to their cash usage and their cash generation along the two dimensions, relative market share and market growth.

Why use a matrix rather than a sheet of figures?

The Boston Matrix shows graphically the positions in terms of relative market share and market growth of a number of products at a glance. Presented in a matrix, it is easier for an executive to see the relationship between a number of different products. It is also a very powerful presentation device for planning purposes.

How is the Boston Matrix used?
Different products have to be managed in ways appropriate to their different business environments and according to their different strengths and weaknesses. There is a need to maintain strong and profitable products. There is a need to invest in new products as existing products mature and die.

The Boston Matrix provides a powerful vehicle for assessing a firm's position as represented by its portfolio of products. Finally, it enables appropriate policies to be developed for each product to ensure continuing growth in sales and profits.

Some examples of the use of the Boston Matrix
The Boston Consulting Group chose picturesque labels to attach to each of the four categories of products to give some indication of the prospects for products in each quadrant:

- Star
- Cash cow
- Question mark
- Dog.

'Cash cows' are leaders in markets where there is little additional growth. They are excellent generators of cash and tend to use little. 'Stars' are leaders in high growth markets. They tend to generate a lot of cash, but also use a lot because of growth market conditions. 'Question marks' have not yet achieved a dominant market position, and so do not generate much cash. They can, however, use a lot of cash because of growth market conditions. Sometimes these are referred to as 'wildcats'. 'Dogs' have little future and are often a cash drain on the company.

The art of portfolio management now becomes clearer. We should be seeking to use surplus cash generated by 'cash cows' to invest in 'stars' and a selected number of 'question marks'.

Figure 5.34 shows a well-balanced product portfolio. There is one large 'cash cow', two sizeable 'stars', and three emerging products in high growth markets. There are only two small 'dogs'.

Figure 5.35 shows a poorly balanced product portfolio. The company has no 'cash cows'. There is only one small 'star'. It has three 'question marks' and three 'dogs', one of which is a sizeable product. This company probably has cash-flow problems.

Figure 5.36 also shows a poorly balanced product portfolio. This company is probably cash-rich, with three sizeable 'cash cows'. However, all the danger signs are evident. There are no new products coming along to replace the 'cash cows', which may well decline in the future.

Exercise 5.4
International Bearings Ltd – directional policy matrix case study

The main business of IBL is the sale of a portfolio of bearings and assemblies based on bearings to a variety of end-use markets in Europe, in which IBL is a very significant and well-established player. IBL manufactures products in five different locations, each making only part of the product range to achieve maximum production cost benefits.

Each country has its own sales organization marketing the whole range. These national organizations have two sales forces, one dealing with original equipment manufacturers (OEMs), the other selling via independent

Figure 5.34
Well-balanced
product portfolio

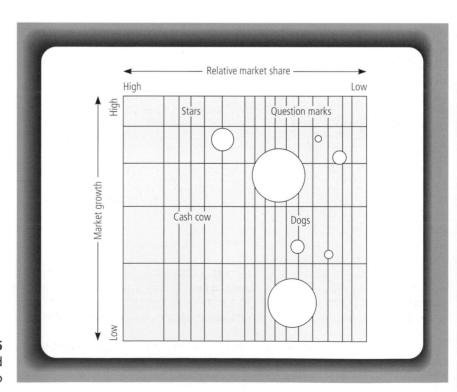

Figure 5.35
Poorly balanced
product portfolio

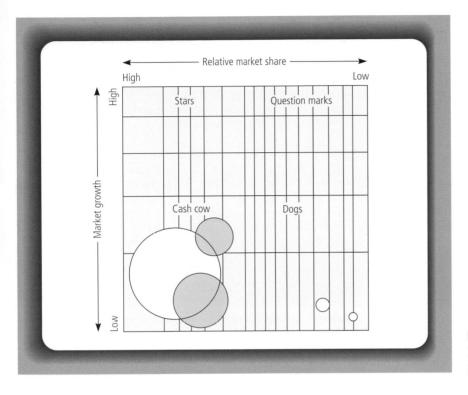

Figure 5.36
Poorly balanced
product portfolio

distributors to the replacement market, except for large customers, who are handled direct.

There is a European marketing organization responsible for strategy in terms of product range development, pricing structures, corporate promotion, etc. Under the European marketing director, it is split into market sector managers (e.g. automotive, electrical machinery, etc.) who develop strategies for their own segments. The European marketing organization reports to the Director-Europe, as do the country general managers, to whom the country sales organizations report.

Early in 2004, a new European marketing director was appointed. His first task was to develop a long-term strategic marketing plan. From a detailed study of past and present performance, he noted that, though historically successful, European market share was hovering at around 28 per cent and that profits, although satisfactory, were mainly stagnant. These results were being caused by lack of growth in some key markets, e.g. automotive, and intensified competition, notably from Japan.

One of the key effects of these market and competitive pressures that he noted as he travelled around Europe was a lack of vision and motivation in the national sales organizations. During the late 1980s/early 1990s, under a policy of decentralization, they had been left largely alone to do the best they could in what were difficult recessionary times.

He concluded that performance could be significantly improved, especially as there were signs that some key segments were becoming buoyant, and he obtained top management approval to develop a long-term plan, 'Going for growth'. The key objective agreed by the board was 'To increase European market share to 35 per cent by the end of the planning period in 3 years'.

In order to achieve this, the European marketing director knew that he would have to look at the product/market portfolio in a different way and to establish realistic strategies in the areas most likely to produce dividends. To help him do this, he decided to construct a directional policy matrix.

As you work through this case study you will observe how the task was tackled. You will appreciate the calculations and the reasons behind decision-making.

The marketing director first set his market research manager the task of selecting SIC (Standard Industrial Classification) categories, based on his current bearing business in order to select those segments best suited for investment. (The governments of most countries keep records of industrial activity under SIC listings. The SIC listings in most countries of the world are comparable for the purpose of comparisons and cross-references.)

His market research manager came up with the information in Table 5.12.

Table 5.12

SIC category	Market size (£ million)	Growth (%)	Competitive intensity	Profitability (%)	Vulnerability
1 Meat-processing	20	12	Low	17	Low
2 Automotive	200	2	High	<10	High
3 Local government	20	4	High	<10	High
4 Food-processing	40	10	Medium	16	Medium
5 Forestry	20	11	Low	20	Medium
6 Electrical	100	0	High	<10	High
7 Agricultural	40	2	Medium	<10	High
8 Chemical	15	15	Low	16	Low

The first stage is to apply the information in Table 5.12, and to establish positions on the vertical scale labelled 'market attractiveness' on the directional policy matrix (DPM). However, before that can be done, some criteria about what constitutes an attractive market for International Bearings have to be established and weighted in terms of their relative importance.

Precisely how this is done is a matter of management judgement, but it is important to follow three golden rules:

1 Never do this in isolation.
2 Make sure your key colleagues are in agreement over the criteria and weightings to be used.
3 Whenever quantitative information, or techniques such as market research, is available, it should be used in preference to opinions, no matter how well founded these opinions might be.

Being aware of these rules, the European marketing director got his marketing team together and they came up with the information in Table 5.13. With this new information available to him, the marketing director was able to begin calculating the market attractiveness 'scores' for different industries.

Table 5.13

Factor	Scoring criteria*			Weighting (%)**
	10–7	*6–3*	*2–1*	
1 Market size (m)	>100	33–100	<33	15
2 Volume growth (units)	>10%	5–9%	<5%	25
3 Competitive intensity	Low	Medium	High	15
4 Profitability	>5%	10–15%	<10%	30
5 Vulnerability	Low	Medium	High	15

* The precise score given is a matter of management judgement.
** The weightings given to each factor are also a matter of management judgement.

From Table 5.12, it will be seen that the market size is £20 m. From Table 5.13, you will see that any category £<33 m is scored in the range 1–2 points, with a weighting of 15, so in this case a score of 1 can be given. It is then multiplied by the weighting of 15 per cent to give a result of 0.15. You will observe from this that you must use your judgement in deciding whether the score should be 1 or 2 (or something in between).

This inevitably means that there will be a range of possible answers. In this case the range could be 0.15 to 0.3.

Bearing this in mind, see if you can complete the market attractiveness scoring for meat-processing in Table 5.14. You can check if your answer is correct by looking at Table 5.15 and comparing your result with that produced by the company.

You will note that the remaining criteria of attractiveness were all high, and, because of that, each carried a score of between 7 and 10. Depending on the actual scores given, the total, after being multiplied by the weighting factor, could fall within the range given in Table 5.15, shown in brackets.

Table 5.14 Meat-processing

	Scoring criteria	Weighting (%)	Total
Market size	1	× 15	= 0.15
Growth	–	× 25	= _____
Competitive intensity	–	× 15	= _____
Profitability	–	× 30	= _____
Vulnerability	–	× 15	= _____
		Total	_____

Table 5.15 Meat-processing

	Scoring criteria	Weighting (%)	Total	
Market size	1	× 15	= 0.15	
Growth	–(7–10)	× 25	= _____	(1.75–2.5)
Competitive intensity	–(7–10)	× 15	= _____	(2.10–3.0)
Profitability	–(7–10)	× 30	= _____	(1.05–1.5)
Vulnerability	–(7–10)	× 15	= _____	(1.05–1.5)
		Total	_____	(6.10–8.65)

It is important that you are clear about how the total market attractiveness score is calculated. If you feel that you would like another opportunity to work at this, see if you can arrive at a score for the automotive industry. All the information you require is in Tables 5.16 and 5.17.

The answer to Table 5.16 is shown in Table 5.17. Again, you will note that there has to be an element of judgement in the scoring.

Table 5.16 Automotive

	Scoring criteria	Weighting (%)	Total
Market size	1	× 15	= _____
Growth	–	× 25	= _____
Competitive intensity	–	× 15	= _____
Profitability	–	× 30	= _____
Vulnerability	–	× 15	= _____
		Total	_____

Table 5.17 Automotive

	Scoring criteria	Weighting (%)	Total	
Market size	–(7–10)	× 15	= _____	(1.05–1.5)
Growth	–(1–2)	× 25	= _____	(0.25–0.5)
Competitive intensity	–(1–2)	× 15	= _____	(0.15–0.3)
Profitability	–(1–2)	× 30	= _____	(0.30–0.6)
Vulnerability	–(1–2)	× 15	= _____	(0.15–0.3)
		Total	_____	(1.90–3.2)

From these two examples, you can see the idea of how the figures are arrived at for *market attractiveness*. As you will see, the final figures are within a minimum and maximum range for each category. For the purpose of this case study, the figures are stated as below:

1 Meat-processing   0.65
2 Automotive   2.35
3 Local government   1.25
4 Food-processing   7.45
5 Forestry   8.05
6 Electrical   2.35
7 Agriculture   2.40
8 Chemical   0.65

Now we will look at how the calculations are made for establishing the relative positions of these markets on the horizontal axis, or *business strengths*, of the DPM.

Two tables, similar to Tables 5.12 and 5.13, are given. The first, Table 5.18, shows factor, scoring criteria, and weighting; and the next, Table 5.19, the marketing team's assessment of the firm's competitive strengths in each of the SIC categories.

Table 5.18

Factor	Scoring criteria*			Weighting (%)**
	10–7	*6–3*	*2–1*	
1 Product advantage	High	Medium	Low	25
2 Image with market	Excellent	Average	Poor	50
3 Ability to supply engineering support	High	Medium	Low	25

*The precise score given is a matter of management judgement.
** The weightings given to each factor are also a matter of management judgement.

Table 5.19 Marketing team's assessment

SIC category	Product advantage	Image	Engineering support
1 Meat-processing	High	Excellent	High
2 Automotive	Low	Excellent	High
3 Local government	Low	Poor	Medium
4 Food-processing	High	Excellent	High
5 Forestry	Low	Poor	Low
6 Electrical	Low	Poor	Low
7 Agricultural	High	Excellent	Medium
8 Chemical	Low	Poor	Medium

Remember the three golden rules still apply:

1 Key colleagues should be in agreement.
2 Do not do this in isolation.
3 Use quantitative techniques to determine criteria whenever available.

There is, of course, a whole range of possible factors which could be viewed as business strengths. However, from International Bearings' point of view, in order to assess the business strengths in each of the eight markets, the marketing director was only concerned with the three key factors given in Table 5.19.

Table 5.19 uses the criteria to assess the firm's competitive strengths. The process to transfer the information from Tables 5.20 and 5.21 is similar to the previous exercise done with Tables 5.12 and 5.13.

Take meat-processing as an example. The product advantage is high in Table 5.19. In Table 5.18, a high assessment may be scored between 7 and 10. The weighting is 25 per cent. You may choose 9 for product advantage, so this, multiplied by the weighting of 25 per cent, gives 2.25 as the score. Table 5.20 shows how the scoring could be completed and the possible range of the end result.

If you would like the practice, work out the score for automotive (Table 5.21). The answer is given in Table 5.22.

Table 5.20 Meat-processing

	Scoring criteria	Weighting (%)		Total
Product advantage	9	× 25	= _____	2.25
Image	–(7–10)	× 50	= _____	(3.5–5.0)
Engineering support	–(7–10)	× 25	= _____	(1.75–2.5)
		Total	_____	(7.0–10)

Table 5.21 Automotive

	Scoring criteria	Weighting (%)		Total
Product advantage	–	× 25	= _____	
Image	–	× 50	= _____	
Engineering support	–	× 25	= _____	
		Total	_____	

Using this technique, the marketing director made the following assessment of the business strengths for the eight product areas:

1 Meat-processing   8.75
2 Automotive   7.75
3 Local government   2.0
4 Food-processing   10.0
5 Forestry   1.0
6 Electrical   1.0
7 Agriculture   9.0
8 Chemical   2.25

Table 5.22 Automotive

	Scoring criteria	Weighting (%)	Total
Product advantage	–(1–2)	× 25	= _____ (0.25–0.50)
Image	–(7–10)	× 50	= _____ (3.5–5.0)
Engineering support	–(7–10)	× 25	= _____ (1.75–8.0)
		Total	_____ (5.5–13.5)

He was now in a position to start plotting the various markets on the directional policy matrix. You will note that, because of the way the scoring and weighting were established, i.e. a maximum of 10 points and the highest weighting being 100 per cent, the highest possible total is 10. Therefore the matrix can be designed with each side being of 10 units' length. Equally, because of this scoring system, 5 represents a genuine mid-point, in the sense that scores above this figure are tending towards the 'more attractive' or 'higher business strengths', whereas those below 5 are, relatively speaking, the poor relations.

The numbers at the intersections refer to the markets as listed above. Thus 1 is meat-processing, 2 automotive and so on (see Figure 5.37).

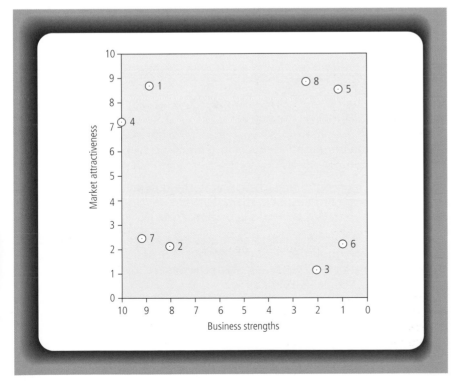

Figure 5.37

The DPM is almost complete. What remains to be done is to indicate the sales volume for each of the markets. This is achieved by drawing a circle proportional to the sales volume at each of the market location points that have just been plotted.

It is often a matter of trial and error to establish the correct basis for drawing these circles. If, for example, the largest sales volume was 1,500 and the smallest was 300, you may decide that every 100 units = 3 mm of diameter. So, 1,500 is shown as 15 units × 3 = 45 mm, and 300 as 3 units × 3 = 9 mm. If this scale is too small or large, then change it to suit the diagram.

This is the sales volume for each category:

SIC	Sales volume
1 Meat-processing	1,500
2 Automotive	1,300
3 Local government	1,000
4 Food-processing	900
5 Forestry	800
6 Electrical	700
7 Agricultural	500
8 Chemical	300

Continuing with the example of 100 units × 3 mm of diameter, we get this representative sales volume for each category:

SIC	Sales volume	Diameter
1 Meat-processing	1,500	45
2 Automotive	1,300	39
3 Local government	1,000	30
4 Food-processing	900	27
5 Forestry	800	24
6 Electrical	700	21
7 Agricultural	500	15
8 Chemical	300	9

Figure 5.38 shows the points representing the sales volume of each category in the correct locations on the matrix.

This form of presentation is superior in terms of the impact and clarity given to the data presentation shown in Tables 5.12, 5.13, 5.18, 5.19. It clearly shows at a glance:

● the relative importance of each market to the business
● the relative attractiveness of each market
● the company's relative strengths in each market.

The same names can be given to each quadrant as are used in the Boston Matrix, although you should note that it is not necessary to give any names at all to each of the boxes. The Boston Matrix names are used here only because you are by now familiar with them.

Faced with the above information, if you were in the marketing director's position, what would be your objectives and strategies for each of the markets?

Write your proposals on a separate piece of paper. When you have completed this task, you can check your answers with those of the marketing director below.

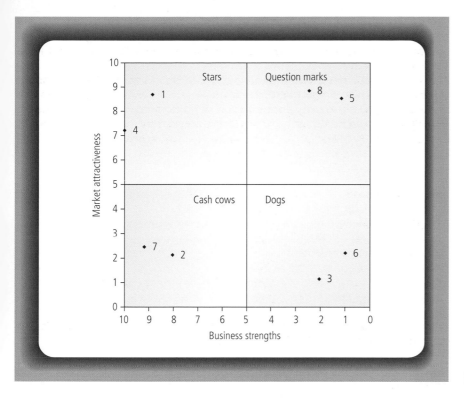

Figure 5.38

Here is how the marketing director of International Bearings used the DPM to arrive at objectives and strategies for each market:

1 In the event, he concentrated much effort on growing the very attractive meat-processing and food-processing segments, because he was well placed to do this and because he was able to add value in so doing. In the next three years, he added a further 2,000 units of very profitable volume to these two segments.

2 Automotive and agriculture were maintained by aggressive pricing whenever he had to in order to keep the business, but he cut down dramatically on costs. In these businesses he succeeded in increasing volume sales from 1,000 to 2,000 units during the next three years. Margins were down, but so were costs.

3 He invested some resources to improve his position in the chemical segment, paying for it by taking money out of the forestry segment. Here he grew his volume from 300 to 700 units.

4 Finally, he did not invest in either local government or electrical, but while he lost market share, with volume dropping from 1,700 to 1,300, he was able to invest some of this revenue in developing a range of bearings for the emerging freezing industry, which promised high margins for the future, i.e. an investment in R&D.

The cumulative result of these strategies was that in Year 3 he had a volume of 9,400 units, i.e. an increase of over 30 per cent, and a well-balanced portfolio of products. There was also the prospect of new business in Europe from the freezing industry.

This case study demonstrates how the DPM can be constructed and used to good effect. Any organization should be able to follow a similar process to that used by International Bearings. The only contentious point is that a company must be clear about how it defines its markets. Any woolly thinking about these will undermine the value of the DPM and will probably generate some downright misleading information.

Anyone with any doubts about market definition would be well advised to look back at Exercise 4.1.

Exercise 5.5

Applying the directional policy matrix to your own organization

Follow these instructions:

1 Choose a product (or group of products) that is bought by many different markets (or segments).
2 List no more than eight of these markets (or segments).
3 Develop a set of criteria for judging:
   ● market attractiveness
   ● your strength in these markets.
4 Develop a scoring and weighting system for these criteria.
5 Evaluate the markets you have chosen, using these criteria.
6 Locate the point of each of these markets on a four-box directional policy matrix.
7 Using an approximate scale of your own choice, make the circle diameter proportional to your current turnover.
8 Comment on the current portfolio.
9 Indicate approximately the size and position of each circle in three years' time.
10 Outline (briefly) the strategies you would pursue to achieve these objectives.

CHAPTER 6

Setting marketing objectives and strategies

Summary

- What marketing objectives are
- How marketing objectives relate to corporate objectives
- How to set marketing objectives
- What competitive strategies are
- How to use competitive strategies to gain competitive advantage
- How to start the process of marketing planning using 'gap analysis'
- New product development as a growth strategy
- What marketing strategies are
- How to set marketing strategies
- Why this step is the most crucial in the marketing planning process
- Exercises to turn the theory into actionable propositions

■ Introduction

From our 'map' of marketing, repeated below as Figure 6.1, we have so far dealt in detail with Box 1, 'Define markets and understand value'.

We also introduced Box 2, 'Determine value proposition' in Chapter 2, when we gave an overview of the marketing planning process.

The purpose of this chapter is to go into some detail about how to set marketing objectives and strategies within the strategic marketing plan and we begin by expanding Box 2, 'Determine value proposition'. The key input to this process is the analysis of customer needs, and the relative attractiveness of different customer segments, which were discussed in detail in Chapters 4 and 5.

Figure 6.1

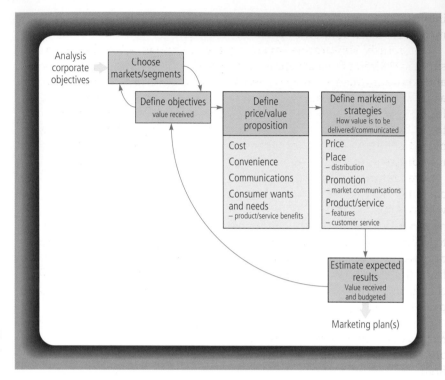

Figure 6.2
Determine value
proposition

The creation of the value proposition to the customer contains five sub-processes, shown in Figure 6.2.

First, using the analysis which flows from the previous process, the range of markets and segments in which the organization is to operate is chosen and prioritized, as explained in Chapters 4 and 5. This will take into account both the market's inherent attractiveness, and the organization's actual and potential ability to meet customer needs within the segment. It will also be shaped by the corporate objectives.

The next two processes define the core of the value proposition to the customer. While they can occur in either order, organizations typically start by defining the value they hope to receive from the segment: 'Define objectives'. This involves defining marketing objectives in terms, for example, of market share, volume, value or contribution by segment, to be discussed in more detail in this chapter.

The other half of the equation is defining the value to be delivered to the customer in return. This price/value proposition can be thought of using the four Cs: 'Cost', 'Convenience', 'Communications' and 'Consumer wants and needs'. These translate the four Ps of marketing from what the organization does to what the customer cares about. For example, the customer is concerned with 'convenience' of purchase, which influences how the organization will 'place' the product through distribution channels. Similarly, instead of 'product', we have 'consumer wants and needs' which are met by the product. Customers are interested in the total 'cost' to them, not necessarily just the upfront 'price'. And finally, 'promotion' translates into two-way 'communications' in which customers declare their require-ments and learn about the organization's offerings.

The fourth sub-process may involve iterations with the third one since, in defining the marketing strategies – how the value is to be delivered and communicated – it may be necessary to reconsider what that value can actually be. We have listed the four major aspects of this process using the four Ps. While separate plans, or plan sections, may be produced for each of these, the decisions are closely intertwined: for example, the choice of distri-bution channel will impact what communications are feasible, what sur-rounding services can be delivered, and what price can be charged.

Some reformulations of the four Ps include others such as 'Provision of customer service', 'People', and 'Processes'. We include customer service within 'Product/service', as it is often difficult to separate the core product or service from surrounding services, but clearly every aspect for the cus-tomer interaction needs to be planned for. 'People' and 'Processes' represent dimensions that certainly need to be planned, but we view them as arising from the consideration of the customer-focused four Ps by asking what changes to people or processes are necessary in order to achieve the desired product offering, price, place or promotions.

Once these issues have been resolved, an estimate of the expected results of the marketing strategies can be made, in terms of the costs to the organization and the impact of the price/value proposition on sales. This final step closes the loop from the original setting of objectives, as it may be that iteration is required if it is considered that the strategies that have been defined are not sufficient to meet the financial objectives.

The output from the 'Determine value proposition' process is typically a strategic marketing plan, or plans, covering a period of at least three years. In some cases, specific plans are produced for aspects of the four Ps, such as a pricing plan, a distribution plan, a customer service plan or a promotions plan. However, even when no plans are produced, the organ-ization is implicitly taking decisions on the offer to the customer and how this offer is to be communicated and delivered. The content of these plans has to be communicated to and agreed with all departments or functions responsible for delivering the customer value spelled out in the plans.

We can now proceed to explain in detail how to set marketing objectives and strategies.

■ Marketing objectives: what they are and how they relate to corporate objectives

There are no works on marketing which do not include at least one para-graph on the need for setting objectives. Setting objectives is a mandatory step in the planning process. The literature on the subject, though, is not very explicit, which is surprising when it is considered how vital the set-ting of ▶ **marketing objectives** is.

▶ **DEFINITION** ◀

A marketing objective is the quantification of what an organization sells (its products) and to whom (its markets)

An objective will ensure that a company knows what its strategies are expected to accomplish and when a particular strategy has accomplished its purpose. In other words, without objectives, strategy decisions and all that follows will take place in a vacuum.

Following the identification of opportunities and the explicit statement of assumptions about conditions affecting the business, the process of setting objectives should, in theory, be comparatively easy, the actual objectives themselves being a realistic statement of what the company desires to achieve as a result of a market-centred analysis, rather than generalized statements borne of top management's desire to 'do better next year'.

> However, objective setting is more complex than at first it would appear to be.

The logical approach to the difficult task of setting objectives is to proceed from the broad to the specific.

Most experts agree that the logical approach to the difficult task of setting marketing objectives is to proceed from the broad to the specific. Thus, the starting point would be a statement of the nature of the business (the mission statement), from which would flow the broad company objectives. Next, the broad company objectives would be translated into key result areas, which would be those areas in which success is vital to the firm. Market penetration and growth rate of sales are examples of key result areas. The third step would be creation of the sub-objectives necessary to accomplish the broad objectives, such as product sales volume goals, geographical expansion, product line extension, and so on.

> The end result of this process should be objectives which are consistent with the strategic plan, attainable within budget limitations, and compatible with the strengths, limitations, and economics of other functions within the organization.

At the top level, management is concerned with long-run profitability; at the next level in the management hierarchy, the concern is for objectives which are defined more specifically and in greater detail, such as increasing sales and market share, obtaining new markets, and so on. These objectives are merely a part of the hierarchy of objectives, in that corporate objectives will only be accomplished if these and other objectives are achieved. At the next level, management is concerned with objectives which are defined even more tightly, such as: to create awareness among a specific target market about a new product; to change a particular customer attitude; and so on. Again, the general marketing objectives will only be accomplished if these and other sub-objectives are achieved.

> It is clear that sub-objectives *per se*, unless they are an integral part of a broader framework of objectives, are likely to lead to a wasteful misdirection of resources.

For example, a sales increase in itself may be possible, but only at an undue cost, so that such a marketing objective is only appropriate within the framework of corporate objectives. In such a case, it may well be that an increase in sales in a particular market sector will entail additional capital expenditure ahead of the time for which it is planned. If this were the case, it may make more sense to allocate available production capacity to more profitable market sectors in the short term, allowing sales to decline in another sector. Decisions such as this are likely to be more easily made against a backcloth of explicitly stated broad company objectives relating to all the major disciplines.

Likewise, objectives should be set for advertising, for example, which are wholly consistent with wider objectives. Objectives set in this way integrate the advertising effort with the other elements in the marketing mix and this leads to a consistent, logical marketing plan.

■ So what is a corporate objective and what is a marketing objective?

A business starts at some time with resources and wants to use those resources to achieve something. What the business wants to achieve is a ▶ corporate objective, which describes a desired destination, or result. Most often this is expressed in terms of profit, since profit is the means of satisfying shareholders or owners, and because it is the one universally accepted criterion by which efficiency can be evaluated, which will, in turn, lead to efficient resource allocation, economic and technological progressiveness and stability. How it is to be achieved is a strategy. In a sense, this means that the only true objective of a company is, by definition, what is stated in the corporate plan as being the principal purpose of its existence.

This means that stated desires, such as to expand market share, to create a new image, to achieve an x per cent increase in sales, and so on, are in fact ▶ strategies at the corporate level, since they are the means by which a company will achieve its profit objectives. In practice, however, companies tend to operate by means of functional divisions, each with a separate identity, so that what is a strategy at the corporate level becomes an objective within each division, or strategic business unit.

> For example, marketing strategies within the corporate plan become operating objectives within the marketing department and strategies at the general level within the marketing department themselves become operating objectives at the next level down, so that an intricate web of interrelated objectives and strategies is built up at all levels within the framework of the overall company plan.

The really important point, however, apart from clarifying the difference between objectives and strategies, is that the further down the hierarchical

▶ **DEFINITION** ◀

A corporate objective describes a desired destination or result. Most often this is expressed in terms of profit

> The only true objective of a company is, by definition, what is stated in the corporate plan as being the principal purpose of its existence.

▶ **DEFINITION** ◀

Corporate strategies define how corporate objectives are to be achieved through the use of its resources

Figure 6.3

chain one goes, the less likely it is that a stated objective will make a cost-effective contribution to company profits, unless it derives logically and directly from an objective at a higher level.

Corporate objectives and strategies can be simplified in the following way:

Corporate objective
- desired level of profitability.

Corporate strategies
- which products and which markets (marketing)
- what kind of facilities (operations, distribution, IT, R&D etc.)
- size and character of the staff/labour force (personnel, finance resource management)
- funding (finance)
- other corporate strategies such as social responsibility, corporate image, stock market image, employee image, etc.

It is now clear that at the next level down in the organization, i.e. at the functional level, what products are to be sold into what markets become *marketing objectives*, while the means of achieving these objectives using the marketing mix are *marketing strategies*. At the next level down, there would be, say, *advertising objectives* and *advertising strategies*, with the subsequent *programmes* and *budgets* for achieving the objectives. In this way, a hierarchy of objectives and strategies can be traced back to the initial corporate objective. Figure 6.3 illustrates this point.

■ How to set marketing objectives

The Ansoff Matrix can be introduced here as a useful tool for thinking about marketing objectives.

A firm's competitive situation can be simplified to two dimensions only – products and markets. To put it even more simply, Ansoff's framework is about what is sold (the 'product'), and who it is sold to (the 'market'). Within this framework, Ansoff identifies four possible courses of action for the firm:

1 Selling existing products to existing markets
2 Extending existing products to new markets
3 Developing new products for existing markets
4 Developing new products for new markets.

The matrix in Figure 6.4 depicts these concepts.

It is clear that the range of possible marketing objectives is very wide, since there will be degrees of technological newness and degrees of market newness. Nevertheless, Ansoff's Matrix provides a logical framework

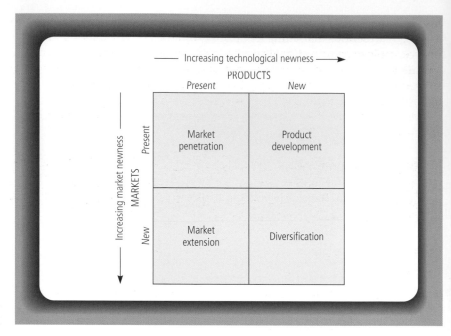

Figure 6.4
Ansoff Matrix

in which marketing objectives can be developed under each of the four main headings above.

> In other words, marketing objectives are about products and markets only.

Common sense will confirm that it is only by selling something to someone that the company's financial goals can be achieved, and that advertising, pricing, service levels, and so on, are the means (or strategies) by which it might succeed in doing this. Thus, pricing objectives, sales promotion objectives, advertising objectives, and the like, should not be confused with marketing objectives.

Marketing objectives are generally accepted as being quantitative commitments, usually stated either in standards of performance for a given operating period, or conditions to be achieved by given dates. Performance standards are usually stated in terms of sales volume or value and various measures of profitability. The conditions to be attained are usually a percentage of market share and various other commitments, such as a percentage of the total number of a given type of distribution outlet.

There is also broad agreement that objectives must be specific enough to enable subordinates to derive from them the general character of action required and the yardstick by which performance is to be judged.

Objectives are the core of managerial action, providing direction to the plans. By asking where the operation should be at some future date, objectives are determined. Vague objectives, however emotionally appealing, are counter-productive to sensible planning, and are usually the result of the

Pricing objectives, sales promotion objectives, advertising objectives, and the like, should not be confused with marketing objectives.

Objectives are the core of managerial action, providing direction to the plans.

human propensity for wishful thinking, which often smacks more of cheerleading than serious marketing leadership. What this really means is that it is unacceptable to use directional terms such as 'improve', 'increase', 'decrease', 'optimize' or 'minimize' as objectives, because it is logical that, unless there is some measure, or yardstick, against which to measure a sense of locomotion towards achieving them, then they do not serve any useful purpose.

Ansoff defines an objective as 'a measure of the efficiency of the resource-conversion process'.

> An objective contains three elements: the particular attribute that is chosen as a measure of efficiency; the yardstick or scale by which the attribute is measured; and the particular value on the scale which the firm seeks to attain.

Marketing objectives, then, are about each of the four main categories of the Ansoff Matrix:

1 *Existing products in existing markets*. These may be many and varied, and will certainly need to be set for all existing major products and customer groups (segments).
2 *New products in existing markets.*
3 *Existing products in new markets.*
4 *New products in new markets.*

Thus, in the long run, it is only by selling something (a 'product') to someone (a 'market') that any firm can succeed in staying in business profitably. Simply defined, product/market strategy means the route chosen to achieve company goals through the range of products it offers to its chosen market segments. Thus the product/market strategy represents a commitment to a future direction for the firm. Marketing objectives, then, are concerned solely with products and markets.

> Marketing objectives are concerned solely with products and markets.

The general marketing *directions* which lead to the above objectives flow, of course, from the life-cycle and portfolio analysis conducted in the audit, and revolve around the following logical decisions:

1 *Maintain*. This usually refers to the 'cash cow' type of product/market and reflects the desire to maintain competitive positions.
2 *Improve*. This usually refers to the 'star' type of product/market and reflects the desire to improve the competitive position in attractive markets.
3 *Harvest*. This usually refers to the 'dog' type of product/market and reflects the desire to relinquish competitive position in favour of short-term profit and cash flow, unless there are sound reasons not to.
4 *Exit*. This also usually refers to the 'dog' type of product/market, also sometimes the 'question mark', and reflects a desire to divest because of a very weak competitive position or because the cost of staying in it is prohibitive and the risk associated with improving its position is too high.
5 *Enter*. This usually refers to a new business area.

The use of pejorative labels like 'dog', 'cash cow', and so on should be avoided.

As already stated, however, great care should be taken not to follow slavishly any set of 'rules' or guidelines related to the above. Also, the use of pejorative labels like 'dog', 'cash cow' and so on should be avoided.

A full list of marketing guidelines as a precursor to objective setting is given in Table 6.1. Figure 6.5 sets out a fuller list which includes guidelines for functions other than marketing. One word of warning, however: such general guidelines should not be followed unquestioningly. They are included more as checklists of questions that should be asked about each major product in each major market *before* setting marketing objectives and strategies.

General guidelines should not be followed unquestioningly.

It is at this stage that the circles in the directional policy matrix can be moved to show their relative size and position in three years' time. You can do this to show, first, where they will be if the company takes no action, and, second, where you would ideally prefer them to be. These latter positions will, of course, become the marketing objectives. Precisely how this is done is shown in Chapter 13. It is, however, the key stage in the marketing planning process.

■ Competitive strategies

At this stage of the planning process, it would be helpful to explain developments in the field of competitive strategies, since an understanding of the subject is an essential prerequisite to setting appropriate marketing objectives.

> One of the principal purposes of marketing strategy is for you to be able to choose the customers, and hence the markets, you wish to deal with.

In this respect, the directional policy matrix discussed in Chapter 5 is particularly useful.

The main components of strategy are:

● the company
● customers
● products/services
● competitors.

So far we have said very little about competitors, although, clearly, if we are to succeed, we need to work hard at developing a sustainable competitive advantage. The important word here is 'sustainable', as temporary advantages can be gained in numerous ways, such as, for example, a price reduction or a clever sales promotion.

If we are to succeed, we need to work hard at developing a sustainable competitive advantage.

Most business people would agree that, as markets mature, the only way to grow the business without diversifying is at the expense of competitors, which implies the need to understand in depth the characteristics of the market and of the main competitors in it. The leading thinker in this field is

Table 6.1 Strategies suggested by portfolio matrix analysis

	Business strengths		
	High		**Low**
High	*Invest for growth* Defend leadership, gain if possible		*Opportunistic* The options are:
	Accept moderate short-term profits and, if necessary, negative cash flow		(i) Move it to the left if resources are available to invest in it
	Consider geographic expansion, product line expansion, product differentiation		(ii) Keep a low profile until funds are available
	Upgrade product development effort		(iii) Divest to a buyer able to exploit the opportunity
	Aggressive marketing posture, viz. selling, advertising, pricing, sales promotion service levels, as appropriate		
Market attractiveness	*Maintain market position, manage for sustained earnings*	*Selective**	*Manage for profit*
	Maintain market position in most successful product lines	Acknowledge low growth	Prune product line aggressively
	Prune less successful product lines, unless necessary to market success	Do not view as a 'marketing' problem	Maximize cash flow
		Identify and exploit growth segments	Minimize market expenditure
	Differentiate products to maintain share of key segments		Maintain or raise prices at the expense of volume
	Limit discretionary marketing expenditure	Emphasize product quality to avoid 'commodity' competition	
	Stabilize prices, except where a temporary aggressive stance is necessary to maintain market share	Systematically improve productivity	(all of these are on the assumption that such products are not essential to market position)
Low		Assign talented managers	

*Selective refers to those products or markets which fall on or near the vertical dividing line in a directional policy matrix.

Main thrust	Invest for growth	Maintain market position, manage for earnings	Selective	Manage for cash	Opportunistic development
Market share	Maintain or increase dominance	Maintain or slightly milk for earnings	Maintain selectively segment	Forgo share for profit	Invest selectively in share
Products	Differentiation – line expansion	Prune less successful Differentiate for key segments	Emphasize product quality Differentiate	Aggressively prune	Differentiation – line expansion
Price	Lead – aggressive pricing for share	Stabilize prices/raise	Maintain or raise	Raise	Aggressive – price for share
Promotion	Aggressive promotion	Limit	Maintain selectively	Minimize	Aggressive marketing
Distribution	Broaden distribution	Hold wide distribution pattern	Segment	Gradually withdraw distribution	Limited coverage
Cost control	Tight control – go for scale economies	Emphasize cost reduction, viz variable costs	Tight control	Aggressively reduce both fixed and variable	Tight – but not at expense of entrepreneurship
Production	Expand, invest (organic acquisition, joint venture)	Maximize capacity utilization	Increase productivity, e.g. specialization/automation	Free up capacity	Invest
R&D	Expand – invest	Focus on specific projects	Invest selectively	None	Invest
Personnel	Upgrade management in key functional areas	Maintain, reward efficiency, tighten organization	Allocate key managers	Cut back organization	Invest
Investment	Fund growth	Limit fixed investment	Invest selectively	Minimize and divest opportunistically	Fund growth
Working capital	Reduce in process – extend credit	Tighten credit – reduce accounts receivable, increase inventory turn	Reduce	Aggressively reduce	Invest

Figure 6.5

Guidelines suggested for different positioning on the directional policy matrix

Michael Porter, of the Harvard Business School, and any reader wishing to explore this vital subject in more depth should refer to his book (*Competitive Strategy*, Free Press, New York, 1980).

Perhaps the best way to summarize this complex subject would be to tell a story.

Imagine three tribes on a small island fighting each other because resources are scarce. One tribe decides to move to a larger adjacent island, sets up camp, and is followed eventually by the other two, who also set up their own separate camps. At first it is a struggle to establish themselves, but eventually they begin to occupy increasing parts of the island until, many years later, they begin to fight again over adjacent land. The more innovative tribal chief, i.e. the one who was first to move to the new island, sits down with his senior warriors and ponders what to do, since none are very keen to move to yet another island. They decide that the only two options are:

1 Attack and go relentlessly for the enemy's territory.
2 Settle for a smaller part of the island and build in it an impregnable fortress.

These two options, i.e. terrain or impregnable fortress (or both), are in fact the same options that face business people as they contemplate competitive strategy. Let's look in turn at each of these options, continuing for a moment longer with the military analogy, and starting with terrain.

Imagine two armies facing each other on a field of battle (depicted by circles). One army has fifteen soldiers in it, the other twelve. Imagine also that they face each other with rifles and all fire one shot at the other at the same time, also that they don't all aim at the same soldier! Figure 6.6 depicts the progress of each side in disposing of the other. It will be seen that after only three volleys, the army on the right has only one soldier remaining, while the army on the left, with eight soldiers remaining, is still a viable fighting unit.

One interesting fact about this story is that the effect observed here is *geometric* rather than *arithmetic*, and is a perfect demonstration of the effect of size and what happens when all things are equal except size. The parallel in industry, of course, is market share.

Just look at what happened in the computer industry when in the 1970s General Electric, Rank Xerox, RCA, ICL and others attacked the giant IBM. The larger competitor was able to win the battle.

So, all things being equal, a company with a larger market share than another should win over a smaller competitor. Or *should* it? Clearly, this is not inevitable, providing the smaller companies take evasive action. Staying with the computer industry, just look at how successful NCR has been with its 'global fortress' strategy (e.g. ATMs for the financial market).

In 1992 and 1993, IBM got caught unawares, with disastrous financial results, by quicker-moving, smarter, smaller competitors. It has now recovered by regrouping and re-segmenting its market, just as Rank Xerox did in the 1970s to recover from the successful entry of the Japanese with small photocopiers. The company has also used its enormous market power and reach to take advantage of the new but substantial markets for services.

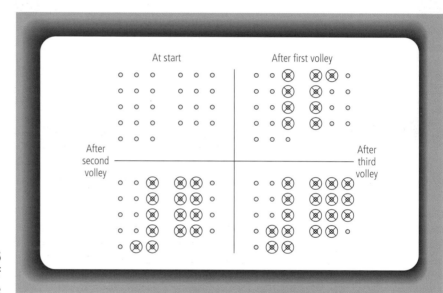

Figure 6.6
The importance of market share

In the banking market, First Direct took a commanding position by means of a differentiated product, dispensing with all the paraphernalia of expensive branches.

In the insurance market, Direct Line has completely changed the rules of warfare by dispensing with brokers, with a consequent saving in premiums for customers.

Put yet another way, look for a moment at the economists' model of supply and demand shown in Figure 6.7. Here we see that when supply is greater than demand, price will fall, and that when demand exceeds supply, the price will tend to rise. The equilibrium point is when supply matches demand. The only way a competitor can avoid the worst effects of such a situation is by taking one of the following actions:

1 Being the lowest-cost supplier
2 Differentiating the product in some way so as to be able to command a higher price.

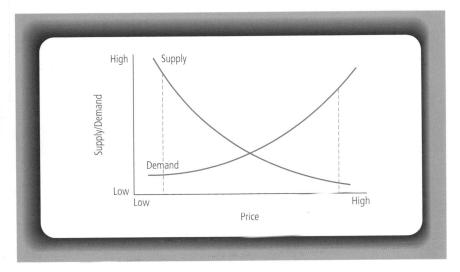

Figure 6.7

Michael Porter combined these two options into a simple matrix, as shown in Figure 6.8. It can be seen that Box 1 represents a sound strategy, particularly in commodity-type markets such as bulk chemicals, where differentiation is harder to achieve because of the identical nature of the chemical make-up of the product. In such cases, it is wise to recognize the reality and pursue a productivity drive with the aim of becoming the lowest-cost producer. It is here that the experience effect described in Chapter 5 becomes especially important.

Many companies, however, such as Mercedes and BMW, could not hope to be the lowest-cost producers. Consequently, their whole corporate philosophy is geared to differentiation and what we have called added value. Clearly, this represents a sensible strategy for any company that cannot hope to be a world cost leader, and indeed many of the world's great companies succeed by means of such a focus (see Box 2). Many of these companies also succeed in pushing themselves into Box 3, the outstanding success box, by occupying what can be called 'global fortresses'. A good example of this is NCR, which dominates the world's banking and retail markets with its focused technological and marketing approach. American Express is another.

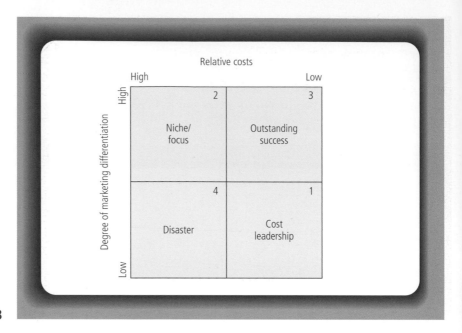

Figure 6.8

Companies like 3M, McDonald's and General Electric, however, typify Box 3, where low costs, differentiation and world leadership are combined in their corporate strategies. Nothing, however, is forever, and readers will be aware of the problems being suffered by McDonald's as a result of the backlash of the health lobby.

Only Box 4 remains. Here we can see that a combination of commodity-type markets and high relative costs will result in disaster sooner or later. A position here is tenable only while demand exceeds supply. When, however, these markets mature, there is little hope for companies who find themselves in this unenviable position.

An important point to remember when thinking about differentiation as a strategy is that you must still be *cost-effective*. It is a myth to assume that sloppy management and high costs are acceptable as long as the product has a good image and lots of added values. Also, in thinking about differentiation, please refer back to the section on benefit analysis in Chapter 4, for it is here that the route to differentiation will be found. It is also clear that there is not much point in offering benefits that are costly for you to provide but which are not highly regarded by customers. So consider using a matrix like the one given in Figure 6.9 to classify your benefits. Clearly, you will succeed best by providing as many benefits as possible that fall into the top right-hand box.

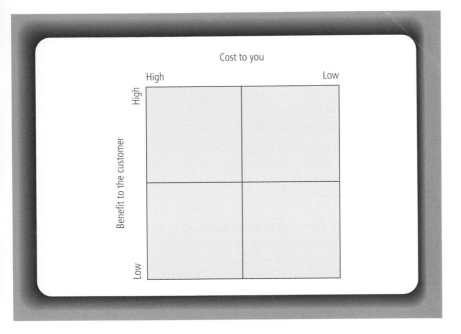

Figure 6.9

ICI is an example of a company that is proactively attempting to change its global strategy by systematically moving away from bulk chemicals in Box 1 (in Figure 6.8) towards speciality chemicals in Box 2 and then going on to occupy a 'global fortress' position in these specialities (Box 3). This, however, is proving extremely difficult in this mature market.

The main point here, however, is that when setting marketing objectives it is essential for you to have a sound grasp of the position in your markets of yourself and your competitors and to adopt appropriate postures for the several elements of your business, all of which *may* be different. It may be necessary, for example, to accept that part of your portfolio is in the 'Disaster' box (Box 4). You may well be forced to have some products here, for example to complete your product range to enable you to offer your more profitable products. The point is that you must adopt an appropriate stance towards these products and set your marketing objectives accordingly, using, where appropriate, the guidelines given in Table 6.1 and Figure 6.5.

Finally, here are some very general guidelines to help you think about competitive strategies:

1   Know the terrain on which you are fighting (the market).
2   Know the resources of your enemies (competitive analysis).
3   Do something with determination that the enemy isn't expecting.

In respect of this last one, the great historian of military strategy, Lanchester, put forward the following equation when applying his findings to industry:

Fighting strength = weapon efficiency (number of men)^2

Let us simplify and summarize this. 'Weapon efficiency' can be elements such as advertising, the sales force, the quality of your products, and so on; '(number of men)^2' is more difficult to explain, but is similar in concept to Einstein's theory of critical mass:

Energy = mass (velocity of light)^2

$E = mc^2$

Let us take as an example the use of the sales force. If your competitor's salesperson calls on an outlet, say, four times a month for six months, he or she will have called twenty-four times. If your salesperson calls eight times a month for six months, he or she will have called forty-eight times. What Lanchester's Square Law says, however, is that the *effect* is considerably more than twice that of your competitor.

An example of this was the Canada Dry attack on the British mixer market. By training the sales force to a high peak of effectiveness (weapon efficiency), and by focusing on specific market segments and out-calling their much larger rival, they were gradually able to occupy particular parts of the market and then move on to the next, until eventually they gained a significant market share. What would have been foolhardy would have been to tackle Schweppes, the market leader, head-on in a major battle. The result would have been similar to the fate of the troops in the Charge of the Light Brigade!

■ Strategic marketing planning: where to start

Understanding the variables

Figure 6.10 illustrates what is commonly referred to as 'gap analysis'.

Essentially, what it says is that if the corporate sales and financial objectives are greater than the current long-range trends and forecasts, there is a gap which has to be filled.

This gap can be filled in six ways:

● by improved productivity (e.g. reduce costs, improve the sales mix, increase prices, reduce discounts, improve the productivity of the sales force and so on)

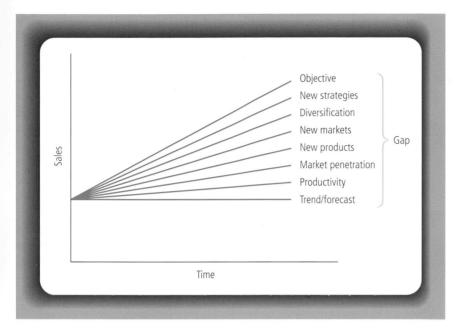

Objective
New strategies
Diversification
New markets
New products
Market penetration
Productivity
Trend/forecast

Figure 6.10

- by market penetration (e.g. increase usage, increase market share)
- by new products
- by new markets (e.g. new user groups, enter new segments, geographical expansion)
- by a combination of new products and markets
- by new strategies (e.g. acquisition, joint ventures, licensing franchising).

Another option, of course, is to reduce the objectives! Gap analysis is best done in two separate steps. Step 1 should be done for sales revenue only so, under the operations gap, above, reducing costs is not relevant as we are only interested in revenue growth. Step 2 should then go through the same stages, but this time looking at the profit and costs implications of achieving the sales growth.

A detailed, step-by-step methodology for completing both steps is given in the exercises at the end of this chapter and in Chapter 13.

If improved productivity is one method by which the profit gap is to be filled, care must be taken not to take measures such as 'to reduce marketing costs by 20 per cent overall'. The portfolio analysis undertaken during the marketing audit stage will indicate that this would be totally inappropriate to some product/market areas, for which increased marketing expenditure may be needed, while for others 20 per cent reduction in marketing costs may not be sufficient.

As for sales growth options, it is clear that productivity improvements and market penetration should always be a company's first option, since it makes far more sense to attempt to increase profits and cash flow from *existing* products and markets initially, because this is usually the least costly and the least risky.

> As for sales growth options, it is clear that market penetration should always be a company's first option.

This is so because, for its present products and markets, a company has developed knowledge and skills which it can use competitively. Associated with this is the growing interest in customer retention and there is now much evidence to show that keeping existing customers can be a source of ever-increasing profits. This is discussed further in Chapter 10.

For the same reason, it makes more sense in many cases to move along the horizontal axis for further growth before attempting to find new markets. The reason for this is that it normally takes many years for a company to get to know its customers and markets and to build up a reputation. That reputation and trust, embodied in either the company's name or in its brands, is not so easily transferable to new markets, where other companies are already entrenched.

The marketing audit should ensure that the method chosen to fill the gap is consistent with the company's capabilities and builds on its strengths.

This is so because, for its present products and markets, a company has developed knowledge and skills which it can use competitively. Associated with this is the growing interest in customer retention and there is now much evidence to show that keeping existing customers can be a source of ever-increasing profits. This is discussed further in Chapter 10.

For the same reason, it makes more sense in many cases to move along the horizontal axis for further growth before attempting to find new markets. The reason for this is that it normally takes many years for a company to get to know its customers and markets and to build up a reputation. That reputation and trust, embodied in either the company's name or in its brands, is not so easily transferable to new markets, where other companies are already entrenched. The famous Wal-Mart entry into Germany is an example of this. For many years they, Wal-Mart, lost hundreds of millions of dollars and was consistently voted Germany's worst supermarket.

The marketing audit should ensure that the method chosen to fill the gap is consistent with the company's capabilities and builds on its strengths.

MARKETING INSIGHT

For example, it would normally prove far less profitable for a dry-goods grocery manufacturer to introduce frozen foods than to add another dry-foods product. Likewise, if a product could be sold to existing channels using the existing sales force, this is far less risky than introducing a new product that requires new channels and new selling skills.

New products should be consistent with the company's known strengths and capabilities. Diversification is the riskiest strategy of all.

Exactly the same applies to the company's operations, distribution and people. Whatever new products are developed should be as consistent as possible with the company's known strengths and capabilities. Clearly, the use of existing operations capacity is generally preferable to new processes. Also, the amount of additional investment is important. Technical personnel are highly trained and specialist, and whether this competence can be transferred to a new field must be considered. A product requiring new raw materials might also require new handling and storage techniques which may prove expensive.

It can now be appreciated why going into new markets with new products (diversification) is the riskiest strategy of all, because *new* resources and *new* management skills have to be developed. This is why the history of commerce is replete with examples of companies which went bankrupt through moving into areas where they had little or no distinctive competence.

MARKETING INSIGHT

This is also why many companies that diversified through acquisition during periods of high economic growth have since divested themselves of businesses that were not basically compatible with their own distinctive competence.

The Ansoff Matrix, of course, is not a simple four-box matrix, for it will be obvious that there are degrees of technological newness as well as degrees of market newness. Figure 6.11 illustrates the point. It also demonstrates more easily why any movement should generally aim to keep a company as close as possible to its present position, rather than moving it to a totally unrelated position, except in the most unusual circumstances.

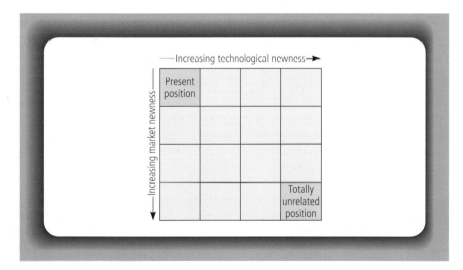

Figure 6.11

Nevertheless, the product life-cycle phenomenon will inevitably *force* companies to move along one or more of the Ansoff Matrix axes if they are to continue to increase their sales and profits. A key question to be asked, then, is *how* is this important decision is to be taken, given the risks involved?

A full list of the possible methods involved in the process of gap analysis is given in Figure 6.12. From this it will be seen that there is nothing an executive can do to fill the gap that is not included in the list. It is worth mentioning again that the precise methodology to implement this concept is given in the final chapter of this book, which provides a marketing planning system.

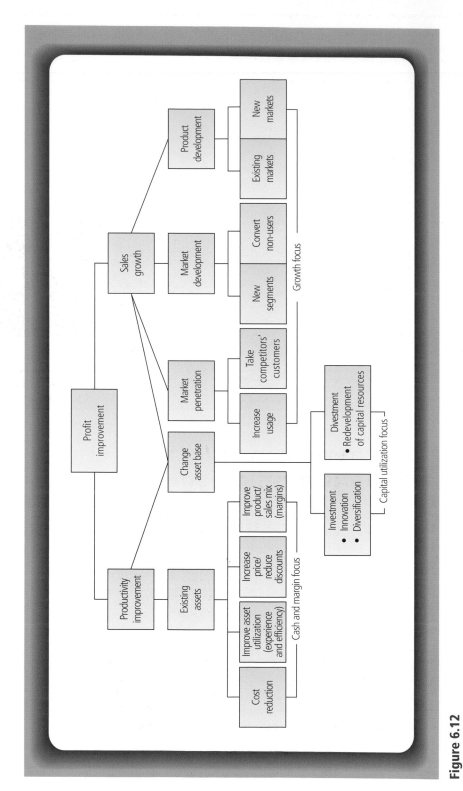

Figure 6.12
Profit/division profit improvement options (after Professor John Saunders, Aston University, used with his kind permission)

At this point, it is important to stress that the 'objectives' point in gap analysis should *not* be an extrapolation, but your own view of what revenue would make this into an excellent business.

MARKETING INSIGHT

The word 'excellent' must, of course, be relative only to comparable businesses. If all the executives in a company responsible for SBUs were to do this, then work out what needed to be done to fill any gaps, it is easy to understand why this would result in an excellent overall business performance. Instead, what often happens is that executives wait until there is a crisis before doing any strategic planning. For many such organizations, alas, during the late 1980s and early 1990s, it was all left too late, and many went bankrupt. In the late 1990s and at the dawn of the new century, countless dotcom businesses jumped on the Internet bandwagon with no properly thought-out strategies, and their demise was inevitable.

One final point to make about gap analysis based on the Ansoff Matrix is that, when completed, the details of exactly *how* to achieve the objectives still need to be worked out. This is the purpose of the strategic marketing plan. So, gap analysis represents a very useful starting point in mapping out the general route, which is why we suggest you start here, rather than going to all the trouble of preparing a strategic marketing plan only to have to change it later. The point is, however, that gap analysis using the Ansoff Matrix is *not* a marketing plan.

Gap analysis using the Ansoff Matrix is *not* a marketing plan.

■ New product development/ market extension/diversification

As stated earlier in this chapter, sooner or later all organizations will need to move along one or both axes of the Ansoff Matrix. How to do this should be comparatively simple if the marketing audit has been completed thoroughly.

It is not the purpose here to explore in detail sub-sets of marketing, such as market research, market selection, new product development, and diversification. What is important, however, in a book on marketing planning is to communicate an understanding of the framework in which these activities should take place.

What we are aiming to do is to maximize *synergy*, which could be described as the 2 + 2 = 5 effect. The starting point is the marketing audit, leading to the SWOT (strengths, weaknesses, opportunities and threats) analyses. This is so that development of any kind will be firmly based on a company's basic *strengths* and *weaknesses*. External factors are the opportunities and threats facing the company.

Once this important analytical stage is successfully completed, the more technical process of opportunity identification, screening, business analysis, and, finally, activities such as product development, testing and entry planning can take place, depending on which option is selected (Figure 6.13 illustrates the process).

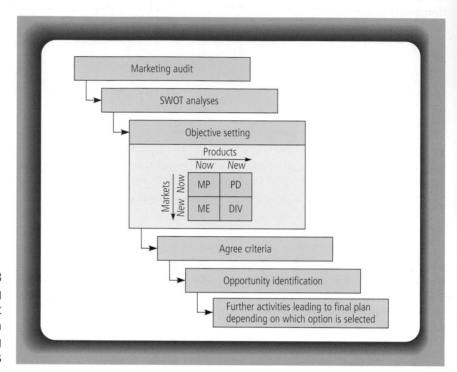

Figure 6.13
Positioning
new product
development in
the marketing
planning process

The important point to remember is that no matter how thoroughly these subsequent activities are carried out, unless the objectives of product development/market extension are based firmly on an analysis of the company's capabilities, they are unlikely to be successful in the long term.

The criteria selected will generally be consistent with the criteria used for positioning products or businesses in the directional policy matrix described in Chapter 5. The list shown in Table 5.2 in Chapter 5, however (which is also totally consistent with the marketing audit checklist), can be used to select those criteria which are most important. A rating and weighting system can then be applied to opportunities identified to assess their suitability or otherwise. Those criteria selected and the weighting system used will, of course, be consistent with the SWOT analyses.

Having said that it is not the purpose of this book to explore in detail any of the sub-sets of marketing such as market research, it would nonetheless be quite useful briefly to outline the process of new product development and its relationship to the gap analysis described above.

After a marketing audit and gap analysis have clarified the place of new product development in a broad company context, the organization must examine the micro-considerations. These involve the range of factors that must be taken into account when a product is assessed in terms of its fit within the product portfolio and its contribution towards objectives.

Figure 6.14 depicts the relationship of the new product development process with the marketing audit and SWOT analyses. New product development can usefully be seen as a process consisting of the following seven steps:

1 *Idea generation* – the search for product ideas to meet company objectives
2 *Screening* – a quick analysis of the ideas to establish those which are relevant
3 *Concept testing* – checking with the market that the new product ideas are acceptable
4 *Business analysis* – the idea is examined in detail in terms of its commercial fit in the business
5 *Product development* – making the idea 'tangible'
6 *Testing* – market tests necessary to verify early business assessments
7 *Commercialization* – full-scale product launch, committing the company's reputation and resources.

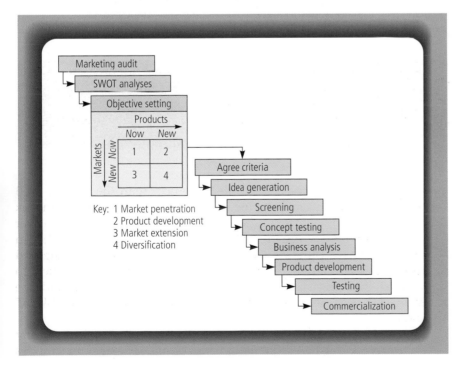

Figure 6.14
The new product development process

■ Marketing strategies

What a company wants to accomplish, in terms of such things as market share and volume, is a marketing objective. How the company intends to go about achieving its objectives is strategy. Strategy is the overall route to the achievement of specific objectives and should describe the means by which objectives are to be reached, the time programme and the allocation of resources. It does not delineate the individual courses the resulting activity will follow.

There is a clear distinction between strategy, and detailed implementation, or tactics.

> ► **Marketing strategy** reflects the company's best opinion as to how it can most profitably apply its skills and resources to the marketplace. It is inevitably broad in scope.

The plan which stems from it will spell out action and timings and will contain the detailed contribution expected from each department.

There is a similarity between strategy in business and strategic military development. One looks at the enemy, the terrain, the resources under command, and then decides whether to attack the whole front, an area of enemy weakness, to feint in one direction while attacking in another, or to attempt an encirclement of the enemy's position. The policy and mix, the general direction in which to go, and the criteria for judging success, all come under the heading of strategy. The action steps are tactics.

Similarly, in marketing, the same commitment, mix and type of resources as well as guidelines and criteria that must be met, all come under the heading of strategy.

For example, the decision to use distributors in all but the three largest market areas, in which company salespeople will be used, is a strategic decision. The selection of particular distributors is a tactical decision.

The following headings indicate the general content of strategy statements in the area of marketing which emerge from marketing literature:

1 Policies and procedures relating to the products to be offered, such as number, quality, design, branding, packaging, positioning and labelling, etc.
2 Pricing levels to be adopted, margins and discount policies
3 Advertising, sales promotion, direct mail, call centres and the Internet, along with the mix of these, the creative approach, the type of media, type of displays, the amount to spend, etc.
4 What emphasis is to be placed on personal selling, the sales approach, sales training, etc.
5 The distributive channels to be used and the relative importance of each
6 Service levels, etc., in relation to different segments.

Strategy is the route to achievement of specific objectives and describes how objectives will be reached.

► **DEFINITION** ◄

Marketing strategies are the means by which a company achieves its marketing objectives and are usually concerned with the four Ps

Thus, marketing strategies are the means by which marketing objectives will be achieved and are generally concerned with the four major
elements of the marketing mix.

These are:

Product   The general policies for product branding, positioning,
              deletions, modifications, additions, design, packaging, etc.

Price   The general pricing policies to be followed for product
              groups in market segments

Place   The general policies for channels and customer service
              levels

Promotion   The general policies for communicating with customers
              under the relevant headings, such as: advertising, sales
              force, sales promotion, public relations, exhibitions, direct
              mail, call centres, the Internet, etc.

The following list of marketing strategies (in summary form), covers the
majority of options open under the headings of the four Ps:

1 *Product*

- expand the line
- change performance, quality or features
- consolidate the line
- standardize design
- positioning
- change the mix
- branding.

2 *Price*

- change price, terms or conditions
- skimming policies
- penetration policies.

3 *Promotion*

- change advertising or promotion
- change the mix between direct mail, call centres, the Internet
- change selling.

4 *Place*

- change delivery or distribution
- change service
- change channels
- change the degree of forward or backward integration.

> Chapters 7–10 are devoted to a much more detailed consideration of promotion, pricing, service and distribution. These chapters describe what should appear in advertising and sales promotion, sales, pricing and place plans. This detail is intended for those whose principal concern is the preparation of a detailed one-year operational or tactical plan.

The relationship of these chapters to the strategic plan is in the provision of information to enable the planner to delineate broad strategies under the headings outlined above. There is no chapter specifically on product management because all the product options have been covered already, particularly in Chapter 5 in the discussion on the product audit.

There are further steps in the marketing planning process before detailed programmes are put together. These are estimating in broad terms the cost of the strategies, and delineating alternative plans. Both of these steps will be covered in more detail in Chapter 11.

Here are some guidelines on what to do in a recession. While not specifically concerned with marketing objectives and strategies, all economies suffer an unexpected downturn from time to time. These guidelines are intended to help managers in such difficult times.

■ Marketing in a downturn

It is pure fiction to imagine that any recession that is happening in America will not affect Western Europe.

The typical reaction to such misfortune is what Andrew Lorenz describes as 'anorexia industrialosa': an excessive desire to be leaner and fitter, leading to emaciation and eventually death. But such a pathetically inadequate response to recession today is doomed to failure, largely because it results in even worse service to customers, and customers just will not stand for this any more.

The rules of competition have changed. The 'make and sell' model has been killed off by a new wave of entrepreneurial technology-enabled competitors unfettered by the baggage of legacy bureaucracy, assets, cultures and behaviours. The processing of information about products has been separated from the products themselves, and customers can now search for and evaluate them independently of those who have a vested interest in selling them. Customers now have as much information about suppliers as suppliers have traditionally accumulated about their customers. *This new state has created a new dimension of competition based on who most effectively acts in the customers' interests.*

On top of these pressures, a new wave of business metrics, such as shareholder value added and balanced scorecards, together with pressure from institutional shareholders to report meaningful facts about corporate performance rather than the traditional, high-level financial reporting that appears every year in corporate accounts, are forcing business leaders to re-examine tired corporate behaviours such as cost-cutting and down-sizing as a route to profitability in recessionary times.

The differing fortunes of Tesco and Marks & Spencer in the UK tell a fascinating story: how can one get it so spectacularly right, the other so dramatically wrong?

Tesco's focus on customers is absolute. Its core purpose, 'to continually increase customer value to earn their lifetime loyalty', is not just a slogan, as so many mission statements are, but actually represents the way the company thinks and acts. It strives constantly to delight its customers with innovative product and service offerings. Marks & Spencer, on the other hand, is a stark reminder of what happens when you take your eye off the customer ball. Only in recent years did it start accepting credit cards and introducing changing booths. So far did the fortunes of the once blue chip M&S fall, that there was at one stage serious doubt about its long-term future.

In a market-driven company such as Tesco, the chief executive and board instil marketing disciplines throughout its core processes and foster cross-functional working, thereby encouraging everyone to focus on the customer.

In times of recession, marketing should be even more centre stage. All that will work is a company-wide focus on market segments and customers with whom we want to work in the long term.

Nonetheless, here are some guidelines for managing in a recession, based on the above:

1 Remember that customers are attracted by promises, but are retained through satisfaction. This means that if you can't describe the value required by customers, you certainly will not be able to deliver it. So, make a special point of understanding their needs.
2 Do not try to cover too many markets, segments and customers. Focus on the ones you want to be with in the long term.
3 Reduce your product portfolio, i.e. do you have too many products, services, pack sizes, etc.?
4 Look carefully at your distribution network. Has it grown too big?
5 Improve the productivity of all your promotional spend, but especially that of the sales force.
6 Get your costs down in unproductive areas of the business. This includes costs associated with serving unprofitable markets and customers.
7 Work out your banker (key) customers. Take them away from the sales force and give one to each of your best managers.
8 Don't let the sales force do big deals – within days *everyone* will have maximum discounts.
9 Selectively attack (focus on) competitors' key customers that are attractive to you. Don't worry if you lose some of your own unprofitable customers.
10 Keep the heart of the business – key products, key markets and key customers.

Above all, follow model 2 rather than model 1 in Figure 6.15.

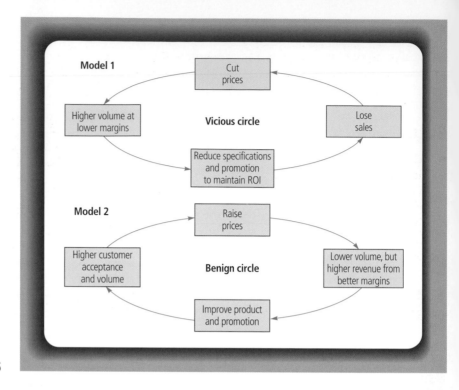

Figure 6.15

■ Marketing objectives, strategies and profitability

Finally, guidelines follow on the *profitability* aspects of setting marketing objectives and strategies.

It is strongly advised, however, that you consult your accountant when considering this section, as the methodology described is quite complex and the implications are very profound for the total organization.

Valuing key market segments

Background/facts

- Risk and required return are positively correlated, i.e. as risk increases, investors expect a higher return.
- Risk is measured by the volatility in expected returns, i.e. the likelihood of making a very good return or losing money. This can be described as the quality of returns.
- All assets are defined as having future value to the organization. Hence assets to be valued include not only tangible assets, like plant and machinery, but intangible assets, such as key market segments.
- The present value of future cash flows is one of the most acceptable methods to value assets including key market segments.

- The present value is increased by:
  - increasing the future cash flows
  - making the future cash flows 'happen' earlier
  - reducing the risk in these cash flows, i.e. improving the certainty of these cash flows (hence the required return).

Suggested approach

- Identify your key market segments. It is helpful if they can be classified on a vertical axis (a kind of thermometer) according to their attractiveness to your company. 'Attractiveness' usually means the potential of each for growth in your profits over a period of between three and five years and according to your relative competitive strengths in each. This will produce a directional policy matrix as detailed in Chapter 5 (see Figure 6.16).

Figure 6.16

- Based on your current experience and planning horizon that you are confident with, make a projection of future net free cash in-flows from your segments. It is normal to select a period such as three or five years. These calculations will consist of three parts:
  - revenue forecasts for each year
  - cost forecasts for each year
  - net free cash flow for each segment for each year.

- Identify the key factors that are likely to either increase or decrease these future cash flows. These factors are likely to be assessed according to the following factors:
  - the riskiness of the product/market segment relative to its position on the Ansoff Matrix
  - the riskiness of the marketing strategies to achieve the revenue and market share
  - the riskiness of the forecast profitability (e.g. the cost forecast accuracy).
- Now re-calculate the revenues, costs and net free cash flows for each year, having adjusted the figures using the risks (probabilities) from the above.
- Ask your accountant to provide you with the overall SBU cost of capital and capital used in the SBU. This will not consist only of tangible assets. Thus, £1,000,000 capital at a required shareholder rate of return of 10 per cent would give £100,000 as the minimum return necessary.
- Deduct the proportional cost of capital from the net free cash flow for each segment for each year.
- An aggregate positive net present value indicates that you are creating shareholder value – i.e. achieving overall returns greater than the weighted average cost of capital, having taken into account the risk associated with future cash flows.

For a full explanation of the above methodology, see *Marketing Due Diligence – Reconnecting strategy to share price*, by McDonald, Smith and Ward (Butterworth-Heinemann, Oxford, 2005).

■ Conclusion

Formulating marketing strategies is one of the most critical and difficult parts of the entire marketing process.

Formulating marketing strategies is one of the most critical and difficult parts of the entire marketing process. It sets the limit of success. Communicated to all management levels, it indicates what strengths are to be developed, what weaknesses are to be remedied, and in what manner.

> Marketing strategies enable operating decisions to bring the company into the right relationship with the emerging pattern of market opportunities which previous analysis has shown to offer the highest prospect of success.

Before proceeding to describe the next stage of marketing planning, i.e. the construction of actual working plans, it should be stressed that the vital phase of setting objectives and strategies is a highly complex process which, if done badly, will probably result in considerable misdirection of resources.

This chapter has confirmed the need for setting clear, definitive objectives for all aspects of marketing, and that marketing objectives themselves have to derive logically from corporate objectives. The advantages of this practice are that it allows all concerned with marketing activities to concentrate their particular contribution on achieving the overall marketing objectives, as well as facilitating meaningful and constructive evaluation of all marketing activity.

For the practical purpose of marketing planning, it will be apparent from the observations above, concerning what was referred to as a hierarchy of objectives, that overall marketing objectives have to be broken down into sub-objectives which, taken all together, will achieve the overall objectives. By breaking down the overall objectives, the problem of strategy development becomes more manageable, hence easier.

A two-year study of thirty-five top industrial companies by McKinsey and Company revealed that leader companies agreed that product/market strategy is the key to the task of keeping shareholders' equity rising. Clearly, then, setting objectives and strategies in relation to products and markets is a most important step in the marketing planning process.

MARKETING INSIGHT

Once agreement has been reached on the broad marketing objectives and strategies, those responsible for programmes can now proceed to the detailed planning stage, developing the appropriate overall strategy statements into sub-objectives

Plans constitute the vehicle for getting to the destination along the chosen route, or the detailed execution of the strategy. The term 'plan' is often used synonymously in marketing literature with the terms 'programme' and 'schedule'. A plan containing detailed lists of tasks to be completed, together with responsibilities, timing and cost, is sometimes referred to as an appropriation budget, which is merely a detailing of the actions to be carried out and of the expected financial results in carrying them out. More about this in Chapters 7–10.

> Those readers who believe they already know enough about promotion, place and pricing, and who are principally concerned with the preparation of a strategic marketing plan can go straight to Chapter 11.

■ Application questions

1 Critically analyse your company's corporate objectives.
2 Critically analyse your company's corporate strategies.
3 Critically analyse your company's marketing objectives.
4 Critically analyse your company's marketing strategies.
5 Has there been any product/market extension during the past ten years which has not been compatible with your company's distinctive competence? If so, state why.
6 Draw up criteria for product/market extension which *are* compatible with your company's distinctive competences.

Chapter 6 review

Corporate objective

This is the desired level of profit the organization seeks to achieve. The *corporate strategy* for doing this covers:

1 Which products and which markets (marketing)
2 What facilities are required (e.g. operations, distribution)
3 The number and character of employees (personnel)
4 What funding is required and how (finance)
5 Social responsibility, corporate image, etc. (other corporate strategies).

Gap analysis

Gap analysis explores the shortfall between the corporate objective and what can be achieved by various strategies.

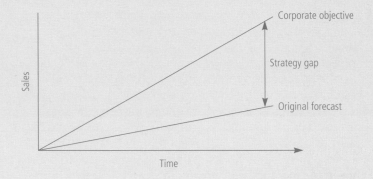

The *operations gap* can be filled by reducing costs, improving the sales mix, increasing market share.

The *strategy gap* can be filled by finding new user groups, entering new segments, geographical expansion, new product development, diversification.   *Try Exercise 6.1*

The marketing audit

This is the systematic collection of data and information about the external environment and about your own company's operations.   *Try Exercise 6.2*

The SWOT analyses

These summarize the marketing audit, which lists:

■ *Internally*, the company's strengths and weaknesses
■ *Externally*, the opportunities and threats facing the company.

Each SWOT analysis should provide strong evidence about what the company should and should not try to set as marketing objectives. It should use strengths to exploit opportunities, while minimizing threats and weaknesses.   *Try Exercises 6.3, 6.4 and 6.5*

Marketing objectives

These are concerned with what is sold (products) and to whom it is sold (markets). There are four possible combinations of products and markets (Ansoff Matrix).

An objective contains three elements:

1   The attribute chosen for measurement, e.g. sales, market share
2   The particular value selected, e.g. 25 per cent market share
3   For a given operating period, e.g. by the end of Year 3.

The matrix suggests four main categories of objectives:

A = market penetration
B = product development
C = market extension
D = diversification.   *Try Exercise 6.6*

Marketing strategies

There are four broad strategies:

1   To invest and grow
2   To extract earnings selectively
3   To harvest
4   To divest.

There are also more specific marketing strategies concerning the four Ps:

1 *Product*
   - expand range
   - improve quality or features
   - consolidate range
   - standardize design
   - reposition product
   - change the mix
   - branding.

2 *Price*
   - change price
   - change terms and conditions
   - penetration policy
   - skimming policy.

3 *Promotion*
   - change advertising
   - change promotion
   - change the mix between call centres, direct mail and the Internet
   - change selling
   - change overall communication mix.

4 *Place*
   - change channels
   - change delivery or distribution
   - change service levels
   - forward or backward integration.

Try Exercise 6.7

Questions raised for the company

1 Q: Who should set the marketing objectives and strategies?
   A: Usually they would be formulated by the marketing director, but they must be agreed at the highest level in the company so that there is genuine commitment to them.

2 Q: Is diversification really a viable objective, bearing in mind the risk in moving into the unknown?
   A: It depends how strong the *factual* evidence is for this step. Clearly it is not a decision to be taken lightly.

3 Q: How secret should marketing objectives and strategies be? Should staff at lower levels know what they are?
   A: Staff are much more committed to a company which 'knows where it is going'. Ideally, subordinates should be given the necessary information to understand their job context.

4 Q: What happens if we get our marketing objectives and strategies wrong?
   A: If the process used for arriving at them was based on facts, the chances are they will not be wrong. Clearly it will be essential to monitor progress and take corrective action when required.

EXERCISES

In these exercises, the most critical part of the marketing planning process will be tackled.

Exercise 6.1 is concerned with carrying out a gap analysis.

Exercise 6.2 is concerned with collecting relevant data about your company and subjecting this to a hard-hitting examination, in summary form, of the opportunities and threats facing your organization.

Exercise 6.3 is concerned with competitor analysis, which clearly is an important part of a marketing audit.

Exercise 6.4 is concerned with carrying out a SWOT analysis.

Exercise 6.5 looks at the assumptions that are made before setting marketing objectives. Clearly, such assumptions should be kept to a minimum, but it is useful to be under no misapprehension regarding what they are, and, just as importantly, the risks attached to making such assumptions.

Exercise 6.6 gets to the heart of the matter and is concerned with setting marketing objectives, while Exercise 6.7 addresses the issue of selecting the most appropriate marketing strategies to match the chosen objectives.

Introduction to Chapter 6 exercises

Revenue
You are asked to complete this two-part exercise. The first part is concerned with *revenue*, the second with *profit*.

Objective
Start by plotting the sales position you wish to achieve at the end of the planning period, point E (Figure 6.17). Next plot the forecast position, point A.

Exercise 6.1
Gap analysis

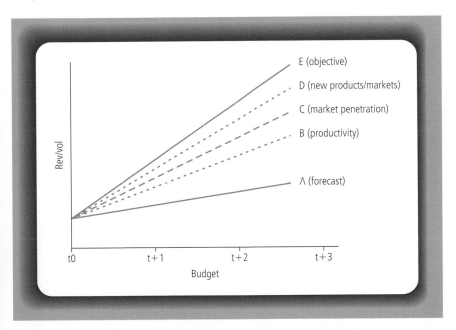

Figure 6.17

Productivity
Are there any actions you can take to close the gaps under the headings in Table 6.2, point B? (These represent cash and margin focus.)

Table 6.2	
Productivity (NB: not all factors are mutually exclusive)	*Revenue*
Better product mix (1)	
Better customer mix (2)	
More sales calls (3)	
Better sales calls (4)	
Increase price	
Reduce discounts	
Charge for deliveries	
Total	

Ansoff product/market (market penetration)
List principal products on the horizontal axis (in Figure 6.18) and principal markets on the vertical axis. In each smaller square, write in current sales and achievable sales during the planning period.

Figure 6.18

Next, plot the market penetration position, point C (Figure 6.17). This point will be the addition of all the values in the right-hand half of the small boxes in the Ansoff Matrix. Please note, revenue from (1), (2), (3) and (4) from the productivity box should be deducted from the market penetration total before plotting point C.

Ansoff product/market matrix (new products/new markets)
Next, list the value of any new products you might develop which you might sell to existing markets (Figure 6.19). Alternatively, or as well, if necessary, list the value of any existing products that you might sell to new markets. Plot the total value of these on Figure 6.17, point D.

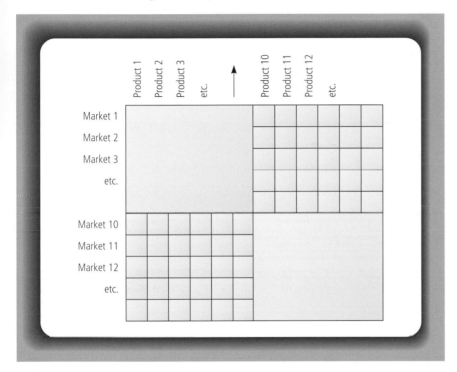

Figure 6.19

Diversification
List the value of any new products you might develop for new markets until point E is reached. (Steps 3, 4 and 5 represent a sales growth focus.)

Capital utilization
If none of this gives the required return on investment, consider changing the asset base. This could be:

(A) Acquisition
(B) Joint venture.

Profit
Objective
Start by plotting the profit position you wish to achieve at the end of the planning period, point E (Figure 6.20).
Next plot the forecast profit position, point A.

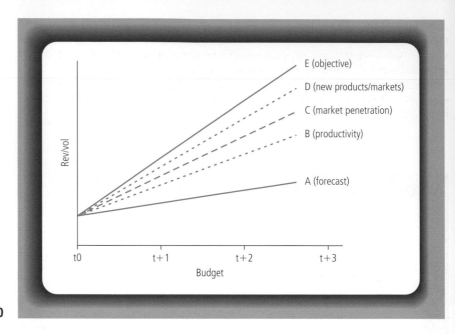

Figure 6.20

Productivity
Are there any actions you can take to close the gap under the headings in Table 6.3? Plot the total profit value of these in Figure 6.20, point B. (These represent cash and margin focus.)

Table 6.3	
Productivity (NB: not all factors are mutually exclusive)	*Profit*
Better product mix	
Better customer mix	
More sales calls	
Better sales calls	
Increase price	
Reduce discounts	
Charge for deliveries	
Reduce debtor days	
Cost reduction	
Others (specify)	
Total	

Ansoff product/market (market penetration)
List principal products on the horizontal axis in Figure 6.20 and principal markets on the vertical axis. In each smaller square, write in current profit and achievable profit value during the planning period.

Next plot the market penetration position, point C, Figure 6.20. This point will be the addition of all the values in the right-hand half of the small boxes in the Ansoff Matrix (Figure 6.21).

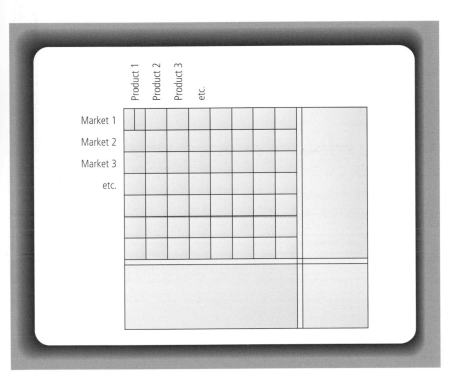

Figure 6.21

Ansoff product/market matrix (new products/new markets)
Next, list the value of any new products you might develop which you might sell to existing markets (Figure 6.22). Alternatively, or as well, if necessary, list the value of any existing products that you might sell to new markets. Plot the total profit value of these on Figure 6.20, point D.

Diversification
List the profit value of any new products you might develop for new markets until point E is reached. (Steps 3, 4 and 5 represent a sales growth focus.)

Capital utilization
If none of this gives the required return on investment, consider changing the asset base. This could be:

(A) Acquisition
(B) Joint venture.

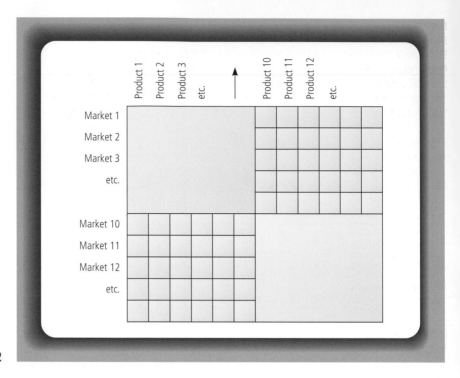

Figure 6.22

Exercise 6.2
The marketing audit

Stage 1 Collecting the data

All the earlier exercises in this book have been designed to improve your understanding of aspects of marketing planning and to discover information about your company and/or its key products and markets. If you completed all the preceding exercises, you should by now be in possession of a fairly comprehensive marketing audit of your organization. However, since every business is in some ways unique, there is a chance that an important piece of information might have been missed. The marketing audit checklist which follows is provided as a safeguard against this happening. (For convenience this is repeated from Chapter 2.)

Use this list to decide whether there is any additional information you would want to add to that you have already collected. When you have completed assembling as much information as you can, you are in a position to progress to Stage 2 of this exercise.

The marketing audit checklist

The following is a list of factors that can affect some businesses. You should only be interested in those that will affect your particular business.

This list doesn't claim to be exhaustive, but it is intended to provide fair coverage of most areas, thereby acting as a guide and stimulus.

External audit

Business and economic environment
Economic
Political/fiscal/legal
Social/cultural
Technological
Intra-company

The market
Total market, size, growth and trends
    (value/volume)
Market characteristics, developments
    and trends
    Products
    Prices
    Physical distribution
    Channels
    Customers/consumers
    Communication
    Industry practices

Competition
Major competitors
Size
Market shares/coverage
Market standing/reputation
Production capabilities
Distribution policies
Marketing methods
Extent of diversification
Personnel issues
International links
Profitability
Key strengths and weaknesses

Internal audit

Marketing operational variables
Own company
Sales (total, by geographical location,
    by industrial type, by customer,
    by product)
Market shares
Profit margins/costs
Marketing procedures
Marketing organization

Marketing information/research
Marketing mix variables, as
    follows:
    Product management
    Price
    Distribution
    Promotion

The marketing audit checklist (fuller details)
EXTERNAL (opportunities and threats)
Business and economic environment

Economic	Inflation, unemployment, energy, price, volatility, materials availability, etc.	as they affect your business
Political/fiscal/ legal	Nationalization, union legislation, human rights legislation, taxation, duty increases, regulatory constraints (e.g. labelling, product quality, packaging, trade practices, advertising, pricing, etc.)	as they affect your business
Social/cultural	Education, immigration, emigration, religion, environment, population distribution and dynamics (e.g. age distribution, regional distribution, etc.), changes in consumer lifestyle, etc.	as they affect your business
Technological	Aspects of product and/or production technology which could profoundly affect the economics of the industry (e.g. new technology, the Internet, cost savings, materials, components, equipment, machinery, methods and systems, availability of substitutes, etc.)	as they affect your business
Intra-company	Capital investment, closures, strikes, etc.	as they affect your business

The market

Total market

Size, growth, and trends (value, volume)

Customers/consumers: changing demographics, psychographics and purchasing behaviour

Market characteristics, developments and trends

Products: principal products bought; end-use of products; product characteristics (weights, measures, sizes, physical characteristics, packaging, accessories, associated products, etc.)

Prices: price levels and range; terms and conditions of sale; normal trade practices; official regulations; etc.

Physical distribution: principal method of physical distribution

Channels: principal channels; purchasing patterns (e.g. types of product bought, prices paid, etc.); purchasing ability; geographical location; stocks; turnover; profits; needs; tastes; attitudes; decision-makers, bases of purchasing decision; etc.

Communication: principal methods of communication, e.g. the Internet, sales force, advertising, direct response, exhibitions, public relations, etc.

Industry practices: e.g. trade associations, government bodies, historical attitudes, interfirm comparisons, etc.

Competition

Industry structure: make-up of companies in the industry, major market standing/reputation; extent of excess capacity; production capability; distribution capability; marketing methods; competitive arrangements; extent of diversification into other areas by major companies in the industry; new entrants; mergers; acquisitions; bankruptcies; significant aspects; international links; key strengths and weaknesses

Industry profitability: financial and non-financial barriers to entry; industry profitability and the relative performance of individual companies; structure of operating costs; investment; effect on return on investment of changes in price; volume; cost of investment; source of industry profits; etc.

INTERNAL (strengths and weaknesses)
Own company
Sales (total, by geographical location, by industrial type, by customer, by product)
Market shares
Profit margins
Marketing procedures
Marketing organization
Sales/marketing control data
Marketing mix variables as follows:

Market research	Samples
Product development	Exhibitions
Product range	Selling
Product quality	Sales aids
Unit of sale	Point of sale
Stock levels	Advertising
Distribution	Sales promotion
Dealer support	Public relations
Pricing, discounts, credit	After-sales service
Packaging	Training

Operations and resources

Marketing objectives
Are the marketing objectives clearly stated and consistent with marketing and corporate objectives?

Marketing strategy
What is the strategy for achieving the stated objectives? Are sufficient resources available to achieve these objectives? Are the available resources sufficient and optimally allocated across elements of the marketing mix?

Structure
Are the marketing responsibilities and authorities clearly structured along functional, product, end-user, and territorial lines?

Information system
Is the marketing intelligence system producing accurate, sufficient and timely information about developments in the marketplace? Is information gathered being used effectively in making marketing decisions?

Planning system
Is the marketing planning system well conceived and effective?

Control system
Do control mechanisms and procedures exist within the group to ensure planned objectives are achieved, e.g. meeting overall objectives, etc.?

Functional efficiency
Are internal communications within the group effective?

Interfunctional efficiency
Are there any problems between marketing and other corporate functions? Is the question of centralized versus decentralized marketing an issue in the company?

Profitability analysis
Is the profitability performance monitored by product, served markets, etc. to assess where the best profits and biggest costs of the operation are located?

Cost-effectiveness analysis
Do any current marketing activities seem to have excess costs? Are these valid or could they be reduced?

Stage 2 SWOT analyses

From the above list you will see that the *external factors* are the sources of all opportunities or threats, whereas the *internal factors* reflect the company's strengths or weaknesses.

In respect of *external factors (opportunities and threats)*, try the following exercise:

Step 1	List the principal *opportunities* (we suggest no more than twenty)
Step 2	Allocate a code to each of these (e.g. A, B, C, etc.)
Step 3	Allocate a number between 1 and 9 to each of them; the number 1 would mean that in your view there is little chance of a particular opportunity occurring within the planning timescale (say three years), while a 9 would mean that there is a high probability of it occurring within the planning timescale
Step 4	Allocate a number between 1 and 9 to indicate the importance of the *impact* each of these opportunities would have on the organization, were it to occur

Step 5 Now put each of your *opportunities* on the *opportunities matrix* (Figure 6.23)

Step 6 You will now have a number of points of intersection which should correspond to your coding system

Step 7 All those in the top left box should be tackled in your marketing objectives and should appear in your SWOT analysis (Exercise 6.4). All the others, while they should not be ignored, are obviously less urgent. The whole exercise should now be repeated for *threats*, using the matrix in Figure 6.24.

Figure 6.23
Opportunities
matrix

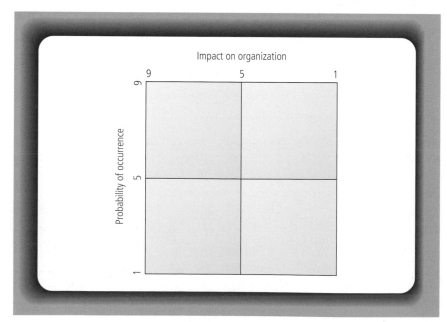

Figure 6.24
Threats matrix

Exercise 6.3 is concerned with summarizing the information gathered about your opportunities and threats in your marketing audit in a more usable format, in the SWOT analysis.

Before moving on to the SWOT analysis (Exercise 6.4), complete the competitor analysis table (Table 6.4) in order to help you to rate yourself more accurately against your competitors.

Guidelines for completing Table 6.4 are given below.

Exercise 6.3
Competitor
analysis

Table 6.4 Competitor analysis

Main competitor	Products/ markets	Business direction and current objectives and strategies	Strengths	Weaknesses	Competitive position

Guide to competitive position classifications

Leadership	● Has major influence on performance or behaviour of others
Strong	● Has a wide choice of strategies
	● Able to adopt independent strategy without endangering short-term position. Has low vulnerability to competitors' actions
Favourable	● Exploits specific competitive strength, often in a product-market niche
	● Has more than average opportunity to improve position; several strategies available
Tenable	● Performance justifies continuation in business
Weak	● Currently unsatisfactory performance; significant competitive weakness
	● Inherently a short-term condition; must improve or withdraw

The following list includes five business directions that are appropriate for almost any business. Select those that best summarize the competitor's strategy.

Business directions

1 *Enter* – allocate resources to a new business area. Consideration should include building from prevailing company or unit strengths, exploiting related opportunities and defending against perceived threats. It may mean creating a new industry.

2 *Improve* – to apply strategies that will significantly improve the competitive position of the business. Often requires thoughtful product/market segmentation.

3 *Maintain* – to maintain one's competitive position. Aggressive strategies may be required, although a defensive posture may also be assumed. Product/market position is maintained, often in a niche.

4 *Harvest* – to relinquish intentionally competitive position, emphasizing short-term profit and cash flow but not necessarily at the risk of losing the business in the short term. Often entails consolidating or reducing various aspects of the business to create higher performance for that which remains.

5 *Exit* – to divest oneself of a business because of its weak competitive position or because the cost of staying in it is prohibitive, and the risk associated with improving its position is too high.

Exercise 6.4
The SWOT analysis

Having completed the marketing audit, your task now is to summarize it into a cogent and interesting analysis of your company's particular situation in each major segment. The SWOT approach (the word SWOT, incidentally, being derived from the initial letters of Strengths, Weaknesses, Opportunities and Threats) will enable you to list in simple terms:

1 Your company's differential strengths and weaknesses vis-à-vis competitors
2 Where the best opportunities exist, i.e. market segments
3 The present and future threats to your business in the market segments.

The SWOT analysis for each segment should only be a few pages in length and should concern itself with key factors only, supported by relevant data.

Some of the most valuable information for the SWOT analysis will come from the life-cycle analysis and the portfolio matrix you prepared in Chapter 5.

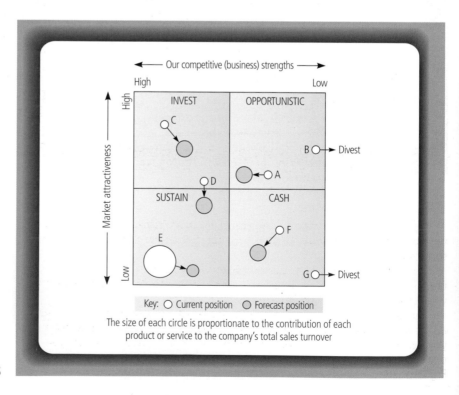

Figure 6.25

The former will give you insights about the prospects for your key products and/or services and this information can then be used on the portfolio matrix, thereby highlighting how the portfolio will change. An example of this is shown in Figure 6.25.

In Figure 6.25, clearly the future portfolio is going to be significantly different from the current one. Products/segments B and G will disappear. The sales volume of A, C and D will increase, while that of E will reduce quite dramatically. All this has a tremendous bearing on how funds are generated, and, again, this is where the portfolio matrix can be helpful in letting one understand what is happening. If you recall, the text explained that different quadrants of the matrix had different characteristics when viewed as sources of funds (Figure 6.26). Although this comes from the Boston Matrix, it is just as relevant to the directional policy matrix shown in Figure 6.26.

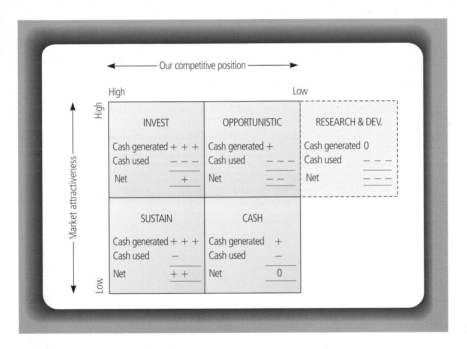

Figure 6.26

The significance of this for any company is to have a balanced portfolio, where there are adequate 'sustains' to fund research and development and selected 'opportunistics'.

The effort and costs associated with keeping the market share for 'invests' makes them unreliable sources of funds. The benefits will be reaped later when today's 'invests' sink into the 'sustain' quadrant.

You can now proceed to complete the pro forma provided in respect of *all your key market segments*. Thus, if you have six key market segments, you will complete six pro formas. In this book, we have provided you with one. If you need more, just repeat the exercise using duplicate forms. See Figure 6.27.

1 SBU description
Here, describe the market for which the SWOT is being done

2 Critical success factors
What are the few key things, from the customer's point of view, that any competitor has to do right to succeed?

1	
2	
3	
4	
5	

3 Weighting
How important is each of these CSFs? Score out of 100

Total	100

4 Strengths/weaknesses analysis
Score yourself and each of your main competitors out of 10 on each of the CSFs. Then multiply the score by the weight

CSF	Comp	You	Competitor A	Competitor B	Competitor C	Competitor D
1						
2						
3						
4						
5						
Total (score x weight)						

5 Opportunities/threats
What are the few key things outside your direct control that have had, and will continue to have, an impact on your business?

	Opportunities		Threats
1			
2			
3			
4			
5			

6 Key issues that need to be addressed

7 Key assumptions for the planning period

1
2
3
4
5
6
7

8 Key objectives

9 Key strategies

Final consequences

Figure 6.27
Strategic planning exercise (SWOT analysis) *Note*: This form should be completed for each product/market segment under consideration

Exercise 6.5
Assumptions

Often it is forgotten that in conducting the SWOT analysis we have had to make assumptions, or educated guesses, about some of the factors that will affect the business – for example, about market-growth rates, about government economic policy, about the activities of our competitors, etc. Most planning assumptions tend to deal with the environment or market trends and as such are critical to the fulfilment of the planned marketing objectives and strategies.

What then are the risks attached to making assumptions? Suppose we get it wrong?

To give some measure of risk assessment, a technique has been developed that looks at the assumption from the negative point of view. It leads one to ask, 'What can go wrong with each assumption that would change the outcome?' For example, suppose the product was an oil derivative and was thus extremely sensitive to the price of oil. For planning purposes, an assumption about the price of oil would have to be made. Using this 'Downside risk' technique, we would assess to what level the price could rise before increased material costs would make our products too expensive and cause our marketing plans to be completely revised.

Now complete the following 'Downside risk assessment form' (Table 6.5) to evaluate some of the key assumptions you used in your SWOT analyses, and which you are now to use as the basis for setting marketing objectives and strategies.

Table 6.5 Downside risk assessment form

Key assumption	Basis of assumption	Confidence in assumption (high/med./low)	What would have to happen to make outcome unattractive?	What is the risk of this happening? (high/med./low)	What would be impact if event occurs?	How far could things be allowed to deviate from plan before action is taken?	What contingency action is planned?

Marketing objectives are solely concerned with *which products go to which markets*, and marketing strategies are concerned with *how* that is done. Therefore, because marketing objectives are only concerned about products and markets, an extremely useful planning aid is provided by the Ansoff Matrix, depicted in Figure 6.28.

This matrix suggests there are four types of marketing objective:

1 Selling established products into established markets (market penetration)
2 Selling established products into new markets (market extension)
3 Selling new products into established markets (product development)
4 Selling new products into new markets (diversification).

Exercise 6.6
Setting marketing objectives

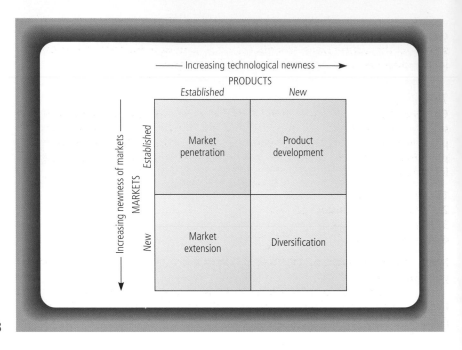

Figure 6.28

Task 1

Using the blank Ansoff Matrix (Figure 6.29), or perhaps using a larger sheet of paper, draw the matrix for your company's products and markets.

Please note that when you consider whether or not a market is new or established, the question you must ask yourself is 'How long does it take to get one's distinctive competence known in this market?' If you have been dealing with the market for anything less than your answer to this question, then that is a new market.

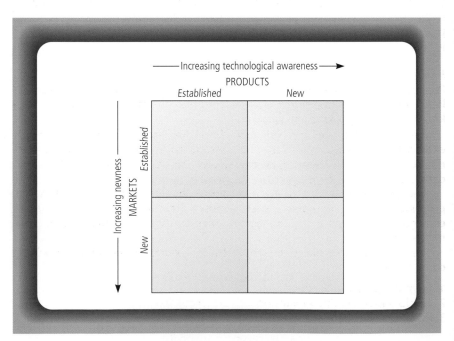

Figure 6.29
The Ansoff Matrix

Similarly, new products are those probably at the early stages of their life-cycles, where the company is still 'learning' how to make them, i.e. it hasn't solved all the operational, scheduling, quality, design and technical problems in the same way as it has for the established products.

Task 2

Combining the information on the Ansoff Matrix with that of your SWOT analyses, pick out those areas of business that offer the best prospects for your company. For each one, summarize your marketing objective for your longer-term planning horizon – i.e. two, three, four or five years. This must be quite explicit in terms of:

1 The product/service
2 The customer/market segment
3 The volume of sales
4 The market share.

Now repeat the exercise, stating the specific objectives for the first year of your planning horizon.

The marketing objectives should be consistent with the information from the product life-cycle analysis and portfolio matrix, completed in Chapter 5. Further guidance is provided in the notes which follow.

Guidelines for setting marketing objectives

Contained within your SWOT analyses will be key information gleaned from your marketing audit. You will know the reasons why customers want your products or services. You will know your best market segments. You will know the 'life' of your products or services and, probably most important of all, the portfolio matrix will have shown you how the various items of your range relate to each other in terms of raising funds.

Creative and intelligent interpretation of the portfolio matrix is the secret behind setting the right marketing objectives for your company. For this to happen, it is important to distinguish the essentially different characteristics of products or services falling into the four quadrants of the matrix. Let us take in turn:

Invest

Products or services in this quadrant are by implication aimed at those markets most attractive to your company. These will almost certainly be the markets with the higher growth rates.

Marketing objectives for such products should be calculated to match or exceed the market-growth rate and thereby hold or extend the company's market share. Since these markets are likely to be attractive to others, the company will have to be aggressive to achieve its objectives.

This marketing posture has to be supported by tight budgeting and control processes to ensure that all resources are used effectively. Concern for present earnings should be subordinate to the main thrust of keeping or extending market share.

The increase in sales looked for in these products or services is likely to come from:

1 Possible geographic expansion
2 Possible product line expansion
3 Possible product line differentiation.

These may be achieved by internal development, acquisition or joint ventures.

Sustain

In these less attractive markets it doesn't make sense to go for aggressive growth as with the invest quadrant – it would prove to be too costly and counter-productive. Instead, the objectives should be aimed at maintaining a profitable position with greater emphasis on present earnings.

The most successful products/services should be maintained, while less successful ones should be pruned. Marketing effort should be aimed at maintaining the market share of key market segments with minimum expenditure. Prices should be stabilized except when a temporary aggressive stance is required to maintain market share.

Sustain products must be managed to be the major source of funding for the company.

Selective

For products/services in this quadrant there are two broad choices:

1 Invest in the products for future earnings, i.e. groom them to be tomorrow's invest products and subsequent sustain products; or
2 Manage them for present earnings.

In practice it is only feasible to 'groom' a limited number of question marks, and so these have to be carefully chosen for their genuine potential. Investment across the range would be prohibitive.

Cash

In effect, there are two kinds of product/service in this quadrant:

1 Genuine cash products (to the right of the quadrant)
2 Select products (to the left of the quadrant, adjacent to the sustain quadrant).

The marketing objectives for *genuine cash products* should be to divest where appropriate or to manage for present earnings. Marketing expenditure should be minimized, product lines pruned and prices stabilized or raised where possible, even at the expense of sales volume.

The marketing objectives for *select products* should acknowledge the low growth/attractiveness of these products and services, but still seek to identify and exploit growth segments, not by flying in the face of reason and trying to restore the product to its previous higher growth rate by costly advertising and promotion, but by emphasizing product quality and looking for improvements in productivity. Judicious marketing expenditure might be reasonable in special circumstances, but the emphasis should be on maximizing present earnings.

Now that the marketing objectives have determined *what* the company must achieve, you have to decide how that might be done by your marketing strategy. Whereas there are only four types of marketing objective, there is a whole range of possible marketing strategies which can be used either singly or in combination with others. A choice of possible marketing strategies is shown in the list below.

Using this list, identify the broad marketing strategies most supportive to each of the marketing objectives you set for the company. Having done this, you will probably find it helpful to refer back to Figure 6.5. The left-hand column of this figure lists the marketing variables that need to be considered, such as pricing, distribution, etc. The other columns represent the key positions on the portfolio matrix and are headed accordingly. Thus it becomes a fairly straightforward procedure to identify the best marketing strategies for your chosen objectives.

Chapters 7–10 will provide you with additional information about advertising, sales promotion, selling, pricing and distribution. Only finalize your marketing strategies after completing these later sections of this book.

Possible marketing strategies
1 Change product performance
2 Change quality or features of product
3 Change advertising
4 Change promotion
5 Change pricing
6 Change delivery arrangements
7 Change distribution channels
8 Change service levels
9 Improve operational efficiency
10 Improve marketing efficiency
11 Improve administrative procedures
12 Change the degree of forward integration
13 Change the degree of backward integration
14 Rationalize product range
15 Withdraw from selected markets
16 Standardize design
17 Specialize in certain products/markets
18 Change sourcing
19 Buy into new markets
20 Acquire new/different facilities
21
22
23
24

Add any other strategies that occur to you in the spaces provided.

Exercise 6.7
Marketing
strategies

CHAPTER 7

The communication plan: 1 The advertising and sales promotion plans

■ Introduction to Chapters 7 to 10

Important note to the readers

Chapters 7–10 define in some considerable detail the contents of the major elements of the marketing mix (the four Ps). Such detail is inappropriate for the *strategic marketing plan*, which will usually only outline the broad strategies intended to achieve marketing objectives. Consequently, we have included here only the summaries of Chapters 7–10. The detailed contents are given in Appendices A to D at the end of the book for readers who wish to understand the detail that needs to be included in one-year operational marketing plans.

Otherwise, please go straight to Chapter 11.

Summary

- The difference between personal and impersonal communications
- Methods for deciding on the communication mix
- How to prepare an advertising plan
- What advertising objectives are and how to set them
- The life-cycle and its relevance to advertising
- How to prepare a sales promotion plan
- How to use a sales promotion plan
- Public relations
- Sponsorship
- Legal issues in marketing communications
- Exercises to turn the theory into practice

Note that the full version of Chapter 7, including the Exercises, can be found in Appendix A to this book.

Chapter 7 review

The communications mix

In order to achieve its marketing objectives, the company has to communicate with *existing* and *potential* customers. It can do this *directly*, face to face, generally using a sales force or call centres, or *indirectly*, using advertising, promotion, electronic media and point-of-sale displays. The choice of communications mix should be determined on the basis of what is going to be most cost-effective in terms of achieving the objectives, i.e. whatever gets the best results per given cost. We will look at direct communication in Chapter 8. Also in the next chapter are guidelines on Integrated Marketing Communications, illustrating how electronic media have affected marketing communication and distribution channels and showing how to determine an integrated communications strategy.

Advertising objectives

There are many possible advertising objectives:

- to convey information
- to alter perceptions
- to alter attitudes
- to create desires
- to establish connections, e.g. egg and bacon
- to direct actions
- to provide reassurance
- to remind
- to give reasons for buying
- to demonstrate
- to generate enquiries.   *Try Exercises 7.1 and 7.2*

Acid test

Is it possible to achieve this objective by advertising alone? If the answer is *No*, then rethink the objective and/or the means of achieving it. If the answer is *Yes*, then go ahead.

The advertising plan

The advertising plan has a number of questions to ask:

- Who is the target audience? What do we know about them? What sort of people are they, etc.?
- What response do we want to achieve? What do we want to say, convey, make them feel, believe or understand, etc.?
- How are we going to proceed? What is our creative platform? Can we be sure this is appropriate?
- Where is the best place to put our communications? Will it be cost-effective? Does it generate the right image, etc.?   *Try Exercise 7.3*
- When will our communications be displayed? Is this the best time? Does it mesh in with other activities, etc.?
- Result – what do we expect to achieve? How will we measure this? Does it mesh in with other activities, etc.?
- Budget – how much is needed? How much is going to be available? How will it be controlled, etc.?
- Schedule – who is going to do what, where and when? What is being spent on what, where and when?   *Try Exercise 7.4*

Sales promotion objectives

Sales promotion seeks to influence:

- salespeople to sell
- customers to buy
- customers to use
- users to buy

- users to use
- distributors to stock

more, earlier, faster, etc.

It is essentially a short-term tactic. In order to achieve these objectives, the promotion can use:

Money	Price reductions, coupons, competitions, etc.
Goods	Free goods, e.g. two for the price of one, trade-ins, free trials, redeemable coupons, etc.
Services	Guarantees, training, prizes for events, free services, etc.

Try Exercise 7.5

The sales promotion plan

The sales promotion plan covers:

- the objectives of the promotion
- background – why the method was chosen
- eligibility – who and where
- timing – opening and closing dates
- support in terms of materials
- administration required
- the sales plan – target, incentives
- sales presentation – points to cover
- monitoring procedure to collect data regarding progress, etc.
- assessment – how will it be evaluated?

Try Exercise 7.6

Questions raised for the company

1 Q: Who should design the advertising?

    A: There is no golden rule and options might be limited by the available budget. Most companies use outside agencies in order to achieve the required level of professionalism. Advertising objectives, however, should *always* be set by you and *not* by an advertising agency.

2 Q: It's been said that 'half the advertising budget is wasted; the problem is to know which half'. Is this true?

    A: It might be for some companies, but, by following the notes and exercises provided here, you should be able to avoid such a problem.

3 Q: Sales promotions aren't used in our business, so would they be a viable marketing tactic for us?

    A: If, by using a promotion, a company breaks new ground, it could give it a differential advantage over competitors.

4 Q: If a sales promotion is successful, should it be kept running?

    A: Once it has achieved its objectives, there seems little point in continuing. It can always be brought back later, and thereby retain its impact and 'freshness'.

CHAPTER 8

The communication plan:
2 The sales plan

Summary

- How important is personal selling?
- The role of personal selling in the marketing mix
- A method for determining the correct number of salespeople required
- How to set quantitative and qualitative sales objectives
- How to improve sales force productivity
- How sales forces should be managed
- How to prepare a sales plan
- How to integrate marketing communications
- Exercises to turn the theory into practice

Note that the full version of Chapter 8, including the Exercises, can be found in Appendix B to this book.

Chapter 8 review

What is the role of personal selling?

This provides the face-to-face element of the communications mix. There are things it can achieve that advertising and promotion can't – for example, salespeople can be flexible in front of the customer and ask for an order. However, personal selling has to be seen in the context of the total communications mix. *Try Exercise 8.1*

How important is personal selling?

Traditionally, companies had sales forces long before marketing was in vogue. Companies still spend more on sales forces than on advertising and promotion combined. Though key parts of the marketing mix, sales departments often act independently of marketing. Thus, in achieving their short-term sales goals, they sometimes fail to achieve the mix of products and markets consistent with the longer-term strategic marketing objectives.

How many salespeople should you have?

Basically salespeople have three activities. They:

- make calls
- travel
- administer.

Their workload should be analysed to establish how many calls it is possible to make in a typical working day. Equally, an assessment of existing and potential customers should be made and the annual total number of calls calculated (bear in mind different customer categories need different call rates).

In the diagram:

    Boxes 1 + 2 = maintenance call rate
    Boxes 4 + 5 = increase effort
    Boxes 3 + 6 = minimum attention
    Boxes 7 + 8 = new strategy
    Box 9 = don't bother.

$$\text{Number of salespeople} = \frac{\text{Annual total calls required}}{\text{Number of working days} \times \text{Cs}}$$

where Cs = all salespeople's calls per day.

	Size of business		
	Large	Medium	Small
Friendly	1	2	3
Average	4	5	6
Hostile	7	8	9

Customer attitude (vertical axis label)

What should they do?

Achieve objectives consistent with the marketing plan in terms of:

- How much to sell (volume)
- What to sell (mix)
- Where to sell (market segments)
- Allowable costs
- Profit margins.

There can be many other types of sub- or enabling objectives, for example:

- Number of telephone contacts
- Number of sales letters written
- Number of calls made
- Use of sales aids
- Number of reports submitted
- Safety record, etc.

Try Exercise 8.2

How are they managed?

To maximize performance, get the optimal balance between incentives and disincentives. Incentives are:

- rewards consistent with performance
- giving praise and recognition where it is due
- minimal boredom and monotony
- freedom from fear and worry
- feeling of belonging
- sense of doing a useful job.

'There are no bad salespeople, only bad sales managers.'   *Try Exercise 8.3*

Questions raised for the company

1 Q: Should sales or marketing be responsible for the sales plan?
   A: Marketing objectives should be agreed first. Then, if there is a separate sales force, sales managers can devise a tactical plan to meet the objectives.
2 Q: Salespeople are sometimes described as notoriously reactive and optimistic. Can they be expected to conform to a sales plan?
   A: Salespeople such as the ones described here are perhaps the salespeople you don't need. The sales plan is designed to make best use of a scarce and expensive resource, a wholly admirable objective. It must not be undermined.
3 Q: Suppose the sales plan requires salespeople to play a different role. Can 'old dogs' be taught new tricks?
   A: Whenever change is introduced, there are often some casualties. However, with well-designed training and sensitive management, the problem is not insurmountable.

CHAPTER 9

The pricing plan

Summary

- Cost-plus pricing approaches and their dangers
- Portfolio management, life-cycle analysis, product positioning and pricing implications
- Costs as an input to pricing decisions
- Pricing for channels
- Pricing for competitive advantage through value-in-use
- How to prepare a pricing plan
- Exercises to turn the theory into practice

Note that the full version of Chapter 9, including the Exercises, can be found in Appendix C to this book.

Chapter 9 review

Reasons for a pricing plan

Pricing is a key part of the marketing mix and needs to be managed intelligently, in the same way as the other parts. Generally, pricing is included as part of product/segment plans and doesn't appear as a separate entity. This can disguise some of the complex issues to be found in pricing.

Cost-plus pricing

Traditionally, pricing has been the remit of accountants. Their concern was mainly about the impact of price on margin and hence revenue. The weaknesses of this approach are as follows:

1 Product can be overpriced because of arbitrary loading of production and other overheads.
2 There is no room for strategic thinking.
3 Products can be eliminated from the range, regardless of their synergy with others.

In contrast, marketers look at price in terms of its influence on demand.

Competitive pricing

The possible pricing spectrum is:

where
A = marginal cost per unit
B = lowest price limit in the market

C = average cost per unit
D = 'going rate' price in the market
E = top end price limit in the market.

Try Exercise 9.1

Pricing and the product life-cycle

Different positions of the life-cycle call for different pricing strategies:

A Introduction	Either (1) price low to win high market share, or (2) price high in recognition of novelty and prestige
B Growth	Price competitively to win market share
C Maturity	As per the growth phase
D Saturation	Stabilize price; consider raising it
E Decline	Raise price

Try Exercise 9.2

Product positioning

Pricing can influence the position of a product in the market, e.g. a high price can convey an image of better quality, design or exclusiveness. Here is one example of product positioning.

Better positioning beats the competition.

Channel discounts

If there are intermediaries, they have to be rewarded in return for their services, i.e. there has to be a total channel margin allowed for in 'price to customer' calculations. Discounts against nominal price lists can be in the form of:

1 Trade discounts
2 Quantity discounts
3 Promotional discounts
4 Cash discounts.

How the total margin is sliced for distributors is a matter of 'trade-offs' of costs versus the added value of using distributors.   *Try Exercise 9.3*

Factors affecting price

Price can be influenced by:

■ marketing objectives
■ the cost structure
■ legal constraints
■ consumer attitudes
■ competition (direct)
■ competition (substitutes)
■ company/product image
■ economic situation.   *Try Exercises 9.4 and 9.5*

Questions raised for the company

1 Q: Is it possible to develop a sound pricing policy if one's costing is suspect?
   A: While 'prices' and 'costs' are separate entities, it is essential that a company has an accurate costing system. Without this there is no point of reference to put pricing into perspective.
2 Q: What is the true price of a product?
   A: Seen by the buyer it is purchase price and cost of introduction; this can include training costs, maintenance, energy consumption, disruption costs, consumables, floor space, etc. However, these items can be a source of differential advantage over competing products, which in effect provides a 'better price' in real money terms.
3 Q: Is it better to price high or low?
   A: It depends on a number of factors, such as market share and so on. It is as well to remember, however, that if you try to have the lowest price, someone will usually try to go even lower. This is a difficult battle to win.

CHAPTER 10

The distribution plan and customer service plan

Summary

- Distribution is not just about physical distribution management
- The several components of the distribution mix
- The several routes to market (channels), including electronic channels
- How to reconfigure the market map
- How to select the most appropriate channels
- Customer retention and profitability
- Customer service and its principal components
- How to prepare a distribution plan
- Exercises to turn the theory into practice

Note that the full version of Chapter 10, including the Exercises, can be found in Appendix D to this book.

Chapter 10 review

Physical distribution

While this chapter applies mainly to tangible products, it also has much relevance to services.
   Physical distribution ensures products get to the right place, on time, and in the right condition. In some businesses, distribution costs can amount to 20 per cent of the selling price. There are five components to manage:

1 *Facilities* – the number, size and geographical location of storage and distribution depots
2 *Inventory* – the stockholding levels throughout the distribution chain consistent with customers' service expectations
3 *Transport* – made up of transport, delivery, schedules, etc.
4 *Communications* – there is also a flow of information, for example order processing, invoicing, forecasting, etc.
5 *Unitization* – the way in which goods are packaged and assembled into large units, e.g. palletization, container loads, etc.

Considerable savings can be made by innovating in this area.

Channels for reaching customers

There is a range of possible distribution channels (see diagram for example).

Which one is best for competitive advantage?   *Try Exercises 10.1 and 10.2*
Routes to market are being reconfigured in five main ways:

1 *Substitute/reconfigured products* (such as e-mails instead of physical post)
2 *Disintermediation* (e-commerce can make intermediaries redundant)
3 *Reintermediation* (a previous intermediary is replaced by a new online intermediary)
4 *Partial channel substitution* (an intermediary's role may be reduced, but not eliminated – as in the case of a car manufacturer providing customer information, but pointing customers to particular outlets)
5 *Media switching/addition* (the links in the chain may remain the same, but communication between them may be partially or fully switched to the Internet from the previous mechanisms).

Market maps need to be reconfigured in the light of e-commerce. Examples of such reconfiguration are given in Chapter 4, in this chapter and in Appendix D.

Availability and customer service package

Customer expectations about product availability will vary from market to market. In theory, 100 per cent availability should be the norm. In practice, a compromise might have to be found, say 95 per cent, because the additional cost of providing that extra 5 per cent can be prohibitive. In addition, often such high levels of customer service are not necessary. Balance the benefits to the customer with cost to you.

Factors which impact on customer service include:

- frequency of delivery
- time from order to delivery
- emergency deliveries when required

- accuracy of paperwork
- stock availability
- reliability of deliveries, etc.

Key factors should be identified and researched with a view to improving them.

Try Exercises 10.3 and 10.4

Distribution planning

The approach should follow these steps:

1 Determine marketing objectives.
2 Evaluate changing conditions in distribution at all levels.
3 Determine the distribution task within marketing strategy.
4 Establish a policy in terms of type, number and level of outlets to be used.
5 Set performance standards for distributors.
6 Obtain performance information.
7 Compare actual with anticipated performance.
8 Make improvements where necessary.

Try Exercise 10.5

Questions raised for the company

1 Q: How important is it to have a distribution plan?
   A: It depends on the type of business. In some industries distribution costs amount to 20 per cent or more of sales revenue. Distribution is the Cinderella of marketing, but can often be the area where a competitive edge can be won – through planning.
2 Q: Can services be distributed? After all, they can't be stocked.
   A: No, but services can be franchised. Once a rational decision has been made to use channels, it is the company's responsibility to work at developing a good business relationship based on trust and mutual respect. It is to both parties' mutual advantage.
3 Q: Are there any new developments in distribution?
   A: Franchising is becoming even more popular. In addition, some transport contractors now also supply warehousing, inventory control and other services, in effect providing the manufacturer with an 'off-the-shelf' distribution facility.

CHAPTER 11

Marketing information, forecasting and organizing for marketing planning

Summary

- Marketing accountability
- The difference between market and marketing research
- How to set the budget for marketing research
- Different forms of marketing research
- Database marketing and segmentation
- Marketing information systems
- The Internet and its strategic implications
- Data warehousing
- Data mining
- Customer Relationship Management (CRM)
- Forecasting techniques
- Different organizational structures for marketing planning
- The implications of corporate culture on marketing planning
- Exercises to turn the theory into practice

■ Introduction

In the next two chapters, we look at one of the most difficult aspects of marketing planning – actually making it all work in practice by means of a system within the company. This is something that most courses and books somehow seem to overlook. Yet no work on marketing planning can be complete without a fairly detailed consideration of how all the structures and frameworks presented in earlier chapters are to be implemented.

The truth is, of course, that the actual *process* of marketing planning is simple in outline. Any book will tell us that it consists of: a situation review; assumptions; objectives; strategies; programmes; and measurement and review. What some books *do not* tell us is that there are a number of contextual issues that have to be considered that make marketing planning one of the most baffling of all marketing problems.

Here are some of those issues:

- *When* should it be done, *how often*, *by whom*, and *how*?
- Is it different in a *large* and a *small* company?
- Is it different in a *diversified* and an *undiversified* company?
- Is it different in an *international* and a *domestic* company?
- What is the role of the *chief executive*?
- What is the role of the *planning department*? Should marketing planning be *top down* or *bottom up*?
- What is the relationship between *operational* (one year) and *strategic* (longer term) planning?

Until issues such as these are understood, the other chapters in this book will remain little more than interesting aspects of marketing planning. So, the purpose of Chapters 12 and 13 is to help us to pick up all the pieces of the jigsaw puzzle and put them together to form a picture we can all see and understand.

First, however, we need to set the scene and, in particular, fill in a few gaps concerning marketing measurement, or accountability, marketing information, and the organizational side of marketing. Our research has shown very clearly that it is important to recognize at the outset what the realistic constraints are likely to be on the implementation of a marketing planning system. Two such major constraints are marketing information and a company's organizational form, which are considered in this chapter. We will then go on in the next chapter to demonstrate how marketing planning can be made to work by means of a system, and will include in this a discussion of the role of the chief executive, and the planning department. In Chapter 13, we provide an actual marketing planning system which will enable you to operationalize the concepts, structures and frameworks described in this book.

This chapter, then, is in three parts:

1 Marketing accountability
2 Marketing information and forecasting
3 Marketing organization.

From our 'map' of marketing, repeated below as Figure 11.1, all that remains to be discussed in more detail is Box 4, 'Monitor value'.

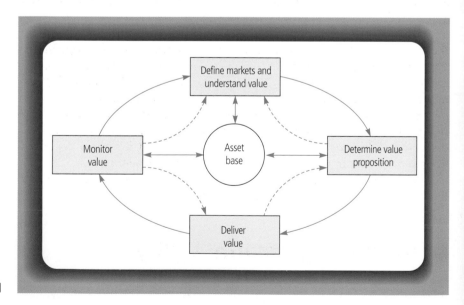

Figure 11.1

There are four main areas where monitoring can occur, corresponding to the main types of information dealt with in the planning processes of 'Understand value' and 'Determine value proposition' (see Figure 11.2).

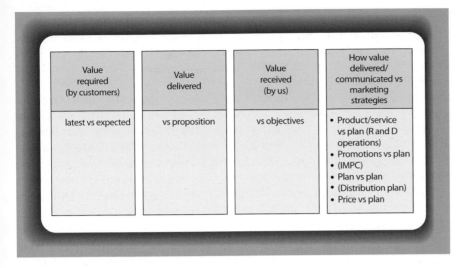

Figure 11.2
Monitor value

First, the organization can monitor whether the value the customers actually require corresponds to the previous analysis of customer requirements carried out as part of 'Understand value'. The information for this may be gained partly from the information gained in the 'Deliver value' process, or it may require special activity such as market research, which is discussed in detail later in this chapter.

Second, the value delivered can be monitored against the value proposition which was defined during 'Determine value proposition'. As all aspects of value are as measured by the customer's perception, this will again involve asking the customer by some means.

The organization will also wish to monitor the value it receives against the marketing objectives defined during 'Determine value proposition'. This is the area that most organizations are best at, through monthly analysis of sales by product, channel and so on (though analysis by segment or customer is often poorer than analysis by product, with customer profitability or lifetime value generally difficult to obtain). But as the financial results are a result of customer satisfaction, monitoring the value delivered to the customer is equally important, and for many organizations, one of the simplest ways of improving performance.

Finally, the overall effectiveness of the marketing strategies by which the value was delivered may be evaluated.

■ Marketing accountability

Three distinct levels for measuring marketing effectiveness

When the author was marketing director of a fast-moving consumer goods (fmcg) company thirty years ago, there were many well tried-and-tested models for measuring the effectiveness of marketing promotional expenditure. Indeed, some of these were quite sophisticated and included mathematical models for promotional campaigns, for advertising threshold and wear-out levels, and the like.

Indeed, it would be surprising if marketing as a discipline did not have its own quantitative models for the massive expenditure of fmcg companies. Over time, these models have been transferred to business-to-business and service companies, with the result that, today, any organization spending substantial sums of shareholders' money on promotion should be ashamed of itself if those responsible could not account for the effectiveness of such expenditure.

However, at this level, accountability can only be measured in terms of the kinds of effects that promotional expenditure can achieve, such as awareness, or attitude change, both of which can be measured quantitatively.

But to assert that such expenditure can be measured directly in terms of sales or profits is intellectually indefensible, when there are so many other variables that affect sales, such as product efficacy, packaging, price, the sales force, competitors and countless other variables that, like advertising, have an intermediate impact on sales and profits.

So, the problem with marketing accountability has never been with how to measure the effectiveness of promotional expenditure, for this we have had for many years. No, the problem occurs because marketing isn't just a promotional activity. As we have stated many times in this book, in world-class organizations where the customer is at the centre of the business model, marketing as a discipline is responsible for defining and understanding markets, for segmenting these markets, for developing value propositions to meet the researched needs of the customers in the segments, for getting buy-in from all those in the organization responsible for delivering this value and for getting them to play their own part in delivering this value, and for monitoring whether the promised value is being delivered.

Indeed, this definition of marketing as a function for strategy development as well as for tactical sales delivery, when represented as a map (see Figure 11.3), can be used to clarify the whole problem of how to measure marketing effectiveness.

From this map, it can be seen that there are three levels of measurement, or metrics.

Level 1 is the most vital of all three, because this is what determines whether or not the marketing strategies for the longer term (usually three to five years) destroy or create shareholder value added. In capital markets, success is measured in terms of shareholder value added, having taken account of the risks associated with the strategies set out in the strategic marketing plan, the time value of money and the cost of capital. This is a totally different measurement from outmoded accounting notions of profit.

It is justified to use the strategic marketing plan for assessing whether shareholder value is being created or destroyed because, as Sean Kelly

Figure 11.3
Map of the marketing domain

agrees:

> The customer is simply the fulcrum of the business and everything from production to supply chain, to finance, risk management, personnel management and product development, all adapt to and converge on the business value proposition that is projected to the customer.
>
> (Sean Kelly, *The Information Wars*, Kogan Page, London, 2005)

Thus, corporate assets and their associated competences are only relevant if customer markets value them sufficiently highly that they lead to sustainable competitive advantage, or shareholder value added. This is our justification for evaluating the strategic plan for what is to be sold, to whom and with what projected effect on profits as a route to establishing whether shareholder value will be created or destroyed.

Once the hype and jargon is cleared away, all marketing plans say the same thing: 'We're going to do these things in this market and make this much profit'. Digging deeper, we can discern three fundamental assertions that lie at the root of all marketing plans:

1. The market we are going for is this big.
2. Our strategy will achieve this much share.
3. That share will result in this much profit.

It is these three assertions that give rise to the three components of business risk:

- market risk – the risk that the market is not as big as you think it will be
- share risk – the risk that your strategy will not deliver the share it promises
- profit risk – the risk that you will not make the margins you promised.

It is comparatively easy to envisage how each of these can be broken down into subcomponents of risk, which can be assessed using the basic tools of marketing such as the Ansoff Matrix, product life-cycle analysis, market segmentation robustness, offer specificity, and so on.

Cumulatively, these three component risks add up to business risk. If all three are certain, then there is no risk and the plan will deliver what it promises. To the extent that there is some uncertainty in one or more areas, the plan is risky and the promised returns must be higher to compensate for the risk. If we could objectively assess business risk, using data in a specific and systematic way, it would help us to create shareholder value in two ways. First, it would allow us to identify the main areas of risk in our strategy and act to reduce that risk. Second, it would give us a tool to sell our strategy to investors, demonstrating in detail that our plan is well thought out and creates shareholder value. The challenge lies in accurately assessing each of those three areas of risk.

The process for doing this has been labelled 'Marketing Due Diligence', based on years of research at Cranfield School of Management.

> In short, Marketing Due Diligence is a process which assesses the probability of a marketing plan delivering its promises. It then adjusts the promised profit to reflect that probability and calculates if, for the firm's cost of capital, the plan would create or destroy shareholder value.

For a full explanation, see M. McDonald, B. Smith and K. Ward, *Marketing Due Diligence*, Butterworth-Heinemann, Oxford, 2006.

Level 3 is the level of micro-promotional measurement we have described above.

Level 2 is another level, however, that few academics or practitioners have addressed to date. We shall describe it briefly here, although once the process of Marketing Due Diligence has been applied to the long-range marketing strategy, it remains central to the issue of marketing metrics and marketing effectiveness. Further, however, let us destroy once and for all one of the great myths of measurement – marketing return on investment. This implies 'return' divided by 'investment' and, for marketing expenditure such as promotional spend, it is an intellectually puerile notion. It's a bit like demanding a financial justification for the wings of an aircraft! (see the points we make above). Also, as McGovern *et al.* (2004) say:

> Measuring marketing performance isn't like measuring factory output – a fact that many non-marketing executives don't grasp. In the controlled environment of a manufacturing plant, it's simple to account for what goes in one end and what comes out the other and then determine productivity.
>
> But the output of marketing can be measured only long after it has left the plant.

Neither is the budget and all the energy employed in measuring it a proxy for measuring marketing effectiveness. Indeed, the sections in Chapter 2 on the unreliably and backward-looking focus of budgets sets out why these can never be a proxy for measuring marketing effectiveness.

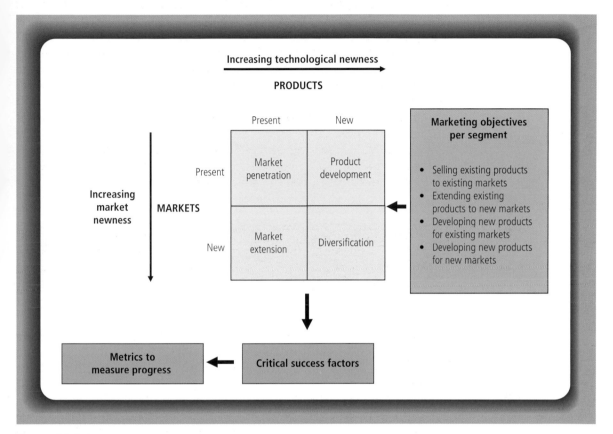

Figure 11.4
The Ansoff Matrix

So, once the Marketing Due Diligence is completed, we can turn our attention to what needs to be measured in the one-year plan.

Figure 11.4 shows the Ansoff Matrix.

Each of the cells in each box (cells will consists of products for segments) is a planning unit, in the sense of objectives which are set for each volume, value and profit for the first year of the strategic plan.

For each of the products for segment cells, having set objectives, the task is then to determine strategies for achieving them. These strategies, or Critical Success Factors (CSFs), will be weighted according to their relative importance to the customers in the segment (Figure 11.5).

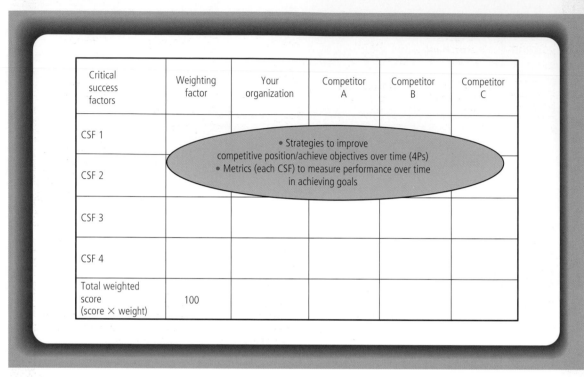

Critical success factors	Weighting factor	Your organization	Competitor A	Competitor B	Competitor C
CSF 1					
CSF 2					
CSF 3					
CSF 4					
Total weighted score (score × weight)	100				

• Strategies to improve competitive position/achieve objectives over time (4Ps)
• Metrics (each CSF) to measure performance over time in achieving goals

Figure 11.5
Critical success factors: in each segment, defined by the segment

It is unlikely that the marketing function will be directly responsible for what needs to be done to improve a CSF. For example, issues like product efficacy, after-sales service, channel management, and sometimes even price and the sales force, are often controlled by other functions, so marketing needs to get buy-in from these functions to improve the CSF scores. There will be other responses that will need to be measured, such as productivity factors and hygiene factors, but to keep it simple we have only shown customer-based critical success factors here.

Figure 11.6 shows another level of detail, i.e. the actions that have to be taken, by whom and at what cost.

Figure 11.7 shows how these actions multiply for each box of the Ansoff Matrix.

Thus, it can be seen how the expenditure on marketing and other functional actions to improve CSFs can be linked to marketing objectives and, ultimately, to profitability, and it becomes clear exactly what must be measured and why. It also obviates the absurd assumption that a particular marketing action can be linked directly to profitability. It can only be linked to other weighted CSFs which, if improved, should lead to the achievement of volumes, value and, ultimately, profits.

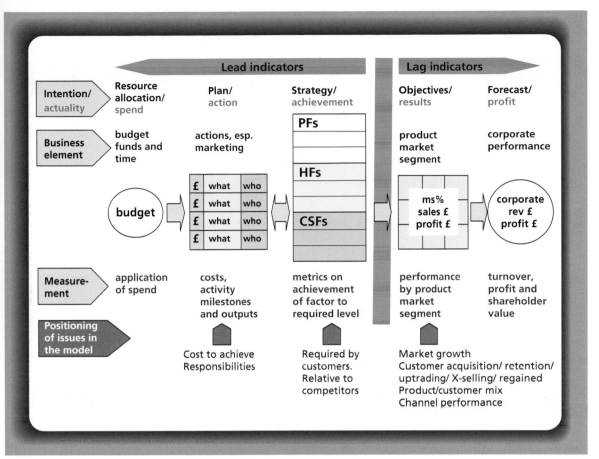

Figure 11.6
The link from objectives and strategies to performance

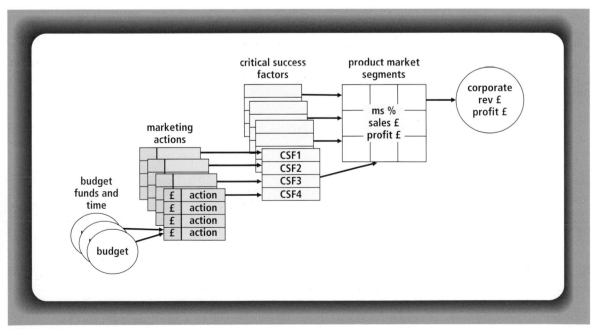

Figure 11.7

We stress, however, that the corporate revenue and profits shown in the right of Figures 11.5 and 11.6 are *not* the same as shareholder value added, which takes account of the risks involved in the strategies, the time value of money and the cost of capital.

The Cranfield RoMI Research Club is committed to researching Level 2 of marketing metrics and accountability. Level 1 was the agenda of the Marketing and Shareholder Value Added Research Club at Cranfield from 2001 to 2003, and the *Marketing Due Diligence* book referred to above explains the detail of the process.

■ Marketing information and forecasting for marketing planning

It will, by now, be obvious that without information it is going to be difficult to do many of the fairly commonsense things we have been discussing so far.

> Any plan can only be as good as the information on which it is based, which is why we have been making sure that we know the right questions to ask, such as: 'Who are our customers?' 'What is our market share?' and so on.

Throughout this book, we have been stressing that the profitable development of a company can only come from a continuous attempt to match the company's capabilities with customer needs. In order that the company can be sure that this matching process is taking place effectively, it is necessary that some type of information flow be instituted between the customer and the firm. This is the role of ► **marketing research**

► **DEFINITION** ◄

Marketing research is concerned with research into marketing processes

The difference between market research and marketing research

► **DEFINITION** ◄

Market research is concerned specifically with research about markets

Put very simply, ► **market research** is concerned specifically with research about markets, whereas marketing research is concerned with research into marketing processes.

> We are concerned here with marketing research, which has been defined by the American Marketing Association as the systematic gathering, recording and analysis of data about problems relating to the marketing of goods and services.

The words in this definition are important. The process has to be systematic, because it is necessary to have a structured interaction between people, machines and procedures designed to generate an orderly flow of pertinent information collected from sources both inside and outside the company, for use as the basis for decision-making in specified responsibility areas of marketing management.

It will be apparent immediately that ▶ **data** by themselves (such as words, figures, pictures, sounds, and so on) are of little use until they are combined with direction and hence become information. But without some purpose in mind, some marketing problem to solve, information is not much use either. Indeed, research has shown that one of the biggest problems facing management today is a *surplus* of data and information, rather than too little.

▶ **D E F I N I T I O N** ◀

Data are words, figures, pictures, sounds, etc.

> Which brings us to our definition of ▶ **intelligence**, which is information consumable and usable by management in converting uncertainty into risk.

▶ **D E F I N I T I O N** ◀

Intelligence is information which is consumable and usable by management in converting uncertainty into risk

Uncertainty, of course, is when any outcome is considered to be equally possible. When a probability can be assigned to certain outcomes, however, we are talking about *risk*, which is just quantified uncertainty. The marketing manager might feel, for example, that a new product has a 90 per cent chance of achieving 30 per cent market share in its first year. Clearly, our ability to make successful decisions is enhanced if we are operating under conditions of known risk rather than uncertainty.

> Conversion of uncertainty into risk and the minimization of risk is perhaps marketing management's most important task, and in this process the role of marketing research is of paramount importance.

How much to spend on marketing research

Before looking at the different kinds of research available to the marketing manager, a book written about marketing planning should surely address the issue of the marketing research budget.

Marketing information has to be produced, stored and distributed, but it has a limited life – it is perishable. Like other resources, information has a value in use; the less the manager knows about a marketing problem and the greater the risk attached to a wrong decision, the more valuable the information becomes. This implies the need for a cost/benefit appraisal of all sources of marketing information, since there is little point in investing more in such information than the return on it would justify.

> But while costs are easy to identify, the benefits are more difficult to pin down. They can best be expressed in terms of the additional profits that might be achieved through identifying marketing opportunities and through the avoidance of marketing failures that could result without the use of information.

It must be stressed, however, that the decision about how much to spend on marketing information is not an easy one. On the one hand, it would, generally speaking, be foolhardy to proceed without any information at all, while, on the other hand, the cost of perfect information would be prohibitive. One way of estimating how much to spend is based on the theory of probability and expected value. For example, if by launching a product you had to incur development costs of 1 million euros and you believed there was a 10 per cent chance that the product would fail, the maximum *loss expectation* would be 100,000 euros (i.e. 1 million euros $\times$ 0.1).

Obviously, then, it is worth spending up to 100,000 euros to acquire information that would help avoid such a loss. However, because perfect information is seldom available, it makes sense to budget a smaller sum for marketing research which effectively discounts the likely inaccuracy of the information. Such an approach can be a valuable means of quantifying the value of marketing research in a managerial context.

Forms of marketing research

Increasing sophistication in the use of the techniques available to the researcher, particularly in the handling and analysis of multivariate data, has made marketing research into a specialized function within the field of marketing management. Nevertheless, any company, irrespective of whether or not it has a marketing department, should be aware of some of the tools that are available and where these may be used.

> Marketing research can be classified either as *external* or *internal*.

| External marketing information gathering should always be seen as a complement to internal marketing analysis.

The former research activity is conducted within the competitive environment outside the firm, whereas much valuable intelligence can be gained from internal marketing analysis in the form of sales trends, changes in the marketing mix such as price, advertising levels, and so on. External marketing information gathering should always be seen as a complement to such internal information.

> Apart from this, there is another basic split between *reactive* and *non-reactive* marketing research.

Non-reactive methods are based upon the interpretation of observed phenomena, or extant data, whereas reactive research involves some form of proactive assessment in the marketplace.

The most widely used method of reactive marketing research involves the asking of questions by means of a *questionnaire* survey, which is indeed a ubiquitous and highly flexible instrument. It can be administered by an interviewer, by telephone, on the Internet, or it can be sent by mail, and so on.

All of these different methods have their advantages and disadvantages, and all have different cost consequences. For example, the greatest degree of control over the quality of the responses is obtained by getting a researcher to administer each questionnaire personally, but this is very expensive and time-consuming. Telephone interviews are quick and relatively inexpensive, but there is a severe limit to the amount of technical information that can be obtained by this means. The postal questionnaire is a much-favoured method, but here great care is necessary to avoid sample bias. For example, is there something special (and possibly therefore unrepresentative of the population) about those who reply to a postal questionnaire?

But, without doubt, the biggest potential pitfalls with the questionnaire lie in its design. Everyone knows about the 'loaded' question or the dangers of ambiguity, yet these are not always easily detectable. Indeed, even the order in which questions are asked can have a distortion effect on the answers.

Such pitfalls can be reduced by *pilot testing* it; in other words, by giving it a trial run on a sub-group of the intended sample to isolate any problems that may arise.

Sometimes it may be more appropriate to gather information not by large surveys, but by smaller-scale, more detailed studies intended to provide qualitative insights rather than quantitative conclusions. *Depth interviews* can provide such insights. These are loosely-structured discussions with a group broadly representing the population in which the researcher is interested, in which a group leader attempts to draw from the group members their feelings about the subject under discussion. Such in-depth interviews can also take place with individuals, a method which is particularly popular when information is required about specialized products or markets.

Experimentation is another type of reactive marketing research which can provide a valuable source of information about the likely market performance of new products or about the likely effects of variations in the marketing mix. Thus, different product formulations, different levels of promotional effort, and so on can be tested in the marketplace to gauge their different effects.

Sometimes, market experimentation can take place in laboratory conditions, particularly in the case of advertising. Samples of the target audience will be exposed to the advertisement, and their reactions obtained. Eye cameras, polygraphs and tachistoscopes are just some of the devices that can be used to record physical reactions to marketing stimuli.

In contrast with such methods are those that are classified as *non-reactive*, in that they do not rely on data derived directly from the respondent.

Best known amongst these are *retail audits* and *consumer panels*, both widely used by consumer companies. Retail audits involve the regular monitoring of a representative sample of stockists. At regular periods, researchers visit the stockists and record the current level of stocks of the product group being audited and the delivery notes for any such goods delivered since their last visit. With the information on stock levels on their last visit, it is now a simple matter to determine sales of the audited items, i.e. opening stock + deliveries between visits – closing stock = sales during the period.

The consumer panel is simply a sample group of consumers who record in a diary their purchases and consumption over a period of time. This technique has been used in industrial as well as consumer markets, and can provide continuous data on usage patterns as well as much other useful data.

> The most important of all marketing research methods is the use of existing materials.

Finally, and, in many respects, the most important of all marketing research methods is the use of existing materials, particularly by means of *desk research*, which should always be the starting point of any marketing research programme.

There is often a wealth of information to be obtained from published information such as government statistics, OECD, EU, the United Nations, newspapers, technical journals, trade association publications, published market surveys, and so on. Two or three days spent on desk research nearly always provides pleasant surprises for the company that believes it lacks information about its markets. When combined with internal sales information, this can be the most powerful research method open to a company.

■ Organizing the information to develop sound plans[1]

The practice of marketing planning is intrinsically difficult. Its main concern is to choose markets to go after and to work out how to win them.

The methods in this book can be applied to make up a plan that describes the marketing objectives and the winning strategies. The trouble is that such a plan could in theory be written without a scrap of supporting evidence; and, in practice, many plans are created upon the flimsiest of evidence.

[1] Figures 11.8, 11.9 and 11.10 and Tables 11.1, 11.2, 11.3, 11.4 and 11.5 are the copyright of Dr Robert Shaw of Shaw Consulting, and are reproduced here with his kind permission.

Two challenges involving evidence and information face executive management.

> The first challenge, faced by companies of any substantial size and diversity, is how to manage the complexity of the planning data.

The question arises, how can the planners know very much about what is happening throughout the geographical regions with all of its products and in all the market segments (see Figure 11.8)? Auditing the market requires its subdivision into many component parts – by geography, by product, by segment, etc. Then, portfolio analysis requires the reassembly of these components into a coherent structure.

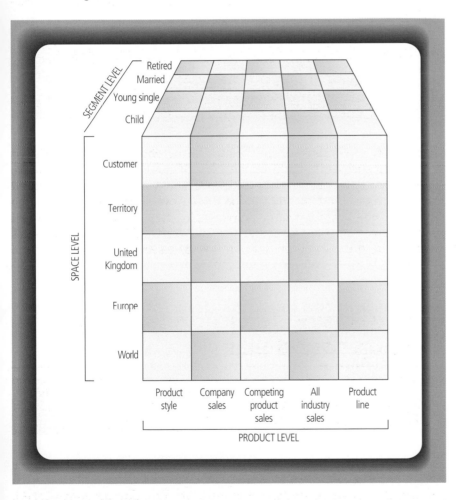

Figure 11.8
One hundred levels of market subdivision and summarization

> The second challenge is how to assess whether a plan is based upon sound evidence, or whether to ignore it as something 'made up', which is based on neither accurate facts nor believable assumptions.

In the process, planners need to match external facts about the market to internal facts and figures to create a clear and harmonious picture (see Figure 11.9). However, it is rare for the same categories to apply internally and externally, which makes the job of the planner especially difficult.

Figure 11.9
Planners must match the internal categories, facts and figures to the external ones

Fortunately, some large companies have found a way to address both of these problems, thanks to increased availability of information on computer databases, and the power of computer software to make complexity more manageable. Planners must, however, understand the limitations and weaknesses of the databases and master the software tools if they are to make the planning decisions sound, as well as easy.

Subdividing the market – data for segmentation

As we saw in Chapter 4, market segmentation is the process that subdivides the market into distinct groups of buyers who might merit separate products and/or marketing mixes. For each segment a profile is developed and, very often, a meaningful and memorable name. Segmentation is only effective when it results in realistic commercial opportunities which can be targeted and measured in practice.

> Market segments change over time, as the buyers' needs evolve and as new product offerings become available. The planner must constantly review new combinations of variables to see which reveal the best new opportunities.

Segments are identified by applying successive variables to subdivide the market. As an illustration, a global telecommunications company is interested in stimulating line usage among low users (segmentation variable: *product usage*). Low users consist of those who fear technology, those who are indifferent and those who are positive towards technology (segmentation variable: *attitude*). Among those who feel positive are those with high incomes who can afford to use more (segmentation variable: *income*). The telecommunications company may decide to target high income people who have a positive attitude, but simply use the competitors' networks.

For segmentation, information needs to be collected about:

- buying and/or usage behaviour
- buyer attitudes to the product category
- buyer characteristics, such as geographics, demographics, psychographics.

As we have seen, this can be obtained from:

- public databases
- proprietary databases (owned by research agencies)
- questionnaires sent by mail
- telephone research
- face-to-face research.

> Note that internal customer data cannot be used in this context because it is not representative of the whole market, unless the company's customers are representative of all areas of the entire market.

Large data samples often need to be collected to cover all combinations of variables. For example, in a survey where the variables are sex, age (split into five categories), geography (ten regions) and products (five categories), with a minimum sample-per-combination of ten people, the survey would need to cover at least 5,000 individuals to cover all combinations of segmentation variables.

A wide range of statistical techniques can be used to identify market segments. These include factor analysis, cluster analysis and multiple regression. More recent techniques which go beyond the traditional limits of statistics include neural networks and pattern-finding algorithms.

Finally, each segment is defined in terms of the key variables. Often the segments are named on the basis of a dominant characteristic.

Analysis options – external agencies or internal resources

Market research has traditionally played an important role in segmentation. However, it has often limited itself to 'field and tab' methods, which are severely limited in their flexibility, and do not support the constant reviewing of new combinations of segmentation variables.

Field and tab methods involve the collection of data on 'field' question-naires, analysis of the data, and presentation of the results as 'tabulations'. This approach is being superseded by in-house analysis, supported by computer systems. There are three reasons for moving in-house: flexibility, competitive advantage and technology.

Flexibility in revising analyses

> The market is changing too rapidly for the traditionally slow process of data collection, data analysis and data presentation. Much data remains unanalysed.

Cost and time limits analysis to the simplest levels – often only hole counts and cross tabulations. There is little opportunity to explore interesting features which emerge from this first stage. As targeted marketing moves closer and closer towards the ultimate market of one person, so the facts produced by the old research are being replaced by models and information on demand.

More than one segmentation scheme will often be needed to fit the strategic objectives at all levels: this covers the advertising and sales promotion plan, the sales plan, the pricing plan and the distribution plan. Cutting the data in many different ways, to explore all the variables, can be prohibitively expensive if done by an external research agency.

British Telecom operates multiple segmentation schemes in the small business market. For advertising and sales promotion they recognize:

- *Enthusiasts*. These people treat telecommunications almost as a hobby and love to be kept up to date with the latest functions and features. All communications with them need to reflect these attitudes.
- *Luddites*. These people hate everything modern and technical. However, give them a few practical examples, and you might get them interested.
- *Corporate executives*. This group includes managers and directors, who respond best to arguments about benefits and competitive advantage.
- *Shopkeepers*. Shopkeepers have very little use for the telephone, so there is little justification for communicating with them.
- *Traditionalists*. These people are interested in ease of use and easy maintenance.

> For sales planning, their targeting is based on the size of revenue opportunity, which is based on a model which combines:
>
> - *Turnover* – larger companies tend to spend more on telecoms
> - *Standard Industry Code (SIC)* – certain industries are bigger telecoms users than others.

Along with inflexibility, lack of control in research is still a problem.

One company commissioned an agency to research who its customers were. The agency decided, without consulting the client, to do the research during school hours, when field-workers would have their children off their hands. Lo and behold, when the results came in, they showed that 1 per cent of customers were under 18 – despite the fact that all previous research showed the figure to be 30–40 per cent. The reason? Most customers shopped during lunch or after school.

MARKETING INSIGHT

Holding the data in-house can enable planners to re-analyse it time after time, without the costs and delays associated with external agencies.

Competitive advantage and unique segmentation schemes

> Standard segmentation schemes bought from external agencies cannot provide significant competitive advantage.

Even if you gain advantage from such standard segmentation schemes today, your competitors can buy them tomorrow and rapidly catch up with you. Unique segmentation schemes are the best solutions to unique problems, yet many agencies continue to offer standardized segmentation products to all their clients.

Table 11.1 gives examples of business objectives and segmentation methods.

Take the automobile industry for example. Henry Ford assumed that price was the dominant segmentation variable, then General Motors started to recognize different income and preference groups in the market. More recently, the Japanese recognized the importance of car size and fuel economy. The success of new entrants into the automobile market has often resulted from discovering new segmentation possibilities in the market.

Yet market research in the automobile market continues to include a widely available off-the-shelf component. The off-the-shelf segments available from agencies are very simple and basic:

- small cars
- medium cars
- large cars.

Table 11.1 Examples of business objectives and segmentation methods

Business objective	Segmentation method	Information source
Market extension ■ new locations ■ new channels ■ new segments	Geodemographics Prospect profiles Survey analysis	Electoral roll (consumer) Companies House (business) Prospect lists and surveys
Market development	Customer profiling Behavioural scoring	Sales ledger and added profile data Models from internal data source
Product development	Factor analysis Qualitative methods	Surveys Panels/discussion groups

MARKETING INSIGHT

The traditional automobile segmentation schemes really do not reflect the market very well, and certainly do not offer competitive advantage. Many products in the market, such as the Land Rover Freelander series or the Renault Clio, have resulted from mould-breaking segmentation schemes.

Other industries, such as financial services, have had their vision of the market blinkered through their adoption of off-the-shelf segmentation. Breaking the traditional rules of segmentation in financial services will almost certainly be a prerequisite to competitive advantage. Customer service is a key characteristic in financial services, and approaches such as First Direct have been based on mould-breaking segmentation schemes.

Developing customized segmentation schemes is often difficult with external agencies, and some companies are doing such analysis in-house to provide a unique segmentation proposition.

Information technology

Technology has provided the means by which planners can break free of the traditional constraints of relying upon external research agencies.

There are three ways in which information technology supports planners:

1 Databases from external and internal sources are alternatives to the data collected by research agencies.
2 Data collected by research agencies is available on computer databases for clients to analyse themselves.
3 Computer software is available to in-house planners and is making data analysis and interpretation easier, faster and more flexible.

All three of these factors are changing the shape of the research industry. However, the industry often regards the information technology explosion as a threat to its own future, as well it may if it fails to respond to the needs of marketing planners.

The marketing audit

As we saw from Chapters 2, 3, 4 and 5, the marketing audit process requires planners to assemble and organize a great number of estimates of market size, structure and dynamics from external sources, and company share and performance from internal sources.

Two major challenges in conducting a marketing audit are:

1 Getting sound data from external and internal sources
2 Matching external and internal categories.

External data sources

> One of the primary tasks in the external audit is to estimate the market size and its breakdown by geography, product and segment.

This should be straightforward, given the vast quantities of market data that do exist.

However, knowing where to begin to collect, store and analyse data presents a real challenge. It helps to differentiate clearly between research on new markets and existing markets. Each presents a very different set of problems in terms of data:

● For *new markets*, data are comparatively scarce, and extrapolation from surveys is often the main source. Carefully designed analysis methods are necessary to resolve uncertainties introduced by small sample sizes. Models based on limited data and plausible assumptions have to be used to infer market size, structure and dynamics.
● For *existing markets*, public and agency-owned data sources can provide a rich and detailed picture. Behavioural data are often widely available on buying patterns; often quite detailed information is available on buyer attitudes and characteristics. Sophisticated statistical techniques that rely on large sample sizes can then be used to infer market size, structure and dynamics.

Some examples of sources of data and segmentation variables are given in Tables 11.2 and 11.3.

Internal data sources and MIS

In theory, the internal audit should be relatively straightforward. Analysis and reporting of company results by region, product and segment should merely involve a bit of computer analysis of the sales ledger.

> In practice, there are problems. Sales ledgers are owned by finance and designed to facilitate billings and collections. Their purpose does not include supporting marketing, and they rarely do so.

Table 11.2 Consumer markets – major external segmentation variables

Variable	External source
What is bought Volume Price Outlets	Government publications provide high-level statistical summaries of many industries. Periodic research by agencies is often published as books of tabulated data. This is obtained by traditional survey methods but also from supermarket scanner data, pharmacy sales data, etc. Such data is often available in computer readable format.

Who buys
Geography
  Postcode
  Population density
  Town or city size
  Driving distance to stores
Demographic
  Age
  Sex
  Income
  Occupation
  Family size
  Family life-cycle
  Race/nationality
Socio-economic
  Social class
  Lifestyle
  personality
	Census data and electoral roll data are the two main sources of geographic and demographic information. The electoral roll can be bought from agencies that collect such data and it covers individual people. Their buying characteristics can be inferred from 'lifestyle' survey databases, built from millions of questionnaires collected from the public over several years. More detailed census data is not available at individual level, but for 100,000 Enumeration Districts (EDs) in the UK. Each ED has hundreds of geodemographic characteristics, which may be of relevance to the planner. Those planners who do not have the time or skill to explore the census data can purchase a pre-segmented coding scheme such as ACORN, which is simpler than the census, but usually less relevant to the user. Most such data can be obtained in computer readable format.
	TV audience data is available from surveys which include a wide rage of profiling details. Magazine circulation data is widely available, and often can be broken down into segments. For limited-circulation magazines, individual reader profiles can be purchased.

Why Attitude towards product Advertising and promotion Readiness stage Benefits sought Perceptions Brand loyalty Preferences	Ad-hoc research can be commissioned and summary data created by a variety of survey methods.

> The information on sales ledgers is incomplete and mis-coded from marketing's viewpoint. Ledgers contain accounts and stock-keeping units, which cannot easily be linked to customers, products, regions or segments.

Collecting, consolidating and using sales-ledger information may also be difficult. Ledgers are designed to do accounting consolidations and analysis, not market consolidation and analysis.

Table 11.3 Industrial markets – major external segmentation variables	
Variable	**External source**
What is bought Volume Price Outlets	Government publications provide a high-level statistical summary of many industries. Periodic research by agencies is often published as books of tabulated data. This is obtained by traditional survey methods. There are few databases in this area.

Who buys
Demographic
   Industry/SIC
   Turnover
   Number of employees
   Financial status
Geography
   Postcode
   Population density
   Driving distance (sales reps)
Organizational
   Job titles
   Department sizes
	Companies House data is the main source of information on industrial firms. Only registered companies are included and data can be out of date and incomplete. Private agencies offer alternative sources of data, sometimes with added details on specific characteristics. In particular, organizational details such as job titles, department sizes, etc. are available. Those planners who do not have the time or skill to explore the data can now purchase a pre-segmented coding scheme similar to ACORN, although its relevance to many planning objectives is unclear. Most of this data can be obtained in computer readable format.

Why Purchasing policies Selection criteria Attitude towards product Advertising and promotion Readiness stage Benefits sought Perceptions Brand loyalty Preferences	Ad-hoc research is the primary source of data. The results of commissioned research can sometimes be obtained on computer media.

An MIS or marketing information system is the solution. Building an MIS involves:

- adding codes to the sales ledger to identify customers and products (in addition to accounts and stock-keeping units)
- summarizing the customer transactions to a level of detail suited to marketing
- extracting the customer/product data
- storing it on a database
- adding extra codes to facilitate segmentation analysis
- obtaining software tools to analyse and report on the database.

This is easy to describe, but, as those who have tried will know, tremendously hard to implement. The main difficulty to overcome is to manage the expectations of computer staff, financial management (who own the sales ledger) and marketing users.

A problem facing anyone contemplating the development of an MIS is whether to hold data at the lowest level of detail or to hold summary statistics. The extra cost of storing and processing detailed data, at customer level, often deters planners. However, only storing summary data is a mistake in most circumstances, for two reasons:

1 Flexibility to analyse and segment by different combinations of variables is only possible if the data is held at the lowest possible levels of detail.

2 Customer data can subsequently be used for implementing the strategy (i.e. for direct mail, telemarketing and field sales call reporting).

Database marketing – reconciling the tactical with the strategic

▶ **D E F I N I T I O N** ◀

A database is a collection of data and information from outside and inside an organization which is stored in such a way that it can be accessed and analysed to provide intelligence for making decisions to achieve the company's objectives

▶ **Databases** have traditionally been too large and expensive, and their performance too slow, for them to be cost-justifiable. Consequently, many of the MIS in use today are summary sales reporting systems. However, with the increased importance attached to direct marketing, telemarketing and sales performance management (using laptop computers), many companies are actively engaged in building customer databases.

Databases often represent a compromise between the strategic requirements of the planners and the tactical requirements of direct marketers, telemarketers and sales managers. Another trouble for newcomers to the world of databases is that they fall prey to the many pitfalls, and believe many of the myths (Table 11.4).

The consequence of these problems is that databases very often hold data that do not fit the purpose of the tacticians, far less the needs of strategic planners.

> The attempt to develop databases that serve both strategic and tactical purposes is often referred to as database marketing.

One of the most acute problems is that of reconciling the internal and external views of the markets. The usual problem is that data retrieved from the sales ledger rarely possess the details needed to link customer records to market segments. Some of the problems are described in Table 11.5.

Fusing together data from external sources and internal data is becoming increasingly common as a solution to the external–internal problem. This is often referred to as data fusion. Where large volumes of data are involved, computer programs, known as de-duplication routines, are used to automate the matching of the data. However, automation rarely achieves more than 80 per cent accuracy in matching, and manual matching has to be applied to the remaining data.

Table 11.4 Myths and realities about databases

Myth	Reality
The database collects what we need	We collect what is easily available
The database measures what matters	We measure what is least embarrassing
The database users understand what data they need	We know what we used last, what the textbooks say and what might be interesting on a rainy day
The database needs to hold more and more data	We feel safer with 'loads a data', even when we haven't a clue how to use it
The database must integrate the data physically	We like neat solutions, whatever the cost
The database will save staff time	We need more and more staff to analyse data
The database will harmonize marketing, finance and sales	We all compete for scarce resources, and this involves fighting
The database is the one source of our market intelligence	We haven't thought through the business problems

Table 11.5 Problems of reconciling internal and external market audits

External audit – variable	Problem with internal
What is bought	Internal systems have rich detail on accounts and stock-keeping units. However, information about products such as colour, style, etc. can often be missing. Information on the outlets or channels through which they sold is very often lacking.
Who buys	Internal systems record who paid the invoice and who received delivery of the goods. They rarely record who made the buying decision, or who influenced it. Even when the buyer details are on the system, it is rarely easy to determine their characteristics such as age, sex, etc. Reconciling external to internal involves: ■ matching accounts to customers ■ matching stock-keeping units to products ■ matching external variables to internal records ■ collecting data from other sources than the sales ledger (e.g. from surveys of sales representatives).
Why	Internal sources of information on why people purchase is scarce. Enquiries can be qualified, using survey techniques, to provide some clues on why people respond to an advertising campaign. Customer satisfaction surveys may also yield clues. Call reports from field sales and telesales can also provide valuable clues, especially if survey disciplines can be observed by the sales staff.

> The cost of matching external and internal market-coding schemes is driving a few companies to collect customer profiles at source. This is either when they first enquire, or when their sales ledger records are first created.

However, the cost of the changes to the sales ledger, and the fact that it is owned by finance, is often a barrier to success. In the future, marketing will need to work much more closely with finance and the IT department if it is to develop databases successfully.

What is the secret of using information successfully?

Information, in the minds of most marketing managers, lies in a strange no-man's land, part way between the nitty-gritty stuff of marketing management and the dizzy abstractions of technologists, cyberneticists and boffins. Widely misunderstood, or equated to 'keyboard literacy' or 'technology awareness', the management of marketing information often ends up neglected or delegated to the most junior member of the marketing team.

Information is not the same as technology, nor is it information technology, nor is it necessarily derived from information technology. There are many myths associated with the use of computers to hold marketing data, as Table 11.4 reveals.

Information is not all hard, objective data; we will not necessarily become better informed by collecting more and more raw data, and storing it until we end up knowing 'everything'. Accounting systems are often seen as a source of hard facts, since most accounting transactions have to be audited and therefore must be reasonably accurate. Yet most accounting data have little direct relevance for marketing strategy.

What information is needed to support a marketing strategy? The answer to this question is something of a conundrum, since the information needed depends upon the marketing objectives that form the strategy. If you change the strategic marketing objectives, then you may need different kinds of information to support your strategy. Table 11.1, earlier in this chapter, illustrates how different objectives require different supporting information.

This observation goes some way towards explaining one of the great puzzles of marketing information:

> Why is it so difficult to specify marketing's information needs? The answer is that, unlike accounting or manufacturing, which have fixed information needs, the information needs of marketing keep changing as a consequence of the evolution of the marketing strategy in response to market changes.

At this point, the sales or marketing director might feel that, because the situation changes so radically every year, there can be no hope for developing an effective system or procedure for obtaining marketing information. Many at this point delegate the need to an office junior, with the result that they are very ill-informed when they come to develop their marketing strategies.

The information needs of marketing keep changing as a consequence of the evolution of the marketing strategy.

For all the problems, there are basic underlying marketing issues with which all companies have to contend. Furthermore, the solutions they have adopted can be seen as variations on relatively few themes. The basic model of a marketing system can be visualized as in Figure 11.10.

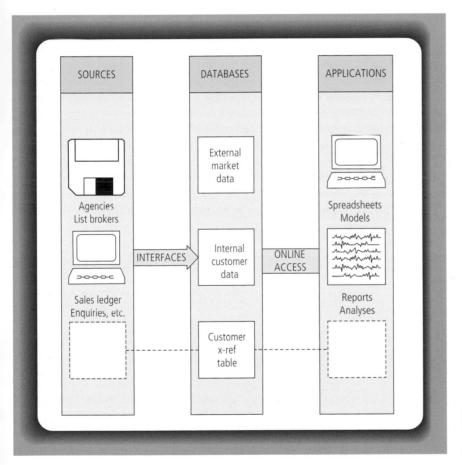

Figure 11.10
Information flows in a marketing system

The main components of the system are as follows:

- *External market data*, purchased from external agencies. These include governmental agencies, market research firms, list brokers, etc.
- *Internal customer data*, collected from the sales ledger and other internal sources such as customer service, field sales, telesales, etc. It is coded and segmented in such a way that market-share figures can be created by comparison with external data.

- *Customer reference table*, needed to make the system work effectively. It identifies customers (as defined by marketing) and provides a cross-reference to sales ledger accounts. Whenever a new sales ledger account is created, the cross-reference table is used to determine the customer associated with that account. This avoids the need for costly manual matching or de-duplication after the account is created. It is also used by marketing applications as a standard reference table for customers.
- *Database* refers to all three of the above data types. It needs to be structured using a technique known as *data modelling*, which organizes the data into the component types that marketing wants, and not the structure that finance or anyone else provides. Usually, the data are held using *relational database* software, since this provides for maximum flexibility and choice of analysis tools.
- *Interfaces* refers to the computer programs that grab the data from the source systems and restructure it into the components to go onto the marketing database. These programs have to be written by the in-house IT staff, since they obtain and restructure data from the in-house sales ledger, and other in-house systems.
- *Applications* are the software programs that the planners use to analyse the data and develop their plans. They include data-grabbing tools that grab the items of data from their storage locations; reporting tools that summarize the data according to categories that marketing defines; and spreadsheets that carry out calculations and what-if analyses on the reported summary data.

■ Software systems in marketing

We have examined the role of the marketing information system in reconciling internal and external information to support decision-making. We now look in more detail at the data held by the marketing information system, and at the applications that can help to analyse it.

Figure 11.11 shows some of the most common data held and manipulated by the marketing function, and some of the most common functions which use this data. A single IT system will support a subset of the data and a subset of the functions. For example, many marketing database products and bespoke systems support more than one of the sales management, direct mailing, telemarketing and electronic commerce functions. Arrows are used to indicate data flow.

Marketing data can broadly be divided into two: operational data, which deal with individual products, customers and transactions; and aggregated data, where the unit of analysis is the market segment, market or product group.

Customer/product level data

At the customer/product level, a variety of data may be held on actual and potential customers. Holding a degree of customer information is

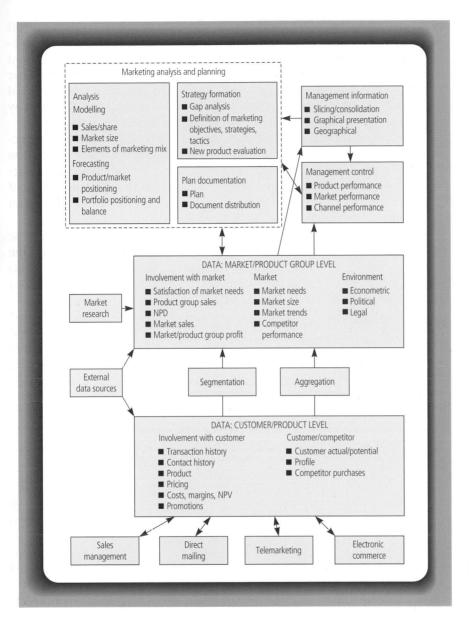

Figure 11.11
Information use in marketing

often taken as the minimal requirement of a marketing database. The information can range from basic reference data (such as name, address and postcode) to demographic data (such as age, sex and income) and psychographic data on attitudes and lifestyle collected from surveys. In industrial markets, information may be richer and more detailed about a smaller number of customers, covering, for example, organizational structure, key contacts and their roles, the customer's value chain, and so on. As well as details of the customer's purchases from the organization, information may be held on their purchases from competitors. Information may relate to both direct and indirect customers, and a similar range of information may be held for distributors and other relevant bodies or individuals such as influencers and sources of referrals.

Information is also typically held in marketing databases on the customer's involvement with the organization. Transaction data can include items such as what products have been purchased at what price, the buying channel used, purchasing frequency and account balance. The transaction data typically references product data, which include product codes, pricing and, in some cases, information on costs and margins and promotions. Contact history information (such as sales contacts, mailings, complaints or service calls) and proposals may also be held. This may include soft data on why customers did or did not buy, aiding analysis of market needs and the extent to which the organization is satisfying them at the aggregated, market level. All this information may be held in a separate marketing database, or it may be integrated into the organization's operational systems.

Customer/product level functions

Drawing on these operational data, most 'marketing database' products and many bespoke systems provide one or more of the following functions:

● *Sales force automation*. This can include sales force productivity tools such as contact management, order entry, checking inventory and order status, diary management, and reporting of expenses. Often now involving notebook computers used by the sales force in the field, the key facility is 'contact management', making all aspects of the contact with the customer available to the salesperson: notes of previous meetings, records of orders placed; notes on service issues and complaints, and so on. Integration with the Internet can include querying online databases to generate leads or find more information about a prospect, as well as e-mail for the sales force to communicate with each other and with back-office staff. Benefits can also include elimination of mistakes in pricing and configuration, and better inventory control. Features can also include management functions such as automated reports on staff performance, sales activity, forecasts versus actuals, and so on.

● *Direct mailing*. Systems supporting direct mailing provide functions such as selecting a subset of a mailing list, customizing letters and address labels, selecting appropriate literature, and tracking and forwarding leads. Management of lists can include facilities such as de-duplication, where two or more lists have been combined, and data quality reporting.

● *Telemarketing*. This typically includes management of call lists, scripting of the dialogue with the prospect, and tracking and forwarding leads or order entry. Again, data management of lists can form a major part of the system.

● *Electronic commerce*. Electronic links between the organization's computers and those of the customer provide an alternative channel for advertising, prospecting, sales and post-sales support, as well as for product/service delivery in some cases. These links may be implemented using the Internet, or other wide-area networks such as those developed for electronic data interchange in cases such as the automotive industry.

Whatever the route to the customer, there is also a need for *campaign management*. Systems that support one or more of the above channels to the customer may support all steps of a campaign, from definition of objectives to recording and analysing campaign results.

There is a growing realization that information needs to be shared across these different means of interacting with the customer, so that all customer information is available to any employee who is in contact with the customer. For many large organizations with complex legacy systems, this integration presents formidable hurdles, and is a major motivation for new systems development. Some organizations are taking advantage of a new generation of integrated off-the-shelf packages, which can support these different means of customer interaction and the various stages of a customer's involvement with the organization, from initial contact through sales to customer service. The term *customer relationship management* (CRM) is currently in vogue for this concept of integrated systems at the customer interface. We discuss CRM in more detail later in this chapter.

Data at the market/product group level

The transaction-level data can be aggregated into data at the level of markets or market segments, and product groups or product-market combinations. This provides information at a sufficiently summarized level for marketing management analysis, planning and control. The data can broadly be regarded as falling into the categories of market information, information about the company's involvement in the market, and the wider economic, political or legal environment. We have discussed the crucial issue of how the segments are defined as a basis for this aggregation earlier in this chapter and in Chapter 4.

Management information and control

Systems focusing on the provision of management information provide facilities for selecting the information required and displaying it in a variety of formats, such as tables and business graphics. The provision of geographic interfaces using maps, and analysis facilities appropriate to geographic data, form a 'Geographic Information Systems' extension found in some cases.

Closely related to management information is management control. Performance against plan for product, market, channel and so on can be tracked through simple graphical display, or through facilities such as exception reporting, where the system highlights areas where the divergence from plan is significant.

Data warehousing

The IT industry has a vested interest in refreshing its vocabulary regularly to ensure that its offerings sound up to date and exciting, and are not tarred with the same brush as the previous generation, which may not have delivered all that was expected. The term ▶ **'data warehouse'** has emerged in recent years as yet another label for a management information system or an EIS (executive information system), most commonly (though not necessarily) focused on marketing. To be fair, the term does reflect some developments from the typical EIS of the late 1980s or early 1990s, which typically summarized a limited amount of key information in a user-friendly format:

1 Data warehouses aim to integrate data from all operational systems, such as order processing and billing, into one database using a single data model. That is, there is a single consistent view of such things as customers and products, so, for example, a customer's name and address will only be stored once, and all the products purchased by a customer can be readily ascertained. The data are refreshed regularly from the operational systems – typically overnight – to keep them up to date. So just as the operational systems at the customer interface are becoming better integrated, data warehousing represents the desire to integrate information better for purposes of management information and analysis.

2 Data warehouses typically hold historical information, not just the current information needed for billing and so on. This has become possible due to the rapidly decreasing cost of computer power and storage.

3 Similarly, increasing capacity allows the information to be held at a fine level of detail. Information can be stored about individual purchases, even for mass consumer markets, over substantial periods.

Taken together, these developments provide a rich store of information which, at least potentially, integrates the two levels of data we have described – customer/product level data, and aggregated data at the level of markets and product groups. As with previous generations, a range of facilities for viewing and tabulating the information may be provided – such as the SQL query language, which allows data to be collected according to specified criteria such as 'All customers with a salary of over £40,000 and an approaching renewal date who are not currently using our highest level of service'. OLAP (online analytical processing) tools – again often previously called EIS or DSS (decision support systems) – allow the data to be browsed graphically and tabulated.

Data mining

The facilities for analysing the data bring us to the next buzzword of the moment. When mining, one may discover unexpected treasures – hence the term ▶ **'data mining'** for searching for relevant patterns in data that had not been anticipated. The term tends, though, to be applied to most forms of data analysis using data warehouses. Some of the analyses of particular relevance to marketing are:

1 Segmentation, such as clustering routines, which we have discussed earlier.
2 Causal, econometric or predictive modelling – predicting the effect on, say, future sales based on predictions of various 'independent variables' such as future price, advertising spend, competitor's price and so on (discussed in the next section).
3 Undirected searching for correlations – asking the system to search for significant correlations between a large number of potentially connected variables, such as consumers' purchases of particular product lines.

> The best-known example is of Wal-Mart, who discovered that a significant customer group was purchasing beer and nappies, and little else, in early evenings in the week. This group turned out to be men who had been asked to buy more nappies, and while doing so had topped up on beer. Once this pattern was observed, the chain could significantly increase sales by placing beer next to the nappies on the shelves.

■ CRM – putting it in its proper context[2]

As this book was being written, billions of dollars were literally being wasted on what has come to be known as Customer Relationship Management – CRM.

It will, however, be blindingly obvious that, no matter what particular definition is given for CRM, and no matter how much money is spent on databases and on systems for accessing and promulgating such data, unless there exists a deep understanding of the market and of the needs of customers within market segments, CRM will become merely the latest fad and will soon wane in importance.

The author and many other critics have berated organizations which embraced TQM, BPR, Balanced Scorecards, Knowledge Management and whichever latest acronym-promoted fad emerged from consultants and business schools. Precisely the same reasoning as we applied in Chapter 1 can and should be used in the case of CRM. CRM is the latest must-have management fad – not, we stress, because there is anything wrong with either the process or with the underlying technology that supports it, but because the fundamental preconditions we outline in Chapters 1–4 are not

[2] The author is grateful to Dr Paul Fifield and Ian Dunbar for their contribution to this section on CRM.

being met in most organizations. We will expand on these conditions later. For now, let us look a little more closely at the latest acronym, CRM.

What is CRM?

Well, it depends. CRM is really too young to be fully formed yet, and what it is rather depends on who you happen to be talking to – or who is trying to sell it to you. Definitions of CRM are everywhere, and different. We offer a selection:

A continuous performance initiative to increase a company's knowledge of its customers.

CRM comprises the organization, processes and systems through which an organization manages its relationships with its customers.

Consistent high-quality customer support across all communications channels and business functions, based on common information shared by employees, their customers and business partners.

A methodology, based on new information technology, that helps companies reach their long-held goals for improved customer satisfaction.

An integrated, multiple-delivery channel strategy that allows companies to capture profitable new customers and improve service.

ERP is from Mars, CRM is from Venus.

The quicker-witted among you will have noted that the IT/systems backbone of CRM keeps peeking through the skin. This is not automatically a bad thing, but we need to recognize CRM, at least as it currently stands, for what it is (see Table 11.6).

At the moment, CRM is being delivered as a method of combining one or more of the IT systems that exist or can be placed into an organization relating to the customer interface. Depending on the source of reference, the following are usually mentioned:

- Data warehouses
- Customer service systems
- Call centres
- E-commerce
- Web marketing
- Operational systems (order entry, invoicing, payments, point-of-sale, etc.)
- Sales systems (mobile representative communications, appointment making, etc.).

Table 11.6 CRM – the features

- Customer analysis
- Market segmentation
- Manage target marketing activities
- Model customer behaviour (predictive)
- Customer service history
- Access self-service patterns
- Customer marketing history
- Measure customer retention
- Measure customer loyalty
- 'Single view' of the customer
- Revenue analysis
- Customer information (demographics and life-cycle/lifestyle)
- Score customer responsiveness to different forms of communication and service
- Identify different forms of product/service in use

We suggest that a more appropriate definition of CRM is:

> The IT-enabled integration of data across multiple customer contact points for the purpose of developing appropriate offers to different groups of customers.

The basic idea, then, is to integrate these systems, thus enabling the organization to manage its customers flawlessly. It goes without saying that having different systems in the same organization that do not and cannot talk to each other is not conducive to efficiency. The fact that marketing doesn't talk to finance or sales is obviously no excuse for the systems to act as badly as the humans. The process of integrating/cleansing/unifying/presenting the diverse data is obviously a 'good thing', no doubt about that, but does it all add up to 'Customer Relationship Management'?

The promised benefits of CRM

Depending on who you are talking to, the benefits of a CRM project might include everything you have ever wanted to know (see Table 11.7) – certainly nothing less than the answer to who buys what and why. At last, the marketing Holy Grail – unpredictable customers reduced to numbers that can be analysed, plotted, planned and categorized. The question is, however, will CRM deliver?

If the answer is 'I don't care, let's give it a go', do you remember the last time you felt like this? When was it, about the time of Business Process Re-engineering, Benchmarking, Customer Service, Investors in People? Or was it even about the time of Total Quality Management or 'Excellence'? None of these initiatives was a bad idea, but very few got anywhere near delivering the benefits that were promised.

Table 11.7 CRM – the benefits

- Identify most profitable customers
- Serve most profitable customers better
- Manage less profitable situations better
- Identify the lifetime value of customers
- Reduce customer 'churn'
- Find profitable prospects
- Market the right products
- Reduce selling and marketing costs
- Improve effectiveness of marketing communications and direct marketing
- Improve customer service
- Focus Internet-e-commerce to the right customers
- Focus marketing to the right customers
- Refine marketing strategy
- Obtain competitive advantage
- Win!

Of course, executives hope CRM will be different. The problem is, this time we do not just risk messing up the back-office processes, now we are playing with customer relationships and if we get CRM wrong, customers leave, never to return.

What is CRM all about?

Ultimately, CRM has to be about *competitive advantage*. This is what organizations want and what the consultants can sell. There is also no doubt that CRM can be a major factor in achieving competitive advantage. Whether CRM is the whole answer is quite another question.

There are three legs to the CRM 'stool': strategy, marketing and IT. Take just one of the legs away and the stool will fall over. Try to build CRM on just one leg alone and you will not even get your organization off the floor.

The simple truth is, CRM projects will spill out enormous amounts of customer data. Whether your organization is able to make those data meaningful and turn them into 'information', then knowledge, depends on whether you know what you want to do with it. Imagine (and this is a real example) you discover that the most important fact (correlation) about the heaviest users of your communication service is that they are likely to be cat owners. Then what? Joint promotions between telecoms and cat food? Too many companies believe that all they have to do is collect large amounts of similarly pointless data and they will finally be able to meet those (ludicrous) cross-selling objectives. The power to annoy more customers, faster and at greater cost is a distinct danger.

Making the small print big print

All of the CRM literature that we have seen does (more or less clearly) state that the success of any CRM project depends on key strategic issues being agreed before any work is done. And, to be fair, those organizations currently marketing CRM solutions do mention the other things that need to be in place before (their version of) CRM will work. Unfortunately, these 'things' are neither small nor particularly easy to put in place. Of course, nobody writes this in red, or inserts health warnings at this point, but it needs to be done.

Perhaps it is time to learn from the pioneers of a previous technological age. Imagine CRM as the railway track. Lay the lines and it will get the train to its destination quickly and efficiently – you may have to knock down a few buildings standing in the way, but that is surely a small price to pay. The eighteenth-century entrepreneurs soon learned (sometimes the hard way) that success existed less in knowing how to lay the lines and more in knowing where people wanted the trains to go. Simple, isn't it?

Pushing the image as far as (or even beyond where) it will go, imagine the company trying to build the first, fastest and best line to – well, any-where really. Customers are taken along for the ride and arrive where none of them ever wanted to be. Exit the customers and exit the business – faster than if it had done nothing in the first place.

So, do you know where your customers want to go?

Find out where you need to be, and then you will begin to understand how CRM might help you get there.

No new technology or TLAs (three-letter acronyms) here, just the same old difficult questions that nobody wants to answer. But with CRM loom-ing, there really is no longer a choice. Tomorrow's battle will not be won by the best CRM system, but by the organizations with the clearest idea of where they are going and how they are going to get there. Simple, maybe, but not easy.

What questions need to be answered?

Where are we now?

Ever since Theodore Levitt's famous 1960 *Harvard Business Review* paper, 'Marketing Myopia', the question of 'What business are we in?' has vexed marketers to the point of forcing them to ignore this most fundamental of all strategic questions. Defining the industry and market within which your organization is going to operate is central to any practical strategy. This is a question all world-class companies are currently asking them-selves. Until it is properly answered, none of the tools and techniques of marketing work. Certainly, CRM will not.

What do our customers want?

Identifying the critical difference between what you are making/selling and what your customers are buying/using identifies your organization's strengths and weaknesses and its real competition. This is the old features–benefits argument. Be very careful. Your customers really do pay good money for the benefits rather than the technical features.

What will our customers want tomorrow?

The objective. Where do we want to be in the future? Not expressed in financial terms; this should describe the ambitions of the organization and the role it expects to be playing in its customers' lives.

Do different customers want different things?

All the CRM vendors make a great play on segmentation as being the key to today's fragmenting and competitive markets. While this is absolutely true, the big problem in all this is that very few are talking about segmentation, preferring to spend more time talking about classifying customers by the data that can be collected from data warehouses. Segmentation is less about which customers do what, and more about why they do it. More meaningful customer data will reduce communications and sales wastage and create competitive advantage. The straightforward method for doing proper segmentation was explained in detail in Chapter 4.

Which customers should we be targeting?

Spotting and serving the most profitable customer has to be the name of the game. Applying segmentation strategically will allow the organization to decide where it needs to focus its activities for greater returns. The time when we could be all things to all people has largely passed. Tomorrow belongs to the credible specialist. An effective CRM process will enable the organization to focus on the customers it wants to retain over the longer term, and will allow the business to develop just those offers that appeal to its target markets.

How do we differentiate our company/brand(s)?

We know a few things about customers – not as much as some would like, but something. We know, for example, that in every developed market (consumer and business-to-business) nine out of ten customers would prefer to buy on non-price criteria. That means the secret to success lies in being different from the rest, not the same – and, for 90 per cent, not the cheapest! Differentiation and owning a unique market position is critical. Do you know how you want to differentiate your offer from the rest? Because if you do not, you might end up with a CRM that only allows you to do the same as everybody else. The inevitable result? Commodity status, price competition and death.

The secret, of course, is careful market segmentation before embarking on expensive and time-consuming CRM projects.

How do we create a CRM process that will work for us, not against us?

The investment involved in agreeing your organization's longer-term ambitions (and therefore the objectives for a CRM project) will be minute compared to the cost of the CRM project itself. If past experience is anything to go by, the IT and organizational costs of CRM are likely to run to many millions – and that is without the potential business costs of getting it wrong. Surely, it must make sense to stop and think through these fundamental questions before committing the organization to an uncertain future.

Very few companies would embark on a major capital project without a feasibility study, or an acquisition without 'due diligence'. So, why set out to spend millions on something that could cause irreparable harm without a CRM audit. What is a CRM audit? As the name implies, it is an unbiased assessment of your organization's current customer position and requirements from any CRM process (see Table 11.8). An audit such as this represents an investment that pays off in two directions: it reduces the downside risks of disaster and increases the upside benefits from success.

The conclusion is probably best summed up by adapting Benjamin Franklin's famous quotation: 'Drive your CRM or it will drive thee'.

Table 11.8 CRM – the audit

- Identification of the market being served; answering 'What business are we in?'
- A quantification of the customer/process dynamics within this market
- An understanding of the competitive environment, including competitor positions and competitive dynamics
- An unbiased (not *a priori*!) segmentation of the market we are interested in serving
- An understanding of customer needs in each segment
- A realistic assessment of the organizational implications of introducing CRM
- An outline plan for the introduction of CRM
- An assessment of the likely costs and benefits of CRM for the organization
- An outline brief for CRM suppliers, especially IT

CRM – some important questions

Before plunging into CRM without agreeing where you want it to take you, think about the following:

Customers

Customers are the name of the game. Without customers there is no business. Levitt said: 'The purpose of a business is to create and keep customers'. Achieving that is not easy, especially as most customers make emotional rather than rational buying decisions and, more often than not, have no idea what they want.

Relationships

How many 'relationships' do you have? How many of those are with commercial organizations? You need to be clear about what is required here. If all you are trying to do is to retain more customers longer to make more money, you can probably do that by making fewer mistakes, so giving fewer excuses for your customers to leave. Building a 'relationship' is quite another matter. But are you sure that your customers want a 'relationship' in the first place? 'Please stop sending me birthday cards, just answer the phone when I ring' is a frequent complaint that we hear. Supplier delusions about the state of customer relationships have reached alarming proportions. Also, do not forget that, just as in our own personal lives the capacity to build close relationships with *all* our friends is limited, so it is with major customers.

Management

Almost everything we read about CRM either talks about (or implies) the organization managing its customers/relationships. Much as it might be the preferred route, it just does not work like that. You do not manage the customer; your customer manages you. At least, that is the impression you should be trying to create. Most customers like to feel in control, so help them. Information flows, systems and processes designed from the customer's perspective might give you a better chance of achieving the results you really want; happy customers spending more and more often. Now, the CRM process that allows customers to manage the organization better to get more of what they want from it certainly would be worth having.

Is CRM just another dangerous management fad or the answer to everyone's prayers? It does not just depend on the CRM providers, but on you and how well you apply the concepts.

Do not be duped into thinking that massaging your own databases will produce the results you want. Remember what most of the real management gurus have said that world-class marketing is over the years. In order of most frequent mention, these are:

● A deep understanding of the market
● Market segmentation
● Differentiation, positioning and branding
● Integrated marketing (marketing planning).

Note the order, and note the expression 'market segmentation', *not* 'your own database segmentation', since your own database segmentation is often a reflection of historical accidents or your own cleverness – in other words, it is what someone sold to someone at some point in time. And since many sales are of products which are the easiest to sell, bought by customers who are the easiest to sell to, this isn't really very promising.

So, before investing in CRM, think about devoting some of the funds set aside for CRM to an audit, or you will waste millions and CRM will join all the other fads.

■ Marketing analysis

We now look at systems that go beyond the provision of information to assisting with its analysis for planning purposes.

Modelling

One way to understand a marketing variable of importance, such as market size or product sales, is to develop a model of the factors affecting the variable. This typically involves defining a mathematical relationship between a number of independent variables and the dependent variable whose variation is to be modelled. For example, a product sales model might include as independent variables consumer spending, product price, competitor's price, and advertising and promotion data. The model can be used to predict future sales, or future market size, on the basis of predictions of the independent variables such as price and advertising spend. Such a 'causal', 'econometric' or 'predictive' model is built by statistical analysis of past data, most commonly through linear regression, although more recently models have also been based on neural nets.

Several software routes are available for the construction of causal models. As well as general-purpose statistical packages such as SPSS, some specialist packages are available that specifically target the business modelling market, such as 4 Thought from Cognos.

The variable being studied does not necessarily vary with time. Cross-sectional analyses may be performed, for example, comparing the effectiveness of distributors or stores, or the attractiveness of possible plan, warehouse or outlet locations. Those based on a time series, however, form a natural basis for forecasting, which is discussed later in this chapter.

Product/market positioning

As well as examining the hard data of sales and market share, systems can assist with assessment of soft data such as a product's positioning in the marketplace. Techniques such as perceptual mapping and Porter's cost/differentiation matrix can be supported by computer to illuminate a strategy debate. A marketing planning system developed by ICL for its own use, for example, included efficiency frontier diagrams to assist with pricing, in which the relative price was plotted against a measure of the product's differentiation.

Portfolio positioning and balance

Portfolio models such as the BCG Matrix and the directional policy matrix have been advocated for over twenty years as a means of assisting with product-market strategy and resource allocation decisions between product-markets. Based on the rationale that their use without specific computer support can be both time-consuming and error-prone, some systems are appearing that help with the mechanics of portfolio analysis, and in some cases generate advice based on textbook marketing theory.

Strategy formation

Systems providing analysis support may also allow the online modelling of the impact of proposed strategies, to provide more active support for strategy formation. Perhaps the simplest form is 'gap analysis' of the gap between the forecast performance and the desired performance. Systems may also provide facilities for exploring possible strategies through 'what-if' amendments to a model. Conclusions reached about marketing objectives, strategies and tactics may be recorded. In theory, the reaction of competitors to the organization's actions can be modelled using ideas such as gaming theory or role-playing, but in practice such active simulation is mainly currently used for training purposes on sample data, using gaming software such as MARKSTRAT.

Systematic schemes for the evaluation of new product proposals have been developed, such as Cooper's NewProd and Cranfield's New Product Manager. These lend themselves to automation as a means of guiding managers through the evaluation process. Systems such as Ideafisher can also be used for new product idea generation.

■ Plan documentation

Having decided on marketing strategies, these may be documented in a marketing plan, or in a plan for one component of the marketing mix. A few systems aim to assist with this process, through automatic generation of a 'template' plan which the user can then edit as necessary. Cranfield's EXMAR[3] system adopts this approach, also including a range of tools for analysis and strategy formation, such as SWOT analysis, perceptual maps, the directional policy matrix and Boston Matrix, Porter's cost-differentiation matrix and gap analysis. Systems may also aid with plan distribution through electronic mail or through adding the numerical data to management information systems.

> The critical issue when building such a system is that it is not self-contained within marketing. It requires interface programs that will alter the systems used by finance, sales and other internal departments, as well as data-feeds from external sources.

[3] EXMAR is a major decision-support tool for strategic marketing planning. For further information, contact Professor Malcolm McDonald, Cranfield University School of Management, Cranfield, Bedford, MK43 0AL, England; email m.mcdonald@cranfield.ac.uk. Alternatively, visit the website: http://www.exmar.com

■ The Internet and marketing strategy[4]

Introduction

We have reviewed the range of IT systems in use within the marketing function, both to support marketing operations and to provide information and analysis for planning purposes. One particular area requires more attention because of its relative newness and far-reaching consequences: the Internet.

If integrated databases provide the means by which information is coordinated and distributed within the organization, wide area networks and in particular the Internet allow this information to be electronically disseminated to customers and, in return, added to as customers interact with the organization via electronic mail and the Web – the two most important Internet applications. Of course, there are plenty of other ways of interacting with customers: face to face, via paper mail, via the telephone, using media advertisements, and so on. But electronic interaction via computer networks provides a new communication channel with quite different advantages and disadvantages from the alternatives. While by no means always appropriate for a given customer interaction, its characteristics have sufficient uses to be irrelevant to none, and for some industries to be a contributor to fundamental reshaping. *Encyclopaedia Britannica* was forced to give up its traditional face-to-face sales approach in the face of competition from Microsoft's multimedia equivalent and the wealth of information available on the Web. The Swedish Post Office has provided every Swedish citizen with an electronic mail address in an attempt to survive the decimation in paper mail that it predicts over the next decade.

The Internet is a *de facto* standard, established by market demand, like Microsoft's Windows and Intel's 86 architecture, rather than by wide industry agreement, like the relational database standards. As such its long-term future is difficult to predict, some believing that it will in time be replaced by other standards, perhaps based on interactive digital TV, which are designed to cope with the high-volume, high-value electronic commerce with which it still struggles. But it is now clearly beyond its initial role as a powerful prototype showing the potential of standardized wide area networks in expanding interactive communication of electronic information.

The 6 Is model

The Internet, then, is an important new way of interacting with customers, but it cannot be considered in isolation: it forms simply one of the channels by which the organization can conduct this interaction. In order to assess

[4]This section on the Internet owes much to the research of Dr Hugh Wilson, principal researcher for the Marketing Information Systems Research Club at Cranfield University School of Management.

its potential contribution, we need a model for the role of IT in marketing more generally. Cranfield's 6 IS model, shown in Figure 11.12, summarizes the ways in which IT can add value to the customer and hence improve the organization's marketing effectiveness. We will discuss the Internet under these six headings.

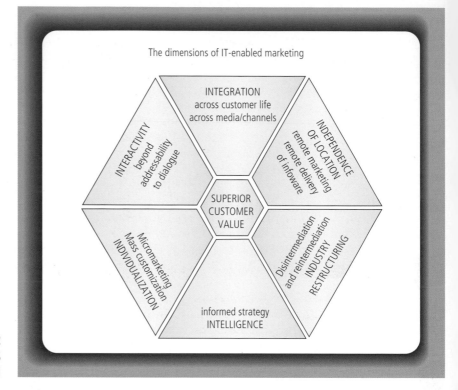

Figure 11.12
Cranfield's 6 IS
model

Integration: know your customer

The need for management of customer relationships implies the need for systems which manage data on the whole of the customer interaction, throughout the customer life-cycle, from initial contact, through configuration and sales, to delivery and post-sales service. The multiple channels by which the consumer demands to be able to reach the supplier imply that these data must also be integrated across communication mechanisms, so a telephone salesperson knows about a service request that was sent yesterday by e-mail, and a sales representative in the field can call on information about previous purchases and customer profitability to assist judgements about discount levels.

This integration is as important with the Internet as with any other communication medium, a fact often lost on companies which delegate the website to enthusiasts in an isolated corner of the organization, or outsource its development and operations with minimal provision for information transfer – hence repeating the mistakes often made in the early days of the call centre. As surveys continue to show, it is all too easy to advertise one's products on the Web with no attempt to gather vital customer information, obtain customer feedback, utilize existing knowledge about the customer or exploit the Web's interactive nature to add value through product configuration, online pricing and so on.

Interactivity: beyond addressability to dialogue

Knowing your customers means closing the loop between the messages sent to them and the messages they send back. IT is supporting an increased use of interactive communication mechanisms such as telephone and the Internet to complement less interactive mechanisms such as mail or media advertisements. It has been said that this is the age of addressability, as organizations have endeavoured to communicate with individual customers through carefully targeted direct mail. Interactivity goes one step further – although there will of course continue to be many occasions when the asynchronous interactivity of the reply coupon is sufficient and appropriate.

A simple example of the appropriate use of the Internet for an interactive dialogue with a known customer is provided by the book market, illustrated in Figure 11.13. Traditionally sold via high-street retailers,

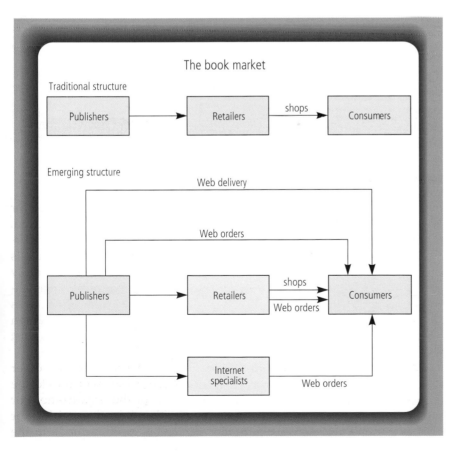

Figure 11.13
Example of interactive dialogue

publishers can now sell books via Internet retailers such as Amazon, or via their own direct Internet service. Naturally, the high-street retailers are looking to protect their business with their own Web channels. There is also, incidentally, an emerging challenge to printed books, provided by electronic publishing, whereby the product is distributed electronically, not just ordered electronically.

On websites such as Amazon, the Web's interactive nature is exploited to provide facilities to the customer such as: searching for books on particular topics; tracking the status of an order placed earlier; asking for recommendations of books similar to a customer's favourite; and reading reviews of a book placed by other customers. The website builds knowledge of the customer, enabling it, for example, to notify the customer by e-mail if a new book appears on a topic of particular interest.

Individualization: information-enabled tailoring

Integrated information about the customer provides the basis for individualizing the product or associated services. A store can produce different versions of their loyalty-card magazine based on the customer's interests. Online newspapers can be tailored to provide the topics you want. Levi's allows jeans to be ordered over the Web to the customer's measurements at a small premium over standard prices. Individualization is closely linked to independence of location – our next topic.

Independence of location: the death of distance

What is the difference between shoes made to measure by the village cobbler and a kitchen made to order by an Internet design service? Both achieve individualization, but the latter combines it with post-industrial revolution economies of scale. It is able to do this because the design service can serve a widely-spread geographical population, using the data transport provided by the Internet and the physical transport of our early twenty-first century infrastructure, plus a database-driven manufacturing facility. Independence of location allows individualization to be achieved economically. Niche products can serve their target markets even if spread globally.

Being able to reach your customers wherever they are may also widen consumer choice and extend consumer power. Software 'agents' are now available that will search the Web for the online bookstore that stocks a particular book at the lowest price, hence outsourcing a time-consuming activity while tending to level prices (as is liable to happen in a given geographical location due to local competition).

The themes of individualization and independence of location are illustrated by Dell, which pioneered a direct sales model for computers (see Figure 11.14). Considerable costs have been taken out by the eradication of local distributors and retail outlets. In Dell's early days, the limited product range could be sold 'off-the-page' by mail order and telephone. But the Web has helped to support a broader range of products, and more

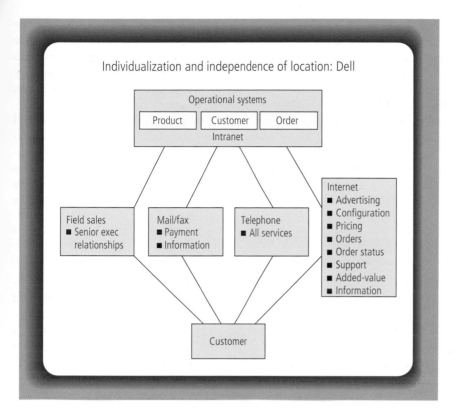

Figure 11.14
Example of mature
Internet usage in a
mixed channel

scope for design of a computer configuration to individual requirements – the kind of well-specified task that computers are good at. Computers are also good at arithmetic, and the customer can see the price of a package interactively as items are added to the bundle. Furthermore, pricing is automatically tailored to the customer, as discounts negotiated by large customers are notified to the pricing algorithm embedded into the website. Further individualization is provided by information services, such as notification by e-mail of new releases of products already held by the customer. All this computer support frees up the expensive individual salespeople for the tasks they are best qualified for: building of individual relationships at senior levels of major accounts.

Intelligence: informed strategy

Better customer data can also improve decisions on marketing strategy. A major computer manufacturer discovered in a marketing planning exercise that the market really segmented according to the application for which the computer was used – accounting, stock control, marketing and so on. However, it had no data on this: all its records were by company name and hence industry segment. Remedying this involved changing its order-taking procedures to track at the time of purchase what use was envisaged by the customer. These extra data had to be gathered through whatever channel was used for placing the order – distributors, direct sales force, telesales or the Internet – illustrating again the importance of data integration. This information could then be aggregated to enable more effective planning, and to support new initiatives to serve particular target segments more effectively.

Segments may also in some cases be derived from the data gathered. A now classic example is Wal-Mart, where a data mining tool discovered a connection between the sales of beer and nappies, which was completely counter-intuitive. This example was quoted earlier in this chapter.

Industry restructuring: redrawing the market map

As already described in some detail in Chapter 10, some industries are being restructured as organizations redefine themselves to take advantage of IT-enabled marketing, or are replaced by newcomers who operate according to the new rules. To take the financial services example, telephone bankers such as First Direct can be seen as the first, comparatively modest step towards the breakdown of the dominance of the 'one-stop-shop' local bank branch. Other challenges to the traditional banks include competitors who are setting up banking services on the Internet, forcing the major clearers to respond with their own Internet services. A 1997 North American study calculated costs of 1 cent for a transaction conducted over the Internet, as opposed to $1.07 for a branch transaction and 27 cents for an ATM. As well as basic transactions, the Internet is being used to replace human advice in product specification. Websites can be used to work out a mortgage's monthly payments, tax and so on using an online form into which the user enters the proposed mortgage size and payment period. New electronic intermediaries are appearing which will search for the best live quote from a range of life insurance companies. The future shape of the retail financial services industry is difficult to predict – one speculative possibility is illustrated by Figure 11.15 – but it is certain to differ from its current configuration. This is a more detailed version of Figure 10.6 from Chapter 10.

Summary of this section on the Internet

We have seen that the Internet can be used as part of a strategy for IT-enabled marketing based on integration of customer data, providing interaction with the customer, allowing individualization of the product or surrounding services, contributing to information needed for planning purposes and reducing the constraints of location. We have also seen how innovative players can use these features to restructure industries to their advantage, as well as that of their customers.

The appropriateness of the Internet for a particular customer interaction will inevitably vary according to circumstances, and in particular according to the characteristics of the segment. As we saw in Chapter 4, the channel may form a primary basis of segmentation, or in other cases a single segment may be served by several channels. Naturally, individual customers will also have their own channel preferences, and often it may

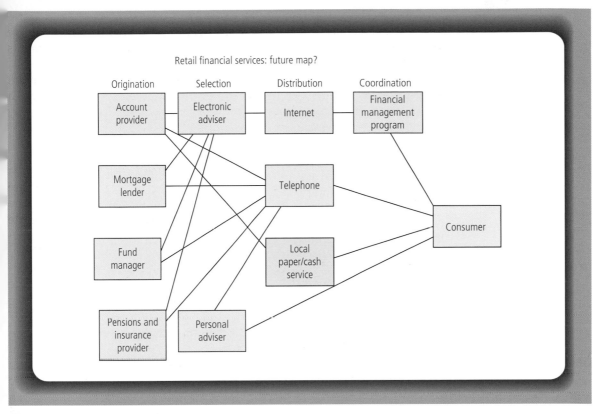

Figure 11.15
Industry restructuring: a possible future for financial services

be necessary to leave the choice to the customer. In general, though, cases where the Internet will be appropriate can be anticipated by considering whether its features match the needs of the interaction. We summarize some of the main features here.

- *Connected subset appropriate.* As long as the Internet is accessible by only a proportion of the population, it is clearly relevant to determine what proportion of the target segment has access. Although users have long since moved beyond the 'nerd' stereotype, there is still a bias towards more highly-educated, younger consumers and, in the business-to-business sector, professionals using computers regularly, such as those in the IT industry.
- *Asynchronous communication at a distance.* Unlike a sales call, the communication can be carried out at any distance, a particular benefit for geographically dispersed markets and those where the cost of sales visits is prohibitive. Asynchronicity means that those communicating do not need to do so at the same time – hence Internet banking can be provided throughout the night without the additional cost of employing

staff at antisocial hours, and product support by electronic mail can be provided when the local staff are next in the office.

- *Interactive*. The Internet is more interactive than direct mail or broadcast media such as traditional television. For the Web, the interactivity differs in nature from that of the telephone or the sales visit, in that the interaction is with a computer rather than a person. This is appropriate for high-volume, repetitive interactions where a computer can be programmed to perform the task.
- *Sight and sound as senses supported*. The Web is mainly a medium of two-dimensional static words and graphics, though this is expanding as bandwidth issues are addressed to include sound and video. This still makes certain products less appropriate for sale over the Internet, such as clothes, where the customer may wish to feel the fabric or try the item on.
- *Cost structure appropriate*. The marginal cost of the Internet as a communication mechanism can be low: the major costs tend to be in the development of appropriate software, such as a website. This balance suits cases where volumes are high. UPS, for example, claims considerable saving from the 60,000 customers per day who check the status of their parcel delivery online, saving 30 cents each time in telephone operator time. The conventional wisdom that one is saved the necessity of advertising is, however, generally false. To grow its market share, Amazon has had to invest heavily in ensuring that its site is given prominent billing by online search engines such as Yahoo and Excite, and service providers such as America Online – online advertisements that have not come cheaply.
- *Privacy and security concerns*. The use of the Internet for the actual placement of an order is being held back by user concerns about security. While these are being addressed through initiatives such as the SET protocol for credit card payments, this is likely to bias Internet sales in the direction of relatively low-value items, and in favour of suppliers with strong brands trusted by the consumer. Users may also have concerns about the privacy of the information they provide. But market research into Internet use suggests that while security and privacy remain genuine concerns, the dominant factors affecting whether the Internet is used remain the traditional factors of shopping experience: price, convenience, service levels, product availability and so on. The more mundane issues of improving the Internet's speed and the quality of websites will be as important as addressing the higher-profile security issues in determining its growth over the next few years.

To summarize, the secrets of success in developing systems for marketing are:

- Understanding what marketing needs and particularly how the internal and external views will be reconciled.
- Developing a strong cost–benefit case for information systems, given that other systems, including financial ones, will have to be altered to accommodate the needs of marketing.

- Working continuously with internal IT staff until the system is built. They are under pressure from other sources, especially finance, and unless marketing maintains momentum and direction, then other priorities will inevitably win.

> Marketing planners need to become far less insular and parochial if they are to obtain the information they require to plan effectively. Cross-functional understanding and cooperation must be secured by marketing if they are to develop the systems they need.

In many companies, marketing staff are, at best, tolerated by their colleagues in finance, operations, IT, and on the board. Building the interdepartmental bridges to secure data, information and knowledge is one of the greatest challenges facing marketing today.

Finally, we have presented an outline process map of the marketing process. Some relevant features of the map are outlined below.

The map is inherently cross-functional. 'Deliver value', for example, involves every aspect of the organization, from new product development through inbound logistics and production to outbound logistics and customer service. Hence, IT support for marketing involves more cross-functional commitment than many other application areas, with important implications for how to organize projects.

The map represents best practice, not common practice. Many aspects of the map are not explicitly addressed by well-embedded processes in even sophisticated companies. Hence, IT projects need to address the issues of how to discover best practice, and how to adapt it to the needs of the organization – issues far outside the expertise of the average computer analyst who is used to analysing an existing process and providing IT support for it.

The map is changing. We have seen that one-to-one communications and principles of relationship marketing demand a radically different sales process from that traditionally practised. Hence, exploiting new media such as the Internet requires a substantial shift in thinking, not just changes to IT and hard processes. It is worth reiterating an illuminating example. Marketing managers at one company related to us their early experience with a website which was enabling them to reach new customers considerably more cost-effectively than their traditional sales force. When the website was first launched, potential customers were finding the company on the Web, deciding the products were appropriate on the basis of the website, and sending an e-mail to ask to buy. So far, so good. But stuck in a traditional model of the sales process, the company would allocate the 'lead' to a salesperson, who would phone up and make an appointment perhaps three weeks' hence. The customer would by now probably have moved on to another online supplier who could sell the product today, but those that remained were subjected to a sales pitch which was totally unnecessary, the customer having already decided to buy. Those that were not put off would proceed to be registered as able to buy over the Web, but the company had lost the opportunity to improve its margins by using the sales force more judiciously. In time the company realized its mistake: unlike those prospects which the company identified and contacted, which might indeed need 'selling' to, many new Web customers were initiating the dialogue themselves, and simply required the company to respond effectively and rapidly. Members of the sales force were increasingly freed up to concentrate on major clients and on relationship building.

Figure 11.16 summarizes and consolidates all of the above. It also consolidates all the previous 'maps' of marketing and IT and, as such, represents a major breakthrough in how IT/IS underpins marketing strategy.

■ Forecasting

> Forecasting is one of the most emotive subjects in the whole field of management. Most managers reckon to be experts, or, at least, are rarely backward in expressing an opinion about the subject, and marketing executives are constantly on the rack, because the one task they inevitably get wrong is the forecast.

While in a book of this kind it is not possible to go into any detail, it would be wrong not to attempt to put this subject into a better perspective than it is currently.

Why is forecasting so difficult?

> The size and complexity of the marketing task in all kinds of enterprise has substantially increased in recent years.

The growing diversity of customer needs in a rapidly-changing environment has resulted in shorter product life-cycles, which have therefore become more difficult to manage profitably.

The growing diversity of customer needs in a rapidly-changing environment has resulted in shorter product life-cycles, which have therefore become more difficult to manage profitably. Distribution patterns have changed dramatically in most markets, and competitive pressures have intensified with the geographical dispersion of operations and the growing internationalization of the scale of businesses, the management of which has become more competent as a result of the growing professionalism of management educators. The socio-cultural, legal and political environments in which managers have to operate have become more volatile and subject to increasingly rapid change. The volume of data and information available has mushroomed, and processing networks have become more sophisticated, while the availability of quantitative techniques to the management of the marketing function has outpaced the ability to use them effectively. Added to this is the ever-present difficulty of measuring the behavioural aspects of marketing, such as social, cultural and psychological.

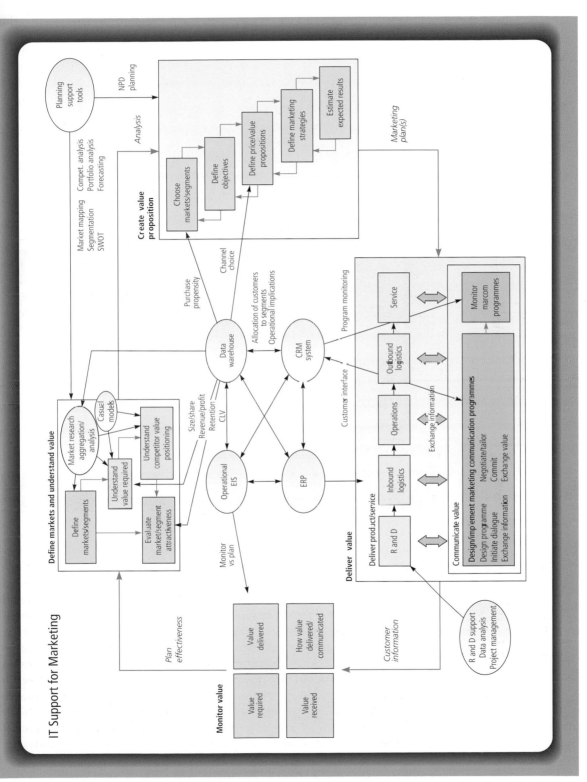

IT Support for Marketing

Monitor value

Value required
Value delivered
Value received
How value delivered/communicated

Define markets and understand value

Define markets/segments
Market research aggregation/analysis
Casual models
Understand value required
Understand competitor value positioning
Evaluate market/segment attractiveness

Create value proposition

Choose markets/segments
Define objectives
Define price/value propositions
Define marketing strategies
Estimate expected results

Deliver value

Deliver product/service
R and D
Inbound logistics
Operations
Outbound logistics
Service

Communicate value

Design/implement marketing communication programmes
Design programme
Initiate dialogue
Exchange information
Negotiate/tailor
Commit
Exchange value
Monitor marcom programmes

Data warehouse
CRM system
Operational EIS
ERP

Planning support tools

Compet. analysis
Portfolio analysis
Forecasting

Market mapping
Segmentation
SWOT

NPD planning

Analysis

Marketing plan(s)

Purchase propensity

Channel choice

Allocation of customers to segments
Operational implications

Program monitoring

Customer interface

Exchange information

Size/share
Revenue/profit
Retention
CLV

Monitor vs plan

Plan effectiveness

Customer information

R and D support
Data analysis
Project management

Figure 11.16

> The result of all this is that it is becoming increasingly more difficult to find and develop profitable markets, and with this comes the difficulty of forecasting with anything like the accuracy that was possible when markets were more stable.

Nevertheless, it has to be done, and it has to be done well, because the consequences of being wrong can be very severe indeed for a company.

This is not the place to go into a detailed description of the many forecasting techniques available to a company. However, it could be useful to discuss briefly the major boundaries of forecasting as outlined in Figure 11.17.

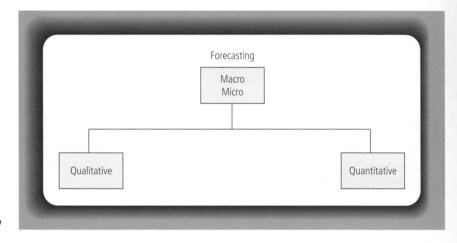

Figure 11.17

> From this, it will be seen that there are two major types of forecasting, which can be loosely described as *macro* and *micro*.

Selection of the appropriate technique is dependent on four main factors, the first of which is the degree of accuracy required. It will be obvious that the greater the risk of the decision that depends on the forecast, the greater will be the accuracy required, hence the cost. Second, the method will depend on the availability of data and information. Third, the time horizon is a key determinant of the forecasting method. For example, are we forecasting next period's sales, in which case quantitative extrapolative approaches may be appropriate, or are we forecasting what will happen to our principal market over the next five years, in which case qualitative approaches may be appropriate? Lastly, the position of the product in its life-cycle will also be a key determinant of the forecasting method. For example, at the introductory stage of a product's life-cycle, fewer data and less information will be available than at the maturity stage, when time series can be a useful forecasting method.

From this, it will be apparent immediately that we must make an important distinction between macro- and micro-forecasting.

> Macro-forecasting is essentially concerned with forecasting markets in total, whereas micro-forecasting is more concerned with detailed unit forecasts.

The discussion of the marketing planning process in Chapter 2 makes it very clear that budgets and plans which are based on little more than trend extrapolations are unlikely to be successful in the long run, since the really key strategic issues relating to products and markets are rarely given due consideration through such a process. Likewise, it will be recalled that our discussion of market segmentation in Chapter 4 stressed that there are inherent dangers in running sophisticated budgeting systems that are based on little more than crude extrapolations of past sales trends and which leave the marketing strategies implicit. Such systems are the ones that cause serious commercial problems when market structures change.

Budgets and plans which are based on little more than trend extrapolations are unlikely to be successful in the long run, since the really key strategic issues relating to products and markets are rarely given due consideration.

> Thus, some form of macro-forecasting has to precede the setting of marketing objectives and strategies, while detailed unit forecasts, or micro-forecasts, should come after the company has decided which specific market opportunities it wants to take advantage of and how best this can be done.

Figure 11.17 also shows that there are basically two major techniques for forecasting, which can be described as *qualitative* and *quantitative*. It would be unusual if either of these methods was used entirely on its own, mainly because of the inherent dangers in each. What we are really talking about is the need to combine an intuitive approach with the purely mathematical approach.

For example, it is comparatively easy to develop an equation which will extrapolate statistically the world population up to, say, the year 2010. The problem with such an approach, however, is that it does not take account of likely changes in past trends. It would be easy to list a whole series of possible events which could affect world population, and then assign probabilities to the likelihood of those events happening.

The main point we are making is that it is the task of management to take whatever relevant data are available to help predict the future, to use on these whatever quantitative techniques are appropriate, but then to use qualitative methods such as expert opinions, market research, analogy, and so on to predict what will be the likely *discontinuities* in the time series. It is only through the sensible use of the available tools that management will begin to understand what has to be done to match its own capabilities with carefully selected market needs. Without such an understanding, any form of forecasting is likely to be a sterile exercise.

■ Organizing for marketing planning

The purpose of this brief section is not to delve into the complexities of organizational forms, but to put the difficult process of marketing planning into the context of the relevant environment in which it will be taking place. The point is that you start from where you *are*, not from where you would like to be, and it is a fact of business that marketing means different things in different circumstances. It is not our intention here to recommend any one particular organizational form. Rather, it is to point out some of the more obvious organizational issues and their likely effect on the way marketing planning is carried out. As a result of the seemingly permanent debate surrounding organizational forms, the author carried out a research study over a two-year period between 1987 and 1989, taking great care in the process to read the literature on the subject of marketing planning.

> The interesting fact to emerge was that most approaches to the subject concentrated almost exclusively on the 'medicine' itself and showed relatively little concern for the 'patient' (if indeed the company can be viewed as being ill and in need of attention).

That this should happen makes about as much sense as a doctor dispensing the same drug to every patient, irrespective of his or her condition. Certainly, the treatment might help a proportion of the clients, but for a vast number it will be at best irrelevant and, at worst, perhaps even dangerous.

> In the case of those promoting the 'marketing planning nostrum', it is particularly ironic to observe how the product has somehow become more important than the customer. Whatever happened to all that good advice about focusing on customers and their situations?

What must be recognized is that there has to be a symbiotic relationship between the patient and the cure. It is the two working together which brings success. Similarly, the 'doctor', if the third-party adviser might be described as such, must be more prepared to take a holistic approach to the situation. Instead of writing an instant prescription, the doctor should first find out more about the patient.

Since the research study referred to above set out to consider how marketing planning might be introduced more effectively into organizations, let us remember that, like the good doctor, we are going to try to understand more about our patients.

■ Organizational life phases

At first sight, every organization appears to be quite different from any other, and, of course, in many ways it is. Its personnel and facilities can never exist in the same form elsewhere. Its products, services, history and folklore also play their part in creating a unique entity.

Yet it is also possible to look at organizations in another way and find that instead of uniqueness, there are also similarities.

What, then, is this commonality all organizations share? As companies grow and mature, it seems that they *all* experience a number of distinct life phases. Certainly, our research experience has convinced us that, once the phases of corporate life are explained to managers, they can readily position their own company on its lifeline.

The significance of this is that the senior executives can then understand the nature of their company's growing pains and how these might contribute to current operational problems and even to a particular organizational culture.

> Moreover, sometimes this culture will be most receptive to marketing planning, at other times less so. Equally, the marketing planning process itself might need to be modified to sit more comfortably within a given corporate culture.

For now, however, let us look at the way companies grow and develop. First, as firms grow in sales, so they tend to go through an organizational evolution. Figure 11.18 shows a firm starting off its existence and growing in turnover over a period of time.

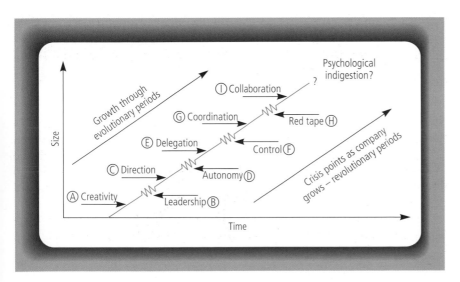

Figure 11.18
(Source: L.E. Greiner (1972) 'Evolution and revolution as organizations grow', *Harvard Business Review*, July/August)

> When such a firm starts off, it is often organized totally around the owner who tends to know more about customers and products than anyone else in the company.

This organizational form can be represented as in Figure 11.19, with all decisions and lines of communication revolving around one person. The point here is that formalized marketing planning by means of systems and written procedures will certainly be less relevant than in, say, a diversified multinational.

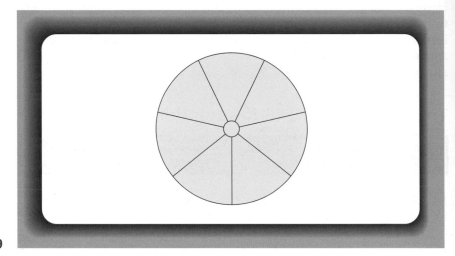

Figure 11.19

The first crisis and the solution

However, as this firm grows in size and complexity, as new products and new markets are added, this organizational form begins to break down and the first crisis appears, which is resolved in one of two ways. Either the owner/entrepreneur sells the business and retires or starts up again, or he or she adopts the more traditional organizational form with which most of us are familiar (Figure 11.20) in which certain functional duties are allocated to individuals to manage by means of their own specialized departments. Some aspects of the work will need to be delegated and systems and procedures will have to be developed to replace the *ad hoc* arrangements of the initial phase. Above all, organizational loose ends have to be tidied up and a new sense of purpose and direction instilled in the employees.

> Thus, a strong leader is required to bring the company out of the leadership crisis phase and into the next, relatively calm period of directed evolution.

Figure 11.20

Here, the leader, who may by now no longer be the founder, directs events from a centralized position. He or she presides over a hierarchical organizational structure which is set up to achieve what the leader prescribes. Again, steady growth can accompany this phase of corporate life until another crisis point is reached. This is the so-called 'autonomy crisis'.

The second crisis and the solution

> Eventually the company will reach a certain size or complexity at which the directive leadership is no longer so appropriate.

Individuals working in their particular spheres of activity know more than the central authority. Not only do they resent being told what to do by someone they perceive to be 'out of touch'; they actually want to have more personal autonomy to influence company policies and operations. The struggle for power at the 'autonomy crisis' can be accompanied by a tightening of central control, which, in turn, exacerbates the problem, causing poor morale and even, perhaps, high staff turnover.

> The crisis is eventually resolved by the company providing a much more delegative style of leadership which does, in fact, generate more autonomy at lower levels. Again a relatively trouble-free, evolutionary growth period follows from this delegated style.

The third crisis and the solution

> However, as growth continues, senior management become increasingly concerned about the high levels of autonomy lower down the organization. They experience feelings of powerlessness and sense the need to regain control.

This control crisis can be another very destabilizing phase of the company's development. Understandable though the feelings of impotence might be for senior management, it seems to be very difficult to turn the clock back to a directive style again. Too much has happened in the intervening years.

> The solution to the control crises seems to be to embark upon a programme for establishing better coordination between the various parts of the organization.

This is often achieved by using such mechanisms as formal planning procedures, centralizing some technical functions, but leaving daily operating decisions at the local level, setting up special projects involving lower-level employees and so on. Thus, another period of relative calm comes with the coordinated evolutionary phase of development.

The fourth crisis and the solution

> With continued growth, there is a tendency for the coordinating practices to become institutionalized, thus planning procedures become ritualized, special projects become meaningless chores and too many decisions seem to be governed by company rules and regulations.

A new crisis point has been reached – the 'bureaucracy' or 'red-tape' crisis. Procedures seem to take precedence over problem-solving.

> The only solution seems to be for the company to strive towards a new phase of collaboration in which, once again, the contributions of individuals and teams are valued as much as, if not more than, systems and procedures.

There has to be a concerted effort to re-energize and re-personalize operating procedures. More emphasis has to be put on teamwork, spontaneity and creativity.

If a company can win through to the collaborative phase of evolution, then, again, a period of relatively trouble-free growth can be expected as a reward. However, as we have seen, this pattern of evolutionary growth followed by a crisis appears to be ever-repeating.

> Each solution to an organizational development problem brings with it the seeds of the next crisis phase.

The fifth crisis?

Thus it is that the collaborative evolutionary crisis will probably end when there is a surfeit of integrating mechanisms and, perhaps, employees begin to lose the ability to function independently.

This last point is purely conjecture, because not many companies seem to have moved far enough along their biographical lifeline for this to be an issue. But from the work we have completed in a number of companies, this idea of company life phases has helped us to understand much more about a client's operating problems and how we might more suitably provide help.

Centralization or decentralization?

Within this second phase of growth, there are basically two kinds of organization, which can be described as either *decentralized* or *centralized*, with several combinations within each extreme.

Looking first at decentralization, it is possible to represent this diagrammatically as in Figure 11.21. The shaded area of the triangle represents the top-level strategic management of the firm. It can be seen from this diagram that the central services, such as market research and public relations, are repeated at the subsidiary company level. It can also be seen that there is a strategic level of management at the subsidiary level, the acid test being whether subsidiary company/unit top management can introduce new products without reference to headquarters.

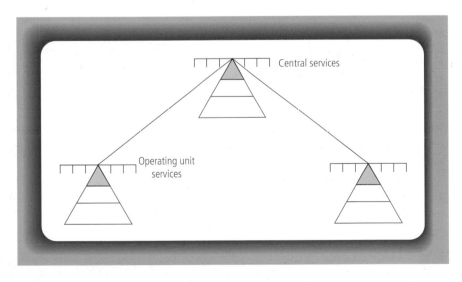

Figure 11.21

The point about this kind of decentralized organizational structure is that it leads inevitably to duplication of effort and differentiation of strategies, with all the consequent problems, unless a major effort is made to get some synergy out of the several systems by means of a company-wide planning system.

MARKETING INSIGHT

One telecommunications company had a range of 1,500 products, and one of those products had 1,300 different variations, all of which was the result of a totally decentralized marketing-orientated approach in the subsidiary companies. It was not surprising that any sensible economies of scale in production were virtually impossible, with the result that the company made a substantial loss.

The same problems apply to marketing research, advertising, pricing, distribution, and other business areas. When someone takes the trouble to find out, it is often very salutary to see the reaction of senior managers at headquarters when they are told, for example, that the very same market problem is being researched in many different countries around the world, all at enormous expense.

MARKETING INSIGHT

It is this kind of organizational structure which, above all others, requires strong central coordination by means of some kind of planning system, otherwise everyone wastes enormous amounts of corporate resources striving to maximize their own small part of the business.

If, however, some system can be found of gaining synergy from all the energy expended, then the rewards are great indeed. The point is that marketing in this kind of system means something different from marketing in other kinds of system, and it is as well to recognize this from the outset.

A centrally controlled company tends to look as depicted in Figure 11.22. Here it will be seen that there is no *strategic* level of management in the subsidiary units, particularly in respect of new product introductions. This kind of organizational form tends to lead to standardized strategies,

Figure 11.22

particularly in respect of product management. For example, when a new product is introduced, it tends to be designed at the outset with as many markets as possible in mind, while the benefits from market research in one area are passed on to other areas, and so on.

> The problem here, of course, is that unless great care is exercised, subsidiary units can easily become less sensitive to the needs of individual markets, and hence lose flexibility in reacting to competitive moves.

The point here, again, is that marketing in this kind of system means something different from marketing in the kind of system described above.

There is a difference between financial manipulation and business management in respect of the headquarters' role. There is a difference between a corporation and its individual components, and often there is confusion about what kind of planning should be done by managers at varying levels in the organization, such confusion arising because the chief executive has not made it clear what kind of business is being managed.

We have looked briefly at two principal organizational forms, both of which consist essentially of a central office and various decentralized divisions, each with its own unique products, processes and markets which complement the others in the group. In enterprises of this type, planning within the divisions applies to the exploration of markets and improved efficiency within the boundaries laid down by headquarters. The problems and opportunities that this method throws up tend to make the headquarters' role one of classifying the boundaries for the enterprise as a whole, in relation to new products and markets that do not appear to fall within the scope of one of the divisions.

In this type of organization, the managers of affiliated companies are normally required to produce the level of profit set by headquarters management within the constraints imposed on them, and such companies need to institutionalize this process by providing a formal structure of ideas and systems so that operating management know what they are expected to do and whether they are doing the essential things.

> The point about these kinds of organization seems to be that some method *has* to be found of planning and controlling the growth of the business in order to utilize effectively the evolving skills and growing reputation of the firm, and so avoid an uncontrolled dissipation of energy.

It is probably easier to do this in a centrally organized firm, but, as we have pointed out, both organizational forms have their disadvantages.

Finally, the *financial trust* type of organization needs to be mentioned briefly, in which the primary concern of central management is the investment of shareholders' capital in various businesses. The buying and selling of interests in various firms is done for appreciation of capital rather than for building an enterprise with any logic of its own. Planning in this type of operation requires different knowledge and skills, and addresses itself to kinds of problems that are different from those in the two organizational forms described above.

Organizing for marketing at board level

Before going on to describe marketing planning systems, there are two further points worth making briefly about organizing for marketing.

> The first is that where marketing and sales are separated at board level, marketing planning is going to be a very different kind of activity from a situation in which both functions are coordinated at board level.

Figure 11.23 illustrates these two different situations.

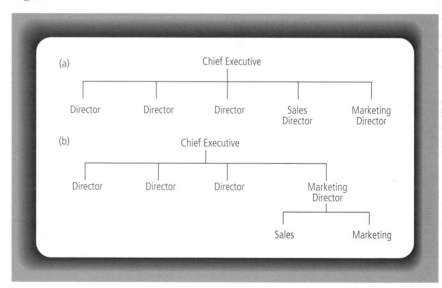

Figure 11.23

In the first of these organizational forms, marketing is very much a staff activity, with the real power vested in the sales organization. While a strong chief executive can ensure that the two activities are sensibly coordinated, unfortunately this rarely happens effectively because he or she is often too busy with production, distribution, personnel, and financial issues to devote enough time to sales and marketing. The point here is that a sales force is quite correctly concerned with *today's* products, problems, customers, and so on, while a marketing manager needs to be thinking about the *future*. The sales force is also quite correctly concerned mainly with *individual* products, problems and customers, while a marketing manager needs to be thinking about *groups* of products and customers (portfolio management and market segmentation).

> The two jobs are closely connected, but fundamentally different, and great care is necessary to ensure that what the marketing department is *planning* is the same as what the sales force is actually *doing* in the field. All too often they are not.

The second kind of organizational form tends to make it easier to ensure a sensible coordination between planning and doing.

> The second and final point about marketing organizational forms is that there are a number of issues that *all* firms have to address.

These are:

- functions (such as advertising, market research, pricing, and so on)
- products
- markets
- geographical locations
- channels.

> Of these, most firms would readily agree that, in most cases, the two main issues are *products* and *markets*, which is why many companies have what are called 'product managers' and/or 'market managers'.

There can be no right or wrong answer to the question of which of these is the better, and commonsense will dictate that it is market circumstances alone that will determine which is most appropriate for any one company.

Each has its strengths and weaknesses. A product manager orientated system will ensure good strong product orientation, but can also easily lead to superficial market knowledge.

MARKETING INSIGHT

Many a company has been caught out by subtle changes in their several markets causing a product to become practically redundant. In consumer goods, for example, many companies are beginning to admit that their rigid product/brand management system has allowed their major customers to take the initiative, and many are now changing belatedly to a system where the focus of marketing activity revolves around major customer/market groups rather than individual products.

On the other hand, a market manager orientated system can easily result in poor *overall* product development.

Ideally, therefore, whatever organizational form is adopted, the two central issues of products and markets constantly need to be addressed. This conundrum can be summarized in the following brief case study.

Northern Sealants Limited manufactures a range of adhesives that fall into two main categories: seals and sealants. The company supplies these products to a large number of markets. However, the main users come under four industry headings: gas, oil and petrochemical refineries; automotive; electrical; and OEM. *Advise how the marketing function should be organized.*

Figure 11.24 illustrates this case diagrammatically in what is often referred to as a *matrix* organization. Figure 11.25 puts this structure into the context of this particular company. Here it will be seen that, organizationally, Northern Sealants has both a product management and a market management structure. The basic role of the product manager is to ensure that the aspects of the product are properly managed, while the role of the market manager is to pay particular attention to the needs of the market. Close liaison between the two is obviously necessary, and a basic principle of this kind of organization is that ultimate authority for the final decision *must* be vested in either one or the other. Even when this is done, however, communications can still be difficult, and great care is necessary to ensure that vested interests are not allowed to dominate the real product/market issues.

Figure 11.24

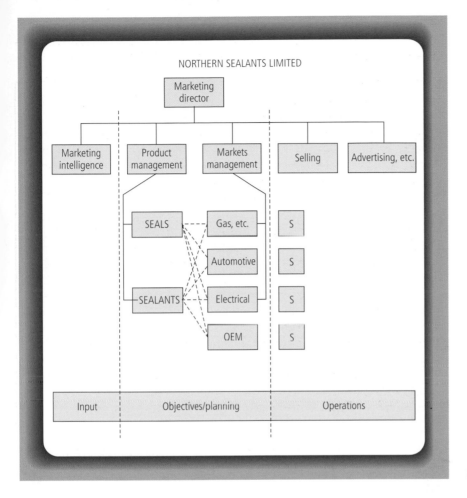

NORTHERN SEALANTS LIMITED

Figure 11.25

Organizing for marketing planning at the operational level

In our experience, the very best marketing plans emerge from an *inclusive* process. Fundamentally, marketing planning is simply a process, with a set of underlying tools and techniques, for understanding markets and for quantifying the present and future value required by the different groups of customers within these markets – what marketers refer to as segments. It is a strictly specialist function, just like accountancy or engineering, which is prescribed, researched, developed and examined by professional bodies such as the Chartered Institute of Marketing in Europe and Asia, and the American Marketing Association in the USA. Sometimes customer-facing activities such as customer service, selling, product development and public relations are controlled by the marketing function, but often they are not, even though many of them are included in the academic marketing curriculum.

In the model in Figure 11.26, representatives from appropriate functions are members of marketing planning teams, with the main body of work being done by the marketing representative who has the professional skills to accomplish the more technical tasks of data and information gathering and market analysis. The team might also include a representative from product development, brand managers, key account managers and so on, depending on circumstances.

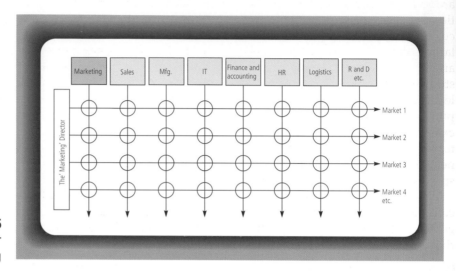

Figure 11.26
Organizing for
marketing planning

The advantages of this approach are as follows:

1   Any plans emerging are based on a deep understanding of the organization's asset base and capabilities.
2   Members of the team 'own' the plan, thus preventing implementation problems later on.
3   The marketing director, or whoever is responsible to the board for integrating and coordinating all the plans emanating from this process, can be sure that he or she is not foisting unwanted plans onto reluctant functional heads.
4   Any strategic functional plans, such as IT, logistics, purchasing, R&D, and so on, will be genuinely market-driven or customer needs-driven rather than production driven.
5   Any business or corporate plans that emerge at a higher level will also be market-driven.

But this is not how most organizations plan for creating superior value. Too often, marketing plans emerge from a marketing 'department' and are developed in isolation and largely ignored by the power brokers.

To summarize, no one particular organizational form can be recommended, commonsense and market needs being the final arbiters. However, the following factors *always* need to be considered:

- marketing 'centres of gravity'
- interface areas (e.g. present/future; salespeople/drawing office; etc.)
- authority and responsibility

- ease of communication
- coordination
- flexibility
- human factors.

Wherever practicable, however, it appears to be sensible to try to organize around customer groups, or markets, rather than around products, functions or geography. Increasingly, firms are organizing themselves around customers or around processes, such as product development. Quite a large 'industry', known as Business Process Redesign (BPR), has grown up around this issue. The Cranfield/Chartered Institute of Marketing research study into the future of marketing has clearly demonstrated that the world's leading companies now organize themselves around customer groups and processes rather than around products. Computer firms, such as AT&T, for example, organize around end-use markets and appoint multidisciplinary teams to focus their attention on their specific needs. The result is personnel, accounting, production, distribution and sales policies that are tailored specifically to a unique set of market needs.

> The world's leading companies now organize themselves around customer groups and processes rather than around products.

While this team-building approach has gone a long way towards overcoming this kind of organizational barrier, of much more importance is to get the task of defining strategic business units (SBUs) right. Let us repeat the definition of an SBU:

> A strategic business unit:
>
> - will have common segments and competitors for most of its products
> - is a competitor in an external market
> - is a discrete, separate and identifiable unit
> - will have a manager who has control over most of the areas critical to success.

But SBUs are not necessarily the same as operating units, and the definition can, and should, be applied all the way down to a particular product, or customer, or group of products or customers, and it is here that the main marketing planning task lies.

What is certain is that one of the major determinants of the effectiveness of any marketing planning which is attempted within a company will be the way that it organizes for marketing. The purpose of this section has been to point out some of the more obvious facts and pitfalls before attempting to outline a marketing planning system, to which we can turn in the final chapter.

■ The marketing planning process and corporate culture

Assuming that marketing planning is acceptable at something deeper than a cosmetic level, it becomes possible to see how the process aligns with different phases of the company's lifeline.

Creative evolution phase

In our research, we did not find a single marketing planner at this stage of development. Most of the companies were still really formulating their business ideas, and the senior executive was in close touch with customers and the company's own staff. The organization had a high level of flexibility to respond to changes in customer needs. In our research, many of these companies were showing high growth, and to introduce marketing planning did not appear to offer any additional benefits.

It has to be recognized that some companies do not have a sufficiently good product or service to develop very far along their life path. The infant mortality rate for businesses is very high.

However, if the company successfully negotiates this initial phase, eventually it reaches the leadership crisis. As we have seen, a strong leader is required who will provide the drive and direction which will lead to the next evolutionary phase.

Directed evolution

Companies at this stage of development fall into two camps. Naturally enough, the underlying style behind the marketing planning process was directive in each case, but the impact and effectiveness was significantly different for each type.

The first type we have referred to as 'Directed Marketing Planning Type 1'. Here, the senior executive took responsibility, or delegated the task of producing a marketing plan. This person would then spend time analysing data, performing a situational review, and so on, until he or she finished up with a document. Generally, an approving mechanism was built into the process. For example, the board of directors would have to vet the marketing plan before it could be issued, but by and large thereafter the plan acts as a directive for the organization.

The second type – 'Directed Marketing Planning Type 2' – involved the appropriate member of staff being told what information to provide about their areas of work, the form in which the information should be provided, and so on.

Thus, in this case, rather than the plan being directed, the process is spelt out carefully. The resulting information is assembled at a senior level and the resulting planning document is issued as before.

Although in both cases all the creative thinking and control takes place at the top level of the organization, the second method holds a prospect of generating more useful data without sacrificing the directive, power-based culture.

Delegated evolution

As a solution to the autonomy crisis which can develop when directive leadership becomes inappropriate, more delegation becomes an operational feature of organizations.

What seemed to be a problem for marketing planning in these companies was that people in the 'front line', or operating units, of large companies were expected to produce marketing plans, but without very much guidance.

As a solution to the autonomy crisis which can develop when directive leadership becomes inappropriate, more delegation becomes an operational feature of organizations.

What seemed to be a problem for marketing planning in these companies was that people in the 'front line', or operating units, of large companies were expected to produce marketing plans, but without very much guidance.

For example, one company had to send its marketing plans to head office, where they were rigorously examined and then given the corporate thumbs up or down. Only through a process of acceptance or dismissal were the criteria for 'good' plans eventually pieced together.

MARKETING INSIGHT

Our conclusion was that a delegated form of marketing planning can lead to some very high-quality inputs, and certainly to high levels of commitment on behalf of those involved. Yet, ultimately, the solely bottom-up planning procedures seem to be difficult to integrate and can be demotivating to those involved. Somehow, the sum of the parts is less in stature than it ought to be.

Coordinated evolution

At this stage, the lessons of the directed and delegated phases seem to have been learned. There is much more emphasis on a plan for planning and a means to incorporate top-down direction and bottom-up quality.

Equally, a coordinated approach enables the company to make best use of its specialized resources and to generate commitment from the staff.

> In many ways, the marketing planning processes, which are the stuff of textbooks and so on, appear to be most suited for a company at this stage of its development.

However, as we have seen, it is possible for the planning process to degenerate from essentially a problem-solving process into a fairly meaningless, bureaucratic ritual. It is at this stage that the planning process will become counter-productive.

Collaborative evolution

Here, the bureaucracy has to make way for genuine problem-solving again. At present we do not have very much evidence about what this means in practice. However, it is possible to speculate that, as business environments change at an ever-increasing pace, so new marketing planning procedures might need to be developed.

Creativity and expediency would appear to be the passwords to this new phase of development.

■ Conclusions

In this chapter, we have discussed the different issues of data, the Internet, forecasting and organization for marketing planning. We have also shown how the acceptance of marketing planning is largely conditioned by the stage of development of the organization and the corporate culture. Thus it is that different modes of marketing planning become more appropriate at different phases of the company's life.

> While the marketing planning process itself remains more or less consistent throughout, *how* that process is managed must be congruent with the current organizational culture. The alternative to this would be to take steps to change the company culture and make it more amenable to a particular planning process.

Since culture tends to act to maintain the existing power structure and the *status quo*, marketing planning interventions in companies must be recognized as having a 'political' dimension and are not purely educational. Not least among the political issues is the question of whether or not a company's management style can adapt sufficiently to enable the marketing planning process to deliver the rewards it promises.

> Can managers who have led a company down a particular path suddenly change track? In other words, is it possible for frogs to change into princes?

The iconoclastic books would claim that they can, because this is a much more optimistic message with which to sell copies. However, those who have carried out academic research, or are experienced consultants, would have some reservations.

We remain open-minded about this issue, believing that, if the business pressures on a company are sufficient, intelligent behaviour will win the day. We might be proved wrong, but, in the meantime, this chapter provides some useful messages for both marketing advisers and senior executives of companies.

While we see our research as being an important step along the road to effective marketing planning, we are also realistic enough to recognize that there is still far to travel.

■ Application questions

1 Do you know:
  - what needs measuring
  - why it needs measuring
  - when it should be measured
  - by whom it should be measured
  - to whom the results should be reported
  - how it should be measured
  - the frequency of measurement?

2 Over what period of time do you forecast in your organization? Is it the right period? Do all relevant managers have an opportunity to make a contribution? If not, say how they could become involved.

3 Is there ever a significant variance between forecasts and sales? If so, how do you explain it?

4 What additional information would you like to help you make more accurate forecasts? How could you obtain such information? Why have you not obtained it in the past?

5 Describe any piece of marketing research that in your view has had a major impact on your company's operations.

6 Describe any major decisions taken which in your view required market research before they were made.

7 Describe what your company's major problems are in the way it uses marketing research.

8 If you were to establish a new marketing information system for your company, say what it would contain. Where is it different from your current one, and how could such a system be organized and made to work?

Chapter 11 review

Marketing accountability
There are three levels of accountability, as shown in Figure 11.3.

Marketing information
Marketing information is at the heart of the company's ability to plan. *Marketing research* is concerned with research into the whole marketing process (*market research* is research about markets).

Try Exercise 11.1

Try answering the first of the Application questions above.

Types of marketing research:

1 Internal – analysis of sales records, advertising levels, price versus volume, etc.
2 External – to complement internal research
3 Reactive – people respond to questionnaires, structured interviews, etc.

4   Non-reactive – interpretation of observed phenomena, e.g. filming customers in a store, listening to customer panels, etc.

There are pros and cons for each type; therefore, a mix can be useful.   *Try Exercise 11.2*

How much to spend
Can be based on the theory of probability and expected value. For example, a product costs 100k euros to develop. There is an estimated 10 per cent chance of failure. The maximum cost therefore = 100k euros $\times$ 0.1 = 10k euros. Therefore, it is worth spending this amount to prevent the loss.

Marketing information system (MIS)
A system to facilitate information flows needs to be developed so that there are appropriate inputs and that correct data gets to the users in a sensible form.

Forecasting
Forecasting can be of two types:

1   *Macro* – forecasting markets in total
2   *Micro* – detailed unit forecasts.

Which to choose depends upon:

- the accuracy required
- the availability of data
- the time horizon
- the position of the product in its life-cycle (macro at early stage).

Techniques for forecasting can be:

- *Quantitative* – based on facts
- *Qualitative* – based on experience and judgement.

Try Exercise 11.3

Organizational barriers
A number of potential barriers exist:

1   *Cognitive* – not knowing enough about marketing planning
2   *Cultural* – the company culture is not sufficiently developed for marketing planning
3   *Political* – the culture carriers feel threatened by marketing
4   *Resources* – not enough resources are allocated to marketing
5   *Structural* – lack of a plan and organization for planning.
6   *Lack of an MIS.*

Centralization versus decentralization
For multi-unit/international organizations there are two possibilities:

1　Marketing function at head office; satellites are just production units
+ = central control
− = remote from local information

2　Marketing decentralized
+ = focused, local identity
− = duplication of information and effort

Choose an approach where the advantages outweigh the disadvantages.　　*Try Exercise 11.4*

Questions raised for the company

1　Q: What influences whether research is carried out internally or by external consultants?
　　A: There can be a number of factors – speed, timing, cost, nature of the research problem, skill requirements, the need for anonymity or objectivity, access of information, etc. Each decision must be taken on its merits.

2　Q: What criteria should be used to assess external researchers?
　　A: Again, there are a number of issues to consider.
　　　(a) *Reputation* – in general, in the industry, for particular types of research, etc.
　　　(b) *Capability and experience* – how long established, quality and qualifications of staff, number of staff, repeat business, recommendations and references, etc.
　　　(c) *Organization* – size, links with sources of information, premises, location, geographical coverage, full-time or part-time interviewers, terms of business, etc.

EXERCISES

To find, maintain or develop a position in any market, it is necessary to have the right information about what is happening in that market. Without having a sensible input of information, the company's decision-making processes will always be suspect.

　　However, collecting and storing information can be both difficult and costly. Moreover, in times of rapid change, information only has a limited 'shelf life'. Generally speaking, companies have an abundance of information at their

Introduction to Chapter 11 exercises

disposal, either in their own records or from easily accessed external sources such as trade associations and government departments.

Yet, in some ways, having too much information can be just as bad as having too little. It becomes difficult to see the wood for the trees. What is required is to cut through what is merely interesting and home in on the information which is necessary, then ensure that it is presented in a usable form.

Exercise 11.1 will investigate just how much marketing information is needed in your company. In addition, it looks at how to get it to the right people, at the right time, in the most appropriate form.

Exercise 11.2 examines the information-gathering techniques at your disposal, their strengths and weaknesses and how you might select one which best meets your requirements.

Exercise 11.3 looks at forecasting in a generalized way so that any confusion about macro- versus micro-forecasting, and qualitative versus quantitative approaches, can be dispelled.

Exercise 11.4 provides ideas about setting up the right marketing organization.

Because all companies are in some ways unique, it follows that there are no easy, 'off-the-shelf', marketing information systems available. Even if they were to exist, the chances would be that they would not work. Instead, the company must assemble its own system, and it must be as simple or as sophisticated as the needs of the situation and the budget allows.

Exercise 11.1
The marketing information system

The starting point for any system must be to assess the company's information requirements.

Information requirements
Already, previous work in this book, and the knowledge you have about your company, will suggest certain information requirements to you. However, to ensure that the whole range of possible information requirements is examined, turn to Worksheet 1 which follows and complete it by following the instructions given.

Current information system
The first worksheet will have highlighted the total information requirements for your company. Put this to one side for the moment and now concentrate on your current system.

Turn to Worksheet 2, and follow the instructions.

Proposal for a new system
Compare the information you gathered in Worksheet 1 and that collected in Worksheet 2. Make a note of the following:

1 Information required but not covered by the current system
2 Areas of information in the current system that are redundant
3 Those areas of information that would be more effective if:
   (a) they were presented differently
   (b) they were directed to different people
   (c) they were provided more or less frequently
4 From the above analysis make recommendations about how your company's marketing information system might be improved. See Worksheet 3.

Worksheet 1 Information requirements (Exercise 11.1)

Below is a list of the areas of business that marketing research could be expected to cover. It doesn't follow that you will need information in all of these areas, but, in the light of your earlier study, *tick those that are relevant*.

Then, in the space provided, specify the nature of the information that would be required.

Areas of business	Relevant	Specific information required
Market size		
Market structure		
Market trends		
Market potential		
Market share		
Company communications		
Company image		
Company structure		
Promotion		
Personal selling		
Distribution channels		
Physical distribution		
Packaging		
Profit		
Costs		
Pricing		
Services		
Market research		
Exporting		
New products		
Technical developments		
Competitor activity		
Competitor prices		
Competitor processes		
Competitor products		
Competitor services		
User attitude/behaviour		
Governmental factors		
Economic factors		
Demographic factors		
Add your own area of business		

Worksheet 2 Current information system (Exercise 11.1)

Consider your existing marketing information system and list the various input data, who uses them, for what purpose, the frequency of use and a judgement about whether or not the data are essential, useful or no longer required.

The form below is designed to help you record your findings.

Note: Remember that journals and magazines can be sources of input data just as much as salespeople's reports and internal control information. You could find it enlightening to include these in your study.

Data input	Used by	Purpose	Frequency	Essential (E), Useful (U), Not req. (X)

Worksheet 3 Proposal for a new system (Exercise 11.1)

Personal notes

Exercise 11.2
Information-gathering techniques

In this exercise you will make a comparative study of various information-gathering techniques and then decide which ones are best suited to solve the company's information requirements.

Step 1   Study Table 11.9 'Information-gathering techniques', and *only proceed to Step 2 when you have read it carefully.*

Step 2   Consider the information gaps you identified in Exercise 11.1 and decide which type of information-gathering technique will be best suited to provide the missing information. In arriving at your answers, you will have to take into account the level of skill in your company and the likely cost.

Exercise 11.3 will also help you in your choice of information-gathering techniques.

If there were no information gaps as a result of completing Exercise 11.1, then review the current information-gathering techniques used in your company and decide if they could be improved upon.

Add any other techniques with which you are familiar and list their strengths and drawbacks.

Personal notes

Table 11.9 Information-gathering techniques

Technique	Main strengths	Drawbacks
Desk research	Can provide quick results, relatively cheap, controllable	Information might not be specific enough – interpretation problems; information can be out of date
Company sales records	Readily accessible	Might not be in a form that can easily be interpreted – mainly historical data
Company financial records	Readily accessible	Might not be easily translated into the required form – mainly historical data
Salespersons' reports	Readily accessible current information about customers	Interpreting narrative into quantified information can be difficult; inadequate records
Journals, etc.	Relatively easy to obtain – libraries, etc.	Information is not exactly what is required, e.g. too general
Trade associations	Have good understanding of specific trade or industry	Quality of information and degree of cooperation from TAs is variable
Government agencies and/or statistics	Vast amount of information, relatively easy access	Need to know way through government systems; can be swamped with useless information
External research	Based on competitive environment – will be current information; provides confidence for decision-making.	Can be costly/time-consuming, samples must be accurate – can be difficult to organize
Questionnaires, face to face	Questioner ensures questions are interpreted correctly – reactions can be noted	Time-consuming; questioner can ask loaded questions; poor design can give rise to misleading results; costly; needs skilled interviewer
Questionnaires, postal	Reach wide audience, relatively cheap	Failure to get replies back on time (or at all); filled in by wrong person; misinterpretation
Questionnaires, telephone	Instantaneous response, relatively cheap; do not take up too much of client's time	Have to be kept brief and so points can be missed; person gives on-the-spot information which might be inaccurate
Depth interviews	Can get to feelings level about products or services; good qualitative information	Needs skilled interviewer; results can be hard to quantify
Experimentation	Can provide 'actual' customer reaction under test conditions	Can be expensive; customer samples must be chosen accurately
Retail audits	Good quantitative information about stock movement	Doesn't explain reasons for stock movements
Consumer panels	Help to establish patterns of purchases and consumption over a period of time	Consumers have to be kept motivated to record activities, etc.
Use MR consultants	Doesn't use up staff time; can produce results in easily digestible form	Can be costly; how do you choose the right consultants?

Exercise 11.3

Forecasting
techniques

There have been many long and heated debates about whether forecasting is a science or an art. The short answer is that it is a bit of both.

If you were asked to forecast what you will be doing in two minutes' time, the chances are you would make a very accurate prediction. The reason for this is obvious, as not very much is going to change in such a short time. Extend the period to tomorrow, next week, a month's time, next year, and your forecasting task becomes increasingly difficult.

Companies are forced to look well ahead in order to plan their investment, launch new products, and so on. Hence their forecasting task is inherently difficult, unless they operate in some backwater unaffected by mainstream change.

The information they require is sometimes very specific (quantitative) and sometimes fairly general (qualitative). Equally, they need to know what is happening in clearly defined areas of their business (micro-forecasting) and sometimes what is happening to total markets (macro-forecasting). These aspects of forecasting can be combined, as in Figure 11.27.

Figure 11.27

The shading indicates the degree of accuracy that can be expected from the various combinations. Thus, the top right-hand corner, quadrant B, demands high accuracy and calls for scientific rigour, whereas the bottom left-hand corner, quadrant C, relies more on feel, intuition and experience.

Collecting information on which to base a forecast can be a costly business; therefore it is important to recognize the nature of the forecasting problem with which one is faced before setting out. It is pointless to measure something to three decimal places if only a rough and ready measurement is required.

Here is a list of 'forecasting problems'. Referring to Figure 11.27, identify whether the nature of each problem is qualitative, quantitative, micro or macro – i.e. falls in quadrant A, B, C or D. Write the appropriate letter in the space provided.

1 What percentage change (in volume) is expected in the ice-cream market in two years' time?   _____

2 What changes in leisure activity are forecast in five years' time?   _____

3 What percentage increase in total sales can we expect in our key market segment over the next twelve months?   _____

4 What would the buyers of our X range want to see as product improvements when we remodel the range next year?   _____

5 What changes are expected in our key technology over the next five years?   _____

6 In what ways will the voting habits of the UK electorate change in three years' time?   _____

7 How many car-users can be expected to be travelling abroad with their vehicles next summer?   _____

8 How many shoppers spending £100 or more can we expect over the next year in our Easthampton store?   _____

The answers are as follows:

1 D
2 C
3 B
4 A
5 A
6 C
7 D
8 B

As a general rule, the margin of error has to be minimal in quadrant B, whereas it is least critical in quadrant C. This clearly has implications for the techniques that are used and the cost of assembling the information.

Look at Exercise 11.2 – 'Information-gathering techniques'

Exercise 11.4
Organizational structure

Business environments are always changing. Demand patterns change, new technology comes in, new legislation is introduced, there is an economic crisis and so on.

Since the key to successful marketing is to have a suitable organization structure, one that can adjust and cope with the environment, it is not surprising that much experimentation has taken place with the different types of structure. Perhaps no-one has yet found the perfect answer to this complex problem of getting the organization right. Nevertheless, research studies have shown that, in certain circumstances, some types of structure are going to be more successful than others.

The accompanying worksheet tries to encapsulate these findings in a fairly crude way, showing that structure will to some extent relate to company size and the diversity of its operations. The degree of formality in the marketing planning process will also be related to these factors.

Please answer the following questions:

1 Where would you place your company on the size/complexity of operations continuum?

2 How does your current structure compare with that suggested on the chart?
3 Do the breakdown signals sound familiar?
4 In what ways do you think your structure ought to change?

Worksheet Organizational structure (Exercise 11.4)

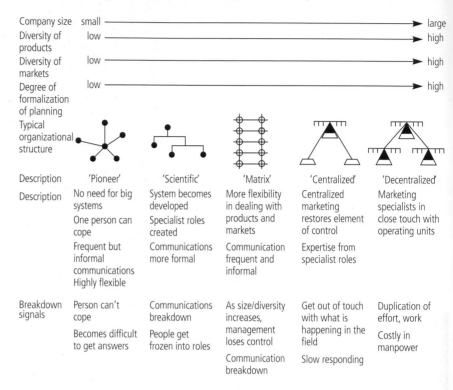

	'Pioneer'	'Scientific'	'Matrix'	'Centralized'	'Decentralized'
Description	No need for big systems	System becomes developed	More flexibility in dealing with products and markets	Centralized marketing restores element of control	Marketing specialists in close touch with operating units
	One person can cope	Specialist roles created	Communication frequent and informal	Expertise from specialist roles	
	Frequent but informal communications Highly flexible	Communications more formal			
Breakdown signals	Person can't cope	Communications breakdown	As size/diversity increases, management loses control	Get out of touch with what is happening in the field	Duplication of effort, work
	Becomes difficult to get answers	People get frozen into roles	Communication breakdown	Slow responding	Costly in manpower

Personal notes

Implementation issues in marketing planning

Summary

- The implications of size and diversity on marketing planning
- A summary of the implications of the main steps in marketing planning
- The role of the chief executive in marketing planning
- The role of the planning department in marketing planning
- The marketing planning cycle
- Marketing planning timescales and horizons
- Exercises to turn the theory into practice

■ Introduction

In Chapter 3, we explained some of the many myths that surround marketing planning and spelled out the conditions that must be satisfied if any company is to have an effective marketing planning system. These are:

1 Any closed-loop marketing planning system (but especially one that is essentially a forecasting and budgeting system) will lead to entropy of marketing and creativity. Therefore, there has to be some mechanism for preventing inertia from setting in through the over-bureaucratization of the system.
2 Marketing planning undertaken at the functional level of marketing, in the absence of a means of integration with other functional areas of the business at general management level, will be largely ineffective.
3 The separation of responsibility for operational and strategic marketing planning will lead to a divergence of the short-term thrust of a business at the operational level from the long-term objectives of the enterprise as a whole. This will encourage a preoccupation with short-term results at operational level, which normally makes the firm less effective in the long term.
4 Unless the chief executive understands and takes an active role in marketing planning, it will never be an effective system.
5 A period of up to three years is necessary (especially in large firms) for the successful introduction of an effective marketing planning system.

Some indication of the potential complexity of marketing planning can be seen in Figure 12.1. Even in a generalized model such as this, it can be seen that, in a large diversified group operating in many foreign markets, a complex combination of product, market and functional plans is possible. For example, what is required at regional level will be different from what is required at headquarters level, while it is clear that the total corporate plan has to be built from the individual building blocks.

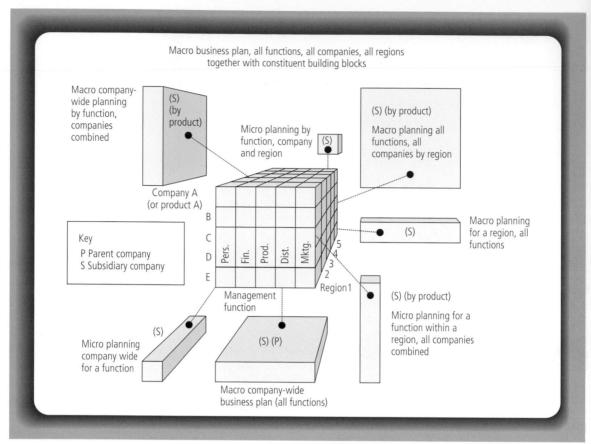

Figure 12.1

Furthermore, the function of marketing itself may be further functionalized for the purpose of planning, such as marketing research, advertising, selling, distribution, promotion, and so forth, while different customer groups may need to have separate plans drawn up.

> Let us be dogmatic about requisite planning levels. First, in a large diversified group, irrespective of such organizational issues, anything other than a systematic approach approximating to a formalized marketing planning system is unlikely to enable the necessary control to be exercised over the corporate identity.
>
> Second, unnecessary planning, or overplanning, could easily result from an inadequate or indiscriminate consideration of the real planning needs at the different levels in the hierarchical chain.
>
> Third, as size and diversity grow, so the degree of formalization of the marketing planning process must also increase. This can be simplified in the form of a matrix (Figure 12.2).

The degree of formalization must increase with the evolving size and diversity of operations. However, while the degree of formalization will

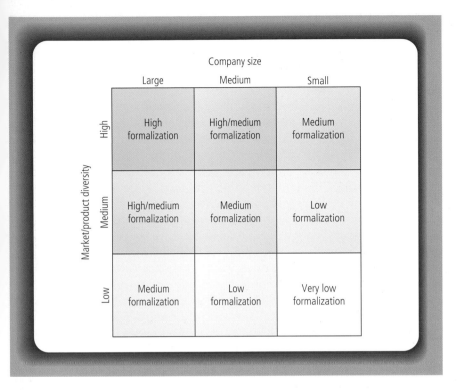

Figure 12.2

change, the need for a complete marketing planning system does not. The problems that companies suffer, then, are a function of either the degree to which they have a requisite marketing planning system or the degree to which the formalization of their system grows with the situational complexities attendant upon the size and diversity of operations.

It has already been stressed that central to the success of any enterprise is the objective-setting process. Connected with this is the question of the design of the planning system and, in particular, the question of who should be involved in what, and how. For example, who should carry out the situation review, state the assumptions, set marketing objectives, and strategies, and carry out the scheduling and costing-out programme, and at what level?

These complex issues revolve essentially around two dimensions – the size of the company, and the degree of business diversity. There are, of course, many other issues, such as whether a company is operating through subsidiary companies or through intermediaries, but these can only be considered against the background of the two major dimensions of size and diversity.

■ Size

Of these two dimensions, size of operations is, without doubt, the biggest determinant of the type of marketing planning system used.

Size of operations is, without doubt, the biggest determinant of the type of marketing planning system used.

> In small companies, there is rarely much diversity of products or markets, and top management has an in-depth knowledge of the key determinants of success and failure.

There is usually a high level of knowledge of both the technology and the market. While in such companies the central control mechanism is the sales forecast and budget, top managers are able to explain the rationale lying behind the numbers, have a very clear view of their comparative strengths and weaknesses, and are able to explain the company's marketing strategy without difficulty. This understanding and familiarity with the strategy is shared with key operating subordinates by means of personal, face-to-face dialogue throughout the year. Subordinates are operating within a logical framework of ideas, which they understand. There is a shared understanding between top and middle management of the industry and prevailing business conditions. In such cases, since either the owner or a director is usually also deeply involved in the day-to-day management of the business, the need to rely on informational inputs from subordinates is considerably less than in larger companies. Consequently, there is less need for written procedures about marketing audits, SWOT analyses, assumptions, and marketing objectives and strategies, as these are carried out by top management, often informally at meetings and in face-to-face discussions with subordinates, the results of which are the basis of the forecasts and budgets. Written documents in respect of price, advertising, selling, and so on, are very brief, but those managers responsible for those aspects of the business know what part they are expected to play in achieving the company's objectives.

> Such companies are, therefore, operating according to a set of structured procedures, and complete the several steps in the marketing planning process, but in a relatively informal manner.

On the other hand, many small companies that have a poor understanding of the marketing concept, and in which the top manager leaves their strategy implicit, suffer many serious operational problems.

These operational problems become progressively worse as the size of company increases. As the number and level of management increase, it becomes progressively more difficult for top management to enjoy an in-depth knowledge of industry and business conditions by informal, face-to-face means. In the absence of written procedures and a structured framework, the different levels of operating management become increasingly less able to react in a rational way to day-to-day pressures. Systems of tight budgeting control, without the procedures outlined in this book, are, in the main, only successful in situations of buoyant trading conditions, are often the cause of high levels of management frustration, and are seen to be a major contributory factor in those cases where eventual decline sets in.

In general, the bigger the company, the greater is the incidence of standardized, formalized procedures for the several steps in the marketing planning process.

■ Diversity of operations

From the point of view of management control, the least complex environment in which to work is an undiversified company. For the purpose of this discussion, 'undiversified' is taken to mean companies with limited product lines or homogeneous customer groups. For example, hydraulic hose could be sold to many diverse markets, or a diverse range of products could be sold into only one market such as, say, the motor industry. Both could be classified as 'undiversified'.

In such cases, the need for institutionalized marketing planning systems increases with the size of the operation, and there is a strong relationship between size and the complexity of the management task, irrespective of any apparent diversity.

For example, an oil company will operate in many diverse markets around the world, through many different kinds of marketing systems, and with varying levels of market growth and market share. In most respects, therefore, the control function for headquarters management is just as difficult and complex as that in a major, diversified conglomerate. The major difference is the greater level of in-depth knowledge which top management has about the key determinants of success and failure underlying the product or market worldwide, because of its homogeneity.

MARKETING INSIGHT

Because of this homogeneity of product or market, it is usually possible for headquarters to impose worldwide policies on operating units in respect of things such as certain aspects of advertising, public relations, packaging, pricing, trademarks, product development, and so on, whereas in the headquarters of a diversified conglomerate, overall policies of this kind tend to be impracticable and meaningless.

The view is often expressed that common planning in companies comprising many heterogeneous units is less helpful and confuses, rather than improves, understanding between operating units and headquarters. However, the truth is that conglomerates often consist of several smaller multinationals, some diversified and some not, and that the actual risk of marketing rests on the lowest level in an organization at which there is general management profit responsibility. Forecasting and budgeting systems by themselves rarely encourage anything but a short-term, parochial view of the business at these levels, and in the absence of the kind of marketing planning procedures described in this book, higher levels of management do not have a sufficiently rational basis on which to set long-term marketing objectives.

Exactly the same principles apply at the several levels of control in a diversified multinational conglomerate, in that, at the highest level of control, there has to be some rational basis on which to make decisions about the portfolio of investments. In our research, the most successful companies were those with standardized marketing planning procedures to aid this process. In such companies, there is a hierarchy of audits, SWOT analyses, assumptions, strategies and programmes, with increasingly more detail required in the procedures at the lowest levels in the organization. The precise details of each step vary according to circumstances, but the eventual output of the process is in a universally consistent form.

The basis on which the whole system rests is the informational input requirements at the highest level of command. Marketing objectives and strategies are frequently synthesized into a multidisciplinary corporate plan at the next general management profit-responsible level until, at the highest level of command, the corporate plan consists largely of financial information and summaries of the major operational activities.

> This is an important point, for there is rarely a consolidated operational marketing plan at conglomerate headquarters.

This often exists only at the lowest level of general management profit responsibility, and even here it is sometimes incorporated into the corporate plan, particularly in capital goods companies, where engineering, manufacturing and technical services are major factors in commercial success.

Here, it is necessary to distinguish between short-term operational plans and long-term strategic plans, both products of the same process. Conglomerate headquarters are particularly interested in the progress of, and prospects for, the major areas of operational activities, and while obviously concerned to ensure a satisfactory current level of profitability, are less interested in the detailed short-term scheduling and costing-out of the activities necessary to achieve these objectives. This, however, is a major concern at the lowest level of general management profit responsibility.

> To summarize, the smaller the company, the more informal and personal the procedures for marketing planning. As company size and diversity increases, so the need for institutionalized procedures increases.

The really important issue in any system is the degree to which it enables *control* to be exercised over the key determinants of success and failure. To a large extent, the issue, much debated in the literature, of where in an international organization responsibility for setting marketing objectives and strategies should lie, is something of a red herring. Of course, in a diversified multinational conglomerate, detailed marketing objectives and strategies for some remote country cannot be set by someone in London. It is precisely this issue – i.e. finding the right balance between the flexibility of operating units to react to changes in local market conditions and centralized control – that a formally designed system seeks to tackle.

The really important issue in any system is the degree to which it enables control to be exercised over the key determinants of success and failure.

Those companies which conform to the framework outlined here have systems which, through a hierarchy of bottom-up/top-down negotiating procedures, reach a nice balance between the need for detailed control at the lowest level of operations and centralized control. The main role of headquarters is to harness the company's strengths on a worldwide basis and to ensure that lower-level decisions do not cause problems in other areas and lead to wasteful duplication.

Figure 12.3 explores four key outcomes that marketing planning can evoke. It can be seen that systems I, III and IV, i.e. where the individual is totally subordinate to a formalized system, or where individuals are allowed to do what they want without any system, or where there is neither system, nor creativity, are less successful than system II, in which the individual is allowed to be entrepreneurial within a total system. System II, then, will be an effective marketing planning system, but one in which the degree of formalization will be a function of company size and diversity.

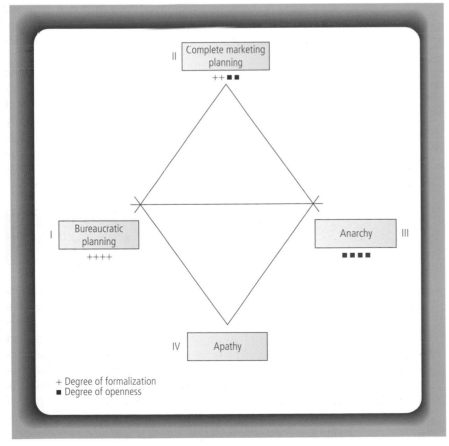

+ Degree of formalization
■ Degree of openness

Figure 12.3

> Creativity cannot flourish in a closed-loop formalized system. There would be little disagreement that in today's abrasive, turbulent, and highly competitive environment, it is those firms that succeed in extracting entrepreneurial ideas and creative marketing programmes from systems that are necessarily yet acceptably formalized, that will succeed in the long run. Much innovative flair can so easily get stifled by systems.

Certainly there is ample evidence of international companies with highly formalized systems that produce stale and repetitive plans, with little changed from year to year and that fail to point up the really key strategic issues as a result. The scandalous waste this implies is largely due to a *lack of personal intervention by key managers during the early stages of the planning cycle.*

> There is clearly a need, therefore, to find a way of perpetually renewing the planning life-cycle each time around. Inertia must never set in. Without some such valve or means of opening up the loop, inertia quickly produces decay.

The critical intervention of senior managers, from the chief executive down through the hierarchical chain, comes at the audit stage.

Such a valve has to be inserted early in the planning cycle during the audit, or situation review stage. In companies with effective marketing planning systems, whether such systems are formalized or informal, the critical intervention of senior managers, from the chief executive down through the hierarchical chain, comes at the audit stage. Essentially, what takes place is a personalized presentation of audit findings, together with proposed marketing objectives and strategies and outline budgets for the strategic planning period. These are discussed, amended where necessary, and agreed in various synthesized formats at the hierarchical levels in the organization *before* any detailed operational planning takes place. It is at such meetings that managers are called upon to justify their views, which tends to force them to be more bold and creative than they would have been had they been allowed merely to send in their proposals. Obviously, however, even here much depends on the degree to which managers take a critical stance, which is much greater when the chief executive takes an active part in the process. *Every hour of time devoted at this stage by the chief executive has a multiplier effect throughout the remainder of the process.* And let it be remembered we are not, repeat not, talking about budgets at this juncture in anything other than outline form.

Until recently, it was believed that there may well be fundamental differences in marketing planning approaches, depending on factors such as the type of business-to-business goods and markets involved, company size, the degree of dependence on international sales, and the methods used to market goods abroad. In particular, the much debated role of headquarters management in the marketing planning process is frequently put forward as being a potential cause of great difficulty.

> One of the most encouraging findings to emerge from our research is that the theory of marketing planning is universally applicable, and that such issues are largely irrelevant.

While the planning task is less complicated in small, undiversified companies, and there is less need for formalized procedures than in large, diversified companies, the fact is that exactly the same framework should be used in all circumstances, and that this approach brings similar benefits to all.

In a multinational conglomerate, headquarters management can assess major trends in products and markets around the world, and is thus able to develop strategies for investment, expansion, diversification and divestment on a global basis. For their part, subsidiary management can develop appropriate strategies with a sense of locomotion towards the achievement of coherent overall goals.

This is achieved by means of synthesized information flows from the bottom upwards, which facilitates useful comparison of performance around the world, and the diffusion of valuable information, skills, experiences and systems from the top downwards. The particular benefits which accrue to companies using such systems can be classified under the major headings of the marketing mix elements as follows:

- *Marketing information* – there is a transfer of knowledge, a sharing of expertise and an optimization of effort around the world.
- *Product* – control is exercised over the product range. Maximum effectiveness is gained by concentrating on certain products in certain markets, based on experience gained throughout the world.
- *Price* – pricing policies are sufficiently flexible to enable local management to trade effectively, while the damaging effects of interaction are considerably mitigated.
- *Place* – substantial gains are made by rationalization of the supply chain management function.
- *Promotion* – duplication of effort and a multitude of different platforms/company images are ameliorated. Efforts in one part of the world reinforce those in another.

The procedures which facilitate the provision of such information and knowledge transfers also encourage operational management to think strategically about their own areas of responsibility, instead of managing only for the short term.

It is abundantly clear that it is through a marketing planning system and planning skills that such benefits are achieved, and that discussions such as those about the standardization *process* are largely irrelevant. Any standardization that may be possible will become clear only if a company can successfully develop a system for identifying the needs of each market and each segment in which it operates, and for organizing resources to satisfy those needs in such a way that best resource utilization results worldwide.

■ A summary of the marketing planning process

The purpose of this section is to summarize the earlier chapters, and to ensure that the many threads developed are seen in their correct context, within the marketing planning process.

> There are many checklists of things you have to do to go through the motions of marketing planning. But pages of figures and marketing prose, well typed, elegantly bound, and retrievably filed, do not make much difference.

They make some, because the requirements of writing a plan demand deep thought. However, it is vital that companies must always search for the *requisite level of marketing planning*, just as, in engineering, you will often seek the requisite level of variety in product or services offered.

It is well to remember, above all else, what the *purpose* of marketing planning is, which is to create sustainable competitive advantage. The following subsections are intended to identify the main barriers to marketing planning and summarize the main points of a requisite marketing planning system, and to provide the basis for the design of a system suitable for any business.

The process itself

'How well should we be doing in present trading conditions?' The answer to this question requires considerable analysis inside and outside the company. Simply looking at the bottom line and saying 'budget achieved' is not enough.

It is quite possible to achieve budget and still lose market share – if the budget is not developed from a proper qualitative assessment of the market *in the first place.*

The real question we should be asking is *'What sales/gross profits should we be achieving in the current trading conditions?'* To answer the above questions, it is necessary to have available a well argued 'common format' in the organization – i.e. a marketing plan.

Undertaking marketing planning is like 'trying to nail a jelly to the wall'; it is a messy process, which evolves over time. In effect, you are attempting to 'control' the future by deciding *what to do about the possible different trading environments*. In undertaking marketing planning, you join the ranks of those who 'make things happen' in the company. The alternative is to be tossed around like a cork in the sea of competition.

The marketing planning process involves the bringing together of minds within the company/group/department, and a 'trading off' between the difficult issues raised. By definition, the marketing planning process starts

Undertaking marketing planning is like 'trying to nail a jelly to the wall'.

from a 'zero base' each year; the 'Ten per cent increase' syndrome must be avoided at all times.

The marketing planning process facilitates, and indeed depends on, interactive communication up and down the organization. If this does not happen, all that results are forecasts projected from history rather than the development of genuine objectives based on what is actually happening inside and outside the company.

Remember, the planning process is first and foremost to help you to help yourself; it is not something you take part in simply to appease your superiors.

It is sometimes difficult for higher echelons in the organization to synthesize and aggregate the SWOTs from lower levels. However, the task is made easier if, for instance, departments are grouped to reflect the structure of the external market.

Once the marketing planning process has developed through to the agreement of a detailed one-year operational plan, and once this budget is agreed, then commitment must be total. If, however, during the course of the ensuing fiscal year, performance begins to fall behind the budget, it is quite legitimate to manipulate any and all elements of the marketing plan in order to correct the deficit. So, there is flexibility in the way the elements of a plan can be altered and manipulated; the budget, however, remains fixed.

The marketing audit

The marketing planning process starts with an *audit* of the company's operating performance and environment. The marketing audit is essentially a *database* of all market-related issues with which the company is concerned. The subsequent SWOT analysis lends structure to the audit in order to facilitate ongoing planning activities.

The company must provide a list of detailed questions which each manager is required to consider for their own area of responsibility. Each manager carrying out an audit will use sales data and the company marketing information system to complete the audit. If the company has a marketing research manager, it is helpful at this stage to issue to all managers a market overview covering major market and product trends, etc.

It will probably be necessary to customize the audit checklist contents according to the level in the organization to which it is addressed. In this way, each particular checklist is made meaningful and relevant to each level. Some brief explanatory definitions may also be necessary.

The audit will inevitably require more data preparation than is finally reproduced in the marketing plan.

Therefore, managers should attempt to start a 'product/market bible' during the year, which can also be used as a reference source at verbal presentations of proposals, etc.

What this means is that the marketing audit should be conducted on a *continuing* (dynamic) basis rather than at a particular point in time. In this way, it becomes a useful information source to draw on for decision-making throughout the year.

Do not try to hide behind vague items in the audit, like 'poor economic conditions'. Even in overall static or declining markets there will be 'growth' points present. Seek these out and decide whether or not to focus/concentrate your efforts on them.

Incorporate product life-cycles and portfolio matrices as an integral part of the audit. The diagrams and the corresponding words should match.

It is suggested that the manager draws a product life-cycle for each of the major products and uses the audit information to attempt to predict the future shape of the life-cycle. It is also suggested that the manager plots these products on a portfolio matrix and uses the audit information to show the future desired position of the products (e.g. for three years ahead, if this is the planning horizon). The matrix may, therefore, have to include some new products not currently in the range.

> The audit can be a useful 'transfer' device for when one manager moves job and another takes over. For example, the incoming manager can quickly pick up an understanding of that department's business.

SWOT analyses

> It is important to remember that it is only the SWOT analyses, *not* the audit, that actually appear in the marketing plan.

This summary of the audit should, if possible, contain not more than one or two pages of commentary focusing on *key* factors only. It should list internal *differential* strengths and weaknesses *vis-à-vis* competitors and key external opportunities and threats. A SWOT should be completed for each segment or product considered to be crucial to that organization's future.

> The SWOT analyses should be interesting to read, contain concise statements, include only the relevant and important data, and give greater emphasis to creative analysis.

A crucial role for marketing management is to differentiate their company from their competitors. The SWOT analysis is a device which assists us to do that.

A SWOT analysis, well done, helps to identify and pin down the real issues which should be addressed in the future as a matter of priority. Too often, however, the SWOT summary is just a smorgasbord of apparently unrelated points (in which case any underlying theme is difficult to discern).

Having listened to someone presenting a SWOT summary, you should end up with a clear understanding of the main thrust of this part of their business.

> If a SWOT is well done, someone else should be able to draft the objectives which logically flow from it. The SWOT analysis should contain clear indicators as to the key determinants of success in the segment being focused on; we can then build on these.

The SWOT statement should, in effect, encapsulate our perception of the marketplace; summarize what we are trying to do; and point out required future actions. If pursued aggressively, this approach will make competitors into followers.

The SWOT is, by definition, a summary of the key issues emanating out of the marketing audit. The SWOT is generated from internal debate; it is not just one person's opinion. The SWOT should provide answers to such questions as:

● What do customers need?
● How do they buy?
● What are our competitors doing?
● How well are we performing against customer needs?

The S and W parts of the SWOT (internal) should be differential. The O and T (external) part of the SWOT is generally non-differential, e.g. the threat of a new sales tax. We have to assess the impact of such a threat (should it happen) earlier than our competitors, and make the appropriate preparations earlier in order to give us the edge.

In writing down each issue in our SWOT summary, we should continually follow with the implied question: 'Which means that . . .?' In this way we are forced to think about the implications of the issue itself.

Finally, agreed budgets (which come at the end of the process) must reflect internal consistency with the issues raised in the original SWOT analyses.

> Often, this internal consistency is not evident because budgets are done first rather than last.

It is difficult to work to a SWOT prepared by another person, unless of course you were involved in the original debate. The quality of a SWOT analysis can suffer if:

1 Each item/issue is over-abbreviated
2 The writer concentrates on micro rather than macro issues.

Remember, it is a great self-discipline to complete a good, tight, but comprehensive, SWOT for each segment in the plan.

Assumptions

These also should appear in the marketing plan. List the major assumptions on which the plan is based. If the plan can be implemented irrespective of any assumption made, then the assumption is unnecessary. They should be few in number and key.

Marketing objectives

These should also appear in the marketing plan. Marketing objectives are about products and markets only (*not* about advertising, etc.). The *words* used should reflect what appears in the product life-cycle and in the portfolio matrix. Any figures used (such as volume, value, etc.) should also reflect this. Please note that there is a detailed explanation of how this should be done in Chapter 13.

Note that if there is, say, a three-year planning horizon, the three-year marketing plan should contain overall marketing objectives with broad revenue and cost projections for the full three-year period. This plan will be required for the long-range corporate plan. The one-year marketing plan should contain the same overall marketing objectives plus the specific objectives for the first year of the planning cycle. Thereafter, the detailed one-year marketing plan should be about the next fiscal year only.

> Ideally the one-year and three-year plans should be separate, but not necessarily so.

At an early stage in the planning process, it is likely that managers will have to discuss their major objectives with their superior prior to final agreement, since that person will probably have a better understanding of the broader company objectives.

It is necessary to set objectives in order to articulate what we are in fact committing ourselves to, and to force us to think about the corresponding resource implications.

Marketing objectives flow from the SWOT analyses and should be fully compatible with the key issues identified in the SWOT. Marketing objectives should be quantifiable and measurable for performance-monitoring purposes; avoid directional terms such as 'improve', 'increase', 'expand', etc. There will be a hierarchy of marketing objectives down through the organization. Try to set priorities for your chosen marketing objectives.

> Many so-called marketing objectives are in fact really marketing strategies – do not mix the two up. Marketing objectives are *what* we want to achieve; marketing strategies are *how* we intend to achieve the set objectives.

In some cases, marketing strategies and detailed marketing *actions* are confused. Actions are the short-term list of activities carried out to a schedule which, in aggregate, amount to a particular strategy.

Marketing strategies

These must also appear in the marketing plan. Strategies are how the objectives are to be achieved:

- *Product* policies, to include functions, design, size, packaging, and so on
- *Pricing* policies to be followed for product groups in market segments
- *Place* policies for channels and customer service levels
- *Promotion* policies for communicating with customers under the relevant headings such as advertising, personal selling, sales promotion, the Internet, etc.

Budget

In the three-year strategic marketing plan, all that is required are the financial implications (budget) of the agreed strategies.

Programmes

Detailed programmes (sometimes referred to as 'appropriation budgets') should appear only in the detailed one-year operational marketing plan.

In a detailed one-year marketing plan, specific sub-objectives for products and segments supported by more detailed strategy and action statements (e.g. what, where, when, costs, etc.) are required. Here, include *budgets* and *forecasts*, and of course a *consolidated budget*. The preparation of budgets and sales forecasts *must* reflect the marketing objectives. In turn the objectives, strategies and programmes *must* reflect the agreed budgets and sales forecasts.

Marketing plans

A written marketing plan (or plans) is the outcome of the marketing planning process. It is effectively a business proposition containing proposed courses of action which in turn have resource implications.

> Written marketing plans verbalize (and formalize) our intuitive model of the market environment within which we operate. Written marketing plans help to make things happen.

The acid test of any marketing plan presentation is to ask yourself, 'Would I put my own life's savings into the plan as presented?' If the answer is 'No', then further work is needed to refine your ideas.

A good discipline in preparing 'internally consistent' marketing plans is to use the following summary format:

SWOT issues → Objective → Strategy → Specific actions and timing

The role of the chief executive in marketing planning

Our research showed that few chief executives have a clear perception of:

- purposes and methods of planning
- proper assignments of planning responsibilities throughout the organization
- proper structures and staffing of the planning department
- the talent and skills required in an effective planning department.

The role of the chief executive is generally agreed as being:

- to define the organizational framework
- to ensure the strategic analysis covers critical factors
- to maintain the balance between short- and long-term results
- to display his or her commitment to planning
- to provide the entrepreneurial dynamic to overcome bureaucracy
- to build this dynamic into the planning operation (motivation).

> In respect of planning, the chief executive's principal role is to open up the planning loop by means of personal intervention. The main purpose of this is to act as a catalyst for the entrepreneurial dynamic within the organization, which can so easily decay through bureaucratization. This is not sufficiently recognized in the literature.

When considering this in the context of the reasons for failures of marketing planning systems, it is clear that, for any system to be effective, the chief executive requires to be conversant with planning techniques and approaches, and to be committed to and take part in the marketing planning process.

The role of the planning department in marketing planning

This raises the important question of the role of the planning department, which is:

- to provide the planning structure and systems
- to secure rapid data transmission in the form of intelligence
- to act as a catalyst in obtaining inputs from operating divisions

- to forge planning links across organizational divisions, e.g. R&D and marketing
- to evaluate plans against the chief executive's formulated strategy
- to monitor the agreed plans.

> The planner is a coordinator who sees that the planning is done – not a formulator of goals and strategies.

The planner's responsibility has three basic dimensions. They are:

1 Directive
2 Supportive
3 Administrative.

In the *directive* role, the planning executive acts on behalf of top management to supervise the planning procedure to promote orderly and disciplined implementation of the planning process. This function can be performed well only when managers have both the *ability* and *willingness* to make it happen. The planning executive is likely to be more effective by acting in a *supportive*, rather than in a *directive*, role.

A *supportive* role brings the planning executive into service as an internal consultant and advisory resource. In this role, the planning executive:

- advises line management on the application of planning principles
- assembles background information to provide insight into the economy, industries, markets, investment alternatives, etc. which are relevant to each business served
- directs or supports forecasting of the economy, industries and end-user markets
- renders assistance in installing progress-monitoring systems and interpreting their output
- renders assistance to line executives in applying advanced methods and procedures
- provides other internal and consulting assistance to line managers in preparing their plans and monitoring their progress.

In their *administrative* role, planners ensure that planning procedures are implemented on schedule and that communications are accurate and rapid. In this role, it is suggested that they have limitations. They can provide coordinating and communicating services, but they cannot enforce them. If line management does not participate willingly, someone else with the appropriate authority must take corrective or disciplinary action.

Again, when this is taken in the context of the failures of marketing planning systems, it is clear that an understanding of the proper role of the planning department is an important determinant of planning success.

The marketing planning cycle

The schedule should call for work on the plan for the next year to begin early enough in the current year to permit adequate time for market research and analysis of key data and market trends. In addition, the plan should provide for the early development of a strategic plan that can be approved or altered in principle.

A key factor in determining the planning cycle is bound to be the degree to which it is practicable to extrapolate from sales and market data, but, generally speaking, successful planning companies start the planning cycle formally somewhere between nine and six months from the beginning of the next fiscal year.

It is not necessary to be constrained to work within the company's fiscal year; it is quite possible to have a separate marketing planning schedule if that is appropriate, and simply organize the aggregation of results at the time required by the corporate financial controller.

Planning horizons

It is clear that, in the past, one- and five-year planning periods have been by far the most common, although three years has now become the most common period for the strategic plan, largely because of the dramatically increasing rate of environmental change. Lead time for the initiation of major new product innovations, the length of time necessary to recover capital investment costs, the continuing availability of customers and raw materials, and the size and usefulness of existing plant and buildings, are the most frequently mentioned reasons for having a five-year planning horizon. Increasingly, however, these five-year plans are taking the form more of 'scenarios' than the detailed strategic plan outlined in this book.

Many companies, however, do not give sufficient thought to what represents a sensible planning horizon for their particular circumstances. A five-year time span is clearly too long for some companies, particularly those with highly versatile machinery operating in volatile fashion-conscious markets. The effect of this is to rob strategic plans of reality. A five-year horizon is often chosen largely because of its universality. Secondly, some small subsidiaries in large conglomerates are often asked to forecast for seven, ten and, sometimes, fifteen years ahead, with the result that they tend to become meaningless exercises. While it might make sense for, say, a glass manufacturer to produce twelve-year plans (or scenarios) because of the very long lead time involved in laying down a new furnace, it does not make sense to impose the same planning timescale on small subsidiaries operating in totally different markets, even though they are in the same group. This places unnecessary burdens on operating management and tends to rob the whole strategic planning process of credibility.

The conclusion to be reached is that there is a natural point of focus into the future, beyond which it is pointless to look. This point of focus is a function of the relative size of a company.

> Small companies, because of their size and the way they are managed, tend to be comparatively flexible in the way in which they can react to environmental turbulence in the short term. Large companies,

on the other hand, need a much longer lead time in which to make changes in direction. Consequently, they tend to need to look further into the future and use formalized systems for this purpose so that managers throughout the organization have a common means of communication.

How the marketing planning process works

There is one other major aspect to be considered. It concerns the requisite location of the marketing planning activity in a company. The answer is simple to give.

Marketing planning should take place as near to the marketplace as possible in the first instance, but such plans should then be reviewed at high levels within an organization to see what issues have been overlooked.

It has been suggested that each manager in the organization should complete an audit and SWOT analysis on his or her own area of responsibility. The only way that this can work in practice is by means of a *hierarchy of* audits. The principle is simply demonstrated in Figure 12.4.

This illustrates the principle of auditing at different levels within an organization. The marketing audit format will be universally applicable. It is only the *detail* that varies from level to level and from company to company within the same group. For example, any one single company can specify without too much difficulty the precise headings under which information is being sought.

In the case of an industrial lubricants company, under an assessment of the market environment, information and commentary was required on capital investment schemes, foreign investments, economic growth rates, health and safety regulations (clearly important in this market), inflation rates, tariff protection, etc., together with an assessment of their effect on the lubricants market.

Under the heading 'market', key product groups and key market sectors were defined (in this case the British Standard Industrial Classification System was used). It was left to each subsidiary to specify what the particular key industries were in their particular territories. Data sheets were provided for this purpose.

In the case of the competitive and the internal audit, each operating unit was merely asked to provide, for each major product, its strengths and weaknesses and those of competitive products; likewise for opportunities and threats. To assist with this process, a checklist was provided which included, *inter alia*, international approvals from original equipment manufacturers, compliance with health and safety regulations, and so on. Some data sheets were provided for market share analysis by key industry, pricing against competitive products, etc.

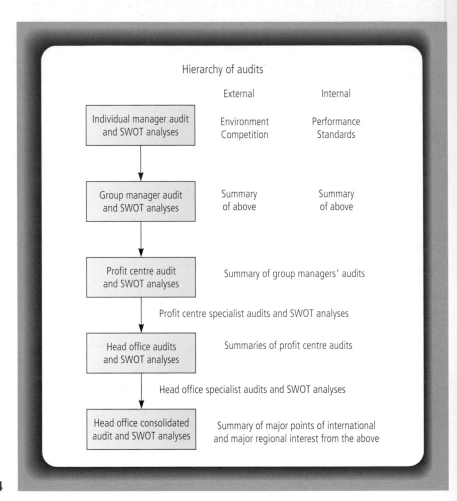

Figure 12.4

At each operating level, this kind of information can be gathered in by means of the hierarchy of audits illustrated in Figure 12.4 with each manager completing an audit for his or her area of accountability. While the overall format can be universal for a large and diversified group, uniformity is only necessary for units engaged in like activities. The advantages which accrue to the several headquarters levels are substantial in terms of measuring worldwide potential for products and market segments. Without such an information-collecting vehicle, it is difficult to formulate any overall strategic view.

> It has to be recognized that information and data are not always readily available in some parts of the world in the sort of format which is required, but given training, resources and understanding between headquarters and units, it is surprising how quickly information links can be forged which are of inestimable value to both sides. The same is also true of agents and distributors, who quickly respond to the give and take of such relationships in respect of audit-type information, which they inevitably find valuable for their own business.

Since, in anything but the smallest of undiversified companies, it is not possible for top management to set detailed objectives for operating units, it is suggested that at this stage in the planning process, strategic guidelines should be issued. One way of doing this is in the form of a *strategic planning letter*. Another is by means of a personal briefing by the chief executive at 'kick-off' meetings. As in the case of the audit, these guidelines would proceed from the broad to the specific, and would become more detailed as they progressed through the company towards operating units. Table 12.1 contains a list of the headings under which strategic guidelines could be set.

Table 12.1 Chief executive's strategic planning letter (possible areas for which objective and strategies or strategic guidelines will be set)

Financial	*Operations*
Remittances:	Land
■ dividends	Buildings
■ royalties	Plant
Gross margin %	Modifications
Operating profit	Maintenance
Return on capital employed	Systems
Debtors	Raw materials supplies
Creditors	Purchasing
Bank borrowings	Distribution:
Investments	■ stock and control
Capital expenditure	■ transportation
Cash flow controls	■ warehousing
Manpower and organization	*Marketing*
Management	Target markets
Training	Market segments
Industrial relations	Brands
Organization	Volumes
Remuneration and pensions	Market shares
	Pricing
	Image
	Promotion
	Market research
	Quality control
	Customer service

Under marketing, for example, at the highest level in a large group, top management may ask for particular attention to be paid to issues such as the technical impact of microprocessors on electromechanical component equipment, leadership and innovation strategies, vulnerability to attack from the flood of products from countries such as India, China and Korea, and so on. At operating company level, it is possible to be more explicit about target markets, product development, and the like.

It is important to remember that it is top management's responsibility to determine the strategic direction of the company, and to decide such issues as when businesses are to be managed for cash, where to invest heavily in product development or market extension for longer term gains, and so on. If this is left to operating managers to decide for themselves, they will tend to opt for actions concerned principally with *today's* products and markets, because that is what they are judged on principally. There is also the problem of their inability to appreciate the larger, company-wide position.

> Nevertheless, the process just described demonstrates very clearly that there is total interdependence between top management and the lowest level of operating management in the objective and strategy setting process.

In a very large company without any procedures for managing this process, it is not difficult to see how control can be weakened and how vulnerability to rapid changes in the business environment around the world can be increased. This interdependence between the top-down/bottom-up process is illustrated in Figures 12.5 and 12.6, which show a similar hierarchy in respect of objective and strategy setting to that illustrated in respect of audits.

Figure 12.5

Having explained carefully the point about *requisite* marketing planning, these figures also illustrate the principles by which the marketing planning process should be implemented in any company, irrespective of whether it is a small exporting company or a major multinational. In essence, these exhibits show a *hierarchy* of audits, SWOT analyses, objectives, strategies and programmes.

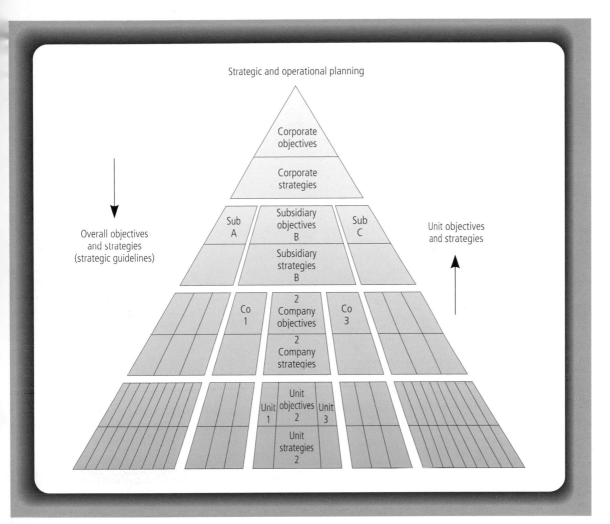

Figure 12.6

Figure 12.7 is another way of illustrating the total corporate strategic and planning process. (This was first shown in Chapter 2.) This time, however, a time element is added, and the relationship between strategic planning letters, long-term corporate plans and short-term operational plans is clarified. It is important to note that there are two 'open loop' points on this last diagram. These are the key times in the planning process when a subordinate's views and findings should be subjected to the closest examination by a superior.

> It is by taking these opportunities that marketing planning can be transformed into the critical and creative process it is supposed to be, rather than the dull, repetitive ritual it so often turns out to be.

These figures should be seen as one group of illustrations showing how the marketing planning process fits into the wider context of corporate planning.

Figure 12.7

Final thought

In conclusion, we must stress that there can be no such thing as an off-the-peg marketing planning system.

> Nonetheless, both our research and our experience have indicated that marketing planning remains one of the last bastions of management ignorance, largely because of the complexity of the process and its organizational, political and cultural implications.

It is for these reasons, and because so many of the readers of the first edition of this book asked for one, that we added a final chapter which contains both a very brief summary of the main points described in the book and a simple, step-by-step system which can become the basis of your own planning procedures. The system provided has been used successfully in businesses ranging from big international business-to-business companies to small domestic service organizations.

> In the end, marketing planning success comes from an endless willingness to learn and to adapt the system to your people and your own circumstances. It also comes from a deep understanding about the *nature* of marketing planning, which is something that in the final analysis cannot be taught.

Success comes from *experience*. Experience comes from making mistakes. We can minimize these if we combine *common sense* and *sweet reasonableness* with the *models* provided in this book. But be sure of *one* thing, above all else. By themselves, the models will not work. However, if you read this book carefully and use the models sensibly, marketing planning becomes one of the most powerful tools available to a business today.

We wish you every success in your endeavours.

■ Application questions

1 Does the principle of hierarchies of audits, SWOTs, objectives, strategies and programmes apply in your company? If not, describe how they are handled.

2 If it does, describe in what ways it differs from the principles outlined here.

3 Design a simple system for your company, or describe in what ways your existing system could be improved.

Chapter 12 review

Conditions that must be satisfied

1 Any closed-loop planning system, especially if it is based just on forecasting and budgeting, will deaden any creative response and will eventually lead to failure.

2 Marketing planning which is not integrated with other functional areas of the business at general management level will be largely ineffective.

3 The separation of operational and strategic marketing planning will lead to divergent plans, with the short-term viewpoint winning because it achieves quick results.

4 The chief executive must take an active role.

5 It can take three years to introduce marketing planning successfully.

Try Exercises 12.1 and 12.2

Ten principles of marketing planning

1 Develop the strategic plan first; the operational plan comes out of this.

2 Put marketing as close as possible to the customer and have marketing and sales under one person.

3 Marketing is an attitude of mind, not a set of procedures.

4 Organize activities around customer groups, not functional activities.

5 A marketing audit must be rigorous. No vague terms should be allowed, and nothing should be hidden. Managers should use tools like portfolio analysis and product life-cycle.

6 SWOT analyses should be focused on segments that are critical to the business; concentrate only on key factors which lead to objectives.

7 People must be educated about the planning process.

8   There has to be a plan for planning.
9   All objectives should be prioritized in terms of their urgency and impact.
10 Marketing planning needs the active support of the chief executive and must be appropriate for the culture.

Planning horizon

There is a natural point of focus in the future beyond which it is pointless to plan for. This can differ from firm to firm, depending on its business. Generally, small firms can use shorter horizons, because they are flexible, to adjust to change. Large firms need longer horizons.

Planning paradox

Companies often set out to achieve the impossible. It is not unknown to see planning objectives which seek to:

- maximize sales
- minimize costs
- increase market share
- maximize profits.

Not only are these incompatible, but they also damage the credibility of the managers who subscribe to such commitments.

Question raised for the company

1   Q Are there different approaches to marketing planning?
    A We believe there are. Please see the following diagram.

The most successful marketing plans are collaborative. Here, relevant executives take part in the process in a caring way, and at the same time planning is done rigorously.

EXERCISES

As the brief notes have indicated, there are a number of conditions to be met if the marketing planning process is not to become a sterile, closed-loop system. The ten principles of marketing planning listed in the notes go a considerable way to ensuring that the process does not degenerate into a ritualized, 'numbers game'. However, there are still some problematical issues to be addressed.

Exercise 12.1 looks at the theory issue of how formalized the planning process should be, and how to take the correct steps to get close to the ideal system for your company.

Exercise 12.2 examines how to set up a timetable for planning. This is particularly useful in getting all contributors to the marketing plan working in unison, and coming up with the necessary information at the appropriate time.

In these exercises, you will focus on the marketing planning system best suited to your company. By way of consolidating on all of your work through this book, you will design an appropriate planning system and lay down the 'ground rules' for its implementation.

Selecting the appropriate approach
Figure 12.8 shows how the degree of formalization of the marketing planning process relates to company size and the diversity of its operations.

Introduction to Chapter 12 exercises

Exercise 12.1
Designing the marketing planning system

		Company size	
	Large	Medium	Small
High	High formalization	High/medium formalization	Medium formalization
Medium	High/medium formalization	Medium formalization	Low formalization
Low	Medium formalization	Low formalization	Very low formalization

Market/product diversity

Figure 12.8
Marketing planning

1 Select a position on this figure which best describes your company's situation.
2 In the space below, write down a few key words or sentences that would best describe the marketing planning system you would need for your company – e.g. high formalization, etc.

Identifying the improvement areas

1 Imagine that it is possible to measure the efficiency of a marketing planning system on a scale 0–100, where 100 is equivalent to 100 per cent efficiency – i.e. the system works well and conforms with your model. How would you rate the current approach to marketing planning in your company? To what extent does it match up with your ideal?

2 Enter your score on Figure 12.9, drawing a horizontal line as shown.

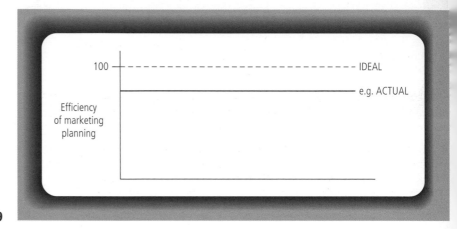

Figure 12.9

The difference between your scoreline and the ideal must represent where there is room for improvement.

Transfer your score line to the worksheet, the force field diagram, then complete the worksheet by following the instructions given below.

Worksheet Force field diagram (Exercise 12.1)

3 Identify all those factors that have 'pushed' your actual efficiency line below the ideal. Add them to the worksheet, showing them as actual forces pushing down. If you can, represent the biggest forces with longer arrows, as shown in Figure 12.10.

You will probably have more than three factors, so list as many as you can. Remember, you should be noting only those that affect the *marketing planning system*, not the company's general approach to marketing. We will call these downward forces 'restraining forces', because they are acting against improvement.

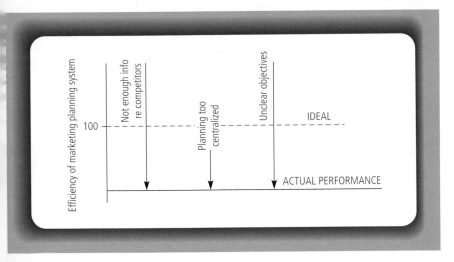

Figure 12.10

4 Now ask yourself, why isn't the actual performance line you have drawn lower than it is? The reason is, of course, that there are several parts of the system that work well, or there are other strengths in your company. Identify these positive forces and add them to the worksheet, as shown in Figure 12.11, again relating the arrow size approximately to the influence of each factor.

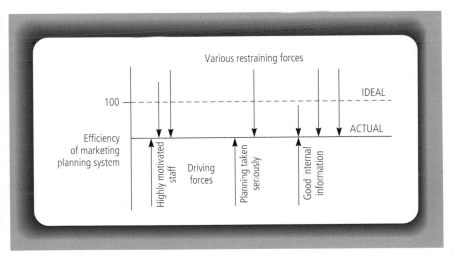

Figure 12.11

Again, the factors shown above are only examples. You will identify many more. We call these 'driving forces' because they are pushing towards improvement.

5 The worksheet should now be complete, showing the two sets of forces lined up against each other. What next? Well, it might have struck you that what you have assembled is somewhat analogous to a ship at sea. Your ship (the marketing planning system) is wallowing below its ideal level in the water but is prevented from sinking by buoyant forces (driving forces). To restore the ship to its correct level, it would be natural to remove or jettison some of the cargo (the restraining forces), not to try to get out and push

from below. As it is for the ship, so it is for your marketing planning system, therefore:

(a) Select the major restraining forces and work out ways that you can reduce their impact, or preferably eliminate them altogether. These will be the source of the greatest improvements, but some remedies might need time to take effect.

(b) So, concurrently, select minor restraining forces and plan to eliminate them also. Although their impact on improvement might be less, you will probably find they respond more quickly to treatment.

(c) Finally, select the smallest driving forces and work out if there are any ways to increase their impact.

6 Assemble your various responses to 5(a), (b) and (c) together into a comprehensive improvement plan, then take steps to get it accepted and acted upon.

Put most of your energy into removing the restraining factors. To focus on the major driving forces (e.g. trying to make highly motivated staff even more motivated) is likely to be counter-productive.

Force field analysis theory

The force field analysis, upon which much of designing a system is based, stems from the work of Kurt Lewin, *Field Theory in Social Science*, Harper, London, 1951). His reasoning, adapted to the programme situation, operates thus:

1 If a company's marketing system is functioning well, then the company could be said to have no problems. Diagrammatically, the efficiency level could be shown at something approaching 100 per cent. See Figure 12.12.

Figure 12.12

2 Few companies reach this happy state of affairs. Without resorting to precise measurement (a consensus of views is generally enough), most companies would 'score' their planning system somewhat lower, as shown in Figure 12.13.

3 Wherever the 'actual' line is drawn, it poses two interesting questions upon which the subsequent analysis hinges, namely:

(a) What causes the performance level to be where it is?

(b) Why doesn't it fall any lower?

4 Clearly the answer to 3(a) is that things are going wrong in the system; that there are missing or malfunctioning areas. Until these are put right, there will always be a drag on the efficiency, holding it down. These negative forces are termed *restraining forces*, because they are restraining improvement.

5 Similarly, the reason that efficiency doesn't drop lower than has been shown is that there must be several parts of the planning system that work quite well. There are many strengths in the system. These positive factors are termed *driving forces*, because they are the forces pushing towards better efficiency.

6 In Figure 12.13, for the efficiency of the planning system to be below the ideal level, then the restraining forces must be greater than the driving forces.

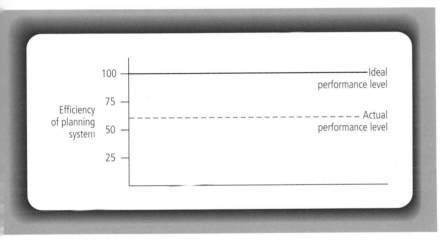

Figure 12.13

7 Let us take a simple illustration. We are driving a car and it is going more slowly than it ought to because the brakes are rubbing (restraining force). If we want to resume driving at normal speed then we have two courses of action open to us:

(a) We can put our foot down on the accelerator (increase the driving force)

(b) We can free the brakes (remove the restraining force).

We can see that by putting our foot down all sorts of troubles are likely to materialize. Unless something is done to free the brakes, then probably they would overheat, perhaps catch fire or jam up completely.

8 A similar overheating could take place in the company's marketing planning system unless it is tackled properly. To get lasting improvements, it will be important to identify all the restraining and driving forces. Indeed, many of the earlier exercises were designed to do just this. Using this information, it will be important *to plan how to reduce or remove the restraining forces and, only when that is done, consider how to plan to boost the driving forces.*

9 Figure 12.14 is an example of how a finished force field diagram might look, although most people will have identified several more factors than shown here. Many of the factors identified by you ought to be unique to your company.

Notes:

1 Remember that only factors that affect the marketing planning process ought to appear in the force field diagram.
2 It is possible to draw the force arrows proportional in length to their influence

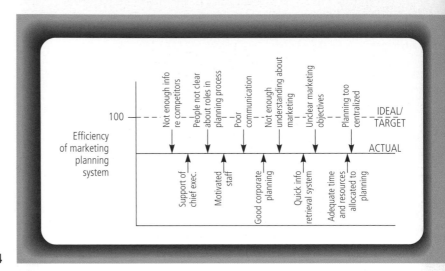

Figure 12.14

Exercise 12.2

Implementing the marketing planning system

Perhaps you will be unable to implement a marketing planning system until your improvement plan from Exercise 12.1 has eliminated the more serious obstacles. Nevertheless, from what you have read in this book, you will know that a successful marketing planning system will have to follow these steps.

1 There will have to be guidance provided by the corporate objectives.
2 A marketing audit must take place.
3 A gap analysis must be completed.
4 A SWOT analysis must be drawn up.
5 Assumptions and contingencies must be considered.
6 Marketing objectives and strategies must be set.
7 Individual marketing programmes must be established.
8 There must be a period of review and measurement.

Because of the work required, all this takes time. Various people might have to participate at different stages. There will certainly have to be several meetings or discussions with other functional departments, either to get information or to ensure collaboration.

Therefore, in order to keep the planning 'train' on the 'rails', it will be in everybody's interest to be clear about the sequencing of these different activities, to have a schedule or timetable.

As the company gets more experienced in planning, then probably the timetable can be tightened up and the whole planning period shortened. However, to get events into perspective, it is often helpful to present a timetable of the planning activities, as shown in Figure 12.15. The circle represents a calendar year and the time periods are merely examples – not to be taken as recommended periods.

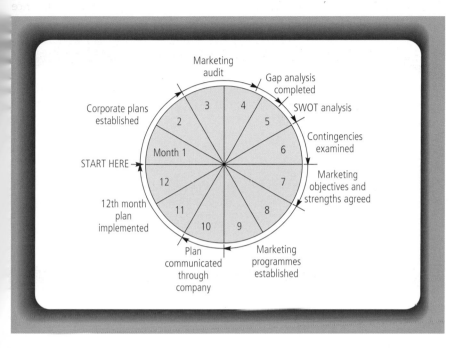

Figure 12.15

In the second planning year, months 11 and 12 could be used to evaluate the first year's plan and thereby prepare information for the next round of corporate planning.

This diagrammatic approach clearly shows how the planning process is a continual undercurrent throughout the year.

Now, as your final task, try drawing up the planning timetable for your company on Figure 12.16.

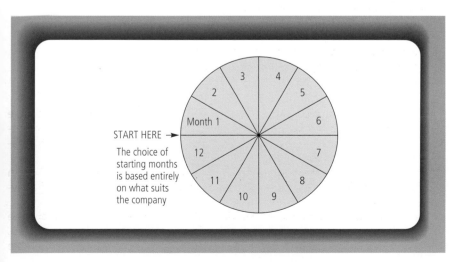

Figure 12.16

CHAPTER 13

A step-by-step marketing planning system

Summary

Part 1:

■ The main barriers to marketing planning

■ How to overcome the main barriers to marketing planning

■ A summary of the contents of a strategic marketing plan

Part 2:

■ A step-by-step approach to preparing a strategic marketing plan

■ A step-by-step approach to preparing a tactical marketing plan

■ A format for those who have to consolidate many strategic marketing plans

■ Forms and templates are provided to turn the theory into practice

Part 1 Marketing planning summary

■ The purpose of marketing planning

The overall purpose of marketing and its principal focus is the identification and creation of competitive advantage.

■ What is marketing planning?

Marketing planning is simply a logical sequence and a series of activities leading to the setting of marketing objectives and the formulation of plans for achieving them.

Why is marketing planning necessary?

Marketing planning is necessary because of:

1 Increasing turbulence, complexity and competitiveness
2 The speed of technological change
3 The need for *you*
    ● to help identify sources of competitive advantage
    ● to force an organized approach
    ● to develop specificity to ensure consistent relationships
4 The need for *superiors*
    ● to inform

5　The need for *non-marketing functions*
- to get support
6　The need for *subordinates*
- to get resources
- to gain commitment
- to set objectives and strategies.

■ Ten barriers to marketing planning

This book has described a number of barriers to effective marketing planning. The ten principal barriers are:

1　Confusion between marketing tactics and strategy
2　Isolating the marketing function from operations
3　Confusion between the marketing function and the marketing concept
4　Organizational barriers – the tribal mentality, for example the failure to define strategic business units (SBUs) correctly
5　Lack of in-depth analysis
6　Confusion between process and output
7　Lack of knowledge and skills
8　Lack of a systematic approach to marketing planning
9　Failure to prioritize objectives
10　Hostile corporate cultures.

The 'Ten S' approach to overcoming these barriers

Figure 13.1 summarizes the 'Ten S' approach developed by the author to overcome each of these barriers. The sections which follow elaborate briefly on each of the 'Ten Ss'. Ten fundamental principles of marketing planning are provided.

Marketing planning – Principle 1. Strategy before tactics
Develop the strategic marketing plan first. This entails greater emphasis on scanning the external environment, the early identification of forces emanating from it, and developing appropriate strategic responses, involving all levels of management in the process.

A strategic plan should cover a period of between three and five years, and only when this has been developed and agreed should the one-year operational marketing plan be developed.

Never write the one-year plan first and extrapolate it.

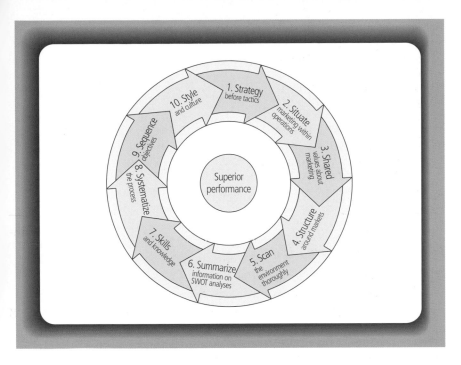

Figure 13.1
Marketing planning for competitive advantage

Marketing planning – Principle 2. Situate marketing within operations

For the purpose of marketing planning, put marketing as close as possible to the customer. Where practicable, have both marketing and sales report to the same person, who should not normally be the chief executive officer.

Marketing planning – Principle 3. Shared values about marketing

Marketing is a management process whereby the resources of the whole organization are utilized to satisfy the needs of selected customer groups in order to achieve the objectives of both parties. Marketing, then, is first and foremost an attitude of mind rather than a series of functional activities confined to the marketing department. However, use the expression 'market-led' or 'customer-driven' to describe the philosophy, *not* 'marketing-driven'.

Marketing planning – Principle 4. Structure around markets

Organize company activities around customer groups if possible rather than around products or functional activities and get marketing planning done in these strategic business units. Without excellent marketing planning in SBUs, corporate marketing planning will be of limited value.

Marketing planning – Principle 5. Scan the environment thoroughly

For an effective marketing audit to take place:

- Checklists of questions customized according to level in the organization should be agreed.
- These should form the basis of the organization's MIS.
- The marketing audit should be a *required* activity.
- Managers should not be allowed to hide behind vague terms like 'poor economic conditions'.
- Managers should be encouraged to incorporate the tools of marketing in their audits, e.g. product life-cycles, portfolios and so on.

Marketing planning – Principle 6. Summarize information in SWOT analyses

Information is the foundation on which a marketing plan is built. From information (internal and external) comes intelligence.

Intelligence describes *the marketing plan*, which is the intellectualization of how managers perceive their own position in their markets relative to their competitors (with competitive advantage accurately defined – e.g. cost leader, differentiation, niche), what objectives they want to achieve over some designated period of time, how they intend to achieve their objectives (strategies), what resources are required, and with what results (budget).

A 'SWOT' should:

- be focused on each specific segment of crucial importance to the organization's future
- be a summary emanating from the marketing audit
- be brief, interesting and concise
- focus on *key* factors only
- list *differential* strengths and weaknesses *vis-à-vis* competitors, focusing on competitive advantage
- list *key* external opportunities and threats only
- identify and pin down the *real* issues – it should not be a list of unrelated points
- enable the reader to grasp instantly the main thrust of the business, even to the point of being able to write marketing objectives
- follow the implied question 'which means that ...?' to get the real implications
- not over-abbreviate.

Marketing planning – Principle 7. Skills and knowledge

Ensure that all those responsible for marketing in SBUs have the necessary marketing knowledge and skills for the job. In particular, ensure that they understand and know how to use the more important tools of marketing, such as:

1 Information
- how to get it
- how to use it

2 Positioning
- market segmentation
- Ansoff
- Porter

3 Product life-cycle analysis
- gap analysis

4 Portfolio management
- BCG Matrix
- directional policy matrix

5 $4 \times$ Ps management
- Product
- Price
- Place
- Promotion

Additionally, marketing personnel require communications and interpersonal skills.

Marketing planning – Principle 8. Systematize the process

It is essential in complex organizations to have a set of written procedures and a well-argued common format for marketing planning. The purposes of such a system are:

1 To ensure that all key issues are systematically considered
2 To pull together the essential elements of the strategic planning of each SBU in a consistent manner
3 To help corporate management to compare diverse businesses and to understand the overall condition of, and prospects for, the organization.

Marketing planning – Principle 9. Sequence objectives

Ensure that all objectives are prioritized according to their impact on the organization and their urgency, and that resources are allocated accordingly.

A suggested method for prioritization is given in Figure 13.2.

Marketing planning – Principle 10. Style and culture

Marketing planning will not be effective without the active support and participation of the culture leaders. But, even with their support, the type of marketing planning has to be appropriate for the phase of the organizational lifeline. This phase should be measured before attempting to introduce marketing planning.

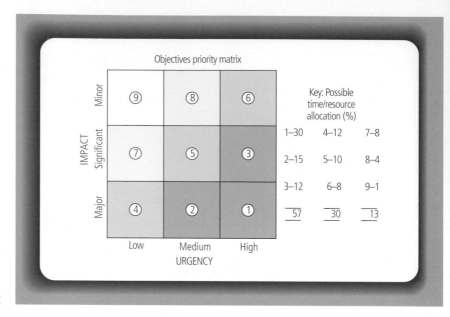

Figure 13.2

■ Conclusion to Part 1

A summary of what appears in a strategic marketing plan and a list of the principal marketing tools/techniques/structures/frameworks which apply to each step is given in Figure 13.3.

It will be understood from the foregoing that marketing planning never has been just the simple step-by-step approach described so enthusiastically in most prescriptive texts and courses. The moment an organization embarks on the marketing planning path, it can expect to encounter a number of complex organizational, attitudinal, process and cognitive problems which are likely to block progress. By being forewarned about these barriers, there is a good chance of successfully using the step-by-step marketing planning system which follows in Part 2 of this chapter, and of doing excellent marketing planning that will bring all the claimed benefits, including a significant impact on the bottom line, through the creation of competitive advantage. If they are ignored, however, marketing planning will remain the Cinderella of business management.

Part 2 A marketing planning system

■ Introduction

This marketing planning system is in three sections. Section A takes you through a step-by-step approach to the preparation of a strategic marketing

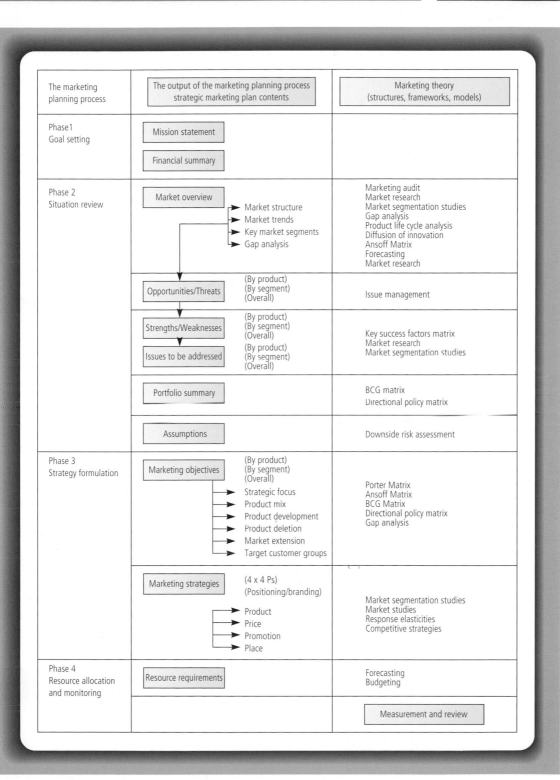

Figure 13.3

plan. What actually appears in the strategic marketing plan is given under the heading 'Strategic marketing plan documentation', which appears later in this chapter.

Section B (page 520) takes you through the preparation of a one-year marketing plan. What actually appears in a one-year marketing plan is given under the heading 'The one-year marketing plan documentation'. Finally, Section C (page 530) refers to the need for a headquarters consolidated plan of several SBU strategic marketing plans and provides a suggested format.

Section A
Step-by-step approach to the preparation of a strategic marketing plan

---

There are four main steps in the planning process (presented in diagrammatic form in Figure 13.4), which any strategic business unit[1] interested in protecting and developing its business must carry out:

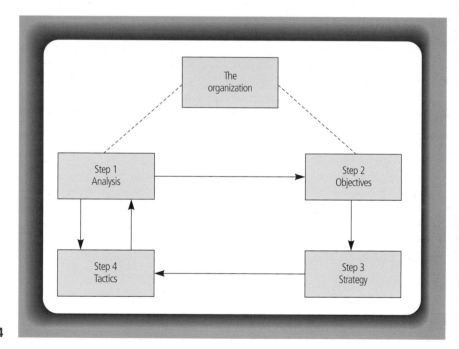

Figure 13.4

---

[1] A strategic business unit:

- will have common segments and competitors for most of its products
- will be a competitor in an external market
- will be a discrete and identifiable unit
- will have a manager who has control over most of the areas critical to success.

SBUs are not necessarily the same as operating units and the definition can, and should if necessary, be applied all the way down to a particular product or customer or group of products and customers.

1 *Analysis* – it must analyse both its marketplace and its own position within it, relative to the competition.
2 *Objectives* – it must construct from this analysis a realistic set of quantitative marketing and financial objectives, consistent with those set by the organization.
3 *Strategy* – it must determine the broad strategy which will accomplish these objectives, conforming with the organization's corporate strategy.
4 *Tactics* – it must draw together the analysis, the objectives and the strategy, using them as the foundation for detailed tactical action plans, capable of implementing the strategy and achieving the agreed objectives.

This process is formally expressed in two marketing plans, the strategic marketing plan and the tactical marketing plan, which should be written in accordance with the format provided in this system. It is designed for strategic business units (SBUs) to be able to take a logical and constructive approach to planning for success.

Two very important introductory points should be made about the marketing plan:

1 *The importance of different sections* – in the final analysis, the strategic marketing plan is a plan for action, and this should be reflected in the finished document. The implementation part of the strategic plan is represented by the subsequent one-year marketing plan.
2 *The length of the analytical section* – to be able to produce an action-focused strategic marketing plan, a considerable amount of background information and statistics needs to be collected, collated and analysed. An analytical framework has been provided in the forms, included in the database section of the 'Strategic marketing plan documentation', which each SBU should complete. However, the commentary given in the strategic marketing plan should provide the main findings of the analysis rather than a mass of raw data. It should compel concentration upon only that which is essential. The analysis section should, therefore, provide only a short background.

■ Basis of the system

Each business unit in the organization will have different levels of opportunity depending on the prevailing business climate. Each business unit, therefore, needs to be managed in a way that is appropriate to its own unique circumstances. At the same time, however, the chief executive officer of the SBU must have every opportunity to see that the ways in which these business units are managed are consistent with the overall strategic aims of the organization.

This system sets out the procedures which, if adhered to, will assist in achieving these aims.

Sections A, B and C set out the three basic marketing planning formats and explain how each of the planning steps should be carried out. They explain simply and clearly what should be presented, and when, in the three-year marketing plan, in the more detailed one-year operational plan and in the headquarters consolidated marketing plan.

The overall marketing planning format is described in Figure 13.5. (Note that, for the sake of simplicity, it has been assumed that the organization's year runs from January to December.) The following sections explain how each of the steps in the planning process should be completed.

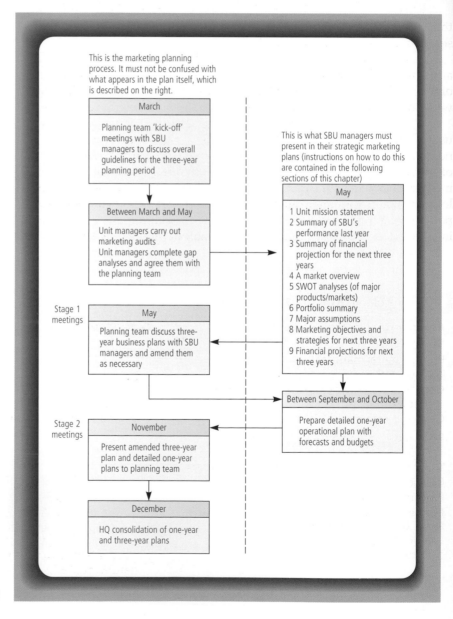

Figure 13.5

■ The marketing audit

(For completion between February and May each year.)

Note: the marketing audit is not for inclusion in the plan or its presentation.

Every market includes a wide variety of customer groups, not all of which will necessarily provide SBUs with opportunities for servicing profitably.

In order to study those areas of the market which are potentially most favourable to the SBU's operations, it is necessary to divide the market into different *market segments* (hereafter just referred to as 'segments') and to analyse sales potential by type of product within each segment.

All SBUs must, therefore, analyse and evaluate the key segments in their market, plus any other segments which have been identified and selected as being of lesser importance to them.

It is appreciated that all the basic information required for this marketing audit may not be readily available. Nevertheless, an analysis and evaluation of the SBU's situation in each of the selected segments, i.e. a marketing audit, will provide the basis from which objectives can be set and plans prepared.

For the purpose of a marketing planning system, it is usual to provide users with an agreed list so that all SBUs using the system use similar nomenclature for products and markets. In this case, we provide an *example* of such a list in Table 13.1. Please note, more detailed criteria for market segmentation should also be used, where appropriate – for example: geographic location; company organization (centralized or decentralized); purchasing patterns (e.g. price sensitivity, fixed annual budget, local autonomy, etc.); integration level; sales channel preference; support requirements; and so on.

Table 13.1 Example of industrial and marine market segments and industrial product groups

Key industrial market segments	Explanatory notes
Primary metal manufacture	
Transportation equipment manufacture	
General mechanical engineering/fabricated metal products	
Glass and ceramics	Glass, glassware, refractory and ceramic goods
Road passenger and freight transportation (specialists)	
Truck and construction equipment distributors	
Building and construction	
Forestry and timber	
Mining and quarrying	
Food, beverage, tobacco processing and manufacture	
Oil and gas	Extraction and processing of mineral oil and natural gas, excluding offshore, which is covered in marine

Table 13.1 Continued

Electricity: power generation and transmission

Bricks and cement | Manufacture of non-metallic mineral products, excluding glass and ceramics

Textiles | Textile industry and the production of man-made fibres

Leather
Pulp and paper
National defence

Central and local government | Excludes national defence

Aviation | Excludes military aviation and aerospace manufacturing industries

Industrial distributors | Wholesale distribution of industrial machinery, industrial spare parts and tools, etc.

Rubber, chemicals, plastics | Excludes rubber plantations

Cosmetics and pharmaceuticals

Key marine market segments

International vessels greater than 4,000 GRT

- Oil tankers
- LPG and chemical tankers
- Containers
- General cargo vessels
- Bulk carriers
- Ferries and roll-on-roll-off vessels
- Miscellaneous vessels

Coastal/international vessels less than 4,000 GRT

- Oil tankers
- LPG and chemical tankers
- Containers
- General cargo vessels
- Bulk carriers
- Ferries and roll-on-roll-off vessels
- Miscellaneous vessels

Fishing

Offshore industry
- Drilling rigs
- Submersibles
- Work units, etc.

Miscellaneous
- Harbour craft
- Inland waterways
- Dredgers
- Military, etc.

Industrial product groups

Automotive products
Engine oils
Transmission fluids and gear oils
Brake fluids
Antifreeze/coolants
Greases
Miscellaneous 'others'

Metalworking products
Cutting oils (soluble)
Cutting oils (neat)
Rolling oils
Heat treatment

Aviation lubricants
Engine oils
Transmission oils
Hydraulic oils
Grease
Other

Other products
White oils
Electrical oils
Process oils
Textile oils
Leather chemicals
Laundry and dry cleaning chemicals

Table 13.1 Continued

Surface treatment products
Corrosion preventives (including DWFs)
Non-destructive testing materials
Industrial cleaning chemicals

Mould releasants
Petroleum jelly
Defoamers

General industrial lubricants
Hydraulic

- fire resistant
- other

Gear oils
Turbine oils
Heat transfer oils
Compressor oils (including refrigerator)
Grease
Circulating oils
Other (e.g. wire rope lubricants, Ss)

All managers carrying out their audit should use internal sales data and the SBU marketing information system to complete their audit. It is helpful at this stage if the various SBU managers can issue to any subordinates involved in the audit a market overview covering major industry and market trends. The audit will inevitably require considerably more data preparation than is required to be reproduced in the marketing plan itself. Therefore, all managers should start a *running reference file* for their area of responsibility during the year, which can also be used as a continual reference source and for verbal presentation of proposals.

It is essential to stress that the audit, which will be based on the running reference file, *is not a marketing plan, and under no circumstances should voluminous documents relating to the audit appear in any business plans.*

■ The contents of a strategic marketing plan

The following sections (1–9) describe what should be presented in strategic marketing plans. These should be completed by the end of May each year.

These sections contain instructions. The actual documentation for the strategic marketing plan is also provided in this section.

1 SBU mission statement

This is the first item to appear in the marketing plan. The purpose of the mission statement is to ensure that the *raison d'être* of the SBU is clearly stated. Brief statements should be made which cover the following points:

1 *Role or contribution of the unit* – for example, profit generator, service department, opportunity seeker.
2 *Definition of business* – for example, the needs you satisfy or the benefits you provide. Do not be too specific (e.g. 'we sell milking machinery') or too general (e.g. 'we are in the engineering business').
3 *Distinctive competence* – this should be a brief statement that applies only to your specific SBU. A statement that could equally apply to any competitor is unsatisfactory.
4 *Indications for future direction* – a brief statement of the principal things you would give serious considerations to (e.g. move into a new segment). A statement about what you *will* consider, *might* consider and *will never* consider can be quite useful.

Note: This is Form 1 in the strategic marketing plan documentation to be found at the end of Section A.

2 Summary of SBU's performance

This opening section is designed to give a bird's-eye view of the SBU's total marketing activities.

In addition to a quantitative summary of performance, as shown in Table 13.2, SBU managers should give a summary of reasons for good or bad performance.

Table 13.2			
	Three years ago	Two years ago	Last year
Volume/turnover Gross profit (%) Gross margin (000 euro)			

Use *constant revenue* (t − 1) in order that the comparisons are meaningful. Make sure you use the same base-year values for any projections provided in later sections in your plan.

Note: This is Form 2 in the strategic marketing plan documentation to be found at the end of Section A.

3 Summary of financial projections

This is the third item to appear in the marketing plan. Its purpose is to summarize, for the person reading the plan, the financial implications over the full three-year planning period. It should be presented as a simple diagram along the lines shown in Figure 13.6. This should be accompanied by

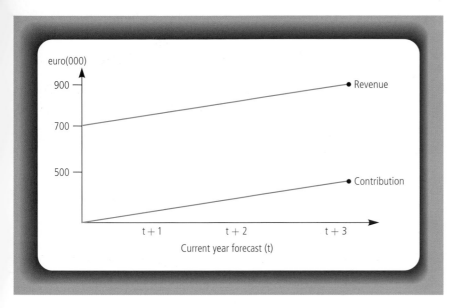

Figure 13.6

a brief commentary. For example: 'This three-year business plan shows an increase in revenue from 700,000 euros to 900,000 euros and an increase in contribution from 100,000 euros to 400,000 euros. The purpose of this strategic plan is to show how these increases will be achieved.'

Note: There is a form, Form 3, in the strategic marketing plan documentation at the end of Section A. In order to comply with this form, it is strongly recommended that the strategic planning (gap analysis) forms (which follow as Forms 4 and 5 in the strategic marketing plan documentation) are completed first. Note that the 'objective' point should be (as a minimum) that point which will enable you to achieve the corporate objectives set for the SBU. *Ideally, however, it should be set at a point which will make this SBU the best of its kind amongst comparable competitive SBUs.* Note that the sales revenue form must be completed first, followed by the profit form.

Forms 4 and 5 should enable you to use an Ansoff Matrix to show diagrammatically where the revenue and profit growth is coming from (i.e. how much from the several products for markets in Box 1, which is existing products in existing markets, broken down by productivity growth, market growth and market share growth; similar for new products for existing markets in Box 2; similar for existing products in new markets in Box 3; and, finally, growth from new products in new markets in Box 4).

4 Market overview

This section is intended to provide a brief picture of the market before descending to the particular details of individual market segments, which form the heart of the marketing plan.

This system is based upon the *segmentation* of markets, dividing these into homogeneous groups of customers, each having characteristics which can be exploited in marketing terms. *This approach is taken because it is the one which is often the most useful for SBU managers to be able to develop their markets.* The alternative, product-orientated, approach is rarely appropriate, given the variation between different customer groups in the markets in which most organizations compete.

The market segmentation approach is more useful in revealing both the weaknesses and the development opportunities than is an exclusively product orientation.

While it is difficult to give precise instructions on how to present this section of the marketing plan, it should be possible (following completion of the marketing audit) to present a market overview which summarizes what managers consider to be the key characteristics of their markets.

In completing this section, SBU managers should consider the following:

1 What are the major products, markets (or segments) which are likely to be able to provide the kind of business opportunities suitable for the organization?
2 How are these changing? That is, which are growing and which are declining?

This section should be brief, and there should be some commentary by the SBU manager about what seems to be happening in their market.

It is very helpful if SBU managers can present as much of this information as possible visually (i.e. as bar charts or pie charts, product life-cycles, etc.). A market 'map' can be extremely useful for clarifying how the market works. (For further details of this technique, see Chapter 4.)

Note: There is a form, Form 6, in the strategic marketing plan documentation at the end of Section A.

5 SWOT analyses of major products/markets

Compiling the SWOT analyses

To decide on marketing objectives and future strategy, it is first necessary to summarize the SBU's *present* position in its market(s). This was done in the previous section.

In respect of the major products/markets (segments) highlighted in the previous section, the marketing audit must now be summarized in the form of a number of *SWOT analyses*. The word *SWOT* derives from the initial letters of the words *strengths*, *weaknesses*, *opportunities* and *threats*. In simple terms:

● What are the unit's differential strengths and weaknesses *vis-à-vis* competitors? In other words, why should potential customers in the target markets prefer to deal with your organization rather than with your competitors?
● What are the opportunities?
● What are the present and future threats to the SBU's business in each of the segments which have been identified as being of importance?

Guidelines for completing the SWOT analysis

The market overview in section 4 above will have identified what you consider to be the key product/market (segments) on which you intend to focus. For presentation purposes, it is helpful if you can present a brief SWOT for each of these key product/market segments. Each of these SWOTs should be brief and interesting to read. Complete SWOTs only for the key segments.

Section I concerns *strengths* and *weaknesses*. Section II, which follows, is intended to indicate how the *opportunities* and *threats* section of the SWOT should be completed. Section III summarizes *key issues to be addressed*. Section IV describes the setting of assumptions, marketing objectives and strategies for each product/market segment. Section V summarizes the position of competitors.

I Some important factors for success in this business (critical success factors)

How does a competitor wishing to provide products or services in this segment succeed? There are always relatively few factors that determine success. Factors such as product performance, breadth of services, speed of service, low costs, and so on, are often the most important factors for success.

You should now make a brief statement about your organization's *strengths and weaknesses* in relation to these most important factors for success that you have identified. To do this, you will probably wish to consider other suppliers to the same segment in order to identify why you believe your organization can succeed and what weaknesses must be addressed in the three-year planning period.

These factors are called critical success factors. A layout such as that shown in Figure 13.7 is useful. You should then weight each factor out of 100 (e.g. CSF1 = 60, CSF2 = 25, CSF3 = 10, CSF4 = 5). It is suggested that you score yourself and each competitor out of 10 on each of the CSFs. Then, multiply each score by the weight. This will give you an accurate reading of your position in each segment *vis-à-vis* your competitors. It will also highlight which are *the key issues that should be addressed* in the three-year planning period.

Great caution is necessary to ensure that you are not guilty of self-delusion. Obviously, it is desirable to have independent evidence from market research in order to be able to complete this section accurately. If you do not have independent evidence, it is still worth doing a SWOT, because it will at least indicate what you need to know. Also, it is quite useful if you can get a number of managers to complete this independently, as, sometimes, it reveals a lot about what they believe to be the factors for success.

II Summary of outside influences and their implications (opportunities and threats)

This should include a brief statement about how important environmental influences such as technology, government policies and regulations, the economy, and so on, have affected this segment. There will obviously be some opportunities and some threats.

Competitors / Critical success factors	Weighting factor	Your organization	Competitor A	Competitor B	Competitor C
CSF1					
CSF2					
CSF3					
CSF4					
Total weighted score	100				

Figure 13.7

III Key issues to be addressed

From I and II above will emerge a number of key issues to be addressed.

IV Assumptions, marketing objectives, marketing strategies

Assumptions can now be made and objectives and strategies set. It should be stressed at this point that such assumptions, objectives and strategies relate only to each particular product/market segment under consideration. These will guide your thinking when setting overall assumptions, marketing objectives and strategies later on (see section below).

Note: There is a form, Form 7, in the strategic marketing plan documentation at the end of Section A. This form incorporates all the points made in I, II, III and IV above, and should be completed for all product/market segments under consideration.

V Competitor analysis

Here you should summarize the findings of the audit in respect of *major competitors* only. For each competitor, you should indicate its sales within the particular product/market segment under consideration, its share now, *and its expected share three years from now*. The greater a competitor's influence over others, the greater its ability to implement its own independent strategies – hence the more successful it is. It is suggested that you should also classify each of your main competitors according to one of the classifications in the guide to competitive position classifications, below, i.e. leadership, strong, favourable, tenable, weak.

Also list their principal products or services. Next, list each major competitor's business direction and current strategies. There follows a list of business directions and business strategies as guidelines. *These should not be quoted verbatim*, as they are only given as guidelines. Next, list their major strengths and weaknesses.

The format shown in Figure 13.8 is useful.

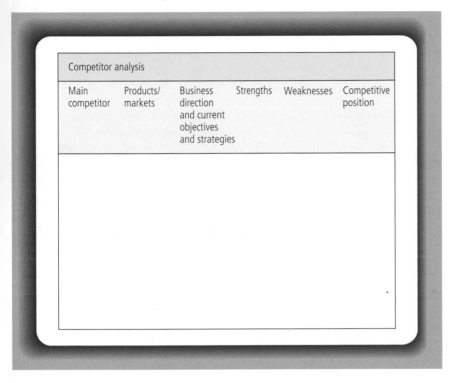

Competitor analysis

Main competitor	Products/ markets	Business direction and current objectives and strategies	Strengths	Weaknesses	Competitive position

Figure 13.8

Note: There is a form, Form 8, in the strategic marketing plan documentation at the end of Section A.

Guide to competitive position classifications:

Leadership	● Has a major influence on the performance or behaviour of others
Strong	● Has a wide choice of strategies ● Is able to adopt an independent strategy without endangering its short-term position ● Has low vulnerability to competitors' actions
Favourable	● Exploits specific competitive strengths, often in a product/market niche ● Has more than average opportunity to improve its position; has several strategies available
Tenable	● Its performance justifies continuation in business
Weak	● Currently has an unsatisfactory performance and significant competitive weakness ● It must improve or withdraw

The following list includes five business directions that are appropriate for almost any business. Select those that best summarize the competitor's strategy.

Business directions:

1 *Enter* – to allocate resources to a new business area. Consideration should include building from prevailing company or division strengths, exploiting related opportunities and defending against perceived threats. This may involve creating a new industry.

2 *Improve* – to apply strategies that will significantly improve the competitive position of the business. Often, this requires thoughtful product/market segmentation.

3 *Maintain* – to maintain one's competitive position. Aggressive strategies may be required, although a defensive posture may also be assumed. Product/market position is maintained, often in a niche.

4 *Harvest* – to relinquish intentionally competitive position, emphasizing short-term profit and cash flow, but not necessarily at the risk of losing the business in the short term. Often, this entails consolidating or reducing various aspects of the business to create higher performance for that which remains.

5 *Exit* – to divest a business because of its weak competitive position, or because the cost of staying in it is prohibitive and the risk associated with improving its position is too high.

6 Portfolio summary (summary of SWOTs)

All that remains is to summarize each of these SWOTs in a format which makes it easy to see at a glance the overall position and relative importance of each of these segments to the organization. This can be done by drawing a diagram in the form of a four-box matrix which will show each of the important product/market segments described earlier. A matrix is shown as Figure 13.9.[2] Some easy-to-follow instructions follow on how to complete such a matrix; more detailed instructions are provided in Chapter 5.

The *portfolio matrix* (referred to as the directional policy matrix in Chapter 5) enables you to assess which products or services, or which groups of customers/segments, will offer the best chance of commercial success. It will also aid decision-making about which products or services (or market segments) merit investment, in terms of both finance and managerial effort.

In this example, market segments are used, although it is possible to use products or services. We recommend that you follow the instructions given below.

This is how you arrive at a portfolio matrix for your SBU.

1 List your market segments on a separate piece of paper and decide which ones are the most attractive. (Note that these 'segments' can be

---

[2] Please note that 'high' is on the left of the horizontal axis because both Michael Porter and the Boston Consultancy Group Matrix put 'high' on the left. It can, if you prefer, be placed on the right of the horizontal axis.

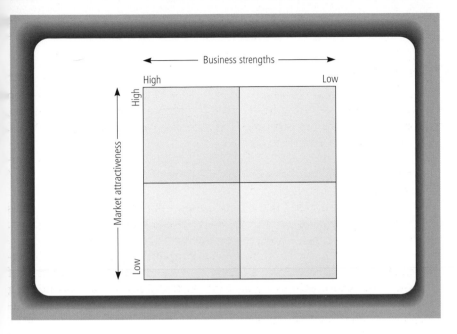

Figure 13.9

countries, divisions, markets, distributors, customers, etc.) To arrive at these decisions, you will no doubt take several factors into account:

- the size of the markets
- their actual or prospective growth
- the margins available to any competitor in this market
- the diversity of needs (which you can meet)
- the amount of competition in terms of quality and quantity
- the supportiveness of the business environment
- technical developments, etc.

Imagine that you have a measuring instrument – something like a thermometer, but which measures market attractiveness rather than temperature. The higher the reading, the more attractive the market is. The instrument is shown in Figure 13.10. Estimate the position on the scale that *each* of your markets would record (should such an instrument exist), and make a note of it as shown by the example below. You should use the methodology outlined in Chapter 5 and the example provided in Table 5.5.

2 Transpose this information on to the matrix in Figure 13.9, writing the markets on the left of the matrix.
3 Still using the matrix, draw a dotted line horizontally across from the top left-hand market as shown in Figure 13.11.
4 Now ask yourself how well your SBU is equipped to deal with this most attractive market. A whole series of questions needs to be asked to establish the company's business strengths, for example:
- Do we have the right products?
- How well are we known in this market?

Figure 13.10

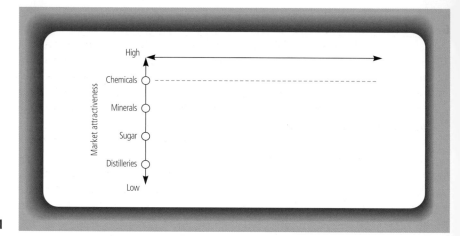

Figure 13.11

- What image do we have?
- Do we have the right technical skills?
- How close are we to this market?
- How do we compare with competitors?

The outcome of such an analysis will enable you to arrive at a conclusion about the 'fitness' of your unit and you will be able to choose a point on the horizontal scale of the matrix to represent this. The left of the scale represents many unit strengths, the right few unit strengths. The analysis completed in the previous section (Section 5 on SWOT analyses) should be used, since you have already completed the necessary quantification. Draw a vertical line from this point on the scale as shown in Figure 13.12, so that it intersects with the horizontal line. (Be certain, however, to use the quantitative method outlined in Chapter 5.)

5 Now *redraw* the circles, this time making the diameter of each circle proportional to that segment's share of your total sales turnover. (Please note that to be technically correct you should take the square root of the volume, or value.)

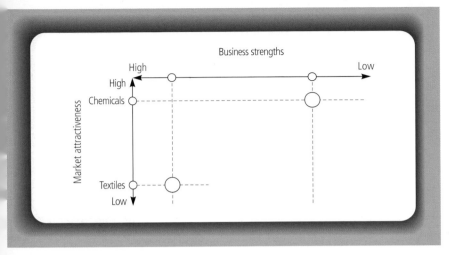

Figure 13.12

6 Now indicate where these circles will be in three years' time and their estimated size. The matrix may, therefore, have to show segments not currently served. There are two ways of doing this. First, in deciding on market or segment attractiveness you can assume that you are at t0 (i.e. today) and that your forecast of attractiveness covers the next three years (i.e. t + 3). If this is your chosen method, then it will be clear that *the circle can only move horizontally along the axis*, as all that will change is your business strength. The second way of doing it shows the current attractiveness position on the vertical axis, based on the past three years (i.e. t − 3 to t0), and then forecasts how that attractiveness position will change during the next three years (i.e. t0 to t + 3). In such a case, the circles can move both vertically and horizontally. This is the method used in the example provided (Figure 13.13), but it is entirely up to you which method you use. It is essential to be creative in your use of the matrix. Be prepared to change the names on the axes and to experiment with both products and markets.

Note: There is a form, Form 9, in the strategic marketing plan documentation at the end of Section A.

7 Overall assumptions

Each SBU must highlight the assumptions which are critical to the fulfilment of the planned marketing objectives and strategies.

Key planning assumptions deal, in the main, with outside features and anticipated changes which would have a significant influence on the achievement of marketing objectives. These might include such things as market growth rate, your organization's costs, capital investment and so on.

Assumptions should be few in number and relate only to key issues such as those identified in the SWOT analyses. If it is possible for a plan to be implemented irrespective of the assumptions made, then those assumptions are not necessary and should be removed.

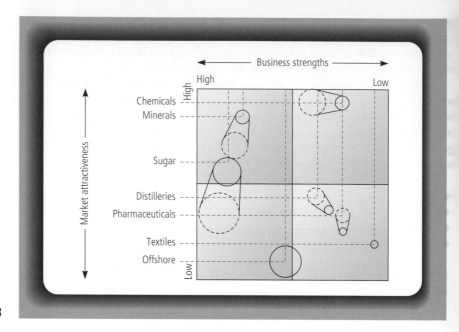

Figure 13.13

You should find that the more detailed lists of assumptions made for each of the principal product/market segments analysed in the SWOT stage (Section 5) will be helpful in deciding what the macro assumptions should be.

Note: There is a form, Form 10, in the strategic marketing plan documentation at the end of Section A.

8 Overall marketing objectives and strategies

Marketing objectives

Following identification and statement of key strengths, weaknesses, opportunities and threats, and the explicit statement of assumptions about conditions affecting the business, the process of setting marketing objectives is made easier, since they will be a realistic statement of what the SBU desires to achieve as a result of market-centred analysis.

As in the case of objective setting for other functional areas of the business, this is the most important step in the whole process, as it is a commitment on an SBU-wide basis to a particular course of action which will determine the scheduling and costing out of subsequent actions.

An *objective* is what the unit wants to achieve. A *strategy* is how it plans to achieve it. Thus, there are objectives and strategies at all levels in marketing – for example, there can be advertising objectives and strategies, pricing objectives and strategies, and so on.

However, the important point about marketing objectives is that they should be about products and markets only, since it is only by selling something to someone that the SBU's financial goals can be achieved.

Advertising, pricing and other elements of the marketing mix are the means (the strategies) by which the SBU can succeed in doing this. Thus, pricing objectives, sales promotion objectives, advertising objectives and so on should *not* be confused with marketing objectives.

If profits and cash flows are to be maximized, each SBU must consider carefully how its current customer needs are changing and how its products offered need to change accordingly. Since change is inevitable, it is necessary for SBUs to consider the two main dimensions of commercial growth – i.e. product development and market development. Marketing objectives are concerned with the following:

- Selling existing products to existing segments
- Developing new products for existing segments
- Extending existing products to new segments
- Developing new products for new segments.

Marketing objectives should be *quantitative*, and should be expressed where possible in terms of *values, volumes, market* shares and, if appropriate, *profitability*. General directional terms such as 'maximize', 'minimize' and 'penetrate' should be avoided unless quantification is included.

The marketing objectives should cover the full three-year planning horizon and should be accompanied by broad strategies (discussed in the following section) and broad revenue and cost projections for the full three-year period.

The one-year marketing plan should contain specific objectives for the first year of the three-year planning cycle and the corresponding strategies which will be used to achieve these objectives. *The one-year and the three-year plans should be separate documents. At this stage, a detailed one-year plan is not required.*

At this point it is worth stressing that the key document in the annual planning round is the three-year strategic marketing plan. The one-year plan represents the specific actions that should be undertaken in the first year of the strategic plan.

Marketing strategies

Marketing strategies should state in broad terms *how* the marketing objectives are to be achieved, as follows:

- The specific product policies (the range, technical specifications, positioning, additions, deletions, etc.)
- The pricing policies to be followed for product groups in particular market segments
- The customer service levels to be provided for specific market segments (such as maintenance support)
- The policies for communicating with customers under each of the main headings, such as sales force, advertising, sales promotion, etc. as appropriate.

Guidelines for setting marketing objectives and strategies are given in Chapter 6. However, the following summarizes some of the marketing objectives and strategies that are available to SBU managers.

Objectives

1 Market penetration
2 Introduce new products to existing markets
3 Introduce existing products to new markets (domestic)
4 Introduce existing products to new markets (international)
5 Introduce new products to new markets.

Strategies

1 Change product design, performance, quality or features
2 Change advertising or promotion
3 Change unit price
4 Change delivery or distribution
5 Change service levels
6 Improve marketing productivity (e.g. improve the sales mix)
7 Improve administrative productivity
8 Consolidate product line
9 Withdraw from markets
10 Consolidate distribution
11 Standardize design
12 Acquire markets, products, facilities.

Guidelines for setting marketing objectives and strategies

Completing a portfolio matrix (which you have done in Section 6) for each major product/market segment within each unit translates the characteristics of the business into visible and easily understood positions *vis-à-vis* each other.

Additionally, each product/market segment's position on the matrix suggests broad goals which are usually appropriate for businesses in that position, although unit managers should also consider alternative goals in the light of the special circumstances prevailing at the time.

The four categories on the matrix are:

● Invest
● Maintain
● Profit
● Selective.

You may prefer to use your own terms, although it should be stressed that it isn't necessary to attach any particular names to each of the quadrants. Each of these is considered in turn.

Invest

Products in this category enjoy competitive positions in markets/segments characterized by high growth rates and are good for continuing attractiveness. The obvious objective for such products is to maintain growth rates at least at the market growth rate, thus maintaining market share and market leadership, or to grow faster than the market, thus increasing market share.

Three principal factors should be considered:

1. Possible geographical expansion
2 Possible product line expansion
3 Possible product line differentiation.

These could be achieved by means of internal development, acquisition, or joint ventures.

The main point is that, in attractive marketing situations like this, *an aggressive marketing posture is required*, together with a very tight budgeting and control process to ensure that capital resources are efficiently utilized.

Maintain

Products in this category enjoy competitive positions in markets/ segments which are not considered attractive in the longer term. Here, the thrust should be towards maintaining a profitable position, with greater emphasis on present earnings rather than on aggressive growth.

The most successful product lines should be maintained, while less successful ones should be considered for pruning. Marketing effort should be focused on differentiating products to maintain share of key segments of the market. Discretionary marketing expenditure should be limited, especially when unchallenged by competitors or when products have matured. Comparative prices should be stabilized, except when a temporary aggressive stance is necessary to maintain market share.

Profit

Products in this category have a poor position in unattractive markets. These products are 'bad' only if objectives are not appropriate to the company's position in the market segment. Generally, where immediate divestment is not warranted, these products should be managed for cash.

Product lines should be aggressively pruned, while all marketing expenditure should be minimized, with prices maintained or where possible raised.

However, a distinction needs to be made between different types of products. The two principal categories are:

- Those which are clearly uncompetitive in unattractive markets
- Those which are quite near to the dividing line.

Products in the first of these categories should generally be managed as outlined above. The others should generally be managed differently. For example, the reality of low growth should be acknowledged and the temptation should be resisted to grow the product at its previous high rates of growth. It should not be viewed as a 'marketing' problem, which will be likely to lead to high advertising, promotion, inventory costs and lower profitability. Growth segments should be identified and exploited where possible. Product quality should be emphasized to avoid 'commodity' competition. Productivity should be systematically improved. Finally, the attention of talented managers should be focused on such products.

Selective

Here, it is necessary to decide whether to invest for future market leadership in these attractive markets/segments or whether to manage for present earnings. Both objectives are feasible, but it must be remembered that managing these products for cash today is usually inconsistent with market share growth and it is usually necessary to select the most promising markets and invest in them only.

Further marketing and other functional guidelines

Further marketing and other functional guidelines which operating unit managers should consider when setting marketing objectives and corresponding strategies are given in Chapter 6.

It should be stressed, however, that there can be no *automatic* policy for a particular product or market, and SBU managers should consider three or more options before deciding on 'the best' for recommendation. Above all, SBU managers must evaluate the most attractive opportunities and assess the chances for success in the most realistic manner possible. This applies particularly to new business opportunities. New business opportunities would normally be expected to build on existing strengths, particularly in marketing, which can be subsequently expanded or supplemented.

Database and summary of marketing objectives

The forms included in the database provide both an analytical framework and a summary of marketing objectives which are relevant to all strategic business unit managers. This summary is essential information which underpins the marketing plan.

Forms included in database

These forms can be found in the strategic marketing plan documentation at the end of Section A.

Form 11	*Market segment sales values*, showing, across a five-year period, total market demand, the business unit's own sales and the market share these represent for the various market segments
Form 12	*Market segment gross profits*, showing, across a five-year period, the business unit's sales value, gross profit, and gross margin for the various market segments
Form 13	*Product group analysis*, showing, across a five-year period, the business unit's sales value, gross profit, and gross margin for different product groups
Form 14	Summary (in words) of main marketing objectives and strategies

9 Financial projections for three years

Finally, SBU managers should provide financial projections for the full three-year planning period under all the principal standard revenue and cost headings as specified by your organization.

Note: There is a form, Form 15, in the strategic marketing plan documentation at the end of Section A.

■ Strategic marketing plan documentation

Form 1

Unit mission statement

This is the first item to appear in the marketing plan.

The purpose of the mission statement is to ensure that the *raison d'être* of the unit is clearly stated. Brief statements should be made which cover the following points:

1 *Role or contribution of the unit*
  e.g. profit generator, service department, opportunity seeker.

2 *Definition of the business*
  e.g. the needs you satisfy or the benefits you provide. Don't be too specific (e.g. 'we sell milking machinery') or too general (e.g. 'we're in the engineering business').

3 *Distinctive competence*
  This should be a brief statement that applies only to your specific unit. A statement that could equally apply to any competitor is unsatisfactory.

4 *Indications for future direction*
  A brief statement of the principal things you would give serious consideration to (e.g. move into a new segment). It helps if these are under the headings:

  Things we WILL do
  Things we MIGHT do
  Things we will NEVER do

Form 2

Summary of SBU's performance

This opening section is designed to give a bird's-eye view of the SBU's total marketing activities.

In addition to a quantitative summary of performance, as follows, SBU managers should give a summary of reasons for good or bad performance.

Use *constant revenue* in order that comparisons are meaningful.

Make sure you use the same base year values for any projections provided in later sections of this system.

	3 years ago	2 years ago	Last year
Volume/turnover			
Gross profit (%)			
Gross margin (000 euro)			

Summary of reasons for good or bad performance

Form 3

Summary of financial projections

This is the third item to appear in the marketing plan.

Its purpose is to summarize for the person reading the plan the financial results over the full three-year planning period. It should be presented as a simple diagram along the following lines:

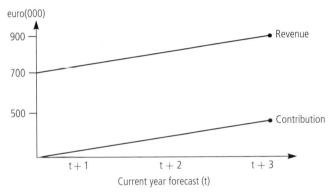

This should be accompanied by a brief commentary. For example:

'This three-year business plan shows an increase in revenue from 700,000 euros to 900,000 euros and an increase in contribution from 200,000 euros to 400,000 euros. The purpose of this strategic plan is to show how these increases will be achieved.'

Form 4

Strategic planning exercise (gap analysis) 1 Revenue

1 Objective
(a) Start by plotting the sales position you wish to achieve at the end of the planning period, Point E
(b) Next plot the forecast position, Point A

2 Gap analysis (1)
Are there any actions you can take to close the gap under the following headings? Plot the total value of these on the gap analysis graph on the left, Point B. (These represent cash and margin focus.) Now proceed to 3 below.

(Productivity)	Value/volume
Better product mix	
Better customer mix	
More sales calls	
Better sales calls	
Increase price	
Reduce discounts	
Charge for deliveries	
Others	
TOTAL	

5 Gap analysis (4)
Finally, list the value of any new products you might develop for new markets until Point E is reached (Steps 3, 4 and 5 represent a sales growth focus).

6 Gap analysis (5)
If none of this gives the required return on investment consider changing the asset base. This could be:
(a) Investment
(b) Divestment
(Step 6 represents a capital utilization focus.)

3 Gap analysis (2)
Ansoff product/market matrix (market penetration)
(a) List principal products on the horizontal axis and principal markets on the vertical axis. In each smaller square write in current sales and achievable sales during the planning period.
(b) Next plot the market penetration position, Point C. This point will be the addition of all the values in the right-hand half of the small boxes in the Ansoff Matrix. If there is a gap, proceed to 4 below.

4 Gap analysis (3)
Ansoff product/market matrix (new products/new markets)
Next, list the value of any new products you might develop which you might sell to existing markets. Alternatively, or as well, if necessary list the products that you might sell to new markets. Plot the total value of these on the gap analysis graph above, Point D. If there is still a gap, proceed to 5.

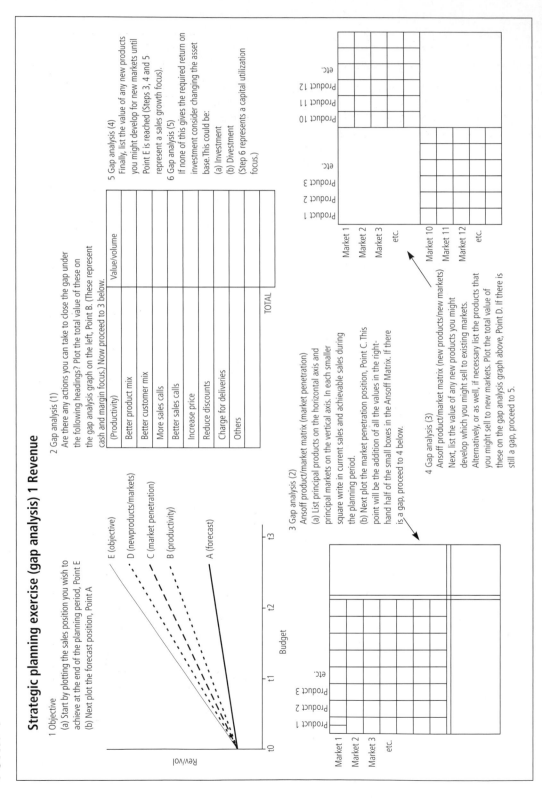

Strategic planning exercise (gap analysis) 2 Profit

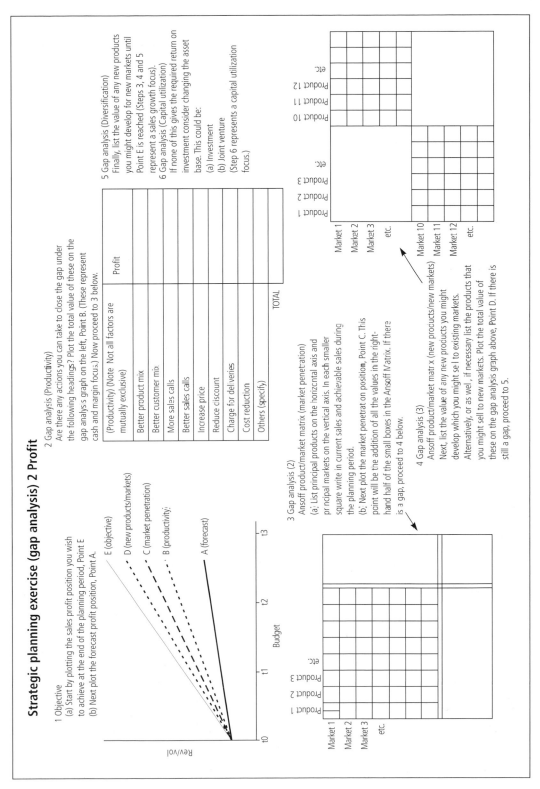

1 Objective
(a) Start by plotting the sales profit position you wish to achieve at the end of the planning period, Point E.
(b) Next plot the forecast profit position, Point A.

E (objective)
D (new products/markets)
C (market penetration)
B (productivity)
A (forecast)

Rev/vol

t0   t1   t2   t3

Budget

2 Gap analysis (Productivity)
Are there any actions you can take to close the gap under the following headings? Plot the total value of these on the gap analysis graph on the left, Point B. (These represent cash and margin focus.) Now proceed to 3 below.

(Productivity) (Note: Not all factors are mutually exclusive)	Profit
Better product mix	
Better customer mix	
More sales calls	
Better sales calls	
Increase price	
Reduce discount	
Charge for deliveries	
Cost reduction	
Others (specify)	
TOTAL	

3 Gap analysis (2)
Ansoff product/market matrix (market penetration)
(a) List principal products on the horizontal axis and principal markets on the vertical axis. In each smaller square write in current sales and achievable sales during the planning period.
(b) Next plot the market penetration position, Point C. This point will be the addition of all the values in the right-hand half of the small boxes in the Ansoff Matrix. If there is a gap, proceed to 4 below.

Market 1
Market 2
Market 3
etc.

Product 1   Product 2   Product 3   etc.

4 Gap analysis (3)
Ansoff product/market matrix (new products/new markets)
Next, list the value of any new products you might develop which you might sell to existing markets. Alternatively, or as well, if necessary list the products that you might sell to new markets. Plot the total value of these on the gap analysis graph above, Point D. If there is still a gap, proceed to 5.

Market 1
Market 2
Market 3
etc.

Product 1   Product 2   Product 3   etc.

Market 10
Market 11
Market 12
etc.

Product 10   Product 11   Product 12   etc.

5 Gap analysis (Diversification)
Finally, list the value of any new products you might develop for new markets until Point E is reached (Steps 3, 4 and 5 represent a sales growth focus).
6 Gap analysis (Capital utilization)
If none of this gives the required return on investment consider changing the asset base. This could be:
(a) Investment
(b) Joint venture
(Step 6 represents a capital utilization focus.)

Form 6

Market overview (with 'market map', if appropriate, together with implications for the organization)

Form 7

Strategic planning exercise (SWOT analysis)

(Note: This form should be completed for each product/market segment under consideration)

1 SBU description
Here, describe the market for which the SWOT is being done

2 Critical success factors
What are the few key things from the customer's point of view, that any competitor has to do right to succeed?

1	
2	
3	
4	
5	

3 Weighting
How important is each of these CSFs? Score out of 100

Total 100

4 Strengths/weaknesses analysis
Score yourself and each of your main competitors out of 10 on each of the CSFs. Then multiply the score by the weight

Comp \ CSF	You	Competitor A	Competitor B	Competitor C	Competitor D
1					
2					
3					
4					
5					
Total (score × weight)					

5 Opportunities/threats
What are the few key things outside your direct control that have had, and will continue to have, an impact on your business?

Opportunities

1	
2	
3	
4	
5	

Threats

6 Key issues that need to be addressed

7 Key assumptions for the planning period

1	
2	
3	
4	
5	
6	
7	

8 Key objectives

9 Key strategies

Financial consequences

Form 8

Note: **This form should be completed for each product market segment under consideration**

Main competitor	Products/markets	Business direction and current objectives and strategies	Strengths	Weaknesses	Competitive position

Form 9

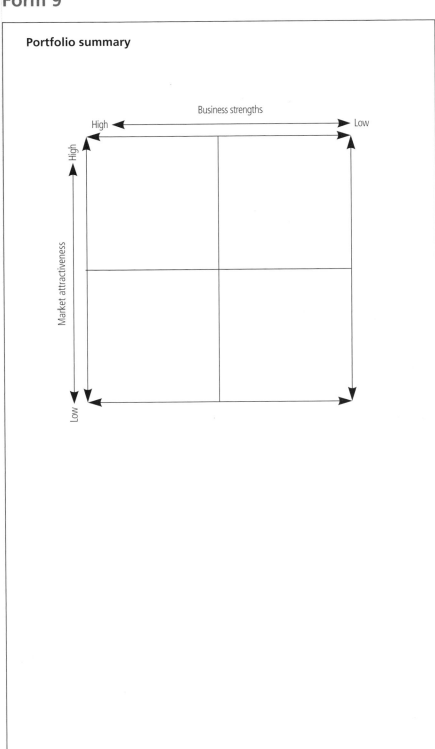

Portfolio summary

Form 10

Assumptions

Form 11

Database and summary of marketing objectives
Market segment sales values

Sales values	Last year (t − 1)	Current year (t0)	Next year (t + 1)	(t + 2)	(t + 3)
Key market segments (list)	Total company market segment sales share	Total company market segment sales share	Total company market segment sales share	Total company market segment sales share	Total company market segment sales share
Total					

Form 12

Database and summary of marketing objectives
Market segment gross values

Sales values	Last year (t − 1)	Current year (t0)	Next year (t + 1)	(t + 2)	(t + 3)
Key market segments (list)	Total company market segment sales share	Total company market segment sales share	Total company market segment sales share	Total company market segment sales share	Total company market segment sales share
Total					

Form 13

Product group analysis

Product groups	Last year (t − 1)		Current year (t0)		Next year (t + 1)		(t + 2)		(t + 3)	
	Sales value	Gross profit	Gross margin (%)	Sales value	Gross profit	Gross margin (%)	Sales value	Gross profit	Gross margin (%)	Sales value	Gross profit	Gross margin (%)	Sales value	Gross profit	Gross margin (%)
Total											

Form 14

Summary (in words and numbers) of main marketing objectives and strategies

Form 15

Financial projections for three years

Section B
The one-year marketing plan

(This should be kept separate from the three-year strategic marketing plan and should not be completed until the planning team has approved the strategic plan in May each year.)

Specific sub-objectives for products and segments, supported by more detailed strategy and action statements, should now be developed. Here, include *budgets* and *forecasts* and a *consolidated budget*. These must reflect the marketing objectives and strategies, and in turn the objectives, strategies and programmes *must* reflect the agreed budgets and sales forecasts. Their main purpose is to delineate the major steps required in implementation, to assign accountability, to focus on the major decision points, and to specify the required allocation of resources and their timing.

If the procedures in this system are followed, a hierarchy of *objectives* will be built up in such a way that every item of budgeted expenditure can be related directly back to the initial financial objectives (this is known as task-related budgeting).

Thus when, say, advertising has been identified as a means of achieving an objective in a particular market (i.e. advertising is a strategy to be used), all advertising expenditure against items appearing in the budget can be related back specifically to a major objective. The essential feature of this is that budgets are set against both the overall marketing objectives and the sub-objectives for each element of the marketing mix.

The principal advantage is that this method allows operating units to build up and demonstrate an increasingly clear picture of their markets. This method of budgeting also allows every item of expenditure to be fully accounted for as part of an objective approach. It also ensures that when changes have to be made during the period to which the plan relates, such changes can be made in a way that causes the least damage to the SBU's long-term objectives.

■ Contingency plan

It is important to include a *contingency plan* in the one-year marketing plan. Notes on this are included below.

■ Guidelines for completion of a one-year marketing plan

Because of the varying nature of strategic business units, it is impossible to provide a standard format for all SBUs. There is, however, a minimum amount of information which should be provided to accompany the financial documentation between September and October. There is no need to supply market background information, as this should have been completed in the three-year strategic marketing plan.

Suggested format for a one-year marketing plan

1 (a) *Overall objectives (see Forms 1 and 2 in the one-year marketing plan documentation)* – these should cover the following:

Volume or value	Value last year	Current year estimate	Budget next year

Gross margin	Last year	Current year estimate	Budget next year

Against each there should be a few words of commentary/ explanation.

   (b) *Overall strategies* – e.g. new customers, new products, advertising, sales promotion, selling, customer service, pricing. For a list of marketing strategies, see Chapter 6.

2 (a) *Sub-objectives (see Form 3 in the one-year marketing plan documentation)* – more detailed objectives should be provided for products, or markets, or segments, or major customers, as appropriate.

   (b) *Strategies* – the means by which sub-objectives will be achieved should be stated.

   (c) *Action/tactics* – the details, timing, responsibility and cost should also be stated.

3 *Summary of marketing activities and costs (see Form 4 in the one-year marketing plan documentation).*

4 *Contingency plan (see Form 5 in the one-year marketing plan documentation)* – it is important to include a contingency plan, which should address the following questions:

   (a) What are the critical assumptions on which the one-year plan is based?

   (b) What would the financial consequences be (i.e. the effect on the operating income) if these assumptions did not come true? For example, if a forecast of revenue is based on the assumption that a decision will be made to buy new plant by a major customer, what would the effect be if that customer did not go ahead?

   (c) How will these assumptions be measured?

   (d) What action will you take to ensure that the adverse financial effects of an unfulfilled assumption are mitigated, so that you end up with the same forecast profit at the end of the year?

To measure the risk, assess the negative or downside, asking what can go wrong with each assumption that would change the outcome. For example, if a market growth rate of 5 per cent is a key assumption, what lower growth rate would have to occur before a substantially different management decision would be taken? For a capital project, this would be the point at which the project would cease to be economical.

5 *Operating result and financial ratios (see Form 6 in the one-year marketing plan documentation).*

Note: This form is provided only as an example, for, clearly, all organizations will have their own formats – this should include:

- Net revenue
- Gross margin
- Adjustments
- Marketing costs
- Administration costs
- Interest
- Operating result
- ROS
- ROI.

6 *Key activity planner (see Form 7 in the one-year marketing plan documentation)* – finally, you should summarize the key activities and indicate the start and finish. This should help you considerably with monitoring the progress of your annual plan.

7 *Other* – there may be other information you wish to provide, such as sales call plans.

■ One-year marketing plan documentation

Form 1

Overall objectives

Product/market/ segment/application/ customer	Volume			Value			Gross margin			Commentary
	(t − 1)	(t0)	(t + 1)	(t − 1)	(±0)	(t + 1)	(t − 1)	(t0)	(t + 1)	

Form 2

Overall strategies

	Strategies	Cost
1		
2		
3		
4		
5		
6		
7		
8		
9		
10		

Comments

Form 3

Sub-objectives, strategies, actions, responsibilities, timing, cost

Product/ market/ segment/ application/ customer	Objective	Strategies	Action	Responsibility	Timing	Cost

Total _____

Form 4

	t − 1	t0	t + 1	Comments
Depreciation				
Salaries				
Postage/telephone/stationery				
Legal and professional				
Training				
Data processing				
Advertising				
Sales promotion				
Travelling and entertainment				
Exhibitions				
Printing				
Meetings/conferences				
Market research				
Internal costs				
Other (specify)				
Total				

Form 5

Suggested downside risk assessment format						
Key assumption	Basis of assumption	What event would have to happen to make this strategy unattractive?	Risk of such an event occurring	Impact if event occurs	Trigger point for action	Actual contingency action proposed

Form 6

	(t − 1)	(t0)	(t + 1)
Net revenue Gross margin Adjustments Marketing costs Administration costs Interest			
Operating result			
Other interest and financial costs			
Result after financial costs			
Net result			

Form 7

Key activity planner

Date/activity	Jan				Feb				March				April				May				June				July				Aug				Sept				Oct				Nov				Dec			
	1	2	3	4	1	2	3	4	1	2	3	4	1	2	3	4	1	2	3	4	1	2	3	4	1	2	3	4	1	2	3	4	1	2	3	4	1	2	3	4	1	2	3	4	1	2	3	4

> **Section C**
>
> Headquarters consolidation of several SBU strategic marketing plans

The author is frequently asked how several SBU strategic marketing plans should be consolidated by senior headquarters marketing personnel. A suggested format for this task is provided below.

■ Directional statement

1 *Role/contribution*. This should be a brief statement about the company's role or contribution. Usually, it will specify a minimum growth rate in turnover and profit, but it could also encapsulate roles such as opportunity seeking service and so on.
2 *Definition of the business*. This statement should describe the needs that the company is fulfilling, or the benefits that it is providing for its markets – for example, 'the provision of information to business to facilitate credit decision-making'. Usually, at the corporate level, there will be a number of definitions for its strategic business units. It is important that these statements are not too broad so as to be meaningless (e.g. 'communications' – which could mean satellites or pens) or too narrow (e.g. 'drills' – which could become obsolete if a better method of fulfilling the need for holes is found).
3 *Distinctive competence*. All companies should have a distinctive competence. It does not have to be unique, but it must be substantial and sustainable. Distinctive competence can reside in integrity, specialist skills, technology, distribution strength, international coverage, reputation and so on.
4 *Indications for future direction*. This section should indicate guidelines for future growth. For example, does the company wish to expand internationally, or to acquire new skills and resources? The purpose of this section is to indicate the boundaries of future business activities.

■ Summary of the main features of the plan

1 Here, draw a portfolio matrix indicating the current and proposed relative position of each of the strategic business units. Alternatively, this can appear later in the plan.
2 Include a few words summarizing growth in turnover, profit, margins, etc.
3 Draw a graph indicating simply the total long-term plan. At least two lines are necessary – turnover and profit.

■ Financial history (past five years)

Include a bar chart showing the relevant financial history, but, at the very least, include turnover and profit for the past five years.

■ Major changes and events since the previous plan

Here, describe briefly major changes and events (such as divesting a subsidiary) which occurred during the previous year.

■ Major issues by strategic business unit

Market characteristics

Here, it might be considered useful to provide a table listing strategic business units, alongside relevant market characteristics. For example:

	SBU1	SBU2	SBU3	SBU4
Market size				
Market growth				
Competitive intensity				
Relative market share				
etc.				

Competitive characteristics

Here, it might be considered useful to list the critical success factors by strategic business unit and rate each unit against major competitors. For example:

Critical success factors/competitors	Our company	Competitor 1	Competitor 2
CSF1			
CSF2			
CSF3			
CSF4			
CSF5			

Key strategic issues

This is an extremely important section, as its purpose is to list (possibly by strategic business unit) what the key issues are that face the company. In essence, this really consists of stating the major strengths, weaknesses, opportunities and threats and indicating how they will be either built on, or dealt with.

Key strategic issues might consist of technology, regulation, competitive moves, institutional changes, and so on.

Strategic objectives by strategic business unit and key statistics

This is a summary of the objectives of each strategic business unit. It should obviously be tailored to the specific circumstances of each company. However, an example of what might be appropriate follows:

Objectives / Strategic business unit	Market share		Relative market share		Real growth		Key statistics				
							Sales per employee		Contribution per employee		etc.
	Now	+5 years	Now	+5 years	+5 years	p.a.	Now	+5 years	Now	+5 years	
SBU1											
SBU2											
SBU3											
SBU4											
SBU5											

Alternatively, or additionally, put a portfolio matrix indicating the current and proposed relative position of each of the strategic business units.

Financial goals (next five years)

Here, draw a bar chart (or a number of bar charts) showing the relevant financial goals. At the very least, show turnover and profit by strategic business unit for the next five years.

■ Appendices

Include whatever detailed appendices are appropriate. Try not to rob the total plan of focus by including too much detail.

■ Timetable

The major steps and timing for the annual round of strategic and operational planning is described in the following pages. The planning process is in two separate stages, which are interrelated to provide a review point prior to the detailed quantification of plans. 'Stage One' involves the statement of key and critical objectives for the full three-year planning period, to be reviewed prior to the more detailed quantification of the tactical one-year plan in 'Stage Two' by 30 November, for subsequent consolidation into the company plans.

Planning team's 'kick-off' meetings (to be completed by 31 March)

At these meetings, the planning team will outline expectations for the following planning cycle. The purpose of the meetings is to give the planning team the opportunity to explain corporate policy, report progress during the previous planning cycle, and to give a broad indication of what is expected from each SBU during the forthcoming cycle. The planning team's review will include an overall appraisal of performance against plan, as well as a variance analysis. The briefing will give guidance under some of the following headings (as appropriate).

1 *Financial*
   - Gross margins
   - Operating profits
   - Debtors
   - Creditors
   - Cash flow
2 *Manpower and organization*
   - Organization
   - Succession
   - Training
   - Remuneration
3 *Export strategy*
4 *Marketing*
   - Product development
   - Target markets
   - Market segments
   - Volumes
   - Market shares
   - Pricing
   - Promotion

- Market research
- Quality control
- Customer service.

This is an essential meeting prior to the mainstream planning activity which SBUs will subsequently engage in. It is the principal means by which it can be ensured that plans do not become stale and repetitive due to over-bureaucratization. Marketing creativity will be the keynote of this meeting.

Top-down and bottom-up planning

A cornerstone of the marketing planning philosophy is that there should be widespread understanding at all levels in the organization of the key objectives that have to be achieved, and of the key means of achieving them. This way, the actions and decisions that are taken by managers will be disciplined by clear objectives that hang logically together as part of a rational, overall purpose. The only way this will happen is if the planning system is firmly based on market-centred analysis which emanates from the SBUs themselves. Therefore, after the planning team's 'kick-off' meetings, audits should be carried out by all managers in the SBUs down to a level which will be determined by SBU managers. Each manager will also do SWOT analyses and set tentative three-year objectives and strategies, together with proposed budgets for initial consideration by their superior manager. In this way, each superior will be responsible for synthesizing the work of those managers reporting to them.

The major steps in the annual planning cycle are listed below and depicted schematically in Figure 13.14.

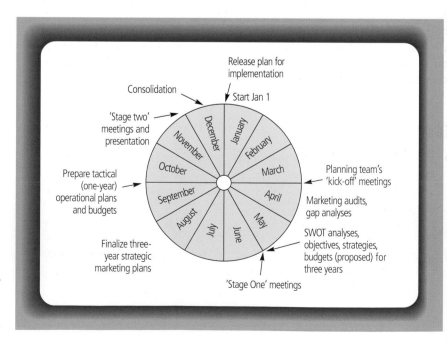

Figure 13.14
Strategic and operational planning cycle

Activity	Deadline
• Planning team's 'kick-off' meetings with SBU managers to discuss overall guidelines for the three-year planning period	31 March
• Prepare marketing audits, SWOT analyses, proposed marketing objectives, strategies and budgets (cover the full three-year planning horizon)	31 May
• 'Stage One' meetings: presentation to the planning team for review	31 May
• Prepare short-term (one-year) operational plans and budgets, and final three-year SBU managers' consolidated marketing plans	31 October
• 'Stage Two' meetings: presentation to the planning team	30 November
• Final consolidation of the marketing plans	31 December

■ And finally, a test to check the quality of your strategic marketing plan

This test has been developed by Dr Brian Smith, Chief Executive of Pragmedic. It is the result of much in-depth research into the output of the process of strategic marketing planning. It consists of twelve tests. Please answer them honestly, otherwise there is no point in doing them.

If you get a high score, congratulations. If you get a low score, you have much work to do, but nothing that cannot be accomplished by implementing what has been written in this book.

Test 1

- Our marketing strategy makes it clear what markets or parts of the market we will concentrate our efforts on
  - If your strategy attacks all of your market sector (e.g. retail groceries, superconducting magnets) equally = 0
  - If your strategy is focused by 'descriptor group' (e.g. ABC1s, large firms, SMEs etc.) = 1
  - If your strategy attacks needs-based segments (e.g. efficacy focused customers with high ego needs) = 2
  - If you don't know = −1.

Test 2

- Our marketing strategy makes clear what actions fit with the marketing strategy and what does not
    - If your strategy allows complete freedom of action = 0
    - If your strategy allows a high degree of freedom of action = 1
    - If your strategy makes most of your action plan decisions for you = 2
    - If you don't know = −1.

Test 3

- Our marketing strategy clearly defines our intended competitive advantage in the target market segments
    - If there is no strong and supported reason why the customer should choose you = 0
    - If there is a reason the customer should buy from you but no strong proof = 1
    - If you can state clearly the reason the customer should buy from you and not the competitor and substantiate that reason = 2
    - If you don't know = −1.

Test 4

- Our marketing strategy allows synergy between the activities of the different parts of the organization
    - If the strategy is a compromise of what each department is capable of = 0
    - If the strategy uses the strengths of only one or two departments = 1
    - If the strategy uses the best strengths of all departments = 2
    - If you don't know = −1.

Test 5

- Our marketing strategy is significantly different from that of our competitors in our key market segments
    - If you attack the same customers with the same value proposition = 0
    - If you attack the same customers OR use the same value proposition = 1
    - If you attack different customers with a different value proposition = 2
    - If you don't know = −1.

Test 6

● Our marketing strategy recognizes and makes full allowance for the needs and wants of our target customers
  - If you only meet the basic functional needs (safety, regulation, efficacy) = 0
  - If you also meet the higher functional needs (efficiency, service, price) = 1
  - If you also meet the emotional and ego needs (brand, confidence) = 2
  - If you don't know = −1.

Test 7

● Our marketing strategy recognizes and makes full allowance for the strategies of our competitors
  - If you are ignoring the strategy of competitors = 0
  - If you are allowing for some of the strategy of competitors = 1
  - If you are allowing for all of the strategy of competitors = 2
  - If you don't know = −1.

Test 8

● Our marketing strategy recognizes and makes full allowance for changes in the business environment that are beyond our control, such as technological, legislation or social change
  - If your strategy is designed for today's conditions = 0
  - If your strategy allows for one or two changes (e.g. technology or demographics) = 1
  - If your strategy considers the combined effects of all the external factors = 2
  - If you don't know = −1.

Test 9

● Our marketing strategy either avoids or compensates for those areas where we are relatively weak compared to the competition
  - If you have taken little or no account of your relative weaknesses = 0
  - If you are trying to fix your relative weaknesses = 1
  - If your strategy means that your relative weaknesses don't matter = 2
  - If you don't know = −1.

Test 10

● Our marketing strategy makes full use of those areas where we are relatively strong compared to the competition
  – If you have taken little or no account of your relative strengths = 0
  – If you are trying to use your relative strengths = 1
  – If your strategy means that your relative strengths become more important = 2
  – If you don't know = −1.

Test 11

● Our marketing strategy, if successfully implemented, will meet all the objectives of the organization
  – If your strategy, fully and successfully implemented, does not deliver your financial or non-financial objectives = 0
  – If your strategy, fully and successfully implemented, delivers only your financial objectives = 1
  – If your strategy, fully and successfully implemented, delivers your financial and non-financial objectives = 2
  – If you don't know = −1.

Test 12

● The resources available to the organization are sufficient to implement the marketing strategy successfully
  – If you have neither the tangible nor the intangible resources to implement the strategy = 0
  – If you have only the tangible or the intangible resources, but not both = 1
  – If you have both the tangible and the intangible resources needed to implement the strategy = 2
  – If you don't know = −1.

How did you score?

● 18–24 – Well done! (are you sure?)
  – Can I buy some shares?
● 12–17 – You will succeed
  – If your competition is weak!
● 6–11 – You will survive
  – If your competition is weak!
● Less than 6
  – Oh dear, it was nice knowing you.

APPENDIX A: CHAPTER 7

The communication plan:
1 The advertising and sales promotion plans

■ Different forms of communication

Now that we have explored the important area of marketing objectives and strategies, let us turn our attention to the question of how we communicate with customers, both current and potential.

It is a fact that organizations communicate with their customers in a wide variety of ways, but it is still possible to distinguish the following two main categories:

1 *Impersonal communications*, e.g. advertising, point-of-sale displays, sales promotions, electronic media and public relations
2 *Personal* (or direct person-to-person) *communications*, e.g. the face-to-face 'meeting' between a salesperson and the customer such as selling and call centres.

So companies have at their disposal an armoury of communication techniques, which may be used either singly or in a combination (the 'communication mix') as the particular situation demands, to achieve maximum effect within given budget constraints.

> Companies with acknowledged professionalism in the area of communicating with customers are continually experimenting with the mix of communicating techniques they employ in an attempt to become more cost-effective in this important, sometimes expensive, part of their business.

A number of the possible means of communicating with customers will now be examined under the two broad headings given above. This chapter will look in more detail at advertising and sales promotion, with the objective of deciding how to go about preparing detailed plans for these important elements of the marketing mix.

In Chapter 8, we will do the same for personal selling and the sales plan.

■ Deciding on the communications mix

Advertising is a popular method of impersonal communications using such media as the press, television, radio, billboard posters, and so on. However, there are a number of problems which need to be carefully considered before any decision can be made about whether to spend any money on advertising at all, let alone *how* to spend it. For example, many people believe that advertising is a waste of money and that media expenditure would be better spent on personal selling.

So, the first question that has to be grappled with is the question of how to determine the communications mix. To help with this question, let us consider two separate surveys on how industry buys. These are shown in Tables 7.1 and 7.2. Even a cursory glance at these will reveal the following information:

1 More than one person has an influence on what is bought
2 Salespeople do not manage to see all the important 'influencers'
3 Companies get the information on which they make their decisions from a variety of sources, only one of which is the salesperson.

Table 7.1 Buying influences by company size

Number of employees	Average number of buying influences	Average number of contacts made by salespeople
0–200	3.42	1.72
201–400	4.85	1.75
401–1,000	5.81	1.90
1,000+	6.50	1.65

Source: McGraw-Hill.

Table 7.2 Sources of information

	% Small companies	% Large companies
Trade and technical press	28	60
Salesperson – calls	47	19
Exhibitions	8	12
Direct mail	19	9

Source: Maclean Hunter.

> The buying process is complicated by the number of people involved and the amount of time taken.

It can be seen, then, that the buying process, but in particular the *business-to-business* buying process, is complicated by the fact that it is not just one person who is involved. Business-to-business buying is a decision-making process which can involve a large number of people and which can take a considerable time. It is possible to split the decision-making process into several distinct steps, as follows:

1 The buyer organization recognizes it has a problem and works out a general solution. For example, the design team of a new plant, or piece of machinery, may decide that they need a specialist component which cannot be provided from within the company or from existing suppliers' stocks.
2 The characteristics and quantity of what is needed are worked out. This is the outline design process specifying performance and particular characteristics such as weight, size, operating conditions, and so on.
3 A specification is then drawn up.
4 A search is made for possible sources of supply. This may merely involve a search of suppliers' catalogues to buy a component from stock, or a complete new product may have to be designed.
5 Potential suppliers will submit plans and products for evaluation.
6 After the necessary trials, suppliers are selected.
7 An order is placed and the product eventually delivered.
8 The goods supplied are checked against specification.

Please note that although this describes an *industrial* purchase process, our research has shown that exactly the same steps are followed in major *service* purchases, such as, for example, in out-sourcing information technology.

Not all these phases are followed in every buying decision. When something is being bought for a new project, all the phases would be followed.

Where it is a case of simply reordering something which has been bought before, the search and even tender processes may not be necessary. The newness of the decision to the buying organization also determines which types of people and how many are involved at each stage. Newness is a function of:

- the complexity of the product
- the commercial uncertainty surrounding the outcome of the purchase.

The higher the 'newness' on both these dimensions, the more people are involved and the higher their status. If product complexity is high but commercial uncertainty low, then the more important role is that of the design engineer and technologist. If newness is low on both dimensions, purchasing officers tend to dominate the process.

> When faced with a new buy situation, the salesperson will be involved with a large number of people over a long period, helping, advising and informing, always trying to influence the decision process and to build up a growing commitment towards their product.

A typical example of this process at work can be seen in the following illustration of the purchase of a telecommunications system:

1 The managing director proposes to replace the company's telecommunications system.
2 Corporate purchasing and corporate telecommunications departments analyse the company's needs and recommend likely matches with potential selling organizations.
3 Corporate telecommunications department and data processing managers have an important say about which system and firm the company will deal with. Other company directors also have a key influence on this decision.
4 All employees who use the telecommunications equipment are 'consulted'.
5 The director of administration selects, with influence from others, the supplying company and the system.

The reason for going into such detail about the business-to-business buying process is simply to illustrate that it is not possible to determine the precise role of advertising versus, say, personal selling, until a company fully understands how its potential customers buy and who are the important people that have to be contacted at the different stages in the buying process. For, clearly, financial and administrative people will be involved at a different stage from, say, the engineers, and they will also require different kinds of information. For example, price, performance characteristics, delivery, before and after sales service, reputation/reliability, guarantees, payment terms, and so on are not relevant to all people at all stages in the buying process.

> The first point, then, is that a firm must understand the buying process of the markets to which it addresses itself.

It is important to identify the people with significant influence on the purchase decision and the specific benefits each influencer wants.

There are many models for helping with this process, but essentially we should use a simple model which answers these questions:

1 Who are the people with a significant influence on the purchase decision?
2 What specific *benefits* does each important influencer want?

Figure 7.1 provides a logical approach to analysing an organization. As can be seen, it can be used equally effectively in either a product or a service company. Having done this analysis for our major customers/potential customers, it should be comparatively easy to:

1 Group them in some way (segmentation)
2 Determine the most cost-effective way of communicating these benefits to each group.

Only then can some qualitative judgements be made about the relative cost-effectiveness of, say, advertising versus personal selling – neither of which,

Figure 7.1
Customer analysis form. Adapted from P. Robinson, C. W. Farris and G. Wind, *Industrial Buying and Creative Marketing*, Allyn and Bacon, 1967

incidentally, will be mutually exclusive in anything but unusual circumstances. Table 7.3 lists some communication objectives.

Table 7.3 Some communication objectives		
Education and information	To . . . Create awareness Inform Get enquiries	
Branding and image building	Get company name in file Create company image Reach personnel inaccessible to salespeople	These objectives contribute towards a total marketing programme, the objective of which is to achieve profitable sales
Affecting attitudes	Ease the selling task Get editorial Overcome prejudice Influence end-users	
Loyalty and reminding	Reduce selling costs Achieve sales	

We can now turn our attention specifically to advertising.

■ Preparing the advertising plan

For many years, people believed that ▶ **advertising** worked in a delightfully simple way, with the advertiser sending a message and the target receiving it and understanding it. Research, however, has shown that in a grossly over-communicated society, the process is more complex. Figure 7.2 gives some indication of the process involved. Advertising, then, is not the straightforward activity that many people believe it to be. It is highly unlikely, for example, that any firm will be able simply to put out an advertisement and expect its sales to increase.

This brings us to perhaps the greatest misconception of all about advertising – that objectives for advertising for the purpose of measuring effectiveness should be set in terms of sales increases. Naturally, we hope that advertising will have an important influence on sales levels, but in most circumstances advertising is only one of a whole host of important determinants of sales levels (such as product quality, prices, customer service levels, the competence of the sales force, and so on).

> Generally, then, it is absurd to set sales increases as a direct objective for advertising.

So, what objectives should be set for advertising? Well, we can start by agreeing that we need to *set* objectives for advertising, for the following reasons:

1 We need to set the budget for advertising.
2 We need to determine who our target audience is.
3 We need to determine the content of advertisements.

▶ **DEFINITION** ◄

Advertising is communication in paid-for media

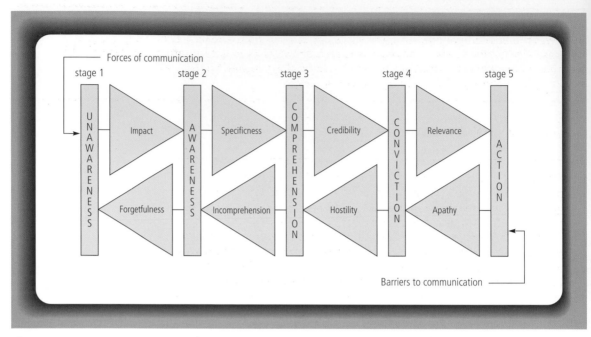

Figure 7.2
Brand loyalty ladder: the five stages of communication

4   We need to decide on what media to use.
5   We need to decide on the frequency of advertising.
6   We need to decide how to measure the effectiveness of our advertising.

These decisions can be summarized as follows:

1   *Why* (objectives)
2   *Who* (target)
3   *What* (copy platform)
4   *Where* (media)
5   *How* (creative platform)
6   *When* (timing)
7   *How much* (budget)
8   *Schedule*
9   *Response*
10   *Evaluation*

The whole edifice, however, depends on the first of these.

Advertising objectives

Research has shown that many companies set objectives for advertising which advertising cannot achieve on its own. Apart from increasing sales, the 'annihilation of the enemy', and other such ridiculously unachievable objectives, are set. For example, it is unreasonable to set as an objective 'to convince our target market that our product is best' if it is perfectly clear to the whole world that someone else's product is better. You cannot blame your advertising agency if this objective is not achieved!

Another example of inadequate thought being given to advertising expenditure was the bus company which spent vast sums advertising the reliability of its bus service, while research showed the real reason sales were deteriorating was that many people thought buses were 'working class'. Again, this is a classic example of scoring a bulls-eye on the wrong target.

One more example should serve to prove the point.

> A machine-tool company could not understand why, after an expensive advertising campaign in Germany in which they emphasized the extremely high quality and reliability of their products, they made little headway in the market. Subsequent market research showed that their target customers already believed this company had the best product. What they were concerned about, and why they were not buying, was their dissatisfaction over *delivery* and *customer service*. This is yet another example of advertising wasted because of ignorance about customer beliefs.

The first step, then, is to decide on reasonable objectives for advertising. The question which must be asked is: 'Is it possible to achieve the objective through advertising alone?' If the answer is *yes*, it is an objective for advertising. If the answer is *no*, it is not an objective for advertising. Advertising through media can do the following:

- convey information
- alter perceptions/attitudes
- create desires
- establish connections (e.g. powdered cream/coffee)
- direct actions
- provide reassurance
- remind
- give reasons for buying
- demonstrate
- generate enquiries.

Setting reasonable, achievable objectives, then, is the first and most important step in the advertising plan. All the other steps in the process of putting together the advertising plan flow naturally from this, and are summarized briefly below.

Who   . . . are the target audience(s)?
           What do they already know, feel, believe about us and our product/service?
           What do they know, feel, believe about the competition?
           What sort of people are they? How do we describe/identify them?

What   . . . response do we wish to evoke from the target audience(s)?
           . . . are these specific communications *objectives*?
           . . . do we want to 'say', make them 'feel', 'believe', 'understand', 'know' about buying/using our product/service?
           . . . are we offering?
           . . . do we *not* want to convey?

	. . . are the priorities of importance of our objectives?
	. . . are the objectives which are *written* down and *agreed* by the company and advertising agency?
How	. . . are our objectives to be embodied in an appealing form?
	What is our creative strategy/platform?
	What evidence do we have that this is acceptable and appropriate to our audience(s)?
Where	. . . is/are the most cost-effective place(s) to expose our communications (in cost terms *vis-à-vis* our audience)?
	. . . is/are the most beneficial place(s) for our communications (in expected response terms *vis-à-vis* the 'quality' of the channels available)?
When	. . . are our communications to be displayed/conveyed to our audience?
	What is the reasoning for our scheduling of advertisements/ communications over time?
	What constraints limit our freedom of choice?
	Do we have to fit in with other promotional activity on other products/services supplied by our company? competitors' products? seasonal trends? special events in the market?
Result	What results do we expect?
	How will we measure results?
	Do we intend to measure results and, if so, do we need to do anything *beforehand*?
	If we cannot say how we would measure precise results, then maybe our *objectives* are not sufficiently specific or are not communications objectives?
	How are we going to judge the relative success of our communications activities (good/bad/indifferent)? Should we have action standards?
Budget	How much money do the intended activities need?
	How much money is going to be made available?
	How are we going to *control* expenditure?
Schedule	Who is to do what and when?
	What is being spent on what, where and when?

The usual assumption is that advertising is deployed in an aggressive role and that all that changes over time is the creative content. But the role of advertising usually changes during the life-cycle of a product.

> For example, the process of persuasion itself cannot usually start until there is some level of awareness about a product or service in the marketplace. Creating awareness is, therefore, usually one of the most important objectives early on in a life-cycle.

If awareness has been created, interest in learning more will usually follow.

Attitude development now begins in earnest. This might also involve reinforcing an existing attitude, or even changing previously held attitudes, in order to clear the way for a new purchase. This role obviously tends to become more important later in the product life-cycle, when competitive products are each trying to establish their own 'niche' in the market.

■ Diffusion of innovation

Also relevant to this is what is known as the 'diffusion of innovation curve', discussed in Chapter 5. To refresh our memories we will repeat the curve in Figure 7.3.

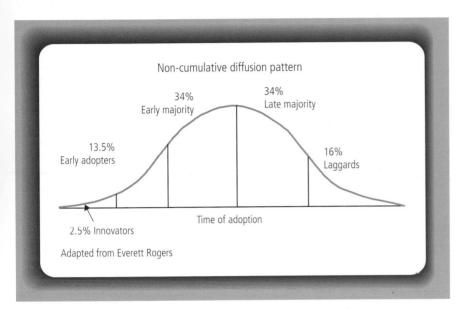

Non-cumulative diffusion pattern

13.5% Early adopters

34% Early majority

34% Late majority

16% Laggards

2.5% Innovators

Time of adoption

Adapted from Everett Rogers

Figure 7.3

Research into any product's progress along the diffusion curve can be very useful, particularly for advertising and personal selling. For example, if we can develop a typology for opinion leaders, we can target our early advertising and sales effort specifically at them. Once the first 3 per cent of innovators have adopted our product, there is a good chance that the early adopters, or opinion leaders, will try it, and once the 8–10 per cent point is reached the champagne can be opened, because there is a good chance that the rest will adopt our product.

We know, for example, that the *general* characteristics of opinion leaders are that they are venturesome, socially integrated, cosmopolitan, socially mobile and privileged. So we need to ask ourselves what are the *specific* characteristics of these customers in our particular industry. We can then tailor our advertising message specifically for them.

Finally, we should remind ourselves that advertising is not directed only at consumers. It can be directed at channels, shareholders, media, employees, suppliers and government, all of whom have an important influence on a firm's commercial success.

■ Sales promotion

The term *advertising* (often referred to as 'above-the-line expenditure') can be defined as all non-personal communication in measured media. This includes television, cinema, radio, print, websites and outdoor media.

▶ **DEFINITION** ◀

Sales promotion is non-face-to-face activity concerned with the promotion of sales. It involves the making of a featured offer to defined customers within a specific time limit

▶ **Sales promotion**, for which the term 'below-the-line expenditure' is often used as a synonym, is not easily defined. For example, Americans use the term to describe all forms of communication, including advertising and personal selling. In Britain, some use the term to describe any non-face-to-face activity concerned with the promotion of sales; some use it to describe any non-media expenditure; while others use it specifically to mean in-store merchandising.

The fact is that none of these definitions is an accurate reflection of how sales promotion works in practice, which is why there is so much confusion about many aspects of this important area of marketing activity.

> In practice, sales promotion is a specific activity, which can be defined as the making of a featured offer to defined customers within a specific time limit.

In other words, to qualify as a sales promotion, someone must be offered something which is featured, rather than just being an aspect of trade. Furthermore, the offer must include benefits not inherent in the product or service, as opposed to the intangible benefits offered in advertising, such as adding value through appeals to imagery.

Seen this way, every other element of the marketing mix, including advertising, personal selling, point-of-sale material, pricing, after-sales service, and so on, can be used as part of a structured activity in order to achieve specified objectives.

Sales promotion in practice

> Sales promotion is essentially a problem-solving activity designed to get customers to behave more in line with the economic interests of the company.

Typical tasks for sales promotion are slow stock movement, counteracting competitive activity, encouraging repeat purchase, securing marginal buyers, getting bills paid on time, inducing trial purchase, and so on.

From this, it will be seen that sales promotion is not necessarily concerned with volume increases. For example, it is often used to assist production and distribution scheduling by persuading customers to bring forward their peak buying from one period to another. To summarize, sales promotion seeks to influence:

- *salespeople* to sell
- *customers* to buy
- *customers* to use
- *users* to buy
- *users* to use

more, earlier, faster, etc.

In recent years, sales promotion activity has increased to such an extent that it now accounts for as much expenditure as above-the-line advertising.

> However, it is important to realize that, on its own, sales promotion will not replace selling, change long-term trends or build long-term customer loyalty.

Nevertheless, while sales promotion is essentially a tactical device, it also has an important strategic role to play, as we shall see later.

Different kinds of sales promotion

The many and varied types of sales promotions are listed in Table 7.4. Each of these different types is appropriate for different circumstances, and each has advantages and disadvantages. For example, with a promotion that consists of a free case bonus, it is possible to measure precisely both the cost of the extra cases

Table 7.4 Types of sales promotions

Target market	Type of promotion					
	Money		**Goods**		**Services**	
	Direct	**Indirect**	**Direct**	**Indirect**	**Direct**	**Indirect**
Consumer	Price reduction	Coupons Vouchers Money equivalent Competitions	Free goods Premium offers (e.g. 13 for 12) Free gifts Trade-in offers	Stamps Coupons Vouchers Money equivalent Competitions	Guarantees Group participation events Special exhibitions and displays	Cooperative advertising Stamps Coupons Vouchers for services Events admission Competitions
Trade	Dealer loaders Loyalty schemes Incentives Full-range buying	Extended credit Delayed invoicing Sale or return Coupons Vouchers Money equivalent	Free gifts Trial offers Trade-in offers	Coupons Vouchers Money equivalent Competitions	Guarantees Group participation events Free services Risk reduction schemes Training Special exhibitions Displays Demonstrations Reciprocal trading schemes	Stamps Coupons Vouchers for services Competitions
Sales force	Bonus Commission	Coupons Vouchers Points systems Money equivalent Competitions	Free gifts	Coupons Vouchers Points systems Money equivalent	Free services Group participation events	Coupons Vouchers Points systems for services Event admission Competitions

and the additional volume resulting from the offer; it is fast and flexible; it is effective where the customer is profit conscious; it can be made to last as long as required; and it is simple to set up, administer and sell. On the other hand, it has no cumulative value to the customer, is unimaginative, and can often be seen as a prelude to a permanent price reduction.

Points schemes are flexible, have wide appeal, do not involve the company in holding stocks of gifts, customers cannot easily value gifts, and they are easy to administer. On the other hand, they offer no advantages in bulk buying, are difficult to budget, and they lack the immediacy of dealer loaders.

Great care is necessary, therefore, in selecting a scheme appropriate to the objective sought.

The strategic role of sales promotion

Because sales promotion is essentially used as a tactical device, it often amounts to little more than a series of spasmodic gimmicks lacking in any coherence. Yet the same management that organizes sales promotion usually believes that advertising should conform to some overall strategy. Perhaps this is because advertising has always been based on a philosophy of building long-term brand franchise in a consistent manner, whereas the basic rationale of sales promotion is to help the company retain a tactical initiative.

> Even so, there is no reason why there should not be a strategy for sales promotion, so that each promotion increases the effectiveness of the next.

In this way a bond between seller and buyer is built up, so that the tactical objectives are linked in with some overall plan, and so that there is generally a better application of resources.

That this is possible can be seen from the sales promotional campaigns involving the Home Pride Flour Graders, who first appeared in the early 1960s; from the 20 million enamel brooches given out by Robertsons since the 1930s; and from Mighty Ajax, Miss Pears, the Ovalteenies, and many other campaigns that have used schemes and devices which have been consistently incorporated into a product's promotional strategy.

More recent schemes, such as the Tesco Clubcard, are proof that it is possible to establish a style of promotion which, if consistently applied, will help to establish the objectives of a product over a long period of time, which are flexible, and which have staying power.

Applying sales promotion to business-to-business products

Business-to-business goods are always sold to other organizations, and this has the effect of changing the emphasis placed on certain elements of the marketing mix, rather than having any fundamental effect on the relevancy of the marketing concept.

> It will not be surprising, then, to learn that, suitably adapted, most consumer goods sales promotional techniques can be applied to business-to-business goods and services.

Yet, in spite of this, sales promotion is comparatively rare in business-to-business markets, perhaps partly from a belief born in the engineering discipline that if a firm has to promote its products, there must be something wrong with them.

In recent years, however, business-to-business companies have begun to take note of the enormous success of sales promotion campaigns, and are becoming more aware of sales promotion as a flexible and competitive tool of marketing.

> One industrial goods company with divisions spanning a range of products from fast-moving industrial goods to high-priced capital goods has developed a range of special promotional schemes which include the following: trade-in allowances, competitions, reciprocal trading schemes, credit arrangements, training schemes, desk-top give-aways, custom-built guarantees – all made as featured offers.

Preparing the sales promotion plan

There is widespread acknowledgement that sales promotion is one of the most mismanaged of all marketing functions. This is mainly because of the confusion about what sales promotion is, which often results in expenditures not being properly recorded. Some companies include it with advertising, others as part of sales force expenditure, others as a general marketing expense, others as a manufacturing expense (as in the case of extra product, or special labels, or packaging), while the loss of revenue from special price reductions is often not recorded at all.

Such failures can be extremely damaging because sales promotion is such an important part of marketing strategy. Also, with increasing global competition, uncertain economic conditions, and growing pressures from channels, sales promotion is becoming more widespread and more acceptable.

Sales promotion is an important part of marketing strategy, but it is one of the most mismanaged of all marketing functions.

> This means that companies can no longer afford not to set objectives, or to evaluate results after the event, or to fail to have some company guidelines. For example, a 1-euro case allowance on a product with a contribution rate of 3 euros per case has to increase sales by 50 per cent just to maintain the same level of contribution.

Failure at least to realize this, or to set alternative objectives for the promotion, can easily result in loss of control and a consequent reduction in profits.

> In order to manage a company's sales promotion expenditure more effectively, there is one essential step that must be taken. First, an objective for sales promotion must be established in the same way that an objective is developed for advertising, pricing, or distribution.

The objectives for each promotion should be clearly stated, such as trial, repeat purchase, distribution, display, a shift in buying peaks, combating competition, and so on. Thereafter, the following process should apply:

- Select the appropriate technique
- Pre-test

- Mount the promotion
- Evaluate in depth.

Spending must be analysed and categorized by type of activity (e.g. special packaging, special point-of-sale material, loss of revenue through price reductions, and so on).

One company manufacturing self-assembly kitchens embarked on a heavy programme of sales promotion after a dramatic reduction in consumer demand. While the company managed to maintain turnover, managers were worried that its sales promotional activity had been carried out in such a haphazard and piecemeal fashion that they were unable to evaluate the cost-effectiveness of what had been done. They were also very concerned about its effect on company image and their long-term consumer franchise. So, the company made a concentrated study of this area of expenditure, which now represented over half its communication budget. Next time round the company had: clear objectives; a clear promotional plan properly integrated into the marketing plan; and an established means of assessment.

As for the sales promotional plan itself, the objectives, strategy, and brief details of timing and costs should be included. It is important that too much detail should *not* appear in the sales promotional plan. Detailed promotional instructions will follow as the marketing plan unfurls. For example, the following checklist outlines the kind of detail that should eventually be circulated. However, only an outline of this should appear in the marketing plan itself.

Checklist for promotional instruction

Heading	Content
1 *Introduction*	Briefly summarize content – What? Where? When?
2 *Objectives*	Marketing and promotional objectives for new product launch.
3 *Background*	Market data. Justification for technique. Other relevant matters.
4 *Promotional offer*	Detail the offer: special pricing structure; describe premium; etc. Be brief, precise and unambiguous.
5 *Eligibility*	Who? Where?
6 *Timing*	When is the offer available? Call, delivery or invoice dates?
7 *Date plan*	Assign dates and responsibilities for all aspects of plan prior to start date.
8 *Support*	Special advertising, point of sale, presenters, leaflets, etc. public relations, samples, etc.
9 *Administration*	Invoicing activity. Free goods invoice lines. Depot stocks. Premium (re)ordering procedure. Cash drawing procedures.
10 *Sales plan*	Targets. Incentives. Effect on routing. Briefing meetings. Telephone sales.

(Continued)

Heading	Content
11 *Sales presentation*	Points to be covered in call.
12 *Sales reporting*	Procedure for collection of required data not otherwise available.
13 *Assessment*	How will the promotion be evaluated?

Appendices

These are usually designed to be carried by salespeople as an aid to selling the promotion:

- Summary of presentation points
- Price structures/profit margins
- Summary of offer
- Schedules of qualifying orders
- Blank order forms for suggested orders
- Copies of leaflets.

Also required by the sales force may be:

- samples of (new) product
- demonstration specimen of premium item
- special report forms
- returns of cash/premiums, etc. issued.

Note: It is assumed that the broad principles of the promotion have already been agreed by other managers affected by it, such as sales managers.

■ Public relations

The sections on PR, sponsorship, and legal issues in marketing communication are indebted to Ardi Kolah.

As the name suggests, 'public relations' is concerned with an organization's relationships with the various groups, or 'publics', that affect its ability to achieve its goals and objectives. The aspects of these relationships which act as a focus for public relations are the image and information a market holds about an organization – in other words, its *position* in the market. At a simple level, this is achieved through publicity in various print and broadcast media. However, the broader views being encouraged by moves towards *relationship marketing* require public relations activities to be more specific in their targeting and objectives. Public relations, therefore, is an important support for both positioning and relationship marketing.

Interest in public relations is also being stimulated by the reducing power and cost-effectiveness of mass media advertising. As the volume of communications aimed at the public increases and media channels proliferate, public relations offers an alternative means of reaching the audiences which an organization would like to influence. A message received, for instance, via an editorial can be up to five times more influential than one received via an advertisement. Public relations, however, is unlikely to replace advertising or other means of communication and

> Public relations messages can be far more influential than advertising.

promotion. A more likely development is that it will increase its significance as an integral part of a communications or promotions mix.

Public relations communications tools

Public relations activities cover a number of different areas:

1 *News generation*. One of the most widely used is the generation of news. News is best structured around a story which can incorporate information about an organization or its products. Stories can be created around discoveries, achievements, personalities or changes. Often surveys or projects are commissioned to provide 'objective' reports about topics of relevance to both the sponsoring organization's products and its position. Thus, toothpaste manufacturers might support dental health research, or a financial services organization might investigate people's attitudes towards saving. News can also be used to make consumers aware of the existence of a product or service in order to stimulate enquiries from interested parties. It must also be remembered, however, that placing news where it will be accepted for publication is as important a skill as spotting and reporting newsworthy activities.

2 *Events*. Organizations can also gain people's attention through staging or sponsoring events. These can range from simple news conferences and seminars to exhibitions, competitive activities, anniversary dinners and stunts. All are likely to gain media coverage and draw attention to the sponsoring organization's name. They can also aid the achievement of credibility or establish images with which an organization would like to be associated. Events are also good opportunities to develop relationships with suppliers, opinion leaders and associates, as well as customers.

3 *Publications*. An organization's publications are another method of communication in which public relations will have an active interest. Sales support material is an obvious example, which can include brochures, manuals and presentations, usable by all personnel who have contact with the outside world. Annual reports, other public interest communiqués, and special publications such as cookery books and children's stories also provide vehicles for influencing both customers and those who can affect customers' perceptions. Internal audiences and significant stakeholders are often addressed by organizational newsletters and magazines.

4 *Support for good causes*. Organizational support for good causes is another means of promoting an image and associating an organization with a certain set of values. This can include charity donations in return for product coupons, the sponsorship of public service activities such as festivals, and individual executives' support for local community interests such as educational establishments, hospitals or crime prevention. All these provide many opportunities for publicity elsewhere.

5 *Expert opinion*. Individuals within an organization can also act as sources of expert opinion for journalists, public enquiries or other forms of research and investigation. Public relations managers may seek to promote the expertise in their organization through the dissemination of contact lists, and by grooming individuals' interviewing and presentational skills.

6 *Visual identity*. Organizations also often seek to establish a visual identity through either conformity of design or logos. While design can make it easier for customers to recognize an organization's products when they come across one, logos and other identification marks can be more important for internal markets as a means of signifying change or commonalty of purpose.

Scope of public relations

Public relations can provide a powerful support for an organization's positioning objectives. As examples, *events* can be used to reinforce brand values, or *publications* can help to draw the public's attention to features such as the stability or innovative nature of an organization. Less directly, but still importantly, public relations can be used to establish credibility for either an organization or its technologies, on the back of which a position can be established. Similarly, public relations may be used to build awareness of new products, new processes or other changes which will enhance an organization's ability to serve its customers. Public relations can thus prepare the way for more direct positioning activities such as sales force campaigns; advertising; pricing mechanisms and packaging.

Public relations is a powerful support to positioning.

Developing *relationships* with both customers and other markets can also benefit from public relations activities. At one level, good relationships involve sharing information, and public relations tools such as sales support materials, specialist publications and research results are useful vehicles here. At another level, relationships should involve demonstrations of commitment – and, again, public relations can provide support. This can be through inviting individuals from targeted markets, be they customer markets, influencer markets, referral markets or third-party intermediaries, to events. Alternatively, this could be achieved by acknowledging their activities with awards, or mentions in press releases, or by referrals of media enquiries to them. These can be further supported by sales force and sales promotions activities.

An additional role for public relations is in dealing with special problems or disasters and *limiting the damage* such events can have on an organization. In this respect, the tobacco industry maintains a vigilant public relations campaign to limit the effects of adverse health publicity and government restrictions on advertising.

An alternative example is provided by Perrier, when it became known that some of their product had become contaminated with poisonous chemicals. To limit the potential damage to its brand names, the company immediately embarked on a widespread public relations campaign to show that this was an isolated event and that the public were in no danger. Coca Cola, however, was not so lucky when it launched Dosani (bottled purified water) in the UK in 2004. First the company just survived the revelation that it was simply tap water, filtered with some additives, with some good defensive PR ('it goes through a sophisticated high-tech filter system'). However, the death knell came a few weeks later when it was revealed that a batch of minerals had contaminated the water with a potentially carcinogenic bromate – something no amount of PR could overcome.

Public relations, then, can be a significant aspect of an organization's promotional mix and can be very influential in shaping attitudes and opinions. Relatively speaking, it is also a cheap means of gaining publicity and access to media channels. As an example, the value to Fuji of advertising on a modern airship was not the direct effect on the people it flew over, but the television coverage it gained from the novelty of the presentation. On a lesser scale, public relations is also very useful for smaller organizations with limited promotional budgets, although the exact results of public relations spending are always hard to quantify.

Public relations can be a powerful means of shaping attitudes and opinions.

■ Sponsorship

Sponsorship has been a popular means of supporting a product or organization's position in its chosen markets since the 1980s. The impetus to seek a wider variety of communication channels to promote a name or product derived mostly from the growing cost of media advertising. In addition, sponsoring the right kind of person or activity often gave global coverage that would have been difficult to achieve elsewhere, and sponsorship also offered tobacco companies exposure that was increasingly difficult to achieve as they were banned from TV advertising.

> Sponsorship can be defined as any commercial agreement by which a sponsor, for the mutual benefit of the sponsor and sponsored party, contractually provides financing or other support in order to establish an association between the sponsor's image, brands or products and a sponsorship property in return for rights to promote this association and/or for the granting of certain agreed direct or indirect benefits.

Types of sponsorship

In general, sponsorship falls into four distinct property types: sport (83 per cent), social (5 per cent), arts and culture (7 per cent) and media (5 per cent) (see Figure 7.4).

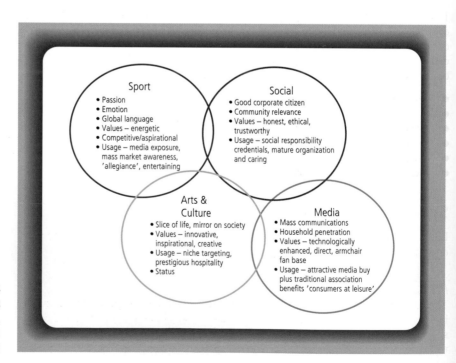

Figure 7.4
Sponsorship types
(*Source*: Ardi Kolah, 2006; personal communication)

Examples of sponsorship activities include:

The Arts	Unilever and the Tate Modern
Social and Community	Tesco's Race for Life
Educational	BT and information technology in schools
Entertainment	T in the Park
Broadcast	Nokia and X-Factor, ITV1
Sports	Emirates and Arsenal FC
Personality	Accenture and Tiger Woods

Sponsorship can be on a local, regional, national, international and global level, ranging from as little as under £100 to over £1 billion and more. Thus, in 2002 Mastercard spent between £20m and £30m as official sponsor of the football World Cup, and several million pounds is required to sponsor a high-profile football team for a year.

Growth of sponsorship

As the twenty-first century unfolds, sponsorship continues to be one of the fastest developing areas of marketing practice in the world today. The global sponsorship market is currently worth over £17 billion and in the UK is set to grow to over £2 billion, largely because of the sponsorship activities around the London 2012 Olympic Games.

For many organizations, sponsorship has established itself as an essential part of the marketing mix as a result of its perceived ability to make a difference, not only to brand awareness but also, more significantly, to a sponsor's 'bottom line'.

Objectives of sponsorship

To use sponsorship well, organizations have to be clear about the outcomes they desire. Simply requiring a better 'bottom line' is inappropriate, since there are few occasions where increased business or acceptance of a price increase can be directly traced to sponsorship. More realistic and potentially more measurable objectives include:

- competitive advantage from association or exclusivity
- alteration or reinforcement of public perception of the sponsor
- associating a business with particular market segments
- involving the company's employees in the community
- generating positive media coverage
- building good will among decision-makers.

Sponsorship processes

Like all positioning support activities, sponsorship needs to be carefully planned and managed, as illustrated in Figure 7.5.

Phase One: Activity review

The existing activity review should include all positioning support activities and how sponsorship can both complement and enhance them. It is important that any sponsorship programme is consistent with the creative aspects used in other communications, and that timings of activities can be coordinated. If, for example,

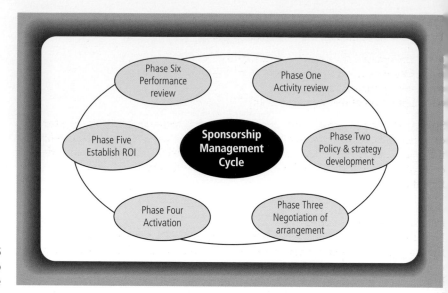

Figure 7.5
Sponsorship
management cycle

sponsorship is for a high-profile event, other communication activities need to support the build-up to the event, and then consolidate the position as the event fades from the public's mind.

Getting the right balance of activities is particularly important if sponsorship is to be used to support brand positioning where consistency of brand values is paramount. Sponsoring a poor performing Formula One racing team, for instance, may not enhance the brand value as much as desired. Similarly, to ensure return on investment, sponsoring a televised event must take into consideration the expected audience profiles and viewing figures to be worthwhile.

Phase Two: Policy and strategy development

A sponsorship strategy needs to be focused on the positioning objectives being pursued. The core decision is what or who should be sponsored, followed by plans for leveraging the association to the maximum cost-effective extent. In the early 2000s, Vodaphone's sponsorship portfolio included Manchester United, the Australian Rugby Union Team and Ferrari. The intended association was excellence on a global scale, and much effort was put into gaining as many spin-off benefits as possible.

Any sponsorship policy and strategy should include:

- measurable objectives (as far as possible)
- audience segmentation (including employees)
- brand essence or image being supported
- fit with desired positioning
- time scales and timings
- geographical requirements
- integration with other communications channels (spin-off opportunities)
- desired impact on behaviour of audiences
- contingency plans for if things change.

The key issue is to ensure a good business case for any sponsorship to avoid serving personal preferences rather than positioning objectives.

Phase Three: Negotiation of arrangement

The objective of the negotiation phase is usually one of the following:

- extension of a sponsorship programme
- extension subject to certain amendments
- a new sponsorship agreement
- termination of the old relationship.

Sponsorship negotiations vary depending on the respective bargaining strengths of the parties involved, as well as the nature of the property involved. Whatever the case, however, it is important to ensure satisfactory legal arrangements, that the costs of sponsorship match the value of the intended returns, and that there is sufficient exclusivity.

Phase Four: Activation

Negotiation of the right to associate with a sponsored property is, however, only the first step in a sponsorship programme. Coca Cola in the US, for instance, spends upwards of four times the sponsorship rights fee in its activation of its FIFA football World Cup and Olympic Games properties. Activation activities based on Nike's sponsorship of US top basketball player, Michael Jordon might include:

- advertising (Michael Jordon wears Nike)
- new media promotions (Nike/Michael Jordon websites)
- hospitality (Come and join us at a Michael Jordon basketball match)
- licensing (Special Michael Jordon Nike shoes)
- public relations (Michael Jordon visits Nike factory in Indonesia)
- promotions (Free entry into a 'Dinner with Michael Jordon' competition with every Nike product purchase).

Phase Five: Establish return on investment

Establishing an overall return on investment (ROI) for a sponsorship programme can be tricky since it will be hard to link sales directly with sponsorship expenditure given the more powerful impact of other marketing activities. However, if measurable objectives have been set as part of the strategy and activation processes, it is possible to ensure the expected returns in other areas are achieved. These could include:

- expected media exposure and audience figures
- increases in awareness, image, affinity etc.
- levels of association
- attendance at sponsored events.

Phase Six: Performance review

Following measurements of the ROI of a programme, all experiences need to be evaluated and any lessons to be learnt established. These might include seeking answers to questions such as: 'did we sponsor too many events?' and 'how did competitors respond to our sponsorships?' Sponsors may decide to withdraw sponsorship of, say, a football team if too many of its players get embroiled in violent conduct. Similarly, a retailer might withdraw from sponsorship of equipment for schools if its competitors find a better way of offering the sponsorship. In the UK in the early 2000s, supermarket giants Tesco and Sainsbury competed by offering vouchers with purchases that could be exchanged for computers and sports equipment respectively by schools. Which will lose momentum first remains to be seen.

■ Legal issues in marketing communications

Marketers and general managers alike will probably know and understand the differences between, say, an Ansoff and a Boston Matrix. It is less likely, however, that they will know the difference between *contract* and *tort* – or, for that matter, between civil and criminal law. More dangerously, they may be completely unaware that a claim in a news release could be subject to review by the Committee of Advertising Practice.

Unfortunately, ignorance of the law as it applies to modern marketing communication is no longer acceptable in today's highly litigious industry, which has only recently (2006) seen two giants of the Mobile world slug it out over the rights to use the colour orange, and the founder of Apple Computers being pursued by the remaining members of the 'Fab Four' (The Beatles) over alleged trademark infringement.

Rules and regulations have a purpose in business, and marketing best practice should comply automatically with the laws of the country in which an organization operates. Thus a business based in London should conform to British and European Union (EU) laws – although it can't always be assumed that it does, given that laws change so frequently. Most law and regulation is based on common sense, so any person who finds him- or herself engaged in activities likely to discredit, rather than enhance, strengthen or protect, an organization's reputation is highly likely to be doing something that is unlawful as well.

However, navigating the legal thicket will require more than just cursory knowledge of basic legal issues, and, with that in mind, a number of resources have been identified that will help. These are listed In Table 7.5.

Table 7.5 Sources of legal information
■ Advertising Standards Authority (www.asa.org.uk)
■ Brand Republic (www.brandrepublic.com)
■ British Copyright Council (www.britishcopyright.org)
■ Committee of Advertising Practice (www.cap.org.uk)
■ European Commission Office (http://europa.eu.int/index_en.htm)
■ Ethics Resource Centre (www.ethics.org)
■ Equal Opportunities Commission (www.eoc.org.uk)
■ Fax Preference Service (www.fpsonline.org.uk)
■ Freedom of Information (www.dca.gov.uk)
■ Human Rights (www.humanrights.gov.uk)
■ Information Commissioner (www.ico.gov.uk)
■ Mailing Preference Service (www.mpsonline.org.uk)
■ Office for Communication (www.ofcom.org.uk)
■ Office of Fair Trading (www.oft.gov.uk)
■ Pinsent Masons (www.out-law.com).

There are three distinct ways in which the laws of England and Wales, and EU laws and regulations, impact the marketing practitioner, and these are illustrated in Figure 7.6.

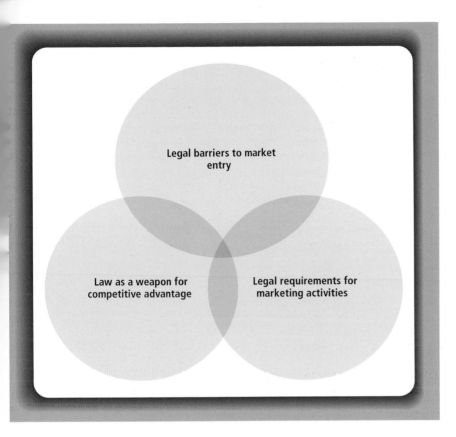

Figure 7.6
Three faces of the law (adapted from Ardi Kolah, 2006; personal communication)

Legal barriers to market entry

Barriers to market entry – such as, for example, the qualifications legally required to practise as a doctor or barrister – are useful. Their existence means that supply of such services is tightly controlled, and as a result they can command a premium price in the market. Conversely, certain products, such as baby clothing, must comply with fire-retardant regulations, which means that baby clothes that don't comply can't be lawfully sold in the market. A legal barrier to market entry therefore makes it difficult for competitors to enter the market, and can help indirectly to protect the market share of existing companies already lawfully trading.

The key legal tools used in marketing to enforce the barrier to market entry are as follows:

- Trademarks – legal protection stops other competitors from using the same or similar marks with protection extending to words (including personal names), designs, letters, numerals and even the shape of goods or their packaging, as is the case for a Coke bottle.
- Passing off – this stops others from producing imitation or fake merchandise, or pretending that their business is in some way linked to your own.
- Copyright – a useful legal measure to prevent competitors using someone's material or ideas without permission. This applies to literature, music, and dramatic and artistic works.

- Personality rights – important for celebrities whose image may be used in an advertising or marketing campaign, as it stops others from using that person's image or endorsement without seeking permission first.

Legal requirements for marketing activities

This is really about staying on the straight and narrow. Some lawyers tend to like this area of the law because it helps them to charge clients large fees by scaring the daylights out of them with the consequences of failing to comply with certain laws and regulations. In some cases, non-compliance can even lead to jail. Laws that place legal requirements on suppliers cover a very wide range of marketing and communications activities, including the following:

- Advertising, sales promotions and direct marketing – the Committee on Advertising Practice (CAP) provides a body of regulations that organizations must comply with. This includes the requirement that all marketing communications should be legal, decent, honest and truthful.
- E-mail and SMS campaigns – under national and EU laws, spamming is an offence and, subject to a few exceptions, businesses must always get the permission of the recipient to send a marketing e-mail or mobile text message that contains an offer or special promotion.
- Using databases for marketing – the Data Protection Act 1998 is possibly the piece of legislation to have had the biggest impact on marketing in the last 100 years. It gives individuals a legal right to know how a third party has obtained, recorded and holds personal data. The 1998 Act also sets out detailed controls on the transmission, retrieval and protection of such data, and makes the staff involved personally liable for any breach of these laws.

Law as a weapon for competitive advantage

The above presents the law as something that is about limiting or controlling the way organizations conduct their marketing activities. However, there are several areas of marketing practice where knowing how to apply the law will make a difference to the nature and content of a business's marketing and communication efforts. As an example, some laws, such as the EU Directive on Comparative Advertising, have legitimized activities previously illegal in some countries. The Directive allows comparative advertising as being in the interests of competition and public information. However, the law also protects competitors from being attacked with untrue comparisons – but not where comparisons are valid. Thus, when British Airways sued Ryanair for an advert that compared prices under the heading 'Expensive B......ds', they were unsuccessful, as the core claim within the advert was substantially true. In a different vein, pharmaceutical companies can gain significant competitive advantage from careful manipulation of patent registrations to extend the life of a drug beyond the initial protection period.

■ Application questions

1 How does your company determine its communications mix (i.e. the relative emphasis given to advertising, sales promotion and personal selling)?

2 Describe the buying process in one of your major customer groups. Who are the key influencers? Critically appraise your strategy for communicating with them.

3 Critically appraise your advertising objectives.

4 Using the checklist given in the text, critically appraise your advertising plan.

5 When you launch a new product/service, do you target your communications specifically at the opinion leaders? Do you know who they are? Can you describe them in terms that are relevant to advertising?

6 Critically evaluate your sales promotional plan.

7 How do you evaluate your sales promotional activities?

EXERCISES

Introduction to Chapter 7 exercises

These exercises look at the topics in the context of a 'communications mix'.

This section starts with an examination of what advertising objectives are (Exercise 7.1). It then goes on to look at how to set advertising objectives for one of your own product/market areas (Exercise 7.2), how to choose the most appropriate advertising media (Exercise 7.3) and how to build up an advertising plan (Exercise 7.4).

Sales promotion is tackled in a slightly different way. The first question that is asked is: 'Is a promotion necessary?' (Exercise 7.5). If the answer to this question is affirmative, then Exercise 7.6 demonstrates how to plan a sales promotion.

Exercise 7.1
What are advertising objectives?

There are two basic questions that advertising objectives should address: 'Who are the people we are trying to influence?' and 'What specific benefits or information are we trying to communicate to them?'

Research has shown that many companies set objectives for advertising which advertising cannot possibly achieve on its own – for example, 'to increase sales' or 'to wipe out the competition'. Equally, it is unrealistic to set an objective 'to convince the target market that our product is best', when any rational analysis would clearly show this not to be true.

Often there is an element of confusion about what advertising objectives are and what marketing objectives are. Remember, marketing objectives are concerned with what products go to which markets, whereas advertising objectives are measurable targets concerned principally with changing attitudes and creating awareness.

Here is a list of marketing or other objectives and advertising objectives mixed up together. Read through this list and write against each objective:

A – if you believe it to be an advertising objective
M – if you believe it to be a marketing or other objective.

Marketing (M) or advertising (A) objectives?[1]
1 To make attitudes more favourable to a particular product
2 To build an image for the product

---

[1] Based on a list provided by Professor David Corkindale (formerly of Cranfield University School of Management) and used with his kind permission.

3 To stop existing users turning to competitive products
4 To get across the idea of a unique product
5 To create a brand leader to help the launch of additional products at a future date
6 To win back previous product users who have defected to a competitive product
7 To expand the whole market
8 To reduce existing negative attitudes
9 To keep building loyalty
10 To establish the brand and position it in a particular way, e.g. as warm and friendly
11 To create a brand leader in a particular market
12 To increase sales among existing users
13 To improve the frequency of purchase
14 To keep new entrants out of the market
15 To convey the idea that the product is 'value for money'
16 To say how much people like the product
17 To improve market share compared with competitors
18 To maintain brand distribution.

The answers to Exercise 7.1 are as follows:

Advertising objectives: numbers 1, 2, 4, 8, 9, 10, 15 and 16

Marketing or other objectives: numbers 3, 5, 6, 7, 11, 12, 13, 14, 17 and 18.

If you made some mistakes in identifying the objectives correctly, go back and have another look at them and see if you can work out where you went wrong.

Exercise 7.2
Setting advertising objectives

Behind all effective advertising there lies a lot of careful thought and planning, and much of it goes into ensuring that the advertising objectives are the right ones. If these are wrong, everything else which follows is doomed to failure.

In this exercise, you are asked to concentrate on just one key market or market segment. It should be a relatively simple matter to repeat the process for other markets at some later date.

Make a note somewhere about which market or segment you will be addressing. Remember, from the Boston Matrix or directional policy matrix, 'stars' will probably be most deserving of the advertising budget.

Now make a note about the marketing objectives which have been set for this market/segment – for example, what products? What quantities? To whom? etc. Having assembled this information, from the list of 'Possible advertising objectives' below:

1 Select the most appropriate objectives, i.e. those that look the most promising to help the company achieve these marketing objectives (tick in the column).
2 From those you have ticked, eliminate any objectives that you believe can only be achieved by personal communication, i.e. by the sales force.
3 List your remaining objectives in rank order, the most important being at the top of the list.
4 Use only the top objective (and perhaps the second) as a basis for your advertising campaign.

Possible advertising objectives

	Tick here		Tick here
• To establish an immediate sale • To bring a prospect closer to a sale • To change customer perceptions • To direct customer action • To support the sales force • To reinforce attitudes of existing customers • To open up distribution • To improve company image • To demonstrate the product capabilities • To generate enquiries • To impart information • To reassure customers • To 'score points' off competitors' advertising • To enter new markets • To give reasons for buying • To create awareness • To support retailers • To convey the idea of 'value for money' • To reach new geographical areas		• To promote the idea of a unique product • To back up promotions • To develop favourable attitudes to a particular product • To counter price competition • To remind customers about our product • To reinforce the company image • To defend market position • To support the launch of a new product/service • To explain new uses for product • To emphasize range and choice • To reinforce brand recognition • To inform about product availability • To educate customers • To communicate company strengths • To build customer loyalty • To say how much people like the product	

If you think this list omits possible advertising objectives for your company, then extend the list by adding your own objectives to it.

The previous exercise should have helped to identify the advertising objectives for your chosen market/segment. The next logical step would be to decide exactly what you want to communicate – your creative platform.

However, such a step does not really lend itself to an exercise. Indeed, copywriting is such a specialized form of communication that most companies engage outside specialists to deal with it. Even so, having decided upon the advertising objectives, you must switch your focus of attention now to the target population you hope to influence:

● Who are they?
● What positions do they hold?
● What is their influence on the purchasing decision?
● What personality traits do they exhibit?
● What socio-economic groupings do they belong to?

Exercise 7.3
Choosing the advertising media

- What lifestyles do they have?
- How old are they? What sex are they? Are they married? and so on.

Please note that it is usually easier to determine the most appropriate media in the case of *business-to-business* customers, although the same logic applies.

You need to assemble as much information as you can about the target population. The more you know about them, the better your chances of selecting the best medium for your advertising platform.

The accompanying worksheet gives a list of possible advertising media Study this list and select what would be the best choice, taking into account your objectives and the profile of the target audience.

In making your choice, you will need to take four factors into account:

1 *The character of the medium* – the geographical coverage it gives, the types of audience it reaches, its frequency of publication or showing, its physical possibilities (such as colour, sound, movement), its power or potential to reach special groups, etc.
2 *The atmosphere of the medium* – its ability to convey an image consistent with your objectives, e.g. hard and punchy, discreet, elegant, exclusive, etc.
3 *The 'size' of the medium* – the number of people exposed to the medium in terms of being aware of the contents – for example, a newspaper might be read by two or three members of a family, whereas a technical journal might be circulated to a large number of managers within a company. Alternatively, a poster might be passed by tens of thousands of people.
4 *The comparative cost* – how much will it cost to reach a specific audience. The cost per 1,000 viewers is often used as a comparative ratio.

There is space on the accompanying worksheet to make notes about these factors, should you be required to keep a record of what influenced your choice of medium.

Worksheet Advertising media (Exercise 7.3)

	Medium	Characteristics	Atmosphere	Size	Comparative cost
Printed media	Local newspapers National newspapers Trade and technical press Magazines and periodicals Direct mail Leaflets Directories (Yellow Pages, buyers' guides, etc.)				
others	Television Posters (static) Transport (on trains, buses, vans, etc.) Cinema Radio Internet Other (specify)				

Having decided what you want to communicate (your advertising objectives, Exercise 7.2), worked out the creative platform of the exact message you wish to convey, and decided on the choice of media (Exercise 7.3), you have assembled the key ingredients of an advertising plan. What remains to be done is to establish when the advertising will be used, who will be responsible for the various activities in bringing what is still an idea into life, how progress will be monitored and the criteria by which success will be judged.

The accompanying worksheet provides a simple format to record all this information. We would recommend that you try using it, and then adapt it to your particular purposes, so that you finish up with something that is genuinely tailor-made.

Exercise 7.4
The advertising plan

Worksheet Advertising plan (Exercise 7.4)

ADVERTISING PLAN FOR _____ (either product or service market or segment)

ADVERTISING OBJECTIVES TO _____

Selected media	Brief description of advert	Timing	Responsibility	Budget	Actual cost	Criteria by which success will be judged	Evaluation comments

Note: Now complete advertising plans for other products/services and market segments.

Sales promotions should be seen as the logical development of the company's marketing strategy. As such, they should be complementary to all other parts of the communications mix and should not be seen as an alternative, or some disconnected activity.

There are three key questions to be answered:

1 How do we decide whether or not to run a promotion?
2 What form should the promotion take?
3 How do we plan it?

The first two questions are addressed by this exercise. The planning element is covered in Exercise 7.6.

In order to give this exercise a clear focus, please select just one of the product/market areas of your portfolio and work with it. Once you have worked through this process you will see how it can be used elsewhere, with other products/markets.

Exercise 7.5
Is a promotion necessary?

Step 1   On a separate piece of paper, write down the problems you see affecting sales of the product or service in the market/market segment you have chosen. If there are no problems, you might question why a sales promotion is being considered in this area. Your efforts might be better spent focusing on another part of your product/service range.

Step 2   Look at the problems you have listed and rank them in order of 'seriousness', 1 being the major problem, 2 the next, and so on.

Step 3   Transfer the information you have just assembled to column 1 of the accompanying worksheet.

Step 4   Taking the major problem first, work across the page on the worksheet and consider the possible solutions to the problem listed there. You will note that there is space to add solutions of your own.

Clearly, a sales promotion is not always going to be the way to resolve a sales problem. However, the economics or convenience of one type of solution compared with another might well sway the argument. For example, the best solution to the sales problem might be to modify the product, but this might be very costly and take time to achieve. In such circumstances, a sales promotion might work in terms of both costs and immediacy.

Therefore, considered judgement has to be used in weighing up the costs and likely chances of success of each possible solution. *Only* when the sales-promotion option looks favourable should you take matters to the next stage of deciding upon the type of promotion.

Step 5   If a sales promotion will not make any impact on the major sales problem, work across the page again for the next problem down. Continue this process for other sales problems until a sales promotion is found which would appear to hold the promise of success.

Ideally, the sales promotion should make impact on a fairly serious sales problem. If it is only going to affect a marginal issue, it raises questions about whether or not it is worth spending the time and effort on the promotion and whether another area might be more deserving of attention.

Worksheet   Deciding if sales promotion will help (Exercise 7.5)

PRODUCT/SERVICE/MARKET SEGMENT
UNDER CONSIDERATION _____

Problems affecting sales	POSSIBLE SOLUTIONS												
	More advertising?		More sales effort?		Change price?		Change product?		Sales promotion?		Other ideas (add your own)		
	Cost	Likely success	Cost	Likely success	Cost	Likely success	Cost	Likely success	Cost	Likely success	Cost	Likely success	Cost	Likely success
Major problem 1														
2														
Problems listed in reducing order 3														
4														
5														

Having established that a sales promotion is a suitable way to have an impact on a particular sales problem, you must now decide on the nature of the promotion.

In broad terms, a promotion can be aimed at three target groups:

1 Customers or consumers
2 Channels/intermediaries
3 Your own sales force.

The promotion can also take one of three forms:

1 It can involve money
2 It can involve goods
3 It can involve services.

You will have to decide first of all which target group needs to be influenced most to make an impact on your sales problem. You might even decide it is more than one group.

Having made that decision, you then have to work out what type of promotion will have maximum appeal to that group. Ideally, you will be able to devise something with maximum appeal, at a modest cost. However, when considering the cost element, you must remember that the promotional costs have to be weighed up against the benefits of reducing the specific sales problem.

Table 7.4 provides a number of ideas about sales promotions and enables you to select the most appropriate type for your purposes.

It is important to ensure that any sales promotion is well coordinated in terms of what happens before, during and after the promotion. At different stages, different people might be participating and special resources might be required. Therefore, a plan needs to be prepared in a simple way that most people can follow. In essence, this is all you need in a plan.

Exercise 7.6
Planning a sales promotion

Heading	Content
Introduction	Briefly summarize the problem upon which the promotion is designed to make impact
Objectives	Show how the objectives of the promotion are consistent with the marketing objectives
Background	Provide the relevant data or justification for the promotion
Promotional offer	Briefly, but precisely, provide details of the offer
Eligibility	Who is eligible? Where?
Timing	When is the offer available?
Date plan	The dates and responsibilities for all elements of the promotion
Support	Special materials, samples, etc. that are required by the sales force, retailers, etc.
Administration	Budgets, storage, invoicing, delivery, etc.

(Continued)

Heading	Content
Sales plan	Briefing meetings, targets, incentives, etc.
Sales presentation	Points to be covered
Sales reporting	Any special information required
Assessment	How the promotion will be evaluated

Using these guidelines, and the accompanying worksheet, try to extend the information you assembled in Exercise 7.5 into a complete promotional plan.

Worksheet Promotion plan (Exercise 7.6)

	Heading	Content
1	Introduction	
2	Objectives	
3	Background	
4	Promotional offer	
5	Eligibility	
6	Timing	
7	Date plan	
8	Support	
9	Administration	
10	Sales plan	
11	Sales presentation	
12	Sales reporting	
13	Assessment	

APPENDIX B: CHAPTER 8

The communication plan: 2 The sales plan

■ Introduction

▶ **Personal selling** has an important strategic role to play in communicating between a company and its customers. To have a chance of success, management must be able to answer the following kinds of question:

- How important is personal selling?
- What is the role of personal selling in the marketing mix?
- How many salespeople do we need?
- What do we want them to do?
- How should they be managed?

These and other questions will be considered in this chapter as important determinants of the sales plan.

▶ **D e f i n i t i o n** ◀

Personal selling is promotion via a person-to-person conversation, whether it be at the customer's premises, on the telephone, or elsewhere

■ How important is personal selling?

Most organizations had an organized sales force long before they introduced a formal marketing activity of the kind described throughout this text. In spite of this fact, sales-force management has traditionally been a neglected area of marketing management.

There are several possible reasons. One is that not all marketing and product managers have had experience in a personal selling or sales management role; consequently, these managers often underestimate the importance of efficient personal selling.

Another reason for neglect of sales-force management is that sales personnel themselves sometimes encourage an unhelpful distinction between sales and marketing by depicting themselves as being at 'the sharp end'. After all, isn't there something slightly daring about dealing with real live customers as opposed to sitting in an office surrounded by marketing surveys, charts and plans? Such reasoning is obviously misleading.

> Unless a good deal of careful marketing planning has taken place before salespeople make their effort to persuade the customer to place an order, the probability of a successful sale is much reduced.

The suggested distinction between marketing 'theory' and sales 'practice' is further invalidated when we consider that profitable sales depend not just on individual customers and individual products but on groups of customers (that is, market segments) and on the supportive relationship of products to each other (that is, a carefully planned product portfolio).

> Another factor to be taken into account in this context is the constant need for the organization to think in terms of where future sales will be coming from, rather than to concentrate solely on present products, customers and problems.

The author of this text has investigated many European sales forces over the last two decades and has found an alarming lack of planning and professionalism.

Salespeople frequently have little idea about which products and which groups of customers to concentrate on, have too little knowledge about competitive activity, do not plan presentations well, rarely talk to customers in terms of *benefits*, make too little effort to close the sale, and make many calls without any clear objectives. Even worse, marketing management is rarely aware that this important and expensive element of the marketing mix is not being managed effectively.

> The fact that many organizations have separate departments and directors for the marketing and sales activities increases the likelihood of such failures of communication.

Although its importance varies according to circumstances, in many businesses the sales force is the most important element in the marketing mix.

MARKETING INSIGHT

In industrial goods companies, for example, it is not unusual to find very small amounts being spent on other forms of communication and very large sums being spent on the sales force in the form of salaries, cars and associated costs.

> Personal selling is also used widely in many service industries where customers are looking for very specific benefits. Insurance companies, for example, do use media advertising, but many rely for most of their sales on personal selling. Customers for insurance policies almost invariably need to discuss which policy would best fit their particular needs and circumstances; it is the task of the salesperson to explain the choices available and to suggest the most appropriate policy.

> Recent surveys show that more money is spent by companies on their sales forces than on advertising and sales promotion combined. Personal selling, then, is a vital and expensive element in the marketing mix.

The solution to the problem of poor sales-force management can only be found in the recognition that personal selling is, indeed, a crucial part of the marketing process, but that it must be planned and considered as carefully as any other element. Indeed, it is an excellent idea for any manager responsible for marketing to go out into a territory for a few days each year and attempt to persuade customers to place orders. It is a good way of finding out what customers really think of the organization's marketing policies!

■ The role of personal selling

Personal selling can be seen most usefully as part of the *communications mix*. (Other common elements of the communications mix, it will be remembered, are advertising, sales promotion, public relations, the Internet, call centres, direct mail, exhibitions, and so on). The surveys set out in Chapter 7 show that organizations cannot leave the communications task only to the sales force. The same question remains, however, as with advertising. This is: how is the organization to define the role of personal selling in its communications mix? Again, the answer lies in a clear understanding of the buying process which operates in the company's markets.

The efficiency of any element of communication depends on achieving a match between information required and information given. To achieve this match, the marketer must be aware of the different requirements of different people at different stages of the buying process. This approach highlights the importance of ensuring that the company's communications reach *all* key points in the buying chain. No company can afford to assume that the actual sale is the only important event.

> The efficiency of any element of communication depends on achieving a match between information required and information given.

> In order to determine the precise role of personal selling in its communications mix, the company must identify the major influencers in each purchase decision and find out what information they are likely to need at different stages of the buying process.

Most institutional buying decisions consist of many separate phases, from the recognition of a problem through to performance evaluation and feedback on the product or service purchased. Furthermore, the importance of each of these phases varies according to whether the buying situation is a first-time purchase or a routine re-purchase. Clearly, the information needs will differ in each case. (This was discussed in some detail in Appendix A – in particular, see Figure 7.1.)

Personal selling has a number of advantages over other elements of the communications mix:

1 It is a two-way form of communication, giving the prospective purchaser the opportunity to ask questions of the salespeople about the product or service.
2 The sales message itself can be made more flexible and, therefore, can be more closely tailored to the needs of individual customers.
3 Salespeople can use in-depth product knowledge to relate their message to the perceived needs of the buyer and to deal with objections as they arise.
4 Most importantly, salespeople can ask for an order and, perhaps, negotiate on price, delivery or special requirements.

Once an order has been obtained from a customer and there is a high probability of a re-buy occurring, the salesperson's task changes from persuasion to reinforcement. All communications at this stage should contribute to underlining the wisdom of the purchase. The salesperson may also take the opportunity to encourage consideration of other products or services in the company's range.

> Clearly, in different markets, different weighting is given to the various forms of communication available. In the grocery business, for example, advertising and sales promotion are extremely important elements in the communications process. However, the food manufacturer must maintain an active sales force which keeps in close contact with the retail buyers. This retail contact ensures vigorous promotional activity in the chain. In the wholesale hardware business, frequent and regular face-to-face contact with retail outlets through a sales force is the key determinant of success. In industries where there are few customers (such as capital goods and specialized process materials), an in-depth understanding of the customers' production processes has to be built up; here,

again, personal contact is of paramount importance. In contrast, many fast-moving industrial goods are sold into fragmented markets for diverse uses; in this area, forms of communication other than personal selling take on added importance.

Many companies in the electronics business use personal selling to good advantage. Word processors, for example, vary enormously in the range of capabilities they offer. Technical details can be supplied in brochures and other promotional material, but the administrative staff likely to be taking the purchase decision often find it difficult to evaluate the alternatives. A good salesperson can ascertain quickly the requirements of a particular client and identify to what extent these will be fulfilled by the company's equipment. For their part, customers can identify quickly whether the company understands their requirements, whether it appears credible, and whether or not it is able to provide the back-up service necessary to install the equipment and establish its use in the organization. Such considerations are likely to be far more influential than the comparison of technical data sheets in a decision to purchase.

■ Determining the requisite number of salespeople

The organization should begin its consideration of how many salespeople it needs by finding out exactly how work is allocated at present. Start by listing all the things the current sales force actually does. These might include opening new accounts; servicing existing accounts; demonstrating new products; taking repeat orders; and collecting debts. This listing should be followed by an investigation of alternative ways of carrying out these responsibilities. For example, telephone selling has been shown to be a perfectly acceptable alternative to personal visits, particularly in respect of repeat business. The sales force can thus be freed for missionary work, which is not so susceptible to the telephone approach. Can debts be collected by mail or by telephone? Can products be demonstrated at exhibitions or showrooms? It is only by asking these kinds of questions that we can be certain we have not fallen into the common trap of committing the company to a decision and then seeking data and reasons to justify the decision. At this stage, the manager should concentrate on collecting relevant, quantified data, and then use judgement and experience to help in making a decision.

Basically, all sales force activities can be categorized under three headings. A salesperson:

● makes calls
● travels
● performs administrative functions.

These tasks constitute what can be called the *workload*. If we first decide what constitutes a reasonable workload for a salesperson, in hours per month, then we can begin to measure how long current activities take, and hence the exact extent of the salesperson's current workload.

This measurement can be performed either by some independent third party or, preferably, by the salespeople themselves. All they have to do for one simple method of measurement is to record distance travelled, time in and out of calls, and the outlet type. These data can then be analysed easily to indicate the average duration of a call by outlet type, the average distance travelled in a month, and the average speed according to the nature of the territory (that is, city, suburbs or country). With the aid of a map, existing customers can be allocated on a trial-and-error basis, together with the concomitant time values for clerical activities and travel. In this way, equitable workloads can be calculated for the sales force, building in, if necessary, spare capacity for sometimes investigating potential new sales outlets.

> This kind of analysis sometimes produces surprising results, as when the company's 'star' salesperson is found to have a smaller workload than the one with the worst results, who may be having to work much longer hours to achieve sales because of the nature of the territory.

> There are, of course, other ways of measuring workloads. One major consumer goods company used its Work Study Department to measure sales force effectiveness. The results of this study are summarized in Table 8.1.
> The table showed the company how a salesperson's time was spent and approximately how much of their time was actually available for selling. One immediate action taken by the company was to initiate a training programme which enabled more time to be spent on selling as a result of better planning. Another was to improve the quality of the sales performance while face-to-face with the customers.

Table 8.1 Breakdown of a salesperson's total daily activity

		Per cent of day	Minutes per day	
Outside call time	Drive to and from route	15.9	81	
	Drive on route	16.1	83	
	Walk	4.6	24	
	Rest and breaks	6.3	32	
	Pre-call administration	1.4	7	
	Post-call administration	5.3	27	
		49.6		254
Inside call time	Business talks	11.5	60	
	Sell	5.9	30	
	Chat	3.4	17	
	Receipts	1.2	6	
	Miscellaneous	1.1	6	
	Drink	1.7	8	
	Waiting	7.1	36	
		31.9		163
Evening work	Depot work	9.8	50	
	Entering pinks	3.9	20	
	Pre-plan route	4.8	25	
		18.5		95
		100.0		8 h 32 min

Armed with this kind of quantitative data, it becomes easier to determine how many salespeople are needed and how territories can be equitably allocated.

■ Determining the role of salespeople

Whatever the method used to organize the salesperson's day, there is always comparatively little time available for selling. In these circumstances, it is vital that a company should know as precisely as possible what it wants its sales force to do. Sales force objectives can be either *quantitative* or *qualitative*.

Quantitative objectives

Principal quantitative objectives are concerned with the following measures:

- how much to sell (the value of unit sales volume)
- what to sell (the mix of product lines to sell)
- where to sell (the markets and individual customers that will take the company towards its marketing objectives)
- desired profit contribution (where relevant and where the company is organized to compute this)
- selling costs (in compensation, expenses, supervision, and so on).

The first three types of objectives are derived directly from the marketing objectives, which are discussed in detail in Chapter 6, and constitute the principal components of the sales plan.

There are, of course, many other kinds of quantitative objectives which can be set for the sales force, including the following:

- number of point-of-sale displays organized
- number of letters written to prospects
- number of telephone calls to prospects
- number of reports turned or not turned in
- number of trade meetings held
- use of sales aids in presentations
- number of service calls made
- number of customer complaints
- safety record
- collections made
- training meetings conducted
- competitive activity reports
- general market condition reports.

Salespeople may also be required to fulfil a coordinating role between a team of specialists and the client organization.

Most objectives are subservient to the major objectives outlined above which are associated directly with what is sold and to whom.

A company selling mining machinery, for example, employs a number of 'good general salespeople' who establish contacts and identify which ones are likely to lead to sales. Before entering into negotiations with any client organization, the company selling the machinery may feel that it needs to call in a team of highly specialized engineers and financial experts for consultation and advice. It is the task of the salesperson in this company to identify when specialist help is needed, and to coordinate the people who become involved in the negotiation.

However, most objectives are subservient to the major objectives outlined above which are associated directly with what is sold and to whom.

Qualitative objectives

Qualitative objectives can be a potential source of problems if sales managers try to assess the performance of the sales force along dimensions which include abstract terms such as 'loyalty', 'enthusiasm', 'cooperation', and so on, since such terms are difficult to measure objectively. In seeking qualitative measurements of performance, managers often resort to highly subjective interpretations, which cause resentment and frustration among those being assessed.

However, managers can set and measure qualitative objectives which actually relate to the performance of the sales force on the job. It is possible, for example, to assess the skill with which people apply their product knowledge on the job, or the skill with which they plan their work, or the skill with which they overcome objections during a sale interview. While still qualitative in nature, these measures relate to standards of performance understood and accepted by the sales force.

Given such standards, it is not too difficult for a competent field sales manager to identify deficiencies, to get agreement on them, to coach in skills and techniques, to build attitudes of professionalism, to show how to self-train, to determine which training requirements cannot be tackled in the field, and to evaluate improvements in performance and the effect of any past training.

> One consumer goods company with thirty field sales managers discovered that most of them were spending much of the day in their offices engaged in administrative work, most of it self-made. The company proceeded to take the offices away and insisted that the sales managers spend most of their time in the field training their salespeople. To assist them in this task, they trained them in how to appraise and improve salespeople's performance in the field. There was a dramatic increase in sales and, consequently, in the sales managers' own earnings. This rapidly overcame their resentment at losing their offices.

■ Improving sales force productivity

> Many salespeople might secretly confess to a proclivity to call more frequently on those large customers who give them a friendly reception, and less frequently on those who put obstacles in their way.

If we classify customers according to their friendliness to us, as well as to their size, it is easy to see how a simple matrix can be developed to help us decide where our major effort should be directed. From Figure 8.1, it can be seen that the boxes which offer the greatest potential for increased sales productivity are Boxes 4 and 5, with Boxes 1 and 2 receiving a 'maintenance' call rate. Boxes 7 and 8 should receive an 'alternative strategy' approach to establish whether hostility can be overcome. If these alternative approaches fail, a lower call rate may be

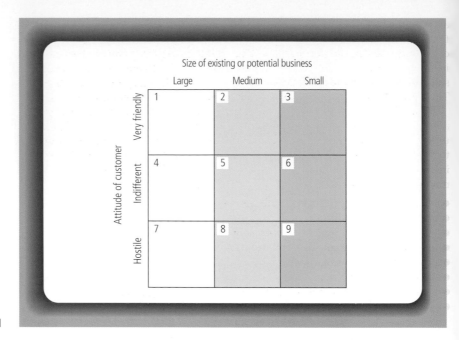

Figure 8.1

appropriate. Box 9 is the 'Don't bother' box, while Boxes 3 and 6 will receive the minimum attention consistent with our goals.

None of this is meant to indicate definitive rules about call frequencies, which will always remain a matter of management judgement. Its sole purpose is to question our assumptions about call frequencies on existing and potential accounts to check that we are not using valuable time which could be more productively used in other directions.

■ Managing the sales force

Sales-force motivation has received a great deal of attention in recent times, largely as a result of the work done by psychologists in other fields of management. There is now widespread appreciation of the fact that it is not sufficient merely to give someone a title and an office and expect to get good results.

> Effective leadership, it is acknowledged, is as much 'follower-determined' as it is determined by management.

If performance is a function of incentives minus disincentives, then the more incentives can be increased and disincentives reduced, the better will be performance.

While for the purposes of this discussion it is not necessary to enter into a detailed discussion of sales-force motivation, it is worth mentioning briefly some important factors that contribute to effective sales-force management.

If a sales manager's job is to improve the performance of the sales force, and if performance is a function of incentives minus disincentives, then the more incentives can be increased and disincentives reduced, the better will be performance.

Research has shown that an important element of sales-force motivation is a sense of doing a worthwhile job. In other words, desire for praise and recognition, the avoidance of boredom and monotony, the enhancement of self-image, freedom from fear and worry, and the desire to belong to something believed to be worthwhile, all contribute to enhanced performance. One well-known piece of research carried out in the USA examined the reasons for the results of the twenty highest producing sales units in one company compared with the twenty lowest producing sales units. The research showed all the above factors to be major determinants of success.

However, remuneration will always be a most important determinant of motivation. This does not necessarily mean paying the most money although, clearly, unless there are significant financial motivations within a company it is unlikely that people will stay. In drawing up a remuneration plan, which would normally include a basic salary plus some element for special effort, such as bonus or commission, the following objectives should be considered:

- to attract and keep effective salespeople
- to remain competitive
- to reward salespeople in accordance with their individual performance
- to provide a guaranteed income plus an orderly individual growth rate
- to generate individual sales initiative
- to encourage teamwork
- to encourage the performance of essential non-selling tasks
- to ensure that management can fairly administer and adjust compensation levels as a means of achieving sales objectives.

A central concept of sales-force motivation is that individual salespeople will exert more effort if managers encourage them to concentrate on:

1 Their expectations of accomplishing their sales objectives
2 The personal benefits derived from accomplishing those objectives.

This theory of sales-force motivation is known as the path–goal approach because it is based on the particular path the salesperson follows to a particular sales objective and the particular goals associated with successfully travelling down that path. The salesperson estimates the probability of success of travelling down various paths or sales approaches, and estimates the probability that superiors will recognize goal accomplishments and will reward him or her accordingly.

> The motivational functions of the sales manager consist of increasing personal pay-offs to salespeople for work-goal attainment, making the path to these pay-offs easier to travel by clarifying it, reducing road blocks and pitfalls, and increasing the opportunities for personal satisfaction *en route*.

Few people would deny that sales-force motivation is a difficult and highly emotive subject, and at the end of the day common sense must prevail. The writer once attended a sales conference which opened with girls dancing to the company song. They were followed immediately by a tawdry-looking marketing manager who spent an hour pointing to bar charts on an overhead projector. Not surprisingly, few of the sales force present remembered much about the central issues of the conference, while the few saleswomen present were offended!

Another common feature of sales conferences is the use of bellicose language, such as 'our plan is to wipe out the enemy …' and so on. The use of such imagery is often in sharp contrast to the day-to-day circumstances of the average salesperson, who gets up on a rainy Monday morning, gets into a small company car, and is rejected on the first call of the week!

Table 8.2 Objectives for the individual salesperson (based on the original work of Stephen P. Morse when at Urwick Orr and Partners)

Task	The standard	How to set the standard	How to measure performance	What to look for
1 To achieve personal sales targets	Sales target or period of time for individual groups and/or products	Analysis of territory potential and individual customers' potential; discussion and agreement between salesperson and manager	Comparison of individual salesperson's product sales against targets	Significant short-fall between target and achievement over a meaningful period
2 To sell the required range and quantity to individual customers	Achievement of specified range and quantity of sales to a particular customer or group of customers within an agreed time period	Analysis of individual customer records of potential and present sales; discussion and agreement between manager and salesperson	Scrutiny of individual customer records; observation of selling in the field	Failure to achieve agreed objectives; complacency with range of sales made to individual customers
3 To plan journeys and call frequencies to achieve minimum practicable selling cost	To achieve appropriate call frequency on individual customers; number of live customer calls during a given time period	Analysis of individual customers' potential; analysis of order/call ratios; discussion and agreement between manager and salesperson	Scrutiny of individual customer records; analysis of order/call ratio; examination of call reports	High ratio of calls to an individual customer relative to that customer's yield; shortfall on agreed total number of calls made over an agreed time period
4 To acquire new customers	Number of prospect calls during time period; selling new products to existing customers	Identify total number of potential and actual customers who could produce results; identify opportunity areas for prospecting	Examination of call reports, records of new accounts opened and ratio of existing to potential customers	Shortfall in number of prospect calls from agreed standard; low ratio of existing to potential customers
5 To make a sales approach of the required quality	To exercise the necessary skills and techniques required to achieve the identified objective of each element of the sales approach; continuous use of sales material	Standard to be agreed in discussion between manager and salesperson related to company standards laid down	Regular observations of field selling using a systematic analysis of performance in each stage of the sales approach	Failure to identify objective of each stage of sales approach, to identify specific areas of skill, weakness, to use support material

A bit of excitement at sales conferences is necessary, of course, but most sales directors and managers would be better occupied providing the sales force with information and tools designed to make the selling task easier, rather than providing entertainment.

Preparing the sales plan

No two sales plans will contain precisely the same headings. However, some general guidelines can be given. Table 8.2 is an example of setting objectives for an individual salesperson. Clearly, these objectives will be the logical result of breaking down the marketing objectives into actual sales targets.

All companies set themselves overall objectives, which in turn imply the development of specific marketing objectives. In this chapter, we have discussed personal selling in the context of the overall marketing activity. This approach leads us to the following hierarchy of objectives: *corporate objectives – marketing objectives – sales objectives*, as outlined in Figure 8.2.

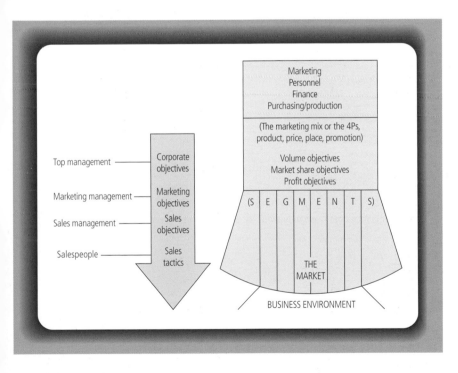

Figure 8.2

The benefits to sales-force management of following this approach can be summarized as follows:

1 Coordination of corporate and marketing objectives with actual sales effort
2 Establishment of a circular relationship between corporate objectives and customer wants
3 Improvement of sales effectiveness through an understanding of the corporate and marketing implications of sales decisions.

> The following example illustrates the main point that a sales force cannot be managed in isolation from broad corporate and marketing objectives. The sales force of a company manufacturing stainless steel containers was selling almost any kind of container to almost anybody who could buy. This caused severe production planning and distribution problems throughout the business, down to the purchase of raw materials. Eventually, the company's profitability was seriously affected. The sales force was finally instructed to concentrate on certain kinds of products and on certain kinds of user industries. This decision eventually led to economies of scale throughout the whole organization.

To summarize, the sales force is a vital but very expensive element of the marketing mix, and as much care should be devoted to its management as to any other area of marketing management. This is most likely to be achieved if intuitive sense, which is associated with experience, can be combined with the kind of logical framework of thinking outlined here (see Figure 8.3).

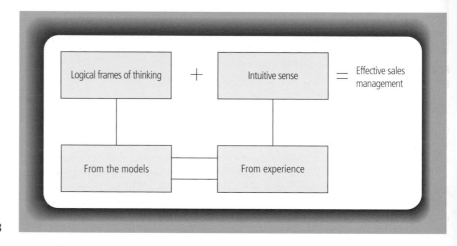

Figure 8.3

■ Integrating marketing communication and distribution channels

The changing nature of promotion and distribution

Promotion and distribution are changing in a number of respects. New channels such as the Internet are emphasizing an already growing trend from mass media such as advertising, through addressable media such as direct mail, to interactive media such as call centres and the Web. Integrating these channels within a coherent strategy is not an easy task. Writers on the new field of Integrated Marketing Communications

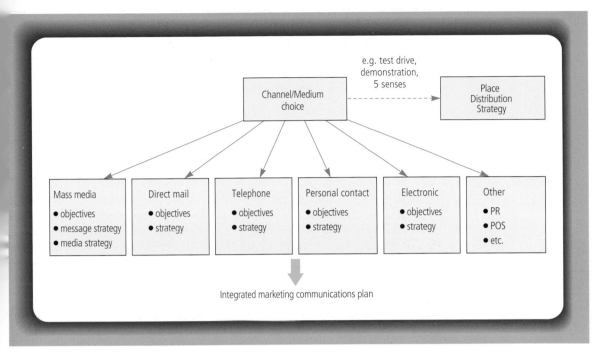

Figure 8.4
Defining a promotion and distribution strategy

(IMC) emphasize that before engaging on detailed planning for each medium – writing sales plans or promotions plans, for example – it is necessary to choose which medium to use for which customer interactions. This is illustrated in Figure 8.4.

The choice of channel/medium is generally a complex one, involving different media for different communications with the same customer. The organization will also frequently wish to leave some options in the hands of the customer. For example, a Dell customer may find out about Dell from colleagues or from press advertising; investigate which product to buy, what the price is and what configuration is required using the Web; print out order details and pass them to the purchasing department to place the order via fax; check on the delivery time via telephone; take delivery via a parcels service; and obtain customer service using e-mail. Customers are no longer content to have the medium dictated by the supplier.

The choice of medium is clearly closely intertwined with the distribution strategy. Distribution channels often have a mix of purposes, providing both a means of conveying a physical product to the customer and a medium for information exchange. A garage, for example, provides information on the model, an opportunity for a test drive, a location where price negotiations can occur, and a step in the physical delivery of the car to the customer. A clothes shop provides a location where the information exchange of trying on a garment and feeling it can occur, in a way which is difficult to replicate using direct marketing approaches. So the focus of promotion on information exchange is closely linked to the often physical issues of distribution. However, considering the two separately can result in new solutions, such as direct banking or web shopping for CDs (which may need to be sampled but won't need to be felt physically), and complementing the sales force with telemarketing and websites for minor transactions or less important customers in business-to-business markets.

Choosing the right medium for the right purpose, then, is not a trivial task. There is increasing recognition that this issue needs to be considered afresh, rather than simply following traditional practice in a given industry. However, although writings on IMC explain the problem, there is little practical help for organizations on how to solve it.

A related problem is the changing nature of the sales process, which we will turn to now.

Marketing operations and the new sales process

Once an overall marketing plan has been drawn up, including a plan for promotions, the plan must be implemented. This is the role of marketing operations – the delivery of the value to the customer which was specified in the planning process. However, during the course of a year, plenty of finer-grained communications decisions need to be taken. To illustrate, we will consider the map of the marketing operations process in Figure 8.6 (this is an expansion of the 'Deliver value' box in the map of the marketing domain in Figure 8.5).

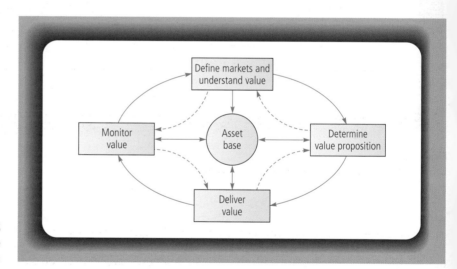

Figure 8.5
Map of the
marketing domain

The starting point for our analysis of this 'Deliver value' process was Porter's value chain (Porter, 1980)[1] This is reflected in the tasks we have listed within 'Deliver the product/service' in the top half of the figure: research and development, leading to inbound logistics, then through operations to outbound logistics and finally to service.

However, we suggest that there are a number of marketing activities that shadow these value chain activities, under the general heading of 'communicate the offer'. Porter placed 'Marketing' after 'Operations' in the value chain, but in today's one-to-one world these communications can occur in parallel with all the tasks involved in value delivery. One might, for example, check a product with customers at the R&D stage – the product may be tailored by the customer, resulting in different components being bought in, assembled and delivered. And so on.

[1] M.E. Porter (1980) *Competitive Strategy*, Free Press, New York.

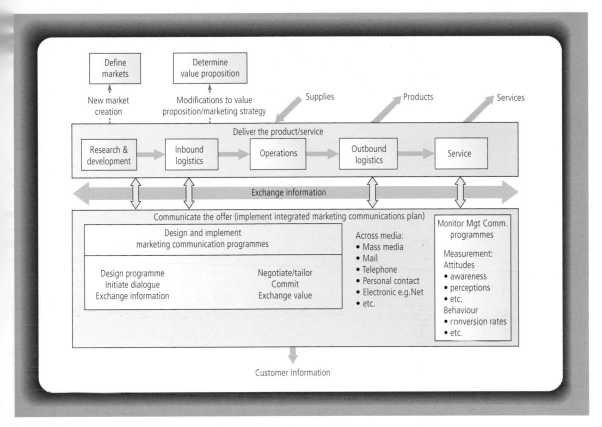

Figure 8.6
Delivering value – a map of marketing operations

Communicating the offer is typically managed by designing, implementing and monitoring a number of marketing communications programmes. A communication programme could be, for example, a direct mail campaign, an advertising campaign, a series of sales seminars, an in-store promotion, and so on. We have also stretched the term 'marketing communication programme' to include management of such media as the sales force, which may be managed in a more continuous way, with annual targets broken down by quarter or month.

Whatever the medium, the campaign will be aiming to contribute to one or more of the tasks within the 'Design/implement marketing communication programmes' box. The tasks may have an unfamiliar look – in order to represent the interactive one-to-one nature of today's marketing we have renamed the classic steps in the sales process. Figure 8.7 illustrates traditional views of the sales and purchasing processes, with this revised interaction perspective between the two.

Traditional 'push-based' models of marketing, in which after the product is made, prospects are found and persuaded to buy the product, are illustrated on the left. The delivery and service that follow are operational functions with little relationship to marketing.

Traditional models of buyer behaviour, illustrated on the right of the figure, assume more rationality on the part of buyers, but underplay the importance of

Supplier perspective			Interaction perspective		Buyer perspective	
Advertising	Selling	Marketing activity	Interaction	Decision theory	Consumer behaviour
		Define markets/ understand value			
			Recognize exchange potential	Problem recognition	Category need
		Create value proposition			
Brand awareness					Awareness
	Prospecting	Initiate dialogue			Attitude
Brand attitude	Provide information	Exchange information		Information search	
• Info *re* benefits					Information gathering and judgement
• brand image					
• feelings					
• peer influence					
	Persuade	Negotiate/tailor		Evaluation of alternatives	
Trial inducement					
	Close sale	Commit		Choice/purchase	Purchase process
	Deliver	Exchange value			
Reduce cognitive dissonance	Service		Monitor	Post-purchase behaviour	Post-purchase experience

Figure 8.7
Re-thinking the sales process

what the buyer says back to the seller. The seller's offer is assumed to be predetermined, rather than developed in conjunction with the buyer.

The stages of the process of communicating value are therefore re-described as follows:

- 'Recognize exchange potential' replaces 'category need' or 'problem recognition'. Both sides need to recognize the potential for a mutual exchange of value.
- 'Initiate dialogue' replaces 'Create awareness' or 'Prospecting'. The dialogue with an individual customer may be started by either party. One feature of the Web, for example, is that on many occasions new customers will approach the supplier rather than *vice versa*.
- 'Exchange information' replaces 'Provide information'. If we are to serve the customer effectively, tailor our offerings and build a long-term relationship, we need to learn about the customer as much as the customer needs to learn about our products.

- 'Negotiate/tailor' replaces 'Persuade'. Negotiation is a two-way process which may involve us modifying our offer in order better to meet the customer's needs. Persuading the customer instead that the square peg we happen to have in stock will fit their round hole is not likely to lead to a long and profitable relationship.
- 'Commit' replaces 'Close sale'. Both sides need to commit to the transaction, or to a series of transactions forming the next stage in a relationship – a decision with implications for both sides.
- 'Exchange value' replaces 'Deliver' and 'Post-sales service'. The 'post-sales service' may be an inherent part of the value being delivered, not simply a cost centre, as it is often still managed.

One-to-one communications and principles of relationship marketing, then, demand a radically different sales process from that traditionally practised. This point is far from academic, as an example will illustrate.

The company in question provides business-to-business financial services. Its marketing managers relayed to us their early experience with a website which was enabling them to reach new customers considerably more cost-effectively than their traditional sales force. When the website was first launched, potential customers were finding the company on the Web, deciding the products were appropriate on the basis of the website, and sending an e-mail to ask to buy. So far, so good.

However, stuck in a traditional model of the sales process, the company would allocate the 'lead' to a salesperson, who would phone up and make an appointment, perhaps three weeks' hence. The customer would by now probably have moved on to another online supplier who could sell the product today, but those that remained were subjected to a sales pitch, complete with glossy materials, which was totally unnecessary, the customer having already decided to buy. Those that were not put off would proceed to be registered as able to buy over the Web, but the company had lost the opportunity to improve its margins by using the sales force more judiciously.

In time, the company realized its mistake, and changed its sales model and reward systems to something close to our 'interaction perspective' model. Unlike those prospects which the company proactively identified and contacted, which might indeed need 'selling' to, many new Web customers were initiating the dialogue themselves, and simply required the company to respond effectively and rapidly. The sales force was increasingly freed up to concentrate on major clients and on relationship building.

The changing nature of the sales process clearly raises questions for the design of marketing communications, such as: Who initiates the dialogue, and how do we measure the effectiveness of our attempts to do so across multiple channels? How do we monitor the effectiveness not just of what we say to customers but what they say back? And how about the role of marketing communications as part of the value that is being delivered and paid for, not just as part of the sales cost?

The trend towards multi-channel communications strategies has been underpinned by developments in CRM technology, which we will briefly consider next.

The need for CRM systems to underpin tailored communications

The market for integrated CRM systems has largely arisen out of the frustration of many companies with their multiple customer databases developed for different tasks – as many as forty, in one recent case. Most major organizations are working towards a unified view of the customer, so that all aspects of the customer interface can be coordinated. In order to achieve this, systems need to manage customer data independently of the task being performed. For example, if customers enter their name and address on a website, they do not wish to be asked the same information on the telephone. This requires all tasks to call on a single module which manages this customer data if a spaghetti-like set of system interconnections is not to result. We term this the principle of *task independent data management*.

This point can clearly be seen in Figure 8.8. The 'task management' layer needs to be separate from the 'data management' layer, rather than systems for each task endeavouring to manage parts of the customer data, as is still often the case.

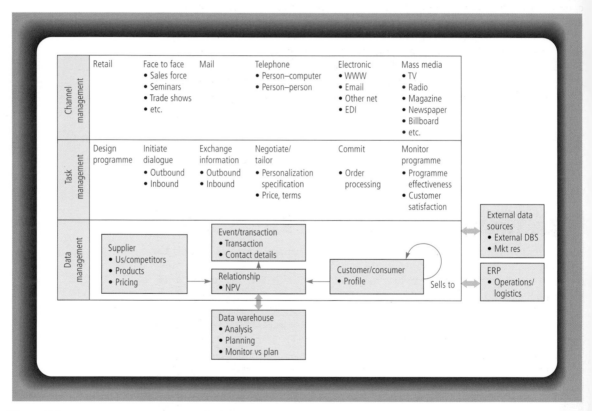

Figure 8.8
Towards a viable CRM architecture

Another point which is clearly illustrated by Figure 8.8 is the importance of *channel independent task management*. The 'channel management' layer of managing different channels or media is often bundled in with particular tasks. A 'direct mail system' will be *the* way in which the organization generates leads; an 'order processing system' will assume that orders come in to an order processing clerk (rather than, say, being made by a website), and so on. Such an architecture is inherently inflexible. An ideal architecture separates the issue of managing the medium from that of managing the task. That way, an order processing system could handle orders that originate over the Web, in-store and from field sales in exactly the same way, without requiring three separate order processing systems.

It is all very well defining ideal architectures that facilitate integrated communications, but organizations more typically are stuck with a set of 'legacy' systems, which they can evolve but rarely replace in one project. Nevertheless, organizations need a sense of direction in their IT projects. From an IMC perspective, they need answers to such questions as: How can organizations find their way round the formidable array of personalization capabilities embedded in today's technology for personalized websites, e-mail campaigns or mobile text messages? How can they decide when to use which, or when to stick with traditional one-to-many approaches? What metrics are required to measure the effectiveness of communications strategies across different media, and how should data be collected and analysed to produce these metrics?

Two examples follow of an attempt by a major global travel company to understand the information-seeking and purchasing processes of different segments. These are given as Figures 8.9 and 8.10. From these two of seven different segments, it can be seen that the behaviour of each is totally different. Without such segmentation knowledge, an integrated communications plan would be impossible.

	Internet	Mobile telephone	iTV	Broadcast TV	Traditional channels
• Recognize exchange potential					
• Initiate dialogue					
• Exchange information					
Negotiate/tailor					
Commit					
• Exchange value					
• Monitor					

Figure 8.9
The Sunlovers

	Internet	Mobile telephone	iTV	Broadcast TV	Traditional channels
• Recognize exchange potential					
• Initiate dialogue					
• Exchange information					
Negotiate/tailor					
Commit					
• Exchange value					
• Monitor					

Figure 8.10
John and Mary Lively

■ Application questions

1. What are the key functions of salespeople in your organization? How is their work coordinated?

2. How is the sales force deployed: by geographical territory; by product range; by type of customer? Is this deployment optimal? What other patterns of deployment should be considered by your organization?

3. Who is responsible for the sales force in your organization? What is the relationship between this post of responsibility and other marketing responsibilities in the organization? Does this cause any problems? Where problems arise, how could they be solved?

4. Can you make a case to justify the present size and type of sales force used? Could you defend your position if you were requested to cut back the sales force by 30 per cent? How would you make your case? What do you believe would be the consequences of a 30 per cent cutback in the sales force?

5. How is your own organization's sales force used? Is this the best possible use of the sales force? In what ways do activities of the sales force complement other forms of marketing communications used? Identify any other ways in which you feel the activities of the sales force could enhance the total marketing communications effort.

6. Critically appraise your company's sales plan. Does it flow naturally from the company's marketing objectives?

7   Using the communications format summarized in Figure 8.7, outline how the role
of the sales force is likely to change in the light of new communications channels.

EXERCISES

While it is quite possible that some companies will not use advertising and
sales promotion, very few fail to have some element of face-to-face selling in
their marketing mix. Often the sales force was in existence long before the
company became concerned about marketing. This sometimes explains why,
in many organizations, sales and marketing are regarded as two separate
functions.

When the total cost of recruiting, managing and providing salespeople
with all the necessary resources and support systems is taken into account, the
sales force is likely to be one of the most costly elements of the company's
marketing activities. In order to obtain value for money, it will be important
to plan how personal selling will be integrated into the 'communications mix',
then organize the logistics to ensure that the right results are achieved.

Exercise 8.1 looks at how the role of the sales force can be established.

Exercise 8.2 tackles the task of how to set quantifiable objectives for the
sales force.

Exercise 8.3 examines issues about managing the sales force and, in particular, how to set the right motivational climate.

Introduction to Chapter 8 exercises

Before attempting to produce a sales plan, we must spend a few minutes getting back to basics and examining exactly what information customers will
require from the sales force.

For different sorts of businesses, the role of the salesperson can be entirely
different. In some they will just be order-takers, in others negotiators, in
others demonstrators, and in others perhaps a composite of these and still
other roles. Clearly, then, to claim that a salesperson 'just sells' is very much an
oversimplification of the role, and sometimes can be downright misleading.

Taking your marketing objectives as the starting point, i.e. which products/
services go to which markets or segments, select one of your key markets/seg-
ments as a study vehicle and focus on the customers. What sort of information
do they require from your sales force?

The next worksheet (page 596) is designed to help with this task. There are
three steps to be tackled:

1 Establish the communication areas that need to be covered.
2 Because of the costs of having a sales force, assess whether there are less
   costly feasible alternatives to personal visits to achieve the same results.
3 List what these alternatives are, together with when and how they will be
   used.

Thus, on completion of the worksheet you will have a complete breakdown
of the personal communications necessary to achieve the company's marketing objectives in your study market segment. In addition, you will have other
information to show how personal visits can be 'back up' to other methods of
contact.

Exercise 8.1
The role of personal communication in the communications mix

Worksheet What information do customers want from sales representatives? (Exercise 8.1)

For study purposes, just consider one market segment. You can repeat the same procedure for the other afterwards.

Recognizing that the sales force plays an important part in the company's communications mix, study the list below and then tick those 'demanded' by customers in column A. Now look carefully at the activities you have just ticked, and, taking each in turn, ask yourself if this information/communication could be provided in a more effective way than by a sales visit. For example, knowing the customer usage of a particular product might make it possible to obtain repeat orders by telephone.

Whenever you see the possibility of an alternative approach, place a tick in column B and make a brief note about the alternative.

Customer info. requirement	A	B	Alternative provision of information

About:
  product range
  product performance
  price
  discounts
  special offers
  promotions
  placing order
  after-sales service
  running cost in use
  guarantees
  spares and accessories
  new developments
  competitor products/performance
  assistance with displays
  assistance with merchandising
  training for own staff
  technical services
  quality assurance
  proof that product/service works
  warehousing/storage
  reordering
  load sizes
  leasing agreement
  delivery arrangements
  franchise agreement
  answers to objections
  joint ventures
  demonstration of product
  long-term contracts
  financial arrangements
 	
Add any other information
requirements that are pertinent
to your business			

Having decided what role the sales force is to play in the communications mix to service your chosen market segment, you can now get down to drawing up some quantifiable objectives. These stem quite logically from the marketing objectives and should cover three main areas:

1 How much to sell (value of unit sales volume)
2 What to sell (the mix of product lines)
3 Where to sell (the markets/segments that take the company towards its marketing objectives).

Please note that in Exercise 8.1 you have already chosen one component, 'where to sell', by selecting an important market or segment.

The sales plan is in effect the translation of these 'ball park' figures into individual targets for each sales representative, taking into account special factors such as their territory size, the size of customers within a particular territory, etc. Thus, how much to sell breaks down into individual targets. The mix of the product lines becomes an individual target. Where to sell becomes a specific customer list.

In addition, there can be other quantifiable objectives, typical examples of which are given on the next worksheet. Using this worksheet, you will be able to devise a set of targets appropriate for each of your sales representatives. The entries towards the end of the worksheet show how the basic targeting can be made somewhat more elaborate if it suits your company to make it so.

If you use one sheet per person, the total will become the sales plan for this particular market segment.

Although some purists might claim this is an oversimplification, the key *management* activities are:

- setting performance standards (both quantifiable and qualitative)
- monitoring achievements against these standards
- helping/training those who are falling behind
- setting the right motivational climate.

The word 'management' has been emphasized because many sales managers perceive themselves to be 'super' salespeople and continue to put most of their energies into selling rather than managing.

Setting performance standards
Exercise 8.2 concentrated on the quantifiable standard – *what* has to be achieved. Equally important are the more subjective elements of *how* the tasks are achieved: the quality of the actions.

Some companies have quite deliberately set out to create a style to which salespeople are expected to conform. This can cover appearance (of people and their property), the layout of letters and reports, the way work is planned, the way customers are addressed, and various other aspects of the work. You might have to give some consideration to this question of 'the way we do things around here'. But please note that in the examples given above, there is a standard to work against and performance is, therefore, measurable.

Place less emphasis on non-measurable factors, such as creativity, loyalty, interest, enthusiasm – relying on them too heavily is to plant the seeds of discord. Such subjective judgements can easily be misconstrued as favouritism by some, and unfairness by others who have been 'scored' lower. Nonetheless, they can be relevant, so we have included a way of 'measuring' these elements in this exercise.

Exercise 8.2
Quantifiable objectives

Exercise 8.3
Managing the sales force

Worksheet Individual sales targets (Exercise 8.2)

Market segment _____

Salesperson _____

Territory _____

Period to which these targets apply,
e.g. year, month, week, call cycle, etc. _____

Target	Number	Qualifying notes (assumptions, special local factors, etc.)
Unit sales volumes		
Product A		
Product B		
Product C		
Product D		
Number of calls planned to be made		
Number of interviews to be secured		
Number of enquiries to be raised		
Number of quotations to be submitted		
Number of orders to be taken		
Call/interview ratio*		
Enquiries/quotation ratio*		
Quotations/order ratio*		
Cost per visit		
Calls per day planned		
Average length of call		
Average daily mileage		
Number of new accounts planned		
Number of letters to be written		
Number of point-of-sale displays to be organized		
Number of meetings to be held, e.g. with trade		
Number of service calls to be made		
Number of customer complaints		
Number of customer training sessions to be run		
Number of competitor activity reports to be submitted		
Number of general market condition reports to be submitted		
Add any others that are relevant to your type of business		

* based on past experience and future expectations.

Monitoring performance

What salespeople are doing can be largely measured by reports, sales figures, internal memos and suchlike. *How* they do things can in most cases only be assessed by being with them and observing their actual performance.

Thus, performance will have to be monitored at these two levels, and the frequency for doing so will depend upon the experience of the salesperson, the newness of the operation and the uncertainty of the situation. As a rule of thumb, the higher the uncertainty surrounding the salesperson, the territory, the product range, the customers, etc., the more frequently should performance be monitored. The appraisal summary (Worksheet 1) provided will enable you to monitor and 'measure' all the relevant quantitative and qualitative elements of your sales force.

Helping/training those whose performance is below par

By having measurable standards of performance, it becomes possible to be quite precise about the area and nature of help that salespeople need. After discussing the problem with them, you will be able to decide if it can be best solved by providing the salespeople with:

- more information (about products, prices, etc.)
- more support (report writing, more joint visits, etc.)
- more training (which generally means improving their skills).

Often training, which can be the most costly solution, is rushed into when other actions would serve the purpose more effectively.

Should training be required, much of it can be carried out on the job by a suitable skilled instructor, who would follow a process like this:

1 Instruction/demonstration by instructor.
2 Practice by the salesperson.
3 Feedback by the instructor.
4 Further practice with feedback until performance is acceptable.

Setting the right motivational climate

Perhaps little of the above will really work unless the motivation of the sales force is right. While this subject could be the basis of a whole book by itself, it is possible to see a fairly straightforward way of cutting through much of the theoretical undergrowth.

By and large, if you can reduce those factors that tend to demotivate your staff and at the same time accentuate those which motivate them, then the motivational climate must improve. In saying this, it is important to recognize the difference between removing a demotivating factor and accentuating a motivating one. Removing a demotivating factor will not of itself bring about motivation; all it will do is to stop the complaints about the situation. In contrast to this, accentuating or adding to the motivating factors will undoubtedly lead to a higher commitment to the work.

Worksheet 2 enables you to establish exactly what these factors will be for your organization.

Worksheet 1   Individual appraisal summary (Exercise 8.3)

SALESPERSON _____

DIVISION _____

TERRITORY _____ YEAR _____

MANAGER _____

Note:
Score between 5 and 1, when 5 represents excellent and 1 represents poor.

Salesmanship	JAN	FEB	MAR	APR	MAY	JUN	JUL	AUG	SEP	OCT	NOV	DEC
Product knowledge												
Pre-planning												
Objectives												
Introduction												
Participation												
Handling objections												
Use of benefits												
Visual aids												
Third-party proof												
Investment merit												
Closing techniques												
Merchandising												
Range selling												
TOTAL												

Organization	JAN	FEB	MAR	APR	MAY	JUN	JUL	AUG	SEP	OCT	NOV	DEC
Territory planning												
Use of time												
Reporting												
Records												
Sales statistics												
New account												
Follow-up												
Care of equipment												
TOTAL												

Attributes	JAN	FEB	MAR	APR	MAY	JUN	JUL	AUG	SEP	OCT	NOV	DEC
Enthusiasm and drive												
Training and self-development												
Appearance												
Punctuality												
Cooperation												
Customer relations												
TOTAL												
GRAND TOTAL												

Worksheet 2 Motivational climate
Get your salespeople to consider the various things, incidents or situations, that have happened to them in their work over the last, say, six months. (You can select the time period.) Then ask them to make brief notes under the headings shown on the form.

Those things I found *DISSATISFYING*	Those things which gave me *SATISFACTION*

Find ways to reduce or eliminate as many of these factors as possible

Find ways to build on or add to these factors. These are the real motivators.

APPENDIX C: CHAPTER 9

The pricing plan

■ Introduction

The first important point to be made about the pricing plan is that very rarely is there a pricing plan in a marketing plan!

The reason is not too hard to find. Promotion, in all its various forms, can be managed and measured as a discrete subset of the marketing mix. So too can distribution. But while the product itself, the price charged, service elements and communication strategies are all part of the 'offer' which is made to the customer, price itself is such an integral part of the offer that it is rarely separated out and put into a plan of its own.

> It is more common to find objectives for a certain group of products or for a particular group of customers, with a pricing strategy attached to it in whatever detail is necessary to indicate what the pricing policy is expected to do to help the company achieve its marketing objectives.

However, we have chosen to address the issue of pricing as a separate element of the marketing mix because this is the only sensible way that all the complex issues relating to pricing can be discussed. We shall, then, refer throughout to a pricing plan as if the intention were to write a separate pricing plan, although it will be structured in such a way that the elements of pricing can be integrated into the individual product/segment plans as appropriate.

The same could, of course, be said for each of the other elements of the marketing mix discussed in this book. How they are all integrated into a total plan is discussed in detail in Chapter 13.

■ Pricing and accountancy

Many people know the story told on pricing courses of the conversation between the restauranteur who decides to put a peanut rack on the end of his counter and his accountant expert. Essentially, the plan is to sell peanuts for 10c a bag, the cost price being 6c.

Unfortunately, the accountant insists that the restaurateur must allocate a proportion of overheads into the peanut operation, including rent, heat, light, equipment, depreciation, decorating, salaries, the cook's wages, window-washing, soap, and so on. These allocated costs, plus a rent for the vacant amount of counter space, amount to €1,563 a year which, on the basis of a sales level of fifty bags of peanuts a week, amount to 60c per bag, so demonstrating that, at a selling price of 10c per bag, the restaurateur would be losing 50 cents on every bag!

Many readers will appreciate the feelings of this imaginary restaurateur and will readily agree that nowhere in an organization are the seeds of potential strife more firmly sown than in the interface between accountants and marketing people, particularly when it comes to pricing issues. Often, however, both parties are equally to blame.

Accountants often fail to understand the essential role that marketing plays in an organization.

> Many accountants know quite a lot about business in general, but very little about marketing, and what little is known tends to be a somewhat jaundiced view.

Somehow, marketing is seen as a less worthy activity than the act of producing goods for society. Marketing's more vocal activities, such as television advertising, are not seen in their total perspective, and it is not always easy to understand the complex decisions that have to be made about an activity that is concerned essentially with human behaviour rather than with things that can be conveniently counted. There is, alas, also the issue of marketers who are unprofessional in the way they manage the marketing function. The 1994 Cranfield/Chartered Institute of Marketing survey into the future of marketing was very critical of the lack of professional qualifications and skills in the marketing community, and an ongoing research database at Cranfield confirms the low regard in which marketing people are held. So the blame lies just as much on the side of marketers.

> For their part, those marketing people who fail to understand both the financial consequences of their decisions and the constraints of money on their decision-making have only themselves to blame for the inevitable internecine disputes that arise.

One area where it all bubbles to the surface is pricing. Our intention here is to explain pricing from a marketing point of view, while still recognizing the financial constraints and implications which accountants face. For one thing is certain. Any team comprising a financially alert marketer and a marketing-orientated accountant will make formidable opposition in any market. 'Demand exists only at a price', so price is an important determinant of how much of a certain product will sell, although it is obviously not the only factor involved. Given its importance, both as an element in the overall marketing mix and as a major factor in determining profitability, it is somewhat surprising to find just how haphazard the pricing policy of so many companies is. More sophistication might be expected.

> One thing is certain. Any team comprising a financially alert marketer and a marketing-orientated accountant will make formidable opposition in the marketplace.

> The pricing decision is important for two main reasons: price not only affects the margin through its impact on revenue; it also affects the quantity sold through its influence on demand.

In short, price has an interactive effect on the other elements of the marketing mix, so it is essential that it is part of a conscious marketing scheme, with objectives which have been clearly defined.

Although in some areas of the economy pricing may be determined by forces which are largely outside the control of corporate decision-makers, prices in the marketplace are normally the result of decisions made by company managements. What should the decision be, however, when on the one hand the accountant wants to increase the price of a product in order to maximize profitability, while on the other the marketer wants to hold or even reduce the net selling price in order to increase market share? The answer would appear to be simple. Get the calculator out and see which proposal results in the biggest 'profit'.

But there are some nagging doubts about the delightful simplicity of this approach.

In order to introduce a structured consideration of such doubts, let us first quote in full the Boston Consulting Group on the issue of the almost defunct British motorcycle industry:

> The fundamental feature is its emphasis on model-by-model profits made. It is seen as essential that throughout the life-cycle, each model, in each market where it is sold, should yield a margin of profit over the costs incurred in bringing it to the market. With this as the primary goal, a number of subsidiary policies follow:
>
> 1   Products should be up-rated or withdrawn whenever the accounting system shows they are unprofitable. Unfortunately, the accounting system will be based on existing methods of production and channels of distribution, not on cost levels that could be achieved under new systems and with different volumes.
> 2   Prices are set at levels necessary to achieve profitability and will be raised higher if possible.
> 3   The cost of an effective marketing system is only acceptable in markets where the British are already established and hence profitable. New markets will only be opened up to the extent that their development will not mean significant front end expense investment in establishing sales and distribution systems ahead of sales.
> 4   Plans and objectives are primarily orientated towards earning a profit on this existing business and facilities of the company, rather than on the development of a long-term position of strength in the industry.

These are the policies that led to the British industry's low and falling share of world markets, to its progressive concentration on higher and higher displacement models. What is more, profitability, the central short-term objective to which these policies have been directed, has in fact deteriorated in the longer term to levels that now call into question the whole viability of the industry.

We now know, of course, that the British motorcycle industry is, to all intents and purposes, dead, and the above viewpoint of the Boston Consulting Group about pricing and profits must be seriously considered at least as a contributing factor. This view is echoed in the National Westminster Bank *Quarterly Review*, which stated:

> The disastrous commercial performance of the British motorcycle industry has resulted from failure to understand the strategic implications of the relationship between manufacturing volumes and the relative cost position.

In contrast, the typical Japanese company makes dedicated efforts to increase its market share, and will often achieve this by cutting its prices, despite the possible short-term penalties of doing so. In other words, there has tended to be a recognition of the pay-off in the longer term from the sacrifice of short-term profitability.

However, there remain some serious doubts even about this point of view. It is a well-known fact that manufacturers and retailers alike have begun to question the value of price cuts, especially when, against a background of falling profitability, research shows that the average shopper, far from having a precise knowledge of prices, has only a general understanding of and feeling towards value and price.

The idea of a price cut, of course, is to increase the quantity sold, as shown in Figure 9.1. The aim is for area B ($p_2 \times q_2$) to be bigger than area A ($p_1 \times q_1$). Additionally, increased volume should lead in theory to cost reductions through the experience effect (explained in Chapter 5). However, what often happens is that market sales do *not* increase enough to balance revenue and costs, with the result that profitability declines. The result is shown in Figure 9.2, area B being less than area A. It is expressed in another way in Figure 9.3.

Figure 9.1

Figure 9.2

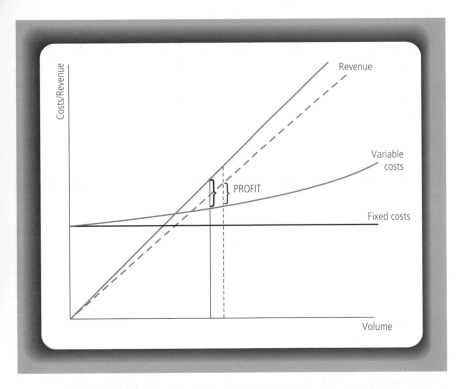

Figure 9.3

This brings into focus the question of *time*, for the shape of demand curves changes over time, depending on a number of factors. There can be little merit in accepting profit reductions in the *long* as well as the *short* term.

It is appropriate, then, to begin to introduce those factors that should be taken into account when trying to resolve the question raised earlier of whether the objective for pricing should be to increase profitability or to increase market share. These factors are:

● Objectives (corporate and marketing) and the product portfolio
● The product life-cycle
● The product's position in the market
● Competitors
● Potential competitors
● Costs (own and competitors')
● Channels of distribution.

■ Objectives and the product portfolio

Unfortunately, many arguments within firms about pricing take place in the sort of vacuum that is created when no one has bothered to specify the *objectives* to which pricing is supposed to be contributing.

We know now that it is important that a company should have a well-defined hierarchy of objectives to which all its activities and actions, including pricing, can be related. For example, corporate objectives may well dictate that the generation of short-term profits is a requirement. (This may well be due to a particular business unit's position in a matrix *vis-à-vis* other units in the same corporation. For example, a group decision may have been taken to invest heavily in one business unit's growth and to fund this growth from one of their 'cash cow' units elsewhere in their portfolio.)

The point is that in reality *corporate* objectives will have an important influence on *marketing* objectives, which were discussed in detail in Chapter 6. In the same way, a company's marketing objectives for a particular product may dictate a short-term emphasis on profitability rather than market share, and this will obviously influence the pricing strategy. This will be a function of that product's position *vis-à-vis* other products in the portfolio. For example, it may well be that a product is one of many 'question marks', and the company has chosen others, rather than this particular one, to invest in. This would naturally result in a wish to make the biggest possible contribution to profits from the product, and the pricing strategy would seek to achieve this.

> The setting of marketing objectives for any particular product, then, is without doubt the starting point in any consideration of pricing.

■ Product life-cycle

The importance of the product life-cycle in determining marketing objectives has already been stressed. For example, for a product estimated to be in the maturity stage of a life-cycle, with only a short time to run, it would probably be unwise to set market-share growth as a marketing objective. Profit contribution would probably be a more appropriate goal, providing of course market share did not slip to a point below which it would jeopardize the company's ability to introduce a new or replacement product.

It will be remembered that when the market reaches saturation level, we could well have a very profitable 'cash cow' on our hands for many years to come.

| The role of pricing will change over a product's life-cycle.

It is also important to stress that the role of pricing will change over a product's life-cycle. For example, during the high-growth phase in the product life-cycle, price tends not to be the customer's primary consideration, since demand is growing at such a rapid rate and it is still relatively 'new'. Here there are plenty of profit opportunities, which have to be carefully balanced against market share considerations.

It is important, then, not to write one's pricing policy on 'tablets of stone'.

> On the other hand, if there is estimated to be plenty of life left in the product, it can often make a lot of sense to reduce the price in order to maintain market share.

MARKETING INSIGHT   There was a period when the policy of Woolworths of Australia was to enter a market later in the product's life-cycle, to price very low, and to promote heavily. However, life-cycle analysis indicated to the company that it unwittingly bought some products early in the life-cycle, *to which they applied exactly the same pricing strategy*. They quickly realized that they were giving profits away unnecessarily and from then on began to be more thoughtful about pricing, devising pricing policies that were appropriate to the product's progress through the life-cycle.

■ Product positioning

The meaning of the term 'product positioning' was explained in Chapter 4. For pricing, it is a highly relevant concept.

> It is clearly foolish, for example, to position a product as a high-quality, exclusive item, and then to price it too low.

Price is one of the clearest signals customers have of the value of the offer that a company is making them, and there has to be a sensible relationship between the two.

Three simple examples will suffice to illustrate this point.

One company launched a new pure juice product on the market after tests had indicated an overwhelming acceptance by consumers. When sales fell far short of expectations, research indicated that consumers simply did not believe that the claims on the can about the product could be true at such a low price. So the company doubled the price and re-launched it, and it was a resounding success.

MARKETING INSIGHT

Jaguar launched a luxury car in the 1960s and priced it on their standard cost-plus basis. Customers were buying the car and re-selling it immediately at a much inflated price. In other words, the *value* of the car to the customer was much greater than the actual price charged.

MARKETING INSIGHT

Likewise, some tertiary educational establishments claim their courses are the best in the world, then charge lower prices than their competitors. Research indicates that for directors and very senior managers in industry a low price is more likely to be counter-productive, because in this particular product field it is considered to be an indicator of quality.

MARKETING INSIGHT

Product positioning, then, is another major consideration in the pricing decision.

■ Competition and potential competition

In spite of product positioning, most products have competitors, and it goes without saying that these must be carefully considered.

It is true, of course, that what are referred to derisively as 'pimply little me-too products' cannot in most circumstances be expected to succeed if they are priced higher than competitive products. It is also true, in such circumstances, that if price is a principal determinant of demand, being higher priced is unlikely to be the right strategy.

This brings into sharp focus again the whole question of product positioning and market segmentation. It will be clear that, wherever possible, a company should be seeking to blend the ingredients of the marketing mix in such a way that their 'offer' to the customer cannot be compared directly with anyone else's 'offer' – for, if two offers *can* be directly compared, it is obvious that the one with the lower price will win most of the time.

Nonetheless, competitive products, in all their forms, clearly have to be taken into account in the pricing decision, as indeed do *potential* competitors.

Some firms launch new products at high prices to recover their investment costs, only to find that they have provided a price 'umbrella' to entice competitors, who then launch similar products at much lower prices, thus moving down the experience curve more quickly, often taking the originating company's market away from it in the process. A lower launch price, with possibly a quicker rate of diffusion and hence a greater rate of experience, may make it more difficult for a potential competitor to enter the market profitably.

> If two products are the same, it is obvious that the one with the lowest price will win most of the time.

■ Costs

Another key factor for consideration is costs – not just our own costs, but those of our competitors as well. There are many cost concepts, and this is not the right medium to go into any detail. However, the two most common cost concepts are *marginal costing* and *full absorption costing*.

The conventional profit-maximizing model of economists tends to indicate that a price should be set at the point where marginal cost equals marginal revenue – i.e. where the additional cost of producing and marketing an additional unit is equivalent to the additional revenue earned from its sale. The theory is indisputable, but in practice this procedure is difficult, if not impossible, to apply. This is largely because the economists' model assumes that price is the only determinant of demand, whereas in reality this is rarely the case.

In practice, the costs of manufacturing (or provision of a service) provide the basis for most pricing decisions – i.e. a 'cost-plus' method. However, as the example given earlier indicates, the trouble with most such 'cost-orientated' pricing approaches is that they make little attempt to reconcile what the customer is prepared to pay with what it costs the company to be in business and make a fair return on its investment of resources.

An example of the 'cost-orientated' approach is when a company targets for a certain return on costs – i.e. the company will set itself a target level of profits at a certain projected level of sales volume. In fact, this type of approach uses a simple form of 'break-even' analysis as depicted in Figure 9.4.

In Figure 9.4, fixed costs are shown as a straight line and all other costs are allocated on a cost-per-unit basis to produce an ascending curve. At point A, revenue covers only fixed costs. At point B, all costs are covered and any additional sales will produce net profit. At point X, Y per cent target profit is being achieved. Obviously, the major problem with such an approach to pricing is that it tends to assume that at a given price a given number of products will be sold, whereas, in reality, the quantity sold is bound to be dependent to a certain extent on the price charged. Also, this model assumes a break-even *point*, whereas in most companies the best that can be said is that there is a break-even *area* at a given level of production. It is, however, quite useful for helping us to understand the relationship between different kinds of costs.

By far the most common way of setting price is to use the cost-plus approach, arriving at a price which yields margins commensurate with declared profit objectives.

When making a pricing decision it is wise to consider a number of different costing options, for any one can be misleading on its own, particularly those that

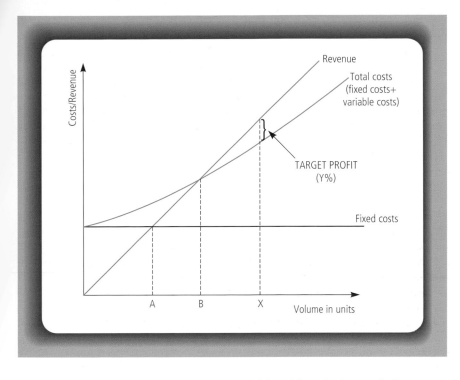

Figure 9.4

allocate fixed costs to all products in the portfolio. Often the basis of allocation is debatable, and an unthinking marketer may well accept the costs as given and easily make the wrong pricing decision.

For example, in difficult economic times, when cost savings are sought, unprofitable products are eliminated from the range. Unprofitable products are identified by the gross or net margins in the last complete trading year, and also by estimates of these margins against estimated future sales. However, because conventional cost accounting allocates the highest costs to high-volume products, they show lower margins, so sometimes these are sacrificed. But product elimination often saves only small amounts of direct costs, so the remaining products have to absorb higher costs, and the next profitability crisis appears. Product elimination also reduces the scale of operations, as well as reducing the product mix, so there is less incentive to invest and the company is less competitive. This approach may be repeated several times under successive management teams, and sometimes leads to the demise of the company.

> In 1989 Andrew Lorenz, writing in the *Financial Times*, used the expression *'anorexia industrialosa'* for this process, which describes an excessive desire to be leaner and fitter, leading to total emaciation and eventually death!

This is not intended to be an attack on any kind of total average costing method. Our intention here is merely to advise caution and a broader perspective when using any kind of costing system as a basis for pricing decisions.

Finally, some account has to be taken of our competitors' costs and an effort made to try to understand the basis of their pricing policies. For, clearly, everything that has been said so far about pricing applies as much to them as it does to us.

Whatever your pricing problem, however, you will never go far wrong if you sit alongside your accountant and discuss all these issues.

■ Channels of distribution

Conventional pricing theory does not help much in determining one's policy towards distributor margins. The intermediaries which constitute a particular marketing channel perform a number of functions on behalf of the supplier which enables the exchange transaction between producer and consumer to be fulfilled. In return for their services, these intermediaries seek to be rewarded; this reward is in effect the 'margin' between the price of the goods *ex* the factory, and the price the consumer pays. However, the total channel margin may have to be shared between several intermediaries and the goods still reach the consumer at a competitive price. Intermediaries, therefore, live or die on the economics of their respective operations. The ideal reward structure in the marketing channel is to ensure that an acceptable rate of return on investment is earned at each level; this situation is often not achieved because of the imbalances of bargaining power present.

There are a number of devices available for rewarding channel intermediaries, most of which take the form of discounts against a nominal price list. These are:

Trade discount	This is discount given against the price list for services made available by the intermediary, e.g. holding inventory, buying in bulk, redistribution, etc.
Quantity discount	A quantity discount is offered to intermediaries who order in large lots
Promotional discount	This is the discount given to distributors to encourage them to share jointly in the promotion of the product(s) involved
Cash discount	In order to encourage prompt payments of accounts, a cash discount of around 2.5 per cent for payment within 10 days is often offered

In the situation where there is a dynamic marketing channel, there will be constant pressure upon suppliers to improve margins. Because of these pressures, the question of margins should be seen at a strategic as well as at a tactical level. This whole area of margin management can be viewed as a series of trade-off type decisions which determine how the total channel margin should be split. The concept of the total channel margin is simple. It is the difference between the level of price at which we wish to position our product in the ultimate marketplace, and the cost of our product at the factory gate. Who takes what proportion of this difference is what margin management is about. The problem is shown in Figure 9.5.

It will be seen that the firm's channel requirements will only be achieved if it either carries them out itself or if it goes some way towards meeting the requirements of an intermediary who can perform those functions on its behalf. The objective of the firm in this respect could therefore be expressed in terms of willingness to trade off margin in order to achieve its marketing goals. Such a trade-off need not lead to a loss of profitability; indeed as Figure 9.6 suggests, the margin is only one element in the determination of profitability, profitability being defined as the rate of return on net worth (net worth being share capital and capital reserves plus retained profits).

Figure 9.5

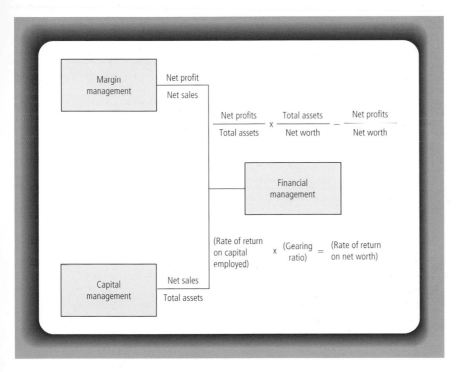

Figure 9.6

It can be seen that by improving the utilization of capital assets (capital management) as well as by using a higher gearing, it is possible to operate successfully on lower margins if this means that marketing goals can be achieved more effectively.

From the foregoing, it becomes apparent that the question of margins (both the margin retained by the firm and thus by implication the margin allowed the distributor) cannot be examined without consideration of the wider implications of overall marketing strategy and the financial policy and capital structure of the firm.

As a general rule, however, a firm should not give away its profits to a distributor. Rather, it should give away only the costs it saves by using an intermediary.

■ Gaining competitive advantage through value-in-use

It is possible to use pricing as a strategic marketing tool to gain a competitive advantage. The 'rules' can be listed as follows:

1 *Reduce the life-cycle/alter the cost mix* – customers are often willing to pay a considerably higher initial price for a product with significantly lower post-purchase costs.
2 *Expand value through functional redesign* – for example:
 ● a product that increases the user's production capacity or throughput
 ● a product that enables the user to improve the quality of reliability of their end product
 ● a product that enhances end-use flexibility
 ● a product that adds functions or permits added applications.
3 *Expand incremental value by developing associated intangibles* – for example, service, financing, 'prestige'.

■ Preparing the pricing plan

We have so far considered some of the main issues relevant to the pricing decision. We can now try to pull all of these issues together. However, let us first recapitulate on one of the basic findings which underpin the work of the Boston Consulting Group.

It will be recalled that, under certain circumstances, real costs reduce the accumulated experience. Figure 9.7 describes this effect. One of the implications of this is that unless a firm accumulates experience at the same or at a greater rate than the market as a whole, eventually its costs will become uncompetitive. Figure 9.8 illustrates this point.

Figure 9.7

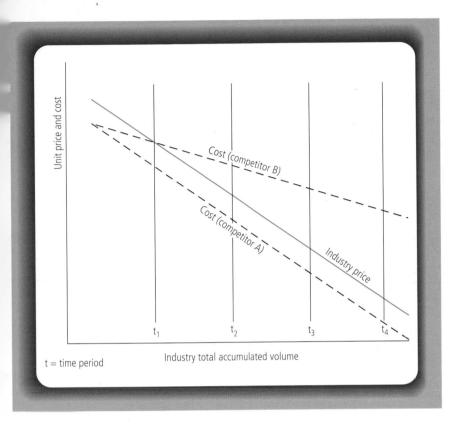

Unit price and cost

Cost (competitor B)

Cost (competitor A)

Industry price

t_1 t_2 t_3 t_4

Industry total accumulated volume

t = time period

Figure 9.8

There is a large range of pricing policies. However, many of these can be simplified into what is referred to either as a *skimming* policy or a *penetration* policy. It is easiest to consider these policies in the context of new product launches.

> Essentially, a skimming policy is a high initial price, moving down the experience curve at a slower rate, while a penetration policy is a low initial price, with a much faster rate of product adoption, and hence a steeper experience curve.

These policies are summarized in Figure 9.9.

The circumstances favouring a skimming policy are as follows:

1 Demand is likely to be price inelastic.
2 There are likely to be different price-market segments, thereby appealing to those buyers first who have a higher range of acceptable prices.
3 Little is known about the costs of producing and marketing the product.

The circumstances favouring a penetration policy are as follows:

1 Demand is likely to be price elastic.
2 Competitors are likely to enter the market quickly.
3 There are no distinct and separate price-market segments.
4 There is the possibility of large savings in production and marketing costs if a large sales volume can be generated (the experience factor).

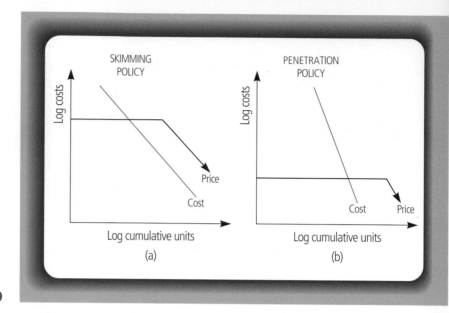

Figure 9.9

However, great caution is necessary whatever the circumstances and, apart from these, all the other factors mentioned above should also be considered.

In conclusion, it must be emphasized that the price charged for the product affects and is affected by the other elements of the marketing mix. It is a common mistake to assume either that the lowest price will get the order, or that we can sell enough of our product at a cost-plus price to give us the required rate of return.

The reality is that pricing policy should be determined after account has been taken of all factors which impinge on the pricing decision. These are summarized in Figure 9.10. The first part shows the discretionary pricing range for a company. The second shows those factors we should take account of in reaching a pricing decision.

■ Application questions

1   When you last introduced a new product or service, how was the price established? Was the pricing decision correct? What additional information could you have used to help you with the pricing decision? What would you do differently given the same circumstances?

2   Describe your pricing strategy for one of your major products. How does it compare with that of your major competitors?

3   Describe how you deal with pricing:
(a) in times of high inflation
(b) at each phase in the product life-cycle.

4   During the past ten years, what trends have occurred in margins in your industry? Are these trends acceptable? What policy has your organization got towards these trends?

5   Are trade margins justified? What is your policy towards trade margins?

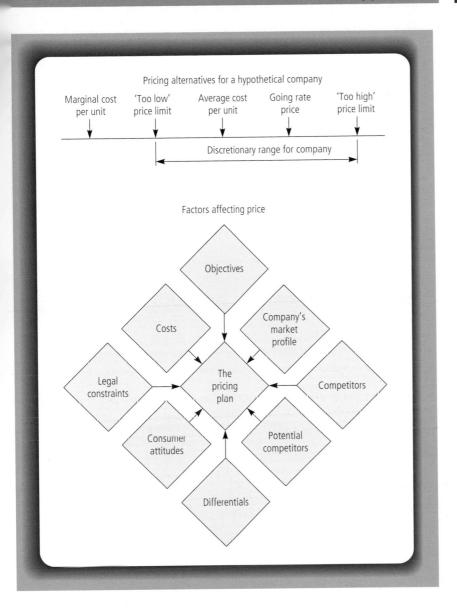

Pricing alternatives for a hypothetical company

| Marginal cost per unit | 'Too low' price limit | Average cost per unit | Going rate price | 'Too high' price limit |

Discretionary range for company

Factors affecting price

Objectives

Costs

Company's market profile

Legal constraints

The pricing plan

Competitors

Consumer attitudes

Potential competitors

Differentials

Figure 9.10

EXERCISES

Clearly, pricing is a marketing 'tool' just as much as advertising, promotions and the use of the sales force. Moreover, it is generally easier and quicker to change a price than it is to alter an advertising campaign, revamp a sales promotion, or deploy the sales force in a different manner.

Pricing decisions not only affect the revenue the company can earn but also influence demand, thereby making an impact on the quantities sold. Yet for all this, few companies have a pricing plan. Indeed, rather than a positive strategy, the very topic often becomes a battleground in a war of apparently conflicting interests between marketers and accountants.

Introduction to Chapter 9 exercises

Exercise 9.1 looks at how to set a competitive price for a product or service taking into account a number of different factors which can have a bearing on the pricing decision.

Exercise 9.2 is concerned with selecting the price.

Exercise 9.3 provides some insights into the real impact of price discounts.

Exercise 9.4 is a self-scoring questionnaire which gives you some assessment about your readiness to get involved in aggressive pricing situations.

Exercise 9.5 poses a number of awkward questions about pricing and gives you an opportunity of testing out your expertise.

Exercise 9.1
Competitive pricing

This exercise will enable you to use pricing in a creative way – one that will support your marketing plan. It will use information from your marketing audit and a few new pieces of data to help you to arrive at a sensible pricing plan for your products or services.

It goes without saying that unless the company has an accurate costing system, one that realistically reflects its internal situation, then it will be impossible to establish anything like a sensible pricing policy. The reason for this will become self-evident as you provide the information requested below.

Figure 9.11 shows some key positions on the costing/pricing continuum. Taking just *one* of your company's major products or services, enter on the worksheet the actual figures that correspond to the numbers 1–5, in the positions marked in Figure 9.11 (i.e. the actual marginal cost, bottom end price limit, etc.).

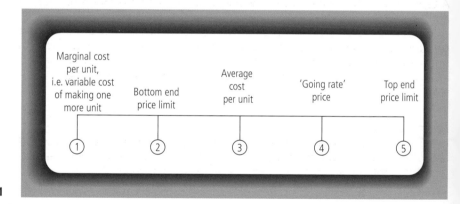

Figure 9.11

When considering the average cost, please remember that costing systems that allocate fixed costs to all products in the range, while being popular, can produce some very misleading results, especially if the basis of cost allocation is somewhat arbitrary. Some products can never survive the cost load they have to carry. Knowing what the customer is prepared to pay for your chosen product/service (the going rate price), consider different costing options, with the objective of getting the average cost per unit as low as possible, thereby providing you with a wider range of pricing options.

Consider other products and services and repeat this process for them. The worksheet is useful in order to establish the range of discretion open to you, but the more important task will be to identify where exactly on this scale to select your price position.

Worksheet Cost price continuum (Exercise 9.1)

PRODUCT/SERVICE	1 Marginal cost per unit	2 Bottom end price limit per unit	3 Average cost per unit	4 Going rate price per unit	5 Top end price limit per unit
Example	£6.50	£8.50	£10	£13	£20

It can be shown that there are a number of factors that can influence your ultimate choice of price. These will be considered in turn.

Exercise 9.2
Selecting the price

Corporate objectives
If the corporate objectives dictate that it will be important to generate short-term profits for your chosen product/service, it would be reasonable to select a high price, somewhere between 4 and 5 on the scale established in Figure 9.11. Alternatively, if the aim is to extend market share, then a position between 3 and 4 would be more suitable.

You can see from this example that whatever the nature of the corporate or marketing objectives for your chosen product or service, it is possible to select a position somewhere on the scale which appears to be most appropriate. Select a position for your chosen product and record the price on the worksheet where indicated.

Portfolio matrix
It has been shown that a different marketing strategy would be required according to which quadrant 'housed' your chosen product. Generally speaking, this would mean that prices should be selected as follows:

1 *'Question mark'* – price competitively to get market share
2 *'Star'* – price to maintain/increase market share
3 *'Cash cow'* – stabilize or even raise price
4 *'Dog'* – raise price.

With these guidelines in mind, select a position on the 1–5 scale for your product/service, and again record the price on the worksheet.

Life-cycle
Your chosen product's position on its life-cycle will also be significant when calculating its price:

1 Introduction stage – either price low to capture market share or, if there is genuine novelty or innovation associated with the product, price high in recognition of its prestige value.

2 Growth stage – price low to get market share.
3 Maturity – as for growth stage.
4 Saturation – stabilize price, consider raising it.
5 Decline – raise price.

Using these suggestions, select a position for your chosen product on the 1–5 scale and, again, note the price on the worksheet.

Product position

Your price will have to take into account the marketing profile you are trying to establish for your chosen product. If yours is the biggest, the best, the most technologically advanced product, then your price ought to echo the fact. Similarly, if your target is just high-income customers, your price should reflect that exclusivity. The converse will be true for down-market economy models, where a lower price would be more consistent with the product position.

Carefully consider your product position and use your judgement to 'score' a position on the 1–5 scale. Record your choice of price on the worksheet.

Current competition

Analyse the prices charged by your competitors for their versions of your product or service. Will these influence your ultimate choice of price?

Where does this information suggest you position the price on the 1–5 scale? Enter your answer on the worksheet.

Potential competition

Another consideration you will have to take into account will be the extent to which your chosen price might either attract or repel competitors. Clearly, if you can get away with charging high prices and making correspondingly high margins, then it will not be long before others become interested in your sphere of business.

Estimate the price you can charge, using the 1–5 scale as a reference. Note the selected price on the worksheet.

Channels of distribution

If your business is one where you need to use intermediaries to reach your customers, then, in return for their services, they will expect a reward in the shape of a 'mark-up' or margin on the goods. Thus the price you charge at the factory gate has to be profitable for you, yet still allow the intermediary a fair margin without leading to an excessively high price for the ultimate consumer. What will this mean for your pricing decision?

Choose a position on the 1–5 scale and enter the price on the worksheet.

Differential benefits

If your product or service provides differential customer benefits which your competitors do not provide, then you could justify a higher price and gain the reward from higher revenue.

Your option for doing this might be limited by some of the other considerations above. For example, it might be better to use your product advantage to gain a larger market share. Nevertheless, if the benefit analysis you carried

Worksheet Factors affecting price (Exercise 9.2)

	Example (based on example on preceding worksheet)	Prod. 1	Prod. 2	Prod. 3	Prod. 4
1 Corporate objectives	£18.00				
2 Portfolio matrix	£16.00				
3 Life-cycle analysis	£16.00				
4 Product position	£10.00				
5 Current competition	£12.00				
6 Potential competition	£10.00				
7 Channels of distribution	Not applic.				
8 Differential benefits	£9.00				
9 Consumer attitudes	£9.00				
Total score	£100.00				
Number of factors	8				
Suggested price average	£12.50				

out in Chapter 4 suggests any room for manoeuvre on pricing, score the new choice on the 1–5 scale and enter the actual figure on the worksheet.

Consumer attitudes
Consumer attitudes to your particular product/service or to your company, because of its name and reputation, might also influence your ultimate choice of price. To what extent will this be the case? Again, select a price position on the 1–5 scale that you believe can be justified as a result of consumer attitudes to your product.

Record the price on the worksheet.
You have now looked at nine different factors that are known to influence pricing. These have been considered in isolation and a notional price position for your product has been calculated against each factor.
The price positions were established by using a cost/price continuum, with key positions numbered 1–5. The actual money value of each of these positions was calculated in the worksheet of Exercise 9.1.
The worksheet in this exercise is a record of the results you have attributed to the various pricing factors. You will now use this information in the following way:

1 Find the average price position for your product by adding up the column of prices and dividing it by the number of factors you used (an example is shown on the worksheet). This average figure would seem to be the 'best fit' when taking all the factors into account, and should therefore be selected as the price for your chosen product, unless, of course, there are other factors known to you which would militate against this decision.
2 Now repeat this process for other products or services.

Critique of example provided on worksheets

This approach to pricing raises many important issues. In the example provided it is quite evident that the corporate objectives are for the product to generate revenue. The positions on the portfolio matrix and life-cycle also appear to support this strategy of pricing high.

But look at some of the other factors. The product position would not appear to justify a high price, as there seem to be few differential benefits and consumer attitudes are not very positive. In addition it looks as if the company will have to price below the 'going rate' if it is going to cope with the competition.

Result A compromise price of £12.50 per unit

Moral If the company wants to price high, it must upgrade the product in terms of providing more differential benefits and work to improve customer attitudes

Alternatively, or in addition, it should carefully re-examine the actual costs and its costing system and by doing so try to improve the margin that would be achievable at £12.50. By these means, it might well obtain results similar to its original objectives of pricing high.

Personal notes

Exercise 9.3

The use of discounts

To give a price reduction, which is really what a discount is, appears on the surface to be a fairly straightforward and easy-to-apply mechanism for stimulating demand. However, it is not always fully appreciated how many extra products have to be sold merely to break even – i.e. to get back to the original situation.

Here is a simple example. Suppose a company had sales of 100 units of a product per week, priced at £10. Thus the total income was £1,000 and this yielded a profit of £200. The marketing director of the company decides that a 10 per cent reduction in price will stimulate a demand in sales. What new level of sales in units would have to be achieved to break even?

Write your answer here_____

Probably this was how you calculated your figure:

	Units	Price	Total income	Profit
Original situation	100	£10	£1,000	£200

Since 100 units yielded £200 profit, profit per unit = £2. With price reduced to £9 (10 per cent reduction), new profit per unit = £1.
Therefore new situation becomes:

	Units	Price	Total income	Profit
New situation	200	£9	£1,800	£200

Thus the company would have to double its sale of units to maintain its existing profit level if it sold at the new lower price. Perhaps some questions would have to be asked about the feasibility of this happening.

To avoid having to make tedious calculations each time you contemplate making a price reduction, Table 9.1 provides an easy-to-use reference.

Table 9.1 Effects of price reductions

| If you cut your price | And your present gross profit is | | | | | | | |
| | 5% | 10% | 15% | 20% | 25% | 30% | 35% | 40% |
	You need to sell this much more to break even							
	%	%	%	%	%	%	%	%
1%	25.0	11.1	7.1	5.3	4.2	3.4	2.9	2.6
2%	66.6	25.0	15.4	11.1	8.7	7.1	6.1	5.3
3%	150.0	42.0	25.0	17.6	13.6	11.1	9.4	8.1
4%	400.0	66.6	36.4	25.0	19.0	15.4	12.9	11.1
5%	–	100.0	50.0	33.3	25.0	20.0	16.7	14.3
6%	–	150.0	66.7	42.9	31.6	25.0	20.7	17.6
7%	–	233.3	87.5	53.8	38.9	30.4	25.0	21.2
8%	–	400.0	114.3	66.7	47.1	36.4	29.6	25.0
9%	–	1,000.0	150.0	81.8	56.3	42.9	34.6	29.0
10%	–	–	200.0	100.0	66.7	50.0	40.0	33.3
11%	–	–	275.0	122.2	78.6	57.9	45.8	37.9
12%	–	–	400.0	150.0	92.3	66.7	52.2	42.9
13%	–	–	650.0	185.7	108.3	76.5	59.1	48.1
14%	–	–	1,400.0	233.3	127.3	87.5	66.7	53.8
15%	–	–	–	300.0	150.0	100.0	76.8	60.0
16%	–	–	–	400.0	177.8	114.3	84.2	66.7
17%	–	–	–	566.7	212.5	100.8	94.4	73.9
18%	–	–	–	900.0	257.1	150.0	105.9	81.8
19%	–	–	–	1,900.0	316.7	172.7	118.8	90.5
20%	–	–	–	–	400.0	200.0	133.3	100.0
21%	–	–	–	–	525.0	233.3	150.0	110.5
22%	–	–	–	–	733.3	275.0	169.2	122.2
23%	–	–	–	–	1,115.0	328.6	191.7	135.3
24%	–	–	–	–	2,400.0	400.0	218.2	150.0
25%	–	–	–	–	–	500.0	250.0	166.7

Example: Your present gross margin is 25 per cent and you cut your selling price by 10 per cent. Locate 10 per cent in the left-hand column. Now follow across to the column headed 25 per cent. You find you will need to sell 66.7 per cent *more* units.

This exercise[1] is really designed for personal insight, but you won't fail to notice that you could use it equally well to analyse your marketing director or chief executive.

Exercise 9.4
Questionnaire

[1]Exercises 9.4 and 9.5 are based on John Winkler's work on pricing and I am indebted to him for the ideas. Readers are recommended to follow this up by reading J. Winkler (1985) *Pricing for Results*, Butterworth-Heinemann, Oxford).

Consider these statements and *quickly* tick the score which most aptly represents your position.

	Very true of me	Usually true of me	No feeling either way	Usually untrue of me	Very untrue of me
1 If a rival company is cheaper, I want to match or beat its price	5	4	3	2	1
2 I would like to talk to competitors about equalizing prices	1	2	3	4	5
3 I'm prepared to start a discount battle any time; I believe the first one in wins	5	4	3	2	1
4 Before quoting a special price I will always ask 'Why?'	1	2	3	4	5
5 I'm prepared to lose some deals on price	1	2	3	4	5
6 I always try to keep it simple if I can! '10 per cent off' is the way to do it	5	4	3	2	1
7 I try not to publish discounts. I prefer to negotiate them individually	1	2	3	4	5
8 I am always prepared to offer bigger discounts than I allow those working for me to offer	5	4	3	2	1
9 I believe that most people will jump at a 10 per cent discount	5	4	3	2	1
10 I believe that people who start savage price wars often live to regret it	1	2	3	4	5

Now add up the total score for all your ticks and write it here _____

Scoring and interpretation of Exercise 9.4

The questions are not very subtle, and so very good scores are required from this exercise. The lowest score for each question is the best, but an extremely low score, *of 12 or less*, might show you to be rather inflexible. You might well be used to working in an industry where the quality content of what you offer is very high, with prices that reflect this. In these circumstances you would tend to avoid price fights as much as you can.

A *score of 13–16* is a good score – you will hold on and make sensible, profitable deals most of the time. Although you might lose out here and there on high volume, you would rather make the largest profits than the largest sales.

Above 25 – you are a potential warmonger, probably used to working at the bottom end of some very tough markets, with some rapacious buyers. There's one other thing, and you might not like to hear this. These buyers are probably taking you to the cleaners.

Here are some hypothetical questions concerning pricing. How would you deal with these situations?

Question 1
You are the Marketing Director of a pharmaceuticals company in a country where there is no equivalent of a National Health Service, and patients have to pay for the drugs they use. Your company produces a life-support drug. Once patients have been treated with it, they must stay on it continuously to survive. This drug has been outdated by a machine which treats new patients and, as a result, your market is gradually eroding. Should you adopt:

(a) A system based on cost-plus?
(b) A system based on what the market will bear?
(c) A system based on some notion of morality?
(d) A system based on what the competition charges?

Question 2
You have an excess of stock of a poor line to clear. You must shift this stock in order to raise money to invest in better products. What is your view of promotional pricing? Do you:

(a) Actively encourage it all the time?
(b) Offer it only to your best customers?
(c) Refuse to use it at all?
(d) Use it sparingly, outside normal markets?
(e) Use it a little, but create an impression that you use it a lot, through advertising, etc.?

Question 3
You want to price aggressively in order to take over a major part of a total market. What level of price discount should you offer in a normal consumer product market, as a minimum, to make the market turn to you in a meaningful way?

(a) 10 per cent off competitors' prices
(b) 15 per cent off competitors' prices
(c) 20 per cent off competitors' prices
(d) 30 per cent off competitors' prices
(e) Between 40 and 50 per cent off competitors' prices.

Question 4
If you average out all the prices of consumer products in a given market, you can arrive at an average price. Yours is the biggest selling brand in this market. Together with your two nearest competitors you share 60 per cent of the market. Measured against the average market price, where would you expect your brand leader product to be positioned?

(a) 10 per cent less than the average price
(b) On, or closely around, the average price
(c) 20 per cent less than the average price
(d) 7 per cent above the average price.

Answers to Exercise 9.5
Question 1
(a) Score +1.
(b) Score −5. They will pay anything to stay alive, but how can you live with yourself?
(c) Score +5.
(d) Score +1.

Question 2
(a) Score 0.
(b) Score +1. A poor tactic because it will make your best customers look for bargains all the time. It might generate some goodwill.
(c) Score +1. Too rigid.
(d) Score +5. Get rid of it altogether if you can, otherwise go for (e).
(e) Score +4. A technique used by some supermarkets. A few loss leaders in reality, but all of them promoted very heavily. But you will still be attracting price cutting in your market, and you will have to advertise your price cuts as well as give the discounts away. This can be expensive unless the volume sales justify it.

Question 3
(a) Score 0.
(b) Score +1.
(c) Score +2.
(d) Score +3.
(e) Score +4.

Question 4
(a) Score 0.
(b) Score +2.
(c) Score −2.
(d) Score +5.

Interpretation of scores
15 or more	You did very well and/or are very experienced
10–14	Think a bit harder before making decisions
Less than 10	Don't engage in pricing decision-making

APPENDIX D: CHAPTER 10

The distribution plan and customer service plan

Introduction

Some readers perceive distribution as outside the scope of marketing.

These readers would, in common with many businesses, tend to think only of physical distribution, or the transportation of goods, rather than of what distribution is really about. In this chapter, we show why distribution is very much the concern of marketers, and what should go into a distribution plan.

The topic of product distribution involves three main decision areas, each of which will be examined in turn:

1. How is the physical movement of our product organized?
2. Through what marketing channels do we reach our customers (or what channels do our customers utilize to acquire our products)?
3. What level of availability of our product do our customers require (and how well do we meet this requirement)?

Physical distribution

The physical distribution function of a firm provides the place and time dimensions which constitute the third element of the marketing mix. This is depicted in Figure 10.1, which also shows its relationship to the other utility-producing elements. The figures on the diagram are illustrative only, although they are realistic for some industries.

If a product is not available when and where the customer wants it, it will surely fail in the market.

Figure 10.1

> If a product is not available when and where the customer wants it, it will surely fail in the market.

To achieve this value-adding function, firms generally have a distributive activit within the corporate organizational structure known variously as physical distr bution management (PDM), traffic management, marketing logistics, or, simply logistics. Today, it is frequently called 'supply chain management'. A generalize model of the entire corporate entity is given in Figure 10.2; this also depicts th position of (finished) product ▶ **distribution** *vis-à-vis* marketing, production, th procurement system, and the financial/accounting systems.

▶ **DEFINITION** ◀

Distribution is the movement of all materials, both prior to production and after production. The term 'logistics' is also used in the same way

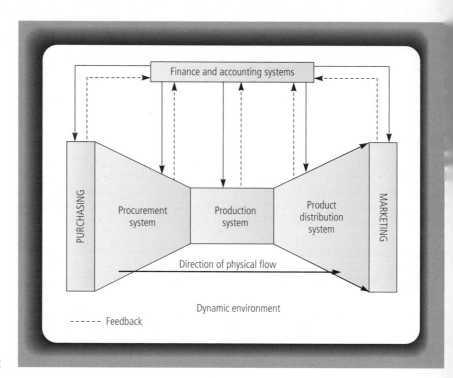

Figure 10.2

The movement of all materials, both prior to production (raw materials, subassemblies, etc.) and after production (finished product), constitutes the total logistics flow of the firm. In this chapter, however, we shall confine our attention to the latter, i.e. finished product distribution.

The distribution mix

In a typical manufacturing company with a formal distribution structure, the responsibility for distribution-related matters is spread across the other functional departments. For example, production may control warehousing and transportation; marketing may control the channels through which the product moves, the levels of service provided to the customer, and communications; and the finance department may control inventory obsolescence, data processing, and inventory costs.

> Such a compartmentalized arrangement leads to each department working to its own objectives, attempting to optimize its own particular activity, oblivious of others or of the good of the whole company.

Introducing a more formalized distribution arrangement into the corporate organizational structure, although not completely eliminating interdepartmental friction, does at least ensure that all distribution-related activities are organized under a more centralized control, thereby gaining focus.

This, then, is the basis of the total distribution concept, because it now becomes possible to seek out potential 'trade-offs', i.e. consciously to incur costs in one area in order to achieve an even larger benefit in another. For example, should a series of field warehouses be maintained, or would one suffice, supplemented by an improved trucking operation? Of course, these types of potential 'trade-off' situations place a heavy burden on the cost-reporting systems of a company.

The professional distribution manager, therefore, has several variables to contend with in the search for trade-offs; taken together these constitute the *distribution mix*. Each of these will now be examined briefly.

Facilities

Decisions in this area are concerned with the problem of how many warehouses and plants should be established and where they should be located. Obviously, for the majority of companies it is necessary to take the location of existing plants and warehouses as given in the short term, but the question does arise in the longer term or, indeed, when new plants or warehouses are being considered.

> The principal marketing task here is to forecast the nature, size and geographical spread of demand.

Increasing the number of field locations will result in an increase in trucking costs and a reduction in retail distribution costs. So, another marketing task is to determine the customer service levels that are likely to be required in order to be able to make a decision about this particular trade-off.

Inventory

A major element in any company's total distribution costs is the cost of holding stock, which is often as high as 30 per cent of its value per annum. This is because of items such as interest charges, deterioration, shrinkage, insurance, administration, and so on. Thus, decisions about how much inventory to hold, where to hold it, in what quantities to order, and so on, are vital issues. Inventory levels are also instrumental in determining the level of service that the company offers the customer.

Transport

The important aspects of the transport decision concern such issues as what mode of transport should be used, whether to own vehicles or lease them, how to schedule deliveries, how often to deliver, and so on. Perhaps of the five distribution variables it is transport that receives the greatest attention within the firm. It is certainly one of the more obvious facets of the distribution task.

Communications

It must always be remembered that distribution not only involves the flow of materials through the distribution channel, but also the flow of information. Here, we are talking about the order processing system, the invoicing system, the demand forecasting system, and so on. Without effective communications support, the distribution system will never be capable of providing satisfactory customer service at an acceptable cost. It is vital that it should be recognized that inefficiency here can lead to a build-up of costs in other areas of the business, such as, for example in emergency deliveries, as well as a permanent loss of sales through customers turning to alternative sources of supply.

Unitization

The way in which goods are packaged and then subsequently accumulated into larger unit sizes (e.g. a pallet-load) can have a major bearing upon distribution economics. For example, the ability to stack goods on a pallet which then becomes the unit load for movement and storage can lead to considerable cost saving in terms of handling and warehousing. Similarly, the use of containers as the basic unit of movement has revolutionized international transport and, to a certain extent, domestic transport as well. Mobile racking systems and front-end pricing by means of scanners are other unitization innovations that have had a dramatic effect upon the way goods are marketed.

Together, these five areas constitute the total cost of distribution within a company.

■ Marketing channels

> The fundamental role of a company's distribution function is to ensure that the 'right product is available at the right time'.

This implies some organization of resources into channels through which the product moves to customers. A marketing channel may therefore be considered as the course taken in the transfer of the title of a commodity (which in turn may be either a product or service) from its original source of supply to its ultimate consumption.

> It is necessary to consider both the route of exchange (and its administrative and financial control) and the physical movement route of the product – they may well be different.

Many companies use multiple marketing channels through which to reach their customers, often involving one or even several 'intermediaries'. The role of an intermediary is to provide the means of achieving the widest possible market coverage at a

ower unit cost. Many intermediaries hold stock and thereby share some of the
inancial risk with the principal (or supplier). Figure 10.3 shows that using an intermediary carries benefits for the manufacturer, but it also involves significant 'costs',
he most important of which is the loss of control which accompanies such a chan-
iel strategy.

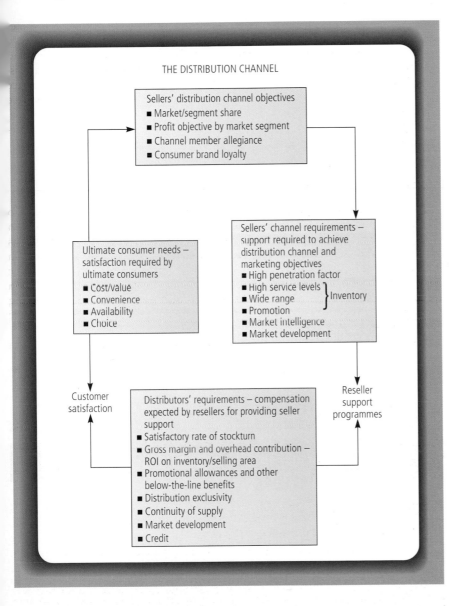

Figure 10.3

Often, too, considerable conflict exists between the respective objectives of suppliers and their distributors; this gives rise to conflict and suspicion in the relationship. Nevertheless, suppliers must evaluate the costs and benefits of each
marketing channel potentially open to them and decide on a combination which
best suits their type of business and the markets they are engaged in. The alternatives depicted in Figure 10.4 quite obviously have different cost/revenue profiles.

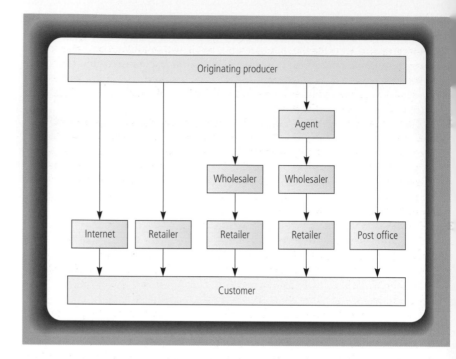

Figure 10.4

Any cost/benefit appraisal needs to be undertaken in the widest context possible. It needs to consider questions of market strategy, the appropriateness of the channel to the product, and customer requirements, as well as the question of the comparative costs of selling and distribution.

Marketing channel decisions are, therefore, key decisions which involve the choice of an intermediary (or intermediaries) and detailed consideration of the physical distribution implications of all the alternatives. The evaluation of intermediaries is, therefore, of significant importance.

■ New channels

It will be recalled that, in Chapter 4, we suggested redrawing the market map to take account of new channels such as the Internet.

There are five main ways in which the market map can be reconfigured:

1 *Substitute/reconfigured products.* An electronic channel may enable the underlying customer need to be satisfied in a different way ('substitute products'). For example, e-mail can substitute for physical post, providing a threat to paper manufacturers, stationers and post offices. Alternatively, customer needs may be bundled into different product configurations ('reconfigured products'). The newspaper, for example, is a bundled product providing job advertisements, weather information, news, consumer-to-consumer advertisements, and so on. It is now competing with Web services which in some cases simply provide one of these components – such as consumer auction sites – or, in others, combine some aspect of the value provided by newspapers with other types of value. For example, a portal such as Yahoo meets some of these needs, such as the day's news, and acts as a gateway to others, such as weather and auction sites, while also satisfying further needs not covered by the newspaper through the ability to search the Web. It can be seen that reconfigured products add complexity to the process, as two market maps from different industries may 'collide' and need to be considered together.

2 *Disintermediation.* As with other IT-enabled channels such as call centres, e-commerce can enable a link to be removed from the market map, by removing intermediaries whose primary function of information transfer can be more effectively performed using the internet. Examples are telephone and Internet banking; direct purchase from clothes manufacturers via websites; and the bypassing of sales agents and distributors by some consumer goods manufacturers who are selling direct to retailers.

3 *Reintermediation.* In some cases, a previous intermediary is replaced by a new online intermediary, rather than bypassed. Online sites which automatically search for the cheapest car insurance are competing with telephone-based brokers, which in turn caused the demise of the AA's high-street shops. General Electric's TPN Register provides an online marketplace between suppliers on the one hand, and GE and its partners on the other.

Predicting what reintermediation will occur is difficult, as the possibilities are numerous. Will a given relationship – say, between CTN (confectioners, tobacconists and newsagents) stores and their suppliers – be a direct one? If so, will the shops buy from a range of suppliers' websites, or will the suppliers respond to tender requests on shop websites? Or will there be a new intermediary acting as a marketplace between the two? As shown in Figure 10.5, possibilities can be placed in an approximate order, from suppliers' websites (such as Japan Airlines, which puts out open invitations to tender to suppliers) at one extreme, to vendors' websites (such as *Harvard Business Review*, which provides an online version at a cost) at the other.

Vendor-controlled	Vendor website	Ernst & Young, HBR
Vendor-oriented	Vendor-run community Consortium distributor Vendor's agent Lead generator Audience broker	Cambridge Information Net Thetrainline Chemdex Auto-by-tel DoubleClick
Neutral	Market maker Shop Mall	EBay, FastParts, priceline RS Components Blackwell's msn.com
Buyer-oriented	Purchaser's agent Purchasing aggregator	Comparenet TPN Register
Buyer-controlled	Buyer website	Japan Airlines

Figure 10.5
Types of intermediaries

Neutral marketplaces are midway between the two. An example is an auction site, which is tied neither to the buyer nor the seller. Somewhat closer to the vendors are intermediaries such as Auto-by-Tel, which passes on leads to a local dealer. A more buyer-oriented intermediary is TPN Register, which we discussed earlier: set up by a consortium of buyers, it acts to ensure that they gain low prices through economies of scale.

Which of these possibilities becomes the dominant trading mechanism in a given relationship depends on the number of vendors and buyers, and the relative power of suppliers and buyers. Where there are few buyers and many suppliers, or buyer power is great, the market will tend towards either individual buyer websites or buyer-oriented intermediaries, such as those being set up by car manufacturers. Conversely, a small number of suppliers selling to large numbers of customers will have the power to control the market through their own websites or through supplier-oriented consortia. Large numbers of both suppliers and buyers will tend to use a neutral marketplace to reduce the search and transaction costs of both parties, though a supplier with a particularly strong brand and/or product differentiation, such as *Harvard Business Review* or the medical journal *The Lancet*, may choose not to participate in such marketplaces.

4 *Partial channel substitution*. This forms a halfway house towards disintermediation. In some cases an intermediary's role may be reduced but not eliminated, through some of their value being provided remotely by the supplier to the intermediary's customer. Websites such as those of car manufacturers may build a brand and provide customer information while pointing customers to traditional outlets for actual purchase.

5 *Media switching/addition*. Finally, the links in the chain may remain the same, but communication between them may be partially or fully switched to the Internet from the previous mechanisms. Examples are Dell's addition of the Internet to its other means of communicating with customers, and RS Components, who have similarly added a Web channel to their dominant telephone sales model, while still selling to the same customers.

Reconfiguring the market map

To reconfigure the market map, therefore, one needs to consider the potential effect of each of these five broad changes in turn. In each case, one needs to:

1 Sketch the effect of the change on the market map.
2 Sketch the resulting effect on the customer's value curve (for each segment).
3 If the effect is positive for some segments, incorporate the transformation in a revised market map.

Whether the effect on the value curve (similar to a customer critical success factor analysis – described below in more detail and with an example provided – is regarded as positive depends on the organization's positioning within the relevant market. In terms of Michael Porter's three generic strategies (low cost, niche or low cost differentiation) this will imply:

● For low-cost strategies, an approximate parity needs to be ensured on non-price criteria, while beating the competition on price.
● For differentiation strategies, excellence needs to be ensured on one or more value-related criteria, while ensuring approximate parity on others.
● For niche strategies, strength needs to be high on criteria important to the target niches.

Table 10.1 contains some additional questions for disintermediation, partial channel substitution and media switching/addition.

Table 10.1 Evaluating potential changes to the market map/value chain

Disintermediation	Does the removal of an intermediary improve physical flows? If so, can information flows or other value-adding services provided by the intermediary be as effectively handled by others in the chain? Can the flow improvements be translated into an enhanced value curve?
Partial channel substitution	Does the addition of an Internet communication channel improve information flows (e.g. cheaper communication with customer)?
Media switching/addition	Within the current structure, can the Internet reduce costs or add value for some communications? Consider the e-marketing mix.

Financial services future market map

An example of a possible reconfigured market map is given for financial services, and this is shown in Figure 10.6.

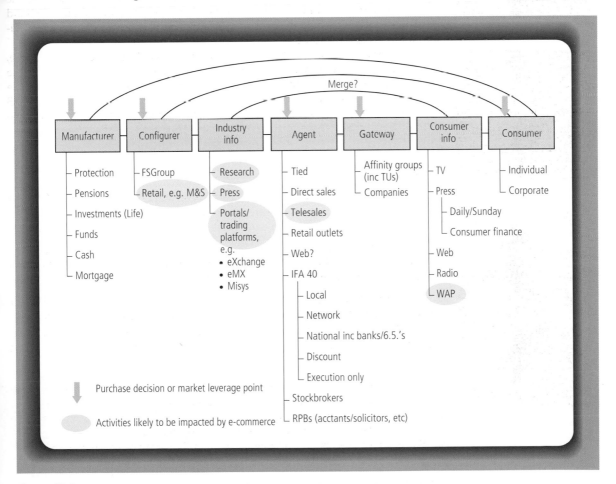

Figure 10.6
Long-term investment: future market

Similar effects of e-commerce can be expected to occur in other markets.

1 *Fund managers go direct.* Fund managers may find that e-commerce makes it easier to sell their products directly to customers. The simplification and transparency of pricing being encouraged throughout the industry should help customers feel more comfortable buying products directly: in fact, they may prefer this route since they will not be swayed by an agent who is receiving a large commission for his advice.

   The ability for fund managers to present clear and easy-to-understand information about their products and their performance online should encourage such direct sales.

2 *The customer becomes the configurer.* Using e-commerce, customers may be able to configure their own investment products from manufacturers. Currently this would be time-consuming, and configurers have a significant amount of regulatory knowledge necessary to undertake this function. However, e-commerce applications that contain this regulatory knowledge as 'rules' would allow customers to undertake this function themselves.

3 *There is a blurring of industry and consumer information.* Currently, information provided to agents and other professional advisers in the market is quite distinct from that provided to consumers. The former is more detailed, and may require specialist knowledge to be understood. However, there are already signs of this blurring happening with insurance exchanges, such as eXchange, eMX and Misys, that have traditionally been wholesale or trade exchanges now providing e-commerce routes to end-consumers.

4 *Affinity groups may become trusted portals.* Consumers in the online world are expected to 'join' communities of interest, such as ThirdAge.com, a community for the over-60s. Such communities may be the route that many choose to buy goods and services online.

5 *There will be a 'dumbing down' of advice.* Currently, many people wishing to buy investment products turn to a well-trained and regulated financial adviser. With e-commerce, a rise of electronic agents offering advice is likely. These will be rule-based algorithms that base product recommendations on the answers to a few simple questions. However, there is a chance that such systems are over-simple and will result in many customers buying the wrong products.

6 *E-commerce could result in great product switching.* The ease of purchasing products via e-commerce, particularly with interactive TV that provides for flow-through sales, may lead to greater impulse buying and hence greater switching when a customer realizes that they have bought an unsuitable product. This is not only unsatisfactory for customers, who stand to lose financially if they withdraw from products aimed at long-term investment, but also for suppliers since they will face a significant administrative burden.

7 *E-commerce may cause cycles in consumers' buying patterns.* In the short-term, many online consumers may be tempted to buy direct from manufacturers. However, after time they may find that they either made the wrong decision, have made a lot of money and now want to protect it, or are suffering from information overload. These factors will cause them to go back to using advisers in their investment decisions.

> A pattern similar to the one described was seen recently in the US, where many consumers transferred to no-load (no upfront fee) funds in which they made a lot of money. They then needed advice on how to ensure these large sums of money were protected.

Another factor resulting in a cyclic approach to financial advice is that of market conditions. Advice is often seen as less important in a rapidly growing bull market, since anyone can invest and make money. However, as markets begin to slow down, consumers will return to sound sources of advice.

8 *Smaller players are more nimble.* Evidence of this in the investment market is already being seen, with small IFAs adopting e-commerce services ahead of larger chains.

9 *E-commerce encourages customers to serve themselves but will not remove face-to-face contact.* By encouraging customers to use online services that require them to register change of address, or bank details or premium amount, customers are effectively undertaking some of the administrative burden of the agent or manufacturer. However, customers that choose to seek advice will still demand face-to-face contact with advisers, particularly for more complex products.

Multi-channel integration

While product innovation continues apace, with the Internet offering many opportunities for providing digitizable products and surrounding services remotely, we believe that the dominant business theme of the next ten years will be innovation in the route to market – the channels by which the customer is communicated with the product delivered. Companies such as Direct Line, First Direct, easyJet, eBay and Amazon all compete by exploiting IT-enabled remote channels to add value, reduce costs, or both.

How organizations should respond to the opportunities and threats of these IT-enabled channels and use them to build profitable customer relationships is the subject of this section. Packages for sales-force automation, direct mail, telemarketing, customer service, e-commerce and marketing analysis have been available for some time, both individually and in combination as integrated customer relationship management suites. But these packages, while providing an essential infrastructure, need to be supplemented by managerial processes to address such questions as which channels to use and how they should work together to deliver customer value.

Our research suggests that companies can select from the following broad channel strategy options:

- A *single-channel provider* provides at least the bulk of the customer interaction through one channel. Direct Line and First Direct both started as primarily telephone operations, while in the Internet world the approach is referred to as 'pure play', represented by Amazon, eBay and so on.
- A *channel migrator* starts with one single channel, but attempts to migrate its customer base onto another channel on the grounds of increased value or reduced cost. EasyJet initially sold tickets by telephone, but now provides financial incentives to its price-sensitive customers to buy online, most of whom now do so.
- An *activity-based strategy* uses different channels in combination to perform different tasks in the customer's life-cycle. Thomas Cook's corporate foreign-exchange business uses the Internet to generate leads, a direct sales force to sign up new clients, and a call centre or the Internet to take orders.
- An *integrated multi-channel* approach involves offering different channels to the customer without attempting to influence which the customer uses. First Direct provides both telephone and Internet banking, as an integrated service. While the Internet has much lower unit costs and also has proved better for cross-selling, First Direct chooses to position itself on customer service and accepts the

higher costs from those customers who primarily use the telephone without penalizing them or rewarding Internet users.

- A *needs-based segmentation strategy* offers different channels to different customer groups to meet their varying needs. Each of these routes to market may use the same brand name, or different names. The insurer Zurich's multiple brands (Allied Dunbar, Zurich, Eagle Star and Threadneedle) have strengths in different routes to market – the direct sales force, independent financial advisers and company pension schemes – in order to serve customer groups with differing needs and attitudes.

- A *graduated customer value strategy* uses channels selectively according to the financial value of the customers. Many IT firms use account managers for high-value customers, and steer smaller customers to lower-cost channels such as the Internet, call centres or value-added resellers. The UK's clearing banks, though, are in danger of doing the precise opposite, offering the high-cost branch network to the lower-value customers who prefer not to bank by phone or Internet.

Which channels will customers choose?

When deciding on a channel strategy, the starting point must be the customers themselves. If we do not offer them the channels they would prefer to use, a competitor will. But with new channels, how can we predict customer take-up in advance? Figure 10.7 shows a simple technique for doing this, which we describe as the 'value curve'.

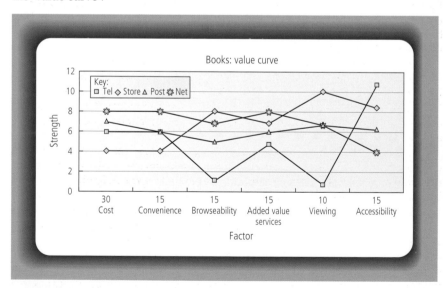

Figure 10.7
Choosing channels – the value curve

The starting-point is to determine the customers' buying factors – the factors that determine which supplier gets their business. These are listed at the bottom of the figure, along with weights out of 100 which represent their relative importance in the buying decision. These factors will vary by customer segment, so the analysis must be done for each one. In the segment illustrated here, the customers are most interested in the cost they pay – the price plus any other charges, such as delivery – but are also concerned with such factors as convenience of purchase and the ability to browse for the book they want.

The ability of each current or future channel to deliver against each factor is then assessed judgementally on a 1–10 basis. In this hypothetical example, the various means by which a book can be purchased are compared. It can be seen that, taking all the factors together, the Internet and physical stores have the best matches to this particular segment. In reality, different segments of the book market are clearly best matched to different channels.

The score of a channel against price-related factors, such as 'cost' in this example, will be affected by the channel economics, which will determine the price which any competitor using the channel chain will be able to offer. One factor in assessing the channel economics is the transaction costs involved. The TPN Register business-to-business exchange set up by General Electric, the first significant e-hub, saves GE 50–90 per cent on processing costs for each order. But acquisition and retention costs should not be forgotten. The dotcom arm of one retail chain recently discovered that customer acquisition through banner advertising was costing £700 per customer, when the average sale was only £50 – good news for this bricks-and-clicks retailer in its competition with pure-play dotcoms, as it could leverage its physical stores for customer acquisition at a cost of just £13 per customer.

How channels work together

This example of physical stores and the Internet working together illustrates a complicating factor. In many markets, customers do not use a single channel. Rather, they use a number of channels in combination to meet their needs at different stages of their relationship with the supplier. To help define how this can best be done, we suggest the use of a tool we term channel-chain analysis, which we illustrate in Figure 10.8.

Channel-chain analysis involves describing which channels are used at which stages of the purchasing and value delivery process. The stages of the process are listed on the left of the diagram, and the channels used to accomplish the stage are listed against each stage. The channel used for one stage will often affect which channel is likely to be used at the next stage, so the relevant boxes are joined with a line.

In this example from the business-to-business PC market, three of the common channel chains being offered by the various competitors are illustrated. The channel chain on the left shows the traditional account management approach, as used by most competitors at the start of the 1990s, when the sales process was largely handled face-to-face by account managers. Still a model used for larger computers or major contracts, it has tended, though, to be complemented by other channel chains which offer better channel economics for smaller deals.

One of these new channel chains was the direct model, illustrated in the middle of the figure. Here, press advertising formed the dominant marketing tool, with further information provided by product brochures and call centre staff. The actual order could be placed by a number of means – often a traditional fax or post order placed by the accounts department.

More recently, many competitors have added the Internet to the channel mix, as illustrated on the right. However, most of these are far from pure-play Internet providers. Account managers might serve major accounts, building relationships and negotiating discount levels. The account managers are freed from the details of product configuration and pricing by the website, while the order itself is as likely to be placed by fax or post as it is on the Web.

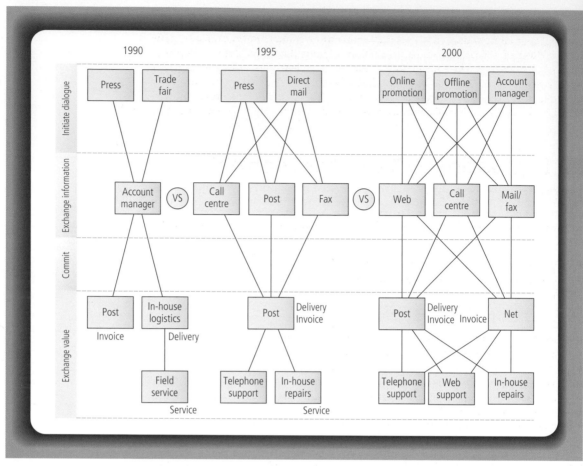

Figure 10.8
Channel-chain analysis: the PC market

Different channels, then, are needed at different points in the sales cycle, and different competitors may adopt different approaches. It is easy to imagine a fourth, pure-play Web channel chain which has a low cost structure and is appropriate to certain price-sensitive segments – and, indeed, competitors adopting this approach exist.

Having drawn the channel chains in current use, the next step is to consider possible future channel chains. This requires experimentation with channel-chain diagrams to think through not just how the sale is to be made, but also how every other aspect of the customer's needs will be satisfied. Will a mobile phone purchaser buying over the Web be able to return a faulty phone to a nearby store? Will an e-hub be able to handle not just price negotiations, but also information flows on stock levels, complaints, returns and product development – and if not, what additional channels will be needed?

The trick is to offer a channel chain that is appropriate to the differing needs of a company's target segments. In other words, the acid test as to whether a channel chain will flourish is whether it represents a better value proposition to some group of customers. To test this, we recommend drawing the value curve we described earlier, but comparing channel chains rather than individual channels.

There is a timing issue to be considered as well. Even if a channel chain offers a theoretically better proposition to customers, they may not yet be ready for it. A channel chain innovation, like a product innovation, is likely to proceed along the lines of Rogers' (1962) bell-shaped diffusion of innovation curve. If one hopes to convert customers to the Internet, for example, it is clearly necessary to consider what proportion of the customer base has Internet access and how mature their use of it is. We recall one department store which wasted millions on an aborted Web service in the mid-1990s because it was simply too far ahead of its market.

■ Evaluation criteria for channel intermediaries

Regardless of the type of intermediary to be used, there are a number of basic evaluation criteria, for example:

- Do they now, or will they, sell to our target market segment?
- Is their sales force large enough and trained well enough to achieve our regional sales forecasts?
- Is their regional location adequate in respect of the retail (and other) outlets serviced?
- Are their promotional policies and budgets adequate?
- Do they satisfy customer after-sales requirements?
- Are their product policies consistent with our own?
- Do they carry competitive lines?
- What are their inventory policies regarding width, depth and cover?
- Are they creditworthy?
- Is distributor management receptive, aggressive, and flexible?

All the above factors, and others, have to be considered when making specific decisions on choice of intermediaries, which in turn is part of the overall channel selection issue.

■ Customer service

The output of a firm's distribution activities is a system organized to provide a continuing link between the first contact with the customer, through to the time the order is received and the goods/services delivered and used, with the objective of satisfying customer needs continuously. It encompasses every aspect of the relationship.

▶ **DEFINITION** ◀

Customer service is a system organized to provide a continuing link between the first contact with the customer, through to the time the order is received and the goods/ services delivered and used, with the objective of satisfying customer needs continuously

However, the provision of ▶ **customer service** in all its various forms is likely to involve the firm in large financial commitments. In fact, it can be demonstrated that once the level of service (defined here as the percentage of occasions the product is available to customers, when and where they want it) increases beyond the 70–80 per cent mark, the associated costs increase exponentially. Figure 10.9 demonstrates the typical relationship between the level of availability and the cost of providing it. From this diagram it will be observed that the cost of increasing the service level by a small amount, say from 95 per cent to 97.5 per cent, results in a sharp increase in inventory costs. The implications of this cost relationship bear closer examination.

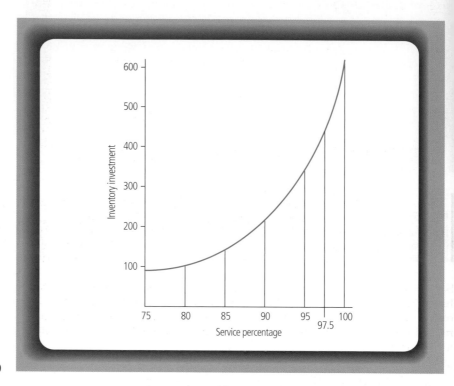

Figure 10.9

> Significantly, many companies appear to be unaware of the level of service they are offering – i.e. there is *no* customer service policy as such. Even where such a policy does exist, the levels are quite often arbitrarily set and are not the result of a careful market analysis.

The question, then, arises: what level of availability *should* be offered? This question is relatively simple to answer in theory, but very difficult to quantify and achieve in practice, since different product groups in different market segments could well demand different levels of customer service. Readers who did not study the short case history on customer service by segment are referred to the end of Chapter 4.

In theory, at least, it is possible to say that service levels can continue to be improved as long as the marketing advantage that results continues to outrun the additional costs incurred. Conceptually, it is possible to draw an S-shaped curve (see Figure 10.10) which suggests that, at very high levels of customer service, customers are unable to distinguish between small changes in the service offered. When a company is operating in this region, it is quite possibly incurring more costs than are necessary for the level of sales being achieved.

For example, marketing and sales managers who insist on offering maximum service to all customers, no matter what the profitability and location of those customers, are quite probably doing their company a disservice.

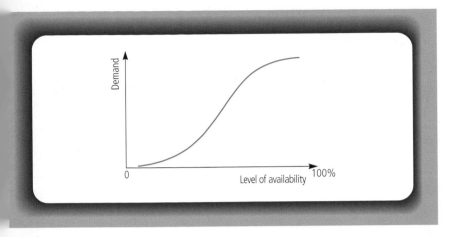

Figure 10.10

By carefully reviewing customer service policy, perhaps even introducing differential service levels for different products or for different customers (at least on a trial-and-error basis), marketing can enhance its contribution to corporate profitability.

Somewhere between the costs and benefits involved in customer service, a balance has to be found.

Somewhere between the costs and benefits involved in customer service, a balance has to be found. It will be at that point where the additional revenue returns for each increment of service are equal to the extra cost involved in providing that incre ment. To attempt to ascertain this point of balance, certain information is required, for example:

1 How profitable is the product? What contribution to fixed costs and profits does this product make and what is its sales turnover?

2 What is the nature of the product? Is it a critical item as far as the customer is concerned, where stock-outs at the point of supply would result in a loss of sales? Does the product have characteristics that result in high stockholding costs?

3 What is the nature of the market? Does the company operate in a sellers' or a buyers' market? How frequently is the product purchased? Are there ready substitutes? What are the stockholding practices of the purchasers? Which markets and customers are growing and which are declining?

4 How profitable are the customers constituting each segment?

5 What is the nature of the competition? How many companies are providing an alternative source of supply to our customers? What sort of service levels do they offer?

6 What is the nature of the channel of distribution through which the company sells? Does the company sell direct to the end-customer, or through intermediaries? To what extent does the company control the channel and the activities of its members, such as the stock levels and order policies?

This basic information is the raw material of the service-level decision. To take an example, the level of service offered is less likely to have an effect on sales if, in fact, the company is the sole supplier of the product, and there are no substitutes. The situation is the case in some industrial markets, and, from a short-term point of view, to offer a higher level of service (say 90 per cent instead of 85 per cent) would probably have the effect of reducing the total profitability of the product.

Customer retention and profitability

Acquiring customers can be expensive. Usually it involves certain one-off costs such as, for example, advertising, promotion, the salesperson's time, and even the cost of entering data into the company's data bank. Thus, every customer represents an investment, the level of which will vary from business to business.

> Retaining customers is extremely profitable.

If they are treated correctly and remain customers over a long period, there is strong evidence that they will generate more profits for the organization each year they maintain the relationship. Across a wide range of businesses this pattern is the same (Figure 10.11).

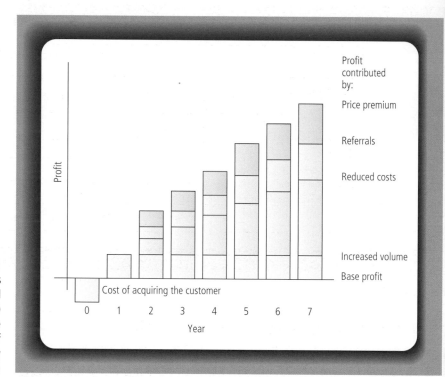

Figure 10.11
Retaining customers pays off (*Source*: Based on F.R. Reichheld (1994) 'Loyalty and the renaissance of marketing', *Marketing Management*, 12(4), 17)

> For example, an industrial laundry almost doubled its profits per customer over five years. A car-servicing business expects fourth-year customers to generate three times the profit of a first-year customer. A distributor of industrial products found that net sales per account continued to rise even into the nineteenth year of the relationship.

This trend holds true for many types of service companies. As the relationship extends, the initial 'contact' costs, such as checking creditworthiness, no longer figure on the balance sheet. In addition, the more that is known about the customer as the relationship develops, the more offers can be tailored effectively to meet that particular customer's needs. Thus, the customer gets greater value, which in turn encourages more frequent and larger purchases.

It follows, therefore, that when a company lowers its customer defection rate, average customer relationships last longer and profits climb. Viewed in this way, the costs of providing enhanced customer service could be seen as an investment in customer retention.

We have evidence at Cranfield that very few organizations bother to measure customer retention on a regular basis, while even fewer measure customer retention by segment. However, as can be seen in the data given in Figure 10.12, this particular organization's best performance is in the least profitable segments and its worst performance is in the market's most profitable segments.

	Total market	Segment 1	Segment 2	Segment 3	Segment 4	Segment 5	Segment 6
Percentage of market represented by segment	100.0	14.8	9.5	27.1	18.8	18.8	11.0
Percentage of all profits in total market produced by segment	100.0	7.1	4.9	14.7	21.8	28.5	23.0
Ratio of profit produced by segment to weight of segment in total population	1.00	0.48	0.52	0.54	1.16	1.52	2.09
Defection rate	23%	20%	17%	**15%**	28%	30%	**35%**

Figure 10.12

Developing a customer service package

In general terms, customer service is normally defined as the service provided to the customer from the time an order is placed until the product is delivered. In fact, it is much more than this.

It actually encompasses every aspect of the relationship between manufacturers and their distributors/customers. Under this definition, price, sales representation, after-sales service, product range offering, product availability, etc. are all dimensions of customer service – i.e. the total activity of servicing one's customer.

However, it is more traditional to think of customer service in distribution-related terms. Under this more restricted definition the key elements of customer service are product availability, overall order cycle time, and order cycle time variation. Research has shown that many companies have poor product availability due to a variety of reasons – e.g. poor forecasting, production difficulties, inadequate inventory controls, etc.

Above all else, it is fundamental for suppliers to derive and make operational their concept of customer service from a study of their customers' real needs rather than their own perceptions of such needs. The following list contains the major components of customer service that should be researched.

> It is fundamental for suppliers to derive their concept of customer service from a study of their customers' real needs.

- Frequency of delivery
- Time from order to delivery
- Reliability of delivery
- Emergency deliveries when required
- Stock availability and continuity of supply
- Orders filled completely
- Advice on non-availability
- Convenience of placing order
- Acknowledgement of order
- Accuracy of invoices
- Quality of sales representation
- Regular calls by sales representatives
- Manufacturer monitoring of retail stock levels
- Credit terms offered
- Customer query handling
- Quality of outer packaging
- Well-stacked pallets
- Easy-to-read use-by dates on outers
- Quality of inner package for in-store handling and display
- Consults on new product/package development
- Reviews product range regularly
- Coordination between production, distribution and marketing.

This will almost certainly mean designing different customer service packages for different market groups. At present, very few manufacturers/suppliers bother to do this. Basically, six steps are involved in this process:

1 Define the important service elements (and sub-elements).
2 Determine customers' viewpoints on these.
3 Design a competitive package (and several variations, if necessary).
4 Develop a promotional campaign to 'sell' the service package idea.
5 Pilot test a particular package and the promotional campaign being used.
6 Establish controls to monitor performance of the various service packages.

> Throughout many types of industry, and especially those that are highly competitive, it is increasingly being recognized that, after all the other terms of trade have been tried and exhausted, it will be customer service considerations that will determine who, in the end, gets the order. The distribution function is becoming as important as that.

■ Developing the distribution plan

Figure 10.13 shows the interrelationship between the process described elsewhere in this book and distribution. Here, we see that product, pricing and promotion decisions are separated from distribution.

Organizationally, it makes a lot of sense to make marketing responsible for distribution, since it is probably in the best position to make the difficult trade-off between very high levels of customer service and the high inventory-carrying costs associated with such levels.

On the other hand, labour relations, wage bargaining, the technical aspects, and so on of distribution also demand specialist attention, and there is a grave danger that such issues may begin to divert too much of the chief marketing officer's

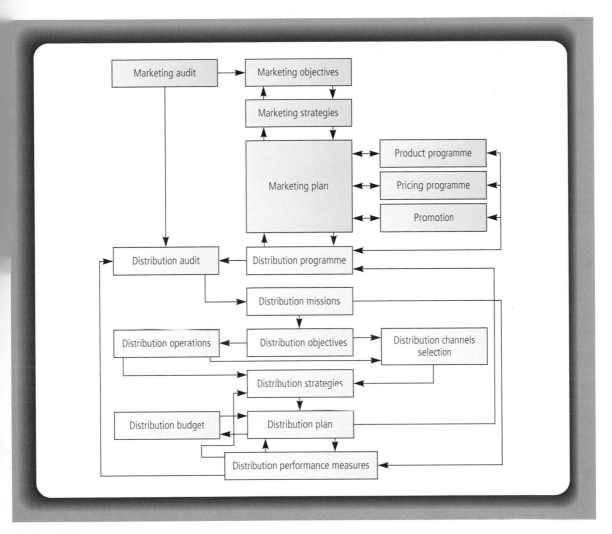

Figure 10.13

attention away from other important marketing areas. The logistics director is one possible answer to this problem. Such a role is to view the whole distribution system in an integrated way.

■ What is integrated distribution management?

▶ **DEFINI**

Integrated d

managem

appro

dist

fi

▶ **Integrated distribution management** is an approach to the distributi mission of the firm whereby two or more of the functions involved in m goods from source to user are integrated and viewed as an interrelated sub-system for purposes of managerial planning, implementation a

Whatever the organizational solution, however, all of the above issues are relevan
and it is necessary to know where to start.

Where to start?

The distribution audit was referred to in Chapter 2. Like the more general market
ing audit referred to there, this is in two major parts – *internal* and *external*. Figure
10.14(a) and (b) illustrate the major components of the distribution audit.

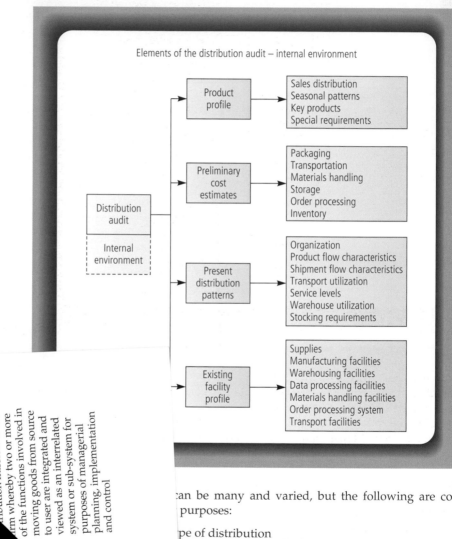

Elements of the distribution audit – internal environment

...can be many and varied, but the following are con-
...purposes:

...pe of distribution
...els to be held
...es promotion activities
...evelopment programmes, e.g. incentives for distributors.

...distribution management approach, it is as well to
...umber of other decisions/trade-offs which need to be
...re depicted in Figure 10.15.

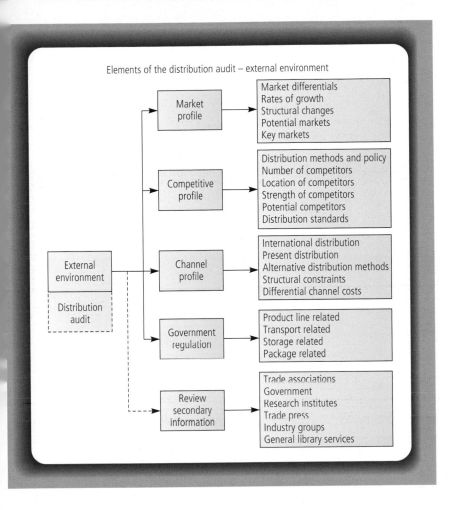

Elements of the distribution audit – external environment

Figure 10.14(b)

Of course, all of these decisions need not necessarily be located in one plan or be made by one person or department, but clearly they need to be made and written down somewhere in the company's plans.

Finally, the following illustrates a simple iterative approach to distribution planning that should help tighten up what is often a neglected area of marketing management.

Distribution planning approach

1 Determine marketing objectives.
2 Evaluate changing conditions in distribution at all levels.
3 Determine distribution task within overall marketing strategy.
4 Determine distribution policy in terms of type, number and level of outlets to be used.
5 Set performance standards for the distribution organization.
6 Obtain performance information.
7 Compare actual with anticipated performance.
8 Adjustment where necessary.

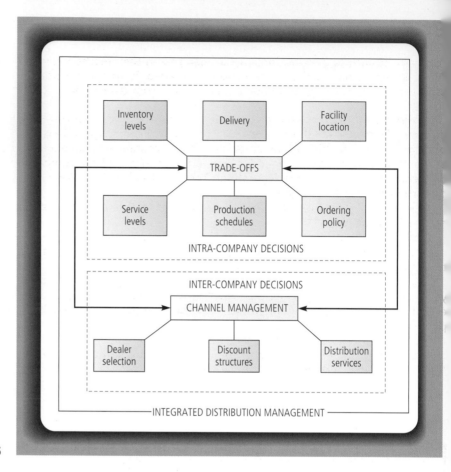

Figure 10.15

■ Application questions

1   What are the advantages and disadvantages of the channels currently used by your company?

2   Are there any cases where the channels used may not be the most appropriate?

3   If your company were new to the market, what channels would you use? How would your recommendations differ from existing arrangements? What prevents you from making these changes?

4   Is logistics adequately represented at board or senior management level in your organization? How could improvements be made?

5   What coordination takes place between physical distribution management and marketing management? How can any problems be minimized?

6   How are decisions currently made concerning customer service levels? How does it compare with competitors?

7   Can you see any way of making savings in your distribution system without reducing customer service?

EXERCISES

For many businesses, distribution plays a small part in their marketing plans. When it is considered, the prime concern seems to focus on the physical aspects, the logistics of getting goods transported from the company to the customer.

Distribution, however, embraces a much broader concept than just the delivery of goods. In addition, it takes into account the strategic importance of distribution channels and the potential value of channel intermediaries. It also ensures that 'customer service' is kept in the forefront of the company's deliberations about its marketing policies. The exercises in this section mirror this broad view of distribution.

Exercise 10.1 helps you to decide whether or not intermediaries are required in your type of business.

Exercise 10.2 explains how intermediaries might be selected.

Exercise 10.3 is designed solely to get you to think about your own customer service from the customer's point of view.

Exercise 10.4 looks at the total customer service package and will enable you to check how yours compares with those of your competitors, and, equally importantly, what steps you will have to take to improve your competitiveness.

Exercise 10.5 addresses the physical aspects of distribution.

Exercise 10.6 invites you to use all the information generated in Exercises 10.1–10.5 and integrate it into a distribution plan.

Introduction to Chapter 10 exercises

At first sight, the choice of distribution channel is deceptively easy. After all, basically there are only three options from which to choose:

1 To sell direct to the customer/user
2 To sell to customers/users through intermediaries
3 To use a combination of 1 and 2, i.e. dual distribution.

The final choice will always be something of a compromise, with, on the one hand, the desire to keep control of the distribution of one's products or services, and, on the other hand, the practical need to keep distribution costs to a bearable level.

The worksheet is designed to help you to make a choice about channels of distribution. This is what you do:

1 Take each product/service in your portfolio in turn and subject them to the algorithm given on the worksheet.
2 Note the decision for each product, i.e. sell direct or use channel intermediaries. Do these seem the best decisions, or can you see good reasons for ignoring them?
3 In working through the algorithm, can you see a case for dual distribution for some products or services? For example, do you sell direct to some customers or regions and sell through intermediaries to others? Remember, the major problem associated with dual distribution is determining a fair division of the market between yourself (as the supplier) and the intermediary (intermediaries).

Exercise 10.1
Do we need channel intermediaries?

Worksheet Distribution channel algorithm (Exercise 10.1)

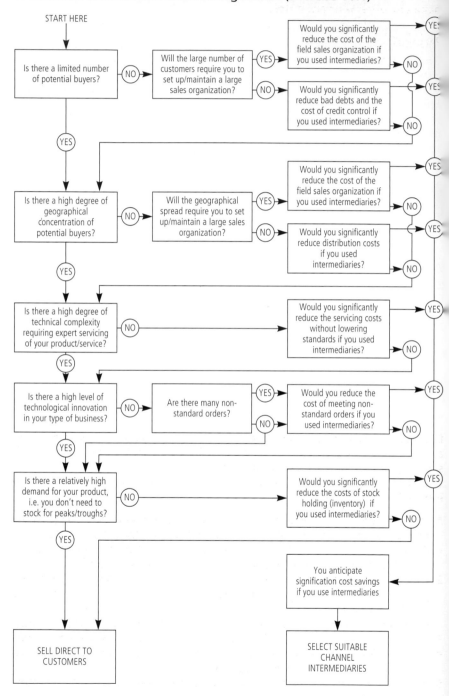

Use the space below to record the decisions from using the worksheet or to make any other relevant notes.

Personal notes

Exercise 10.1 helped to answer the question of whether or not an intermediary is required. Assuming the answer is affirmative, you are now faced with selecting a suitable candidate to play that role.

The worksheet should help you in your decision-making. Here are the instructions for using it:

1 Make a note of organizations that, on the surface, appear to be possible choices as intermediaries. (You will see that the worksheet allows for comparisons between just three prospective intermediaries. You should, of course, draw up your own form to include as many as you like.)
2 Looking at the list of evaluation criteria, take criterion 1 and apply it to all the prospective channel intermediaries. Place scores in columns A, B and C – a number between 0 and 10, depending on whether the intermediary is a very poor fit against this criterion (zero score) or an extremely good fit (10 points).
3 Continue down the list of evaluation criteria, repeating this scoring process.
4 Add any further criteria that are relevant for your business to the bottom of the list and score them likewise.
5 Add up the scores in each column. The highest total represents the most suitable intermediary.

You may decide that some criteria are more important than others on this list. In this case use a points weighting system which takes importance into account. An example of a weighting system is given in Exercise 4.2.

Exercise 10.2
Selecting a suitable intermediary

Worksheet Criteria for selecting intermediaries (Exercise 10.2)

Evaluation criteria	Prospective intermediaries		
	A	B	C
1 Currently deals with our target market segment			
2 Is prepared to deal with target market segment			
3 Sales force is sufficiently large			
4 Sales force is well trained			
5 Regional locations well positioned			
6 Promotional policies consistent with ours			
7 Budgets are adequate			
8 Can provide customer after-sales service			
9 Product policies consistent with ours			
10 Does not carry competitor lines			
11 Prepared to carry adequate stocks			
12 Prepared to carry range/cover			
13 Suitable storage facilities			
14 Is creditworthy			
15 Management attitudes compatible with ours			
16 Has suitable reputation (Add others that are relevant)			
17 _____			
18 _____			
19 _____			
20 _____			
21 _____			
22 _____			
23 _____			
24 _____			
25 _____			
26 _____			
27 _____			
28 _____			
29 _____			
30 _____			
Total			

Exercise 10.3
Customer service audit[1]

Before getting into more detail about customer service, start by completing this customer service audit. If you have 'No' in more than three questions, or if you have difficulty answering the open-ended questions, you may have a serious customer service problem in your organization. It is preferable if you can complete this exercise for each segment of the market in which you compete.

[1] This audit is based on an audit constructed by Professor Martin Christopher of Cranfield University School of Management, and is used with his kind permission.

1 Do you have a written customer service policy?

Yes _____

No _____

2 Is this given a wide circulation within the company?

Yes _____

No _____

3 Do customers receive a copy of this policy?

Yes _____

No _____

4 What are the three most crucial aspects of customer service as they impinge upon your marketing effectiveness?

1 _____

2 _____

3 _____

5 Is any attempt made to monitor your customer service performance on these three dimensions?

Yes _____

No _____

6 Do you monitor competitive customer service offerings?

Yes _____

No _____

7 Do you believe that within your company there is adequate knowledge of the true costs of providing customer service?

Yes _____

No _____

8 Which function(s) has responsibility for customer service management?

_____

_____

9 Where does customer service management fit in relation to the marketing function? (Draw an organizational chart if necessary.)

10 Do you have an established method of communications for your customers to contact you about some aspect of their order after the order has been entered?

Yes _____

No _____

11 Do you (a) have a single point of contact for customers or (b) do certai[n]
departments handle different types of inquiries/complaints?

Yes (a) (b)

No   (a) (b)

12 What do you think are the major areas of weakness in your curren[t]
approach to customer service management?

_____

_____

_____

_____

_____

Exercise 10.4

The customer service package

Customer service has been defined as the percentage of occasions the product
or service is available to the customer *when* and *where* he or she wants it.
Obviously, to operate service levels at 100 per cent might, and often does,
impose a crippling cost on the supplier, yet to drop below an acceptable level
is to surrender one's market share to a competitor.

Research has shown that to improve one's service level by even a small
amount when it is already at a high level can become expensive (the law of
diminishing returns). Therefore, the marketer will have to be certain about
the actual levels of customer service provided and to have a greater understanding of customer expectations and needs. It will be highly likely that different market segments will require different levels of customer service.

The ultimate choice of service level for a specific product will be tempered
by other influential factors:

1 The contribution to fixed costs – for example, can it bear the cost of an
upgraded service level?
2 The nature of the market – for example, are there substitute products?
3 The nature of the competition – for example, do they offer better service
levels?
4 The nature of the distribution channel – for example, do we sell direct or
through intermediaries?

The key to marketing success is for your company to develop a customer service package – one that embraces product availability, with attractive order
cycle times, and mechanisms for minimizing customer inconvenience arising
from order cycle variations.

The worksheet is designed to help you to arrive at a more competitive customer service package or, if this is too expensive, to devise an alternative. The
instructions are provided on the worksheet. The space below is for any notes
you might wish to make about these issues.

Worksheet Developing a customer service package (Exercise 10.4)

Take one of your market segments and decide what would make the best 'package' by putting a tick against the appropriate items in column 1, i.e. what does your marketing strategy suggest?

In column 2 tick the items that go to make the best competitor package.

In column 3 estimate whether the provision of your item is Better, Equal or Worse than the best competitor.

In column 4 indicate the relative cost of improving where you compete unfavourably with the best competitor, i.e. High, Medium or Low.

In column 5 list improvement actions to upgrade the service package to match the best competition.

In column 6 consider alternative packages, i.e. to fight on different grounds.

Repeat this process for all other market segments.

Components of customer service	(1) Market strategy suggestions	(2) Best comp.	(3) Better, Equal, Worse	(4) Comp. cost H, M, L	(5) Actions to upgrade cust. serv.	(6) Alt. package
Frequency of delivery						
Time from order to delivery						
Reliability of delivery						
Emergency deliveries when required						
Stock availability						
Continuity of supply						
Advice on non-availability						
Convenience of placing orders						
Acknowledgement of orders						
Accuracy of invoices						
Quality of sales representation						
Regularity of calls by sales reps						
Monitoring of stock levels						
Credit terms offered						
Handling of customer queries						
Quality of outer packaging						
Well-stacked pallets						
Easy-to-read use-by dates on outers						
Clear handling instructions on outers						
Quality of inner package for handling						
Quality of inner package for display						
Consultation on new developments, e.g. products or packaging						
Regular review of product range coordination between production, distribution and marketing						
Add others which are relevant for your business						

Personal notes

Exercise 10.5
Physical
distribution

It has been shown that there are five areas to be considered when it comes to physical distribution, the so-called 'distribution mix'. They are: facilities, inventory, transport, communications and unitization.

Facilities
Having established the level of customer service required by each market segment, you must reappraise the location of your own plants and warehouses in order to ensure they are situated in geographically suitable positions *vis-à-vis* the customers. If the nature of demand and the location of major customers are forecast to change dramatically, then relocating manufacturing units and/or warehouses is an option that, in the long term, can lead to savings due to reduced distribution costs.

Such decisions cannot be taken lightly. For most organizations their facilities are taken as fixed, certainly in the short term.

Inventory
The holding of stock, whether by design or accident, is always a costly business. Therefore, it is important to know the comparative costs of holding stocks of different products in order to arrive at a sensible stockholding policy.

Worksheet 1 enables you to calculate the various components of inventory cost for each of your major products and thereby produce the necessary cost data. Once in possession of this information, it might become necessary for you to revise the customer service package or indeed earlier deliberations about channel intermediaries.

Transport
This is the area that many people are familiar with, and, as such, has traditionally received most management attention. Worksheet 2 shows a typical way of calculating the merits or demerits of various forms of transporting goods to customers. Try it, using some of your own products as study vehicles.

While cost is an important determinant in the choice of transport, frequency of service and reliability are often just as important. Regular monitoring of transport costs is to be recommended if distribution costs are to be held in check.

Communications

It is often overlooked that accompanying the flow of materials through the distribution channel there is also a flow of information in the form of orders, invoices, demand forecasts, delivery schedules, etc. Each of these 'communications' is likely to be an integral part of your customer service package, and yet, in all probability, they were set up for your own company's administrative convenience.

Look at all your communications associated with distribution and put yourself in the customer's shoes. For example, how sensible does your ordering system seem when viewed from the other end? Get out and speak to some actual customers and seek their views. Anything that can be done to simplify or speed-up communications must be to your company's benefit – and it doesn't have to cost you money to improve the situation.

Unitization

Assess whether or not it is possible to make your products more acceptable to users or intermediaries – for example, for handling or stacking, by pack-aging them into different-sized units such as shrink-wrapped bulk packs, pallet loads, container loads, etc. It is often possible to win substantial cost savings in terms of handling or warehousing by considering this aspect of distribution.

Worksheet 1 Comparative inventory costs (Exercise 10.5)

Area of cost	Product				
	(1)	(2)	(3)	(4)	(5)
Warehouse costs (rent, rates, heat, light, etc.)					
Labour costs					
Losses/shrinkage					
Deterioration/damage					
Insurance					
Interest (on funds tied up in stock)					
Administrative costs					
Other costs relevant to your specific business					
_____					
_____					
_____					
_____					
_____					
_____					
_____					
_____					
_____					

For the purpose of this worksheet take the cost per item, or unit; or you can, if you prefer, just express the costs as a percentage of the book value of the stock.

Worksheet 2 Comparative physical distribution costs (Exercise 10.5)

Method of physical distribution	Product/service				
	(1)	(2)	(3)	(4)	(5)
Use own transport					
Contract hire					
Use carriers					
Other forms of road transport					
_____					
_____					
_____					
Passenger rail train					
Freight train					
Red Star Parcel					
Other forms of rail transport					
_____					
_____					
_____					
Boat on deck					
Boat in hold					
Sea Cat					
Others forms of sea transport					
_____					
_____					
_____					
Air parcel					
Air freight					
Other forms of air transport					
_____					
_____					
_____					
1st class post					
2nd class post					
Parcel post					
Other postal methods					
_____					
_____					
_____					
Other transport methods					
_____					
_____					
_____					
_____					
_____					

From the foregoing study material you will by now have highlighted several ways of improving distribution in your company or have confirmed that existing practices were well chosen. In order that your effort is not wasted, it will be important to encapsulate your major findings in the distribution plan. Here is a suggestion for how this can be done:

1 Show how, in the light of the company's marketing objectives and strategy, the distribution task needs to be defined.
2 From your work, show where current practice supports this definition of the distribution task and where it does not.
3 Using the data you have assembled, recommend:
   (a) a distribution policy in terms of type, number and level of outlet to be used
   (b) performance standards for the distribution organization
   (c) where changes in the distribution organization are required
   (d) ways of monitoring performance as the plan unfolds.

Personal notes

Exercise 10.6
The distribution plan

Index

An asterisk (*) before page numbers indicates the inclusion of a marginal note of definition on those pages

Above-the-line expenditure, see Advertising
Absolute market share, 250–1
Accountancy, 605–9
ACORN (A Classification of Residential Neighbourhoods), 139, 179
Action/tactics, 521, 525
Added value, 188, 287
Administrative role of planners, 457
Advertising, 541–5, *545
  European Union Directive on Comparative Advertising, 564
  legal requirements, 564
  marketing confused with, 12
  media, exercise, 567–9
  objectives, 332, 545–8
    exercises, 565–7
  plan, 332, 545–8
    exercise, 569
Analysis, in strategic marketing plan, 485
'Anorexia industrialosa', 613
Ansoff Matrix, *94, 279–82, 307, 361
  see also Gap analysis
Applications (software programs), 382
  see also Computer programs
Appropriation budgets, 305, 455
Assumptions, 55, 454, 494
  exercise, 322–3
  overall, strategic marketing plan, 499–500, 514
Asynchronous communication, 403–4
Audits, hierarchy of, 459–63
Autonomy crisis, 413
Availability, product, 350–1, 645–6
Average cost, 620

Banks, marketing and, 11
Barriers to marketing planning, 478–82
  'Ten S' approach to overcoming, 478–82
Below-the-line expenditure, see Sales promotion
Benefit analysis, 144, 288–9
  exercise, 169–71

Benefit package analysis, exercise, 242–6
Benefit segmentation, 142–4
Benefits, categories, 143–4
Bipolar maps, 190, 191
Board-level organization, 418–21
Boston Consulting Group, 207–10, 607
Boston matrix, 116, *210–17, 241
  developments, 215–17
  exercise, 249–59, 260–1
  principles, 258
  weaknesses, 213–14
  see also Directional policy matrix
Bottom-up planning, 534
Brand functionality, 192–3
Brand loyalty ladder, 546
Brand personality, 191–3
Brand positioning, 190–1
Brand strategy, 190
Brands, *186–97
  vs commodities, 188
  company as, 194
  components, 190–4
  corporate, 194, 195
  functionality, 192–3
  global vs local, *194–7
  'me-tooism', 193, 197
  pseudo brands, 189
  successful/unsuccessful, 188–90
Break-even analysis, 612, 613
British Telecom, 372–3
Budget, 31–4, 57–8, *80, 455
  appropriation budgets, 305, 455
Budgeting, 80–1, 520
  operating problems and, 81
Bureaucracy crisis, 414
Business definition, 51, 530
Business directions, 319–20, 496
Business environment, 7–8, 19, 53, 315
Business Process Redesign (BPR), 423
Business risk, 359–60
Business strengths/position, 215–16, *219, 222–5
Business success, 6–7, 87–8
  influencing factors, 86

Business-to-business marketing, 14–15
  demographic descriptors, 140
Business-to-business products
  buying process, 542
  influencers of purchase decision, 544
  sales promotion, 552–3
Buying process, 542–5
  see also Customers

Campaign management, 385
Capabilities
  company, 4–5, 19
  exercise, 22
'Cash cows', 212, 259, 281, 282
Cash discount, 614
Cash flow, 210
'Cash' products, 326, 503
Category management (CM), 235–8
  challenges for the future, 237–8
  evolution, 238
  growth of, 236–7
  limitations of, 237
Centralization, 415–18, 428–9, 438
Channel discounts, 345
Channels, see under Distribution
Chief executive, 448
  role, 98, 100, 456
  weak support from, 89–91
Closed-loop marketing planning system, *100, 448
Clustering, 145–7
Collaborative evolution, 411, 414, 425–6
Committee on Advertising Practice, 564
Commodities, vs brands, 188
Commodity slide, 187
Communication, 10
  communications mix, 331, 541–5
  elements of, 576
  personal communication in, exercise, 595–6
  personal selling as part of, 337, 576–8
  with customers, 331

Communication (*continued*)
  distribution mix, 349, 632–3, 634, 663
  forms of, 541
  integrating marketing communication and distribution channels, 586–94
  legal issues in marketing communications, 562–4
  objectives, 545
  task independent data management, 592
  see also Advertising; Personal selling; Sales promotion
Company benefits, 143, 169
Company capabilities, 4–5, 19
  exercise, 22
Company situation, quiz, 23–6
Competence, distinctive, 51–2, 215, 293, 530
Competition, 53, 315, 316
  potential, 611–12
  and pricing, 611–12, 622
Competitive advantage, 40
  CRM and, 390
  gaining through value-in-use, 616
  law as a weapon for, 563, 564
  marketing planning for, 479
  sustainable, 282
  and unique segmentation schemes, 373–4
Competitive characteristics, 531
Competitive position classifications, 495
Competitive pricing, 343–4
  exercise, 620–1
Competitive strategies, 282–90
Competitor analysis
  exercise, 319–20
  strategic marketing plan, 494–6, 512
Competitor value positioning, understanding, 115, 116
Competitors, 7
Computer industry
  marketing and, 11
  microprocessors, 7–8
Computer programs
  applications, 382
  de-duplication routines, 378, 382
  software systems, 382–7
Consolidation of several SBU marketing plans, 481, 530–5
  appendices, 533
  directional statement, 530
  financial goals, 532
  financial history, 531

major changes and events, 531
major issues by SBU, 531
  competitive characteristics, 531
  key strategic issues, 532
  market characteristics, 531
  strategic objectives by SBU, 532
summary of main features, 530
Consultants, 185, 435
Consumer attitudes, and pricing, 623
Consumer marketing, 14–15
Consumer markets, segmentation, 376
Consumer panels, 368, 435
Consumers
  vs customers, *116–18, 161
  final users, 128–33
Contact history information, 384
Contingency plan, 520, 521–2, 527
Control crisis, 413–14
Coordinated evolution, 411, 414, 425
Copyright, 563
Core product, 186, 187, 239
Corporate branding, 194, 195
Corporate culture, 423–6, 481
Corporate objectives, 44–5, 52, *277, 306
  financial, 43–4
  and marketing objectives, 275–9, 610
  and pricing, 621
Corporate plan/planning, 43–6
  failure to integrate marketing planning into, 98
  and marketing planning, 41–9
Corporate strategies, 43, *277, 279, 306
Cost decline, 208–9
Cost-effectiveness, 288
Cost-plus pricing, 343, 605–9, 612
Cost/price continuum, 620
Costing
  full absorption costing, 612
  marginal, 612
  product elimination and, 613
Costs, *30
  average, 620
  costs/marketing differentiation matrix, 287–9
  customer relationship management (CRM), 392–3
  customer service, 645–7, 649
  Internet, 402, 404
  inventory, 663
  physical distribution, 664
  pricing and, 612–14
  summary, 521, 526
Creative evolution, 411
Crises, 412–15
Critical purchase influencers, 159

Critical Success Factors (CSFs), *144–5, 159, 161, 361–3, 493, 494
  exercise, 165–6
  importance of, 145
Culture
  corporate, 423–6, 481
  social/cultural environment, 53, 315
Current market growth, 250
Customer analysis form, 544
Customer audit, exercise, 171–6
Customer focus, 238
Customer loyalty, 157–8
Customer reference table, 382
Customer relationship management (CRM), 385, 387–94, 591–4
  audit, 393, 394
  benefits, 389–90, 391
  competitive advantage, 390
  costs, 392–3
  features, 389
Customer retention, 648–9
Customer satisfaction, 157–8
Customer service, 10, 350–1, *645–50
  audit, exercise, 658–60
  costs, 645–7, 649
  factors impacting on, 350–1
  marketing confused with, 12
  package, 350–1, 649–50
    exercise, 660–2
  plan, 349–51
Customers
  analysis of attributes, 135–6, 138–40
  analysis of behaviour, 142–3, 162
  analysis of purchases, 136–8, 162
  benefits sought, 142–4
  choice of channel, 642–3
  communication with, 331
  vs consumers, *116–18, 161
  direct, 117
  internal customer data, 375–8, 381
  MIS
    data, 382–4
    functions, 384–5
  targeting of, 392
  wants, 8–10, 13, 19, 391–2
  see also Market segmentation

Damage limitation, 557
Data, *365
  marketing data, 382–4
Data fusion, 378
Data mining, *386–7
Data modelling, 382
Data Protection Act 1998, 564
Data warehousing, *386

Database, *378, 382, 504
    forms included in, 515–18
    myths and realities, 379
Database marketing, 378–80
    legal requirements, 564
Decentralization, 415–18, 428–9, 438
De-duplication routines, 378, 382
Definition of the business, 51, 530
Delegated evolution, 411, 412, 424–5
Delegation of planning to a planner,
    98–100
Demographic characteristics, *138,
    139, 177, 178
Depth interviews, 367, 435
Desk research, 368, 435
Detail, too much, 94–6
Determiners, see Key Discriminating
    Features
Differential benefits, 143–4, 169–70
    and pricing, 622
Differentiation, product, 35–6, 287–9,
    392
Differentiators, see Key
    Discriminating Features
Diffusion of innovation, *203–6, 240,
    549
Direct mailing, 384
Direct marketing, legal requirements,
    564
Directed evolution, 411, 413, 424
Directional policy matrix (DPM), 116,
    215–17, 241, 282, 284
    analysis team, 218–19
    case studies, 230–5, 259–70
    exercises, 259–70
    portfolio analysis, 303
    process, 219–27
    steps in producing, 219
    what should be plotted, 218
Directional statement, 530
Directions
    business, 319–20, 496
    marketing, 281
Directive role of planners, 457
Discounts, 345, 614
    exercise, 624–5
Disintermediation, 147, 350, 637, 639
Distinctive competence, 51–2, 215,
    293, 530
Distribution, 10, 200, 631–65, *632
    audit, 43, 652, 653
    channel independent task
        management, 592–3
    channel intermediaries, 614–16,
        634–5, 636
        evaluation criteria, 645
        exercises, 655–8

    types of, 637–8
    channels, 350, 634–6
        changing nature of, 586–8
        channel-chain analysis, 643–5
        customer choice of channel,
            642–3
        integrating marketing
            communication and, 586–94
        multi-channel integration, 641–2
        new channels, 636–45
        and pricing, 614–16, 622
    choice of, 587–8
    integrated distribution
        management, *651–4
    mix, 349, 632–3
    objectives, 652–3
    physical distribution, 349, 631–4
        costs, 664
        exercise, 662–4
    planning, 349–51, 650–1, 653
        exercise, 665
    see also Customer service
Diversification, 5, 279–81, 292–3,
    295–7, 323
    undiversified companies, 445
Diversity of operations, 442, 445–9
'Dogs', 212, 259, 281–2
Driving forces, 469, 471
Due Diligence, see Marketing Due
    Diligence

e-commerce, see Electronic commerce
Ecological strategy model, 42
Economic environment, 7, 53, 315
Economies of scale, 208
Effectiveness, and efficiency, 37–8
Efficient Customer Response (ECM),
    235–6, 238
80/20 rule (Pareto effect), *122–3, 176
Electronic commerce (e-commerce),
    384–5
    distribution plan, 636–45
    marketing audit, 147–9
Email, legal requirements, 564
Emotional appeal, 192
'Enter' marketing/business direction,
    281, 319, 496
Environment, see Business
    environment; Economic
    environment; Intra-company
    environment; Marketing
    environment; Social/cultural
    environment; Technological
    environment
European Union Directive on
    Comparative Advertising, 564
Events, staged/sponsored, 556, 557

Evolution of organizations, 411
Existing markets, 375
'Exit' marketing/business direction,
    281, 320, 496
Experience effect, *208
Experimentation, 367, 435
Expert opinion, 556
External audit, 52–3, 315–16
External market data, 375, 381

Facilities (plants/warehouses), 349,
    633, 662
Features of products, 136–7
Final users, 128–33
Financial audit, 43
Financial goals, 532
Financial history, 531
Financial objectives, *83
Financial projections
    summary of, 490–1, 507
    for three years, 505, 519
Financial ratios, 522, 528
Financial services, 402, 403
    market map, 639–41
Financial trusts, 417–18
Firmographic characteristics, 138
Five Forces model, 221
Force field analysis, 470–2
Forecast market growth, 250
Forecasting, 225, 226, 406–9, 428
    exercise, 436–7
    marketing information and, 364–8
    sales, 31–4, *80–1
        operating problems and, 81
Formalization, 442–3, 447
Four Cs, 274
Four Ps, 3, 56, 274–5, 299, 308, 449
Franchising, 351
Full absorption costing, 612
Functionality of brand, 192–3

Gap analysis, 290–5, 306
    exercise, 309–14
    strategic marketing plan, 491, 508–9
Generic mission statement, 51
Generic strategies matrix, 35–6
Geodemographic characteristics, 138,
    139, 179
Geographic characteristics, *138, 178,
    178–9
Global brands, *194–7
Global fortresses, 287, 289
Global sponsorship, 559
Globalization, 125
Good causes, 556
Government policy, 7, 53, 315
Growth rate, 220

'Harvest' marketing/business direction, 281, 320, 496
Hierarchy
  of audits, 459–63
  of objectives, 277–9, 585, 609–10
  of strategies, 279

IBM, 7–8, 285–6
Ignorance, 80–5, 101
Impersonal communications, 541
Implementation issues, 438
  diversity of operations, 445–9
  hierarchy of audits, 459–63
  marketing planning cycle, 457–8
  planning horizons, 44, 61, 458–9, 466
  role of chief executive, 456
  role of planning department, 456–7
  size of operations, 442–3, 443–5
  summary of marketing planning process, 450–65
'Improve' marketing/business direction, 281, 319, 496
Incentives, sales force, 339, 582–3
Independence of location, 398, 400–1
Individualization, 398, 400
Industrial markets
  buying process, 542–5
  market audit exercise, 167–8
  sales promotion, 553
  segmentation, 377, 487–9
Industry attractiveness, 215–16
Industry restructuring, 398, 402, 403
Influencers, 130, 131, 136, 159
Information, see Contact history information; Management information; Marketing information
Information-gathering techniques, 366–8
  exercise, 434–5
  strengths and drawbacks, 435
Information technology, 374–5
  see also Internet; Marketing information system
Innovation, diffusion of, *203–6, 240, 549
Integrated distribution management, *651–4
Integrated marketing communications (IMC), 586–94
Integration, 398–9
  multi-channel, 641–2
Intelligence, *365, 398, 401–2, 480
Interaction perspective model, 589–91
Interactivity, 398, 399–400
Interfaces, 382

Internal audit, 52–3, 315, 316–17
Internal customer data, 375–8, 381
International Standards Organization (ISO), *6, 9
Internet, 397–406
  costs, 402, 404
  independence of location, 398, 400–1
  individualization, 398, 400
  industry restructuring, 398, 402, 403
  integration, 398–9
  intelligence, 398, 401–2
  interactivity, 398, 399–400
  main features, 403–4
  6 IS model, 397–8
Interpretative strategy model, 42
Intra-company environment, 53, 315
Inventory, 349, 633, 662
  costs, 663
'Invest' products, 325–6, 502–3
ISO (International Standards Organization), *6, 9

Jargon, 94

Key account, *63
Key account planning, 63–4
  position of, in strategic marketing planning, 64
Key activity planner, 522, 529
Key Discriminating Features (KDFs), *136–7, 141
Key market segments, 302–4
Key strategic issues, 532
Knowledge, 108, 480–1

Lanchester's Square Law, 290
Leadership crisis, 412–13
Learning curve, 207
Legal issues in marketing communications, 562–4
  barriers to market entry, 563
  competitive advantage and, 563, 564
  requirements for marketing activities, 563, 564
  sources of information, 562
Leverage points, 134–5
Life-cycle, of product, see Product life-cycle
Life phases, organizational, 411–23
  collaborative evolution, 411, 414, 425–6
  coordinated evolution, 411, 414, 425
  corporate culture and marketing planning process, 423–6
  creative evolution, 411, 424

delegated evolution, 411, 424–5
  directed evolution, 411, 424
Line management, 53
  lack of skills, 92, 99
  lack of support from, 92–3, 102
Local brands, 194–7
Location, independence of, 398, 400–1
Logical incremental strategy model, 42
Logistics, *632

Macro business plan, 441–2
Macro forecasting, 408–9, 428, 436
'Maintain'
  marketing/business direction, 281, 320, 496
  products/services, 326, 503
Management audit, 43, 44
Management information and control, 385
Manufacturers/retailers power shift, 236
Margin turnover, 9
Marginal costing, 612
Marine markets, segmentation, 487–9
Market, *119
Market attractiveness, 216, *219, 220–2, 227–9, 283
  factors contributing to, 217
Market audit, exercise, 167–8
Market characteristics, 316, 531
  external audit, 53
  new and existing markets, 375
  overview, 491–2, 510
Market definition, 115, 119–21, 125–7, 150
  exercise, 163–5
Market entry, legal barriers to, 563–4
Market extension, 279–81, 295–7, 323
Market growth, 207, 210, 252–3
  current, 250
  forecast, 250
  see also Boston Matrix
Market leverage points, 134–5
Market map/mapping, 54, *127–35
  advanced, 135
  reconfiguring the market map, 638–41
Market maturity, 202, 248–9
Market orientation, see Marketing concept
Market overview, 54
Market penetration, 279–81, 291–2, 323, 617–18
Market positioning, 395
Market research, *193, *364, 427
  vs marketing research, 364–5

Market risk, 359–60
Market screening, 164
Market segmentation, 10, 14, 54, *123–5, 162
  analysis of purchases, 136–8
  benefit analysis, 144
  business objectives and segmentation methods, 374
    analysis options, 371–5
  case histories, 150–61
  clustering process, 145–7
  consumer markets, 376
  criteria for viable segments, 124
  customer behaviour, 142–3
  data, 370–1, 385
    unique segmentation schemes, 373–4
  impact of e-commerce, 147–9
  industrial markets, 377, 487–9
  objectives, 150
  strategic marketing plan, 484, 491–2, 515–16
  valuing key market segments, 302–4
  vital in marketing planning, 149–50
  see also Micro-segments
Market segments, *145
  gross profits, 504, 516
  sales values, 504, 515
Market share, 118–21, 161
  absolute, 250–1
  importance of, 286
  relative, 250
  return on investment and, 118
  unit costs and, 207–10
Market size, accessible, 220
Marketing, 1–25, 114–15
  aspects of, 46–7
  business-to-business, consumer and service, 14–15
  confusion about, 11–13
  definition, 4, 18, 20
  direct, legal requirements, 564
  expense, 59
  quiz on company situation, 23–6
  in a recession, 300–2
  role in business, 6–7
Marketing accountability, 357–64, 427
Marketing activities
  legal requirements for, 563, 564
  summary of, 521, 526
Marketing audit, 52–4, 113–14, 306, 451–2, 459, 480
  checklist, 314–17
  data, 375–8
    external data sources, 375–8
    internal data sources, 375–8

reconciling internal and external sources, 378–80
  exercise, 314–18
  form of, 52–3
  line managers and, 53
  in marketing planning system, 487–9
  need for, 52
  relevance of product life-cycle analysis and portfolio management to, 230
  timing, 53
Marketing channels, see Distribution
Marketing concept, *3, 18
Marketing data, 382–4
Marketing department
  necessity for, 15–17, 19
  and sales force, 418
Marketing directions, 281
Marketing Due Diligence, 360
Marketing effectiveness, measuring, 357–64
Marketing environment, 7–8, 19, 53, 315
  exercise, 22–3
  monitoring for changes in, 8
Marketing function, 3, 4, 18
Marketing information, 10, 427–8, 449
  analysis, 395–6
  and forecasting, 364–8
  as foundation of marketing plan, 480
  information-gathering techniques, 366–8
    exercise, 434–5
  Internet, 397–406
  organizing to develop sound plans, 368–82
  plan documentation, 396
  software systems, 382–7
  using successfully, 380–2
Marketing information system (MIS), 377–8, 427–8
  customer/product level data, 382–4
  customer/product level functions, 384–5
  data at market/product group level, 385
  exercise, 430–4
  management information and control, 385
  reconciling internal and external data, 378–80
  strategy formation, 396
  successful use of information, 380–2
  support for marketing, 407
Marketing managers, 418–19

Marketing map, 114, 183, 358–9
Marketing mix, 3, 10
  product life-cycle and, 199–201
Marketing objectives, 56, 225, 226, *275, 281, 307, 454–5, 494
  and corporate objectives, 275–9, 610
  one-year marketing plan, 521, 523
  and profitability, 302–4
  by SBU in consolidated plan, 532
  sequencing, 481
  setting, 276, 279–82
    exercise, 323–7
    guidelines, 282, 283–4, 325–6, 502–4
  strategic marketing plan, 500–4, 518
  sub-objectives, 276, 305, 521, 525
Marketing operations, 588–91
Marketing orientation, 16–17, 18
  exercise, 20–1
Marketing planning, 27–110
  barriers to, 478–82
    'Ten S' approach to overcoming, 478–82
  benefits, 65, 87
    exercise, 72–3
  and corporate planning, 41–9
  cycle, 457–8
  defining, 29–30, 64–5
  documentation, 396
  effectiveness of, 40–1
  essential nature of, 30–6
  failure to integrate into corporate planning, 98
  formal aspect of, 50
  horizons, 44, 61, 458–9, 466
  ignorance of, and operational problems, 80–5, 101
  in marketing context, 46–9
  model, 107–10
  naivety about, 86–8
  necessity for, 477–8
  organizational issues, exercise, 104–10
  organizing for, 410
  principles of, 465–6, 478–82
  process, see Marketing planning process
  purpose of, 477
  role of chief executive, 456
  role of planning department, 456–7
  strategic, see Strategic marketing plan
  in strategic planning context, 41–3
  symptoms of lack of, 103
  tactical, see Operational marketing planning
Marketing planning managers, 99–100

Marketing planning process, 49–58, 80, 85–6, 87, 450–65
  alternative plans, 57
  assumptions, 55, 454
  budget, 57–8, 455
  and corporate culture, 423–6
  corporate objectives, 52
  estimate of expected results, 57
  first year detailed implementation programme, 58
  how the process works, 459–64
  market overview, 54
  marketing audit, 52–4, 451–2
  marketing objectives, 56, 454–5
  marketing strategies, 56, 455
  mission statement, 50–2
  programmes, 455
  questionnaire, 67–71
  SWOT analyses, 54–5, 452–4
  written marketing plans, 455–6
Marketing planning systems, 482–538
  basis of, 485–6
  closed-loop system, *100, 448
  consolidated plan, 481, 530–5
  design and implementation problems, 60, 88–100, 101–2
    confusion over planning terms, 94
    delegation to planners, 98–100
    failure to integrate corporate and marketing planning, 98
    lack of line management support, 92–3
    lack of a plan for planning, 91–2
    numbers instead of written objectives and strategies, 94
    once-a-year ritual, 96
    over-planning, 94–6
    separation of operational and strategic planning, 96–8
    weak support from executive, 89–91
  designing, exercise, 467–72
  formalization in, 442–3, 447
  implementing, exercise, 472–3
  marketing audit, 487–9
  planning cycle, 533–5
  planning team's 'kick-off' meetings, 533–4
  steps in, 472
  strategic marketing plan, *see* Strategic marketing plan
  timetable, 472–3, 533–5
  see also One-year marketing plan
Marketing plans, written, 455–6
Marketing research, *364, 427–8
  expenditure, 365, 428

  forms of, 366–8, 427–8
  vs market research, 364–5
  see also Marketing information
Marketing strategies, 56, 225, 226, 279, *298–300, 307–8, 455, 494
  exercise, 327
  formulating, 304
  Internet and, 397–406
  and profitability, 302–4
  setting, 298–300, 502–4
  strategic marketing plan, 500–4, 518
Marks & Spencer, 301
Matching process, 5, 7, 8, 82
  exercise, 22
Matrix organization, 438
Media switching/addition, 350, 638, 639
Micro forecasting, 408–9, 428, 436
Micro-segments, *135–6
  clustering, 145–7
  defining by need, 144–7
  developing, 140–2
  exercise, 176–80
  profiling component, 138
  recording, 141
Microprocessors, 7–8
Mission statement, 50–2, 489, 505
  exercise, 72
Modelling, 395, 396
MOSAIC, 180
Motivation of sales force, 582–5, 599, 601
  path–goal approach, 583
Motorcycle industry, British, 607
Multi-channel integration, 641–2

Naivety, 86–8
Neighbourhoods, classification of, 139, 179
New distribution channels, 636–45
New markets, 375
New product development, 279–81, 292–3, 295–7
  steps in, 297
News generation, 556
Non-reactive marketing research, 366–7, 367–8
Numbers, 82–3, 94

Objectives, 485
  advertising, 546–8
    exercises, 565–7
  corporate, *see* Corporate objectives
  definition, 281
  distribution, 652–3
  elements of, 281, 307
  financial, *83

  hierarchy of, 277–9, 585, 609–10
  marketing, *see* Marketing objectives
  numbers in lieu of written, 94
  pricing and, 609–10
  prioritization, 481, 482
  sales force, 580–1
    exercise, 597–8
    individuals' objectives, 584
  sales promotion, 332–3, 553–4
  setting, 31–3, 44, 81
  sponsorship, 559
  in strategic marketing plan, 485
Off-licence chain, case history, 150–1
Once-a-year ritual, 96
One-year marketing plan, 478, 484, 501, 520–9
  contingency plan, 520, 521–2, 527
  documentation, 523–9
  format, 521–2
  guidelines for completion, 520–2
  key activity planner, 522, 529
  operating result and financial ratios, 522, 528
  overall objectives, 521, 523
  overall strategies, 521, 524
  sub-objectives, strategies and tactics, 521, 525
  summary of marketing activities and costs, 521, 526
Operating result, 522, 528
Operational marketing planning, 421–3
  in planning cycle, 533–5
  and strategic planning, 463–4
  timetable, 533–5
  see also One-year marketing plan
Operational planning, and strategic planning, 96–8
Operational problems, 80–5, 101
Operations audit, 43
Opinion leaders, 142, 204, 549
Organizations, 411–23
  barriers, 428
  board-level organization, 418–21
  corporate culture and marketing planning, 423–6
  crises, 412–15
  evolution, 411
  issues in marketing planning, 104–10
  life phases, *see* Life phases, organizational
  operational-level organization, 421–3
  structure, 415–23, 428–9, 479
    exercise, 437–8

Outsourcing, 14
Over-planning, 94–6

Pareto effect, *122–3, 176
Partial channel substitution, 147, 350, 638, 639
Passing off, 563
Pattern matching, 146
Penetration policy, 617–18
People, 3, 90–1
Performance
    sales force, 598–9, 600
    summary of SBUs, 490, 506
Personal communications, 541
Personal selling, 337, *575
    advantages of, 577–8
    importance of, 337, 575–6
    role, 576–8
    see also Sales force
Personality of brand, 191–3
Personality rights, 564
Personnel audit, 43
Physical distribution, 349, 631–4
    costs, 664
    exercise, 662–4
PIMS (Profit Impact of Marketing Strategy) project, 40–1
'Pioneer' organizational structure, 438
Place, 3, 56, 299, 308
    see also Distribution; Marketing mix
Plan documentation software, 396
Plan for planning, lack of, 91–2
Planners, 98–100
Planning cycle, 96, 457–8, 533–5
    key account planning in, 63–4
Planning department, role, 456–7
Planning horizon, 44, 61, 458–9, 466
Planning model of strategy formation, 41
Planning paradox, 466
Planning team, 'kick-off' meetings, 533–4
Planning terms, confusion over, 94
Plans, 305
Policy, government, 7, 53, 315
Political strategy model, 42
Porter, Michael, 35, 285, 287, 588
    Five Forces model, 221
Portfolio, product, see Product portfolio
Portfolio management
    product life-cycles and, 229–30
    relevance to marketing audit, 230
Portfolio matrix, *235, 496–9, 502–4
    analysis, strategies suggested by, 283
    and pricing, 621

Positioning, 158
    brand, 190–1
    competitor value, 115, 116
    market, 395
    portfolio, 395–6
    product, 395, 611
        and pricing, 344, 611, 622
Potential competition, 611–12
    and pricing, 622
Presentationality of brand, 193
Price, 3, 56, 144, 299, 308
    see also Pricing
Pricing, 449
    and accountancy, 605–9
    competition, 611–12, 622
    competitive, 343–4
    competitive advantage through value-in-use, 616
    cost-plus, 343
    costs and, 612–14
    discounts, 345, 614
        exercise, 624–5
    distribution channels and, 622
    distributor margins, 614–16
    factors affecting, 345, 621–3
    marketing strategies and, 299, 308
    objectives and product portfolio, 609–10
    price reductions, 607–9, 624–5
    price selection, exercise, 621–4
    product life-cycle and, 199–200, 344, 610, 621–2
    product positioning and, 344, 611, 622
    questionnaire, 625–6, 627–8
Pricing plans, 343–5, 603–28
    preparation of, 616–18
Privacy on the Internet, 404
Problem formulation, framework for, 84–5
Process, 3
Procter & Gamble, 118
Product, 3, 56, 299, 308
Product availability, customer expectations, 350–1
Product development, 279–81, 292–3, 295–7, 323
Product groups, 385, 487–9
    analysis, 504, 517
Product life-cycle, *197–202, 239–40
    analysis
        exercise, 246–9
        relevance to marketing audit, 230
    diffusion of innovation, *203–6, 240
    marketing mix and, 199–201
    phases, 198, 240
    and portfolio management, 229–30

and pricing, 199–200, 344, 610, 621–2
Product management, 10, 183–270
    importance of brand, 186–97
    marketing confused with, 11–12
Product managers, 419
Product portfolio, *206–7, 240–1
    Boston matrix, *210–17, 241
        exercise, 249–59
    DPM approach, see Directional policy matrix
    MIS and, 395–6
    objectives and, 609–10
    portfolio creation, 217–29
    portfolio management, 229–30
    portfolio summary, 227–9, 496–9, 513
    preparation, 218
    and pricing, 621
Product positioning, pricing and, 344, 611, 622
Product surround, 186, 187, 239
Productivity, increased, 10
Products, *184, 449
    analysis of purchases, 136–8
    availability, 350–1, 645–6
    core/surround, 186, 187, 239
    differentiation, 35–6, 287–9, 392
    features of, 136–7
    marketing strategies and, 299, 308
    MIS, functions, 384–5
    mix of, 35–6
    nature of, 184–6, 239
    positioning, 395, 611
        and pricing, 344, 611, 622
    product elimination and costing, 613
    substitute/reconfigured products, 350, 636–7
Profiling, 138–40
    of benefits, 177–8
    of individuals, 178–80
Profit, *30
Profit Impact of Marketing Strategy (PIMS) project, 40–1
Profit improvement options, 294
Profit potential, 220–1
'Profit' products, 503–4
Profit risk, 359–60
Profitability, 9, 82
    customer retention and, 648–9
    market share and, 209
    marketing objectives, strategies and, 302–4
    pricing and, 606–7, 608
Programmes, 305, 455

Promotion (of products), 3, 56,
199–200, 299, 308, 449
see also Advertising; Marketing mix;
Sales force; Sales promotion
Promotional discount, 614
Pseudo brands, 189
Psycho-social customer, 142
Psychographic characteristics, *138,
140, 178, 179–80
Public relations, 555–7
activities, 556
communications tools, 556
damage limitation and, 557
scope of, 557
Publications, 556, 557
Purchases
analysis of, 136–8
see also Buying process
Purpose statement, 51–2

Qualitative forecasting, 409, 436
Qualitative sales objectives, 581
Quality, *see* ISO
Quantitative forecasting, 409, 436
Quantitative sales objectives, 580–1
exercise, 597–8
Quantity discount, 614
'Question marks', 211–12, 259, 281
Questionnaires, 367, 435

Rational appeal, 192
Rational customer, 142
Reactive marketing research, 366–7
Recession, 300–2
Reconfigured/substitute products,
350, 636–7
Red-tape crisis, 414
Reference theory, 203
Reintermediation, 147–9, 350, 637–8
Relationships, 394
developing, from public relations
activities, 557
see also Customer relationship
management
Relative market share, 250, 252–3
see also Boston Matrix
Remuneration, sales force, 583
Representationality, 192, 193
Requisite marketing planning, 100–1,
459–64
Research, external, 435
Research and development,
technology/market-driven, 13
Research clubs, xiii
Residential neighbourhoods,
classification of, 139, 179
Restraining forces, 469–70, 471

Restructuring, industry, 398, 402, 403
Retail audits, 368, 435
Retailers/manufacturers power shift,
236
Retention of customers, 648–9
Return on investment, 30
and market share, 118
Revenue, *30
Risk, 359–60
Ritual, once-a-year, 96
Rogers, Everett, 203
Running reference file, 489

Sales, marketing confused with, 11
Sales force
activities, 337–8, 578–9
automation, 384
incentives, 339, 582–3
individuals' objectives, 584
managing, 339, 581, 582–5
exercise, 598–601
marketing department and, 418
motivation, 582–5, 599, 601
objectives, 338, 580–1
exercise, 597–8
productivity improvement, 581–2
remuneration, 583
reports, 435
role, 580–1
size of, 337, 578–9
workload, 337–8, 578–9
see also Personal selling
Sales forecasting, 31–4, *80–1
operating problems and, 81
Sales plan, 337–9
Sales promotion, *549–55
business-to-business products,
552–3
changing nature of, 586–8
checklist for promotional
instruction, 554–5
exercise, 569–71
industrial products, 553
legal requirements, 564
objectives, 332–3, 553–4
plan, 333, 553–4
exercise, 571–2
in practice, 550–1
promotion and distribution
strategy, 587
strategic role, 552
types of, 551–2
Sales/selling, 12
changing nature of sales process,
588–91
personal, *575
plan, 585–6

see also Sales force
Schedules, 305
'Scientific' organizational structure,
438
Security on the Internet, 404
Segment attractiveness, 158
Segmentation schemes, unique, 373–4
'Selective' products, 326, 504
Selling, personal, *see* Personal selling
Senior managers, critical intervention,
448
Sensual appeal, 192
Sequencing objectives, 481
Service, *184
Service marketing, 14–15, 185
Service segmentation, case study,
153–60
Share risk, 359–60
Shared values, 479
6 IS model, 397–8
Size of operations, 442–3, 443–5
Skills, 480–1
Skimming policy, 617, 618
SMS campaigns, legal requirements,
564
Social/cultural environment, 53, 315
Socio-economic groups, 139
Sodium tri-poly phosphate (STPP),
case history, 152
Software systems, 382–7
Sponsorship, 558–61
activation, 561
activity review, 559–60
definition, 558
establish return on investment, 561
examples, 559
global, 559
growth of, 559
management cycle, 560
negotiation of arrangement, 561
objectives, 559
performance review, 561
policy and strategy development,
560
processes, 559–61
types of, 558–9
Standard benefits, 143, 169
Standard Industrial Classification
(SIC), *140, 177, 262
'Stars', 212, 259, 281
Strategic business units (SBUs),
217–18, 423, 484
consolidation of several SBU
strategic marketing plans, 481,
530–5
mission statement, 489, 505
summary of performance, 490, 506

see also Strategic marketing plan
Strategic guidelines, 461–2
Strategic marketing plan, 478, 482,
    483, 484–519
  basis of system, 485–6
  contents, 58–60, 65, 489–505
    financial projections, 490–1, 507,
        519
    market overview, 491–2, 510
    marketing objectives and
        strategies, 500–4, 518
    overall assumptions, 499–500, 514
    portfolio summary, 496–9, 513
    SBU mission statement, 489–90,
        505
    SBU performance, 490, 506
    SWOT analyses, 492–6, 511–12
  documentation, 505–19
  marketing audit, 487–9
  and operational planning, 62, 96–8,
      463–4
  in planning cycle, 533–5
  preparation, 484–5
  vs tactical plan, *36–9, 478
  test for quality, 535–8
Strategic marketing planning, 60–3
  barriers to integration of, 61
  position of key account planning,
      64
  timetable, 533–5
  understanding the variables, 290–5
Strategic planning letter, 461
Strategic thinking, *81
Strategies, 485
  brand strategy, 190
  competitive, 282–90
  corporate, 43, *277, 279
  definition of strategy, 298
  hierarchy of, 279
  marketing, see Marketing strategies
  MIS and strategy formation, 396
  numbers in lieu of written, 94

operational marketing plan, 521,
    524, 525
  sales promotion, 552
  setting, 44
  in strategic marketing plan, 485
Strategy-forming models, 41–2
Structure
  organizational, 415–23, 428–9, 479
    exercise, 437–8
Sub-markets, 10
Sub-objectives, 521, 525
Substitute/reconfigured products,
    350, 636–7
Success, business, 6–7, 87–8
  influencing factors, 86
Supply and demand model, 286–7
Supply chain management, see
    Distribution
Supportive role of planners, 457
Surveys, 367
Survival matrix, exercise, 67, 73–5
'Sustain' products, 326
SWOT analyses, 54–5, 306–7, 317–18,
    452–4, 480
  exercise, 320–2
  guidelines for completing, 493–6
    assumptions, objectives and
        strategies, 494, 511
    competitor analysis, 494–6, 512
    key issues, 494
    opportunities and threats, 493
    strengths and weaknesses, 493
  summary of, 496–9, 513
Synergy, maximization of, 295
Systematization, 481
  see also Marketing planning
      system

Tactical marketing plan
  vs strategic plan, *36–9, 478
  see also Operational marketing
      planning

Tactics, in strategic marketing plan,
    485
Tactics/action, 521, 525
Task independent data management,
    592
Task-related budgeting, 520
Technological environment, 7–8, 53,
    315
Telemarketing, 384
'Ten S' approach, 478–82
Tesco, 301
Thinking, strategic, *81
Timetable, planning, 472–3, 533–5
Top-down planning, 534
Top management, weak support from,
    89–91
Trade discount, 614
Trademarks, 563
Transaction data, 384
Transport, 349, 633–4, 662

Uncertainty, 365
Unit costs, and market share, 207–10
Unitization, 349, 634, 663

Value(s)
  added value, 188, 287
  shared, 479
  understanding value required by
      customer, 115–16
Value curve, 638, 642–3
Value-in-use, 616
Value map, 148–9
Value proposition, 47–8, 273–5
Visionary leadership model, 42
Visual identity, 556

'Wildcats', 212, 259
Workload, salesperson's, 578–9

Zero-based budgeting, 57, 58

LIFT ATTENDANT

LOCAL BANK MANAGER

BRICKLAYER

TOOL-MAKER

SENIOR PARTNER IN A
FIRM OF SOLICITORS

SCHOOL TEACHER

GROUP CHAIRMAN

COMPUTER PROGRAMMER

MACHINE OPERATOR

ELDERLY GRANNY

SALES MANAGER

SELF-EMPLOYED PLUMBER

FAMILY SALOON

EXECUTIVE TRANSPORT

SECOND CAR

ECONOMY CAR

ESTATE CAR

SPORTS CAR